Indian Railway Acts and Rules 1849-1895

Railway Construction in India: Select Documents (1832-1900)

Indian Railway Acts and Rules 1849-1895

Volume IV

General Editor
Amiya Kumar Bagchi

Editor
Bhubanes Misra

Research Assistant
Kanchan Mandal

Indian Council of Historical Research
35, Ferozeshah Road, New Delhi

in association with

Anamika Publishers & Distributors (P) Ltd.

ANAMIKA PUBLISHERS & DISTRIBUTORS (P) LTD.
4697/3, 21A, Ansari Road, Daryaganj, New Delhi 110002
Phone: 2328 1655, 23270239; Fax.: 011-27868035
E-mail : anamikapublishers@yahoo.co.in

First Published 2009

ISBN 978-81-7975-285-2

PRINTED IN INDIA

Published by Anamika Publishers & Distributors (P) Ltd. 4697/3, 21A, Ansari Road Daryaganj, New Delhi 110002. Typset by Aadil Printographics, Delhi 110092 and Printed at Nagri Printers, Delhi.

Dedicated
to
all those Indian workers
who constructed our railways

CONTENTS

Documents

PART I

ACTS OF INCORPORATION AND AMALGAMATION OF INDIAN RAILWAY COMPANIES (1849-1885)

PART II

Indian Railway Acts and Rules (1850-1895)

PART III

Land Acquisition Acts and Rules (1857-1894)

FOREWORD

I have great pleasure in presenting the fourth volume of documents on 'The History of construction and operation of railways in India under British rule' beginning with the pre-construction period, planning and ending with Indian independence in 1947. The first three volumes related to the planning and the process of construction of Indian railways from the 1830s to 1900 [Bhubanes Misra (ed), *Railway Construction in India: Select Documents (1832-1900)*, vols I, II and III, New Delhi: Indian Council of Historical Research and Northern Book Centre].

One major reason for ICHR taking the initiative to publish these volumes is that railways became the grid on which the imperial structure was consolidated by the British Indian rulers, and then they served as the network for connecting the diversities of the South Asian subcontinent. The British Empire, at least in its upper reaches, was governed by law. Law was used to serve both imperial and private British interests, however arbitrary the assumptions behind the enactment of those laws might be. The laws reflected, not just the imperial interest or the interests of British private capital, but also the way a public good such as the railway network was sought to be regulated in Britain, even if the network was managed for private profit.

A close reading of the way the laws changed over the half century covered by this volume will also help illuminate the changes in policy thinking by the British Indian rulers. They will also help us understand how the rulers responded to the new demands thrown up by the displacement of subsistence reserves by the overriding imperatives of the market in every corner in India. Some historians have tried to argue that railways had completely integrated the different parts of the Indian economy already by the 1880s. In that case, there would have been no room for the private railway companies promoted by district or provincial authorities.

In the final part of the current volume, land acquisition Acts passed by the government have been collected. A network like the Indian railway system could not have been constructed without riding rough-shod over the claims of private users or owners and, in many cases, those of whole communities whose rights were either not recognized by the rulers or simply pushed aside by them. The more intensive exploitation of natural resources as well as of human has often needed the construction of new transport and communication networks. The overriding of the interests of the losers was, of course, much easier under a structure of imperial governance than it is within a democratic polity.

With these preliminary remarks, out of the way, I now move on to sketch the general outline of the current volume. The current volume comprises three parts. The first part contains the Acts of Incorporation of the seven oldest railway companies. The second part contains Indian Railway Acts passed between 1850 and 1895. The third part contains the land Acquisition Acts for Indian railways and for public purposes passed between 1850 and 1894. This volume is of great interest for several different reasons.

As I have already mentioned, the documents often reflect the concerns of the British government, the way in which it sought to regulate a public utility, such as the railways, in the public interest and transmission and adaptation of that concern by the British Indian government. That public interest was, of worse, generally seen to be synonymous with the interest of the imperial authorities. However, the documents also reflect the conflicts of interest between the British government as the representative, basically of the propertied class, and those of the people they governed. It is significant that William Ewart Gladstone, the great champion of Liberalism in Britain had to resign because the British parliament buckled under the pressure of the propertied interest when Gladstone wanted to regulate railways in public interest.

In colonial India, of course, the British Indian government did not have to listen to any popular voice because the representation of that voice was extremely narrow and its power virtually non-existent. Even then the government had to pay some attention to the public interest in an indirect fashion, because the cost to the exchequer of the guarantee given to virtually unregulated companies kept mounting. So the state stepped in for a time to construct its own railways. Furthermore, the different companies pursued different strategies of trade, traffic rules and so on because they were monopolistic in railway carriage in their own areas, and railway carriage was virtually without any competitor in long distance transport in most areas of India. Hence an Act had to be passed in 1890 to eradicate some of the arbitrariness in the behaviour of different railway companies. The state had been stepping in earlier with similar interventions, but the 1890 Act was more stringent in its regulatory provisions than the earlier ones. That is why four major railway companies protested against the 1890 Act but ultimately the Government of India overruled their objections. This story should be an object lesson to some of the champions of unregulated private enterprise of even today, as the mention of a public interest has become virtually a taboo in certain quarters.

Finally, the volume contains a series of Acts for acquisition of land. As in many other cases, the state had to overrule private interest to promote public interest. However, the colonial state often interpreted the 'public interest' as being synonymous with the interest of the private and the state railway companies, and of the exchequer of the colonial government. But the necessity of overriding private interests cannot be ignored in some cases, even in a situation where the state is run by a popular government. The Act of 1894 relating to land acquisition acquires added significance because it tackles the issue of compensation for compulsory acquisition of land, an issue which has gained a new significance in the current political-economic environment of India.

These brief comments, I hope, will substantiate a claim that documents of the kind incorporated in Volume IV relating to the construction and operation of railways in India are not merely of historical significance. They can be of great help also in understanding the complexities of many issues that are confronting the public and the political authorities today.

Amiya Kumar Bagchi
General Editor
Documents on Economic History
of British Rule in India 1858-1947

PREFACE

I welcome the publication of the Volume since I am sure that research into the process and organization of railway construction in India will be substantially enriched by the publication of the present collection of documents. I welcome the publication also because it is a long awaited outcome of a project that the ICHR had undertaken in 1993. The work of collection of documents on the period 1849-1895 was partly completed by 1999 when the then authorities of the ICHR decided to suspend the work of the project. After this unfortunate interruption of work for about five years, it was revived at the end of 2004 and Professor A.K. Bagchi of Kolkata kindly accepted the responsibility of being the General Editor. Now before us is the output of the project in the form of this Volume which complements the three Volume collection published earlier by the ICHR. These Volumes comprising more than 1600 pages documented railway construction in India from the inception of that enterprise in 1832 *(Railway Construction in India,* Volumes I-III, New Delhi, 1999). It gives me great satisfaction to note that now, with the publication of Volume IV, this project has been nearly completed.

This collection of documents is particularly useful because the original documents collected and reproduced in this volume are dispersed in several archives such as those of the Railway Board, the National Rail Museum, the National Archives of India, the British Library in London etc. The documents are, of course, to be read in the light of the contemporary context and other documents which are naturally not covered by this particular documentation project. For instance, when one reads the Acts conferring extraordinary powers on the Government of India for purposes of land acquisition (e.g. document No. 2, Part III, Act of 1863), we might bear in mind how the economies of India, Britain and United States of America were affected by the global scarcity of raw cotton during the American Civil War of 1864, driving forward railway construction for raw cotton export from India. Likewise, guaranteed interest in the railway documents (e.g. document No. 5, Part I, Act of 1855)—that is to say, the East India Compnay's promise to pay interest "at the rate of five pounds per centum per annum"—it brings to mind the peculiar colonial device of private investment at public risk. That arrangement, at the cost of the Indian tax payer, was the subject of a vast literature to which Indian public spokesmen like R.C. Dutt and Dadabhai Naoroji contributed. Or again, the documents in this Volume (Part II) on state construction of railways, roughly between 1869 and 1882, are to be situated in the context of the great debate that occurred about that time due to a conflict between the railway capitalists' lobby and a government anxious to save itself from the financial consequences of the contracts which had been signed in the 1850s. We find in Mayo's private papers letters from the Secretary of State Argyll who was plainly scared of the powerful railway lobby: "It will be well to keep the question very private at present. Many interests will be alarmed by the proposals." (Argyll to Mayo, February 1869, Mayo papers, manuscript bundle No. 47, No. 7, National Archives of India). In all such instances the readers of the present Volume will naturally look for a briefing on the background to these documents. Fortunately, a part of that need is fulfilled by the introduction written by the Editor, Dr. Bhubanes Misra. I will like to record my thanks to him for having completed the present Volume under the able guidance of Professor A.K. Bagchi.

Sabyasachi Bhattacharya
Chairman
Indian Council of Historical Research

ACKNOWLEDGEMENTS

The publication of the present volume represents a long journey which would not have been possible without the assistance and cooperation of many individuals and institutions. In this journey first I would like to express my sincere gratitude to Professor D.N. Tripathi, the Chairman and Dr. P.K. Shukla, the Member Secretary, Indian Council of Historical Research (ICHR), New Delhi. Under the project 'The Documents on Economic History of British Rule in India 1850-1947', the ICHR provided necessary research funding. I also owe a debt of gratitude to Professor Irfan Habib, the former Chairman of the ICHR for his valuable suggestions and encouragement.

Professor Amiya Kumar Bagchi, General Editor of the project and Director of the Institute of Development Studies, Kolkata (IDSK) guided me with his visionary leadership, invaluable comments and suggestions. May I express my deep gratitude to him.

Dr. Ramkrishna Chatterjee, Assistant Secretary, IDSK provided infrastructural support and many other helps. I am very thankful to him. Professor Pabitra Giri, Director of the Centre for Urban Economic Studies (CUES), University of Calcutta, provided necessary space and sitting arrangements for me and my research assistant going beyond the normal custom. I am sincerely thankful to him also. In editing the present book I was also benefited for comments and other help from Dr. Uttam Bhattacharya, IDSK. I am thankful to him for his kind cooperation.

Without cordial cooperation from Professor Sudhendu Mondal, Director, Mr. Mazharul Islam, Library and Information Centre and Mr. Ashim Mukhopadhya, Library Information Assistant, National Library, Kolkata it would not have been possible to collect full texts of official documents for the present book. I express my sincere gratitude to them. The staff of the National Archives of India, New Delhi and National Library, Kolkata, provided all sorts of cooperation. I convey my thanks to them. I convey my thanks to the Director of the State Archives of West Bengal, Kolkata for his kind cooperation.

Sri Kanchan Mandal, Research Assistant of the project, and Tonmoy Mazumdar, who copied official documents in long hand from the National Library and the State Archives of West Bengal, Kolkata performed admirably for preparing the present volume for publication.

I convey my thanks to them. I also convey my thanks to Mr. Dipankar Chatterjee and Pranab Kumar Das for typing all the documents.

I still remember the cordial cooperation and immense help which I received in the past from Professor Sabyasachi Bhattacharya and Professor Sougata Mukhopadhyaya when I was preparing the first three volumes on Railway Construction in India under British Rule 1832-1900, published by the ICHR in August 1999. I express my deep gratitude to them also on the occasion of the publication of the present volume.

My wife Smt. Kshowni and my son Sriman Kankadeb extended every support to me when I was preoccupied with the present work; they calmly tolerated and excused my long absence from the family representatives and allowed me to carry on my work uninterrupted. I shall be happy if the outcome satisfies them.

However, I remain solely responsible for the remaining errors. Moreover, views expressed in the 'Introduction' are exclusively my own, and these should not be ascribed to the Institutions that supported the project or to the individuals whose help or assistance is acknowledged here.

Bhubanes Misra
Editor

ABBREVIATIONS

A.	Acre (standard land measurement)
A.E.	Assistant Engineer
An.	Anna
Asstt.	Assistant
B.	Bigah, beegha (standard land measurement)
C.	Cottah (standard land measurement)
c.	Chapter
Ch.	Chittack (standard land measurement)
Coll.	Collector
EIC	East India Company
GIP	Great Indian Peninsula
Govr. Genl.	Governor General
Govt.	Government
h.	Hour
m.	Minute
Major Genl.	Major General
Messrs.	Messieurs
No.	Number
Offg.	Officiating
P.W.D.	Public Works Department
R.	Rood (standard land measurement)
R.A.	Railway Administration
R.E.	Railway Engineer, Royal Engineer
Rs.	Rupees
P.	Pole (standard land measurement)
Ps.	Paise
s.	Section
ss.	Sections

Sd	Signed
Sects.	Sections
Secy.	Secretary
Vic.	Victoria
Vict.	Victoria
V.C.	Victoria Cross
&C.	etc. (et cetera)

DOCUMENT INDEX

(Numbering in continuation with vol. III)

INTRODUCTION

The economic history of India under British rule has been the subject of many controversies, involving both concepts and facts. India's development or lack of it, under imperial hegemony is central to any visualization of the shaping of modern India. However, a major constraint encountered by research scholars is the paucity of access to the relevant primary source material in this area. Herein lies the importance of the compilation of the volumes of select documents on major areas of colonial economic history including documents on railway construction in India under British rule, 1832-1900. The project entitled, "The Documents on Economic History of British Rule in India", was undertaken by the Indian Council of Historical Research, New Delhi and was revived in 2004 under the general editorship of Professor Amiya Kumar Bagchi, Director of the Institute of Development Studies, Kolkata. This project aims at meeting the long-felt academic need for easy access to some of the basic documents relating to the economic history of India.

Three volumes on *Railway Construction in India: Select Documents (1832-1900)* were published in August 1999. Many documents related to railway acts, railway agreements and railway statistics were collected during the first phase of this project (1993-1999). The aim of the present volume is to provide a chronological as well as a thematic documentation of the acts related to the Indian railways passed by the British Parliament and the Government of India during 1849-1900.

In order to get a clear idea of railway construction in India from 1832 to 1900, the period has been divided into three distinct phases, according to the change in the nature and pattern of ownership and management of railway construction and development in India:

(a) Railway construction by private companies under the guaranteed interest system 1849-1868;

(b) Railway construction under joint ventures by the State and the private sector, during 1869-1882, when the main lines were operated by the private companies while the Government of India concentrated on auxiliary lines. It is also marked by a controversy over the cost of construction and operation of railways built by two sets of organizations and management;

(c) Railway construction by private companies under a modified guaranteed interest system during 1883-1900. This period was characterized by State ownership of the railways and control over the capital expenditure of the private railways, with the management resting with the private companies. With the introduction and development of railways in India, the legislation was amended and modified gradually, according to the needs of the situation. Accordingly fresh agreements were signed with the railway companies and new acts were passed by the government;

In the previous three volumes, we covered the early correspondence (1832-1849) and the protracted controversy between persons and groups interested in railway construction on the one hand, and the Court of Directors of the East India Company, the Board of Control headed by a British Cabinet Minister and the Government of India on the other. In the formative stage, especially from 1844 to 1849, the question of guarantee on capital and selection of routes occupied the pride of place. The centre of activity in this phase was London. The documents also include minutes of various Governors General, official notes on railway policy, reports of the consulting engineers, and despatches between the Court of Directors, the Secretary of State for India, the Government of India and the Indian native states. Recommendations and notes of dissent regarding the railway policy, selection of routes of construction, written by engineers and government officials of the day have also been included therein. In the later phases (1849-1900), the flows of correspondence between the Secretaries of State for India, the Government of India, the Court of Directors and the various railway companies on the questions of granting guaranteed interest, sanctioning of free land for railway purposes, selection of routes, choice of gauge, extension of lines, their control and management, rates and fares and various other factors came into prominence. This correspondence revealed the interests and motives of the different parties involved.

Apart from these documents, there were legal papers, related to the powers and rights of the government and the railway companies respectively, conferred by the Parliament, regarding the construction, administration, management, finance, conveyance and safety of the passengers. The acts of incorporation of the Indian railway companies by the British Parliament, the railway agreements between the Government of India and the railway companies, the different pieces of railway legislation and the acts on land acquisition for Indian railways passed by the Government of India reveal the legal powers and responsibilities of the different parties. Herein lies the importance of the compilation of the acts of incorporation, railway acts and agreements and land acquisition acts passed during 1849-1900. These acts had a far-reaching effect upon the later course of development of railways and the economy of India. These acts and agreements analyzed how the lines were constructed and were operated under the government supervision and specified the type of controlling authority the government had assumed for itself. The documents also focused on how the promoters and shareholders of various railway companies utilized the opportunities to protect their interests under such legal bindings and limitations.

The present book on the Indian Railways Acts 1849-1900, Volume IV, consists of 49 documents and is divided into three parts.

Part I. Nine Acts that include Acts of Incorporation of the seven oldest private railway companies by the Parliament during the first decade (1849-1858) of the Indian railway system; the Act for the Amalgamation of the Great Southern of India Railway Company and the Carnatic Railway Company into the South Indian Railway Company passed in the British Parliament on 16 July 1874; and, as appendix to part I, the Indian Tramways Act of 1885 (Act No. XI of 1886), passed by the Governor-General of India in Council, which received the assent of the Governor-General on 12 March 1886.

Part II. Thirty-four documents that include Acts and Rules on Indian railways passed between 1850 and 1900 by the Government of India; and, as appendices to part II, list of Repealing of Acts on Indian Railways passed between 1854 and 1890 by the Governor General of India, two Indian Telegraph Acts (1885, and 1888), four memoranda/statement of protest on behalf of the four oldest guaranteed railway companies against the third Indian Railway Act (Act IX of 1890), reply to these from the Secretary of State for India to the Government of India, and two notes from Legal Adviser, India Office.

Part III. Six Acts on Land Acquisition for Indian railways and other public works introduced between 1850 and 1900 by the Government of India.

The source material on the railway acts, railway agreements and acts on land acquisition is unevenly distributed in different archives and libraries in India and abroad. These include the National Archives of India, the Railway Board Library, the National Rail Museum Reference Library, the British Council Library (New Delhi), the National Library and the State Archives of West Bengal (Kolkata), the British Library, London and several other Archives in India and U.K.

In the present volume, original documents are reproduced unaltered. In several original documents, many words were printed in bold letters and in italics. The style was maintained in the process of reproduction. In the Rules for Land Acquisition for Railways and other Public Purposes of 1889 several lines could not be printed owing to indistinctness and unreadability in the original documents. However, the gaps do not appear to hamper the sense and meaning of the document.

Railway construction by the British private entrepreneurs was declared as 'public work' in Act XLII of 1850 by the Government of India. In addition, by the Indian Railway Servants Act of 1867, the Government of India declared that "Every officer and servant of a Railway Company shall be deemed a public servant within the meaning of Sections 161, 162, 163, 164 and 165 of the Indian Penal Code." It also promulgated that for the purpose of this act "the definition of legal remuneration contained in the said Section 161 the word 'Government' shall be deemed to include a Railway Company." Moreover, in the railway documents all employees and workers (mostly Indians) except the railway officers (all Europeans) engaged in the railways were termed as 'servants' and treated accordingly.

Throughout the nineteenth century, the authorities of the day encouraged the British businessmen and traders to believe that there was no limit to the possibility of profitable development of economic relations with British India. However, they noted that the British trade with India was unimpressive and failed to attain the dimensions expected. In order to expand British trade with India, the British mercantile houses were eager to utilize two principal achievements of the Industrial Revolution – the steamships and the railways. Their campaign for steam shipping (1820s-1830s) from England to India got materialized with the foundation of the Oriental Steam Navigation Company (the celebrated P & O) at the end of the 1840s on the basis of an agreement of annual subsidies from both the British Government and the East India Company. The campaign for achieving the second goal was started in India seriously from the early 1840s. The relatively low level of Britain's trade with India was attributed to the absence of proper and modern transport network, and fastened on the railways as the best means of remedying the situation. The British Government was also aware that the British regime in India would be powerfully assisted by the expansion of commerce in and with India. They regarded the railways as the best means of ensuring quick and cheaper means of transportation. In advanced capitalist countries, railways were constructed by popular demand. In the case of India, construction of railways preceded rather than followed the expansion of commerce. The construction of railways also allowed private British capital to enter massively into a vast empire, and satisfy the demand for more raw materials at home and create larger outlets for their finished products outside. With such objectives in mind, the British promoters and investors, under the full protection of Her Majesty started construction of railways in India. The study of the construction of railways in India becomes necessary for analyzing its wide impact on agriculture and industry as well as the political and social life of this country.

PART I

Acts of Incorporation and Amalgamation of Indian Railway Companies (1849-1885)

A brief history of railway construction in England will help us better understand the circumstances, motives and purposes of the governments of England and India behind the introduction of the acts of incorporation of Indian railways by the Parliament, and the associated rules and regulations for operating the railways, and legislation related to land acquisition for railways and other purposes.

The influential British businessmen and merchants in England and in India who pioneered the drive for railway construction in India in the 1840s realized from their past experience at home that it was essential to ensure the aid and full support of the governments of England and India. The gradual elimination of the commercial privileges of the East India Company (EIC) by the Parliament between the years 1813 and 1833 emboldened the dominant interest groups in Britain to dispense with direct involvement of the EIC in any business ventures. Analyzing the deplorable state of economic conditions in India, the British officials, publicists and businessmen came to the conclusion that Britain's low level of trade with India was the result of lack of proper internal transport network. In addition to this, referring to the East India Company's humiliating disaster in the Afghan war in 1842 and the bitter war with the Sikhs in Punjab in the late 1840s, the promoters of Indian railways strove to convince the higher authorities that introduction of railways into India would not only reduce government expenses in India but also strengthen its political and military supremacy and power.

Britain's early experience with railways at home had decisive influence in setting the policy and pattern for the introduction of railway construction in India. During her first 25 years of railway construction (1824-1848), England faced many problems related to the choice of trunk lines to build up a sound infrastructure for national network, control of railway finance, rates and fares, prevention of monopolistic practices, etc. By the 1840s it became clear in the UK that whatever might be the ownership, the railways were quasi-public enterprises and should be placed under some kind of government control. Debates raged regarding the form regulations should take. The pioneers and promoters of Indian railways were very conscious about these policy debates. The proponents of strict government control over Indian railways were particularly anxious not to allow India as to become a free ground of malpractices and monopolistic abuses of the promoters, which had characterized the first 25 years of operation of British railways at home. In England by 'private' acts of the Parliament, the railway companies were granted corporation rights, authorized to raise capital for specific projects and empowered to compel the people to sell their lands when needed by the railways. The only restriction placed was on limiting annual dividends to 10 percent, and that was imposed only on the Manchester-Liverpool line. Facing strong criticism about the railway companies' unregulated, haphazard and frenzied pattern of monopolistic activities, a Parliamentary Committee in 1839-40 undertook a general review of the whole railway affairs of England. The Committee recommended several measures which included the setting up of a Railway Department at the Board of Trade, and empowering the Department to exercise some control over railway construction and adopt steps to prevent accidents.

William E. Gladstone, then a rising young leader of the Tory party and the Chairman of the Parliamentary Committee, made a determined effort to set up a system of state control of railway companies and railway finance. In 1844, he introduced a bill in the Parliament for comprehensive regulation of all new railway companies not yet chartered by the Parliament. The provisions of the bill empowered the UK government either to buy up any new railway 15 years after it had been chartered, or to alter the rates and fares of such railways, as had earned 10 percent profit for three consecutive years. In the latter case, the government would possess authority to exert a strict control over profitable lines. All the vested railway interests at home were mobilized against the bill and these declared the State control over the private railways as 'Un-English'. The members of the Manchester School of publicists and the newspaper 'Economist' strongly backed the *laissez fare* position of the private railway enterprises.

The railway interest groups were ready to provoke a Parliamentary crisis over the bill. To avoid the crisis, the Cabinet under the Prime Minister Robert Peel put pressure on Gladstone and all the key financial provisions in the bill were so weakened that the law enacted became fatuity. Gladstone resigned from his office in early 1845 in despair and Dalhousie became the head of the Railway Department of the Board of Trade. Dalhousie struggled hard for almost three years (1845-1847) to impose a significant degree of government control over the chaotic British railway system. But the British railway lines and system virtually remained uncontrolled till the commercial crash of 1847-48. The Railway Department and the Cabinet failed to impose any sort of State control on British railways at home.

The lesson derived from the construction and operation of domestic railways had a decisive influence in setting the policy, pattern and modalities for the construction of railways in India. Keeping in mind the commercial and political interests of the British trading community in India, the government of Great Britain decided that no individual or company would be legally permitted to make any agreement with the government of British India for construction of railways, without prior incorporation by the Parliament. After incorporation, the company could enter into an agreement or contract with the government (then the East India Company). Through the Act of Incorporation, the Parliament set out in outline the terms of agreement between the EIC government and railway companies, and the provisions for Indian railway acts for performing all such matters and deeds necessary or convenient for carrying into effect the objects and purposes of making and constructing, working and maintaining railways in India. Using the Act of Incorporation as a guideline, the British government in India entered into agreements, prepared railway legislation and passed land acquisition acts at different times according to the perceived need of the situation. The agreements were framed and formulated in a manner premeditating the chances of the government or any individual railway company becoming involved in disputes centring on the powers and rights conferred on both the parties respectively by the Parliament. The provisions incorporated in the Act of Incorporation distinctly demarcated the jurisdiction and area of operation of the government and the respective companies related to the construction and management of railways.

The powers conferred on the government of India by the Parliament for controlling the activities of the railway companies were:

1. to supervise, direct, regulate and order the railway company for its finance, works, contracts, accounts, byelaws, acts, proceedings, transactions and affairs of the company in England and in India,
2. to appoint an ex-officio director as representative of the government (whether qualifying by holding shares or not) of the company in the place of any ordinary director and to regulate powers including a right to veto at the board of directors meeting,
3. to compel the company to conform to and fulfil all directions related to finance and management given by the government,
4. to appoint the agent of the railway company in India and elsewhere and to determine and regulate the powers and duties of such agent,
5. to settle dispute through arbitrators,
6. to acquire land for railway purposes, and
7. to terminate any agreement or to purchase any railway company after a period to be mentioned in the agreement.

The rights attributed to the railway companies by the Parliament for performing their activities independently were:

1. to make agreements with the Government of India for constructing and maintaining

railways and telegraph lines connected therewith,
2. to get interest on the capital invested in the railway, i.e., to get guaranteed interest on invested capital from the Indian revenue,
3. to acquire as much lands to be required for the railway purposes at free of cost,
4. to secure rights, facilities and advantages related to railway,
5. to collect tolls, receipts and profits and application of such rights,
6. to deposit subscribed capital of the company to the treasury of the government in due time,
7. to borrow on bonds but not on mortgagee any amount of sum sanctioned by the government for railway purposes,
8. to surrender or sale the railway company to the government at any future time to be mentioned in the agreement, and
9. to claim property of the company with the payment of money to the government.

It may be noted that in case of amalgamation or extension or opening of any branch line by any company similar Act of Incorporation became essential. The Act of Incorporation had direct influence on the formulation of the provisions of the Deed of Agreements, Indian Railway Acts and Land Acquisition Acts. Judging the indirect control and supervision of the Parliament as well as the Government of Great Britain on the Indian railways the Acts of incorporation of seven oldest railway companies, incorporated during the first decade (1849-1858) of Indian railway system, are presented in this volume. Besides, the Act for the Amalgamation of the Great Southern of India Railway Company and the Carnatic Railway Company into the South Indian Railway Company passed in the British Parliament on 16 July 1874 is also reproduced here. In appendix to part I, the Indian Tramways Act of 1885 (Act No. XI of 1886), passed by the Governor-General of India in Council, which received the assent of the Governor-General on 12 March 1886, is also given. Moreover, as these documents are rare, these also carry a historical value and importance. Readers will find a close relationship between these four types of acts, namely the Acts of Incorporation by the Parliament, Deed of Agreements with Government of India (not incorporated in the present volume, will be published in the next volume), Indian Railway Acts and Indian Land Acquisition Acts passed between 1849 and 1900.

PART II
Indian Railway Acts and Rules (1850-1895)

1. Railway Acts Passed During the Guaranteed Interest Term (1849-1869)

The first act related to railways in India was passed by the government of India (GOI) in March 1853, for the Great Indian Peninsula Railway Company in Western India under the title Railway Act III of 1853. After three months in July 1853, it was supplemented by the Railway Act XII of 1853. The act was introduced mainly for preventing fraud in the said company and for punishment of certain offences which could endanger the safety of the passengers travelling in the said railways. No such act was passed for the East Indian Railway

Company which began operating in the same year in Eastern India.

The first legislation on the operation of Indian railways was Act XVIII of 1854. This act practically did little more than gave legal effect to regulations such as were then in force on English railways. The Act dealt with the provisions related to the pre-payment of fares, production of tickets, prohibition of smoking, fraudulent attempts, trespass, obstruction, recovery of fines for breach of rules, handling of luggage and non-liability of the railway companies as to luggage and valuable property. There were provisions to erect and maintain good and sufficient fences on both sides of the line and failing therein, to be liable to a fine of Rs. 50/- for every offence. But the act did not give the list of 'definitions' of offences. The act was inadequate and defective, particularly because of its omission to provide safety for the workers, protection of the public against undue preference, measures for inspection of lines and inquiry into accidents. The government of India soon realized some of these shortcomings and tried to fill the gaps by issuing official resolutions and circulars from time to time.

Indian Railway Act IX of 1860 was introduced for a speedy determination of disputes on wages between the employers and servants of railways and other public works by the government. Using sections 161, 162, 163, 164 and 165 of the Indian Penal Code, the Indian Railway Servants Act of 1867 sought to criminalize certain offences committed by the railway servants.

There was a defect in the Act of 1854 as to the recovery of fines from a railway company and an amendment of this act was necessary. The opinion of the provincial governments was invited with this regard and to any other defects that might have appeared in the working of this Act. The Public Works Department (PWD) of government of India passed a resolution on 19 August 1865 with regard to a new act for Indian railways. The resolution stated that the act of 1854 made railway companies liable for loss or injury only when such had been caused by the gross negligence or misconduct of their servants. It should be laid down, however, that loss or injury occurred was sufficient proof of negligence and the railway companies should be liable in all such cases. More stringency was suggested to deal with accidents, and lay down a careful procedure for preventing haphazard opening of railway traffic before proper checking of fitness for traffic conveyance. The provision of a sufficient number of level crossings and the need for more measures in dealing with cattle trespasses were also suggested.

But no action was taken for framing a comprehensive railway act for India although there was a mass of correspondence related to the question of competency of the government to override any rights of the railway companies by any new act. In 1870 and 1871 two short acts were passed to meet certain urgent questions including the control and reporting of accidents and cattle trespasses. Indian Railway Act XIII of 1870, a supplement to the first Indian Railway Act XVIII of 1854, dealt with the definition of several words related to railways. Indian Railway Act XXV of 1871, a substitution of Act XVIII of 1854, dealt with the conveyance of passengers and goods, duty and responsibility of the railway officers and servants and punishment for breach of railway rules by passengers and persons employed in railways.

2. Railway Acts Passed During the Period of State Construction and Management (1869-1882)

On 12 March 1871 the GOI issued a resolution, which could be regarded as a new and important departure in the direction of the construction and working of state railways. It stated that it was evident that the law of the land relating to railway construction should be the same to whomsoever such railway might belong and the law that governed the railway companies' lines must also govern the railways under state construction. Thus the question as to the liability of the railway administration as distinguished from that of their servants, imposition of fines, etc., which were manifestly inapplicable to the state railways, according to the present modified bill, rendered it necessary to reconsider the greater portion of the bill. In January 1873 the GOI, however, declared that there was no pressing need for a further legislation, because the government, under the agreements, possessed large executive powers of supervision and control both on the working of railways and in determination of rates and fares, etc. They suggested that it would not be sound and wise policy to introduce any change in the existing railway legislation of the country at a time when the state was going to undertake railway construction on its own. Thus the need of a comprehensive railway act was allowed to remain in abeyance again.

But in 1873 the GOI passed General Rules and Regulations for the Rajputana State Railways which was applicable to all railways owned by the state. The rules comprised in this code were divided into 19 sections with 236 provisions. It dealt with the general regulations related to the construction and management of railways, the servants of the railway companies, different types of signals and signalling systems to be used and followed in the stations and lines, duties and responsibilities of the station masters and clerks in charge of the station, the guards, the enginemen and firemen, the railway policemen, pointsmen and signalmen, the gatemen at railway level crossings, and free passes to be issued only to the railway officers (and not to the general railway workers) and the forms to be signed by the railway employees without stamp duty. It also incorporated certain regulations for inspectors, foremen, mistries and labourers engaged in repairing the permanent lines and works and for ballast trains or wagons.

Public General Statutes for Indian Railway Companies, 1873 was introduced for enabling various railway companies to issue and register shares and securities in India. At the same time Public General Statutes for Indian Guaranteed Railway Companies, 1873 was formulated to permit guaranteed railway companies to raise capital on shares and debentures for further extension of railways. Simultaneously the Act for Indian Railway Companies, 1873 was passed for enabling and facilitating the railway companies to establish their offices in India for the issue, registration and transfer of shares, stocks, bonds and securities of the companies.

In 1875 an accident occurred on the Oudh and Rohilkhand Railway, in which a village near the line caught fire from a locomotive engine. The company was sued for compensation and it was discovered that the railways in India had no statutory power to run steam locomotives. As a consequence the questions of further legislation became evident.

Though several acts, rules and regulations on Indian railways were passed between 1850 and 1875, they were not enough to handle the problems and difficulties faced by the railway companies as well as the government in their administration and management. Therefore, in 1876 a bill was introduced in the Viceroy's Council, and after being subjected to numerous comments and suggestions, it was passed on 13 March 1879 as the second Indian Railway Act IV of that year and came into force on 1 July 1879. Its provisions were extended to the whole of British India and the native states as well.

The previous acts of 1854, 1867, 1870 and 1871 were repealed by the new act. It was more elaborate and detailed than the first Indian Railway Act XVIII of 1854. It incorporated certain new provisions and contained 54 clauses divided in six chapters. The Carriers Act of 1865 was declared no longer applicable to carriage by railway. All types of railway administration, whether of the state or of the companies, or of the native states, were brought under the purview of the new act. Provisions were laid down for powers to run locomotives, opening of new lines after their checking and inspecting by special officers, reporting of accidents and defining the classes into which they should be divided, and punishment of hackney carriage and omnibus drivers in case of obstruction or misbehaviour at railway stations. The new act empowered the government to extend it or any portion of it to any tramway worked by steam. Railway administration was empowered as before to frame general rules and byelaws for the working of a line.

In 1879 Indian Guaranteed Railways Act was passed by the British Parliament. It enabled the guaranteed railway companies in India and the Secretary of State for India to enter into agreements with respect to the working of railways and telegraphs and conferring upon the companies additional powers with respect to their undertakings. This measure was felt necessary in consequence of the railway companies being unable to work and manage other lines than their own, or to surrender or sell any portion of their undertakings or telegraphs connected therewith. The act empowered the railway companies, subject to the approval of the Secretary of State for India, to work any ferry, construct any bridge used in connection with railways and supply the means of communication required for the convenience of traffic on any railway. Most probably this act was prompted by, or was indicative of, the change in the attitude of the Government of Great Britain towards the use of private enterprises again in Indian railways. The further introduction of private railway companies in a new form came into effect largely as a consequence of these powers and authority conferred on them. Simultaneously Indian Railway Act VI of 1879 was introduced for the construction of a steam tramway between Darjeeling and Siliguri. In the same year the East Indian Railway Purchase Act was passed.

3. Railway Acts Passed During the Revival of Private Railway Companies under a Modified Guaranteed System (1883-1902)

The period 1883-1902 was very important in the history of Indian railway acts as it was characterized by the introduction of comprehensive (third) Indian Railway Act IX of 1890 and the Land Acquisition Rules for 1889 for railways under private and state control. The Act IV of 1879 was defective as regards the inspection of railways both before and after their opening up. Therefore, the General Rules and Regulations of 1880 was made in conformity with the provision 8 [that section specified the power of the railway administration to make general rules for regulating the mode and speed at which carriages and wagons to be used, the maximum number of passengers to be carried, accommodation and conveyance of passengers, precaution for carrying dangerous goods, and the travelling upon and use, working and management of railways] of the second Indian Railway Act IV of 1879. The new General Rules and Regulations were divided into 19 sections with 394 provisions (paragraphs). The provisions laid down in the General Rules and Regulations of 1880 were more or less similar with the sections of the General Rules and Regulations of 1873 introduced for the Rajputana State Railways, except for several rules newly incorporated in this set of rules for working the lines on certain new systems.

Indian Railway Act IV of 1883 empowered the GOI, to take action for the protection of public against dangers from inefficient management of a railway and to appoint officers for periodical inspection. The law also provided for the framing of rules by the GOI for the inspection of all railways, instead of a state line only, prior to their being opened for traffic conveyance. The government then passed a resolution that legal authorities would inspect all railways prior to their being opened for public. One month's notice of the intended inspection would be given, and the inspecting officer would be supplied at the same time with full information regarding the manner of the construction of the line, and certificates would be given after inspection.

Apart from the acts related to railways, the Indian Telegraph Act XIII of 1885 has been incorporated in the present volume as it had a direct relation with the railway industry. The act dealt with the privileges and powers of the government for establishing, maintaining, working and placing of telegraph lines and posts, and for imposing penalties for breaking the act and for damage control. Indian Railway Act XI of 1887 was passed for regulating traffic on the Sindh-Pishin section of the North Western Railway. Indian Telegraph Act XI of 1888 was an addition to the Telegraph Act XIII of 1885.

A need for a new general railway act had long been recognized, mainly owing to disputes arising from interchange of traffic, preferential rates and fares and settlement of disputes between railways by arbitration. On 5 November 1884 the GOI circulated a draft bill, and a copy was sent to the Secretary of State for India for opinion. The discussion on the bill extended over five years in England and India. The passing of the Railway and Canal Act of 1888 in England influenced the criticism of the bill and ultimately led to a complete change in the character of the bill. The principal feature of the bill was the introduction of clauses for the settlement of disputes between railway companies through arbitration. Nearly every clause of Act IV of 1879 was modified in the bill of 1884. The Secretary of State for India on 4 July 1889 intimated the GOI that he had doubts as to the applicability of this method under the peculiar conditions of the Indian railway system. Considering the large power of control over all the railway lines vested with the government, which would give exceptional scope for dealing with the action of the railway companies, the Secretary of State for India gave a somewhat partial sanction to the provision of Commission, so that instead of a permanent tribunal, the bill finally empowered the government to appoint a special Commission whenever circumstances so required.

On 21 March 1890 the modified draft bill of 1884 was passed as the third Indian Railway

Act IX and came into force on 1 May 1890. The act represented largely the policy of the Government of India as regards railway and its proper administration and management. The principal object of the act was to empower the Governor-General in Council to take action for the protection of the public against dangers arising from the inefficient maintenance of a railway and to appoint officers for the purpose of making periodical inspection with this object. Thereafter no new railway legislation on management and administration was passed till the end of 1900. The only exception was the Indian Railway Act X of 1895, which related to the payment by railway companies (registered under Indian Companies Act of 1882) of interest out of capital during the period of construction.

The first chapter of Act IX of 1890 consisted of usual and necessary definitions. The second chapter dealt with inspection of the railways but differed little from the act of 1879. The third chapter, on the construction and maintenance of work, was practically a new one. Its provisions established the powers and responsibilities of railway administration as regards the construction and maintenance of the lines and accommodation works. The fourth chapter, relating to the opening of railways for traffic, dealt with passenger and goods traffic.

The fifth chapter was wholly new. It dealt with the traffic facilities, undue preference and the institution of a Railway Commission. The interesting point is that provisions of this chapter were mostly copied from the 'Railway and Canal Traffic Act of 1888' of England. The difference between the two acts was that the Indian Commissions for tribunals were purely temporary in character and were to be appointed by the Governor-General in Council when the Council might consider it required and fit. Moreover, the contrast between the standing Railway Commission in England and the temporary Railway Commission in India was marked by the anomaly that in the Indian Act IX of 1890, the decision as to the necessity for appointing a Commission and the selection of its members was left in the hands of the government executives. As the owner of most of the railways and co-partner in other railways, the GOI, from a legal point of view, could hardly be regarded as an impartial executor in those important initiatory steps. However, Sections 42 and 46 of this chapter were remarkable as providing, for the first time in India, for reasonable traffic facilities and protection against undue preference.

Chapter six relating to the working of railways was more or less similar to those in Act IV of 1879. But in the new sections of this chapter, powers were given to the government to determine arrangements or disputes regarding a common terminus or junction and proportion of the cost of the same to be shared by each line. In accordance with an important section of this chapter, every railway company would henceforth have to submit annual returns regarding its capital, revenue transactions and traffic, in prescribed form.

The seventh chapter defined responsibilities of railway administrations as carriers. But it surprisingly exempted the railway companies from the responsibility for loss or damage in case of contracting to carry goods by voyage under the conditions of the ordinary bill of landing. The eighth chapter relating to accidents laid down detailed rules, and duties of a railway administration in case of accidents. Chapter nine dealt with offences and penalties of railway companies, railway servants, travellers, and traders. Under Sections from 87 to 98 of this act, penalties were to refer to private railway companies only, and the officials of the state railways were thus excluded. Who would deal with the offences and penalties occurred on the State lines was not mentioned.

The Select Committee, appointed by the GOI to look into the objections against the new Act, unanimously opined that no saving clause regarding the rights of the companies should be inserted, for such a clause might bring each company under a different law and would certainly cause great inconvenience. Each company might claim to interpret the act according to its own view of its rights under the agreement and any attempt to do this, even if unsuccessful, would seriously impair the operation of those portions of the act, which dealt with the creation of traffic facilities and prevention of undue preferences.

When the bill was passed as Act IX of 1890, the home boards of directors of the four oldest guaranteed railway companies lodged protests to the Secretary of State for India against the infringement of their rights. They held that as regards the guaranteed companies, the passing of Act IX was 'ultra vires' on the part of the GOI. Their main objection was related to chapter five which dealt with traffic facilities, control and modification of rates and fares, measures against undue preference and the appointment of Railway Commission for the settlement of disputes. They stated that the act was an ill-advised attempt to transplant into India the legislation, which was not adapted to its conditions. They opined that the Railway and Canal Traffic Act of 1888 of England was compatible with the conditions under which private railway companies existed in England, as they were merely statutory commercial enterprises with which the Government had neither privity nor contract.

The Secretary of State for India forwarded these representations of the railway companies, along with the opinion of the legal advisor of the India Office, to the GOI for final decision. Thereupon the GOI in April 1891 took a firm stand, refuted the allegation that the act was ultra vires and deprecated the suggestion that a further reference on the subject should be made to the law officers of the Crown. It assured the railway companies that no undue preference would occur and unless it could be shown that very unreasonable encroachment on the rights enjoyed under the agreement had resulted, the companies should have no reason to complain.

The implementation of Act IX of 1890 was a matter of more difficulty and delicacy in the Indian native states. Particularly, in the case of railways wholly confined in a native state, the government had no direct concern with that railway otherwise as the paramount power. In their case railway management was in fact administration within foreign territory. But when such lines (as happened in many cases) formed part of a thorough route, it became evident that civil and criminal jurisdiction for damage or offences under this act must lie with the GOI. This end was attained after a considerable negotiation, on behalf of most of the native states with the Secretary of State for India and the Government of India.

The general tenor and intention of railway legislation in India was to follow more or less closely the example of Great Britain, and provisions were laid down accordingly. There were but few indications, either in the proceedings of the GOI or in the enactments, of any desire to go beyond this or to regard the circumstances and habits of the common Indian people as requiring any special treatment, whether of restraint or protection in their dealings with the railway administration. The only direction where special legislation was noticeable was the Land Acquisition Act of 1870, for the construction of railways and other public works, where the government was principal party and in most cases acted as selling itself in one department and buying in another, the only point to be dealt with being the equitable compensation of the tenants.

PART III
Land Acquisition Acts and Rules (1857-1894)

Land acquisition played an important and significant role in the rapid growth of railway infrastructure and reshaping the economy of India where agriculture was the backbone of national income. The Indian railway industry seized a large amount of land for construction of a railway network throughout India. The GOI provided strong legal and financial support for the development of the plantation and construction of railway industries under private British entrepreneurship. In the case of tea industry large tracts of waste and fallow lands were leased for 99 years to various British sterling and rupee tea companies without any rent. In the history of industrial world, tea was the only industry which was started by the Government of British India in 1833 in Assam, and after successful experiment it was handed over to a private British sterling concern (Assam Tea Company) in 1834. So, the GOI was a pioneer in the selling of a public enterprise to a private concern.

Prior to the beginning of the railway construction, several land acquisition acts were passed between 1824 and 1850. These acts were introduced for public works such as digging of canals for irrigation and navigation, making of pucca roads, bridges and drainage. However, railway lines required far bigger tracts of land than these public works, which were carried out by the Public Works Department (PWD) of the GOI. But the public works 'for most of public utility' were very limited and mostly confined in cities and towns, and in the case of irrigation canals to a few regions before the 1850s. Judging the importance of land for the railways, six land acquisition acts (of 1850, 1857, 1861, 1863, 1870 and 1894) were passed between 1850 and 1900, and four of them are incorporated in the present volume along with Land Acquisition Declaration, 1889 and the Rules for Land Acquisition 1889, all under the Land Acquisition Act X of 1870.

When the East Indian Railway Company (EIR) began its construction work from 1849, the Governor General of India passed the Act XLII of 1850 by which it instructed the district magistrates of the Bengal Presidency to acquire any private land by forcing the person or persons interested in that land to surrender it to the government without any delay, as and when needed by the EIR. Thereafter Land Acquisition Act VI of 1857 was passed. This Act laid down the procedure to be followed for the acquisition of land and determination of the amount of compensation to be made to the owner or owners of the acquired land by the government. The act was amended in 1861, under the title Land Acquisition Act II of 1861, without incorporating any new provision.

Thereafter Land Acquisition Act XXII of 1863 was introduced. It dealt with the official procedures to be followed by the railway companies or promoters to obtain any land from the government for any construction work for public utility. It empowered the government to inspect and monitor the construction of railways, roads, bridges, canal, drainage and electric telegraph for railways on the acquired land in case these would cause any danger to the public. In this act the word 'Lands' included messuages, lands, tenements and hereditaments of any tenure. To keep vigilance on the construction, provisions were incorporated in the act that any public work project, including railways, should first be registered with the local government where the proposed work would be carried out. After registration with the government, the company concerned would be permitted to take possession of the acquired land.

The acts passed between 1850 and 1863 for acquisition of land, were general, superficial and indistinct in many areas. It was felt that the acts did not serve the interests of various railway companies and the government as well, as they liked. Moreover, the demand for land for railways began to increase from the late 1860s, when several new railway companies began to construct new lines on a large scale in different regions of India. To eliminate the gaps and indistinctness of the previous land acquisition acts it became necessary to pass a more comprehensive land acquisition act.

To meet the need of the changed situation, the GOI passed the Land Acquisition Act X of 1870. It was formulated in seven parts. It dealt with the definition of the act, the procedure to be followed for the acquisition of land, the reference to the court by the district collector about enquiry on land and procedure to be followed thereafter, the apportionment of compensation, the payment of compensation, the temporary occupation of land and several other miscellaneous matters. Act X of 1870 was passed to acquire land by the local governments for general public works including railways.

When the GOI decided to construct its own railways from 1869, it became essential to formulate rules for acquisition and use of land for the private and state railways separately. But it took two decades to prepare separate rules for land use by the two sectors. In August 1889, the GOI promulgated special rules under section 59 (power of the local government to make rules for the guidance of officers in all matters) of Act X of 1870: the Board of Revenue issued general rules for the guidance of public officers in the administration of land acquisition and special rules for public officers when taking up land for guaranteed railways, railways to be constructed by assisted or private companies, and for State railways. Prior to that, in March 1889, the Government of India under section 6 (declaration by the local government for acquisition of any particular land for a public purpose) of the Land Acquisition Act X of 1870 passed Land Acquisition Declaration for the Assam Behar State Railway. It dealt with fifty-one declarations of the Lieutenant Governor of Bengal for acquiring lands in different villages, mouzahs, parganahs and districts of Bengal and Bihar for the said state railway.

However, in section I of the Rules for Land Acquisition for Public Purposes 1889, the government declared general rules to be followed by the public officers (district Collector, deputy Collector, Commissioner, deputy Commissioner, etc.) engaged in the administration of land acquisition. In section II, part 1, lands to be required for guaranteed railways and railways to be constructed by assisted or private companies were divided into four categories A, B, C, and D. Class A land comprised the land required for the permanent construction of a railway which would be supplied by the government free of cost. The occupation of this type of land was so far permanent that it only ceased when their agreement would be terminated or surrendered to the government. Class B land was also provided free of cost but only for temporary occupation by the private railway companies. Class C land contained the land for the preparation of railway materials and for other miscellaneous objects, which the private railway companies had to provide at its own cost. Class D land was provided free of cost but it did not come directly into the possession of the railway companies. This category of land would be exclusively used for roads leading to the railway stations or to permanent store-yards or workshops detached from the main works, division or changes of old roads made necessary for railway works.

In part II of section II, lands to be used by the state railways were divided into two classes. Class A land was required permanently for the construction works related to lines, bridges, embankments, cuttings, fencings, stations and station buildings, storehouse, workshops, sidings, dwellings, testing the diversion of water courses and other works, roads leading to the stations, for water supply, and for preparation of railway materials and other works. Class B land was required temporarily for roads for access to works, storehouses, side cuttings, spoil banks, brick fields, quarries, ballast pits, temporary diversion of streams, highways and other works.

By introducing the Land Acquisition Rules of 1889, the government specifically defined the use of land by the private and state railways and thereby tried to stop the misuse of land by the railway companies. But it could not stop the railway companies acquiring huge amounts of land free of cost as there was no provision in these rules or acts or agreements about the limit of acquisition. As a result, enormous expanses of land possessed by the railway companies remained unused and thereby caused loss to the Indian revenue. Thus both the private and state railways misused the most important resource of the railway industry.

The Land Acquisition Act of 1894 was passed for the "acquisition of land needed for public purposes and for companies and for determining the amount of compensation to be made on account of such acquisition". The act dealt with the acquisition, declaration of intended acquisition, enquiry into measurement, value and claims and award by the collector, taking possession of land, reference to the court in case of objection related to the measurement of land or amount of compensation or the apportionment of compensation, method of payment of compensation, temporary occupation of land (not exceeding three years), acquisition of land for companies and several miscellaneous clauses related to this act. By the introduction of the Land Acquisition Act of 1894, the Land Acquisition Act of 1870 and section 74 of the Punjab Courts Act of 1884 were repealed.

It is interesting to note that during the passed 113 years (1894-2007), no new land acquisition act was passed. The result of which at present, both the Government of India and various state governments are often facing serious administrative, judicial and law and order problems including strong protest from the Indian peasantry whenever any land is declared by the government to be acquired for industrial and infrastructural developments either under public or private sector.

The government took the initiative in land acquisition and shouldered all the burdens of acquisition of lands from the people by force of law. Simultaneously, the government assured the railway companies that interest would be paid on their capital invested in this industry from the Indian revenue. Thus the British railway pioneers and promoters from the very beginning were freed from two major risk factors of the industry namely, the burden of occupation of land and the risk of low profitability of their investment. The railway companies naturally took much more time to complete any construction than originally specified in their agreements with the government.

The deeds of agreement signed between various railway companies and the GOI during 1849-1900 will be published in volume V. But it may be useful to sketch some of the provisions of these agreements for us to grasp the understanding that developed between the British Cabinet, the Parliament, GOI and railway companies operating in India over the period. Reader will understand why land acquisition acts were passed under the pretext of 'public purposes'.

Major Subjects of Agreements with the Railways

The acts of incorporation of the EIR and the Great Indian Peninsula Railway Company were passed into law in the Parliament on 1 August, 1849. The protracted official negotiations of six years from 1844 to 1849 had at last culminated in an historic investment agreement. Later, many British-owned railway companies were incorporated in the Parliament and agreements were signed between the GOI and the railway companies. In case of extension of existing lines, or construction of any new route, joint venture for construction of a junction station to be used by the respective railway companies, or construction of lines in the native states by private railway, or construction of state lines by private railway companies, fresh agreements were signed between the GOI and the native states and the respective railway companies. Most of these agreements contained 27 to 29 clauses governing the following major subjects:

1. Government control and supervision on raising and expenditure of capital,
2. Acquisition of land and construction of lines,
3. Operation of the line and traffic control and charges,
4. Keeping of annual accounts and distribution of net receipts, and
5. Provisions for eventual transfer of the railway company to the government through annuity commutation and for turn back the lines with full compensation.

Government Control and Supervision on Raising and Expenditure of Capital

The respective railway company was required to deposit its capital in sterling in the treasury of the in the England. The company could not draw on its deposited capital for construction works without sanction of the government. In all matters, except legal proceedings, the railway companies were to be subject to the supervision, superintendence and control of the government. The government would exercise its power and control through its representative, who as an ex-officio director, would sit with the board of directors of each railway company, and as government nominee would possess the right to veto its decision except in legal affairs. The government representative should not receive any salary and should not own any share of the railway company. The railway company should submit statements of expenditure regularly and only those were to be allowed which the government had approved. A capital account would also be kept recording the cost of construction of the line, and once the line was opened for public conveyance a separate revenue account would also be maintained. The guaranteed interest would be paid from the day on which the said railway company deposited its capital into the government treasury for a period of 99 years.

Acquisition of Land and Construction of Lines

Land required for the construction of lines and for all works connected therewith had to be provided by the government to each railway company free of cost under a lease of 99 years by acquiring it from the people of India (without obtaining their consent, of course). The government had the absolute authority to determine, fix upon and select or alter the route and direction of a railway line to be constructed, to stipulate whether the line was to be single or double tracked and to lay down the specification of various engineering works, including the gauge to be used.

Operation of the Line and Traffic Control and Charges

As soon as the construction of a line was completed, the said line would be opened for the conveyance of passengers and goods subject to the satisfaction of the government. The opened line would be maintained properly with sufficient rolling stocks, wagons and other plant and machinery for working of the line. Engines, carriages, number of running trains and their schedules and rates and fares had to be approved and sanctioned by the government. All government mails and employees connected therewith would be carried free when they would be on duty, while army personnel, officers and artisans on the business of the government, military stores, guns and ammunitions and government goods would be charged at reduced rates.

Keeping of Annual Accounts and Distribution of Net Receipts

After deducting the cost of operating, maintaining, repairing and restoring of the rolling stock, wagons, plant and machinery and for establishing a reserve fund for future requirement, the remaining net receipts would be applied first towards the discharge of the current interest charges so as to exonerate the government. If any residue still remained, it would be divided in the following manner: One half of the moiety would go to the government for repayment of guaranteed interest which was given as advance in previous years to the railway company, and the other half would go to the railway company for its own use. When the government had been repaid in full from the net receipts for all guaranteed interest amount, then the railway company would have the right to enjoy the entire surplus. If net receipts exceeded 10 per cent upon the outlay, the government could ask the said railway company to reduce the rates and fares and toll charges so that the net receipts should not exceed 10 per cent per annum.

Transfer of Railway Company to the Government of India through Annuity Commutation

At the end of the said lease term of 99 years, the railway company and all its works, buildings, land, fixed machinery, telegraph conveniences, plans, surveys, books, printing, writing, document and sections whatsoever, which were anywise connected with the undertaking, would automatically and without any compensation become the property of the government. The only payment, which would then be received by the railway company, would be for its plant, machinery and rolling stock. Any land in England which might then be held by the railway company for the purpose of its business, should be sold and money to be so earned by such sale, should be paid to the government. But the next provision of each agreement was quite interesting where it stated that each railway company had the right to turn back its line and works at any time up to the final six months of the 99 years, in such a way as to receive compensation in full for all capital expended. This meant any railway company in the 98th year of the agreement could prevent the provision of 'without compensation' from ever coming into effect.

In other provisions the government had the power of purchasing the line within six months at the end of the first 25 years, or the first 50 years. If a railway company proved unable to raise its stipulated capital, or applied its money improperly, or defaulted on its obligations under the agreement, or failed to work its line satisfactorily, or failed to maintain the line properly when open, the government could terminate the agreement with that railway company, or take possession of the line on payment of the capital expended and unused capital minus debts and liabilities. In all cases where the government might have to return part or all of the capital, it could do so either by lump-sum payment in full, or by an annuity to continue for the remainder of the 99 years. Finally, the government was bound itself to promote such legislation as might be necessary to enable the railway companies to fulfil the objects of their undertakings.

At a first glance these acts and agreements may create an impression that the GOI had established absolute authority and control over the railway companies. The provisions in the acts and agreements were so laid down that at the end of the lease period, each railway company would automatically surrender all their lines, works, buildings, etc. to the government without any compensation. But a minute reading of the acts and agreements would reveal that the interests of the British capitalist class and promoters were very well protected.

The key provisions regarding the government power of control and supervision over the railway companies were more than counterbalanced by other provisions like absolute guaranteed interest which the government was bound to pay from the Indian revenue on all capital deposited with it by the railway companies. The shareholders shouldered absolutely no risk in investing in Indian railways. S. Laing, the Finance Member of the Viceroy's Council, pointed out in 1861 that the guarantee system was proving uneconomic from the point of view of the government. The real companies were 6000 miles away from the place of construction, the management was non-resident, had no incentive to minutely examine the productivity of the outlay on the works, and looked almost exclusively to the guarantee. Moreover, having no regulations as to how and when the lines were to be constructed and opened, the railway companies very cleverly utilized the loopholes of the acts and agreements. They simply supplied the capital and enjoyed guaranteed interest and did not bother about the cost and the operating result of their undertakings. The system of guaranteed interest killed incentives for economy, prompted recklessness and involved the country in liabilities much beyond what the Indian people could bear, or needs of the time could justify.

Moreover, the provisions related to automatic surrender without compensation at the end of 99 years, the government's power to purchase at the end of first 25 years, and the railway companies' right to surrender at any time with full compensation had different meanings and implications. A qualitative difference can be noticed regarding the exercise of power by the government and use of right by the railway company. The government had to wait at least for first 25 years for exercising its power while the railway company could enjoy its right at any time after opening the line. This meant the supreme power became legally powerless up to the first 25 years, while the subordinate railway company had greater liberty of using its right at any time than the government.

In addition, centring on the question of administration and management there were some quasi-political problems, including the real meaning of the public sector in a colonial country. In British India, unlike in European countries, private railway companies had been controlled by foreign businessmen. On the other side, the state had not been accountable to the Indian people. Similarly, the question of separation of railway finance from the general budget, which was raised as early as 1880s, did not reach its final solution till 1930. But such separation was highly desirable to check many of the evils of state management. The question of terminal charges also remained unsettled. What was needed was final decision on uniform rates and fares, which could secure full and fair rates for all state lines, but those rates and fares remained subject to bureaucratic turf-fighting and manipulation by influential British businessmen.

Similarly, as we pointed out, the provision for automatic surrender of the railway company to the government without any compensation at the end of 99 years became meaningless by another provision under which any railway company, if it wished, could surrender its lines and works at anytime, and could receive compensation in full. This unconditional right of anytime surrender with full compensation gave the railway companies enormous power over the government. Thus if any railway company considered that the government control was too irksome, or its profits were not sufficient as was expected, or if more attractive ventures appeared than investment in railways, it could easily withdraw from this enterprise and shift to other more remunerative undertakings. Practically, the provision of unconditional right of anytime surrender with full compensation gave the railway companies some sort of liberty to carry out their construction and operation exactly as they liked at their own will. The promoters and shareholders were happy because they got the better share of their bargain and the railway companies were granted more than they demanded. They compelled the government to underwrite their annual dividends at the cost of Indian revenue. Railway undertakings in India were pre-eminent examples of private profit at public risk, to recall a famous formulation of Daniel Thorner.

The British businessmen and the British government (and the British Indian government) had similar outlook towards railway construction in India but from two different angles. While the promoters were anxious about protecting and profiting from their investment, the governments of England and India were equally worried about their political and economic stability and authority and control over the private enterprises in India. These acts and agreements were the reflection of some sort of compromise between the apparently conflicting views of the three parties and the provisions laid down in these legal papers gave the parties what they originally asked for. Basically, these acts and agreements were nothing but the papers of give and take which were legalized and accepted by the State and the private sectors. The state gave the right to enjoy absolute guaranteed interest and acquisition of huge amounts of land, and in exchange got the power of full control over the biggest and largest private sector in India. Authority was purchased by money and profit was earned at the cost of the Indian public. One can hardly say that problems like those of policy and management, rates and fares, financial administration, carriers' responsibility in transportation, better statutory protection to the users of rail, claims for safety arrangements, proper assessment of compensation for land acquisition, etc, were properly dealt within these legal papers. These acts and agreements were the legal documents that protected the interests of the dominant parties involved.

The railways of England greatly facilitated her industrialization; while in nineteenth century India, they further decimated indigenous industry by cheapening the distribution of imported machine-made commodities from Europe. The history of human civilization is replete with examples of institutions and instruments which may be progressive in one context but regressive in another. A discerning reader might get examples of such phenomenon from these documents and legal papers. Readers would find it a matter of political significance that the power lobbies and interest groups backing the Indian railways were more persistent in their diplomacy and opinion building than the British Cabinet and the GOI. The promoters succeeded in promoting a belief among the investing public that the ironclad guarantee of state aid was the only means of mobilizing resources for railways in India and taught them to put their faith in the state guarantee but not in unaided private enterprise. The guarantee system and unconditional right of anytime surrender with full compensation not only minimized the risk of private investment but also ensured all the public expenditure needed to satisfy the greed of the investors. Even if private investment in the railways on its own turned out to be unprofitable, the investing public would provide them with capital so long as the interest on that capital was guaranteed.

Moreover, railways helped in meeting the demand for Indian primary products to meet the growing needs of the industrial economy in England and Europe. On the other side, railways helped to push British products into the Indian market. More particularly, railway construction and operation in India expanded the market for the British steel industry. The higher cost of British steel as compared with Continental European steel was further aggravated by the exchange problem caused by the depreciation of the value of silver and of the Indian rupee during the last quarter of the nineteenth century. A large component of the so-called Home Charges was interest on railway debt.

The Indian people and Indian commodities also faced discrimination in railway freight policy. Goods on the long haul and carried by more than one railway system paid lower freight than goods transported for short distances. The transfer from one system to another was also costly. In this way the flow of manufactured goods from the port cities to the interior and of primary goods from the centres of production to the port cities for export was facilitated, while the inter-regional flow of goods became disadvantaged. This discouraged regional specialization and independent production centres for the development of a capitalist production system in India.

Moreover, by legal fiat the GOI treated the Indian employees and workers engaged in the railways, who constituted more than 95 percent of the total workforce of the railway industry, as 'servants'. They were then covered by the draconian Masters and Servants' legislation and were denied the rights of unionization, for example. Instead of the state being servant of the public as in democratic countries, the British power made the people of India 'servants' not of the state only but also of the British-managed private sector.

Hopefully, the previous three volumes and the present one would serve a significant academic purpose in restructuring the history of railway construction in India. Indeed an easy access to the published works should facilitate fresh interpretations of events that might unfold many untold stories with a significant bearing on various phases of the development of the Indian railways and the Indian economy.

Bhubanes Misra
Editor

PART I

Acts of Incorporation and Amalgamation of Indian Railway Companies (1849-1885)

361. Act of Incorporation of the East Indian Railway Company, 1849
362. Act of Incorporation of the Great Indian Peninsula Railway Company, 1849
363. Act of Incorporation of the Madras Railway Company, 1853
364. Act of Incorporation of the Bombay, Baroda, and Central India Railway Company, 1855
365. Act of Incorporation of the Scinde Railway Company, 1855
366. Act of Incorporation of the Eastern Bengal Railway Company, 1857
367. Act of Incorporation of the Great Southern of India Railway Company, 1858
368. The South Indian Railway Act, 1874 (Act for the Amalgamation of the Great Southern of India Railway Company and the Carnatic Railway Company into the South Indian Railway Company)

    Appendix to Part I
369. Indian Tramways Act, 1885

361

Act of Incorporation of the East Indian Railway Company, 1849

Source: Acts on Railways, London, 1886

ANNO DUODECIMO & DECIMO TERTIO
VICTORIÆ REGINÆ

Cap. XCIII

[An Act for incorporating the East Indian Railway Company, and for other purposes connected therewith. Act 12 and 13 Vic., Cap. 93, 1st August 1849]

Gist: The Act of Incorporation of the East Indian Railway Company passed in the British Parliament in August 1849 has 11 sections and legalizes the formation of the said company formed on 11 June 1845 in London with Roger Hunt and Thomas Harris Devonshire as trustees and the rest of members as shareholders, for constructing railways in India. The Act details the indenture of settlement made for the company between shareholders on 9 April 1847, objects of the company, powers of the General Body Meeting of shareholders, quorum, change of share values, conversion of debentures into shares, number of directors and change if any in their number, settlement of disputes by arbitration, and jurisdiction of suits if occurring. The initial capital was four million Pounds Sterling money of the United Kingdom of Great Britain and Ireland, divided into 80,000 shares of 50 Pounds each. It was made lawful for the company to enter into contracts and agreements with the East India Company (EIC) on behalf of the Government of India to construct railways, any telegraphs connected therewith, and any other facilities. This Act was enacted as a Public Act.

Whereas by an Indenture of Settlement bearing Date the Ninth day of April One thousand eight hundred and forty-seven, and made or expressed to be made between the several Persons whose Names and Seals are or shall be thereunto subscribed and affixed of the First Part, and Roger Hunt and Thomas Harris Devonshire, Gentlemen, of the Second Part, after reciting that on or about the Eleventh Day of June One thousand eight hundred and forty-five a Company was formed in the City of London for the Purpose of undertaking the Construction of Railways in India, under the Style or Title of the "East Indian Railway Company" and the Provisional Formation of the said Company by a certain Indenture or Subscription Contract bearing Date, the Day and Year last above mentioned, and made between the Several Persons whose Names and Seals were thereunto subscribed and affixed of the one Part and John Sims Weir, Gentleman, and the said Roger Hunt of the other Part, and that the Number of the Shares in the said Company taken or to be taken by the Persons / Parties to the said Indentures or Settlement now in recital of the First Part respectively was written opposite to their Names and Seals respectively subscribed and affixed to the same Indenture, it was witnessed, that for the Purpose of forming the Company, each of them the said several Persons / Parties to the said Indenture now in recital of the First Part covenanted with the said Roger Hunt and Thomas Harris Devonshire, who were Trustees on behalf of the Company, their Executors and Administrators, in manner following; (that is to say,) that the several Persons / Parties thereto of the First Part, and the several other Persons who should become Proprietors as therein-after mentioned, should, while holding Shares in the Capital of the Company, be and continue, until it should have been dissolved under the Provisions for that Purpose therein-after contained, a Company under the Names or Style of the East Indian Railway Company for the Purpose of acquiring and holding Lands in the East Indies and Great Britain, and making, acquiring, and working One or more Railway or Railways in India, with all necessary Works, Stock, and Conveniences, and of doing and performing all such Matters and Things as are generally done by Persons or Companies engaged in Business of the like and as extensive a Nature as might be deemed advisable or desirable for efficiently carrying into effect the Objects and Purposes aforesaid, including therein the working of Mines of Coal, Iron, and other Minerals in the East Indies, and manufacturing the Produce thereof, and the erecting and carrying on all necessary and convenient Works, Furnaces, Forges, Smelting-Houses, and Gasworks for furthering the Objects of the Company, and selling and disposing of such of the Produce thereof as from Time to Time should not be wanted or necessary for the making, repairing, or carrying on any Railway of the Company; and it was by the said Indenture now in recital further agreed, that the Capital of the Company should, in the first instance, and subject to the Powers therein-after given to increase the same by the issue of new Shares, consist of the Sum of Four million Pounds Sterling Money of the United Kingdom of Great Britain and Ireland, and be divided into Eighty thousand Shares of Fifty Pounds each, and it was further provided that the Board of Directors of the said Company might from Time to Time, as and when and on such terms as they should think fit, allot and issue, either to Proprietors of Shares in the said Company or to any Person or Persons whomsoever, any of the said Eighty thousand Shares which should not have been subscribed for, and might also, at such Times and such Prices and on such Conditions as they might think proper, sell, issue, and otherwise dispose of, either to Proprietors for the Time being of Shares in the Company or to any Person or Persons whomsoever, all or any of the Shares in the Company, whether original or created in pursuance of the Powers therein-after contained and herein-after mentioned, and further that the principal Place for carrying on the Business of the Company should be in London, and further, that subject and without Prejudice to the Powers therein-after given to the General Meetings of Proprietors, the Affairs of the Company should be conducted by and under the Superintendence and Direction of a Board of Directors, and Powers were thereby given to the Board of Directors on behalf of the said Company to enter into and conclude such Contracts, Agreements, and Arrangements as therein mentioned;

and it was by the said Indenture of Settlement further provided, that the said Board of Directors should, when and so soon as the same Indenture should have been executed by the Proprietors of One equal Fourth of the Number of the said Eighty thousand original Shares, have Power from Time to Time or at one Time by a Resolution or Resolutions to increase the capital of the Company by an Amount not exceeding Ten million Pounds of lawful Money of Great Britain, so that the Capital might amount to Fourteen million Pounds, by the Creation of a Number of new or additional Shares of Fifty Pounds each, over and above the said Number of Eighty thousand original Shares; and it was by the said Indenture of Settlement further provided, that after Nine-Tenths of the original Shares in the Company, and of the new or additional Shares therein-after authorized as aforesaid to be created for increasing to Capital of the Company, should have been taken or subscribed for, it should be lawful for any Extraordinary General Meeting of the Proprietors, to be specially called for the Purpose, from Time to Time to authorize the Board of Directors further to increase the Capital of the Company by such an Amount not extending Six millions as should be determined upon from Time to Time by any such Meeting or Meetings, by creating further new Shares in the Company, of such Amount per Share as by such Extraordinary General Meeting should from Time to Time be deemed expedient: And whereas the greater Part of the said Eighty thousand original Shares of Fifty Pounds each in the Capital of the said Company were taken and subscribed for prior to the Month of June One thousand eight hundred and forty-seven, and the Subscribers for the same respectively executed the said recited Deed of Settlement, and the said Company was, on or about the Fifteenth day of May One thousand eight hundred and forty-seven, completely registered at the Office of the Registrar of Joint Stock Companies appointed under the Act passed in the Session of Parliament held in the Seventh and Eighth Years of the Reign of Her present Majesty, intituled An Act for the Registration, Incorporation, and Regulation of the Joint-Stock Companies: And whereas, in pursuance of the Power contained in the said recited Indenture of Settlement, the Board of Directors of the said Company, at a Board or Meeting of Directors duly held at the Office of the Company on the Second Day of June One thousand eight hundred and forty-seven, came to a Resolution that the Capital of the Company, as originally constituted, should be extended from Four million Pounds to Twelve million Pounds Sterling, and that One hundred and sixty thousand new Shares of Fifty Pounds each in the constituted Company should be created and issued to represent such Extension capital: And whereas a considerable Number of the said One hundred and sixty thousand new Shares of Fifty Pounds each in the increased Capital of the said Railway Company have also been taken and subscribed for; and by an Indenture bearing Date the Sixth Day of September One thousand eight hundred and forty-seven; and made or expressed to be made between the several Persons whose Names and Seals are or shall be thereunto subscribed and affixed, being respectively Persons who have taken and subscribed for new Shares in the said increased Capital of the Company, of the First Part, and the said Roger Hunt and Thomas Harris Devonshire of the Second Part, each of them the said several Persons Parties thereto of the First Part hath covenanted with the said Roger Hunt and Thomas Harris Devonshire, their Executors and Administrators, as Trustees on behalf of the Company, that the several Persons Parties of the First Part had become Proprietors in the said East Indian Railway Company in respect of such of the said new or Extension of Shares as had been taken by them, as in the same Indenture is mentioned, and would, whilst holding Shares in the Capital of the Company, be and continue Proprietors and Partners in a Company, and would fully and punctually observe and perform and abide by and conform to, in all respects so far as they related to or concerned him, her, or them, or the Shares held by him, her, or them in the Capital of the Company, all and every Covenants, Agreements, Regulations, and Stipulations contained in the said recited Indenture of Settlement of the Ninth Day of April One thousand eight hundred forty-seven: And whereas the Board of Directors of the said Company is now composed of the following Persons, (that is to say,) Henry Aglionby Aglionby, Bazett David Colvin, Joseph Baxendale, Robert Merttins Bird, Charles Dashwood Bruce, John Cattley, James Denis De Vitre, Thomas Seddon Kelsall, John Pascal Larkins, Alexander Nairne, John Stewart, Ronald Macdonald Stephenson, and Robert Wigram Crawford, which said Persons are the present Directors of the Company: And whereas Negotiations have been commenced and are still in progress between the said Railway Company and the East India Company, with a view to the Construction by the former of a Line of Railway in India, upon such Terms and Conditions as shall be mutually agreed between them; but the Objects and Purposes of the same Railway Company cannot be effectually carried out without the Incorporation of the said Railway Company and the Authority of Parliament: May it therefore please Your Majesty that it may be enacted; and be it enacted by the Queen's most Excellent Majesty, by and with the Advice and Consent of the Lord's Spiritual and Temporal, and Commons, in this present Parliament assembled, and by the Authority of the same, That the said Directors, and the several other Persons and Corporations who are Proprietors and Shareholders, and the several other Persons and Corporations who shall become Proprietors and Shareholders in the said Railway Company, and their respective Executors, Administrators, Successors, and Assigns, shall be and are hereby united into one Body Corporate under the Name of "The East Indian Railway Company," for the purpose of making and constructing, working and maintaining such Railway or Railways in the East Indies, including all necessary, accessory, or convenient Extensions, Branches, Stocks, and Works as may be agreed upon by the said Railway Company and the East India Company, and also of doing and performing all such Matters and Things necessary or convenient for carrying into effect the Objects and Purposes aforesaid, as may also be agreed upon by the said Railway Company and East India Company; and the Company hereby incorporated by the Name aforesaid shall have perpetual Succession and a Common Seal, and by that Name shall and may sue and be sued as well in the Territories now under the Government of the East India Company as elsewhere, and shall have Power to purchase, take, and hold Lands in the said Territories, and in Great Britain, for the Purposes aforesaid, without incurring any Penalties or Forfeitures, and shall have such other Powers as herein-after mentioned.

II. And be it enacted, That all Property, Real and Personal, and all Deeds, Books, and Writings, belonging to the Company or which have been conveyed to or are held by any Person in trust for the Company, and all Rights and Powers of the Company, subject to any Engagements affecting the same, shall be vested in the Company, without the Necessity of any Transfer or connecting Title other than this Act; and all Contracts, Covenants, Engagements, and Liabilities now existing with or by the said Railway Company, or any Director, Trustee, or Person on behalf of the said Railway Company, other than any of the Covenants of the said Deed of

Settlement which are superseded by the Provisions herein-after contained, shall and may be binding, fulfilled, and enforced by, with, and against the Company hereby incorporated, and such incorporated Company shall and may sue and be sued in respect thereof, in the same Manner as if such incorporated Company had been Party thereto.

III. And be it enacted, That the said Company incorporated by this Act shall be and continue to be regulated by the said Deed of Settlement bearing Date the Ninth Day of April One thousand eight hundred and forty-seven, and the said Deed bearing Date the Sixth Day of September One thousand eight hundred and forty-seven, save and except so far as the same or either of them are or is altered or varied by this Act, or may be altered, varied, or affected by any Agreement, Contract, or Arrangement made under the Powers and Provisions of this Act, but shall be subject to and have the Benefit of the Clauses and Provisions of the "Companies Clauses Consolidation Act, 1845," as if the same Act had been expressly made applicable to such a Case as is intended to be provided for by this Act, in respect to the Construction of this Act, and with respect to the Distribution of the Capital of the Company into Shares, the Certificates of Proprietorship of Shares being admissible in all Courts in India as prima facie Evidence of Title, as in the other Courts referred to in the Companies Clauses Consolidation Act, and the Consolidation of the Shares into Stock, and with respect to the Payment of Subscriptions and the Means of enforcing the Payment of Calls, and with respect to the Forfeiture of Shares for Nonpayment of Calls, and which Provisions of the said last-mentioned Act, and no others, are hereby extended to and incorporated with this Act.

IV. And be it enacted, That it shall and may be lawful for the Company from Time to Time to enter into and conclude with the East India Company, on account of the Government of India, such Contracts, Agreements, and Arrangements as the respective Parties may think fit and agree upon for making any Railway or Railways in India, and any Telegraphs connected therewith, and for maintaining and working the same, and for the other Objects and Purposes aforesaid, including, so far as the said respective Parties may agree thereto, all or any of the Provisions following; (that is to say,) any Provisions for securing to the East India Company any Facilities, Rights, and Advantages in relation to the said Railways and Premises respectively; and any Provisions as to the Tolls, Receipts, and Profits, and any Provisions for giving to the East India Company, and to say of their Officers, Servants, or Agents, any absolute or other Rights of supervising, controlling, directing, regulating, and ordering the said Railway Company, and the Works, Contracts, Accounts, Byelaws, Acts, Proceedings, Transactions, and Affairs of the said Railway Company, as well in England as elsewhere; and any Provisions for enabling the East India Company to appoint an ex-officio Director of the said Railway Company, whether qualified by holding Shares or not, in the Place of any One of the ordinary Directors of the said Company or otherwise; and any Provisions for regulating the Powers, including even a Right of Veto at the Board of Directors, and the Duties and Proceedings and the Liabilities of any such official Director; and any Provisions for binding the said Railway Company to conform to and fulfill all or any Directions which may be given by the East India Company or their authorized Officers and Agents touching all or any of the Matters aforesaid; and any Provisions for the Appointment of Agents of the said Railway Company in India or elsewhere, and for determining and regulating the Powers and Duties of such Agents as aforesaid; and any

Provisions for depositing with or paying to the East India Company all or any Part of the subscribed Capital of the Company, upon any Terms (as to Interest or otherwise) to be agreed upon; and any Provisions with regard to any Land which may be granted or leased to the Company by the East India Company or otherwise, and any Provisions for charging all or any Part of the Property of the Company with any Sum or Sums of Money upon any Terms to be agreed upon; and any Provisions for the Surrender or Sale to the East India Company, or to any other Person or Persons, of the said Railway or Railways or any part thereof, and of all or any Part of the Property of the Company at any future Period; and any Provisions for referring Disputes to Arbitration; and any Provisions intended to enforce or secure the due performance of any Contract or Engagement to be made by the Company; and generally all such Provisions and Stipulations in relation to the Matters aforesaid and any of them, and in relation to the Undertaking of the Company and the Encouragement and Promotion thereof, and the eventual or contingent Transfer of the same or any Part thereof to the East India Company, as the said respective Parties shall think fit and agree upon, and from Time to Time to vary and alter such Contracts, Agreements, and Arrangements and to enter into new or other Contracts, Agreements, and Arrangements, in relation to the Premises, all which Contracts, Agreements, and Arrangements (whether the same shall or not be within the Objects originally contemplated by the said Company, or in accordance with the Provisions and Clauses by which the Company would otherwise be governed) shall be valid and effectual, and binding to all Intents and Purposes whatsoever, and full Effect shall be given to the same accordingly; and in case there shall be included in any such Contract, Agreement, and Arrangement, any Provisions for referring Disputes to Arbitration, the Arbitrators or their Umpire shall, so far as there shall be no Provision to the contrary in any such Contract, Agreement, or Arrangement, have all such Powers as are given to Arbitrators or their Umpire by the Provisions in that Behalf included in the Clauses contained in the said Clauses Consolidation Act with respect to the Settlement of Disputes by Arbitration.

V. Provided always, and be it enacted, That in all Cases in which it is or shall be for any Purpose required by the said Deed of Settlement, bearing Date the Ninth day of April One thousand eight hundred and forty-seven, or otherwise, that any Notice should be given to the Proprietors of the Company, it shall not be necessary to give such Notice by sending a Circular Letter to each Proprietor, but it shall be sufficient from and after the passing of this Act, to cause an Advertisement giving such Notice to be inserted in any Two Newspapers published at least Six Days in the Week in London or Westminster.

VI. Provided always, and be it enacted, That until more than Twenty Pounds each shall have been called up on the original Fifty Pounds Shares in the Company the said Company shall have Power at any Time after the passing of this Act, by a Resolution or Resolutions of a Board or Boards of Directors, to reduce and alter the Shares in the Company from Fifty Pounds to Twenty Pounds each, and to make a new Division of the Capital of the Company into Shares of Twenty Pounds each, and on such Division shall and may allot and apportion to every Shareholder for the Time being in the Company, One of such Twenty Pounds Share previously held by such Shareholder, and to issue and dispose of the Remainder of the Shares necessary to make up the Capital of the Company in such Manner, on such Terms, and at such

Time or Times as they shall see fit, and to number such Shares anew, and thenceforth every Holder of a Twenty Pounds Share shall be entitled to attend at General Meetings and to give one vote in respect of such Share, but in all other Cases where any Number of Shares is necessary to give to a Shareholder a Qualification for any office, or to entitle him to give any Number of votes more than One at a General Meeting or Ballot, or to any other Privilege or Power, he must hold a Number of Such Twenty Pounds Shares in the Proportion of Two and a Half for every Fifty Pounds Shares which have been required to give him or them such Qualification or such Number of Votes or other Privilege or Power; any/every such Holder of or Person entitled to a Twenty Pounds Share shall be subject and liable in respect thereof to all the Covenants, Engagements, and Liabilities to which he was before subject or liable in respect of his Fifty Pounds Shares to the Extent of such Share of Twenty Pounds, and to the Calls and Installments that may be or may have been made or become payable upon or in respect of such Share, whether of Fifty Pounds or Twenty Pounds; and every Person being a Holder of or entitled to a Share of Fifty Pounds shall remain and continue liable to all Covenants, Engagements, Liabilities, Calls, and Installments in respect thereof so long as the same shall continue to be held as a Share of Fifty Pounds.

VII. And be it enacted, That it shall and may be lawful for the said Company, by a Resolution or Resolutions of a Board or Boards of Directors from Time to Time after the Reduction of Fifty Pounds Shares into Twenty Pounds Shares, to create and issue Half Shares of Ten Pounds each or Quarter Shares of Five Pounds each, and to prescribe Time and Mode of Payment of the Amount of such Shares by One or more Installment or Installments; and all and every the Powers contained in the said Deed of Settlement relating to Shares, and also the said Clauses and Provisions in the said "Companies Clauses Consolidation Act" with respect to the Payment of Subscriptions and the Means of enforcing the Payment of Calls, and to the Forfeiture of Shares, and Consolidation of the Shares into Stock, shall extend and apply to the said Shares of Ten Pounds and Five Pounds to be created and issued under the Powers herein contained; and the Proprietor of Two Shares of Ten Pounds and Four Shares of Five Pounds each shall have the like Powers of voting and otherwise as a Proprietor of One Twenty Pounds Share, and shall also be entitled from Time to Time to Interest or Dividends on the said Shares ratably with the Proprietors of other Shares on the Amount for the Time being paid up on the said Half or Quarter Shares.

VIII. And whereas the Board of Directors of the said Company are empowered and authorized by the said Deed of Settlement to issue Debentures to the Amount of Shares not for the Time being taken or subscribed for in Sums of Fifty Pounds to One thousand Pounds each, convertible into Shares as therein mentioned; Be it enacted, That it shall be lawful for the Board of Directors of the said Company for the Time being to issue such convertible Debentures for any sum not less than Five Pounds each, and that all and every Powers contained in the said Deed of Settlement in regard to convertible Debenture of Fifty Pounds and upwards shall extend equally to the Debenture of Five Pounds and upwards authorized by this Act: Provided that every Debenture made or issued under the Provisions of this Act shall be chargeable with and duly stamped for devoting the Payment of the *ad valorem* Stamp Duty payable upon a Mortgage for a like Amount, and that every Transfer or Assignment of any such Debenture shall be by

Deed duly stamped, wherein the Consideration for the same shall be truly stated.

IX. And be it enacted, That any Declarations which by the said Companies Clauses Consolidation Act are authorized to be made before a Justice or before a Master in Chancery shall be of the same Force and Effect if made before a Justice of the Peace or Magistrate in India, or before any Officer authorized to take an Affidavit or Declaration in the Supreme Court of any of the Presidencies.

X. And whereas by the said Deed of Settlement it is provided, that it shall be lawful for the Proprietors at any Extraordinary General Meeting to be held after the First General Meeting of the Company to alter and vary the Number of Directors, so as the same shall not be reduced below Twelve nor increased beyond Twenty-four, and so from Time to Time; and that in case of any Alteration in the then present Number of Eighteen Directors, it should be lawful for the Proprietors of any General Meeting to make such Alterations as they should judge fit in the Number of Directors required to constitute a Quorum, or to do any Acts, and for which a Board of Directors was or should be required: Be it enacted, That it shall be lawful for the Proprietors at any General Meeting to alter and vary the Number of Directors so as the same shall not be reduced below Six nor increased beyond Eighteen, and so from Time to Time; and in case of any Alternation in the Number of Directors by which the Number shall be made other than Eighteen, it shall be lawful for the Proprietors at any General Meeting to make such Alternations as they shall judge fit in the Number of Directors required to constitute a Quorum, or to do any Acts for which a Board of Directors is or shall be required.

XI. And be it enacted, that this Act shall be a Public Act, and shall be judicially taken notice of as such, and may be amended or repealed in this present Session of Parliament.

London: Printed by George Edward Eyre and William Spottiswoode, Printers to the Queen's most Excellent Majesty, 1858.

362

Act of Incorporation of the Great Indian Peninsula Railway Company, 1849

Source: Acts on Railways, London, 1886

ANNO DUODECIMO AND DECIMO TERTIO
VICTORIÆ REGINÆ

Cap. LXXXIII

[An Act to incorporate the Great Indian Peninsula Railway Company, and for other Purposes connected therewith. Act 12 and 13 Vic., Cap. 83, 1st August 1849]

Gist: The Act of Incorporation of the Great Indian Peninsula Railway Company passed in the British Parliament on 1 August 1849 is a Public Act with 20 sections. This is made a registered company, with deed of settlement signed on 16 April 1849, for establishing railway connection between Bombay and other parts of India on terms mutually agreeable to the company and East India Company (EIC). Seed capital was five lakh Pounds with one lakh shares of 5 Pounds each. There were 9 founder directors with number of them flexible between 8 and 19. Provisions are there for legal suits, jurisdiction of suits, rotation of directors, power to purchase and hold lands (including in Great Britain), necessary extensions, branches, stocks and works, conversion of borrowed money into capital, and consolidation of shares into stock. Section 5 of the Act provides more powers to the EIC.

Whereas under or by virtue of a Deed of Settlement bearing Date the Sixteenth Day of April One thousand eight hundred and forty-nine, made in conformity with the Act passed in the Seventh and Eighth Years of Her Majesty, intituled An Act for the Registration, Incorporation, and Regulation of Joint Stock Companies, and of the Act for amending the same, the several Persons hereinafter named are associated together with certain other Persons as a Company (completely registered), under the Name of the Great Indian Peninsula Railway Company, for the Purpose of establishing Railway Communication between Bombay and other Parts of India on such Terms and Conditions as may be agreed upon by the said Railway Company and the East India Company, and with Powers reserved by the said Deed to the said Railway Company of extending and varying their Undertaking; and by the said Deed the Capital of the said Railway Company is fixed at the Sum of Five hundred thousand Pounds (but subject to be increased to the Sum of One million Pounds in certain Events), and is divided into One hundred thousand

Shares of five Pounds each, of or to which the Persons herein-after named and other Persons aforesaid are or are entitled as the registered Shareholders of the said Railway Company; and the said Deed of Settlement contains Covenants on the Part of the Shareholders, Parties thereto, the they will remain associated in a Company for the Business or Purpose of making, constructing, working, and maintaining a Railway as therein mentioned, according to the Provisions of the said Act for the Registration, Incorporation, and Regulation of Joint Stock Companies, and the said Act for amending the last-mentioned Act, and with and subject to all the Powers, Rights, and Privileges which under or by virtue of the said Acts of the Company shall lawfully have, exercise, and be liable to on its complete Registration being certified according to the same Acts, and under and subject to the Provisions in the said Deed of Settlement contained, which Provisions are contained in certain Clauses and numbered respectively from One to Ninety-seven inclusive: And whereas the Directors of the said Railway Company are now the Right Honourable the Lord Wharncliffe, and William John Hamilton, Frederick Ayrton, Robert Wigram Crawford, John Griffith Frith, Robert William Kennard, Cornelius Nicholson, William Nicol, and Melvil Wilson, Esquires: And whereas Negotiations are still in progress between the said Railway Company and the East India Company with a view to the Construction by the said Railway Company of the said Railway, and the establishing of such Railway Communication as aforesaid, upon such Terms and Conditions as shall be mutually agreed upon between them, which Terms and Conditions may in some respects vary from what was contemplated at the Date of the said Deed of Settlement: And whereas the Objects and Purposes of the said Railway Company cannot be effectually carried out without the Incorporation of the said Railway Company and the Authority of Parliament: May it therefore please Your Majesty that it may be enacted; and be it enacted by the Queen's most Excellent Majesty, by and which the Advice and Consent of the Lord's Spiritual and Temporal, and Commons, in this present Parliament assembled, and by the Authority of the same, That the Right Honourable the Lord Wharncliffe, William John Hamilton, Frederick Ayrton, Robert Wigram Crawford, John Griffith Frith, Robert William Kennard, Cornelius Nicholson, William Nicol, and Melvil Wilson, Esquires, and the several other Persons and Corporations who are or shall become Proprietors and Shareholders in the said Railway Company, and their respective Executors, Administrators, Successors and Assigns, shall be and are hereby united into One Body Corporate, under the name of "The Great Indian Peninsula Railway Company," for the Purpose of making and constructing, working and maintaining such Railway or Railways in the East Indies, including all necessary convenient, or accessory Extensions, Branches, Stocks, and Works as may be agreed upon by the said Railway Company and the East India Company, and also of doing and performing all such Matters and Things necessary or convenient for carrying into effect the Objects and Purposes aforesaid as may also be agreed upon by the said Railway Company and the East India Company; and the Company hereby incorporated by the Name aforesaid shall have perpetual succession and a Common Seal, and by the Name aforesaid shall and may sue and be sued, and shall have Power to purchase, take, and hold Lands for the Purposes aforesaid (including Lands in Great Britain for the Purpose of the Business of the same Company) without incurring any Penalties or Forfeitures, and shall have such other Powers as hereinafter mentioned.

II. And be it enacted, That the following Words and Expressions in this Act shall have several Meanings hereby assigned to them, unless there be something in the Subject or Context repugnant to such Construction; (that is to say,) Words importing the Plural Number only shall include the Plural Number, and words importing the Plural Number only shall include the Singular Number; Words importing the Masculine Gender only shall include Females; the Expression "this Act" shall include all clauses and Provisions incorporated therewith; the Expression "the Consolidation Act" shall mean the Companies Clauses Consolidation Act, 1845; the Expression "the Company" shall mean the said Railway Company incorporated by this Act; the Expression "the Directors" shall mean the Directors of the Company having the management in Great Britain of the Affairs of the Company; the word "Shareholder" shall mean Shareholder, Proprietor, or Member of the Company; and in referring to any such Shareholder Expressions properly applicable to a Person shall be held to apply to a Corporation.

III. And be it enacted, That all Property, real and Personal, and all Deeds, Books, and Workings, belonging to the Company, or which have been conveyed to or are held by any Person in trust for the Company, and all Rights and Powers of the Company subject to any Engagements affecting the same, shall be vested in the Company without the Necessity of any Transfer or connecting Title other than this Act; and all Contracts, Covenants, Engagements, and Liabilities now existing with or by the said Railway Company, or any Director, Trustee, or Person on behalf of the said Railway Company (other than any of the Covenants of the said Deed of Settlement which are superseded by the Provisions herein-after contained), shall and may be enforced by, with, and against the Company hereby incorporated, and such incorporated Company shall and may sue and be sued in respect thereof in the same Manner as if such Company had been Party thereto.

IV. And be it enacted, That the Provisions of the said Act of the Seventh and Eighth Years of Her Majesty, and of the said Act for amending the same, so far as the same Provisions are by the said Deed of Settlement made applicable to the said Company and the Affairs of the same, shall no longer be of force or effect as applied to the said Company; and also that the said several Clauses of the said Deed numbered respectively from one to Ninety-seven shall no longer be of any Force, but shall be and the same are hereby superseded (without Prejudice to any Resolution, Acts, Matters, or Things already passed, made, done, or transacted under or by virtue of the same or confirmed by the same), and that in lieu of and in addition to the same Clauses (without Prejudice as aforesaid) the Company shall be subject to the Clauses and Provisions of "The Companies Clauses Consolidation Act, 1845," as if the same Act had been expressly made applicable to such a Case as is intended to be provided for by this Act with respect to the Matters following; (that is to say,) the Distribution of the Capital of the Company into Shares, the Transfer or Transmission of Shares, the Payment of Subscriptions and the Means of enforcing the Payment of Calls, the Forfeiture of Shares for Non-payment of Calls, the Remedies of Creditors of the Company against the Shareholders, the Conversion of the borrowed Money into Capital, the Consolidation of the Shares into Stock, the General Meetings of the Company and the Exercise of the Right of voting by the Shareholders, the Appointment and Rotation of Directors, the Powers of the Directors and the Powers of the Company to be exercised only in General Meetings, the Proceedings and Liabilities of the Directors, the Appointment and Duties of the Auditors, the Accountability of the Officers of the Company, the keeping of Accounts and the Right of Inspections thereof by the Shareholders, the making of Dividends, the making of Byelaws, the giving of Notices, and the Provision to be made for affording Access to the special Act by all Parties interested, save so far as the same Provisions are expressly varied by the Provisions herein contained; and that as to the said Clauses with respect to the Distribution of the Capital of the Company into Shares, the Certificate of the Proprietorship of Shares shall be admissible in the Supreme Courts of Judicature in India as prima facie Evidence of Title as in the Courts mentioned in the same Clauses; and that as to the said Clauses with respect to the Payment of Subscriptions and the Means of enforcing the Payment of Calls, the Supreme Courts of Judicature in India shall have jurisdiction in Cases where the Company shall sue Shareholders in India for the Amount of Calls, and the same Course of Procedure shall be adopted in all Actions and Suits in the said Supreme Courts as in Actions and Suits in England in the like Matters under the last mentioned Clauses; and that as to the said Clauses with respect to the Remedies of Creditors against the Shareholders, the Supreme Courts of Judicature in India shall have Power to order Execution to be issued against Shareholders residing in India, such Shareholders being entitled to such Reimbursement as in the said last-mentioned Clauses is provided; and that as the said Clauses with respect to the Proceedings and liabilities of the Directors, every Entry signed by the Chairman of a Meeting as in the same Clauses mentioned shall be admissible as Evidence in Supreme Courts of Judicature in India as well as the Courts mentioned in the same Clauses; and that as to be the said Clauses with respect to the Accountability of the Officers of the Company, Justices of Peace or Magistrates in India shall, in all matters occurring in India, have the same Powers as under the same Clauses are exercisable by Justices in England in Matters occurring there; and that as to the said Clauses with respect to the making of Byelaws, Byelaws have to effect in India shall be not repugnant to the Laws of India; and that as to the said Clauses with respect to the giving of Notices, the Reference in the same Clauses to any Act for the Relief of Insolvent Debtors shall be construed to include the Act or Acts of Parliament for the Time being in force relating to the insolvent Debtors in India; and the Secretary or Treasurer of the Company shall have Power to authorize by Letter of Attorney some other Officer in India of the Company to represent the Company in all Cases of Bankruptcy or Insolvency in India, and to act therein in like Manner as it shall be lawful for the Secretary or Treasurer of the Company to act under the last-mentioned Clauses in like Cases in England; and the Provision made by the same Clauses for the Tender of Amends shall be held to apply to Tender of Amends in India; and that as to the said Clauses with respect to the Provision to be made for affording Access to the Special Act by all Parties interested, a copy of the Special Act shall be kept in the principal Place of Business in England; and that any Declarations which by the Consolidation Act are authorized to be made before a Justice or before a Master in Chancery shall be of the same Force and Effect if made before a Justice of the Peace or Magistrate in India, or before any Officer authorized to take an Affidavit or Declaration in any of the Supreme Courts of Judicature in India.

V. And be it enacted, That it shall and may be lawful for the Company from Time to Time to enter into and conclude with the East India Company on account of the Government of India such Contracts, Agreements, and Arrangements as the respective Parties may think fit and agree upon for making any Railway or Railways in India and any Telegraphs connected therewith, and for maintaining and working the same, and for other Objects and Purposes aforesaid, including, so far as the respective Parties may agree thereto, all or any of the Provisions following: (that is to say,) any Provisions for securing to the East India Company any Facilities, Rights and Advantages in relation to the said Railways and Premises respectively; and any Provision as to the Tolls, Receipts, and Profits thereof, and the Application of such Tolls, Receipts, and Profits; and any Provisions for giving to the East India Company, and to any of their Officers, Servants, or Agents, any absolute or other Rights of supervising, controlling, directing, regulating, and ordering the Company, and the Works, Contracts, Accounts, Byelaws, Acts, Proceedings, Transactions, and affairs of the Company as well in England as elsewhere; and any Provisions for enabling the East India Company to appoint an ex officio Director of the Company, whether qualified by holding of Shares or not, in the Place of any One of the ordinary Directors of the Company, or otherwise; and any Provisions for regulating the Powers, including a Right of Veto at the Board of Directors, and the Duties and Proceedings and Liabilities of any such official Director; and any Provisions for binding the Company to conform to and fulfil all or any Directions which may be given by the East India Company or their authorized Officers and Agents touching all or any of the Matters aforesaid; and any Provisions for the Appointment of Agents of the Company in India or elsewhere, and for determining and regulating the Powers and Duties of such Agents as aforesaid, and any Provisions for depositing with or paying to the East India Company all or any Part of the subscribed Capital of the Company upon any Terms (as to interest or otherwise) to be agreed upon; and any Provisions with regard to any Land which may be granted or leased to the Company by the East India Company or otherwise; and any Provisions for charging all or any Part of the Property of the Company with any Sum or Sums of Money upon any Terms to be agreed upon; and any Provisions for the Surrender or Sale to the East India Company or to any other Person or Persons of the said Railway or Railways, or any Part thereof, and all or any Part of the Property of the Company, at any future Period; and any Provisions for referring Disputes to Arbitration; and any Provisions intended to enforce or secure the due Performance of any Contract or Engagement to be made by the Company; and generally all such Provisions and Stipulations in relation to the Matters aforesaid and any of them, and in relation to the Undertakings of the Company and the Encouragement and Promotion thereof, and the eventual or contingent Transfer of the same or any Part thereof to the East India Company, as the said respective Parties shall think fit and agree upon, and from Time to Time to vary and alter such Contracts, Agreements, and Arrangements, and to enter into new or other Contracts, Agreements, and Arrangements in relation to the Premises; all which Contracts, Agreements, and Arrangements (whether the same shall or not be within the Objects originally contemplated by the said Company, or in accordance with the Provisions and Clauses by which the Company would otherwise be governed) shall be valid and effectual and binding to all Intents and Purposes whatsoever, and full Effect shall be given to the same accordingly.

VI. And be it enacted, That the Capital shall be in the first instance the said existing Capital of Five hundred thousand Pounds in One hundred thousand Shares of Five Pounds each.

VII. And be it enacted, That Three Calendar Months at the least shall be the Interval between successive Calls on the said Shares respectively, and no such Call shall exceed Twenty Shillings per Share.

VIII. And be it enacted, That the General Meetings of the Shareholders shall be held in London and the Ordinary General Meetings of the Shareholders shall be held in the Months of April and October in each year, or at such other stated Periods as shall be appointed for that Purpose by an Order of a General Meeting of the Shareholders, and the First Ordinary Meeting shall be held in April one thousand eight hundred and fifty.

IX. And be it enacted, That it shall be lawful for the Company from Time to Time to consolidate into any less Number the Shares into which the capital for the Time being, or any Part thereof, of the Company shall for the Time being be divided; and such consolidated Shares shall be Shares within the Meeting and Intent of the Provisions to which Shares are subject by this Act, or by virtue thereof: Provided always, that as to any aliquot Part of such Capital whereof the Shares shall be so consolidated, which aliquot Part shall not after such consolidation represent an entire consolidated Shares in such Capital, it shall be lawful for the Company to purchase such aliquot part, or the then existing original Share representing such aliquot Part, at the Value of such original Share at the Time of making of such Consolidation, and the aggregate of such purchased Capital may be re-issued in the consolidated Shares in such Manner and on such Terms as the Company shall think fit.

X. And be it enacted, That in event of any Agreement being made between the Company and the East India Company by which any Amount of Interest shall be guaranteed to the Company, it shall be lawful for the Directors to attach to any Certificates of paid-up Shares in the Capital for the Time being of the Company or of any Capital Stock of the Company, any subsidiary Certificate in the Nature of Interest Warrants or Coupons payable pursuant thereto, due regard being had to the Nature of such Agreement as aforesaid.

XI. And be it enacted, That when and so soon as from Time to Time the whole of the Capital for the Time being of the Company shall have been subscribed for, and One Half of such Capital shall have been paid-up, it shall be lawful for the Company from Time to Time, by Order of a General Meeting, to borrow Money to an Amount in the whole equal to One Third Part of such Capital for the Time being, and such Money shall be borrowed in the Manner provided by the said Clauses with respect to the Conversion of the borrowed Money into Capital, or shall be borrowed in any such other Manner and subject in all respects to such Provisions, as the East India Company shall from Time to Time approve; and such of the Clauses or Provisions of the Consolidation Act with respect to the borrowing of Money by the Company on Mortgage or Bond as make Provision for the Powers of borrowing, and for sufficient Evidence of the Fact of the Capital required to be subscribed or paid-up having been so subscribed or paid-up, and of the Order for borrowing Money having been made, and for the granting of the Certificate therein mentioned in that Behalf, shall extend to the borrowing of Money hereby authorized.

XII. And be it enacted, That the Quorum to be present, either personally or by Proxy, in order to constitute a Meeting of the Shareholders, shall be Shareholders holding in the aggregate not less than One Fiftieth of the Capital of the Company, and being in Number not less than Twenty.

XIII. And be it enacted, That (notwithstanding anything in the Consolidation Acts contained to the contrary) the Power of authorizing Proxies contained in the Consolidation Act shall, as to the Proxies authorized by Shareholders resident out of the United Kingdom, extend to the authorizing of Proxies to vote at all or any Meetings in the United Kingdom to be held thereafter within such Period from the Date of the Instrument of Proxy as shall be mentioned therein, and such Instrument of Proxy shall not be liable to any Stamp Duty to which the Instrument of Proxy authorized by the Consolidation Act, if executed by such Shareholders out of the United Kingdom, would not be liable: Provided always, that no Person shall be Proxy for more than Twenty Shareholders: Provided also, that no Person shall be entitled to vote by way of Proxy unless the Instrument of Proxy have been transmitted to or lodged with the Secretary or Clerk of the Company not less than Forty-eight Hours before the Time appointed for holding every Meeting at which the same is to be used.

XIV. And be it enacted, That the Number of Directors shall be Nine, and the said existing Directors shall be the First Directors of the Company.

XV. And be it enacted, That it shall be lawful for the Company from Time to Time increase or reduce the Number of the Directors within the limits of the Numbers Nineteen and Eight.

XVI. And be it enacted, That the Number of Shares of which a Person shall be possessed in order that he may be capable of being a Director shall be Fifty at least.

XVII. And be it enacted, That (notwithstanding anything in the Consolidation Act contained to the contrary) the existing Chairman and Deputy Chairman of the Directors shall be First Chairman and Deputy Chairman of the Directors held after each annual Appointment of Directors the Choice of the Chairman of the Directors and of the Deputy Chairman shall be in all respects according to the Provisions in this Behalf of the Consolidation Act.

XVIII. And be it enacted, That the Newspaper in which Notices shall be advertised shall be some Newspapers published at least Six Days in the Week in London or Middlesex.

XIX. And whereas the said Capital of Five hundred thousand Pounds was fixed upon with a view to making in the first instance a Railway from Bombay to Callian, and the Company may under Agreements with the East India Company be empowered to make Railways of much greater Extent, and for which the said Capital of Five hundred thousand Pounds would be insufficient: Be it enacted, That in case, under any such Agreement or Agreements to be so made with the East India Company, the Company shall be enabled to make any Railway or Railways of Greater Extent in the whole than a Railway from Bombay to Callian, it shall be lawful for the Directors and they shall have Power (notwithstanding anything in the Consolidation Act contained) to increase the Capital of the Company to the Sum of One million Sterling; and further, that in case the Company shall under any Agreement or Agreements with the East India Company be empowered to make or carry on any Railway or Railways or Works in India, it shall be lawful for the Company, by the Order of any General Meeting at which there shall have been present, either personally or by Proxy, Shareholders holding in the aggregate not less than One Twentieth of the Capital of the Company, and being in Number not less than Fifty, to increase the Capital of the Company to any Amount which shall be certified by the East India Company to be proper and desirable, having regard to the Extent of the Undertakings in which the Company shall not for the Time being be engaged; and every such Increase of Capital as aforesaid shall be raised by creating new Shares, to be subject to the

Provisions of the Consolidation Act with respect to the Conversion of the borrowed Money into Capital, and to be within the Meeting and Intent of the same Act and of this Act accordingly, or shall be raised as to so much of such Increase of Capital as shall at once be paid up, or any Part thereof, without creating such new Shares, but by the Creation and Issue of a Capital Stock to the Amount of such Increase or such Part thereof, such Creation and Issue to be made with the Consent and in manner by the Consolidation Act directed in the Case of the Conversion of paid-up Shares into Stock; and such Capital Stock so created shall be Stock within the Meaning and Intent of the Provisions of the same Act with respect to the Consolidation of the Shares into Stock.

XX. And be it enacted, That this Act shall be a Public Act, and shall be judicially taken notice of as such, and may be amended or repealed in this present Session of Parliament.

London: Printed by George Edward Eyre and William Spottiswoode, Printers to the Queen's most Excellent Majesty, 1877.

363

Act of Incorporation of the Madras Railway Company, 1853

Source: Acts on Railways, London, 1886

ANNO DECIMO SEXTO
VICTORIÆ REGINÆ

Cap. XLVI

[An Act for incorporating the Madras Railway Company, and for other Purposes connected therewith. Act 16 Vic., Cap. 46, 14 June 1853]

Gist: The Act of Incorporation of the Madras Railway Company passed in the British Parliament on 14 June 1853 has provisions for the establishment of telegraphs also. The Act has 8 sections, besides the preliminary paragraph. The company was formed with Roger Hunt and Thomas Harris Devonshire as trustees and had eight present directors. EIC has kept the right to appoint ex-officio director, and also rights to use staff and facilities of the company as and when needed. The company with indenture of settlement dated 26 July 1852 and deed of settlement dated 11 September 1852 was registered at the Office of the Registrar of Joint Stock Companies. The indenture of agreement was signed between EIC and the company on 22 December 1852. The company had the power to hold lands in East Indies and Great Britain.

Whereas by an Indenture of Settlement bearing Date the Twenty-sixth Day of July One thousand eight hundred and fifty-two, and made or expressed to be made between the several Persons whose Names and Seals are or should be thereunto subscribed and affixed of the First Part, and Roger Hunt and Thomas Harris Devonshire, Gentlemen, of the Second Part, after reciting that a Company had been provisionally formed in the City of London for the Purpose of undertaking the Construction of Railways in India, under the Style or Title of "The Madras Railway Company," and that the Number of Shares in the said Company taken or to be taken by the Persons / Parties to the said Indenture of Settlement of the First Part respectively was written opposite to their Names and Seals respectively subscribed and affixed to the same Indenture, it was witnessed, that for the Purpose of forming the Company each of them the said several Persons / Parties to the said Indenture now in recital of the First Part covenanted with the said Roger Hunt and Thomas Harris Devonshire, who were Trustees on behalf of the Company, their Executors and Administrators, in manner following; (that is to say,) that the several Persons/Parties thereto of the First Part, and the several other Persons who should become Proprietors as thereinafter mentioned, should, while holding Shares in the Capital of the said Company, be and continue, until it should have been dissolved under the Provisions for that Purpose thereinafter contained, a Company, under the Name or Style of "The Madras Railway Company," for the Purpose of acquiring and holding Lands in the East Indies and Great Britain, and making, acquiring, and working One or more Railway or Railways in India, with all necessary Works, Stock, and Conveniences, and of doing and performing all such Matters and Things as are generally done by Persons or Companies engaged in Business of the like and as extensive a Nature as might be deemed advisable or desirable for efficiently carrying into effect the Objects and Purposes aforesaid; and it was by the said Indenture further agreed, that, subject and without Prejudice to the Powers therein-after given to the General Meetings of Proprietors, the Affairs of the Company should be conducted by and under the Superintendence and Direction of a Board of Directors, on behalf of the said Company, to enter into and conclude such Contracts, Agreements, and Arrangements as in their Discretion they might see fit with Her Majesty's Government in this Country or in India, or with the Honourable East India Company, for the Purpose of making and maintaining such One or more Line or Lines of Railway as aforesaid, and for other Purposes therein particularly mentioned: And whereas the greater Part of the said Shares in the Capital of the said Company were taken and subscribed for prior to the Month of September One thousand eight hundred and fifty-two, and the Subscribers for the same respectively executed the said Deed of Settlement, and the said Company was on or about the Eleventh Day of September One thousand eight hundred and fifty-two completely registered at the Office of the Registrar of Joint Stock Companies appointed under the Act passed in the Session of Parliament held in the Seventh and Eighth Years of the Reign of Her Present Majesty, intituled An Act for the Registration, Incorporation, and Regulation of Joint Stock Companies: And whereas the Board of Directors of the said Company is now composed of the following Persons; (that is to say,) Nathaniel Brindley Acworth, John Alves Arbuthnot, Robert Cannon, Morgan Charles Chase, Alexander Mackenzie, Duncan Montgomery, Duncan Sim, and James Walker, which said Persons are the present Directors of the said Company: And whereas by an Indenture of Agreement bearing Date the Twenty-second Day of December One thousand eight hundred and fifty-two, and made between the said East India Company of the one Part, and the said Madras Railway Company on the other Part, it was agreed that the said Railway Company should make, construct, and maintain an Experimental Line of Railway, to be determined and fixed upon by the said East India Company, to commence at or near Madras, and to take Direction towards the Western Coast of India, including all necessary and convenient Extensions and Branches thereof, together with the Stocks and Works necessary for the same, upon such Terms and Conditions as in the said Agreement were mutually agreed upon: And whereas the Objects and Purposes of the said Railway Company cannot be fully and effectually carried out without the Incorporation of the said Railway Company and the Authority of the Parliament: May it therefore please Your Majesty that it may be enacted; and be it enacted by the Queen's most Excellent Majesty, by and with the Advice and Consent of the Lord's Spiritual and Temporal, and Commons, in this present Parliament assembled, and by the Authority of the same, as follows; (that is to say,)

I. That the said Directors; and the several other Persons and Corporations who are Proprietors and Shareholders, in the said Railway Company, and their respective Executors, Administrators, Successors, and Assigns, shall be and hereby united into One Body Corporate under the Name of "The Madras Railway Company," for the Purposes of making and constructing, working and maintaining such Railway or Railways in the East Indies, including all necessary, accessory, or convenient Extensions, Branches, Stocks, and Works; as have already been agreed upon or may hereafter be agreed upon between the said Railway Company and the East India Company, and the Company hereby incorporated by the Name aforesaid shall have perpetual Succession and a Common Seal, and by that Name shall and may sue and be sued, as well in the Territories now under the Government of the East India Company as elsewhere, and shall have Power to purchase, take, and hold Land in the said Territories and in Great Britain for the Purposes aforesaid, without incurring any Penalties or Forfeitures, and shall have such other Powers as are hereinafter mentioned.

II. That all Property, Real and Personal, and all Deeds, Books, and Writings belonging to the said Railway Company, or which have been conveyed to or are held by any Person in trust for the said Railway Company, and all Rights and Powers of the said Railway Company, subject to any Engagements affecting the same, shall be vested in the Railway Company hereby incorporated, without the Necessity of any Transfer or connecting Title other than this Act; and all Contracts, Covenants, Engagements, and Liabilities now existing with or by the said Railway Company, or any Director, Trustee, or Person on behalf of the said Railway Company, other than any of the Covenants of the said Deed of Settlement which are superseded by the Provisions herein-after contained, shall and may be binding, fulfilled, and enforced by, with, and against the Company hereby incorporated, and such incorporated Company shall and may sue and be sued in respect thereof in the same Manner as if such incorporated Company had been Party thereto.

III. That the said Company incorporated by this Act shall be and continue to be regulated by the said Indenture of Settlement bearing Date The Twenty-sixth Day of July One thousand eight hundred and fifty-two, save and except so far as the same is altered or varied by this Act, or may be altered, varied, or affected by any Agreement, Contract, or Arrangement made under the Powers and Provisions of this Act; and the Clause of "The Companies Clauses Consolidation Act, 1845," with respect to the Matters following, (that is to say,)

With respect to the Construction of the said Act and of this Act,

With respect to the making of Byelaws, and the Recovery of Penalties imposed by any Byelaws,

With respect to the Consolidation of Shares into Stock,

With respect to the Payment of Subscriptions and the Means of enforcing the Payment of Calls otherwise than by Forfeiture,

Shall be incorporated with this Act: Provided always, that from and after the passing of this Act the said Railway Company shall cease to be subject to any of the Provisions or Enactments of the said Act for the Registration, Incorporation, and Regulation of Joint Stock

Companies, except only the several Provisions in the said Act relating respectively to the making and accepting and endorsing of Promissory Notes and Bills of Exchange, and to the balancing and auditing of the Company's Accounts, which are particularly referred to in and by the said Deed of Settlement of the said Company; and that the last-mentioned Provisions of the said Act so referred to in and by the said Deed of Settlement shall be deemed to be Part of the said Deed of Settlement, and shall have no further or higher Authority than they would have had if they had been expressed and contained in the said Deed of Settlement only; and that such Provisions, and also any other Provisions contained in the said Deed of Settlement, may be from Time to Time varied or repealed by Two Extraordinary General Meetings of Proprietors of the said Railway Company; provided that Two Thirds of the Votes at each such Meeting be in favour of the same; and provided that it shall not be lawful for any Meeting to vary the Proportion of Liabilities and Profits of Shareholders, to increase the Amount payable by any Shareholder in respect of any Share, or to vary the Provisions for the Dissolution of the said Railway Company.

IV. That, notwithstanding the Provisions in the said Deed of Settlement contained requiring Directors from Time to Time to go out of Office, it shall be lawful for any Extraordinary General Meeting of Proprietors of the said Railway Company to appoint the Directors for the Time being, or any of them, to continue in Office for any longer period not exceeding Five Years.

V. That any Penalties to be imposed by any Byelaw of the said Railway Company may be recovered in India by summary Proceeding before Two Justices of Peace or Magistrates, in the same Manner, as nearly as may be, as by "The Companies Clauses Consolidation Act" is provided for the Recovery of Penalties in England before Two Justices, and under and subject to the same or the like Limitations and Provisions.

VI. That all Contracts, Covenants, Agreements, and other Engagements, of what Nature or Kind so ever, which at the Time of the passing of this Act shall have been entered into between the East India Company and the said Railway Company, and especially the said Indenture of Agreement of the Twenty-second Day of December One thousand eight hundred and fifty-two, shall be and continue as valid and effectual, to all Intents and Purposes whatsoever, as if the said Railway Company had been incorporated at the respective Times when the same were entered into, and as if this Act had been passed before the making of such Contracts, Covenants, Agreements, and other Engagements; and all such Contracts, Covenants, Agreements, and other Engagements are hereby confirmed, and shall and may be enforced by and against the said Company hereby incorporated.

VII. That it shall and may be lawful for the Company hereby incorporated from Time to Time to enter into and conclude with the East India Company, on account of the Government of India, such Contracts, Agreements, and Arrangements as the respective Parties may think fit and agree upon, for making any Railway or Railways in India, and any Telegraphs connected therewith, and for maintaining and working the same, and for the other Objects and Purposes aforesaid, including, so far as the said respective Parties may agree thereto, all or any of the Provisions following; (that is to say,) any Provisions for securing to the East India Company any Facilities, Rights, and Advantages in relation to the said Railways and Premises respectively; and any Provisions so as to the Tolls, Receipts, and Profits thereof, and the Deposit, Custody, and Application of such Tolls, Receipts, and Profits; and any Provisions for giving to the East

India Company, and to any of their Officers, Servants, or Agents, any absolute or other Right of supervising, controlling, directing, regulating, and ordering the said Railway Company, and the Works, Contracts, Accounts, Byelaws, Acts, Proceedings, Transactions, and Affairs of the said Railway Company, as well in England as elsewhere; and any Provisions for enabling the East India Company to appoint an ex-officio Director of the said Railway Company, whether qualified by holding Shares or not, in the Place of any One of the ordinary Directors of the said Railway Company, or otherwise; and any Provisions for regulating the Powers, including even a Right of Veto at the Board of Directors, and the Duties and Proceedings and the Liabilities of any such Official Director; and any Provisions for binding the said Railway Company to conform to and fulfil all or any of the Directions which may be given by the East India Company, or their authorized Officers and Agents touching all or any of the Matters aforesaid; and any Provisions for the Appointment of Agents of the said Railway Company in India or elsewhere, and for determining and regulating the Powers and Duties of such Agents as aforesaid; and any Provisions for depositing with or paying to the East India Company all or any Part of the subscribed Capital of the said Railway Company, upon any Terms (as to Interest or otherwise) to be agreed upon; and any Provisions with regard to any Land which may be granted or leased to the said Railway Company by the East India Company or otherwise; and any Provisions for charging all or any Part of the Property of the said Railway Company with any Sum or Sums of Money, upon any Terms to be agreed upon; and any Provisions for the Surrender or Sale to the East India Company, or to any other Person or Persons, of the said Railway or Railways or any Part thereof, and of all or any Part of the Property of the said Railway Company, at any future Period; and any Provisions for referring Disputes to Arbitration; and any Provisions intended to enforce or secure the due Performance of any Contract or Engagement to be made by the said Railway Company; and generally all such Provisions and Stipulations in relation to the Matters aforesaid and any of them, and in relation to the Undertakings of the said Railway Company, and the Encouragement and Promotion thereof, and the eventual or continual Transfer of the same Undertakings, and the Property of the said Railway Company or any Part thereof, to the East India Company, as the said respective Parties shall think fit and agree upon; from Time to Time to vary and alter such Contracts, Agreements, and Arrangements, and to enter into new or other Contracts, Agreements, Arrangements (whether the same shall or not be within the Objects originally contemplated by the said Railway Company, or in accordance with the Provisions and Clauses by which the said Railway Company would otherwise be governed,) shall, subject to the Provisions of this Act, be valid and effectual and binding to all Intents and Purposes whatsoever, and full Effect shall be given for the same accordingly; and in case there shall be included in any such Contract, Agreement, and Arrangement any Provisions for referring Disputes to Arbitration, the Arbitrators or their Umpire shall, so far as there shall be no Provision to the contrary in any such Contract, Agreement, or Arrangement, have all such Powers as are given to Arbitrators or their Umpire by the Provisions in that Behalf included in the Clauses contained in the said "Companies Clauses Consolidation Act" with respect to the Settlement of Disputes by Arbitration.

VIII. Provided always, that in all Cases in which it is or shall be for any Purpose required by the said Deed of Settlement or otherwise that any Notice should be given to Proprietors of the Company hereby incorporated, it shall not be necessary to give such Notice by sending a Circular Letter to each Proprietor, but it shall be sufficient to cause an Advertisement giving such Notice to be inserted in any Two Newspapers published at least Six Days in the Week in London or Middlesex.

London: Printed by George Edward Eyre and William Spottiswoode, Printers to the Queen's most Excellent Majesty, 1857.

364

Act of Incorporation of the Bombay, Baroda, and Central India Railway Company, 1855

Source: Acts on Railways, London, 1886

ANNO DECIMO OCTAVO & DECIMO NONO
VICTORIÆ REGINÆ

Cap. CXIII

[An Act for incorporating the Bombay, Baroda, and Central India Railway Company; and for other Purposes connected therewith. Act 18 & 19 Vic., Cap. 113, 2nd July 1855]

Gist: The Act of Incorporation of the Bombay, Baroda, and Central India Railway Company passed in the British Parliament on 2 July 1855 has 20 sections, besides the preliminary paragraph. The company was provisionally formed in London as per indenture of settlement dated 24 April 1855 with Edward Lowther and John Frederick Freegard as trustees. The company was formed with the purpose of acquiring and holding lands in East Indies and Great Britain, making one or more railways with necessary approaches, works, stocks and conveniences, and for working of mines of coal, iron and other metals in East Indies, under terms mutually agreeable to EIC and the company. The company was registered at the Office of the Registrar of Joint Stock Companies with 8 present directors. EIC retained the right to appoint ex-officio director and right to veto in the Board of Directors. Provisions are there to issue bonds and debentures. Some sections (10 to 13) deal with book and register keeping for shares and debentures. Jurisdiction of suits is India and England.

Whereas by an Indenture of Settlement, bearing Date the Twenty-fourth Day of April One thousand eight hundred and fifty five, made or expressed to be made between the several Persons whose Names and Seals are or should be thereunto subscribed and affixed, of the First Part, and Edward Lowther and John Frederick Freegard of the Second Part, after reciting that a Company had been provisionally formed in the City of London for the Purpose of undertaking the Construction of Railways in India, under the Name or Style of "The Bombay, Baroda, and Central India Railway Company," and that the Number of Shares taken or to be taken by the Persons / Parties to the said Indenture of Settlement of the First Part respectively was written opposite to their Names and Seals respectively subscribed and affixed to the same Indenture, it was witnessed that, for the Purpose of forming the Company, each of them the said several Persons / Parties to the said Indenture of the First Part covenanted with the said Edward Lowther and John Frederick Freegard, who were Trustees on behalf of the Company, their Executors and Administrators, in the following manner; (that is to say,) that the several Persons / Parties thereto of the First Part, and the several other Persons who should become Proprietors as thereinafter mentioned, should, while holding Shares in the Capital of the said Company, be and continue, until it should have been dissolved, under the Provisions for that Purpose thereinafter contained, a Company, under the Name and Style of "The Bombay, Baroda, and Central India Railway Company," for the Purpose of acquiring and holding Lands in the East Indies and Great Britain, and making, acquiring, and Working One or more Railway or Railways in India, with all necessary Approaches, Works, Stock, and Conveniences, and of doing and performing all such Matters and Things as are generally done by Persons or Companies engaged in Business of the like and as extensive a Nature, and as might be deemed advisable or desirable for efficiently carrying into effect the Objects and Purposes aforesaid, including therein the acquiring and working of Mines of Coal, Iron, and other Minerals and Metals in the East Indies, and manufacturing the Produce thereof, and the erecting and carrying on all necessary and convenient Works, Furnaces, Forges, Smelting Houses, Water works, Gasworks for furthering the Objects of the Company, and selling disposing of such of the Produce thereof as from Time to Time shall not be wanted or necessary for the making, repairing, or carrying on any Railway of the Company: And whereas the said Company has been completely registered at the Office of the Registrar of Joint Stock Companies, appointed under the Act passed in the Session of Parliament held in the Seventh and Eighth Years of the Reign of Her present Majesty, intituled An Act for the Registration, Incorporation and Regulation of Joint Stock Companies; And whereas the Board of Directors of the said Company is now composed of the following Directors; (that is to say,) Patrick Theodor French, Henry Vansittart, Henry Harrington Thomas, Robert Scott, Arther James Lewis, John Pitt Kennedy, the Right Honourable William Earl of Devon and William Walter Cargill, which said Persons are the present Directors of the Company: And whereas Negotiations have been commenced and are now in progress between the said Railway Company and the Honourable East India Company with a view to the Construction by the former of One or more Line or Lines of Railway, in India in such Direction and upon such Terms and Conditions as shall be mutually agreed upon between them; but the Objects and Purposes of the said Railway Company cannot be fully and effectually carried out without the Incorporation of the said Railway Company and the Authority of Parliament: May it therefore please Your Majesty that it may be enacted; and be it enacted by the Queen's most Excellent Majesty, by and with the Advice and Consent of the Lord's Spiritual and Temporal, and Commons, in this present Parliament assembled, and by the Authority of the same, as follows:

I. The Expression "the Company" in this act shall mean "The Bombay, Baroda, and Central India Railway Company."

II. The said Directors and the Several other Persons and Corporations who are or shall Proprietors and Shareholders in the Company, and their respective Executors, Administrators, Successors, and Assigns, shall be and hereby united into One Body Corporate, and under the Name of "The Bombay, Baroda and Central India Railway Company," for the Purpose of making and constructing, working and maintaining such Railway or Railways in India, including all necessary, convenient, or accessory Extensions, Branches, Stocks, and Works as may be agreed upon by the Company and the East India Company, and also of doing and performing all such Matters and Things necessary or convenient for carrying into effect the Objects and Purposes aforesaid, as may be agreed upon by the Company and the East India Company; and the Company hereby incorporated by the Name aforesaid shall have perpetual succession and a Common Seal, and by such Name shall and may sue and be sued, and shall have Power to purchase, take, and hold Lands for the Purposes aforesaid, (including Lands in Great Britain for the Purposes of the Business of the same Company,) without incurring any Penalties or Forfeitures, and shall have such Powers as hereinafter mentioned.

III. All Property, Real and Personal, and all Deeds, Books, Plans, Surveys, Estimates, and Writings belonging to the Company, subject to any Engagements affecting the same, shall be vested in the Company hereby incorporated, without the Necessity of any Transfer or connecting Title other than this Act; and all Contracts, Covenants, Engagements, and Liabilities now existing with or by the Company, or any Director, Trustee, or Person on behalf of the Company, other than any of the Covenants of the said Deed of Settlement which are superseded by the Provisions herein-after contained, shall and may be enforced by, with, and against the Company hereby incorporated, and such incorporated Company shall and may sue and be sued in respect thereof in the same Manner as if such Company had been Party thereto.

IV. The Company shall be and continue to be regulated by the said Deed of Settlement bearing Date the Twenty fourth Day of April One thousand eight hundred and fifty-five, save and except so far as the same is altered or varied by this Act, or may be altered, varied, or affected by any Agreement, Contract, or Arrangement made under the Powers and Provisions of this Act, and the Clauses of "The Companies Clauses Consolidation Act, 1845," with respect to the Matters following, (that is to say,) with respect to the Construction of the said Act and of this Act, with respect to the making of Byelaws, with respect to the Consolidation of Shares into Stock, with respect to the Payment of Subscriptions and the Means of enforcing the Payment of Calls otherwise than by Forfeiture, shall be incorporated with this Act: Provided always, that after the passing of this Act the Company shall cease to be subject to any of the Provisions or Enactments of the said Act for the Registration, Incorporation, and Regulation of Joint Stock Companies, except only the several Provisions in the said Act relating respectively to the making and accepting and endorsing of Promissory Notes and Bills of Exchange, and to the balancing and auditing of the Company's Accounts which are particularly referred to in and by the said Deed of Settlement of the Company, and that any Provisions contained in the said Deed of Settlement may be from Time to Time varied or repealed by Two Extraordinary General Meetings of Proprietors of the Company, provided that Two Thirds of the Votes at each such Meeting be in favour of the same; provided that it shall not be lawful for any Meeting to vary the Proportion of Liabilities and Profits of Shareholders to increase the Amount payable by any Shareholder in respect of any Share, or to vary the Provisions for the Dissolution of the Company.

V. The Company may from Time to Time enter into and conclude with the East India Company on account of the Government of India such Contracts, Agreements, and Arrangements as the respective Parties may think fit and agree upon for making any Railway or Railways in India, and any Telegraphs connected therewith, and for maintaining and working the same, and for the other Objects and Purposes aforesaid, including the making of Surveys and other preliminary Arrangements for any Railway or Railways in India, although at the Time there shall be no Contract for the making such Railway or Railways; and such Contracts or Agreements shall include, so far as may be necessary or as the said respective Parties may agree thereto, all or any of the Provisions following; (that is to say,) any Provisions for securing to the East India Company any Facilities, Rights and Advantages in relation to the said Railways and Premises respectively; and any Provision as to the Tolls, Receipts, and Profits thereof, and the Application of such Tolls, Receipts, and Profits; any Provisions for giving to the East India Company, or any of their Officers, Servants, or Agents, any absolute or other Rights of supervising, controlling, directing, regulating, and ordering the Company, and the Works, Contracts, Accounts, Byelaws, Acts, Proceedings, Transactions, and Affairs of the Company, as well in England as elsewhere; and any Provisions for enabling the East India Company to appoint an ex-officio Director of the Company, whether qualified by holding Shares or not, in the place of any of the ordinary Directors of the Railway Company or otherwise; and any Provisions for regulating the Powers, including a Right of Veto at the Board of Directors, and the Duties and Proceedings and the Liabilities of any such official Director; and any Provisions for binding the Railway Company to conform to and fulfil all or any Directions which may be given by the East India Company or their authorized Officers and Agents touching all or any of the Matters aforesaid; and any Provisions for the Appointment of Agents of the Company in India or elsewhere, and for determining and regulating the Powers and Duties of such Agents as aforesaid; and any Provisions for depositing with or paying to the East India Company all or any Part of the subscribed Capital of the Company upon any Terms (as to Interest or otherwise) to be agreed upon; and any Provisions with regard to any Land which may be granted or leased to the Railway Company by the East India Company or otherwise; and any Provisions for charging all or any Part of the Property of the Company with the Payment of any Sum or Sums of Money upon any Terms to be agreed upon; and any Provisions for the Surrender or Sale to the East India Company, or to any Person or Persons, of the said Railway or Railways, or any Part thereof, and of all or any Part of the Property of the Company, at any future Period; and any Provisions for referring Disputes to Arbitration; and any Provisions intended to enforce or secure the due Performance of any Contract or Agreement to be made by the Company; and generally all such Provisions and Stipulations in relation to the Matters aforesaid and any of them, and in relation to the Undertakings of the Company and the Encouragement and Promotion thereof, and the eventual or contingent Transfer of the same or any Part thereof to the East India Company, as the said respective Parties shall think fit and agree upon; and from Time to Time to vary and alter such Contracts, Agreements, and Arrangements, and to enter into new or other Contracts, Agreements, and Arrangements in relation to the Premises, all which Contracts, Agreements, and Arrangements shall be subject to the Provisions of this Act, and of any other Law or Statute for the Time being in force, valid and effectual, and binding to all Intents and Purposes whatsoever, and full Effect shall be given to the same accordingly.

VI. It shall be lawful for the Company at any Time or Times to increase the Capital of the Company by such an Amount as may be deemed necessary for carrying into effect any Contract or Contracts of the Company with the East India Company by the Creation of a Number of new additional Shares of Eighteen Pounds each, and to issue and allot all or any of such new or additional Shares when so created either to Proprietors for the Time being of Shares in the Company, or to any other Person or Persons whomsoever who shall respectively be willing to take the same, upon such Terms and subject to such Regulations and Conditions as to the Distribution of Profits or otherwise as at the Time of any such Issue shall be deemed expedient, and in all other respects such new and additional Shares and the Holders thereof shall be subject to the same Laws, Regulations, and Provisions as relate to the existing Shares in the Company.

VII. It shall be lawful for the Board of Directors, to such an Extent, as may be agreed upon by and between the Company and the East India Company, to issue from Time to Time in England Bonds, or elsewhere, or in India Debentures of the Company, in Sums from Eighteen Pounds to One thousand Pounds, each payable at such Period and bearing such Interest, not exceeding Five Pounds per Centum per Annum, as may be agreed upon; and all and every the Powers and Provisions contained in the said Deed of Settlement as to convertible Debentures shall and shall be deemed to apply to the Debentures hereby authorized to be issued.

VIII. The Board of Directors of the Company for the Time being may establish in India one or more Office or Offices for the Issue, Registration, and Transfer of Shares, Stock, and Securities of the Company at such Place or Places as they shall think fit, and from Time to Time may remove or alter the Place or Places of any such Office or Offices, and from Time to Time may make such Regulations as to the said Board may seem fit and expedient for enabling the Issue, Transfer, and Registration at such Office or Offices, or any of them, of such Shares, Stock, and Securities, or of any of the said Shares, Stock, and Securities to be described in such Regulations; and all and every Powers and Provisions contained in the Deed of Settlement and this Act in relation to the Issue, Transfer, and Registration of Shares, Stock, and Securities to be issued, transferred and registered in India at such Office or any of such Offices, except so far as the same are inconsistent with the Provisions of this Act.

IX. The said Board of Directors may nominate and appoint such Person or Persons as they shall approve to issue and dispose of Shares, Stock, and Securities of the Company at such Office or Offices in India, and from Time to Time may remove such Person or Persons and appoint any other Person or Persons in his or their Place, and may delegate such Person or all or any of such Persons respectively all or any of the Powers of the Directors or other Officers of the Company in relation to the Issue, Transfer, and Registration of Shares, Stock, and Securities of the Company which the said Board shall think necessary or expedient for the Issue, Transfer, and Registration of such Shares, Stock, and Securities in India; and the said Board may from time to Time make such Provisions and Regulations as they shall think fit for the Conduct, Government, and Management of the Person or Persons so to be appointed, and for the Issue, Transfer, and Registration of such Shares, Stock, and Securities as aforesaid, and may cause an Official Seal to be prepared for each such Office which shall be so established in India as aforesaid, to be used by such Person or Persons in lieu of the Common Seal of the Company, and may from Time to Time vary and renew any such Seal, and all Documents duly sealed with any such Official Seal, in pursuance and exercise of the Powers to be conferred on such Person or

Persons, shall have the same Force and Effect as if they had been sealed with the Common Seal of the Company.

X. The said Board of Directors shall cause to be kept at each Office which may be so established in India as aforesaid a Book to be called "The ________ Register of Shareholders" (the Blank in the above prescribed Title being filled up with the Name of the Place where the Office shall be established), and also if any Shares shall be converted into Consolidated Stock, a Book for the Registry at such Office of Holders of Consolidated Stock to be called "The ________ Register of Consolidated Stock" (the Blank being filled up in manner aforesaid), and also a Book for the Entry at such Office of Transfer of Shares and Stock to be called "The ________ Register of Transfers" (the Blank being filled up in manner aforesaid), and also if deemed necessary, Books to be called respectively "The _______ Register of Mortgages and Bonds," and, "The ________ Register of Debentures," (the Blanks being filled up in manner aforesaid), and shall cause Accounts of all Entries and Alterations made in such Books respectively to be from Time to Time transmitted to the principal Office of the Company in London.

XI. All Transfers of any Shares, Stock, and Securities as aforesaid shall be made at the Office at which the same respectively shall for the Time being be registered, and none of such Shares, Stock, or Securities shall ever be on the Registry of more than One Office at one and the same Time.

XII. Subject to such Regulations and Conditions as the said Board of Directors may think fit and prescribe as to all or any of such Shares, Stock, and Securities as aforesaid, the Registry of any Shares, Stock, or Securities of the Company may and shall, on Notice in writing by the Holder or Holders thereof being given to the Person for the Time being acting in the Capacity of Secretary or principal Clerk at the Office of the Company, either in London or in India, where such Shares, Stock, or Securities shall for the Time being be registered, be transferred from the Register thereof at such Office to the corresponding Register at any other Office of the Company where for the Time being a Register shall be kept, to be appointed and named in such Notice Advice thereof shall be transmitted to the Office to which such Transfer is directed to be made.

XIII. For the Purpose of determining any Question as to the Place or Jurisdiction within which any Shares, Stock, or Securities of the Company shall be deemed to be or to have been situated at any given Time, the Locality, whether in India or in Great Britain, of the Register in which such Shares, Stock, or Securities shall be or have been actually registered for the Time being, shall be deemed to be or to have been at such Time the Locality of such Shares, Stock, or Securities, and so soon as Notice shall have been given as aforesaid for the Transfer of the Registry of any Shares, Stock, or Securities from either or any of the said Registers to any other Register, such Shares, Stock, or Securities shall for the Purpose aforesaid be deemed to be actually registered in such last-mentioned Register.

XIV. And whereas the East India Company have agreed to guarantee Interest upon a certain Portion of the Capital of the Company at the rate of Five Pounds per Centum per Annum, upon condition that when the said Railway or Railways should become profitable the net Profits thereof should be applicable to the Payment of the current Interest, and the Repayment of the Interest therefore paid: And whereas upon the Issue of further Capital from Time to

Time Arrangements may be entered into for the Payment by the East India Company of Interest thereon at another Rate or other Rates: And whereas it is expedient to provide for the Application and Division of the Profits of the Company in manner following: Be it enacted, That, subject to any Agreement or Arrangement that may hereafter be made to the contrary, the whole of the Interest payable and therefore paid by the East India Company upon the whole Capital of the Company shall be from Time to Time charged upon and payable out of the net Profits of the Company, or upon and out of such Portion thereof as shall be agreed upon by the East India Company, and the Company to be charged with the Payment thereof respectively, or any Part thereof respectively, and that the Residue of the said Profits shall be applied for the rateable Benefit of all the Shareholders entitled to Dividend, and divided accordingly.

XV. And whereas by the said Deed of Settlement it is provided that Annual General Meetings of Proprietors shall be held in the month of May, or within Twenty Days thereafter, in every Year, and that a Half-yearly General Meeting of Proprietors shall also be held in every Year at Expiration of Six Calendar Months after each such Ordinary Annual General Meeting, or as near thereto as conveniently may be: And whereas the Periods within which the said Meetings are to be held have been found inconvenient, and it is desirable that the said Company should have Power to alter the same: Be it enacted, that the Annual General Meetings of Proprietors of the said Company may be held in either of the Months of March, April, May, or June, and the Half-yearly Meetings at Periods as nearly Six Calendar Months after each such Annual General Meeting as may be deemed convenient or expedient.

XVI. And whereas by the said Deed of Settlement it is provided that Two at least of the Directors shall certify by writing the due Annexation of the Seal of the Company to any Act, Deed, Matter, or Thing, together with the Date of such Annexation: And whereas Inconvenience has been found to result from such Provision: Therefore whenever the Seal of the Company shall be set or affixed to any Act, Deed, Matter, or Thing by the Authority of a Board of Directors; it shall not be necessary for any Director to certify the due Annexation thereof, or the date of such Annexation, but such Act, Deed, Matter, or Thing shall be valid and effectual if the Seal of the Company be set or affixed thereto.

XVII. Notwithstanding the Provisions in the said Deed of Settlement contained requiring Directors from Time to Time to go out of Office, it shall be lawful for an Extraordinary General Meeting of Proprietors of the Company to appoint the Directors for the Time being or any of them to continue in Office for any longer Period not exceeding Five Years.

XVIII. Any Penalties to be imposed by any Byelaw of the Company may be recovered in India by summary Proceeding before Two Justices of Peace or Magistrates in the same Manner as nearly as may be as by "The Companies Clauses Consolidation Act 1845," is provided for the Recovery of Penalties in England before Two Justices, and under and subject to the same or the like Limitations and Provisions.

XIX. Provided always, That in all Cases in which it is or shall be for any Purpose required by the said Deed of Settlement or otherwise that any Notice should be given to the Proprietors of the Company, it shall not be necessary to give such Notice by sending a Circular Letter to each Proprietor, but it shall be sufficient to cause an Advertisement giving such Notice to be inserted in any Two Newspapers published at least Six Days in the Week in London or

Middlesex.

XX. In citing this Act for any Purpose whatever it shall be sufficient to use the Expression "The Bombay, Baroda, and Central India Railway Act, 1855."

London: Printed by George Edward Eyre and William Spottiswoode, Printers to the Queen's Most Excellent Majesty, 1855.

365

Act of Incorporation of the Scinde Railway Company, 1855

Source: Acts on Railways, London, 1886

ANNO DECIMO OCTAVO & DECIMO NONO
VICTORIÆ REGINÆ

Cap. CXV

[An Act for incorporating the Scinde Railway Company, and for other Purposes connected therewith. Act 18 and 19 Vic., Cap. 115, 2nd July 1855]

Gist: The Act of Incorporation of the Scinde Railway Company passed in the British Parliament on 2 July 1855 has 20 sections, besides the initial paragraph. The Scinde Railway Company with indenture of settlement bearing the date of 6 March 1855 was formed for the construction of railway and related accessories between Karachi seaport and Hyderabad both in Sind province, now in Pakistan. The company with William Patrick Andrew and Francis Horsley Robinson as trustees was registered on 31 March 1855 as a Joint Stock Company having its principal office in England. EIC has the right to appoint ex-officio director and right to veto in the Board of Directors. EIC has also the right to use all the conveniences of the railway company.

Whereas by an Indenture of Settlement bearing Date the Sixth Day of March One thousand eight hundred and fifty-five, and made or expressed to be made between the several Persons whose Names and Seals are or should be thereunto subscribed and affixed, except William Patrick Andrew, of Forty-one, Bryanstone Street in the County of Middlesex, Esquire, of the Honourable the East India Company's Service, and Francis Horsley Robinson of Queen Street, May Fair, in the said County, Esquire, of the Honourable the East India Company's Service, of the First Part, the said William Patrick Andrew and Francis Horsley Robinson of the Second Part, and John Hollams of the Commercial Sale Rooms, Mincing Lane, in the City of London, Gentleman, of the Third Part, after reciting that a Company had been provisionally formed in the City of London for the Purpose of undertaking the Construction of Railways in India, under the Style or Title of "The Scinde Railway Company," and that the Number of Shares taken or to be taken by the Persons / Parties to the said Indenture of Settlement of the First Part respectively was written opposite to their Names and Seals, respectively subscribed and affixed to the same Indenture, it was witnessed, that for the Purpose of forming the Company each of them the several Persons / Parties to the said Indenture of the First Part covenanted with the said William Patrick Andrew and Francis Horsley Robinson, who were Trustees on behalf of the Company, their Executors and Administrators, and the said William Patrick Andrew and Francis Horsley Robinson covenanted with the said John Hollams in manner following; (that is to say,) that the several Person / Parties thereto of the First Part, and the several other Persons who should become Proprietors as thereinafter mentioned, should, while holding Shares in the Capital of the said Company, be and continue, until it should have been dissolved under the Provisions for the Purpose therein-after contained, a Company under the Name or Style of "The Scinde Railway Company" for the Purpose of acquiring and holding Lands in the East Indies and Great Britain, and making, acquiring, and working One or more Railway or Railways in India, and in particular and in the first instance a Railway to commence at or near the seaport of Kurrachee, and to proceed to a Point at or near Hyderabad, both in the Province of Scinde, together with all necessary Works, Stocks, and Conveniences, and of doing and performing all such Matters and Things as are generally done by Persons or Companies engaged in Business of the like and as extensive a Nature, and as might be deemed advisable or desirable for efficiently carrying into effect the Objects and Purposes aforesaid, including therein the acquiring and working of Mines of Coal, Iron, and other Minerals and Metals in the East Indies, and manufacturing the Produce thereof, and the erecting and carrying on all necessary and convenient Works, Furnaces, Forges, Smelting Houses, and Gasworks, for furthering the Objects of the Company, and selling and disposing of such of the Produce thereof as from Time to Time should not be necessary or wanted for the making, repairing, or carrying on any Railway of the Company: And whereas the greater Part of the said Shares in the Capital of the said Company were taken and subscribed for prior to the Month of March One thousand eight hundred and fifty-five, and the subscribers for the same respectively executed the said Deed of Settlement, and the said Company was on or about the Thirty-first Day of March One thousand eight hundred and fifty-five completely registered at the Office of the Registrar of Joint Stock Companies appointed under the Act passed in the Session of Parliament held in the Seventh and Eighth Years of the Reign of Her Present Majesty, intituled An Act for the Registration, Incorporation and Regulation of Joint Stock Companies: And whereas Negotiations have been commenced and are still in progress between the said Railway Company and the East India Company, with a view to the Construction by the former of the said Line of Railway in the Province of Scinde, herein-before mentioned, upon such Terms and Conditions as shall be mutually agreed between them; but the Objects and Purposes of the said Railway Company cannot be effectually carried out without the Incorporation of the said Railway Company, and the Authority of Parliament: May it therefore please Your Majesty that it may be enacted; and be it enacted by the Queen's most Excellent Majesty, by and with the Advice and Consent of the Lord's Spiritual and Temporal, and Commons, in this present Parliament assembled, and by the Authority of the same,

I. That in citing this Act for any Purpose whatever it shall be sufficient to use the Expression "The Scinde Railway Act, 1855."

II. That the Expression "the Company" in this Act shall mean the Scinde Railway Company.

III. That the several Persons and Corporations who are or shall become Proprietors and Shareholders in the Company, and their respective Executors, Administrators, Successors, and Assigns, shall be and are hereby united into One Body Corporate, under the said Name of "The Scinde Railway Company," for the Purpose of making and constructing, working and maintaining such Railway or Railways in India, including all necessary, convenient, or accessory Extensions, Branches, Stocks, and Works as may be agreed upon by the Company and the East India Company, and also of doing and performing all such Matters and Things necessary or convenient for carrying into effect the Objects and Purposes of the Company, as may be agreed upon by the Company and the East India Company; and the Company hereby incorporated by the Name aforesaid shall have perpetual Successors and a Common Seal, and by such Name shall and may sue and be sued, and shall have Power to purchase, take, and hold Lands for the Purposes aforesaid (including Lands in England for the Purposes of the Business of the same Company), without incurring any Penalties or Forfeitures, and shall have such other Powers herein-after mentioned.

IV. That all Property, Real and Personal, and all Deeds, Books, and Writings belonging to the Company, or which have been conveyed to or are held by any Person in trust for the Company, and all Rights and Powers of the Company, subject to any Engagements affecting the same, shall be vested in the Company hereby incorporated, without the Necessity of any Transfer or connecting Title other than this Act; and all Contracts, Covenants, Engagements, and Liabilities now existing with or by the Company, or any Director, Trustee, or Person on behalf of the Company, other than any of the Covenants of the said Deed of Settlement which are superseded by the Provisions herein-after contained, shall and may be binding, fulfilled, and enforced by, with, and against the Company hereby incorporated, and the Company hereby incorporated shall and may sue and be sued in respect thereof, in the same Manner as if the Company hereby incorporated had been Party thereto.

V. That the Company shall be and continue to be regulated by the said Indenture of Settlement bearing Date the Sixth Day of March One thousand eight hundred and fifty-five, save and except so far as the same is altered or varied by this Act, or may be altered, varied, or affected by any Agreement, Contract, or Arrangement made under the Powers and Provisions of this Act, and the Clauses of "The Companies Clauses Consolidation Act, 1845," with respect to the Matters following, (that is to say,) with respect to the Construction of the said Act and of this Act, with respect to the making of Byelaws, and Recovery of Penalties imposed by any Byelaws, with respect to the Consolidation of Shares into Stock, with respect to the Payment of Subscriptions, and to the Means of enforcing the Payment of Calls otherwise than by Forfeiture, shall be incorporated with this Act: Provided always, that from and after the passing of this Act the Company shall cease to be subject to any of the Provisions or Enactments of the Said Act for the Registration, Incorporation, and Regulation of Joint Stock Companies, except only the several Provisions in the said Act relating respectively to the making and accepting and endorsing of Promissory Notes and Bills of Exchange, and to the balancing and auditing the Company's Accounts, which are particularly referred to in and by the said Deed of Settlement of the Company; and that any Provisions contained in the said Deed of Settlement may be from Time to Time varied or repealed by Two Extra ordinary General Meetings of the Proprietors of the Company; provided, that Two Thirds of the Votes at each such Meeting be in favour of the same; and provided, that it shall not be lawful for any Meeting to vary the Proportion of Liabilities and Profits of Shareholders to increase the Amount payable by any Shareholder in respect of any Share, or to vary the Provisions for the Dissolution of the Company.

VI. That it shall and may be lawful for the Company from Time to Time to enter into and conclude with the East India Company, on account of the Government of India, such Contracts, Agreements, and Arrangements as the respective Parties may think fit and agree upon, for making any Railway or Railways in India, and the Telegraphs connected therewith, and for maintaining and working the same, and for the other Objects and Purposes aforesaid, including the making of Surveys and other preliminary Arrangements for any Railway or Railways in India, although at the Time there shall be no Contract for the making such Railway or Railways; and such Contracts or Agreements shall include, so far as may be necessary, or as the said respective Parties may agree thereto, all or any of the Provisions following; (that is to say,) any Provisions for securing to the East India Company any Facilities, Rights, and Advantages in relation to the said Railways and Premises respectively; and any Provisions as to the Tolls, Receipts, and Profits thereof, and the Application of such Tolls, Receipts, and Profits; and any Provisions for giving to the East India Company, or to any other Officers, Servants, or Agents, any absolute or other Right of supervising, controlling, directing, regulating, and ordering the Company, and the Works, Contracts, Accounts, Byelaws, Acts, Proceedings, Transactions, and Affairs of the Company, as well in England as elsewhere; and any Provisions for enabling the East India Company to appoint an ex-officio Director of the Company, whether qualified by holding Shares or not, in the Place of any One of the ordinary Directors of the Company or otherwise; and any Provisions for regulating the Powers (including a Right of Veto at the Board of Directors) and the Duties and Proceedings and the Liabilities of any such official Director; and any Provisions for binding the Company to conform to and fulfil all or any Directions which may be given by the East India Company, or their authorized Officers and Agents, touching all or any of the Matters aforesaid; and any Provisions for the Appointment of Agents of the Company in India or elsewhere, and for determining and regulating the Powers and Duties of such Agents as aforesaid; and any Provisions for depositing with or paying to the East India Company all or any Part of the subscribed Capital of the Company, upon any Terms (as to interest or otherwise) to be agreed upon; and any Provisions with regard to any Land which may be granted or leased to the Company by the East India Company or otherwise; and any Provisions for charging all or any Part of the Property of the Company with the Payment of any Sum or Sums of Money, upon any Terms to be agreed upon; and any Provisions for the Surrender or Sale to the East India Company, or to any other Person or Persons, of the said Railway or Railways or any Part thereof, and all or any Part of the Property of the Company at any future Period; and any Provisions for referring Disputes to Arbitration; and any Provisions intended to enforce or secure the due Performance of any Contract or Engagement to be made by the Company; and generally, all such Provisions and Stipulations in relation to the Matters aforesaid and any of them, and in relation to the Undertakings of the Company, and the Encouragement and Promotion thereof, and the eventual or contingent Transfer of the same or any Part thereof to the East India Company, as the said respective Parties shall think fit and agree upon; and from Time to Time to vary and alter such Contracts, Agreements, and Arrangements in relation to the Premises; all which Contracts, Agreements, and Arrangements shall, subject to the Provisions of this Act, and of any other Law or Statute for the Time being in force, be valid and effectual and binding, to all Intents and Purposes whatsoever, and full Effect should be given to the same accordingly.

VII. That it shall be lawful for the Company, at any Time or Times, to increase the Capital of the Company by such an Amount as may be deemed necessary for carrying into effect any Contract or Contracts of the Company with the East India Company, by the Creation of a Number of new or additional Shares of Twenty Pounds each, and to issue and allot all or any of such new or additional Shares, when so created, either to Proprietors for the Time being of Shares in the Company, or to any other Person or Persons whomsoever who shall respectively be willing to take the same, upon such Terms, and subject to such Regulations and Conditions as to the Distribution of Profits or otherwise, as at the Time of any such Issue shall be deemed expedient; and in all other respects such new and additional Shares, and the Holders thereof, shall be subject to the same Laws, Regulations, and Provisions as relate to the existing Shares in the Company and the Holders thereof.

VIII. That it shall be lawful for the Board of Directors, to such an Extent as may be agreed upon by and between the Company and the East India Company, to issue from Time to Time, in England or elsewhere, or in India, Debentures of the Company, in Sums from Twenty Pounds to One thousand Pounds each, payable at such Period, and bearing such Interest, not exceeding Five Pounds per Centum per Annum, as may be agreed upon; and that all and every the Powers and Provisions contained in the said Deed of Settlement as to convertible Debentures shall and shall be deemed to apply to the Debentures hereby authorized to be issued.

IX. That the Board of Directors of the Company for the Time being may establish in India One or more Office or Offices for the Issue, Registration, and Transfer of Shares, Stock, and Securities of the Company, at such Place or Places as they shall think fit, and may from Time to Time remove or alter the Place or Places of any such Office or Offices, and may from Time to Time make such Regulations as to such Board may seem fit and expedient for the Issue, Transfer, and Registration, at such Office or Offices or any of them of such Shares, Stock, and Securities, or any of the said Shares, Stock, and Securities to be described in such Regulations; and that all and every the Powers and Provisions contained in the Deed of Settlement and in this Act in relation to the Issue, Transfer, and Registration of Shares, Stock, and Securities in Great Britain shall apply and be in force as to the Shares, Stock, and Securities to be issued, transferred, and registered in India, at such Office or any of such Offices, except so far as the same are inconsistent with the Provisions of this Act.

X. That the said Board of Directors may nominate and appoint such Person or Persons as they shall approve to issue and dispose of Shares, Stock, and Securities of the Company at such Office or Offices in India, and may from Time to Time remove such Person or Persons, and appoint any other Person or Persons in his or their Place, and delegate to such Persons, or all or any of such Persons respectively, all or any of the Powers of the Directors or other Officers of the Company in relation to the Issue, Transfer, and Registration of Shares, Stock, and

Securities of the Company, which the said Board shall think necessary or expedient for the Issue, Transfer, and Registration of such Shares, Stock, and Securities in India; and the said Board may from Time to Time make such Provisions and Regulations as they shall think fit for the Conduct, Government, Management of the Person or Persons so to be appointed; and may cause an Official Seal to be prepared for each such Office which shall be so established in India as aforesaid, to be used by such Person or Persons in lieu of the Common Seal of the Company; and may from Time to Time vary and renew any such Seal; and all Documents duly sealed with any such Official Seal, in pursuance and exercise of the Powers to be conferred on such Person or Persons, shall have the same Force and Effect as if they had been sealed with the Common Seal of the Company.

XI. That the said Board of Directors shall cause to be kept at each Office which may be so established in India as aforesaid a Book to be called "The _______ Register of Shareholders" (The Blank in the above prescribed Title being filled up with the Name of the Place where the Office shall be established), and also if any Shares shall be converted into Consolidated Stock, to be called "The _______ Register of Consolidated Stock" (the Blank being filled up in manner aforesaid), and also a Book for the Entry at such Office of Transfers of Shares and Stock, to be called "The ______ Register of Transfers" (the Blank being filled up in manner aforesaid), and also if deemed necessary, Books to be called respectively "The _____ Register of Mortgages and Bonds" and "The ______ Register of Debentures," (the Blanks being filled up in manner aforesaid), and shall cause Accounts of all Entries and Alterations made in such Books respectively to be from Time to Time transmitted to the Principal Office of the Company in England.

XII. That all Transfers of any such Shares, Stock, and Securities as aforesaid shall be made at the Office at which the same respectively shall for the Time being be registered; and that none of such Shares, Stock or Securities shall ever be on the Registry of more than One Office at One and the same Office.

XIII. That, subject to such Regulations and Conditions as the said Board of Directors may think fit and prescribe as to all or any of such Shares, Stock, and Securities as aforesaid, the Registry of any Shares, Stock, and Securities of the Company may and shall, on Notice in writing by the Holder or Holders thereof being given to the Person for the Time being acting in the Capacity of Secretary or Principal Clerk at the Office of the Company, either in England or in India, where such Shares, Stock, and Securities shall for the Time being be registered, be transferred from the Register thereof at such Office to the corresponding Register at any other Office of the Company where for the Time being a Register shall be Kept, to be designated or named in such Notice, and as soon as conveniently may be after giving of such Notice Advice thereof shall be transmitted to the Office to which such Transfer is directed to be made.

XIV. That, for the Purpose of determining any Question as to the Place or Jurisdiction within which any Share, Stock, or Securities of the said Company shall be deemed to be or to have been situated at any given Time, the Locality, whether in Great Britain or in India, of the Register in which such Share, Stock, or Securities shall be or actually have been registered for the Time being shall be deemed to be or to have been at such Time the Locality of such Share, Stock, or Securities; and so soon as Notice shall have been given as aforesaid for the Transfer of the Registry of any Share, Stock, or Securities from either or any of the said Registers to any other Register, such Share, Stock, or Securities shall for the Purpose aforesaid be deemed to be actually registered in such last-mentioned Register.

XV. And whereas by the said Deed of Settlement it is provided, that Two at least of the Directors shall certify by writing the due Annexation of the Seal of the Company to any Act, Deed, Matter, or Thing, together with the Date of such Annexation: And whereas Inconvenience has been found to result from such Provision: Be it enacted, That whenever the Seal of the Company shall be set or affixed to any Act, Deed, Matter, or Thing, by the Authority of a Board of Directors, it shall not be necessary for any Director to certify the due Annexation thereof, or the Date of such Annexation, but such Act, Deed, Matter, or Thing shall be valid and effectual if the Seal of the Company be set or affixed thereto.

XVI. That, notwithstanding the Provisions in the said Deed of Settlement contained, requiring Directors from Time to Time to go out of Office, it shall be lawful for an Extraordinary General Meeting of Proprietors of the Company to appoint the Directors for the Time being, or any of them, to continue in Office for any longer Period not exceeding Five Years.

XVII. That any Penalties to be imposed by any Byelaw of the Company may be recovered in India by summary Proceeding before Two Justice of the Peace or Magistrates, in the same Manner, as nearly as may be, as by "The Companies Clauses Consolidation Act" is provided for the Recovery of Penalties in England before Two Justice, and under and subject to the same or the like Limitations and Provisions.

XVIII. Provided always, That in all Cases in which it is or shall be for any Purpose required by the said Deed of Settlement or otherwise that any Notice should be given to the Proprietors of the Company, it shall not be necessary to give such Notice by sending a Circular Letter to each Proprietor, but it shall be sufficient to cause One Advertisement giving such Notice to be inserted in any Two Newspapers published at least Six Days in the Week in London or Middlesex.

XIX. And whereas the East India Company have agreed to guarantee Interest upon a certain Portion of the Capital of the Company, at the Rate of Five Pounds per Centum per Annum, upon condition that when the said Railway or Railways should become profitable the net Profits thereof should be applicable to the Payment of the current Interest, and the Repayment of the Interest therefore paid: And whereas upon the Issue of further Capital from Time to Time Arrangements may be entered into for the Payment by the East India Company of Interest thereon at another Rate or other Rates: And whereas it is expedient to provide for the Application and Division of the Profits of the Company in manner following: Be it enacted, That, subject to any Agreement or Arrangement that may hereafter be made to the contrary, the whole of the Interest payable and therefore paid by the East India Company upon the whole Capital of the Company shall be from Time to Time charged upon and payable out of the net Profits of the Company, or upon and out of such Portion thereof as shall be agreed upon by the East India Company and the Company to be charged with the Payment thereof respectively or any Part thereof respectively, and that the Residue of the said Profits shall be applied for the rateable Benefit of all the Shareholders entitled to Dividend, and dividing accordingly.

XX. That the Costs, Charges, and Expenses of applying for, obtaining, and passing this

Act, or in any way incidental thereto, shall be paid by the Company.

London, Printed by George Edward Eyre and William Spottiswoode, Printers to the Queen's most Excellent Majesty, 1877.

366

Act of Incorporation of the Eastern Bengal Railway Company, 1857

Source: Acts on Railways, London, 1886

ANNO VICESIMO & VICESIMO PRIMO
VICTORIÆ REGINÆ

Cap. CLIX

[An Act for incorporating the Eastern Bengal Railway Company, and for other Purposes. Act 20 and 21Vic., Cap. 159, 25th August 1857]

Gist: The Act of Incorporation of the Eastern Bengal Railway Company passed in the British Parliament on 25 August 1857 was intended to build a railway link between Calcutta and Dacca. The Act has 48 sections, besides first paragraph. Initial capital was 1 million Pounds in 50,000 shares of 20 Pounds each. The company can sue and be sued in England, India and elsewhere. The company has the responsibility to build all requisites including ferries and floating bridges, telegraphs, etc. The company had 7 directors, and they should not be fewer than 4 and more than 12 if their number is changed. General meetings and Directors meetings are to be held only in England. Company has provisions of issuing shares, giving dividends, and conversion of debts into capital. The costs of passing the Act had been borne by the company.

Whereas several Persons lately associated themselves together for promoting the Establishment of a Company (to be called the Eastern Bengal Railway Company) for making and maintaining a Railway (to be called the Eastern Bengal Railway) from Calcutta on the Left Bank of the Hooghly, through the Districts of Kishnaghur, Jessore, and Pubna, to the Right Bank of Ganges at Kooshtee, and ultimately to the City of Dacca, and with Power to raise in the first instance for the Purpose of the Railway a Capital of One million Pounds in Fifty thousand Shares of Twenty Pounds each, and afterwards to raise such further Capital as might be requisite for the Extension to Dacca: And whereas the Promoters of the Undertaking have obtained from the East India Company a Guarantee of Interest upon the Capital to be raised in the first instance: And whereas it is expedient that a Company be incorporated for the Purposes of Undertaking, with the Powers for carrying those Purposes into effect: And whereas the Objects of this Act cannot be attained without the Authority of Parliament: May it therefore please Your Majesty that it may be enacted; and be it enacted by the Queen's Most Excellent Majesty, by and with the Advice and Consent of the Lord's Spiritual and Temporal, and Commons, in this present Parliament assembled, and by the Authority of the Same, as follows:

I. This Act may be cited for all Purposes as "The Eastern Bengal Railway Act, 1857."

II. In this Act, the following Words and Expressions have the following Meanings, unless excluded by the Subject or Context; (to wit,)

The Expression "East India Company" means and includes the Honourable East India Company and Other (if any) the Supreme Government from Time to Time of India, by whomsoever or under whatsoever Authority or in the whatsoever Part of India the Functions of the Supreme Government are from Time to Time discharged:

The word "India" means and includes the Territories now and from Time to Time hereafter under the Government of the East India Company:

The Expression "the Railway" means and includes all Railways, Works, and Conveniences from Time to Time belonging to the Company, and all Lands from Time to Time acquired by the Company for the Purposes thereof:

The world "Land" means and includes Messuages, Lands, Tenements, and Hereditaments of whatsoever Tenure, and Easements, Rights, Powers, and Privileges in, over, and effecting Messuages, Lands, Tenements, and Hereditaments of whatsoever Tenure:

The word "Share" includes Stock:

The word "Shareholder" includes Stockholder.

III. "The Companies Clauses Consolidation Act, 1845" is incorporated with this Act, and applies to the Company in India and elsewhere as well as in England, and the several Powers and Provisions thereof shall be construed and have effect accordingly; and in the Construction of that Act for the Purposes of this Act the following Words and Expressions have the following Meanings, unless excluded by the Subject or Context; (to wit,)

The Expression "Superior Courts" includes Her Majesty's Supreme Courts of Judicature at the several Presidencies in India respectively, and the Courts of the East India Company:

The word "Justice" and the Expression "Master in Chancery" respectively include a Justice of Peace or Magistrate in India, or any Officer authorized to take an Affidavit or Declaration in the Supreme Court of any Presidency in India:

The Expression "Two Justices" means with respect to India any One Justice of the Peace or Magistrate in India, and whatsoever Proceedings or Act for the Purposes of this Act if had or done in England might be had or done by, under, before, or with respect to Two Justices may, if had or done in India, be had or done by, under, before, or with respect to any One Justice of the Peace or Magistrate in India.

IV. Except as is by this Act otherwise expressly provided, the several Words and Expressions to which by the Act incorporated with this Act Meanings are assigned have in this Act the same respective Meanings, unless excluded by the Subject or, Context.

V. John Farley Leith, William Anderson, William Walter Cargill, James Fargusson, James Thompson Mackenzie, Robert Guthrie Macgregor, and William Miller, and all other Persons who have already subscribed or hereafter subscribe for Shares in the Capital of the Company, and all other Persons who become Shareholders in the Company, and their respective Successors,

Executors, Administrators, and Assigns, shall be and are by this Act united into One Body Corporate by the Name of "The Eastern Bengal Railway Company," with perpetual Succession and a Common Seal, and with Power by that Name to sue and be sued in England, in India, and elsewhere, and to purchase, take, hold, and dispose of Lands in India for the Purposes of this Act, and to make, maintain, regulate, work, and use the Eastern Bengal Railway as now proposed, or any Railway in India wholly or partly in lieu thereof, and any Extensions of and Branches from the same, and any Works and Conveniences connected therewith including all requisite Ferries and connexions by means of Floating Bridges or otherwise across Rivers and Waters, and other Means of Communication by Water and Telegraphs, and to enter into and carry into effect all Contracts for those Purposes and in all other respects to carry this Act into execution.

VI. The Company may prepare a Seal for Use in India in lieu of the Common Seal of the Company, and from Time to Time may vary and renew it, and make Regulations for its User; and except as is by this Act otherwise expressly provided, every Document sealed with such Seal in conformity with such Regulations, or in pursuance of any Order of the Directors, or of any Authority given by the Company under their Common Seal, shall be as Valid and effectual as if the Common Seal were affixed thereto.

VII. The Company from Time to Time may negotiate for, conclude, enter into with the East India Company, and carry into effect Contracts, and Arrangements with respect to all or any of the following Matters; (to wit,)

1. The making, maintaining, regulating, working, and using by the Company of the Eastern Bengal Railway as now proposed, or any Railway in India wholly or partly in lieu thereof, and any Extensions of and Branches from the same respectively, and any Works and Conveniences connected therewith:
2. The acquiring by the Company of Lands in India for the Purposes of their Undertaking:
3. The obtaining by the Company from the East India Company of any Guarantee of Interest on the Capital of the Company, and any other Support, Countenance, and Facilities for the Purposes of the Undertaking:
4. The securing to the East India Company of any Facilities, Rights, and Advantages with respect to the Railway:
5. The making of Provision with respect to the Classification of Shares in the Capital of the Company, and the Rate of Dividend thereon respectively, and the Conversion of Debt into Capital, and the Amounts and Times of Calls on Shares, and the Transfers of Shares, including Restrictions on the Transfer of Shares not fully paid up, and the Tolls, Charges, Revenue, and Profits of the Company, and the Deposit, Custody, and Application thereof respectively:
6. The giving to the East India Company, and to any of their Officers, Agents, Servants, of any absolute or other Rights of supervising, controlling, and regulating the Company, and the Works, Contracts, Accounts, Byelaws, Proceedings, Acts, and Affairs of the Company in England, in India, and elsewhere respectively:
7. The enabling of the East India Company to appoint an ex-officio Director of the Company (whether qualified by holding Shares or not) in the Place of any ordinary

Director of the Company or otherwise:

8. The regulating of the Powers (including a Right of Veto) at the Board of Directors, and the Duties, Proceedings, and Liabilities of any such ex-officio Director:
9. The binding of the Company to conform to and fulfil any Directions given by the East India Company, or by their Officers or Agents in that Behalf authorized, touching all or any of the Matters aforesaid:
10. The appointing of Agents of the Company in India or elsewhere, and the determining and regulating of their Powers, Duties, and Remuneration:
11. The depositing with or paying to the East India Company of all or any Part of the subscribed Capital or other Money of the Company upon any Terms as to Interest or otherwise agreed on:
12. The making of Provision with respect to any Land granted or leased to the Company by the East India Company or otherwise:
13. The charging of all or any Part of the Property of the Company with any Sum of Money on any Terms agreed on:
14. The surrendering or selling at any future Period to the East India Company, or to any other Persons, of the Railway, or any Part thereof, or of all or any Part of the Property of the Company, and the winding up of the Affairs of the Company, and the Distribution of net Assets of the Company among the Shareholders:
15. The referring of Differences to Arbitration:
16. The making of Provision for enforcing or securing the due Performance of any Contract or Arrangement made by the Company:
17. The uniting of all or any Part of the Railway, or of the Undertaking of the Company, or both, with any other Railway or Undertaking:
18. Generally all such Provisions and Stipulations with respect to the Matters aforesaid or any of them, and the Undertaking of the Company, and the Encouragement and Promotion thereof, and the eventual or contingent Transfer of the same or any Part thereof to the East India Company, or to any other Persons as the East India Company and the Company think fit and mutually agree on:

And so far as any such Contract or Arrangement affects the Interest of the Shareholders, or of any Class of the Shareholders, they shall be bound thereby.

VIII. The Company and the East India Company respectively from Time to Time may negotiate for, conclude, and enter into any Contracts and Arrangements for any of the Purposes of this Act in addition to or by way of Repeal or Modification of any Contracts or Arrangements theretofore entered into by them under this Act.

IX. If there be in any such Contract or Arrangement any Provision for referring Differences between the Company and the East India Company to Arbitration, then, except so far as is by the Contract or Arrangement otherwise provided, the Provisions with respect to the Settlement of Disputes by Arbitration of "Companies Clauses Consolidation Act, 1845," shall extend and apply to every Arbitration so provided for.

X. The Company from Time to Time may demand, take, and recover such Tolls and Charges with respect to the User of the Railway as the East India Company sanction.

XI. The First Ordinary Meeting of the Company shall be held within Twelve Months after the passing of this Act, and all the General Meetings of the Company shall be held in England in such Months as the Company from Time to Time resolve; and Notice of a General Meeting shall be sufficient if given only in England.

XII. The Number of Directors shall be Seven, but by the Resolution of a General Meeting, the Number may from Time to Time be increased or reduced, but not to be fewer than Four or more than Twelve.

XIII. The Qualification of a Director shall be the possession in his own Right and as the sole Holder thereof of Twenty-five Shares.

XIV. All the Meetings of the Directors shall be held in England.

XV. The Quorum of the Meetings of the Directors shall be such Number as the East India Company and the Company mutually determine, but until they otherwise determine shall be Three.

XVI. John Farley Leith, William Anderson, William Walter Cargill, James Fargusson, James Thompson Mackenzie, Robert Guthrie Macgregor, and William Miller shall be the First and present Directors of the Company.

XVII. The Directors appointed by this Act shall continue in Office until the First Ordinary Meeting, and at that Meeting the Shareholders present, personally or by Proxy, may either continue in Office the Directors appointed by this Act, or elect a New Body of Directors to supply their place, the retiring Directors being in qualified, eligible for Re-election.

XVIII. The Company from Time to Time may appoint and remove such Committees, Person, or Persons as the Company think fit to act on behalf of the Company in India or elsewhere, with respect to the making, maintaining, managing, working, and using of the Railway, and the Disposal of Issue, Registration, and Transfer of Shares and of Bonds, and the Registration of Transfer of Shares and of Bonds, and the Registration of Shareholders, and the Control and Conduct of any of the Affairs, in India of elsewhere, or the Company, and may delegate to any such Committee, Persons, and Person respectively all or any of the Powers of the Company, and of the Directors and Officers thereof, which the Company think it expedient that such Committee, Persons, and Person respectively should possess for the Purposes of them and his respective appointment.

XIX. The Company from Time to Time determine the Quorum of any such Committee or Persons, and may determine and regulate the Authority, Duties Procedure, Liabilities, and Remuneration of any such Committee, Persons, and Person respectively, and generally may make such Provisions and Regulations for their and his respective Government and Conduct as the Company think expedient.

XX. All the Proceedings and Acts of such Committees, Persons, and Person respectively within their and his respective Authority shall (but subject to any Regulations of the Company requiring such Proceedings and Acts or any of them to be confirmed by the Directors) be as valid and effectual as if they were Proceedings and Acts of the Directors.

XXI. The Committees, Persons, and Person respectively so from Time to Time appoint shall, with respect to all their and his respective lawful Proceedings and Acts within the Limits of the Authority conferred on them and him respectively, have the like Discretions and Indemnities as if they and be respectively were or was Directors or a Director of the Company.

XXII. It shall not be requisite for any Auditor to have any Share in the Undertaking.

XXIII. The original Capital of the Company shall be One million Pounds.

XXIV. The Company, with the sanction of a General Meeting, may from Time to Time increase the Capital to any Amount not exceeding in the whole One million five hundred thousand Pounds, or, with the Sanction of the East India Company and of a General Meeting, to any Amount not exceeding in the whole Six million Pounds.

XXV. The additional Capital from Time to Time created by the Company shall be Part of their general Capital; and except as is by this Act otherwise expressly provided, all such Rights, Privileges, Liabilities, and Incidents shall attach to and be conferred by the additional Capital and the Shares therein as to and by the original Capital and Shares therein.

XXVI. The Shares in the original Capital shall be Fifty thousand Shares of Twenty Pounds each, and the Shares in any additional Capital shall be, of such Amount as consistently with the Provisions of this Act, the Company think fit.

XXVII. The Company from Time to Time, with the sanction of at least Three Fifths of the Votes of the Shareholders present, personal or by Proxy, at a General Meeting specially convened for the Purpose, may and issue the Shares in the additional Capital, either of One Class and with the like Privileges, or of several Classes and with different Privileges, and respectively with any fixed, fluctuating, preferential, perpetual, terminable, redeemable, or other Dividend, and with such Privileges and subject to such Restrictions (if any), as the Company think fit: Provided always, that all the Shares of the same Class be of the like Amount, and all the Shares of the same Class shall bear like Dividend and confer like Privileges, and be subject to like Restrictions (if any): Provided also, that no Preference in Payment of Dividend shall be created to the Prejudice of any Preference Payment of Dividend previously created.

XXVIII. The additional Capital shall be divided into shares of such Amount as conveniently allows the same to be apportioned among the then Shareholders in proportion to the existing Shares held by them respectively.

XXIX. The new Shares shall be offered to the then Shareholders in that proportion, and the Offer shall be made by Letter under the Hand of the Secretary or his substitute authorized by the Directors, given or sent by Post addressed to every Shareholder according to his address in the Shareholders Address Book, or left at his usual or last known Place of Abode.

XXX. The new Shares shall vest in and belong to the Shareholders who accept the same and pay the Value thereof to the Company at the Times and by the Instalments fixed by the Company: Provided always, that if any Shareholder fail, if he be in England, for One Month, or if he be in India for Four Months, after such Offer of new Shares, to accept the same and pay the instalments called for in respect thereof, the Company may dispose of such New Shares as they think fit.

XXXI. Certificates of the Proprietorship of Shares registered in England, shall have the Common Seal of the Company affixed thereto, and if issued in India, shall have the Common Seal of the Company and the Seal (if any) for India respectively affixed thereto.

XXXII. Notice of every Call made on Shares registered in England shall be sufficient if given only in England, and Notice of every Call made on Shares registered in India shall be sufficient if only given in India.

XXXIII. The Company may borrow on Bond but not on Mortgage any Sums, but, unless with the Sanction of the East India Company, not exceeding in the whole One Third Part of the Capital from Time to Time subscribed for, and whereof One Half is actually paid up.

XXXIV. The Bonds if issued in England, shall have the Common Seal of the Company affixed thereto, and, if issued in India, shall have the Common Seal of the Company and to Seal (if any) for India respectively affixed thereto.

XXXV. All Claims of the East India Company against the Company shall have Priority over all Claims of the all Obligees in the Bonds, except only with respect to Bonds issued with the Sanction of the East India Company, or so far as the East India Company from Time to Time consents to waive such Priority.

XXXVI. The Company from Time to Time may establish at such Place in India as they think fit an Office for the Issue, Registration, and Transfer of Shares and Bonds, and the Registration of Transfers of Shares and Bonds, and the Registration of Shareholders, and may alter the Place of any such Office, and may make such Regulations consistent with the Provisions of this Act as they think fit for enabling the Issue, Registration, and Transfer of Shares and Bonds, and the Registration of Transfers of Shares and Bonds, and the Registration of Shareholders at such Office; and all the Provisions of this Act with respect to the Issue, Registration, and Transfer of Shares and Bonds, and the Registration of Transfers of Shares and of Bonds, and the Registration of Shareholders, and to Shares, Bonds, and Transfers, and to Shareholders, Bondholders, the Company, and all other Persons with respect to the same, shall be construed and have effect accordingly.

XXXVII. The Company shall keep at such Office in India Books to be called respectively "the India Register of Shareholders," and "the India Shareholders Address Book," and "the India Register of Transfers," and, if the Capital or any Part thereof be consolidated into Stock, another Book to be called "the India Register of Holders of Consolidated Stock," and also Book for the Registration of Bonds and Transfers of Bonds, and the Books so kept shall be of the like Validity and Effect as the Books kept for like Purposes by the Company in England.

XXXVIII. Provided always, That if and when the Company have Offices in India at more Places than One, then the Company shall substitute for or add to the Word "India" in the Titles of the Registers kept at every such Office the Name the Place at which the respective Office is established.

XXXIX. No Share or Bond shall be on the Register of more than One Office at one and the same Time: Provided always, that the Company may keep in England Duplicates of any Books of Register kept in India, but no such Duplicate Book shall be deemed a Register.

XL. The Entry of a Transfer of a Share or of a Bond shall be made only at the Office at which the Shares or the Bond is registered.

XLI. Subject to the Regulations from Time to Time made by the Company with respect to the Issue, Registration, and Transfer of Shares and Bonds respectively, and the Registration of Transfers of Shares and of Bonds respectively, the Company may and shall, on Notice in Writing by the Holder of any Share or Bond to the Person acting as Secretary or principal Clerk at the

Office in England or in India where the Share or Bond is then registered, transfer the Share or Bond from the Register thereof at that Office to the corresponding Register at any other Office, and so soon as conveniently may be after the Receipt of any such Notice such Secretary or principal Clerk shall transmit Advice thereof to the Office to which the Transfer is directed to be made.

XLII. For the Purpose of determining any Question as to the Place or Jurisdiction at or within any Share or Bond shall be deemed to be at any Time situated, the Locality, whether in England or in India, of the Register in which the Share or Bond is or was actually registered, shall be deemed the then Locality of the Share or Bond; and so soon as Notice for the Transfer of any Share or Bond from one Register to another is given according to this Act, the Share or Bond shall for the Purpose of this Section be deemed to be actually registered in the Register to which it is so directed to be transferred.

XLIII. The Newspapers for Advertisements in England shall be a London Daily Morning Newspaper, and the Newspaper for Advertisements in India shall be a Newspaper published and commonly circulated in the Presidency of Bengal.

XLIV. All Notices by the Company which, if given in England, would be published in the London Gazette shall, if given in India, be sufficient if published in the Newspaper in India in which official Notices by the East India Company are usually published.

XLV. The Byelaws from Time to Time made by the Company to have effect in India shall not be repugnant to the Laws of that Part of India where they are to have effect, and shall be approved by the East India Company, or by such Judicial or other Authority as the East India Company think fit.

XLVI. The Justice or Magistrate by whom any Penalty or Forfeiture is imposed in India may award to the Company such Part thereof as he does not award to the Informer.

XLVII. The Appeal from any Determination or Adjudication of any Justice or Magistrate in India may be made to the Court having ordinary Jurisdiction over his Adjudications, and the Court may hear, proceed on, and determine the Appeal accordingly.

XLVIII. All the Costs, Charges, and Expenses of and incident to the obtaining and passing of this Act, and the Formation and Establishment of the Company, shall be borne and paid by the Company.

London, Printed by George Edward Eyre and William Spottiswoode, Printers to the Queen's most Excellent Majesty, 1861.

367

Act of Incorporation of the Great Southern of India Railway Company, 1858

Source: Acts on Railways, London, 1886

ANNO VICESIMO PRIMO & VICESIMO SECUNDO
VICTORIÆ REGINÆ

Cap. CXXXVIII

[An Act to incorporate and regulate the Great Southern of India Railway Company, and for other Purposes connected therewith. Act 21 and 22 Vic., Cap. 138, 2nd August 1858]

Gist: The Act of Incorporation of the Great Southern of India Railway Company passed in British the Parliament on 2 August 1858 has 40 sections, besides the first paragraph. The company was constituted under the Joint Stock Companies Act, 1856 with principal office in London and the company had borne costs of passing the Act. The Great Southern of India Railway Company (Limited) was formed to construct railways and accessories including tramways if needed in places mostly included in the southern parts of present Kerala and Tamil Nadu. Initial capital was 1 million Pounds in 50,000 shares of 20 Pounds each. Provisions are also there for Indian office, registers and seal, ex-officio director besides shareholder directors, and auditors by rotation.

Whereas a Company has been duly constituted under "The Joint Stock Companies Act, 1856," by a Memorandum of Association filed in accordance with the said Act, by the Name of "The Great Southern of India Railway Company (Limited)," for the Purpose of affording Railway Communication to the Provinces of Southern India, including, among other Places, Salem, Trinchinopoly, Tanjore, Majore, Madura, Tinnivelly, Tuticorin, Travancore, and such other Places as the said Company might from Time to Time determine, and the doing of all such other Things as were identical or conducive to the above Object; and it was thereby declared, that their registered Office was to be established in England, and that their Capital was One million Pounds, divided into Fifty thousand Shares of Twenty Pounds each, and the Articles of Association of the said Railway Company have been duly registered, and the said Company were thereby empowered, with the sanction of a General Meeting of the Shareholders, to increase their Capital, without any Restriction as to the Amount of such Increase: And whereas the said Company as constituted under the said Memorandum and Articles of Association, had Power to borrow any Sums of Money; And whereas the Execution of the Undertaking of the said Company would be of great public Advantage not only to the Inhabitants of India, but also to commerce in general, and the Honourable East India Company have sanctioned a guarantee of Interest to the said Company; but the Objects aforesaid cannot be fully effected without the further Incorporation of the Company by the Authority of Parliament, nor without other Powers which can only be conferred by the same Authority: May it therefore please Your Majesty that it be enacted; and be it enacted by the Queen's most Excellent Majesty, by and with the Advice and Consent of the Lord's Spiritual and Temporal, and Commons, in this present Parliament assembled, and by the Authority of the same, as follows; that is to say,

I. This Act may be cited for all Purposes as "The Great Southern of India Railway Act, 1858."

II. The following Words and Expressions shall in this Act have the several Meanings hereby assigned to them, except where the Subject or Context shall be inconsistent therewith; that is to say,

The Expression "the original Company" means the "Great Southern of India Railway Company (Limited)," as constituted immediately before the passing of this Act:

The Expression "The Company" means the Company incorporated by this Act:

The Expression "The East India Company" means and includes the Honourable East India Company and their Successors, and other, if any, the Supreme Government from Time to Time of India:

The Word "Lands" means and includes Messuages, Lands, Tenements, and Hereditaments of any Tenure, and Easements, Rights, Powers, and Privileges in, over, and affecting Messuages, Lands, Tenements, and Hereditaments of any Tenure:

The Word "Share" includes Stock:

The Word "Shareholder" includes Stockholders.

III. From and after the passing of this Act the said Memorandum and Articles of Association shall be void and of no further effect.

IV. Notwithstanding the Avoidance of the said Memorandum and Articles of Association, and except only as is by this Act otherwise expressly provided, everything before the passing of this Act done and suffered respectively under that Memorandum or those Articles shall be as valid as if this Act were not passed; and such Avoidance and this Act respectively shall accordingly be subject and without Prejudice to everything so done and suffered respectively, and to all Rights, Liabilities, Claims, and Demands, both present and future, which, if any such Avoidance had not happened and this Act were not passed, would be incident to and consequent on any and every thing so done and suffered respectively; and with respect to all such Rights, Liabilities, Claims, and Demands, the Company shall to all Intents and Purposes represent the original Company: Provided always, that the Generality of this Enactment shall not be restrained by any of the other Provisions of this Act.

V. Notwithstanding the Avoidance of the said Memorandum and Articles of Association, all Contracts, Covenants, Agreements, or Obligations executed, entered into, or granted by, with, to, or in favour of the original Company, and now in force, shall be as good, valid, subsisting, and effectual for, in favour of, against, and in respect to the Company and their Successors, and may be claimed, enforced, and acted on as fully and effectually to all Intents and Purposes, as if instead of the original Company the Company had been Party thereto or named or referred to therein.

VI. Notwithstanding the Avoidance of the said Memorandum and Articles of Association, any Action, Suit, Prosecution, or other Proceeding whatsoever commenced before the passing of this Act, either by or on behalf of or against the original Company, shall not cease, abate, be suspended, or discontinued, but shall continue valid and in force, and shall take effect in favour of or against the Company, as the Case may be, in the same Manner in all respects as the same would or might have continued and remained in force or taken effect in favour of or against the original Company if this Act had not been Passed.

VII. Notwithstanding the Avoidance of the said Memorandum and Articles of Association, all Persons who, immediately before the passing of this Act, owed any Sum of Money to the original Company, or to any Person on their Behalf, shall pay the same, with all Interest (if any) due and payable or accruing for the same, to the Company; and all Debts and Moneys which, immediately before the passing of this Act, were due or owing by or recoverable from the original Company, or for the payment of which the original Company were or but for the Repeal of this Act would be liable, shall be paid, with all Interest (if any) due and payable or accruing for the same, by or be recoverable from the Company.

VIII. The several Persons who immediately before the passing of this Act were respectively the Holders of Shares in the original Company shall become and be Shareholders in the Company, and they, and all other Persons who shall from Time to Time become Shareholders in the Company, and their Executors, Administrators, Successors, and Assigns respectively, shall, while respectively continuing to be such Shareholders, be united into and be a Company for the Purposes herein mentioned by the Name of "The Great Southern of India Railway Company," and by that Name shall be a Body Corporate, with a Common Seal, with perpetual Succession in England, in India, and in all other Places, and shall have Power to purchase and hold Lands for the Purposes of the Undertaking, subject to the Restrictions herein contained.

IX. The Business and Objects of the Company, and for which they are incorporated, are to afford Railway Communication to the Provinces of Southern India, and such other Places as they may from Time to Time determine, by constructing, maintaining, and working Railways, and by the Performance of all other Matters and Things incidental or conducive thereto.

X. The Company may purchase by Agreement and hold such Lands in England as they may require for the Purposes of their Undertaking not exceeding One Rood.

XI. All Property, real and Personal, and all Debts, Books and Writings, belonging to the original Company, or which have been conveyed to or are held by any Person in trust for the original Company, and all Rights and Powers of the original Company, subject to any Engagements affecting the same, shall be vested in the Company without the Necessity of any Transfer or connecting Title other than this Act; and all Contracts, Covenants, Engagements, and Liabilities now existing with or by the original Company, or any Director, Trustee, or Person duly authorized by and on behalf of the original Company, shall and may be enforced by, with, and against the Company, and the Company shall and may sue and be sued in respect thereof in the same Manner as if the Company had been Party thereto.

XII. The Registrations of "The Joint Stock Companies Acts, 1856-1857," and the Memorandum of Association and Articles of Association of the Company, shall no longer apply to the Company, but "The Companies Clauses Consolidation Act, 1845" (in this Act called "the incorporated Act,") shall be incorporated with and form Part of this Act, and shall extend and apply, so far as applicable, and not hereinafter varied or altered, to all Acts and Proceedings in India, in the same Manner as in England; and in the incorporated Act the Expression "lawful interest," and all analogous Expressions, shall be held to mean Interest as the rate of Five Pounds per Centum per Annum.

XIII. The Byelaws made by the Company under the Provisions of the incorporated Act to have Effect in India shall not be repugnant to the Laws of India; and as to the Clauses of the incorporated Act with respect to the Payment of Subscriptions, and the Means of enforcing Payment of Calls, the Supreme Courts of Jurisdiction in India shall have Jurisdiction in Cases where the Company shall sue Shareholders in India for the Amount of Calls; and the same Course of Procedure shall be adopted in all Actions and Suits in the said Supreme Courts as in Actions and Suits in England in the like Matters under the last-mentioned Clauses, or as near thereto as the Laws or Rules of the said Supreme Court will allow; and as to the Clauses with respect to the Forfeiture of Shares for Non-payment of Calls, the Notice of Forfeiture in the same Clauses directed to be given before a Declaration of Forfeiture is made shall, with respect to the Forfeiture of Shares held in India, be duly given in the Government Gazette published at Madras, and also in some Newspapers published there; and as to the Clauses with respect to the giving of Notices, the Reference in the same Clauses to any Act for the Relief of Insolvent Debtors shall be construed to include the Act or Acts of Parliament for the Time being in force relating to Insolvent Debtors in India, and the Managing Director, Secretary, or Treasurer of the Company shall have Power to authorize by Letter of Attorney some other Officer in India of the Company to represent the Company in all Cases of Bankruptcy and Insolvency in India, and to act therein in like Manner as it shall be lawful for the Managing Director, Secretary, or Treasurer of the Company to act under the last-mentioned Clauses in like Cases in England; and the Provision made by the same Clauses for the Tender of Amends in India; and as to the Clauses with respect to Provision to be made for affording Access to the Special Act by all Parties interested, a printed Copy shall be kept in the principal Place of Business in India of the Company, as well as their principal Place of Business in England; and any Declarations which by the incorporated Act are authorized to be made before a Justice or before a Master in Chancery shall be of the same Force and Effect if made before a Justice of the Peace or Magistrate in India, or before any Officer authorized to take an Affidavit or Declaration in any of the Supreme Courts of Judicature in India; and for the Purpose of this Act the Expression "Supreme Courts" in the incorporated Act shall extend to the Supreme Courts of Jurisdiction in India, and the Word "Justice" in the same Act shall extend to any Justice of Peace or Magistrate in India or other Person in India duly authorized to act as a Justice of the Peace or Magistrate in India, and the Expression "General Quarter Sessions" in the same Act shall extend to any Courts or Sessions of the Peace in India.

XIV. It shall be lawful for the Company from Time to Time to enter into and conclude with the East India Company on account of the Government of India, and to carry into effect, such Contracts, Agreements, and Arrangements as the respective Parties may think fit and agree upon, for or connected with, or incident to, or respecting all or any or either of the Objects and Purposes aforesaid, including the making of Surveys and preliminary Arrangements for any Works, Railways, Tramways, and other Means of Transit, although there shall be at the Time no Contract for the Execution of the same, and also including, so far as the said respective Parties may agree thereto, all or any of the Provisions following; (that is to say,) any Provision for enabling the East India Company to guarantee Interest on the Capital and Loan of the Company, and to afford any other Support, Countenance, and Facilities for the Purposes of their Undertaking; and any Provisions for securing to the East India Company any Rights and Advantages in relation to all or any of the said Works, Railways, Tramways and Premises respectively, and the Revenues, Royalties, Rents, Tolls, Receipts, Dues, and Profits thereof, or to be derived therefrom, and the Application of such Revenues, Royalties, Rents, Tolls, Receipts, Dues, and Profits, or for giving to the East India Company, or to any of their Officers, Servants, or Agents, any absolute or other Rights of supervising, controlling, directing, regulating, and ordering the Company, and the Works, Contracts, Accounts, Byelaws, Acts, Proceedings, Transactions, and Affairs of the Company, as well in England as elsewhere; and any Provisions for enabling the East India Company to appoint an ex officio Director of the Company, whether qualified by holding Shares or not, in addition to the ordinary Directors of the Company, or otherwise; and any Provisions for regulating the Powers (including a Right of Veto at the Board of Directors), and the Duties and Proceedings, and the Liabilities of any such Official Director, and for binding the Company to conform to and fulfil all or any Directions which may be given by the East India Company, or their authorized Officers and Agents, touching all or any of the Matters aforesaid, and for the Appointment of Agents of the Company in India or elsewhere, and for determining and regulating the Powers and Duties of such Agents as aforesaid, and for depositing with or paying to the East India Company all or any Part of the subscribed Capital of the Company, upon any Terms (as to Interest, Guarantee, or otherwise) to be agreed upon; and any Provisions with regard to any Land which may be granted or leased to the Company by the East India Company or otherwise, and for charging all or any Part of the Property of the Company with the Payment of any Sum or Sums of Money upon any Terms to be agreed upon; and any Provisions for entering into and fulfilling any Arrangements with any other Company or Body with reference to the Construction and Use of connecting Lines and Works, the Use of Railways of the Company, and the Conveyance of Passengers and Traffic, which may be deemed expedient for the public Advantage; and also Provisions for the Surrender, leasing, or Sale to the East India Company, or to any Person or Persons, of the Works, Railways, Tramways, and Premises of the Company, at any future Period, either absolutely or for any Term or Terms of Years or other Period; and any Provisions referring Disputes to Arbitration; and any Provisions intended to enforce or secure the due Performance of any Contract or Engagement to be made by or to the Company; and generally all such Provisions and Stipulations in relation to the Matters aforesaid, or any of them, and in relation to all or any or either of the Objects of the Company, and the Encouragement and Promotion thereof, and the immediate, eventual, or contingent leasing, Sale, or Transfer of the Undertaking, or any Part thereof, to the East India Company, or, with Consent of the East India Company, to any other Company or Corporation, Person, or Persons, as the said respective Parties shall think fit and agree upon; and from Time to Time to vary and alter or rescind such Contracts, Agreements, and Arrangements, and to enter into new or other Contracts, Agreements, and Arrangements, in relation to the Premises; all which Contracts, Agreements, and Arrangements (the same being within the Objects authorized by this Act, and in accordance with the Provisions and Clauses by which the Company would otherwise be governed,) shall be valid and effectual and binding to all Intents and Purposes whatsoever, and full Effect shall be given to the same accordingly.

XV. The Capital of the Company shall be Sum of One million Pounds Sterling (being the Amount of the existing Capital of the original Company), in Fifty thousand Shares of Twenty Pounds each, but subject to increase as hereinafter provided.

XVI. Every Person who, immediately before the passing of this Act, was the Holder of a Share or Shares in the original Company, shall immediately after the passing of this Act, become entitled to and be registered as the Holder of the same Number of Shares in the Company as he previously held in the Capital of the original Company, which Shares shall be indicated in the Register by the same Number as, and be made in all respects to correspond as nearly as possible with, those held by him in the original Company.

XVII. It shall be lawful for the Company at any Time or Times to increase the Capital of the Company by an Amount not exceeding Two million Pounds Sterling, for carrying into effect any Contract or Agreement with the East India Company, by the Creation of a Number of new or additional Shares of Twenty Pounds each, and to issue and allot all or any of such new Shares or additional Shares, when so created, either to Proprietors for the Time being of Shares in the Company, or to any other Person or Persons whomsoever who shall respectively be willing to take the same, upon such Terms, and subject to such Regulations as to the Distribution of Profits or otherwise, as at the Time of such Issue shall be deemed expedient; and in all other respect such new and additional Shares, and the Holders thereof, shall be subject to the same Laws, Regulations, and Provisions as the existing Shares in the Company.

XVIII. Three Calendar Months at least shall be the Interval between every Two successive Calls, and Five Pounds per Share shall be the greatest amount of any One Call which shall be made in respect of such Shares, and not more than Three-Fourths of the Amount of any Share shall be called up in any One Year.

XIX. The principal Office and corporate Domicile of the Company shall be in London.

XX. The Ordinary General Meetings of the Shareholders shall be held in London in the Months of April or October, or at such other stated Periods as shall be appointed for that Purpose by an Order of a General Meeting of the Shareholders; and the First Ordinary General Meeting shall be held in the Month of April in the Year One thousand eight hundred and fifty-nine, and so long as there shall be but One Ordinary General Meeting in the Year, the Balance Sheet to be produced at each such Meeting, or any Adjournment thereof, shall embrace and extend to the Transactions of the whole preceding Year.

XXI. The Quorum to be present, either personally or by Proxy; in order to constitute a Meeting of the Shareholders, shall be Shareholders holding in the aggregate not less than One

Fiftieth of the Capital of the Company, and bearing in Number not less than Twenty: Provided nevertheless, that no Business shall be proceeded with after the Chair shall be vacated.

XXII. A Poll shall not be taken unless demanded in writing by at least Five Shareholders, and if demanded shall be taken in such Manner as the Chairman of the Meeting shall direct, but so that the same be concluded within One Month at least from such Meeting.

XXIII. The Number of Directors (exclusive of the ex-officio Director, if any, and of any Directors from India alone) shall be Five, and the Persons who immediately before the passing of this Act were the Directors of the original Company shall be the First Directors of the Company.

XXIV. The Qualification of a Director (other than any Director for India alone) shall be the Possession in his own Right of Fifty Shares at the least.

XXV. The Board of Directors in London may appoint Persons in India (not exceeding Three in Number), being Shareholders, to be Directors in and for India alone, and may from Time to Time fix the Rotation and Retirement of such Directors, and supply or authorize them to supply Vacancies in their Number, and the Qualification of every such Director shall be the Possession in his own Right of Twenty-five Shares at least, and Three of such Indian Directors shall constitute a Board; and any such Director being absent from India for Six consecutive Months, or ceasing to hold in his own Right Twenty-five Shares, shall cease to be a Director.

XXVI. Candidates for the Office of the Directors or Auditor shall give Notice in writing of their intention to offer themselves for Election, by sending the same, addressed to the Directors, at the Company's principal Office in England, Thirty Days at least before the Ordinary Meeting at which the Election is to take place.

XXVII. There shall be Two Auditors of the Company, but it shall not be necessary for any Auditor to be a Shareholder, One of such Auditors (to be determined, in the first instance, by Ballot between themselves, unless they shall otherwise agree, and afterwards by Seniority) shall go out of Office at the First Ordinary Meeting in each Year, but the Auditor so going out shall be immediately re-eligible, and after any such Re-election shall, with respect to the going out of Office by Rotation, be deemed a new Auditor.

XXVIII. When and so soon as the whole of the said Capital of One million Pounds Sterling shall have been subscribed for, and One Half of such Capital shall have been paid up, it shall be lawful for the Company from Time to Time, by Order of a General Meeting, to borrow on Mortgage or Bond any Sums not exceeding in the whole Three hundred and thirty thousand Pounds, subject in all respects to such Provisions as the East India Company from Time to Time approve; and when and as from Time to Time the Capital of the Company shall be increased under the Powers of this Act in that Behalf, the Company may, by such Order and subject to such Provisions as aforesaid, borrow on Mortgage or Bond any further Sums not exceeding in the whole One Third of the Amount of the additional Capital beyond One million Pounds Sterling for the Time being subscribed for, and of which additional Capital One Half shall have been paid up.

XXIX. The Directors in London of the Company may establish in India One Office for the Issue, Registration, and Transfer of Shares, Stock, and Securities of the Company, and the Payment of Dividends and Interest, at such Place as they shall think fit, and from Time to Time may remove or alter the Place of such Office, and from Time to Time may make such Regulations as to the said Board may seem fit and expedient for enabling the Issue Transfer, and Registration at such Office of such Shares, Stock, and Securities, or of any of the said Shares, Stock, and Securities to be described in such Regulations, and the Payment of Dividends and Interest at such Office; and all and every the Powers and Provisions contained in this Act and in the incorporated Act in relation to the Issue, Transfer, and Registration of Shares, Stock, and Securities in Great Britain, shall apply and be in force as to the Shares, Stock, and Securities to be transferred and registered in India at such Office, except so far as the same are inconsistent with the Provisions of this Act.

XXX. The Directors in London of the Company may by Power of Attorney, under the Seal of the Company, nominate and appoint such Person or Persons as they shall approve to issue and dispose of Shares, Stock, and Securities of the Company, and pay Dividends and Interest at such Office in India, and from Time to Time may by Resolution remove such Person or Persons and appoint any other Person or Persons in his or their Place, and may, by Power of Attorney as aforesaid, delegate to such Person or all or any of such Persons respectively all or any of the Powers of the Directors or other Officers of the Company in relation to the Issue, Transfer, and Registration of Shares, Stock, and Securities of the Company, and Payment of Dividends and Interest, which they shall think necessary or expedient for the Issue, Transfer, and Registration of such Shares, Stock, and Securities, and Payment of such Dividends and Interest in India; and the said Board may from Time to Time make such Provisions and Regulations as they shall think fit for the Conduct, Government, and Management of the Person or Persons so to be appointed, and for the Issue, Transfer, and Registration of such Shares, Stock, and Securities, and Payment of Dividends and Interest as aforesaid, and may cause an Official Seal to be prepared for the Office which may be established in India as aforesaid, to be used by such Person or Persons in lieu of the Common Seal of the Company, and may from Time to Time destroy or vary and renew any such Seal; and all Documents duly sealed with such Official Seal, in pursuance and exercise of the Powers to be conferred on such Person or Persons, shall have the same Force and Effect as if they had been sealed with the Common Seal of the Company, except where by this Act the Common Seal of the Company is also required to be affixed thereto.

XXXI. The Directors shall cause to be kept at the Office which may be so established in India as aforesaid a Book, to be called "The Indian Register of Shareholders" and also (if any Shares shall be converted into Consolidated Stock) a Book for the Registry at such Office of Holders of Consolidated Stock, to be called "The Indian Register of Consolidated Stock," and also a Book for the Entry at such Office of Transfer of Shares and Stock, to be called "The Indian Register of Transfers," and also, if deemed necessary, Books to be called respectively "The Indian Register of Mortgages and Bonds," and "The Indian Register of Debentures," and shall cause Copies of all Entries and Alterations made in such Books respectively to be from Time to Time transmitted to the principal Office of the Company in London.

XXXII. Certificates of Shares and Securities issued in India shall have affixed thereto both the Common Seal of the Company and the Official Seal of the Office in India.

XXXIII. There shall be made in such Books respectively such Entries in respect of the Shares, Stock, and Securities issued at or from such Office, or for the Time being registered there as herein-after mentioned, as under the Provisions of the Act incorporated herewith are directed to be made in the corresponding Books in England; and for the Purposes of any Proceeding, or of entitling any Shareholder to participate in the Profits of the Undertaking, any Entry or Alteration which may subsequently be made in any of the corresponding Books in England, so as to make the same accord with the Books kept in India, shall be deemed to have been made at the Time when the corresponding Entry was made in the Register in India.

XXXIV. All Transfers of any Shares, Stock, and Securities as aforesaid shall be made at the Office at which the same respectively shall for the Time being be registered at the Office in India shall, on the Registers in England, be distinguished in such Manner as the Director shall determine.

XXXV. Subject to such Regulations and Conditions as the said Board of Directors may think fit and prescribe as to all or any of such Shares, Stock, and Securities as aforesaid, the Registry of any Shares, Stock, or Securities of the Company may and shall, on Notice in Writing by the Holder or Holders thereof being given to the Person for the Time being acting in the Capacity of Secretary or Principal Clerk at the Office of the Company, either in London or in India, where such Shares, Stock, or Securities shall for the Time being be registered, be transferred at the Expense of the Person giving such Notice from the Register thereof at such Office to the corresponding Register at the other Office of the Company; and as soon as conveniently may be after the giving of such Notice, Advice thereof shall be transmitted to the Office to which such Transfer is directed to be made, and the Secretary or Clerk receiving such Notice shall forthwith make or cause to be made in the proper Book in his Office, opposite the Name of the Person giving such Notice, an Entry of such Notice.

XXXVI. For the Purpose of determining any Question as to the Place or Jurisdiction within which any Shares, Stock, or Securities of the Company shall be deemed to be or to have been situated at any given Time, the Locality, whether in India or in Great Britain, of the Register in which such Shares, Stock, and Securities shall be or have been actually registered for the Time being shall be deemed to be or to have been at such Time and Locality of such Shares, Stock or Securities; and so soon as Notice shall have been given as aforesaid for the Transfer of the Registry of any Shares, Stock, or Securities from either of the said Registers to any other Register, such Share, Stock, or Securities shall for the Purpose aforesaid, be deemed to be actually registered in such last-mentioned Register.

XXXVII. Notwithstanding anything in the incorporated Act contained to the contrary, the Power of authorizing Proxies contained in that Act shall, as to Proxies authorized by Shareholders resident out of the United Kingdom, and notwithstanding their subsequent Death, extend to the authorizing of Proxies to vote at all or any Meetings in the United Kingdom to be held thereafter of the Shareholders within such Period from the Date of the Instrument of Proxy as shall be mentioned therein, until revoked or repealed by the Executors, Administrators, Assigns, or other proper legal Personal Representative of the Person giving the same; Provided always, that no Person shall be entitled to vote by way of Proxy, unless the Instrument of Proxy shall have been transmitted to or lodged with the managing Director, Secretary, or Clerk of the Company, or at the Office in London of the Company, not less than Forty-eight Hours before the Time appointed for holding the First Meeting at which the same is to be used.

XXXVIII. The Newspapers in which the Notices relating to the Proceedings of the Company shall be advertised shall be, as regards Proceedings in Great Britain, some Newspaper published Six Days in the week in London or Middlesex, and as regards Proceedings in India, some Newspaper published in the Presidency of Madras; and Notices affecting only Stock, Shares, and Securities registered in India shall be sufficient if given only in India.

XXXIX. The Company may from Time to Time enter into any Contract with any other Company, being Owners, Lessees, or in possession of any other Railway, for the Passage over or along the Railways of the Company of any Engines and Carriages of such other Company, or which shall pass over any other Line of Railway, or for the Passage over any other Line of Railway of any Engines and Carriages of the Company, or which shall pass over their or any of their Railways, upon the payment of such Tolls, and under such Conditions and Restrictions, as may be mutually agreed upon; and for the Purpose aforesaid it shall be lawful for the respective Parties to enter into any Contract for the Division or Apportionment of the Receipts, or any Part of the Receipts, upon their respective Railways.

XL. The Cost, Charges, and Expenses of and incident to obtaining and passing this Act shall be paid by the Company.

London: Printed by George Edward Eyre and William Spottiswoode, Printers to the Queen's most Excellent Majesty, 1858.

368

The South Indian Railway Act, 1874 (Act for the Amalgamation of the Great Southern of India Railway Company and the Carnatic Railway Company into the South Indian Railway Company)

Source: Acts on Railways, London, 1886

Cap. CXII

[An Act for the Amalgamation of the Great Southern of India and Carnatic Railway Companies, and for enabling the amalgamated Company to make Agreements with the Secretary of State in Council of India; and for other Purposes.
Act 37 and 38 Vic., Cap. 112, 16th July 1874]

Gist: The Act for the Amalgamation of the Great Southern of India Railway Company and the Carnatic Railway Company into the South Indian Railway Company passed in the British Parliament on 16 July 1874 has 20 sections, besides the preliminary paragraphs. The costs of passing the Act had been borne by the amalgamated company. This Act was taken to be effective from 1 July 1874, though passed later. Here also, railway includes the telegraphs and works connected therewith. Three million and eight hundred thousand pounds, the aggregate amount of the nominal capitals of the two dissolved companies, was nominal guaranteed capital of the amalgamated company. The qualification of a Director shall be possession of not less than fifty shares, or one thousand pounds stock in the ordinary capital of the amalgamated company. The quorum for general meetings of shareholders shall be twenty shareholders, present in person or by proxy.

Whereas the Great Southern of India Railway Company (herein called "the Great Southern Company") and the Carnatic Railway Company, Limited, (herein called "the Carnatic Company") were respectively incorporated in the manner and for the purposes appearing by the recitals of the agreement, a copy of which is contained in the schedule to this Act:

And whereas it is expedient that the Great Southern Company and the Carnatic Company should be united into one undertaking, and that the two companies should be amalgamated under the title of "The South Indian Railway Company," on the terms and with the powers herein-after provided:

And whereas the said agreement has been come to between the Secretary of State in Council and the said Railway Company, and it is expedient that such agreement should have effect and be binding on the Secretary of State in Council and the amalgamated Company:

And whereas the said objects can not be effected without the authority of Parliament:

May it therefore please Your Majesty that it may be enacted; and be it enacted by the Queen's most Excellent Majesty, and by and with the advice and consent of the Lord's Spiritual and Temporal, and Commons, in this present Parliament assembled, and by the authority of the same, as follows:

1. This Act may be cited for all purposes as "The South Indian Railway Act, 1874."

2. In this Act the following words and expressions have the following meanings, unless excluded by the subject or context; (to wit,)

The expression "the amalgamated Company" means "the South Indian Railway Company":

The word "India" has the same meaning in this Act as in the Act passed in the twenty-first and twenty-second years of the reign of Her present Majesty, intituled "An Act for the better Government of India":

The expression "Secretary of State in Council" means the Secretary of State in Council of India:

The word "railway" includes a railway and the telegraphs and works connected therewith:

The word "Shareholder" includes stockholder.

3. "The Companies Clauses Consolidation Act, 1845," and Part V. of "The Railways Clauses Act, 1863," relating to amalgamation, are, except where expressly varied or modified by this Act, or by either of the Acts recited in the agreement in the schedule to this Act, or by that agreement, incorporated with this Act, and apply to the Company, in India and elsewhere, as well as in England, and shall be construed and have effect accordingly; and in the construction of those Acts for the purposes of this Act the following words and expressions have the following meanings, unless excluded by the subject or context; (to wit,)

The expression "superior courts" includes Her Majesty's high courts of judicature at the several presidencies in India respectively:

The word "justice" and the expression "master in chancery" respectively include a justice of peace or magistrate in India, and whatsoever proceedings or acts for the purposes of this Act if had or done in England might be had or done by, under, before, or with respect to two justices, may if had or done in India be had or done by, under, before, or with respect to any one justice of the peace or magistrate in India.

4. Except as is by this Act otherwise expressly provided, the several words and expressions to which by "The Companies Clauses Consolidated Act, 1845,"[1] meanings are assigned have in this Act the same respective meanings, unless there be in the subject or context something repugnant to or inconsistent with such construction.

5. The undertaking of the Great Southern Company and of the Carnatic Company to which the provisions of this Act shall apply, are hereby declared to be the several railways, branches,

1. The reference is to The Companies Clauses Consolidation Act, 1845.

extensions, stations, sidings, approaches, buildings, fixed plant, telegraphs, and all other works, whether complete or incomplete, and all the land and all other property, estate, moneys, and effects, whether real or personal, and whether in England or India, which immediately before the time appointed for the commencement of this Act shall belong to or be vested in the said two companies respectively, or which they respectively shall then have power to execute or acquire, and also the right, interest, or estate which the same companies, or either of them, shall then possess in any railways, stations, or works, jointly or in common with any other company, and also all rights, powers, and privileges, interest, or estate, which the said companies, or either of them, shall then enjoy or be entitled to exercise over other undertakings.

6. At and from the time appointed for the commencement of this Act, the Shareholders in the Great Southern Company and in the Carnatic Company shall be united into one company, under the name of "the South Indian Railway Company," and by that name shall be a body corporate, with perpetual successors in England, in India, and all other places, and a common seal, and with power to purchase, take, hold, and dispose of lands and other property, and their undertaking shall be called "the South Indian Railway."

7. At and from the time appointed for the commencement of this Act the Great Southern Company and the Carnatic Company shall be dissolved, and their undertakings as herein before defined, and all their estate, right, title, and interest in and to the said undertakings, and all the right, privileges, easements, powers, and authorities incident to or affecting the same respectively, shall, subject to the existing charges, debts, covenants, contracts, obligations, and liabilities of the said companies then affecting the same, become and be absolutely vested in the amalgamated Company, and shall and may be held, possessed, enjoyed, used, exercised, and executed by the amalgamated Company in the same manner and to the same extent as they respectively were or could, or might, if this Act had not been passed, have been held, possessed, enjoyed, used, exercised, or extended by the said two companies respectively, and thereupon and thenceforth the undertakings of the said two companies respectively shall be amalgamated, and shall be and constitute one united undertaking, and shall be deemed to be and shall be undertaking of the South Indian Railway Company.

8. And whereas it is expedient to make provision for the conversion and exchange of the existing stock and shares of and in the Great Southern Company and the Carnatic Company respectively into and for the stock and shares of and in the amalgamated Company, in such manner that each proprietor of stock of the Great Southern Company, or of the Carnatic Company, which carries the right to interest at the rate of five per centum per annum, shall be entitled to a corresponding amount of stock of the amalgamated Company carrying interest at the like rate, and each proprietor of stock of the Great Southern Company which carries the right to interest at rate of four and three quarters per centum per annum, shall be entitled either to a corresponding amount of stock of the amalgamated Company carrying interest at the like rate, or, at his option, instead of such last-mentioned stock, to an amount of stock of the amalgamated Company carrying interest at the rate of five percent per centum per annum, in the proportion of ninety-five of the latter stock to one hundred of the former stock, and that each proprietor of shares in the Great Southern Company or in the Carnatic Company shall be entitled to corresponding shares in the amalgamated Company, credited with the like amount

as shall have been paid upon his existing shares: Now be it further enacted, that the limit of the nominal guaranteed capital of the amalgamated Company, exclusive of capital not bearing interest, shall be the sum of three millions eight hundred thousand pounds, being the aggregate amount of the nominal capitals of the two dissolved companies; and at and from the time appointed for the commencement of this Act the shares and stocks of the dissolved companies shall be converted respectively into shares and stocks of the amalgamated Company, so that each proprietor of ordinary stock of either of the dissolved companies, in respect of which or in respect of the capital represented by which interest at the rate of five percent per centum per annum is guaranteed by the Secretary of State in Council, shall in lieu thereof become the proprietor of an equal amount of stock of the amalgamated Company, on which interest will be payable at the rate of five percent per centum per annum, and so that each proprietor of ordinary four and three quarters per centum stock of the Great Southern Company, in respect of which or in respect of the capital represented by which interest at the rate of four and three quarters per centum per annum is guaranteed by the Secretary of State in Council, shall become the proprietor of an equal amount of stock of the amalgamated Company, on which interest will be payable at the rate of four and three quarters per centum per annum, or, at the option of such last-mentioned proprietor, (such options to be declared according to the terms of the notice herein-after directed,) he shall in lieu of such stock as last aforesaid become the proprietor of stock of the amalgamated Company on which interest will be payable at the rate of five per centum per annum, in the proportion of ninety-five pounds of the latter stock for one hundred pounds of the former stock; and each proprietor of a share of either of the dissolved companies not fully paid up shall in lieu thereof become the proprietor of a share of the same nominal amount in the amalgamated Company credited as paid up to the amount paid up on the first-mentioned share, and the holder for the time being of the share so substituted shall be liable to calls for the amount not paid up as if he had subscribed for the share; and a share in or stock of the amalgamated Company hereby substituted for a share in or stock of either of the dissolved companies shall be subject and liable to the trusts, provisions, agreements, charges, lines, and incumbrances (if any) which immediately before the substitution affected the share or stock for which the same is substituted, and in any testamentary instrument taking effect after the substitution words referring to the last-mentioned share or stock shall be deemed to refer to the share or stock substituted for the same, unless a different intention is expressed.

9. Within three months after the time appointed for the commencement of this Act, the amalgamated Company shall send to every shareholder of either of the dissolved companies a notice, addressed to his last known place of abode, stating that on or after a day to be therein named (being not later than three months from the date thereof) he may exchange the certificate of his share or stock for a certificate of the substituted share in or stock of the amalgamated Company, at such place as the notice shall specify, and upon application according to the notice the exchange shall be so made: Provided, that until such exchange the certificate for any share in or stock of either of the dissolved companies shall be deemed to be a certificate for the share in or stock of the amalgamated Company.

10. The Secretary of State in Council and the amalgamated Company are hereby empowered to carry into effect the agreement (a copy of which is contained in the schedule to

this Act), and such agreement shall from and after the time appointed for the commencement of this Act be binding on the Secretary of State in Council and the amalgamated Company, and shall, until the same shall be cancelled or modified under the powers given by this Act, have complete legal effect as between these parties as if the provisions therein contained were inserted in and enacted by this Act.

11. From and after the time appointed for the commencement of this Act the amalgamated Company may from time to time negotiate for, conclude, enter into with the Secretary of State in Council and carry into effect any contract or agreement for any of the following purposes, in addition to the purposes for which power is given to make contracts and agreements by "The Great Southern of India Act, 1858," (that is to say,)

A. The cancellation, surrender, or modification of any existing contracts (including the agreement in the schedule to this Act), leases, rights, or guarantees relating to any of the amalgamated Company's undertakings, and the substitution therefore of any new contracts, leases, rights, or guarantees relating to the same undertakings, or any of them:

B. The construction, establishment and maintenance of any new railway or other works in India as part of and in connexion with the amalgamated undertaking of the Company.

C. The obtaining from the Secretary of State in Council of a guarantee of interest on the share capital of the Company and moneys raised for the purposes thereof:

D. The application of the revenue of the amalgamated Company:

E. The surrendering or selling at any future period to the Secretary of State in Council or any other persons of the railways, or any part thereof, or all or any part of the property of the amalgamated Company, and the winding up of the affairs of the same Company, and the distribution of the net assets of the amalgamated Company among the shareholders:

F. The settlement of any question arising between the amalgamated Company or any class of shareholders therein and the Secretary of State in Council in respect of the amalgamation:

G. Generally all such provisions and stipulations with respect to the matters provided for by this Act, or any of them, and the purposes of the amalgamated Company, and the encouragement and prosecution thereof, and the eventual or contingent transfer of the same or any part thereof to the Secretary of State in Council, or to any persons as the Secretary of State in Council and the amalgamated Company may think fit and mutually agree on.

12. The Act (thirty-first Victoria, chapter twenty-six), intituled "An Act to enable certain guaranteed Indian Railway Companies to raise money on debenture stock," shall apply to the amalgamated Company as if it had been one of the railway companies named in the same Act: Provided, that notwithstanding anything in that Act or in Part III of "The Companies Clauses Act, 1863," contained, the interest of all debenture stock at any time after the passing of this Act created and issued by the amalgamated Company shall rank *pari passu* with the interest of all mortgages at any time after the passing of this Act granted by the amalgamated Company, and shall have priority over all principal moneys secured by such mortgages.

13. The persons who immediately before the time appointed for the commencement of this Act were directors of the dissolved companies shall be the first directors of the amalgamated Company, and directors retiring by rotation shall be qualified for re-election, but no vacancy in the number of the present directors caused by death, resignation, or disqualification, or

incompetency to act as director, or ceasing to be a director from any other cause than that of retiring by rotation, shall be filled up until the whole number of the directors (exclusive of the Government director) shall be reduced below five, after which time the number of directors (exclusive as aforesaid) shall never exceed five.

14. The qualification of a Director shall be possession in his own right of not less than fifty shares, or the amount of one thousand pounds stock in the ordinary capital of the amalgamated Company.

15. The persons who immediately before the time appointed for the commencement of this Act were auditors of the dissolved companies shall be the first auditors of the amalgamated Company, and auditors retiring by rotation shall be qualified for re-election, but no vacancy in the number of the present auditors caused by death, resignation, disqualification, or incompetency to act as an auditor, or ceasing to be an auditor from any other cause other than that of retiring by rotation, shall be filled up until the number of the auditors shall be reduced to one, after which time the number of auditors shall never exceed two.

16. All powers of the Great Southern Company and of the Carnatic Company respectively as to the raising of further moneys by borrowing on mortgage or bond, or by the issue of debenture stock, which immediately before the time appointed for the commencement of this Act were subsisting, shall thenceforth cease to be exercisable, and the amalgamated Company may from time to time with the sanction of the Secretary of State in Council, borrow or raise on mortgage or bond or by the issue of debenture stock any moneys, at such times, in such amounts and manner, or such terms, and to be applied in such mode and for such purposes as may be agreed upon the by Secretary of State in Council and the amalgamated Company.

17. The quorum for general meetings of shareholders shall be twenty shareholders, present in person or by proxy.

18. From and after the time appointed for the commencement of this act "The Great Southern of India Railway Act, 1858," as amended by "The Great Southern of India Railway Amendment Act, 1860," and also the lastly-mentioned Act shall, except where varied by or inconsistent with this Act, or the agreement in the schedule to this Act, extend and apply to the amalgamated Company, and all rights and powers by the said Acts or either of them conferred on and immediately before the time appointed for the commencement of this Act vested in the Secretary of State in Council and the Great Southern Company respectively, in relation to the undertaking of the Great Southern Company, shall be enjoyed and exercised by the Secretary of State in Council and the amalgamated Company in relation to both the undertakings of the dissolved companies.

19. This Act shall be taken to have come into operation on the first day of July one thousand eight hundred and seventy four and shall take effect accordingly.

20. All costs, charges, and expenses of and incident to the preparing for, obtaining, and passing of this Act, or otherwise in relation thereto, shall be paid by the amalgamated Company.

Appendix to Part I

Indian Tramways Act, 1885

Source: Henry Edward Trevor: Railway in British India, London, 1891

Act No. XI of 1886

[An Act to facilitate the construction and to regulate the working of Tramways. Act No. XI of 1886; Passed by the Governor-General of India in Council; Received the assent of the Governor-General on the 12 March 1886]

Gist: The Indian Tramways Act of 1885 (Act No. XI of 1886), passed by the Governor-General of India in Council, which received the assent of the Governor-General on 12 March 1886, has 50 sections with numerous subsections and clauses. The sections of the Act are classified into subtitles such as: Preliminary (sections 1 to 3), Orders authorising the construction of tramways (sections 4 to 10), Construction and maintenance of tramways (sections 11 to 13), Traffic on tramways (14-16), Licences to use tramways (17-18), Discontinuance of tramways (19-20), Insolvency of promoter (21), Purchase of tramways (22), Working of tramways owned by Local Authorities (23), Rules (24-26), Offences (27-34), Settlement of differences (35), Recovery of tolls (36-38), Savings (39-41), and Supplemental provisions (42-50). The land required is to be procured as per the Land Acquisition Act, 1870.

Whereas it is expedient to facilitate the construction and to regulate the working of tramways; it is hereby enacted as follows: –

Preliminary

1. (1) This Act may be called the Indian Tramways Act, 1886; and
   (2) It shall come into force at once.
2. (1) It extends in the first instance to the whole of British India, except the territories administered by the Governor of Fort Saint George in Council, the Governor of Bombay in Council, and the Lieutenant-Governor of Bengal.
   (2) But the Governor of Fort Saint George in Council, the Governor of Bombay in Council, or the Lieutenant-Governor of Bengal may, by notification in the official Gazette, extend this Act to the whole or any part of the territories under his administration.

3. In this Act, unless there is something repugnant in the subject or context, –

(1) "Local authority" means a municipal committee, district board, body of port commissioners or other authority legally entitled to, or entrusted by the Government with the control or management of a municipal or local fund;

(2) "Road" means the way of a road, street, thorough fare, passage or place along or across which a tramway authorised under this Act is, or is intended to be, laid, and includes the surface-soil and sub-soil of a road, and the footway, beams, drains and ditches and a road, and any bridge, culvert or causeway forming part of a road:

(3) "Road authority" in relation to a road means –

(*a*) If a local authority maintains and repairs the road, then that authority;

(*b*) If a local authority does not maintain and repair the road, and the road is neither vested in her Majesty nor maintained and repaired by the Government, then the person in whom the road is vested; and

(*c*) If a local authority does not maintain and repair the road, and the road is vested in her Majesty or maintained and repaired by the Government, then the Local Government:

(4) "Circle" in relation to a local authority or road authority, means the area within the control of that authority:

(5) "Tramway" means a tramway, or any part of a tramway, or any siding, turnout, connection, line or track belonging to a tramway:

(6) "Order" means an order authorizing the construction of a tramway under this Act, and includes a further order substituted for, or amending, extending or varying, that order:

(7) "Promoter" means a local authority or person in whose favour an order has been made, and includes a local authority or person on whom the rights and liabilities conferred and imposed on the promoter by this Act and by the order and any rules made under this Act as to the construction, maintenance and use of the tramway, have devolved:

(8) "Undertaking" includes all moveable and immoveable property of the promoter suitable to and used by him for the purposes of the tramway:

(9) "Carriage" in the case of a tramway on which steam power or any other mechanical power is used, includes an engine worked on the tramway for the purpose of producing that power:

(10) "Toll" includes any charge leviable in respect of the use of a tramway:

(11) "Lessee" means a person to whom a lease has been granted of the right of user of a tramway and of demanding and taking the authorised tolls:

(12) "District magistrate" includes an officer empowered by the Local Government by name or by virtue of his office to discharge within any local area all or any of the functions of a district magistrate under this Act:

(13) "District Court" means a principal civil Court of original jurisdiction, and includes a High Court having ordinary original civil jurisdiction:

(14) "Collector" means the chief officer in charge of the revenue-administration of a district, and includes an officer empowered by the Local Government by name or by virtue of his office

to discharge within any local area the functions of a Collector under this Act: and

(15) "Prescribed" means Prescribed by rules made by the Local Government under this Act.

Orders Authorising the Construction of Tramways

4. (1) The local Government may make an order authorising the construction of a tramway in a circle on application made:

   (*a*) By the local authority of the circle with the consent of the road authority of any road or part of a road which is to be traversed by the tramway and of which the local authority is not itself the road authority; or

   (b) By any person with the consent of the local authority of the circle, and of the road-authority of any road or part of a road which is to be traversed by the tramway and of which the local authority is not the road-authority:

   Provided that, if any part of the proposed tramway is to traverse land which is not included within the limits of a municipality or of a cantonment, the Local Government shall not make the order without the previous sanction of the Governor-General in Council.

   (2) A local authority shall not make an application for an order or be deemed to consent to an application being made by any person for an order, unless the making of the application or the giving of the consent has been approved by the local authority in manner prescribed.

5. When it is proposed to lay a tramway in two or more circles, and a local authority or road-authority having control in either or any of the circles does not consent thereto, or attaches conditions to its consent, the Local Government may, nevertheless, make an order authorizing the construction of the tramway in the circle, or by the order impose on the promoter any conditions which it deems fit, if, after considering the reasons of the authority for withholding its consent or attaching the conditions thereto, it is satisfied that the construction of the tramway in the circle is expedient, or, as the case may be, that the conditions attached by the authority to its consent ought not to be imposed.

6. (1) The Local Government on receiving an application shall consider it, and, if satisfied as to the propriety of proceeding thereon, publish in the official Gazette and in such other manner as it deems sufficient for giving information to persons interested, a draft of a proposed order authorising the construction of the tramway.

   (2) A notice shall be published with the draft stating that any objection or suggestion, which any person may desire to make with respect to the proposed order, will, if submitted to the Local Government on or before a date to be specified in the notice, be received and considered.

   (3) If, after considering any objections or suggestions which may have been made with respect to the draft on or before the date so specified, the Local Government

is of opinion that the application should be granted, with or without addition or modification, or subject, or not to any restriction or condition, it may make an order accordingly.

(4) Every order authorising the construction of a tramway shall be published in the official Gazette in England, and in the other prescribed language or languages, if any; and that publication shall be conclusive proof that the order has been made as required by this section.

7. (1) An order made under section 6 shall empower the promoter therein specified to construct and maintain the tramway therein described in the manner therein provided, and shall specify the time within which the tramway shall be commenced and the time within which it shall be completed and opened for public traffic.

(2) The order may also provide, in manner consistent with this Act, for all or any of the following, among other matters, that is to say: –

(*a*) A period before the expiration of which the tramway shall not be commenced, and the conditions subject to which the local authority, when it is not itself the promoter, may, within that period, elect to be substituted in the place of the promoter, in respect of the undertaking of so much thereof as is within its circle; and the limits of the time within which, and the terms upon which, the local authority may, after the tramway has been constructed, require the promoter to sell to it the undertaking or so much thereof as is within its circle;

(b) The acquisition by the promoter of land for the purposes of the tramway, and the disposal by him of land, which has been acquired but is no longer required for these purposes;

(c) The conditions subject to which roads may be opened and broken up for the purposes of the construction or maintenance of the tramway or any part thereof, and the methods of, and materials to be used in, the re-instating of the roads, and the approval of the method and materials by the Local Government or the road authority before the commencement of the works.

(d) The conditions on which the tramway may be constructed over a bridge or across a railway or tramway when the carriage-way over the bridge is to form part of the tramway or when the tramway is to cross a railway or another tramway on the level;

(e) The space which shall ordinarily intervene between the outside of the carriage-way on either side of a road whereon the tramway is to be constructed and the nearest rail of the tramway, and the conditions on which a smaller space may be permitted;

(f) The gauge of the tramway, the rails to be used, and the mode in which and the level at which, they shall be laid and maintained; and the adoption and application by the promoter of such improvements in the rails, and in their situation, and in the substructure upon which they rest, as the local government may from time to time require;

(g) The portion of the road or roads traversed by the tramway to be kept in repair by the promoter; the maintenance by the promoter to the satisfaction of the local government or the road authority, or both, of that portion of the road or roads; and the liability of the promoter, on the requisition of the Local Government, from time to time to adopt and apply such improvements in the tramway as the Local Government may consider necessary or desirable for the safety or convenience of the public, and to alter the position or level of the tramway to suit future alterations in the road or roads;

(h) The application of material excavated by the promoter in the construction or maintenance of the tramway;

(i) The provision of such crossings, passing-places, sidings, junctions and other works, in addition to those specified in or authorised by the order, as may from time to time be necessary or convenient to the efficient working of the tramway;

(j) The powers which may from time to time be exercised by the Local Governments, the local authority, the road authority or any person in respect of powers, drains, telegraph lines, gas pipes, water pipes or other things in or on land occupied by the tramway; the notice (if any) to be given of the intended exercise of those powers the manner in which the powers shall be exercised; and the extent to which the tramway and the traffic thereon may be interfered with in the exercise thereof;

(k) The conditions subject to which the promoter may from time to time interfere with, or alter or require the alteration of the position of, drains (not being sewers or main drains), telegraph lines, gas-pipes, water pipes or other things as aforesaid;

(l) The provision of a temporary tramway in place of a part of a tramway which has been removed, or of which the use has been discontinued, by reason of the execution of any work affecting a road along which the part of the tramway was laid, or by reason of the use of the road being interrupted by floods or other cause;

(m) The motive power to be used on the tramway, and the conditions on which steam-power or any other mechanical power may be used;

(n) The nature, dimensions, fittings, appliances and apparatus of the carriages to be used on the tramway, and the inspection and examination thereof by officers of the Local Government or the local authority, and the liability of the promoter or lessee, on the requisition of the Local Government, from time to time, to adopt and apply such improvements in the carriages, and in the fittings, appliances and apparatus, as the local government may consider necessary or desirable for the safety or convenience of the public;

(o) The traffic which may be carried on the tramway, the traffic which the promoter or lessee, shall be bound to carry, and the traffic which he may refuse to carry; the tolls to be leviable by the promoter or lessee and the periodical revision thereof by the Local Government; and the regulation of the traffic and of the levy of tolls;

(p) The use of the tramway free of toll by the local authority, with its own carriages, for specified purposes, during specified hours, with power to the local authority to make such sidings and other works as may be necessary for communication between its premise and the tramway;

(q) The conditions subject to which the promoter may transfer the undertakings, or any part thereof, by sale, mortgage, lease, exchange or otherwise; and the conditions subject to which the local authority may be the transferee;

(r) The performance by the Local Government or by the local authority or road authority of any work required by the Act or the order to be done by the promoter; and

(s) The penalty to be incurred by the promoter or lessee for failure to observe any condition or direction contained in the order, and the application of the penalty when recovered.

(3) The Local Government may, in providing in the order for the acquisition of land for the purposes of a tramway of which the promoter is not a company, direct that land may be acquired for the promoter under the provisions of the Land Acquisition Act, 1870, in the same manner and on the same conditions as it might be acquired for the purposes of the tramway if a company were the promoter.

(4) The order shall imply the condition –

(a) In the case of a tramway of which the local authority is the promoter, that a lease thereof shall be granted only in manner by this Act provided; and

(b) In the case of a tramway of which a local authority is not the promoter, that a lease thereof shall be only of the right of user and of demanding and taking the authorised tolls, and shall not confer or impose on the lessee any of the powers or duties of the promoter in respect of the construction or maintenance of the tramway.

8. (1) The Local Government may on the application of the promoter, revoke, amend, extend or vary the order by a further order.

(2) An application for a further order shall be made in the same manner and subject to the same conditions as an application for an order.

(3) The Local Government may, in its discretion, either grant or reject the application.

(4) If it grants the application, it shall make the further order in the same manner as an order, except that no addition to, or modification of, the rights, powers and authorities asked for in the application, or restriction or condition with respect thereto, shall be made or imposed by the further order without the consent in writing of the promoter.

9. (1) Subject to, and in accordance with, the provisions of this Act, the local government may, on a joint application, or on two or more separate applications make an order empowering two or more local authorities, respectively, jointly to construct

the whole, or separately to construct parts of a tramway, and jointly or separately to own the whole or parts thereof.

(2) All the provisions of this Act, which relate to the construction of the tramways, shall extend and apply to the construction of the whole and the separate parts of the tramway, and the form of the order may be adapted to the circumstances of the case.

10. (1) If a promoter authorised by an order to construct a tramway –

(*a*) does not within the time specified in the order substantially commence the construction of the tramway, or

(b) having commenced the construction, suspends it without a reason sufficient in the opinion of the Local Government to warrant the suspension, or

(c) does not within the time specified in the order complete the tramway and open it for public traffic, the following consequences shall ensue: –

(i) The powers given by the order to the promoter for constructing the tramway and otherwise in relation thereto shall, unless the local government, by special direction in writing, prolongs the time or condenses the suspension, cease to be exercised except as to so much of the tramway as is then completed;

(ii) As to so much of the tramway as is then completed, the Local Government may either permit, or refuse to permit, the powers given by the order to continue;

(iii) If the Local Government refuses to permit the powers to continue, then so much of the tramway as is then completed may be dealt with, under the provisions of this Act relating to the discontinuance of the tramways, as a tramway of the working whereof the discontinuance has been proved to the satisfaction of the Local Government.

(2) A notification published by the Local Government in the official Gazette to the effect that on a date specified in the notification the construction of a tramway had not been substantially commenced or a tramway had not been completed and opened for public traffic, or that the construction of a tramway had been suspended without sufficient reason, shall, for the purposes of this section, be conclusive proof of the matter stated therein.

Construction and Maintenance of Tramways

11. A tramway shall be constructed and maintained in the manner provided by the order.

12. A tramway or portion or extension of, or addition to, a tramway, shall not be opened for public traffic until an engineer appointed in this behalf by the Local Government has inspected it and certified it to be fit for such traffic.

13. Subject to the provisions of any order for the time being in force with respect to the matters mentioned in section 7, sub-section (2), clause (g), the road-authority and the

promoter may from time to time enter into agreements as to the keeping in repair of the whole or a part of a road traversed by a tramway, and as to the proportion to be paid by either of them of the expense of keeping the road or part in repair.

Traffic on Tramways

14. (1) The promoter of a tramway shall, subject to the provisions of sub-section (2) and to the other provisions of this Act and of the order, have the exclusive use of the tramway for carriages with flange-wheels or other wheels suitable to run on the rail described in the order as the rail to be used on the tramway:
Provided that nothing in this Act or in the order or any rule made under this Act shall affect the right of any person authorised to use a tramway or railway to pass across a tramway constructed under this Act with carriages having wheels suitable to run on the rail thereof.

(2) The public shall have a right to pass along or across any part of a road along or across which a tramway is constructed, whether on or off tramway, with carriages not having flange-wheels or other wheels suitable to run on the rail of the tramway:

Provided –

(a) That this sub-section shall not apply where the tramway is constructed on land the right to the exclusive possession of which has been acquired by the promoter; and

(b) That the Local Government may by an order authorise the construction of a tramway on any part of a road with rails raised above the surface of the road, if it is satisfied that the convenience of the public will not be injuriously affected thereby.

15. (1) The promoter or lessee may demand and take, in respect of the tramway, tolls not exceeding the limits in specified in or determinable under the order, or, if the order contains no provision in this behalf, then such sums as may from time to time be fixed by the promoter or lessee with the previous sanction of the Local Government.

(2) A list of all the tolls authorised to be levied shall be exhibited, in such languages as the district magistrate may direct, in a conspicuous place inside and outside each of the carriages used upon the tramway.

16. (1) A person shall not be entitled to carry or to require to be carried, on a tramway constructed under this Act, any goods of a dangerous or offensive nature.

(2) A person taking such goods with him on the tramway shall, before entering the carriage, give notice of their nature to the servant of the promoter or lessee in charge of the carriage.

(3) A person sending such goods by the tramway shall distinctly mark their nature on the outside of the package containing them, or otherwise give notice thereof in writing to the servant of the promoter or lessee with whom he leaves them for the purpose of their being sent by the tramway.

(4) Any servant of the promoter or lessee may refuse to carry upon the tramway a parcel which he suspects to contain goods of a dangerous or offensive nature, and, if any such parcel has been received for the purpose of being carried upon the tramway, may stop the transit thereof until he is satisfied as to the nature of its contents.

(5) When a servant of the promoter or lessee refuses under sub-section (4) to carry a parcel which has been received for the purpose of being carried upon the tramway, he shall, as soon as may be, give notice of his refusal to the consignor or consignee if he refuses at a time when neither of them is present.

Licences to use Tramways

17. If, at any time after a tramway or part of a tramway has been for three years opened for public traffic in a circle, the local authority of the circle represents in writing to the Local Government that the public is deprived of the full benefit of the tramway or of the part thereof, the Local Government may, if after considering any statement which the promoter or lessee or both may desire to make, and after such further enquiry as it deems necessary, it is satisfied as to the truth of the representation, grant a licence to any person to use the tramway conformably to this Act and to the order and the rules made under this Act, subject to the following provisions, namely:–

(a) the licence shall be for a period not less than one year or more than three years from the date of the licence, but local government may in its discretion renew it;

(b) the licence shall be to use the whole of the tramway for the time being opened for public traffic, or such part or parts of the tramway as the local government having regard to the cause for granting the licence, thinks fit:

(c) the licence shall specify the number of carriages which the licence shall run upon the tramway, the mode in which, and times at which, the carriages shall be run, the tolls to be paid to the promoter or lessee by the licensee for the use of the tramway, and the tolls, being those for the time being leviable by the promoter or lessee, which the licensee may demand and take for the use of his carriages;

(d) the licensee and his officers and servants shall permit one person, duly authorized for that purpose by the promoter or lessee, to travel free of toll in or upon each carriage of the licensee run upon the tramway for the whole or any part of a journey;

(e) any provision of this Act, or of the order or rules made under this Act, relating to the functions of a servant of a promoter or lessee shall be construed, so far as may be, as referring to a servant of the licensee; and

(f) The local government may revoke, alter or modify the licence for any cause sufficient in its opinion to warrant the revocation, alteration or modification thereof.

18. A licence shall, on demand, give to an officer or servant authorised in that behalf by the promoter or lessee an exact account in writing, signed by the licensee, of the number of passengers, or number or quantity of goods, conveyed by any and every carriage used by him on the tramway.

Discontinuance of Tramways

19. If it is proved to the satisfaction of the Local Government, at any time after the opening of a tramway for public traffic, that the working of the tramway, or any part thereof, has been practically discontinued, for the space of three months, without a reason sufficient, in the opinion of the Local Government, to warrant discontinuance, the Local Government, if it thinks fit, may, by notification in the official Gazette, declare that the powers of the promoter and of the lessee, if any, in respect of the tramway or the part thereof of which the working has been so discontinued shall, from the date of the notification, be at an end; and the reason the said powers shall cease and determine, except in so far as they may be purchased by local authority in manner by this Act provided.

20. (1) Where a notification has been published under section 10, the road-authority may, at any time after the expiration of two months from the date of the notification, remove the tramway or part of the tramway of which the working has been so discontinued and use the materials thereof in reinstating the road.
(2) The promoter shall pay to the road-authority the cost incurred by that authority in removing the tramway or the part thereof and in reinstating the road.
(3) The cost shall be entitled by an officer of the road-authority, and his certificate, countersigned by the district magistrate, shall be conclusive proof as to the cost incurred.
(4) If the promoter does not pay the amount so certified within one month after the delivery to him of the certificate or of a copy thereof, the road-authority may, without any previous notice to the promoter and without prejudice to any other remedy which it may have for the recovery of the amount, sell and dispose of such materials of the tramway or part thereof removed as it has not used in reinstating the road, either by public auction or by private sale, and for such sum or sums, and to such person or persons, as it thinks fit, and may, out of the proceeds of the sale, pay and reimburse itself the amount of the cost aforesaid and of the expenses of the sale, and shall pay over the residue (if any) of the proceeds of the sale to the promoter.

Insolvency of Promoter

21. (1) If, at any time after the opening of a tramway in a circle for public traffic, it appears to the road-authority or local authority of the circle that the promoter of the tramway is insolvent, so that he is unable to maintain the tramway, or to work it with advantage to the public, and either of these authorities makes a representation to that effect to the Local Government, the Local Government may, if after considering any statement which the promoter may desire to make, and after such further inquiry as it deems necessary, it is satisfied as to the truth of the representation, declare, by notification in the official Gazette, that the powers of the promoter shall, at the expiration of six months from the publication of the notification, be at an end; and the powers of the promoter shall cease and determine at the expiration of that period, except in so far as they may be purchased by a local authority in manner by this Act provided.

(2) Where a notification has been published under sub-section (1), the road authority may, at any time after the expiration of six months from the date thereof, remove the tramway in the same manner, and subject to the same provisions as to the payment of the cost of the removal and to the same remedy for recovery of the cost, in every respect as in cases of removal under section 20.

Purchase of Tramways

22. (1) Where the promoter of a tramway in a circle is not the local authority, the local authority, with the previous sanction of the local government, may –

(a) Within such limits of time as may be specified in this behalf in the order, or
(b) If a time was not specified in the order, then within six months after the expiration of a period of twenty-one years from the date of the order, and within six months after the expiration of every subsequent period of seven years, or
(c) Within two months after the publication of a notification under section 19 or within six months after the publication of a notification under section 21, by notice in writing, require the promoter to sell to the local authority his under-taking or the part thereof which is within the circle of the local authority; and thereupon the promoter shall sell the same upon the terms specified in the order, or, if the terms were not specified in the order, then upon the terms of paying the then value of the undertaking or of the part thereof, exclusive of any allowance for past or future profits of the undertaking or any compensation for compulsory sale or other consideration whatsoever.

(2) A requisition shall not be made under sub-section (1) unless the making thereof has been approved by the local authority in manner prescribed.
(3) When a sale has been made under this section, all the rights, powers and authorities of the promoter in respect of the undertaking or part thereof sold, or, where a notification has been published under section 19 or section 21, all the rights, powers and authorities of the promoter previous to the publication of the notification in respect of undertaking Or part thereof sold, shall be transferred to the authority to whom the undertaking or part has been sold, and shall vest in, and may be exercise by, that authority in the same manner as if the tramway had been constructed by it under an order made under this Act.
(4) Subject to, and in accordance with, the preceding provisions of this section, two or more local authorities may jointly purchase an undertaking or so much thereof as is within their circles.

Working of Tramways owned by Local Authorities

23. (1) When a local authority has under the authority of an order completed a tramway, or has under the provisions of this Act or of an order acquired possession of a

tramway, it may, by a lease to be approved by the Local Government, let to any person the right of user of the tramway and of demanding and taking the authorized tolls.

(2) On the determination of a lease, the local authority may from time to time let the right for such further term and on such conditions as the local government may approve.

(3) Every lease made under this section shall imply a condition of re-entry if at any time after the making thereof it is proved to the satisfaction of the Local Government that the lease has practically discontinued the working of the tramway leased, or of any part thereof, for the space of one month without a reason sufficient, in the opinion of the Local Government, to warrant the discontinuance.

(4) Notice of the intention of the local authority to make a lease shall be given in manner prescribed.

(5) If the local authority can not by means of a lease obtain what it deems to be a fair rent for the tramway, it may itself, with the previous sanction of the Local Government and for such term as the Local Government directs, place and run carriages upon the tramway, and demand and take the authorized tolls in respect of the use of the carriages.

Rules

24. (1) In addition to any other power to make rules expressly or by implication, conferred by this Act, the local government may make rules consistent with this Act –

(a) As to the form in which an application for an order shall be made;

(b) As to the costs to be paid by an applicant in respect of an order, and the time when, and the place where, those costs shall be paid;

(c) As to the payment of money or lodgement of securities, by way of deposit, by the applicant for an order before the order in published under section 6, sub-section (4), or a further order is made under section 8; the investment of money so paid; the disposal of interest or dividends from time to time accruing due on money or securities so paid, lodged or invested; the application of the money or securities or the produce thereof to the discharge of any liability incurred by the promoter; and the forfeiture, repayment of return of the money or securities;

(d) As to the phases and sections of any works to be deposited by applicants for orders or by promoters;

(e) For regulating the use of steam power or any other mechanical power on a tramway;

(f) As to any matter specified in section 7, sub-section (2), clauses (c), (d), (e), (j) and (k), as a matter which may be provided for in an order, when that matter has not been so provided for, or has not, in the opinion of the Local Government, been effectually so provided for;

(g) As to the periodical submission by promoters, lessees, licensees, of accounts of traffic and receipts to the Local Government or as that government directs, and as to the forms in which those accounts are to be submitted;
(h) As to the accidents of which report is to be made to the Local Government or as that government directs;
(i) As to any matter respecting which rules may be made under this section by a local authority or a promoter or a lessee; and
(j) Generally, as to any other matter or thing in respect of which it may seem to the local government to be expedient to make rules for carrying out the purposes of this Act.

(2) A local authority may, from time to time, with the previous sanction of the Local Government, make rules consistent with this Act and with the order and any rules made by the Local Government under this Act for regulating –

(a) The rate of speed to be observed in travelling upon a tramway within the circle of the local authority;
(b) The use of animal power on the tramway;
(c) The distance at which carriages using the tramway are to be allowed to follow one after the other;
(d) The stopping of carriages using the tramway and the notice to be given to the public of their approach;
(e) The manner in which carriages using the tramway after sunset and before sunrise are to be lighted;
(f) The traffic on roads along or across which the tramway is laid;
(g) The number of passengers, which may be carried in any carriage;
(h) The licensing and control of drivers, conductors and other persons having charge of the carriages of the promoter or lessee or a licensee; and
(i) Generally, the mode of use of the tramway.

(3) The promoter or lessee of a tramway may, from time to time, with the previous sanction of the local government, make rules consistent with this Act and with the order and any rules made under this Act –

(a) For preventing the commission of any nuisance in or upon any carriage, or in or against any premises, belonging to him; and
(b) For regulating the travelling in any carriage belonging to him.

(4) The Local Government may cancel any rule made by a local authority or by a promoter or lessee under this section.

25. The authority making any rule under section 24 may direct that a breach of it shall be punishable with fine, which may extend –

(a) If the authority making the rule is the Local Government, to two hundred rupees, and

(b) If that authority is a local authority or a promoter or lessee, to twenty rupees; and when the breach is a continuing breach, with a further fine which may extend –

(c) If the authority making the rule is the local government, to fifty rupees, and

(d) If that authority is a local authority or a promoter or lessee, to five rupees, for every day after the first during which the breach continues.

26. (1) Every authority having power to make rules and any section of this Act shall, before making the rules, publish a draft of the proposed rules for the information of persons likely to be affected thereby.

(2) The publication shall be made, in the case of rules made by the Local Government, in such manner as may in its opinion be sufficient for giving information to persons interested, and in the case of rules made by a local authority or by a promoter or lessee, in manner prescribed.

(3) There shall be published with the draft a notice specifying a date, not earlier than the expiration of one month after the day of publication, at or after which the draft with be taken into consideration.

(4) The authority shall received and consider any objection or suggestion which may be made by any person with respect to the draft before the date specified.

(5) The publication in the official Gazette of a rule purporting to be made under this Act shall be conclusive proof that it has been duly made.

Offences

27. If a promoter –

(a) constructs and maintains a tramway otherwise than in accordance with the order, or

(b) opens the tramway for traffic, or permits it to be so opened, before it has been inspected and certified in manner required by section 12, or

(c) fails to observe any requirement or condition of the order for neglect or breach whereof no penalty has been expressly provided in the order, or if a promoter, lessee or licensee runs a carriage on a tramway otherwise than in accordance with the order, he shall (without prejudice to the enforcement of specific performance of the requirements of this Act or of the order, or to any other remedy which may be obtained against him in a Court of civil judicature), on complaint made by the Local Government or by the local authority or road-authority or by the district magistrate or, with the previous sanction of the district magistrate, by any person injuriously affected by the act or omission, be punished with fine which may extend to two hundred rupees, and in the case of a continuing offence to a further fine which may extend to fifty rupees for every day after the first during which the offence continues to be committed.

28. If any person without lawful excuse, the burden of proving which shall lie upon him,

wilfully obstructs any person acting under the authority of the promoter in the lawful exercise of his powers in constructing or maintaining a tramway, or injures or destroys any mark made for the purpose of setting out the line of the tramway, he shall be punished with fine which may extend to fifty rupees.

29. If any person without lawful excuse, the burden of proving which shall lie upon him, wilfully does any of the following things namely: –

    (a) Interferes with removes or alters any part of a tramway constructed under this Act, or of the works connected therewith, or
    (b) Places or throws upon or across any such tramway any wood, stone, refuse or other thing or
    (c) Does anything in such a manner as to obstruct any carriage using any such tramway, or
    (d) bets within the meaning of the Indian Penal Code the doing of, or attempts to do, anything mentioned in clause (a), clause (b) or clause (c), he shall (without prejudice to any other remedy which may be obtained against him in a Court of Civil Judicature) be punished with fine, which may extend to one hundred rupees.

30. If any person, except under a lease from, or by agreement with, the promoter, or under license from the Local Government granted under this Act, uses on a tramway, otherwise than as permitted by section 14, a carriage having flange-wheels or other wheels suitable to run on the rail of the tramway, he shall be punished with fine which may extend to two hundred rupees.

31. (1) If any person travelling or having travelled in a carriage of the promoter or lessee or of a licensee evades or attempts to evade payment of toll, or if any person having paid toll for a certain distance wilfully proceeds in any such carriage beyond that distance and does not pay the additional toll for the additional distance or attempts to evade payment thereof, or if any person wilfully refuses or neglects on arriving at the point to which he has paid toll to quit the carriage, he shall be punished with fine which may extend to ten rupees.

    (2) When a person commits an offence under this section and refuses on demand of a servant of the promoter, lessee or licensee to give his name and residence, or gives a name or residence which the servant has reason to believe to be false, he may be arrested and taken to the nearest police station by the servant or any person when the servant may call to his aid.

    (3) When the person is taken to the police-station he shall with the least possible delay be forwarded to the nearest magistrate, unless his true name and residence are ascertained, in which case he shall be released on his executing a bond for his appearance before a magistrate if so required.

32. If any person takes or sends by a tramway any goods of a dangerous or offensive nature without giving the notice required by section 16, he shall be punished with fine, which may extend to fifty rupees.

33. (1) If a licensee fails on demand to give the account mentioned in section 18 or, with intent to evade the payment of tolls, gives a false account when he is called upon to give an account under this section, he shall be punished with fine which may extend to fifty rupees.

(2) The fine shall be in addition to any tolls payable by the licensee to the promoter or lessee in respect of the passengers or goods conveyed by the carriage or carriages used by the licensee on the tramway.

34. Nothing in this Act shall prevent a person from being prosecuted under any other law for an act or omission which constitutes an offence against this Act or the rules made under it, or from being liable under that other law to any other or higher punishment or penalty than that provided by this Act or the rules made under it; Provided that a person shall not be punished twice for the same offence.

Settlement of Differences

35. (1) If any difference arises between the promoter or lessee on the one hand and the Local Government, or the local authority, or the road-authority, or a person having the charge of any sewers, drains, telegraph-lines, gas-pipes, water-pipes or other things in or on land occupied by the tramway, on the other hand with respect to any interference or control exercised or claimed to be exercised by, or on behalf of, either party by virtue of this or any other Act,. or of the order or the rules made under this Act, or with respect to the propriety of, or the mode of, the execution of any work, or with respect to any compensation to be made by or to the promoter or lessee, or on the question whether any work is such as ought reasonably to satisfy the Local Government or the road-authority or both, or with respect to any other subject or thing regulated by, or comprised in, this Act or the order or the rules made under this Act, and not otherwise expressly provided for therein, the matter in difference shall, except where the parties elect to proceed under section 523 of the Code of Civil Procedure, be settled, on the application of either party, by a referee.

(2) Where the difference is –

(a) between the promoter or lessee on the one hand and the Local Government, either as such or as the road-authority, on the other, or

(b) between the promoter on the one hand and the local authority on the other, with respect to the sum to be paid by the local authority for an undertaking or part of an undertaking which that authority has required the promoter to sell under section 22, the referee shall be the district Court within the jurisdiction of which the tramway is situated, or, where the tramway is within the jurisdiction of more than one district Court, the district Court within the jurisdiction of which, the greater part of the tramway is situated.

(3) In other cases, the referee shall be appointed by the Local Government.

(4) Except where referee is district Court, the powers and procedure of the referee may be prescribed.

(5) In the case of the difference between a promoter on the one hand and the local authority on the other, with respect to the sum to be paid by the local authority for an undertaking or part of an undertaking which that authority has required the promoter to sell under section 22, an appeal shall lie to the High Court from the award of the referee as from an original decree of the district Court.

(6) In the case of every other difference the award of the referee shall be final.

Recovery of Tolls

36. Any of the following moneys, namely, any rent due to a local authority from a lessee, any penalty receivable from a promoter or lessee under an order, any sum payable by a promoter or lessee under an award of a referee, the cost of the performance under this Act by the Local Government or by a local authority or road-authority of any work required by this Act or by an order to be done by a promoter and the cost incurred by a road-authority in removing a tramway and reinstating a road under this Act, may, without prejudice to any other remedy that the authority to which the money is due may have by suit or otherwise, be recovered by that authority, on application made in this behalf to the Collector, as if the sum due were an arrear of land-revenue due by the promoter or lessee or his surety (if any):

Provided that nothing in this section shall authorise the arrest of the promoter or lessee or his surety in execution of any process issued by the Collector.

37. (1) If a licensee fails to pay on demand the tolls due for the use of a tramway, the promoter or lessee to whom the tolls are due may without prejudice to the remedy which he may have by suits apply to a magistrate to recover the amount of the tolls, and the magistrate may, after giving notice to the licensee (if possible) and allowing him an opportunity of being heard, proceed to recover the amount by distress and sale of any carriage or other moveable property of the licensee which may be leased on the tramway or on premises connected therewith.

(2) When a licensee has failed to pay on demand the tolls due from the promoter or lessee to whom the tolls are due may seize any carriage or other moveable property of the licensee on the tramway or on premises connected therewith, and detain the same for forty-eight hours unless the tolls are sooner paid.

(3) When application is made to a magistrate under sub-section (1) he may make an interim order of distraint pending his final decision.

38. Any toll due to a promoter, lessee or licensee from a passenger may be recovered either by suit or, on application to a magistrate have jurisdiction within any local area in which any part of the tramway is laid, by distress and sale of any moveable property belonging to the passenger within the local limits of the jurisdiction of the magistrate.

Savings

39. (1) Notwithstanding anything contained in this Act, or in an order or any rule made under this Act, a promoter shall not require any right other than that of user only over a road along or across which he lays a tramway nor shall anything contained in this Act, or in an order or any rule made under this Act, exempt the promoter of a tramway, or any other person using the tramway, from the payment of such charges as may lawfully be levied in respect of the use of a road or bridge along or across which the tramway is laid.

(2) The Local Government may, if it thinks fit, fix rates at which a promoter or lessee or licensee may compound for the charges payable in respect of the use of a road or bridge.

40. (1) Nothing in this Act, or in an order or any rule made under this Act, shall take away or abridge any power which a road-authority, local authority or other person has by law to break up, widen, alter, divert or improve a road, rail-road or tramway along or across which a tramway is laid.

(2) The road authority, local authority or other person executing any work referred to in sub-section (1) shall not be liable to pay to a promoter, lessee or licensee any compensation for injury done to a tramway by the execution of the work or for loss of traffic occasioned by the reasonable use of any power lawfully exercised for the execution thereof.

41. Nothing in this Act, or in an order or any rule made under this Act, shall affect the powers of a local authority or of a Magistrate or police-officer to regulate the passage of traffic along or across a road along or across which a tramway is laid; and the authority, magistrate or other aforesaid may exercise its or his powers as well on as off the tramway and with respect as well to the traffic of a promoter, lessee or licensee as to the traffic of other persons.

Supplemental Provisions

42. A promoter, lessee or licensee shall be answerable for all injuries happening through his act or default, or through the act or default of any person in his employment, by reason or in consequence of any of his carriages or works and shall save harmless all authorities and persons collectively and individually and their officers and servants, from all damages and costs in respect of injuries so happening.

43. For the purpose of this Act, want of funds shall not be deemed to be a sufficient reason for the suspension of the construction, or the discontinuance of the working, of a tramway by a promoter or lessee.

44. When a tramway is constructed under this Act within the limits of a municipality, the Local Government may exempt the animals, plant, rolling-stock, yards, workshops, engine-sheds and depots of the promoter, lessee or licensee, for such period as it thinks fit, from all or any municipal taxes leviable within these limits.

45. (1) The fund to or with the control or management of which the local authority of a

municipality, cantonment or district is entitled or entrusted shall, notwithstanding anything in any enactment respecting the purpose to which that fund may be applied, be applicable, subject to the control of the Local Government, to the payment of expenses incidental to the exercise of the powers and functions which may be vested in or exercised by a local authority under this Act.

(2) The fund shall also be applicable, with the previous sanction of the Local Government, to a guarantee of the payment of interest on money to be applied with the concurrence in writing of the local authority, within the limits of the local area under its control, to any of the purposes to which the fund might be applied by the local authority under sub-section (1).

46. The Local Government may, with the consent of the local authority and road authority and of the promoter and his lessee (if any), extend any part of this Act or any rules made under this Act, either with or without modification, to the whole or any part of the tramway constructed, or authorised by the Local Government to be constructed, before the passing of this Act, and may withdraw any part of the Act or any rules extended.

47. (1) A tramway of which the construction has not been authorised by the Local Government before the passing of this Act shall not, after the passing of this Act, be constructed for public traffic in any place to which this Act extends, except in pursuance of an order made under this Act.

(2) A person constructing a tramway in contravention of sub-section (1) of this section. or after the passing of this Act maintaining or using for public traffic, otherwise than in pursuance of an order made under this Act, a tramway which was not constructed, or authorised by the Local Government to be constructed before the passing of this Act,

shall be liable, on the complaint of the Local Government or local authority, to double the penalty to which a promoter acting otherwise than in accordance with an order is liable under section 27.

48. If at any time a local area comprising a tramway to which this Act or any part thereof or any rule thereunder applies ceases to be included in the circle of a local authority, the functions of that authority under this Act or the part thereof or the rule thereunder, and under the order (if any), shall in respect of that local area, devolve on the Local Government or, if that Government so directs, on the local authority of the circle in which the tramway has been included.

49. (1) In section 54 of the Indian Railway Act, 1879, the word "tramway" shall have the meaning assigned to it by section 3 of this Act.

(2) In the same section of that Act, after the words "by steam" the words "or other mechanical power" shall be added.

50. All powers conferred by this Act on a Local Government may be exercised from time to time as occasion requires.

S. HARVEY JAMES,
Offg. Secy. to the Govt. of India

Ref. Gazette of India, January-June, 1886.

PART II

Indian Railway Acts and Rules (1850-1895)

370. Act 42 of 1850 for Railway, Road, Canal and other Public Works
371. Railway Act 3 of 1853 for the Great Indian Peninsula Railway Company
372. Supplementary Railway Act 12 of 1853 for the Great Indian Peninsula Railway Company
373. An Act Relating to Railways in India (Act 18 of 1854)
374. Indian Railway Act 9 of 1860 for the Determination of Disputes on Wages and Price of Work between the Railway Employers and Employees
375. Indian Railway Servants' Act, 1867
376. Indian Railway (Amendment) Act XIII of 1870
377. The Repealing Act, 1870
378. Indian Railway Act XXV of 1871, Substitution of the Act XVIII of 1854
379. General Rules and Regulations for the Rajputana (State) Railways, 1873
380. Act for the Indian Railway Companies to Issue and Register Shares and Securities in India, 1873
381. Public General Statutes for Indian Guaranteed Railway Companies, 1873
382. The Great Indian Peninsula Railway Company Rules for General Passengers, 1873

383. The Repealing Act, 1874
384. The Indian Railway Act, 1879
385. Indian Guaranteed Railways Act, 1879
386. The Darjeeling Steam Tramway Act, 1879
387. East Indian Railway Company Purchase Act, 1879
388. General Rules and Regulations for all Railways in India, 1880
389. The Indian Railway Act, 1883
390. The Sindh-Pishin Railway Act, 1887
391. The Indian Railways Act, 1890
392. General Rules for all Railways in India, 1890
393. The Indian Railway Companies Act, 1895

Appendices to Part II

394. Repealing of Acts on Indian Railways passed between 1854 and 1890 by the Governor General of India
395. The Indian Telegraph Act, 1885
396. The Indian Telegraph Act, 1888
397. Memorandum from the Great Indian peninsula Railway Company dated 27 June 1890, upon the Indian Railways Act, 1890 submitted to the Secretary of State for India
398. Memorandum from the East Indian Railway Company dated 10 July 1890, upon the Indian Railways Act, 1890 submitted to the Secretary of State for India
399. Memorandum from the Madras Railway Company dated 14 July 1890, upon the Indian Railways Act, 1890 submitted to the Secretary of State for India
400. Statement of the Bombay, Baroda and Central India Railway Company dated 14 July 1890, upon the Indian Railways Act, 1890 submitted to the Secretary of State for India
401. Letter from the Secretary of State for India, the India Office, London to the Governor General of India in Council (the Government of India) dated 28 August 1890
402. Note by Legal Adviser, India Office dated 18 June 1890 regarding the Indian Railway Act IX of 1890
403. Note by Legal Adviser, India Office dated 30 July 1890 regarding the Indian Railway Act IX of 1890

370

Act 42 of 1850 for Railway, Road, Canal and other Public Works passed by the Governor General of India[1]

Source: P.W.D. Railway Department, Railway Proceedings, September 1845 to November 1851, Vol. I.

Act No. XLII of 1850

Passed by the Honourable the President of the Council of India in Council on the 20th December 1850, with the assent of the most Honourable the Governor General of India

[An Act for giving additional facilities for Public Works in Bengal. Act No. 42 of 1850]

Gist: The Act 42 of 1850 was passed on 20 December 1850 in the Council of India, in order to remove all hurdles in delay including acquiring lands for public works such as railway road and canal. This was introduced to strengthen Regulation 1 of 1824 of the Bengal Code. The Act has 11 sections besides introduction, and provides modalities of survey, compensation, arbitration, and punishment for obstruction.

Whereas by Regulation 1, 1824, of the Bengal Code, power was given for taking any land in the territories subject to the Presidency of the Fort William in Bengal, which is needed for any public purpose, according to the forms there in prescribed, but it is expedient for hindering needless delay in making the Railway about to be constructed in the said Presidency under the sanction of government, and also in any other public work that more summary power should in certain cases be given for gaining immediate possession of the land needed for such public work.

It is declared and enacted as follows:

I. Any Railway made in the said territories under the sanction of Government, is a public work within the meaning of the said Regulation.

II. The persons employed in any public work, with their servants and workmen, may enter upon any land for surveying the ground, and in the case of a road, canal or railway for setting out the intended line thereof, and in the case of any intended road, canal or railway may mark the intended line by cutting a trench or placing land marks along the line, and where otherwise the survey cannot be completed, and the line marked, may, with the sanction of the

Government, or of any officer appointed by Government for this purpose, cut down and clear away any part of any jungle or tape of trees in the direction of the intended line. Provided that no person shall enter the curtilage of any house under colour of this Act without consent of the occupier, unless between sunrise and sunset, and after due notice given to such occupier.

III. It shall be the duty of the officer so appointed by the Government to take account of all necessary damage done as aforesaid, that it may be allowed for in awarding compensation to the owners and occupiers of land.

IV. Whoever wilfully obstructs any person in lawfully setting out the line of any road, canal or railway, or wilfully destroys, damages, or displaces any such landmark, or effaces, or fills any such trench, shall be liable to be imprisoned for any term not exceeding six months, and also to fine not exceeding two hundred rupees.

V. Whenever the said officer shall have recorded his opinion that the land in dispute is needed immediately for the purpose of the public work, he shall be empowered to take immediate possession thereof on behalf of the Government, leaving the amount and distribution of the consideration to be paid for it, if not agreed to by private bargain to be afterwards ascertained according to the said Regulation, and such possession may be enforced and the obstruction of it punished in like manner as if the land so taken had been sold in execution of the decree of a Civil Court : and all Collectors, Magistrates and other officers shall, if necessary, give the like aid as they would be bound to give for enforcing the speedy and complete execution of any such decree.

VI. If the said officer is opposed or impeded in taking immediate possession of any such land as in his opinion is immediately needed, he shall apply to the Magistrate of the district, who shall enforce the surrender of the land.

VII. The powers of the said Regulation and of this Act shall extend in the case of any road, canal or railway, to authorise the temporary occupation of any land not more than one hundred yards from the centre line of the road, canal or railway, as marked on the ground, for taking earth or other materials for making or repairing the road, canal or railway, or for depositing thereon superfluous earth or other materials, or erecting temporary buildings and workshops thereon, or any land which may be needed for making temporary roads from any public road to the intended line of railway; and for the temporary occupation of any such land, and for any permanent damage done by such occupation and use of the land, including the full value of all clay, stone, gravel, sand and other materials taken thence, compensation shall be paid to and among all persons having an interest therein, to be ascertained in case of disagreement in the same manner as compensation for land permanently taken.

VIII. The local Government, if it thinks fit, may empower any such officer to execute any award made under the said Regulation, and to do all things necessary for completing the business, of taking and paying for the said land, and for setting all disputes concerning it, without sending any report to the local Government.

IX. In every case in which any land has been or shall be taken by the Government for any public work, otherwise than according to the said Regulation, such land after the lapse of five years, without any claim preferred for the recovery thereof in any competent Court, or under the said Regulation I, 1824, or this Act shall vest absolutely in the East India Company, freed and discharged from all other claims thereunto.

X. The said term of five years shall be reckoned from the date of this Act, in the case of land heretofore taken, and in the case of land hereafter taken from the time of taking possession thereof.

XI. If within the said term of five years any suit is begun upon which final judgement shall be obtained establishing the right of the plaintiff to any interest in any such land, then instead of the said land, there shall be paid to the person obtaining such judgement the value of his interest in the said land, at the time when possession thereof was taken, with interest thereon at the usual and lawful rate, to be ascertained and settled in case of dispute by arbitration in the manner described for disputed claims by the said Regulation.

Fort William
26th December 1850

1. The letter from W. Grey, the officiating Secretary of the Government of India, to I.P. Grant, the Secretary of the Government of Bengal, dated 24 December 1850 (PWD Railway Department, Railway Proceedings, September 1845 to November 1851, Vol. I) refers to Mr. Secretary Halliday's letter, and says that he is directed to forward 5 copies of Act XLII of 1850 "for giving additional facilities for Public Works in Bengal," and to request that the Railway Commissioner may be instructed to make immediate use, if necessary, of the provisions of that law in taking such lands as may be required for the Railway. Though this Act deals mainly with land acquisition, it is not included in the Part III, because it is enacted to remove all hurdles in the delay of public work.

371

Railway Act 3 of 1853 for the Great Indian Peninsula Railway Company

Source: The Calcutta Gazette, Saturday, March 12, 1853

> **Gist**: The Railway Act III of 1853 for the Great Indian Peninsula (GIP) Railway Company has 24 sections besides preliminaries. It was enacted for preventing frauds on the GIP railway company in the Presidency of Bombay, and for the punishment of certain offences, which may endanger the safety of persons travelling in the railway. Evading the requirement for second reading, Governor General of India in Council passed this legislation at once into Law. The Act has rules and regulations regarding fares and luggage, penalties for various illegal actions such as ticketless travel, trespassing, and acts of nuisance, intoxication and indecency in railway premises or carriage. Provisions are also made to fine and imprison railway officers and servants in case of wilful negligence of duties.

Fort William, Home Department, Legislative,
The 11th March 1853.

The following Act is brought up before the Legislative Council this day, the Governor General of India in Council being desirous that no time should be lost in passing the Act.

Resolved, —that the rule requiring that no draft of a law shall be ordered to be published till at least one week shall have elapsed from the day on which it was first laid before the Council of India in its Legislative Department, and that the Rules requiring that all Acts of the Governor General of India in Council shall be brought up for second reading in two months, or in three months, from the date of the first reading, be suspended in respect to the following proposed Act, and that it be at once passed into Law:

Act No. III of 1853

An Act relating to the Railway belonging to the Great Indian Peninsula Railway Company in the Presidency of Bombay.

Whereas it is expedient before the opening of any part of the Railway belonging to the Great Indian Peninsula Railway Company, in the Presidency of Bombay, to provide rules for regulating the said Railway, for preventing frauds upon the said Company, and for the punishment of certain offences which may endanger the safety of persons travelling upon the said Railway; It is enacted as follows:

I. No passenger shall enter any Carriage used on the aforesaid Railway, without having first paid his fare and obtained a ticket. Each passenger, on payment of his fare, shall be furnished with a ticket, specifying the class of Carriage and the distance for which the fare has been paid; each passenger shall, when required, show his ticket to any servant of the said Company duly authorized to examine the same, and shall deliver up such ticket upon demand, to any of the Company's servants duly authorized to collect tickets. Any passenger, not producing or delivering up his ticket as aforesaid, shall be liable to pay the fare from the place whence the train originally started, unless he can prove that he has travelled a less distance only, and has paid his fare for such less distance.

II. At the intermediate stations, the fares shall be deemed to be accepted, and the tickets furnished only upon condition that there shall be room in the train for which the tickets shall be furnished. In case there shall not be room for all the passengers to whom tickets shall be furnished, those who shall have obtained tickets for the longest distance shall have the preference, and those who shall have obtained tickets for the same distance shall have the preference according to the order in which they shall have received their tickets.

III. Any person, who shall attempt to defraud the Company by travelling, or attempting to travel, upon the Railway without having previously paid his fare, or by riding in or upon a Carriage of a highest class than that for which he shall have paid his fare, or by continuing his journey in or upon any of the Carriage of the Company beyond the place for which he shall have paid his fare, without previously paying the fare for the additional distance, and with intent to avoid payment thereof, or who shall knowingly and wilfully refuse or neglect, on arriving at the point to which he shall have paid his fare, to quit such Carriage, or who shall in any other manner whatever, attempt to evade the payment of his fare, is hereby subjected to a penalty, not exceeding Twenty Rupees.

IV. Any passenger, who shall get into or upon, or attempt to get into or upon, or shall quit or attempt to quit any Carriage while such Carriage is in motion, or who shall ride or attempt to ride on the steps or any other part of the Carriage except on those parts which are intended for the accommodation of passengers, shall be liable to a penalty, not exceeding Twenty Rupees.

V. Any person other than the engineman and fire-man, who shall ride or attempt to ride upon any locomotive engine or tender, and any person other than the guard or breaksman, who shall ride or attempt to ride upon any luggage van or goods waggon, without the special licence of the Superintendent of Locomotives, shall be liable to a penalty, not exceeding Twenty Rupees for each offence.

VI. No person shall smoke either on the Company's premises, or in or upon any of their Carriages (except in places of Carriages which may be specially provided for the purpose); any person infringing this regulation is hereby subjected to a penalty not exceeding Twenty Rupees, and any person persisting in such infringement after being warned to desist by any of the Company's servants, in addition to incurring the penalty above mentioned, may immediately, or at the first opportunity, be removed from the Company's premises and shall forfeit his fare.

VII. Any person, who shall be found in any Railway Carriage, or any part of the Company's premises, in a state of intoxication, or committing any nuisance, or act of indecency, or shall wilfully and without lawful excuse interfere with the comfort of any passenger on the Railway, shall be liable to a penalty not exceeding Twenty Rupees; and in addition to such liability the offender may immediately, or at the first opportunity of travelling, be removed from the Company's premises, and shall forfeit his fare.

VIII. If any special Carriage, or portion of a Carriage, or any private room or apartment shall be provided for the exclusive use of females, any male person who shall enter such Carriage or portion of a Carriage, or any such room or apartment, knowing the same to be exclusively appropriated as aforesaid, or who shall remain therein after having been informed of its exclusive appropriation, shall be liable to a penalty not exceeding Twenty Rupees, and may be immediately removed therefrom, and also from the Company's premises, and shall forfeit his fare.

IX. The Company shall not in any case be answerable for passengers' luggage, unless it shall have been booked and separately paid for.

X. If any person shall fail to pay on demand any sum due for the conveyance of any goods conveyed upon the Railway, it shall be lawful for the Company to detain and sell all or any part of such goods, or if the same shall have been removed from the premises of the Company, it shall be lawful for them to detain and sell any other goods on their premises belonging to the party liable to pay such sum, and out of the money arising from such sale to retain the sum payable as aforesaid, and all charges and expenses of such detention and sale, rendering the overplus, if any, of the money arising by such sale and such of the goods as shall remain unsold, to the person entitled thereto, or the Company may recover any such sum by action at law.

XI. The owner or person having the care of any goods which shall have been carried upon the said Railway, or shall be brought on to the premises of the said Railway Company for the purpose of being carried on their Railway, shall, on demand by any servant of the Company appointed to receive goods to be carried on that part of the Railway on which such goods shall have been carried, or shall be about to be carried, deliver to such servant an exact account in writing signed by him of the number or quantity of such goods.

XII. If any such owner or person as aforesaid shall fail to give such account to such servant of the Company demanding the same, or if he shall give a false account thereof, he shall for every such offence, forfeit to the Company a sum not exceeding Fifty Rupees for every ton of goods, or for any parcel exceeding one hundred weight, (as the case may be), in addition to the sum payable for the carriage of such goods.

XIII. No person shall be entitled to carry, or to require the Company to carry, upon the Railway, any goods which in the judgement of the Company shall be of a dangerous nature; and if any person shall cause any dangerous goods to be carried upon the said Railway, without distinctly marking their nature on the outside of the package containing the same for otherwise giving notice in writing the Book-keeper, or other servant of the Company to whom the same shall be delivered for the purpose of being so carried, he shall forfeit to the Company Two Hundred Rupees for every such offence; and it shall be lawful for the Company to refuse to carry any parcel that they may suspect to contain goods of a dangerous nature, or to require the same to be opened to ascertain the fact previously to carrying the same.

XIV. Any person, who shall wilfully obstruct or impede any officer or servant of the Company in the discharge of his duty on the Railway, or any of works, stations or premises connected therewith, shall be liable to a penalty, not exceeding Fifty Rupees.

XV. Any person who shall trespass upon the Railway, or any of the lands, stations or other premises belonging to the Company, shall be liable to a penalty not exceeding Twenty Rupees; and if any such person shall refuse to leave such premises on being requested to do so by any officer, servant or other person on behalf of the Company, he shall be liable to a penalty not exceeding Fifty Rupees, and may be immediately removed from such premises by such officer, servant or other person as aforesaid.

XVI. Any person who shall ride, or drive upon or across the said Railway, or any part thereof, any beast or animal, (except in directly crossing the said Railway at any road or place appointed for that purpose, at a time at which he shall be lawfully authorized so to do,) shall be liable to a penalty not exceeding Fifty Rupees for each offence.

XVII. The owner of any animal, which shall be found straying on the Railway, or on any lands belonging to the Company, shall be liable to a penalty not exceeding Ten Rupees for each animal.

XVIII. Any person who shall unlawfully and wilfully remove or deface the number-plates, or remove or extinguish any lamp on any carriage belonging to the said Company, or shall wilfully damage or injure any carriage, engine, waggon, truck, warehouse, building, machine, fence or any other matter, or thing belonging to the Company, shall be liable to a penalty not exceeding Fifty Rupees, in addition to the amount of damage done.

XIX. If any person for whose use or accommodation any gate shall have been set up by the said Company on either side of the said Railway, or any other person, shall open such gate, or pass, or attempt to pass, or drive or attempt to drive any animal across the said Railway, at a time when any engine or train passing along the same shall be in sight, or who shall at any time omit to shut and fasten such gate as soon as he and any carriage, cattle or other animals or things under his carriage, shall have passed through the same, he shall forfeit for every such offence a sum not exceeding Fifty Rupees.

XX. If any person shall commit any offence against this Act to which any penalty is attached, and the name and address of such person shall be unknown, any officer or servant of the Company, or any Police Officer, may lawfully apprehend and detain such person until he can conveniently be taken before a Magistrate, or other officer having jurisdiction over the offence, or until he shall be otherwise discharged by due course of law.

XXI. Whoever shall wilfully do any act or omit to do what he shall be legally bound to do, intending by such act or omission to cause, or knowing that he is thereby likely to cause, any engine, tender, carriage, or truck upon the said Railway to be obstructed, mismanaged, overthrowing, or damaged in its passage upon the said Railway, and the life or limb of any person to be thereby endangered, shall be liable to be transported beyond sea for the term of his life, or to be imprisoned with or without hard labour, for any term not exceeding seven years.

XXII. If any officer or servant of the said Company shall wilfully or negligently omit to do what he should be legally bound to do, and if, in consequence of such omission the life or limb of any person shall be endangered, such officer or servant shall be liable to be imprisoned, with or without hard labour, for any term not exceeding three years.

XXIII. If any officer or servant of the said Company shall be in a state of intoxication whilst actually employed upon the Railway, or any of the works connected therewith, in the discharge of any duty, the omission or negligent performance of which would be likely to endanger the life or limb of any person, such officer or servant shall be liable to imprisonment, with or without hard labour, for a term not exceeding one year.

XXIV. In the construction of this Act every officer or servant of the Company shall be deemed to be legally bound to do everything which he shall be required to do by any regulation having regard to public safety which shall be made by the said Railway Company, and allowed by the Government of Bombay, and of which such officer or servant shall have notice.

J.P. Grant,
Secy. to the Govt. of India

Supplementary Railway Act 12 of 1853 for the Great Indian Peninsula Railway Company

Source: The Calcutta Gazette, Saturday, July 30, 1853

Gist: The Supplementary Railway Act 12 of 1853 for the Great Indian Peninsula Railway Company was passed as a supplementary to Act No. III of 1853 on 22 July 1853, fixing what officers are eligible to punish certain offences through pecuniary penalties and forfeitures.

Fort William, Home Department, Legislative,
The 22nd July 1853.

The following Act, passed by the Governor General of India in Council on 22nd July 1853, is hereby promulgated for general information: -

Act No. XII of 1853

An Act supplemented to Act No. III of 1853, relating to the Great Indian Peninsula Railway Company in the Presidency of Bombay.

Whereas by Act No. III of 1853, certain offences are made punishable by pecuniary penalties or forfeitures, and doubts have arisen whether such offences are punishable by Magistrates of Police in the Island of Bombay and Colaba, and it is expedient to remove such doubts, and also to define by what Officers such offences shall be punishable; It is enacted as follows:

I. Any person who shall be guilty of any offence for which, according to the provisions of the said Act, such person shall be liable to any pecuniary penalty or forfeiture, shall be punishable for such offence by any Magistrate of Police, Justice of the Peace, Magistrate, Joint Magistrate or person lawfully exercising the powers of a Magistrate, within the local limits of whose jurisdiction such offence shall be committed, and any person hereby made punishable by a Magistrate of Police or Justice of the Peace, shall be punishable upon summary conviction.

II. Any Deputy or Assistant Magistrate, and any district or joint Police Officer, may, to the extent of the powers conferred upon him by the general Regulations of the Bombay Code, and by the Acts of the Governor General of India in Council, exercise the powers conferred upon a Magistrate by this Act, coupled with Act No. II of 1839.

III. Payment of any fare to which any passenger not producing or delivering up his ticket shall be liable under Section 1 of the said Act No. III of 1853 may be enforced in the same manner as any penalty under this Act.

Geo. Plowden,
Offfg. Secy. to the Govt. of India

373

An Act Relating to Railways in India (Act 18 of 1854)

Source: The Calcutta Gazette, July to December 1854

Gist: The Indian Railway Act 18 of 1854 with 43 sections got the assent of the Governor-General of India on 12 August 1854. The Act provides for ticket, checking of tickets, order of preference of seats for valid ticket holders, preference of EIC staff over the public, penalty for evading payment of fare, boarding and quitting carriage in motion, riding on engine, tender or luggage van, smoking in prohibited areas, intoxication, nuisance, and entering private room or carriage, rules regarding luggage charges, ban on dangerous goods, rules for railway crossings, measures against trespassing of animals, defacing number plates, damaging railway property and machinery, and against negligent behaviour of staff. It also details fines warrants, custody and jail imprisonment and the competent authorities to do so. With this Act, the Acts 3 and 12 of 1853 are repealed. Section 29 gives importance to public safety. Sections 41 and 42 suggest how the railway company should work in tandem with the local government in case of accidents. Last section (43) provides for the need of exhibiting documents in vernacular language of the district where the station is situated.

Legislative Council,
12th August, 1854

The following Act, passed by the Legislative Council, received the assent of the Most Noble the Governor-General of India, on the 12th August 1854, and is hereby promulgated for general information: -

Act No. XVIII of 1854
An Act relating to Railways in India

Whereas it is expedient, that all Railways, which have been, or shall be opened by any Railway Company, under the superintendence and control of the East India Company, for the public conveyance of passengers or goods in any part of the territories in the possession and under the Government of the said Company, should be subject to the same regulations; It is enacted as follows: -

I. No person shall enter any carriage used on any such Railway, for the purpose of travelling therein, without having first paid his fare, and obtained a ticket. Every person desirous of travelling on such Railway shall, upon payment of his fare, be furnished with a ticket, specifying the class of carriage and the distance for which the fare has been paid, and shall, when required, show his ticket to any servant of the said Company, duly authorised to examine the same, and shall deliver up such ticket upon demand, to any of the Company's servants duly authorised to collect tickets. Any person, not producing or delivering up his ticket, as aforesaid, shall be liable to pay the fare from the place whence the train originally started, unless he can prove, that he has travelled a less distance only, in which case he shall be liable to pay the fare only from the place whence he has travelled.

II. At the intermediate Stations, the fares shall be deemed to be accepted, and the tickets furnished only upon condition that there be room in the train for which the tickets shall be furnished. In case there shall not be room for all the passengers to whom tickets shall have been furnished, those who shall have obtained tickets for the longest distance shall have the preference; and those who shall have obtained tickets for the same distance shall have the preference, according to the order in which they shall have received their tickets. Provided, that all Officers and troops of Her Majesty, or of the East India Company, on duty, and all other persons on the business of the East India Company, who, by virtue of any contract with the East India Company, shall be entitled to be conveyed on such Railway in preference to, or in priority over the public, shall be entitled to such preference and priority without reference to the distance for which, or the order in which they shall have received their tickets.

III. Any person who shall defraud or attempt to defraud any such Railway Company, by travelling, or attempting to travel upon such Railway, without having previously paid his fare; or by riding in or upon a carriage of a higher class than that for which he shall have paid his fare; or by continuing his journey in or upon any of the carriages of the Company beyond the place for which he shall have paid his fare, without previously paying the fare for the additional distance, and with intent to avoid payment thereof; or who shall knowingly and wilfully refuse or neglect, on arriving at the point to which he shall have paid his fare to quit such carriage; or who shall in any other manner whatever, attempt to evade the payment of his fare, shall be liable to a fine not exceeding fifty rupees for each offence.

IV. Any passenger, who shall get into or upon, or attempt to get into or upon, or shall quit or attempt to quit any carriage upon any such Railway, while such carriage is in motion, or who shall ride or attempt to ride upon any such Railway, on the steps, or any other part of a carriage except on those parts which are intended for the accommodation of passengers; shall be liable to a fine, not exceeding twenty rupees for each offence.

V. Any person other than the engine-man and fire-man, and assistant fire-man, if any, who without the special licence of the Superintendent of locomotives, shall ride or attempt to ride upon any locomotive engine or tended upon any such Railway; and any person other than the guard or brakesmen, who, without such licence as aforesaid, shall ride, or attempt to ride upon such Railway, in or upon any luggage van or goods- waggon, or other vehicle not appropriated to the carriage of passengers, shall be liable to a fine not exceeding twenty rupees for each offence.

VI. If any person shall smoke, either on the premises, or in or upon any of the carriages belonging to any such Railway Company, except in places or carriages which may be specially provided for the purpose, he shall be liable to a fine not exceeding twenty rupees for each offence; and if any person persist in infringing this regulation after being warned to desist by any of the servants of the Company such person, in addition to incurring the liability above mentioned, may be removed by any of the servants of the Company from any such carriage, and from the premises of the Company, and shall forfeit his fare.

VII. Any person who shall be in a state of intoxication, or shall commit any nuisance or act of any indecency in any Railway carriage, or upon any part of the premises of any such Railway Company; or who shall wilfully and without lawful excuse interfere with the comfort of any passenger on such Railway, shall be liable to a fine not exceeding twenty rupees; and in addition to such liability the offender may be removed by any of the servants of the Company from any such carriage, and also from the premises of the Company and shall forfeit his fare.

VIII. If any special carriage, or portion of a carriage, or any private room or apartment, shall be provided by any such Railway Company for the exclusive use of females, any male person who without lawful excuse shall enter such carriage, or portion of a carriage, or any such room or apartment, knowing the same to be exclusively appropriated as aforesaid, or shall remain therein after having been informed of its exclusive appropriation, shall be liable to a fine not exceeding one hundred rupees, and may be removed therefrom, and also from the premises of the Company by any of the servants of the Company, and shall forfeit his fare.

IX. No such Railway Company shall in any case be answerable for loss or injury to any passengers' luggage, unless it shall have been booked and separately paid for.

X. No such Railway Company shall in any case be answerable for loss of, or injury to any gold or silver, coined or uncoined, manufactured or unmanufactured, or any precious stones, jewellery, watches, clocks or time-pieces of any description, trinkets, Government securities, bills of other exchange, promissory notes, Bank-notes, orders or other securities for payment of money, Government stamp paper, postage stamps, maps, writings, title deeds, paintings, engravings, pictures, plated articles, glass, china, silks in a manufactured or unmanufactured state, and whether wrought up or not wrought up with other materials, shawls, lace or any of them contained in any parcel or package which shall have been delivered to such Railway Company, either to be carried for hire or to accompany the person of any passenger, unless the value and nature of such articles shall have been declared by the person or persons sending or delivering the same and an increased charge for the safe conveyance of the same shall have been accepted by some person specially authorised to enter into the engagements on behalf of the said Railway Company.

XI. The liability of such Railway Company for loss or injury of any articles or goods to be carried by them other than those specially provided for by this Act, shall not be deemed or construed to be limited or in any wise affected by any public notice given, or any private contract made by them; but such Railway Company shall be answerable for such loss or injury when it shall have been caused by gross negligence or misconduct on the part of their agents or servants.

XII. If any person shall fail to pay on demand any sum due to any such Railway Company for the conveyance of any goods, it shall be lawful for the Company to detain all or any part of such goods, or, if the same shall have been removed from the premises of the Company, any other goods of such person which shall then be on their premises, or shall thereafter come into their possession; and also to sell by public auction sufficient of such goods, to realize the sum payable as aforesaid and all charges and expenses of such detention and sale, and out of the proceeds of the sale to retain the sum so payable together with the charges and expenses aforesaid, rendering the overplus, if any, of the money arising by such sale, and such of the goods as shall remain unsold, to the person entitled thereto; or the Company may recover any such sum by action at law.

XIII. The owner or person having the care of any goods which shall have been carried upon any such Railway, or shall be brought on to the premises of any such Railway Company for the purpose of being carried on their Railway, shall, on demand by any servant of the Company appointed to receive goods to be carried on that part of the Railway on which such goods shall have been carried, or shall be about to be carried, deliver to such servant an exact account in writing signed by him of the number or quantity and description of such goods.

XIV. If any such owner or person as aforesaid, shall wilfully fail to give such account to such servant of the Company; or if he shall wilfully give a false account thereof, he shall, for every such offence, be liable to a fine not exceeding fifty rupees for every ton of goods, or for any parcel exceeding one Hundred weight; and to a fine not exceeding twenty rupees for any quantity of goods less than a ton or for any parcel less than one hundred weight.

XV. No person shall carry upon any such Railway any dangerous goods; or be entitled to require any such Railway Company to carry upon such Railway, any luggage or goods which, in the judgement of the Company or any of their servants, shall be of a dangerous nature; and if any person shall carry upon such Railway any dangerous goods, or shall deliver to such Railway Company any such goods for the purpose of being carried upon such Railway, without distinctly marking their nature on the outside of the package containing the same, or otherwise giving notice in writing of the nature thereof to the book-keeper or other servant of the Company to whom the same shall be delivered for the purpose of being so carried, he shall be liable to a fine not exceeding two hundred rupees for every such offence; and it shall be lawful for any such Company or any of their servants to refuse to carry any luggage or parcel that they may suspect to contain goods of a dangerous nature, and to require the same to be opened to ascertain the fact previously to carrying the same; and in case any such luggage or parcel shall be received by the Company for the purpose of being carried on the Railway, it shall be lawful for the Company or any of their servants to stop the transit thereof, until they shall be satisfied as to the nature of the contents of the baggage or parcel.

XVI. Any person, who shall wilfully obstruct or impede any officer or servant of the Company in the discharge of his duty on such Railway, or any of the works, stations or premises connected therewith, shall be liable to a fine not exceeding fifty rupees.

XVII. Any person who shall trespass upon any such Railway, or upon any of the lands, stations, or other premises belonging to the Company, shall be liable to a fine not exceeding twenty rupees; and if any such person shall refuse to leave such Railway or premises on being requested to do so by any officer or servant of the Company, or by any other person on behalf of the Company, he shall be liable to a fine not exceeding fifty rupees, and may be immediately removed from such Railway or premises by such officer, servant, or other person as aforesaid.

XVIII. Any person who shall wilfully ride, lead, or drive upon or across any such Railway, any animal, except in directly crossing the said Railway at any road or place appointed for that purpose, at a time at which he shall be lawfully authorised so to do, shall be liable to a fine not exceeding fifty rupees for each offence.

XIX. If the Railway cross any public carriage road on a level, the Railway Company shall erect, and at all times maintain good and efficient gates, either across the Railway, or across the road on each side of the Railway where the same shall communicate with the road, and shall employ proper persons to open and shut such gates; if such gates be across the road they shall be kept constantly closed, except during the time when horses, cattle, carts, or carriages, passing along the same, shall have to cross the Railway, and the gates shall be of such dimensions and so constructed as when closed to fence in the Railway, and prevent cattle, carriages, or passengers from entering upon the Railway: provided that it shall be lawful for the local Government in any case to order that the gates shall be across the road or across the Railway as the Government may think fit, and in such case the gates shall be erected, maintained, and closed accordingly. If any Railway Company shall wilfully fail to comply with the provision of this Section they shall forfeit a sum not exceeding two hundred rupees for each offence, and any Magistrate or Justice of the Peace may, in case any such gates be not erected or maintained the same within a time to be specified in the order, and in case of wilful failure on the part of the Railway Company to comply with such order, they shall be liable to a fine not exceeding two hundred rupees for every day that they shall wilfully fail so to do.

XX. Every such Railway Company shall be bound to erect and maintain good and sufficient fences on each side of their Railway; or, failing therein, shall be liable to a fine not exceeding fifty rupees for every offence; and it shall be lawful for a Magistrate or Justice of the Peace to order the Company to erect or repair any such fence within a time to be specified in the order, and upon failure of the Company to comply with such order they shall be liable to a fine not exceeding fifty rupees for every day that they fail so to do.

XXI. The owner of any animal which shall trespass or stray upon any such Railway, or upon any lands belonging to such Railway Company, except for want of the erection or maintenance of any fence or gate which the Company is bound to erect and maintain shall be liable to a fine not exceeding ten rupees for each animal; and it shall be lawful for the Company, or any of their servants, to take or drive every animal which shall be found so trespassing to the nearest Police Station, there to be detained until the highest amount of the fine incurred by such trespass and the expense of feeding and keeping the animal be paid, or until a Magistrate shall otherwise order. A Magistrate may, upon proof of the trespass, cause such animal to be sold by public auction, and the proceeds of the sale, after deducting therefrom such fine or such a sum not exceeding ten rupees for each animal, as the Magistrate shall award to be paid in lieu of the fine to which the owner is hereby made liable, and such further sum as the Magistrate shall order to be paid for the expense of detaining, feeding, and selling such animal, shall be returned to the owner of the animal on demand.

XXII. Any person who shall unlawfully and wilfully remove or deface the number plates, or remove, or extinguish any lamp on any carriage belonging to any such Railway Company, or shall wilfully or negligently damage or injured any carriage, engine, waggon, truck, warehouse, building, machine, fence or any other matter or thing belonging to such Railway Company, shall be liable to a fine not exceeding fifty rupees.

XXIII. If any person for whose use or accommodation any gate shall have been set up by any such Railway Company on either side of such Railway, or any other person, shall open such gate; overpass, or attempt to pass, or drive, or attempt to drive any carriage, cattle, or other animal or dog across the said Railway at a time when any engine or train approaching along the same shall be in sight; or shall at any time omit to shut and fasten such gate, as soon as he and any carriage, cattle, or other animal or thing under his carriage, shall have passed through the same, he shall be liable to a fine not exceeding fifty rupees.

XXIV. If any person shall commit any offence here be made punishable by fine, and the name and address of such person shall be unknown, or there be reason to believe that the offender will abscond, any officer or servant of the Company, or any police officer, or other person whom such officer or servant may call to his aid, may, without any warrant or written authority, lawfully apprehend and detain such offender until he can be taken before a Magistrate or other officer having jurisdiction over the offence, or shall give sufficient security for his appearance before such Magistrate or other officer, or shall be otherwise discharged by due course of law.

XXV. Whoever shall wilfully do any act, or shall wilfully omit to do what he is legally bound to do, intending by such act or omission to cause, or knowing that he is thereby likely to cause the safety of any person travelling or being upon any such Railway to be endangered, shall be liable to be transported beyond sea for the term of his life, or to be imprisoned, with or without hard labour, for any term not exceeding seven years.

XXVI. If any officer or servant of such Railway Company shall wilfully do any act which he is legally prohibited from doing; or shall wilfully or negligently omit to do what he is legally bound to do, and if, in consequence of such act or omission, the safety of any person travelling or being upon such Railway shall be endangered, such officer or servant shall be liable to be imprisoned, with or without hard labour, for any term not exceeding three years, or to fine, or to both.

XXVII. Any officer or servant of such Railway Company who shall be in a state of intoxication, whilst actually employed upon the Railway, or any of the works connected therewith, in the discharge of any duty, and any officer or servant of such Company who negligently shall omit to perform his duty, or shall perform the same in an improper manner, shall be liable to a fine not exceeding fifty rupees; and if the duty in any of the cases in this Section above-mentioned be such, that the omission or negligent performance thereof would be likely to endanger the safety of any person travelling or being upon such Railway, such officer or servant shall, on conviction before a Magistrate, be liable to imprisonment, with or without hard labour, for a term not exceeding one year, or to fine, or to both.

XXVIII. If any person shall rashly or negligently and without lawful excuse do any act, which shall be likely to endanger the safety of any person travelling or being upon such Railway, he shall, upon conviction before a Magistrate, be liable to imprisonment, with or without hard labour, for a term not exceeding one year, or to fine, or to both.

XXIX. In the construction of this Act, every officer and servant of such Railway Company, shall be deemed to be legally bound to do every thing necessary for, or conducive to the safety of the public which he shall be required to do by any Regulation which shall be made by the Company, and allowed by the Governor General of India in Council, and of which Regulation such officer or servant shall have notice; and every such officer and servant shall be deemed to be legally prohibited from doing every act which shall be likely to cause danger, and which by any such Regulation he shall be prohibited from doing; and every person employed by or on behalf of such Railway Company to do any act upon the Railway, shall be deemed to be a servant of the Company.

XXX. Any person, whether a European British subject or not, who shall be guilty of any offence, for which, according to the provisions of this Act, he shall be liable to a fine only, shall be punishable for such offence by any Justice of the Peace for any of the Presidency Towns of Calcutta Madras and Bombay, Magistrate, Joint Magistrate, or person lawfully exercising the powers of a Magistrate, whether the offence shall have been committed within the local limits of the jurisdiction of such officer or not, and any person hereby made punishable by a Justice of the Peace, shall be punishable upon summary conviction.

XXXI. No conviction, order, or judgement of any Justice of the Peace, shall be quashed for error of form or procedure, but only on the merits; and it shall not be necessary to state on the face of the conviction, order, judgement, the evidence on which it proceeds; but the depositions taken, or copy of them, shall be returned with the conviction, order, or judgement, in obedience to any writ of *certiorari*, and if no jurisdiction appears on the face of the conviction, order, or judgement, but the depositions taken supply that defect, the conviction, order, or judgement shall be aided by what so appears in such depositions.

XXXII. A Magistrate may refer for trial and decision any charge of an offence hereby made punishable by fine only to any of his Assistants, or to any Deputy Magistrate lawfully appointed to exercise the powers of a covenanted assistant, and in such case every such Assistant or Deputy Magistrate may exercise all the powers vested in a Magistrate, subject to all the rules applicable to criminal cases deputed to such Assistants or Deputy Magistrate, acting judicially.

XXXIII. The local Government may give general authority to any such Assistant or Deputy Magistrate to exercise, without reference by a Magistrate, any of the powers which they are hereby rendered competent to exercise upon reference by a Magistrate, subject to appeal to the Magistrate from any conviction by such Assistant or Deputy Magistrate, within one month from the date of conviction. Provided that a Magistrate may at any time call from any of his Assistants, or from any Deputy Magistrate subordinate to him, any case pending before such assistant or Deputy Magistrate.

XXXIV. All fines imposed under the authority of this Act for offences punishable by fine only by any Justice of the Peace, Magistrate, Joint Magistrate, or person lawfully exercising the powers of a Magistrate, or by any Assistant to a Magistrate, or Deputy Magistrate may, in case of non-payment thereof, be levied by distress and sale of the goods and chattels of the offender, by warrant under the hand of any of the above-named officers; and in case any such fine shall not be forthwith paid, any such officer may order the offender to be apprehended and detained in safe custody until the return can be conveniently made to such warrant of distress, unless the offender shall give security to the satisfaction of such officer for his appearance at such place and time as shall be appointed for the return of the warrant of distress, and such officer may take such security by way of recognizance or otherwise; and if upon the return of such warrant it shall appear that no sufficient distress can be had whereon to levy such fine, and the same shall not be forthwith paid, or in case it shall appear to the satisfaction of such officer, by the confession of the offender or otherwise, that he has not sufficient goods and chattels whereupon such fine or sum of money could be levied if a warrant of distress were issued, any such officer may, by warrant under his hand, commit the offender to prison, there to be imprisoned only, or to be imprisoned and kept to hard labour, according to the discretion of such officer, for any term not exceeding two calendar months when the amount of the fine shall not exceed fifty rupees, and for any term not exceeding four calendar months when the amount shall not exceed one hundred rupees, and for any term not exceeding six calendar months in any other case, the commitment to be determinable in each of the cases aforesaid on payment of the amount.

XXXV. The heads of district police and *ameens* of police in the Presidency of Madras, and district or joint police officers in the Presidency of Bombay, may punish, to the extent of the powers conferred upon them respectively in petty offences, any offence hereby made punishable by fine not exceeding twenty rupees.

XXXVI. Payment of any fare to which any passenger not producing or delivering up his ticket shall be liable under Section I of this Act, may be enforced in the same manner as any fine imposed by this Act.

XXXVII. Every person who shall be guilty of any offence mentioned in this Sections XXV, XXVI, XXVII, and XXVIII of this Act, may be lawfully apprehended without any warrant or written authority, by any servant or officer of the Company, or by any other person whom such officer or servant shall call to his aid, or by any police officer of such grade, as shall, by any law in force for the time being, be entrusted in any case with the power of arrest without a warrant; and every person so apprehended shall, with all convenient despatch, be carried and conveyed before a Magistrate or Justice of the Peace, or other officer lawfully authorised to punish the offender or to commit him for trial.

XXXVIII. In the construction of this Act, unless where a contrary intention appears from the context, the word "Magistrate" shall include a Joint Magistrate, and any person lawfully exercising the powers of a Magistrate,-words in the singular number shall include the plural, words in the plural shall include the singular; and words in the masculine gender shall include the feminine; and the word "fine" shall include a sum of money due upon a forfeited recognizance.

XXXIX. Acts No. III of 1853 and No. XII of 1853, are hereby repealed, except as to acts done, offences committed, and the liabilities incurred before the passing of this Act.

XL. Every Railway with the said territories used for the public conveyance of passengers or goods shall, until the contrary be proved, be presumed to be a Railway within the meaning of this Act, and every Company to whom any such Railway shall belong, shall, until the contrary be proved, be presumed to be a Railway Company within the meaning of this Act.

XLI. Every such Railway Company shall, within forty-eight hours after the occurrence upon the Railway belonging to such Company of any accident attended with serious personal injury, give notice thereof to the local Government; and if any such Company omit to give such notice, they shall forfeit the sum of fifty rupees for every day during which the omission to give the same shall continue.

XLII. The local Government may order and direct any such Railway Company to make up and deliver to them a return of serious accidents occurring in the course of the public traffic upon the Railway belonging to such Company, whether attended with personal injury or not, in such form and manner, as the Government shall deem necessary and require for their information, with a view to the public safety, and if any such returns shall not be so delivered within fourteen days after the same shall have been required every such Company shall forfeit the sum of fifty rupees for every day during which the said Company shall neglect to deliver the same.

XLIII. A copy of this Act, and of the General Regulations, Time Tables, and Traffic of Charges which shall from time to time be published by any Railway Company, with the sanction of the local Government, shall be exhibited in some conspicuous place at each Station of every Railway so that they may be easily seen and read; and all such documents shall be so exhibited in English and in the Vernacular language of the district in which the Station is situated, and in such other language, if any, as shall be required by order of the local Government.

W. Morgan,
Clerk of the Council

374

Indian Railway Act 9 of 1860 for the Determination of Disputes on Wages and Price of Work between the Railway Employers and Employees

Source: The Calcutta Gazette, 4th April 1860

Gist: The Indian Railway Act 9 of 1860 was passed to rationalize wages and resolve disputes on wages between the employers and employees in railway and other public works. The Act has nine sections, which provides for the authority (magistrates and officers) and jurisdiction to decide on disputes and fines on non-compliance.

Act No. IX of 1860

"An Act to make provision for the speedy determination of certain disputes between workmen engaged in Railway and other public works and their employers."

WHEREAS it is expedient to make provision for the speedy determination of certain disputes between workmen engaged in Railway and other public works and their employers; It is enacted as follows: -

I. It shall be lawful for the Executive Government of any Presidency or place within the British Territories in India to invest any Magistrate or other Officer exercising the powers of a Magistrate with power to enquire into and decide disputes on account of wages, hire of carriage, or the price of work, between any workmen employed in the construction of any Railway, Canal, or other public work, the construction of which is or shall be sanctioned by Parliament or by any such Executive Government, and the person or persons by whom such workmen are employed.

II. Magistrates empowered to decide disputes under the preceding Section shall have jurisdiction only in case the amount in dispute shall not exceed the sum of two hundred Rupees, and the claim is preferred within six months from the date on which the cause of action arose.

III. The Executive Government shall fix, and may, from time to time, alter the local limits of the jurisdiction of any Magistrate invested with jurisdiction under Section I of this Act. A Magistrate so invested may hold a Court for the investigation of disputes of the nature described in the said Section, at any place within the local limits of his jurisdiction.

IV. The rules for the institution of suits as provided in Act VIII of 1859 (for simplifying the Procedure of the Courts of Civil Jurisdiction not established by Royal Charter) shall, as far as circumstances will allow, be followed in the investigation of disputes under the preceding Sections, and the procedure adopted shall be that provided for the cases in which the suit may be disposed of at the first hearing.

V. There shall be no appeal against any decision passed under this Act.

VI. The Magistrate having heard and decided the case, shall make an order for the payment of such sum of money (if any) as shall appear to him to be justly due: and if the person ordered to pay shall make default in the payment of such sum immediately or within such time as the Magistrate shall direct, the Magistrate shall issue his warrant to levy the money by distress and sale of the goods and chattels of the defaulter.

VII. If any question shall arise whether any goods or chattels seized under the warrant of distress belong to the defaulter, or are liable to be distrained and sold as aforesaid, the same shall be determined in the manner provided by the said Act VIII of 1859 for the determination of the like questions arising in the execution of decrees.

VIII. Any person who shall voluntarily engage for a stipulated period to work on any Railway, Canal, or other public work, the construction of which is or shall be sanctioned in the manner specified in Section I of this Act, or to execute any specific work in connection with such public work, and who shall wilfully and without lawful or reasonable excuse neglect or refuse to perform the work so stipulated for, shall be liable, on conviction before a Magistrate, to a fine not exceeding twenty Rupees. The Magistrate may, at the request of the complainant or of any one authorized to act on his behalf, instead of fining such person, under him to perform or get performed the work according to the terms of his contract or engagement; and if he shall fail to comply with the order, the Magistrate may, upon proof to his satisfaction of such non compliance, sentence such person to be imprisoned with or without hard labour for any term not exceeding two months.

IX. This Act shall take effect only in those Districts or places to which it shall be extended by order of the Governor-General of India in Council, or of the Executive Government of any Presidency or place.

M. WYLIE,
Clerk of the Council

Indian Railway Servants' Act, 1867

Source: The Gazette of India, 13th July 1867

Gist: The Indian Railway Servants' Act, 1867 (Act 31 of 1867) was passed to render penal certain offences of the railway servants, as per the Indian Penal Code.

ACT No. XXXI of 1867

To render penal certain offences committed by servants of Railway Companies.

WHEREAS it is expedient to extend certain provisions of the Indian Penal Code relating to public servants to persons in the employment of Railway Companies; It is hereby enacted as follows: -

1. In this Act "Railway Company" means the proprietors for the time being of every railway or tramway situated in the territories vested in Her Majesty or her successors under the Statutes 21 and 22 Vic., Cap. 106 (*An Act for the better Government of India*), or (so far only as regards British subjects within the dominions hereinafter mentioned) situated in the dominions of Princes and States in the East Indies in alliance with Her Majesty or her successors, and the lessees, representatives and assigns of such proprietors.
2. Every officer and servant of a Railway Company shall be deemed a public servant within the meaning of Sections 161, 162, 163, 164 and 165 of the Indian Penal Code.
3. In the definition of legal remuneration contained in the said Section 161 the word 'Government' shall, for the purposes of this Act, be deemed to include a Railway Company.
4. This Act shall be called "The Railway Servants' Act 1867."

WHITLEY STOKES,
Asstt. Secy. to the Govt. of India,
Home Department (Legislative)

Indian Railway (Amendment) Act XIII of 1870

Source: The Gazette of India, Part IV, 9th April 1870

Gist: The Indian Railway (Amendment) Act 13 of 1870 was enacted to make apply Act 18 of 1854 relating to railways in India, with changes in wordings and overall change in section 29.

ACT No. XIII of 1870

An Act to apply the provisions of Act No. XVIII of 1854 to Railways belonging to, or worked by, Government.

1. Act No. XVIII of 1854 (relating to Railways in India) shall apply to all Railways now or hereafter belonging to Government, but worked by a Railway Company, in the same manner as if such Railways belonged to the Company and had been opened by the Company in manner mentioned in the preamble to the said Act.
2. Subject to the modifications hereinafter mentioned, the said Act shall apply to all Railways now or hereafter worked by Government in the same manner as if such Railways had been opened by a Railway Company in manner aforesaid.
3. In applying the said Act to any Railway now or hereafter worked by Government, the expressions "servant of the Company," "such servant," "such servant of the Company," "servant of the said Company," "Company's servants," "servants of the Company," "their servants" and "any of their servants" shall mean a servant or servants employed on such Railway: the expressions "officer or servant of such Railway Company," "officer or servant of such Company," "officer or servant of the Company," "servant or officer of the Company," and "such officer or servant" shall mean an officer or servant employed on such Railway: the expressions "the premises of any such Railway Company," "the premises of the Company," "premises belonging to the Company," "land belonging to such Railway Company," and "lands, stations or other premises belonging to the Company" shall mean the premises, lands or stations (as the case may be) occupied by or for such Railway: the expression "delivered to such Railway Company" shall mean "delivered to an officer on behalf of Government," and the expression "engagements on behalf of the said Railway Company" shall mean engagements on behalf of Government: sections nine and ten shall be read as if, for the expression "No such Railway Company shall," the expression "The Government

shall not" were substituted: the expression "any such Railway Company," "such Railway Company," "any such Company," and "the Company" shall mean, in sections three, six, eight, eleven, twelve, fifteen, twenty-two, twenty-seven and thirty, the Government; but in sections seventeen, nineteen, twenty, twenty-one, twenty-three, forty-one and forty-two, the expressions "Railway Company," "such Railway Company," "the Company" and "they" (when referring to a Company) shall mean the officer for the time being entrusted with the control of such Railway: in section twenty the expression "their railway" shall mean such Railway: and section twenty-nine shall be read as follows: -

"XXIX. In the construction of this Act, every officer and servant employed on such Railway shall be deemed to be legally bound to do every thing necessary for or conducive to the safety of the public, which he shall be required to do by any regulation made by the officer for the time being entrusted with the control of such Railway and allowed by the Governor General of India in Council, and of which regulation such officer or servant shall have notice; and every such officer and servant shall be deemed to be legally prohibited from doing every act which shall be likely to cause danger and which by any such regulation he shall be prohibited from doing; and every person employed by or on behalf of the Government to do any act upon the Railway shall be deemed to be a servant employed on such Railway."

WHITLEY STOKES,
Secy. to the Council of the Govr. Genl.
for making Laws and Regulations

377

The Repealing Act, 1870

Source: The Gazette of India, Part IV, 9th April 1870

Gist: The Repealing Act, 1870 (Act 14 of 1870) was passed to repeal certain enactments (that ceased to be in force) mentioned in the Schedule to the Act 14 of 1870, if this does not affect other provisions of the said Act. Section 39 of Act 18 of 1854, section 1 of Act 8 of 1860, section 22 of Act 16 of 1861, and the whole of Act 8 of 1868 are repealed.

ACT No. XIV of 1870

An Act for repealing certain enactments which have ceased to be in force, or have become *unnecessary*.

WHEREAS it is expedient that certain enactments (mentioned in the schedule to this Act) which have ceased to be in force otherwise than by express and specific repeal, or have by lapse of time and change of circumstances become unnecessary, or which merely repeal prior enactments, should be expressly and specifically repealed; It is hereby enacted as follows: -

1. The enactments mentioned in the schedule to this Act are hereby repealed to the extent specified in the third column of the same schedule:

   Provided that the repeal by this Act of any enactment shall not affect any Act or Regulation in which such enactment has been applied, incorporated or referred to:

   And this Act shall not affect the validity or invalidity of anything already done or suffered, or any indemnity already granted, or any right or title already acquired, or accrued, or any remedy or proceeding in respect thereof, or the proof of any past act or thing:

   Nor shall this Act affect any principle or rule of law, or established jurisdiction, form or course of pleading, practice or procedure, or existing usage, custom, privilege, restriction, exemption, office or appointment, notwithstanding that the same respectively may have been in any manner affirmed, recognized, or derived by, in or from, any enactment hereby repealed:

   Nor shall this Act provide or restore any jurisdiction, office, usage, custom, privilege, restriction, exemption, usage or practice not now existing, or in force.
2. This Act may be called "The Repealing Act, 1870."

SCHEDULE
PART I - STATUTES

Number and Year	*Title*	*Extent of repeal*
XVIII of 1854	An Act relating to Railways in India	Section thirty-nine
VIII of 1860	An Act for regulating the establishment and management of Electric Telegraphs in India	Section one
XVI of 1861	An Act for licensing and regulating stage carriages	Section twenty-two
VIII of 1868	An Act for repealing certain enactments which have ceased to be in force or have become unnecessary	The whole

WHITLEY STOKES,
Secy. to the Council of the Govr. Genl.
for making Laws and Regulations

378

Indian Railway Act XXV of 1871, Substitution of the Act XVIII of 1854

Source: The Calcutta Gazette, 25th October 1871

Gist: This is the Act 18 of 1854, as amended by the Act 25 of 1871. This Substitution Act has 44 sections, of which sections 1, 18 to 21, 26 and 29 are substituted, section 39 is repealed, and section 44 is added. Relevant provisions of the Cattle Trespass Act, 1871 are used in this Act. The Act provides for ticket, checking of tickets, order of preference of seats for valid ticket holders, penalty for evading payment of fare, boarding and quitting carriage in motion, riding on engine, tender or luggage van, smoking, intoxication, nuisance, and entering reserved room, rules regarding luggage, ban on dangerous goods, rules for railway crossings, measures against trespassing of animals, damaging railway property, and negligent behaviour of staff. It also details on fines warrants, custody and jail imprisonment, and the need of exhibiting documents in vernacular language in stations.

Act XVIII of 1854

[As Amended by Act XXV of 1871]

An Act relating to Railways in India

Whereas it is expedient that all Railways which have been, or shall be, opened by any Railway Company, under the superintendence and control of the East India Company, for the public conveyance of passengers or goods in any part of the territories in the possession and under the Government of the said Company, should be subject to the same regulations; It is exacted as follows:

I. *[Substituted by Act XXV of 1871.]*
For the purposes of this Act, 'Railway' includes land within the fences or other boundary-marks prescribed under section twenty-one, and all Lines of rail, sidings, or branches, worked over by locomotive engines for the purposes of, or in connexion with, a Railway; also all Stations, offices, ware-houses, fixed machinery, and other works constructed, or being constructed for the purposes of, or in connexion with, a Railway.

No person shall enter any carriage used on any such Railway, for the purpose of travelling therein, without having first paid his fare, and obtained a ticket. Every person desirous of travelling on such Railway shall, upon payment of his fare, be furnished with a ticket, specifying the class of carriage and the distance for which the fare has been paid, and shall, when required, show his ticket to any servant of any said Company duly authorized to examine the same, and shall deliver up such ticket upon demand, to any of the Company's servants duly authorized to collect tickets. Any person not producing or delivering up his ticket, as aforesaid, shall be liable to pay the fare from the place whence the train originally started, unless he can prove that he has travelled a less distance only, in which case he shall be liable to pay the fare only from the place whence he has travelled.

II. At the intermediate stations, the fares shall be deemed to be accepted, and the tickets furnished only upon condition that there be room in the train for which the tickets shall be furnished. In case there shall not be room for all the passengers to whom tickets shall have been furnished, those who shall have obtained tickets for the longest distance shall have the preference; and those who shall have obtained tickets for the same distance shall have the preference according to the order in which they shall have received their tickets. Provided that all officers and troops of Her Majesty, or of the East India Company, on duty, and all other persons on the business of the East India Company, who, by virtue of any contract with the East India Company, shall be entitled to be conveyed on such Railway in preference to, or in priority over the public, shall be entitled to such preference and priority without reference to the distance for which, or the order in which they shall have received their tickets.

III. Any person who shall defraud or attempt to defraud any such Railway Company by travelling, or attempting to travel, upon such Railway, without having previously paid his fare; or by riding in or upon a carriage of a higher class than that for which he shall have paid his fare; or by continuing his journey in or upon any of the carriages of the Company beyond the place for which he shall have paid his fare, without previously paying the fare for the additional distance, and with intent to avoid payment thereof; or who shall knowingly and wilfully refuse or neglect, on arriving at the point to which he shall have paid his fare, to quit such carriage; or who shall, in any other manner whatever, attempt to evade the payment of his fare, shall be liable to a fine not exceeding fifty rupees for each offence.

IV. Any passenger, who shall get into or upon, or attempt to get into or upon, or shall quit or attempt to quit any carriage upon any such Railway, while such carriage is in motion; or who shall ride or attempt to ride upon any such Railway, on the steps, or any other part of a carriage, except on those part which are intended for the accommodation of passengers, shall be liable to a fine not exceeding twenty rupees for each offence.

V. Any person other than the engine-man, and fire-man, and assistant fire-man, if any, who, without the special license of the Superintendent of Locomotives, shall ride or attempt to ride upon any locomotive engine or tender upon any such Railway; and any person other than the guard or breaksmen, who, without such license as aforesaid, shall ride or attempt to ride upon such Railway, in or upon any luggage-van or goods-waggon, or other vehicle not appropriated to the carriage of passengers, shall be liable to a fine not exceeding twenty rupees for each offence.

VI. If any person shall smoke, either on the premises, or in or upon any of the carriages belonging to any such Railway Company, except in places or carriages without may be specially provided for the purpose, be shall be liable to a fine not exceeding twenty rupees for each offence; and if any person persist in infringing this regulation after being warned to desist by any of the servants of the Company, such person, in addition to incurring the liability above mentioned, may be removed by any of the servants of the Company from any such carriage and from the premises of the Company, and shall forfeit his fare.

VII. Any person who shall be in a state of intoxication, or shall commit any nuisance or act of indecency in any Railway carriage, or upon any part of the premises of any such Railway Company; or who shall wilfully and without lawful excuse interfere with the comfort of any passenger on such Railway, shall be liable to a fine not exceeding twenty rupees; and in addition to such liability the offender may removed by any of the servants of the Company from any such carriage, and also from the premises of the Company, and shall forfeit his fare.

VIII. If any special carriage, or portion of a carriage, or any private room or apartment, shall be provided by any such Railway Company for the exclusive use of females, any male person, who without lawful excuse shall enter such carriage, or portion of a carriage, or any such room or apartment knowing the same to be exclusively appropriated as aforesaid; or shall remain therein after having been informed of its exclusive appropriation, shall be liable to a fine not exceeding one hundred rupees, and may be removed therefrom, and also from the premises of the Company, by any of the servants of the Company, and shall forfeit his fare.

IX. No such Railway Company shall in any case be answerable for loss or injury to any passenger's luggage unless it shall have been booked and separately paid for.

X. No such Railway Company shall in any case be answerable for loss or injury to any gold or silver, coined or uncoined, manufactured or unmanufactured, or any precious stones, jewellery, watches, clocks or time-pieces, of any description, trinkets, Government securities, bills of exchange, promissory notes, bank notes, orders, or other securities for payment of money, Government stamp-paper, postage stamps, maps, writings, title-deeds, paintings, engravings, pictures, plated-articles, glass, china, silks in a manufactured or unmanufactured state, and whether wrought up or not wrought up with other materials, shawls, lace, or any of them contained in any parcel or package which shall have been delivered to such Railway Company, either to be carried for hire or to accompany the person of any passenger, unless the value and nature of such articles shall have been declared by the person or persons sending or delivering the same, and an increased charge for the safe conveyance of same shall have been accepted by some person especially authorized to enter into such engagements on behalf of the said Railway Company.

XI. The liability of such Railway Company for loss or injury to any articles or goods to be carried by them other than those specially provided for by this Act, shall not be deemed or construed to be limited or in anywise affected by any public notice given, or any private contract made by them; but such Railway Company shall be answerable for such loss or injury when it shall have been caused by gross negligence or misconduct on the part of their agents or servants.

XII. If any person shall fail to pay on demand any sum due to any such Railway Company for the conveyance of any goods, it shall be lawful for the Company to detain all or any part of such goods, or, if the same shall have been removed from the premises of the Company, any other goods of such person which shall then be on their premises or shall thereafter come into their possession; and also to sell by public auction sufficient of such goods to realize the sum payable as aforesaid, and all charges and expenses of such detention and sale, and out of the proceeds of the sale, to retain the sum so payable, together with the charges and expenses aforesaid, rendering the overplus, if any, of the money arising by such sale, and such of the goods as shall remain unsold, to the person entitled thereto; or the Company may recover any such sum by action at law.

XIII. The owner or person having the care of any goods which shall have been carried upon any such railway, or shall be brought on to the premises of any such Railway Company for the purpose of being carried on their Railway, shall, on demand by any servant of the Company appointed to receive goods to be carried on that part of the Railway on which such goods shall have been carried, or shall be about to be carried, deliver to such servant an exact account in writing signed by him of the number or quantity and description of such goods.

XIV. If any such owner or person as aforesaid shall wilfully fail to give such account to such servant of the Company, or if he shall wilfully give a false account thereof, he shall for every such offence be liable to a fine not exceeding fifty rupees for every ton of goods, or for any parcel exceeding one hundred weight; and to a fine not exceeding twenty rupees for any quantity of goods less than a ton, or for any parcel less than one hundred weight.

XV. No person shall carry upon any such Railway any dangerous goods, or be entitled to require any such Railway Company to carry upon such Railway any luggage or goods which, in the judgement of the Company or any of their servants, shall be of a dangerous nature; and if any person shall carry upon any such Railway any dangerous goods, or shall deliver to such Railway Company any such goods for the purpose of being carried upon such Railway, without distinctly marking their nature on the outside of the package containing the same, or otherwise giving notice in writing of the nature thereof to the book-keeper or other servant of the Company to whom the same shall be delivered for the purpose of being so carried, he shall be liable to fine not exceeding two hundred rupees for every such offence; and it shall be lawful for any such Company or any of their servants to refuse to carry any luggage or parcel that they may suspect to contain goods of a dangerous nature, and to require the same to be opened to ascertain the fact previously to carrying the same; and in case any such luggage or parcel shall be received by the Company for the purpose of being carried on the Railway, it shall be lawful for the Company or any of their servants to stop the transit thereof, until they shall be satisfied as to the nature of the contents of the baggage or parcel.

XVI. Any person, who shall wilfully obstruct or impede any officer or servant of the Company in the discharge of his duty on such Railway, or any of the works, stations, or premises connected therewith, shall be liable to a fine not exceeding fifty rupees.

XVII. Any person who shall trespass upon any such Railway, or upon any of the lands, stations, or other premises belonging to the Company, shall be liable to a fine not exceeding twenty rupees; and if any such person shall refuse to leave such Railway or premises on being requested to do so by any officer or servant of the Company, or by any other person on behalf of the Company, he shall be liable to a fine not exceeding fifty rupees, and may be immediately removed from such Railway or premises by such officer, servant, or other person as aforesaid.

XVIII. *[Substituted by Act XXV of 1871.]* The word 'cattle' shall have the meaning attached to it in the Cattle Trespass Act, 1871, and the expression 'public road' in sections eleven and twenty-six of the said Act, shall be deemed to include a Railway. Any person employed on a Railway may exercise the powers of seizure provided by the said section eleven.

XIX. *[Substituted by Act XXV of 1871.]* The owner or person in charge of any cattle trespassing or straying on any Railway provided with fences suitable for the exclusion of cattle shall, on conviction before a Magistrate, be liable to a fine not exceeding ten rupees for each animal, in addition to any amount that may be recovered under the Cattle Trespass Act.

XX. *[Substituted by Act XXV of 1871.]* Whenever cattle are wilfully driven or knowingly permitted to be on any Railway provided with fences suitable for the exclusion of cattle, otherwise than for the purpose of crossing the Railway at a gate or bar provided for public use, the person in charge of such cattle, or, if he cannot be identified, then the owner of the said cattle, shall, on conviction before a Magistrate, be liable to a fine not exceeding fifty rupees for each animal, in addition to any amount that may be recovered under the said Act.[1] Fines imposed under this or the preceding section may be recovered in the manner provided by section twenty-five of the said Act.

XXI. *[Substituted by Act XXV of 1871.]* The Governor General in Council, or the Local Government with the sanction of the Governor General in Council, shall make rules, and may in like manner, from time to time, vary the same, for the provision of boundary-marks or fences for any Railway or any part thereof, and for roads constructed in connection therewith, and of gates or bars at places where any Railway crosses a road on the level, and for the employment of persons to open and shut such gates or bars; and may be such rules determine what kind of fences shall, for the

1. The Cattle Trespass Act, 1871.

purpose of sections nineteen and twenty, be deemed to be suitable for the exclusion of cattle.

XXII. Any person who shall unlawfully and wilfully remove or deface the number plates, or remove or extinguish any lamp on any carriage belonging to any such Railway or Company, or shall wilfully or negligently damage or injure any carriage, engine, waggon, truck, ware-house, building, machine, fence, or any other matter or thing belonging to such Railway Company, shall be liable to a fine not exceeding fifty rupees.

XXIII. If any person, for whose use or accommodation any gate shall have been set up by any such Railway Company on either side of such Railway, or any other person, shall open such gate, or pass, or attempt to pass, or drive, or attempt to drive, any carriage, cattle, or other animal or thing across the said Railway at a time when any engine or train approaching along the same shall be in sight; or shall at any time omit to shut and fasten such gate, as soon as he and any carriage, cattle or other animal or thing under his charge shall have passed through the same, he shall be liable to a fine not exceeding fifty rupees.

XXIV. If any person shall commit any offence hereby made punishable by fine, and the name and address of such person shall be unknown, or there be reason to believe that the offender will abscond, any officer or servant of the Company, or any police officer, or other person when such officer or servant may call to his aid, may, without any warrant or written authority, lawfully apprehend and detain such offender until he can be taken before a Magistrate or other officer having jurisdiction over the offence, or shall give sufficient security for his appearance before such Magistrate or other officer, or shall be otherwise discharged by due course of law.

XXV. Whoever shall wilfully do any act, or shall wilfully omit to do what he is legally bound to do, intending by such act or omission to cause or knowing that he is hereby likely to cause the safety of any person travelling or being upon any such Railway to be endangered, shall be liable to be transported beyond sea for the term of his life, or to be imprisoned, with or without hard labour, for any term not exceeding seven years.

XXVI. *[Substituted by Act XXV of 1871.]* Every Railway Company or, in the case of a Railway not managed by a Company, the officer for the time being entrusted with the control of such Railway, shall make general rules and regulations for the use, working, and general administration of the Railway, and may, in like manner, from time to time, vary the same.

All such general rules and regulations or variations thereof shall be submitted to the Governor General in Council for sanction, and, when sanctioned, shall be published in the "*Gazette of India*," and shall be otherwise notified to the public and to the officers and persons employed upon such Railway in such a manner as the Governor General in Council from time to time directs.

Any such rule and regulation may contain a provision that any person committing a breach of it shall be liable to a fine not exceeding fifty rupees, or, in default of payment of such fine, to imprisonment of either description for a term which may extend to two months.

The Governor General in Council may at any time cancel any rule or regulation so sanctioned.

Any justice of the Peace may try an European British subject for an offence under this section and on conviction award a sentence within the limits thereby prescribed for such offence.

XXVII. Any officer or servant of such Railway Company, who shall be in a state of intoxication whilst actually employed upon the Railway, or any of the works connected therewith, in the discharge of any duty, and any officer or servant of such Company, who negligently shall omit to perform his duty, or shall perform the same in an improper manner, shall be liable to a fine not exceeding fifty rupees, and if the duty in any of the cases in the section above mentioned be such that the omission or negligent performance thereof would be likely to endanger the safety of any person travelling or being upon such Railway, such officer or servant shall on conviction before a Magistrate, be liable to imprisonment, with or without hard labour, for a term not exceeding one year, or to fine, or to both.

XXVIII. If any person shall rashly or negligently, and without lawful excuse, do any act, which shall be likely to endanger the safety of any person travelling or being upon such Railway, he shall upon conviction before a Magistrate be liable to imprisonment, with or without hard labour, for a term not exceeding one year, or to fine, or to both.

XXIX. *[Substituted by Act XXV of 1871.]* If any officer or person employed upon a Railway endangers the safety of any person by

(1) disobeying any general rule or regulation sanctioned and notified in the manner prescribed by section twenty-six, or

(2) disobeying any rule or order not consistent with the general rules or regulations aforesaid, and which he was bound by the terms of his service to obey, and of which he had notice, or

(3) by any rash or negligent act or omission, he shall be liable to imprisonment of either description for any term not exceeding three years, or to fine not exceeding five hundred rupees, or to both.

XXX. Any person, whether a European British subject or not, who shall be guilty of any offence for which, according to the provisions of this Act, he shall be liable to a fine only, shall be punishable for such offence by any justice of the Peace for any of the Presidency Towns of Calcutta, Madras, and Bombay, Magistrate, Joint Magistrate, or person lawfully exercising the powers of a Magistrate, whether the offence shall have been committed within the local limits of the jurisdiction of such officer or not; and any person hereby made punishable by a Justice of the Peace, shall be punishable upon summary conviction.

XXXI. No conviction, order, or judgement of any Justice of the Peace shall be quashed for error of form or procedure; but only on the merits; and it shall not be necessary to state on the face of the conviction, order, or judgement, the evidence on which it proceeds; but the depositions taken, or a copy of them, shall be returned with the conviction, order, or judgement, in obedience to any writ of "*certiorari,*" and if no jurisdiction appears on the face of the conviction order, or judgement, but the depositions taken simply that defect, the conviction, order, or judgement shall be aided by what so appears in such depositions.

XXXII. A Magistrate may refer for trial and decision any charge of an offence hereby made punishable by fine only to any of his Assistants, or to any Deputy-Magistrate lawfully appointed to exercise the powers of a Covenanted Assistant, and in such case every such Assistant of Deputy-Magistrate may exercise all the powers vested in a Magistrate, subject to all the rules applicable to criminal cases deputy to such Assistants or Deputy-Magistrate, acting judicially.

XXXIII. The Local Government may give general authority to any such Assistant or Deputy-Magistrate to exercise, without reference by a Magistrate, any of the powers which they are hereby rendered competent to exercise upon reference by a Magistrate, subject to appeal to the Magistrate from any conviction, by such Assistant or Deputy-Magistrate, within one month from the date of conviction: Provided that a Magistrate may at any time call from any of his Assistants, or from any Deputy Magistrate subordinate to him, any case pending before such Assistant of Deputy Magistrate.

XXXIV. All fines imposed under the authority of this Act for offence punishable by fine only by any Justice of the Peace, Magistrate, Joint-Magistrate, or person lawfully exercising the powers of a Magistrate, or by any Assistant to a Magistrate or Deputy-Magistrate, may, in case of non payment thereof, be levied by distress and sale of the goods and chattels of the offender, by warrant under the hand of any of the above-named officers, and in case any such fine shall not be forthwith paid, any such officer may order the offender to be apprehended and detained in safe custody until the return can be conveniently made to such warrant of distress, unless the offender shall give security to the satisfaction of such officer for his appearance at such place and time as shall be appointed for the return of the warrant of distress, and such officer may take such security by way of recognizance or otherwise; and if upon the return of such warrant it shall appear that no sufficient distress can be had whereon to levy such fine, and the same shall not be forthwith paid, or in case it shall appear to the satisfaction of such officer, by the confession of the offender or otherwise, that he has not sufficient goods and chattels whereupon such fine or sum of money could be levied if a warrant of distress were issued, any such officer may, by warrant under his hand, commit the offender to prison, then to be imprisoned only, or to be imprisoned and kept to hard labour, according to the discretion of such officer, for any term not exceeding two calendar months when the amount of the fine shall not exceed fifty rupees, and for any term not exceeding four calendar months when the amount shall not exceed one hundred rupees, and for any term not exceeding six calendar months in any other case, the commitment to be determinable in each of the cases aforesaid on payment of the amount.

XXXV. The heads of district police and ameens of police in the Presidency of Madras, and district or joint police officers in the Presidency of Bombay, may punish, to the extent of the powers conferred upon them respectively in petty offences, any offences hereby made punishable by fine not exceeding twenty-rupees.

XXXVI. Payment of any fare to which any passenger not producing or delivering up his ticket shall be liable under section one of this Act, may be enforced in the same manner as any fine imposed by this Act.

XXXVII. Every person who shall be guilty of any offence mentioned in sections twenty-five, twenty-six, twenty-seven, and twenty-eight of this Act, may be lawfully apprehended without any warrant or written authority, by any servant or officer of the Company, or by any other person whom such officer or servant shall call to his aid, or by any police officer of such grade, or shall by any law in force for the time being be entrusted in any case with the power of arrest without a warrant; and every person so apprehended shall, with all convenient despatch, be carried and conveyed before a Magistrate or Justice of the Peace, or other officer lawfully authorized to punish the offender or to commit him to trial.

XXXVIII. In the construction of this Act, unless where a contrary intention appears from the context, the word "Magistrate," shall include a Joint-Magistrate and any person lawfully exercising the powers of a Magistrate; words in the singular number shall include the plural; words in the plural shall include the singular: and words in the masculine gender shall include the feminine; and the word "fine" shall include a sum of money due upon a forfeited recognizance.

XXXIX. *"Repealed by the Repealing Act XIV, 1870."*

XL. Every Railway within the said territories used for the public conveyance of passengers or goods, shall, until the contrary be proved, be presumed to be a Railway within the meaning of the Act, and every Company to whom any such Railway shall belong, shall, until the contrary be proved, be presumed to be a Railway Company within the meaning of this Act.

XLI. Every such Railway Company shall, within forty-eight hours after the occurrence upon the Railway belonging to such Company of any accident attended with serious personal injury, give notice thereof to the local Government; and if any such Company omit to give such notice, they shall forfeit the sum of fifty rupees for every day during which the omission to give the same shall continue.

XLII. The Local Government may order and direct any such Railway Company to make up and deliver to them a return of serious accidents occurring in the course of the public traffic upon the Railway belonging to such Company, whether attended with personal injury or not, in such form and manner as the Government shall deem necessary and require for their information with a view to the public safety; and if any such returns shall not be so delivered within fourteen days after the same shall have been required, every such Company shall forfeit the sum of fifty rupees for everyday during which the said Company shall neglect to the deliver the same.

XLIII. A copy of this Act, and of the General Regulations, Time Tables, and Tariff of charges, which shall from time to time be published by any Railway Company, with the sanction of the Local Government, shall be exhibited in some conspicuous place at each station of every Railway, so that they may be easily seen and read; and all such documents shall be so exhibited in English and in the Vernacular language of the district in which the station is situated, and in such other language, if any, as shall be required by order of the Local Government.

XLIV. *[Added by the Act XXV of 1871.]* The Governor General in Council may from time to time, by notification in the "*Gazette of India*," declare what Government shall be deemed to be the Local Government in respect of the whole or any part of a Railway for the purposes of this Act.

H.S. CUNNINGHAM,
Offg. Secy. to the Council of the
Govr. Genl. for making Laws and Regulations

379

General Rules and Regulations for the Rajputana (State) Railways, 1873

Source: The Gazette of India, Part 1, 12th April 1873

Gist: General Rules and Regulations for the Rajputana (State) Railways, 1873 contains the general rules and regulations for the use, working, and general administration of the Rajputana (state) Railways, as sanctioned by the Governor General in Council on 3 April 1873, under section XXVI of Act 18 of 1854, as applied by Act 13 of 1870, and amended by Act 25 of 1871. It has 236 rules spread in 19 larger sections. While section I lists general regulations relating to construction and management, section II deals with regulations generally applicable to the servants of the railway. Sections from III to X are concerned with various kinds of signals. Sections XI to XIV deal on the duties and responsibilities respectively of stationmasters or clerks in charge of stations; guards; enginemen and firemen; and policemen, pointsmen and signalmen. Other sections provide rules on gatemen at level crossings, free passes, forms to be signed by the railway servants, regulations for inspectors, foreman, mistries and labourers engaged in repairing the permanent-way and works, and regulations for ballasting.

RAILWAY

The 3rd April 1873

No. 1. The following general Rules and Regulations for the use, working, and general administration of the Rajpootana (state) Railway have been sanctioned by His Excellency the Governor General in Council, under section XXVI of Act XVIII of 1854, as applied by Act XIII of 1870, and amended by act XXV of 1871.

INDIAN STATE RAILWAYS

The Rules comprised in this code shall be held applicable, and are to be observed on all Lines of Railway owned by the State, unless specially exempted by the Governor General in Council.

The Officer entrusted with the control of each Railway may hereafter make such subsidiary Rules as he may find necessary, or may deem expedient, provided always that no subsidiary Rule shall be at variance with the General Rules.

The catch words[1] in the margin of this Code have been added merely for the purpose of facilitating reference to the different clauses. They are not to be held either as an integral part of the Code, or as in any way giving an interpretation to the clauses to which they may be annexed.

SECTION I
GENERAL REGULATIONS RELATING TO CONSTRUCTION AND MANAGEMENT

1. Every Line of Railway intended to be worked by Engine power, for the conveyance of Passengers, shall be provided with an Electric Telegraph.
2. Trains moving on a single line, shall invariably pass each other at the Stations, and no Engine, with or without a Train, shall be permitted to leave one Station for another until it shall have been ascertained, by means of the Electric Telegraph, that the Line between those two Stations is clear of Engines and Trains, and of all impediments, so far as can be known.

   The **Station Master is responsible** that no Engine or Train is permitted to leave Station until it has been thus ascertained that the **Line is clear**, and the **Engineman and Guard** are jointly and severally responsible that their Engine or Train does not leave any Station without a **Written permission from the Station Master** stating that the **Line is clear**.

   This Rule is not intended to prevent an Engine being sent cautiously along the Line, to assist a Train disabled by accident, if asked for by the Guard of such Train. See Rule 117, Section XII, and Rule 140, Section XIII.
3. No Special Train or Pilot Engine shall leave a Station, or pass along a Railway, unless previous notice shall have been sent by Electric Telegraph, and shall have been acknowledged at every Station throughout the distance to which such Engine or Train is intended to proceed. Special Trains shall be subject to the Rules prescribed in the preceding clause, and the utmost caution shall be used whenever such Trains are run.
4. No Train shall be allowed to move from any Station, unless it be provided with efficient means of communication, whilst in motion, between the Engine-driver and the Guard, or other Officer in charge of the Train reciprocally.
5. To enable the Guard to call the attention of the Driver, there shall, unless otherwise directed by the Governor General in Council, be suspended on some convenient part of each tender a bell, with a lever arm, to which shall be attached a cord, passing through spring brackets fixed on the top, or along the sides of all the Carriages in the Train, and terminating in the Guard's Van; and no Carriage, Truck, or Horse-box shall be attached to a Passenger Train unless it be provided with brackets to carry the cord above-mentioned. When the Guard may have occasion to call the attention of the Engine-driver, he will put the cord and sound the bell.
6. No Passenger Train shall be allowed to move from any Station unless it be provided with an arrangement by which the Guard in charge can communicate with, and make his way to, any and every Carriage in the Train.
7. In part of every Train for the conveyance of Passengers, there shall be a loaded Van or Truck interposed between the tender of the Engine and the first Passenger Carriage.

8. No Locomotive Engine shall, on any account, be employed to push a Train from behind, except in shunting from a Main Line to a siding, or in the event of an accidental obstruction obliging a Train to return to the nearest Station, or in assisting a crippled Train (see Rule 140). This rule does not apply to portion of Lines on an incline steeper than 1 in 100; nor to Sections of Lines that are ordered to be worked as such inclines by the Governor General in Council.
9. No Train shall be despatched from any Station without one or more Brake-vans, and one or more Guards, and all the necessary Lamps and other appliances specified in Rule 106, Section XII.
10. Whenever or wherever Trains or Engines are run in to dusk, or by night, the Station Lamps shall be lighted as soon as it becomes dusk, and during the twilight both the Day and Night Signals shall be used. The Signal Lamps shall not be put out in the morning until broad day-light.
11. **No Engine** shall be driven **tender foremost** on the Main Line (unless when shunting into a siding), without the written order of the Locomotive Superintendent, for which he will be held responsible, or from unavoidable necessity, which the Engine-driver will be required to establish. See Rule 151, Section XIII.
12. No Engine, Carriage, or Wagon shall cross or shunt on or from the Main Line, until the proper Signal has been sent back, or exhibited both up and down the Line.
13. The Statistics of Traffic shall be recorded in the fullest detail and on a uniform system according to such forms as are now or may hereafter be prescribed for general adoption.

SECTION II
REGULATIONS GENERALLY APPLICABLE TO THE SERVANTS OF THE RAILWAY

14. Each person is to devote himself exclusively to the Railway Service, attending at such hours as may be appointed, and residing wherever he may be required.
15. **He** is to obey promptly all instructions he may receive from persons placed in authority over him, and must strictly conform to all their orders, in addition to the General Rules and Regulations which may be furnished.
16. He must not quit the service without having given one month's previous notice in writing of his intention, excepting such servants as have several agreements to the contrary. In case of his quitting without such notice, all claims for pay due will be forfeited.
17. **He** will be subject to immediate **dismissal** for **disobedience of order**, **negligence**, **misconduct**, or **incompetency**, or for any neglect of these Regulations, and will moreover be held liable for all damages occasioned by misconduct or negligence. The pay of each man will always include his services during all such hours, whether early or late, as may be determined from time to time by his Foreman, and which hours will be so arranged as to give each man a fair average day's work.
18. No instance of **intoxication** on duty will ever be overlooked, and besides being **dismissed**, the offender will be liable to a **fine** not exceeding **fifty rupees**, or in default

of payment of such fine, to **imprisonment** of either description for a term not exceeding **two months**.

19. The first and most important duty of all the officers and servants of the Railway Department is to **provide for the Public safety**; to prevent any obstruction on the Main Line, which can be avoided, and to remove it instantly should it occur; to take special care at all times that the "Danger" Signals, as hereafter denoted, are properly worked, to protect Trains standing on the Line, and that **Signals are shown** in sufficient time to warn all parties of the obstruction before any Engine, Carriage, Wagon, Truck, Horse-box, or other vehicle, or other obstruction be placed on, or crossed over Main Line, and also during the time that impediments (of any description) to the safe passage of trains may exist.
20. In order to secure the observance of Rule 19, it is required that the Clerk or person in charge of any Station or Siding, as well as the Signalman, shall be first apprized verbally by any servant of the Railway, whose duty it may be to remove any Engine, Carriage, Wagon, Truck, or anything which may obstruct any passage of Train into or across the Main Line, that he is about to do so; and the person in charge of such Station or place shall thereupon personally attend to that business, in order to see that the proper signals of danger have been shown, and he shall attend to this duty until the Line shall again be quite clear or unobstructed.
21. The responsibility of any other servant of the Railway Department, than those specified in the last Rule, is no way lessened by it, and **all persons** whose duty calls them to assist, or who are present on any such occasion as those specified above, will be held **individually responsible for** the exhibition of **proper Signals** for the protection of the Engine, Train, Carriage, or Wagon from interruption or danger, and for **keeping the line clear**, unless properly protected by Signals.
22. The conduct of all the servants of the Railway Department is to be regulated by a prompt, civil, courteous, and obliging attention to every person with whom they may have intercourse; they must at all times make full and satisfactory answers to all inquiries, and invariably give their names and occupations to persons who may require to know them; and any instance of **rudeness, incivility**, or want of proper attention to Passengers, will meet with instant **dismissal**.
23. No money or gratuity in the shape of fee, reward, or remuneration, is allowed to be taken from the passengers or other persons, by any servant of the Railway Department under any pretence whatever, even though the regulated hours of duty shall have expired. Any **servant receiving any gratuity** will be immediately **dismissed** from the service.
24. Swearing and immoral and indecorous language are strictly prohibited, and also violent altercation and threats.
25. The authorities of the Railway reserve the right to deduct from the pay of their servants such sums as may be awarded as fines for neglect of duty, which will be appropriated to a sick-fund, or for such other purpose as the Governor general in Council may think fit.

26. No person is allowed under any circumstances to absent himself from his duty without permission from the Head of his Department.
27. Smoking is strictly prohibited in the carriages and in all parts of the Railway premises; the use of Beer and Spirituous Liquors is in like manner forbidden, except in the Refreshment-rooms or other places set apart for that purpose.
28. No person, except he be in the service of the Railway Department, is allowed to walk along any part of the Railway without a written license from the Resident Engineer, or the Head of the Engineering Department of the Railway.
29. Any person having occasion to walk along the Railway is to **walk clear** of the **Rails** altogether, unless this duty should require him to pass between them. **Any** person who may be obliged to **walk through a tunnel** is to keep close to the wall on his **right hand**.
30. In case of accident or obstruction to the Train, the safety of the passengers must be deemed of the greatest importance. The most prompt mode of communicating the circumstance to the next Stations and to Headquarters must be adopted, and all possible assistance may be demanded from, and must be promptly rendered by, any servant of the Railway whose services may be of use under such circumstances.
31. Every person receiving uniform must wear it on duty clean and neat, and if any article of dress, tools, or other things provided by the Railway Authorities shall have been improperly used or damaged, the person receiving it will be required to make it good. On leaving the Railway service, each article of dress, tools, or other things which have been supplied must be delivered up.
32. Every servant of the Railway Department is required to report immediately to his superior Officer any infringement of the Rules and Regulations which may come to his knowledge.
33. The Book of Rules in English is to be kept in the possession of every Engineman, Fireman, Guard, Switchman, Policeman, Platelayer, Gauger and Foreman, and such other servants understanding English, to whom it may be delivered, and any such servant found without one will be fined by the Head of his Department such a sum as he may think proper. It must be produced when required, and if defaced or torn, a new one will be supplied at the cost of the owner; and any person who may have lost his copy of the Rules, is required immediately to any degree responsible for the safety of the Passengers, the Railway property, or that of their fellow-servants, must be thoroughly and perfectly conversant with all the Rules contained in this Book, their special attention being directed to those which refer to their own particular duties; and in every case where the assistance is required of persons who are not conversant with all such Rules, these persons must be strictly prohibited from doing any act or work on or within 10 feet of the Main Line, except in the presence of, and under the immediate directions of, some officer or servant who is perfectly conversant with all the Rules and Regulations of the Railway.
34. Each Native Subordinate who may be unacquainted with the English language will be provided with a translation into his own tongue of these Rules, or of the Section

relating to his peculiar duties. He will be required to make himself thoroughly acquainted with its contents, to carry it about with him, to produce it when called upon to do so, and if lost, to take the measures for replacing it prescribed in the foregoing clause.

35. The **Head of each Department** shall be held personally **responsible** for satisfying himself that every subordinate employed in that Department has a thorough **knowledge** of his **duties**, and is competent to perform them. Each **Contractor**, or his responsible Agent, employed on the Railway, shall be similarly personally **responsible** for the knowledge and competence of his subordinates.
36. Any articles found by any of the Railway servants in any of the Carriages, or at a Station, or on any other part of the Railway property, must be immediately sent to the person in charge of the nearest Station, by whom it is to be forwarded to the Traffic Manager's Office, for registration. Any breach of this Rule will be visited with severe punishment.
37. Should any servant think himself aggrieved, he may memorialize the Government or the officer entrusted with the control of the Railway, but in every such case the Memorial must be sent through the Head of his Department.
38. When any accident occurs on any part of the Line, it must be immediately reported to the nearest Station Master or Station Clerk, and as soon as possible to the Locomotive Superintendent and Chief Engineer.
39. Every servant of the Railway Department is specially invited to communicate to his superior Officer anything circulated to promote the interests of the Railway, or the safety and convenience of the public.
40. **Reports** or other communications are, if practicable, to be **made in writing**; verbal messages are strictly prohibited, except in cases where writing materials are not procurable.

SECTION III
SIGNALS

41. **Red** is a Signal of Danger to "**Stop**". **Green** is a Signal of Caution to "**Proceed slowly**". **White** is a Signal of All right to "**Go on**".
42. The Signals will be made by Flags in the day-time and by Lamps at night.
43. In addition to this, any **Signal**, or the **Arm**, **waved violently** denotes "**Danger**", and the necessity of stopping immediately.

SECTION IV
HAND SIGNALS BY DAY

44. When the line is clear, or nothing to impede the progress of any Engine or Train, the Policeman will stand erect with his Flag in his hand, thus: -

ALL CLEAR

45. If it is necessary to proceed with caution, the Green Flag will be elevated thus: -

CAUTION

Or in the absence of the Flag, one Arm will be held up thus:

CAUTION

46. If it is necessary to proceed with **caution**, from any defect in the Road or Rails, the Green Flag will be depressed thus: -

CAUTION (RAILS)

47. If required **to Stop**, the Red Flag will be shown and waved to and fro, the Policeman facing the Engine thus: -

STOP

Or in the absence of a Flag, by both Arms being held up thus:

STOP

48. Engine Drivers seeing a Red Signal, whether it be by Flag, Lamp, or any other contrivance, are required, under all circumstances, and without exception, to Stop their Engine as soon as possible.
49. As soon as the Engine passes, the Policeman will bring his Flag to his shoulder.

SECTION V
DETONATING SIGNALS

50. **Detonating Signals** are to be used in addition to the regular Day and Night Signals in cases of **fog, dust-storms, obstructions, or obstacles** and a supply of not less than twelve shall be kept at each Station, in a place known to all servant, so that they may be obtainable at all times. These Signals are to be placed on the Rail (label upwards), by binding the lead clip round the upper flange of the Rail. When the Engine passes over the Signal, it explodes with a loud report, when the Engineman must act as directed in rule.
51. Every person in charge of Detonating Signals must see that they are kept in good

order and free from damp, and that they are **periodically tested** at intervals of one month during the rainy season, and three months at other times.

SECTION VI

FIXED SIGNALS BY DAY – SEMAPHORE SIGNALS

52. The Signals are constructed with either one or two Semaphore Arms.
53. The Signal is invariably made on the **left hand side** of the Post, as seen by an approaching Engine Driver.
54. **All right** is indicated by the **Left hand side** of the post being clear, the Arm being within the post thus: -

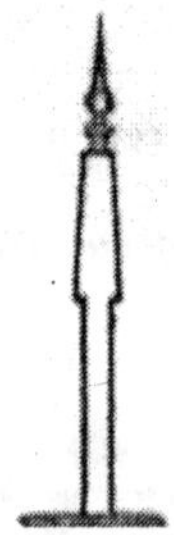

55. The **Caution** Signal to slacken speed is shewn by the Semaphore Arm on the **left hand side** being raised to an angle of 45 degrees, thus:

which must always be shewn where the Danger Signal is temporarily lowered to allow of the passage of an Engine or Train within **15 minutes** of the passage of a preceding Engine or Train.

56. The **Danger** Signal to stop is shewn by the Arm being raised to the horizontal position, thus:

which must always be kept up and only turned off to allow a Train to pass, after which it must be immediately turned on again.

57. When the two **Arms** are raised horizontally, both Lines are obstructed.

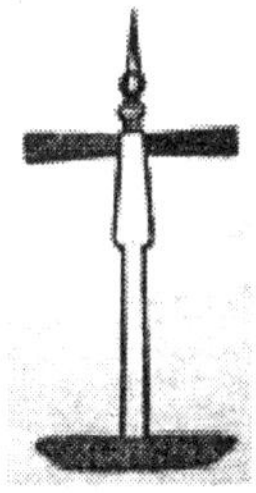

SECTION VII
FIXED SIGNALS BY NIGHT

58. The **All Right** signal is shewn by the **White Light**.
59. The **Caution** signal is shewn by the **Green Light**. This must always be shewn when an Engine or Train is allowed to pass within **15 minutes** of the passage of a preceding Engine or Train.
60. The **Danger** Signal by the **Red Light** must always be shewn, and is to be turned off only to allow an Engine or Train to pass.

SECTION VIII
TRAIN SIGNALS

61. No Engine or Train shall start from any Station between sun-set and sun-rise without the Red Head and Tail Lamps being lighted, and these Lamps must be examined wherever the Train stops, to see that they are still attached and burning clearly.

SECTION IX
STATION SIGNALS

62. When the line is single, the "**Danger**" **Signal** on both sides of the Station must be always kept "**On**", and only turned off to allow a Train to come up to the platform, after which it must be turned on again. Should a second Train arrive from either direction, the Pointsman having given his Signal, the "Danger" Signal shall be turned off until the newly arrived Train shall have passed the Points to the Main Line, where it will remain protected by the two "Danger" Signals until the Train at the Platform has moved out. The Train on the Main Line will then shunt or back to the Points, and be passed to the Platform.
63. Every Train and Engine will stop at all Stations, and will only be allowed to pass when the Signal "All Right" is shewn.

SECTION X
JUNCTION SIGNALS

64. At the Junction of two Lines of Railway, separate Signals Posts will be provided for each.
65. All the **Signals at Junctions** must be **kept** to show "**Danger**", except when an engine or Train approaches which it is not necessary to stop, in which case the Signal on the Line in which such Engine or Train is coming must be lowered to "Caution", all the other Signals being kept "Danger". Engines or Trains on the Main Line must have the preference of, and be allowed to precede, any Engine or Train on the Branch Line; the Signals at Junctions must never, on any account, be lowered below "Caution", and after the passing of any Engine or Train they must be kept at "Danger", and only moved from this position to allow Engines or Trains to pass.
66. The Signals levers and switch handles at junctions shall be brought together and so arranged that no conflicting signals can be given.
67. A Red Board or an additional Tail Lamp attached to the back of an Engine or Train denotes that a special Train is to follow, and care must be taken to attach such Board or Lamp to any Train starting from a Station where notice has been given of a Special Train to follow.
68. If any Signal is out of order, it must be immediately reported to the Traffic Manager and to the nearest Station Master.

SECTION XI
STATION MASTERS OR CLERKS IN CHARGE OF STATIONS

69. Station Masters will receive orders from, and report to, the Traffic Manager. Clerks in charge of Stations will be under the immediate orders of the Traffic Manager, or under those of neighbouring Station Master, as may be ordered in each case.
70. Every Officer in charge of a Station has control over all the Servants of the Railway Department attached to the Station, or to the Points and Signals connected with it.
71. It will be the special duty of every Officer in charge of a Station to attend to the arrival, despatch, and departure of Trains. He will be held answerable for the Station buildings and the property attached to them. He is also to be responsible for the faithful and efficient discharge of the duties devolving upon all the Railway servants at the Station. He will bring fully to the notice of his official superior all misconduct and inefficiency on the part of his subordinates. He is to take care that all Signals gates, and points are in complete working order by day and night, and shall give notice to the Inspector of Permanent Way of the Division immediately on any repairs being required thereto, and in case any part becomes deranged or broken, he must immediately order the nearest Plate-layer to get the same made perfectly safe, and he will be held responsible for the consequence of any accident that may occur from the defective state of the signals, gates, or points under his charge, unless the same shall have been previously reported as hereby required.

72. He is to see that all general and other orders are duly entered and executed and that all books and returns are regularly written up and kept.
73. He is to see that all the servants obey the rules and regulations, and is to pay particular attention to the Signals and to the rules respecting them, and to see that whenever Engines or Trains are run in the dusk or by night, the Signal Lamps are lighted as soon as it becomes dark, and during the interval between the dust of the evening and dark, **both** the Day and Night Signals must be used. The Signal Lamps must not be put out until broad day-light.
74. Every Officer in charge of a Station shall be held personally responsible that **no one** shall **handle points** or perform any duty connected with the service of the Railway, who is **not thoroughly competent** for such duty.
75. Every officer in charge of a Station shall see that the tail and side lamps of Engines and Trains are in good order and burning brilliantly and if any oversight be made in calling attention thereto before the departure of the Engine or Train, notice must be sent by telegraph to the next Station that the lights may be made perfect.
76. He is to inspect daily all the rooms, platforms and places connected with the Station, in order to see that they are neat and clean.
77. He is to see that all the servants at his Station come on duty clean in their persons and clothes.
78. He must be careful that all stores supplied for the Station are prudently and economically used, and that there is no waste of oil, stationery, & c.
79. He is responsible for having the name of the Station distinctly called out from end to end of every Train stopping at the station.
80. In case of obstruction or accident, he is to obtain all necessary assistance as soon as possible, and report such occurrence to head-quarters immediately.
81. He is to take care that the establishment is on the alert, and that there shall be **no obstruction on the main line** near his Station **when any Train is due.**
82. He is to see that all Carriages or **Wagons** which may be left **standing** in the **sidings** are securely **scotched,** and the brakes down.
83. He is to see that when a private carriage is loaded into a Railway Carriage Truck care is taken that the wheels of the Truck are securely scotched before commencing to load or unload. As a rule, the carriage must be run with its back to the Engine.
84. **Every exertion must be made** for the expenditures despatch of the Station duties, and **for ensuring punctuality** in the Trains and no Trains shall be started before the time stated in the Tables.
85. As a general rule, passenger trains are to take the precedence of goods trains.
86. The Station Masters must leave to the discretion of the Engineman to determine the load that may be sufficient for his Engine, but each case of refusal to take freight that the Station Master may which to forward must be reported to the Traffic Manager.
87. The Clerks of the several Stations are to deliver tickets to all persons booking their places for conveyance by the Railway, and no one is to be allowed to pass into the platforms unless a ticket is produced.

88. If a Guard or Station Clerk have reason to suspect that any passenger has been travelling on the Railway without having paid the proper fare, he may require such person to produce his ticket, and if any passenger shall refuse to show his ticket, or to deliver the same up when required, or shall commit any other offence against the rules and regulations of the railway, the case shall immediately be investigated by the Chief Clerk of the station where the occurrence may take place, who is to exercise his discretion as to the proceedings to be taken, always reporting to head-quarters what has been done.
89. The power of **detention** is **to be exercised with great caution,** and never where the address of the person to known and his position such as will afford reasonable security for his appearance to answer the charge, or where adequate security is offered for such appearance. When it shall be necessary to detain any person, such detention shall not continue for a longer period than is absolutely necessary, but he shall be conveyed before a Magistrate with as little delay as possible.
90. As it is the **intention to defraud** which **constitutes the offence**, it is very desirable that the power of detention should be exercised with caution and discretion, as cases may frequently occur of persons travelling unintentionally beyond the distance for which they have paid their fare, or even against their wish, and the right of detention is only applicable, in cases of what is termed over-riding to persons who knowingly and wilfully proceed beyond the place to which they are booked, and that not only without previously paying the additional fare for the original distance, but also with intent to avoid payment thereof.
91. Passengers not producing their tickets are required to deposit the amount of the whole fare from whence the train started until enquiry can be made in order to ascertain whether the fare has been actually paid or not; in every case the circumstance must be inquired into without delay and reported to head-quarters.
92. An account of all unclaimed luggage, and any property or articles fund on the line and on the railway premises, must be kept by the clerk in charge, and all such articles or things must be sent to the Traffic Manager's Office at the end of each week, together with a list thereof.
93. Persons in charge of stations must be careful in seeing that the station clocks are kept at the proper time and in working order.
94. No station master is allowed to absent himself from the duties of his office unless with leave from the Traffic Manager, except from illness, in which case he must immediately inform his superior, and in the meantime, he must take care that some competent person is entrusted with his duties.
95. Smoking is not allowed either in the carriages, or at the stations. In the event of any person being drunk and disorderly, or conducting himself to the annoyance of others, the station master is to use all gentle means to stop the annoyance, and if the offender persists, the station master is to remove him from the railway premises.
96. Each officer in charge of a station shall be accountable for the tickets entrusted to him, and for the money collected is his station, unless he shall have been relieved of that

responsibility, and it shall have been separately vested in some other officer by special order in writing.

97. No person suffering from a contagious disease, such as Small-pox, Cholera, Measles, Scarlet Fever, Diphtheria and Hooping Cough, shall enter a railway carriage without previously notifying to the station master that he is so suffering.

98. Any one having in charge a person suffering from a contagious disease shall be subjected to the same restrictions while travelling by railway as if he himself were suffering from the disease.

99. If any railway carriage has been entered by a person suffering from a contagious disease, such carriage shall be disinfected within 12 hours after it has arrived at its destination, in the manner prescribed below (Rule No. 102), and no passenger shall be allowed to travel in it until this disinfection has been carried out.

100. The Railway Authorities, if called upon not less than six hours before the departure of the train shall provide, at the usual rate of fare charged for an entire Carriage or Compartment a separate Carriage or a separate Compartment in a Lower Class Carriage for the conveyance of any person suffering from a Contagious Disease, such compartment to have no communication with the other compartments of the same Carriage.

101. If, on the arrival of a train at any Station, it shall become known to the Station Master thereof that any person travelling by that train is suffering from any Contagious Disease, such Station Master shall at once proceed to remove **other** travellers from the Carriage or Compartment.

102. The rules regarding persons suffering from Contagious Disease shall also apply to the conveyance of the dead body of any person who may have died of a Contagious Disease; excepting the rate which may be specially fixed for corpses.

103. Any Compartment which has been used for the conveyance of a person suffering from a Contagious Disease, or of the body of a person who has died of such disease, shall be disinfected in the following manner.

104. Every portion of the interior of the carriage shall be washed over with boiling-water, containing in each gallon a wine-glass full of carbolic acid, after which sulphur shall be burnt in each Compartment, and the doors and windows kept closed on the sulphur fumes for two hours.

SECTION XII
GUARDS

105. Every Guard must be in attendance at the Station at least half an hour before the time appointed for his Train to start.

106. Each Guard is to take with him the following Articles, viz.: -

1 Time Table.
1 Monkey Wrench.
1 Ramps.

1 Cross-cut Saw.
1 Large Crowbar.
1 Small Crowbar.
1 Axe.
1 Whistle.
1 Hammer.
1 Carriage Screw Jack.
1 Fire Buckets.
1 Red Tail Board.
1 Case of Detonating or Fog Signals.
6 Sprags and Scotches.
1 Spare Side Lamp.
1 Spare Tail Lamp.
1 Hand Signal Lamp.
1 Can of Oil and Oiling Apparatus
1 Time-piece and Bell.
A Complete set of Signal Flags.
2 Couplings.
1 Tail Rope.
30 Yards one-inch Rope.

107. He shall receive instructions from the Station Master, to whom he is to make known whether is wanting.

108. He is to see that his Brake is in good working order, and that the Lamps of the Train are in good order, and that they are lighted between sun-set and sun-rise, and also that the Carriages and Wagons in his Train are in good order and properly coupled; that the communication with the Driver is in proper working condition, and also that the Axle bearings of all the Vehicles are oiled.

109. The Train when in motion will be under the control of the **First Guard** (in case there are two, the first shall ride on the Van or Carriage furthest from the Engine or Tender). The Passengers and property in the Train will be under his charge, he will be **responsible for the safety and regularity** of the whole, he is to keep the time as given to him by the Station Master at the principal Terminus, by which he is to regulate his Time-piece daily, and which time he is to give to the clerks at the intermediate Stations, he is to see every Carriage detached which may be destined for any intermediate Station; he is to attend to the Luggage and enter up his **Way Bill** correctly.

110. When a **second Guard** goes with a Train, he is to attend to the instructions of the first Guard, and to assist him in any way that may be required. At the same time he will be held **jointly responsible** with the Head Guard for the proper observance and execution of these Rules and Regulations.

111. Guards must regularly signal to the Engineman that all is right; but when anything is wrong, they must give the "Caution" or "Danger" Signal, and if not observed, they must use the communication prescribed in Rule 5. When **two short sharp whistles**

are given by the Drivers, they are to be taken as a signal of **Danger**, and the Guards must immediately apply their **Brakes.**

112. On arrival at a Terminus, the Guard or Guards are not to leave the Platform until they have delivered over all Parcels and Luggage to the person appointed to take charge of them, and if any article is missing, they are to report the same to the Officer in charge of the Station.
113. The Guard is also to report any unusual circumstances which he may have observed during the journey, and any Carriage, Wagon, &c., complained of as being uneasy, or which may require examination.
114. The doors of the Carriages on the side furthest from the platform are always to be locked, and the Guards are charged to request Passengers to keep their seats in case of any stoppages on the road.
115. Guards are to exert themselves to prevent any breach of any Regulations by Passengers or others, and to report such cases if they occur. With regard to persons intending to defraud the Railway, they are referred to Rules for Station Masters, Sc., Nos. 88, 89, 90, and 91.
116. When a Train comes to a stand-still, and it becomes necessary to send for assistance, the Guard is to see that the Under Guard and Fireman or competent persons be sent, both back and forward, placing detonating signals every **150 yards** until a distance of **600 yards** has been reached (or **800 yards** on a **descending gradient** steeper than 1 in 100), when they will place two detonating signals 5 yards apart, and **stand** 20 yards behind them, exhibiting either a **Red Flag** by day, or a **Red Lamp** by night, until re-called by the signal whistle of the Driver, when they must leave the two detonating signals on the Rails at 600 yards distance and return, taking up on their way the intermediate detonating signals, but exhibiting all the time their lamp or flag signal. The Guard in the discharge of his duty must use every exertion for the protection of the Train under these circumstances, and in case of emergency, he must go with a Signal himself the required distance; he is, however, except on such an emergency, to remain with his Train.
117. When assistance is required, the Guard must ask for it **in writing,** and despatch the message by some competent person: and when assistance has been asked for, the Engine or Train is **on no account to move until the assistance has arrived.**
118. If any part of a Train becomes **detached** when in motion, care must be taken **not to stop** the portion in front **before** the **detached part has stopped,** and it is duty of the Guard of such detached part to apply his Brake in time to prevent a collision with the vehicles in front in the event of their stopping.
119. When it is necessary for the Guard to make a Signal to the Engineman, he must use the communication prescribed in Rule 5, but should this apparatus get out of order, the Brake may be applied, or a Flag or Lamp is to be waved to attract the Fireman's attention.
120. The Guard must not allow any Passenger or parcel to be carried by the Train unless properly booked, and if he has reason to suspect that any Passenger has not paid

his Fare, he is to request such person to show him his Ticket, and in default thereof, he is to report such case to the Clerk at the next Station, and enter it in his report. When the Passenger wishes to change from an inferior to a superior Carriage, the Guard must have this done by the Clerk at the first Station, to whom the difference is to be paid.

121. It is the Guard's duty to see that each Passenger is seated in the class of Carriage corresponding to his Ticket.

122. Prisoners and persons who are afflicted with Insanity, or who from any like causes, may be disagreeable to the other Passengers, must be placed in a compartment by themselves.

123. When a Guard is in charge of a Train to which Goods Wagons are attached he must **carefully examine** the **loading,** and see that it has no or not moved, and is well protected and secured, and especially that it does not **over-hang the sides.**

124. He must see that goods of a combustible nature, such as might possibly take fire from a spark or hot cinder, shall be completely sheeted and tied down.

125. He is to be careful in delivering all invoices, letters, despatches, and other things lawfully committed to his care.

126. He is to examine the Tickets on the Wagons and compare them with the Way Bill, and must have any discrepancy rectified before starting.

127. He shall not permit any person to ride in the Guard's Van or Brake Van without a special order.

SECTION XIII
ENGINEMEN AND FIREMEN

128. Every Engineman must be with his Engine at least 45 minutes before the time appointed for starting with the Train, to see that his Engine is in proper order and sufficiently supplied with Fuel, Water, Signals, Lamps, &c., &c., and every Fireman must, for the same purpose, be with his Engine at least one hour before such Train is to start.

129. **Firemen** must obey the orders of Enginemen in all particulars, at the same time they will be held **jointly responsible** with Enginemen for the proper observance and execution of these Rules and Regulations.

130. At five minutes before the hour of starting with any Train, and not sooner, the Engineman must place his Engine in front of the Train; often that time, and until the end of the journey, he will receive his orders from the Guard in all matters affecting the starting, stopping, or movement of the Train; and he must **promptly obey all orders or signals** given to him, whether **by the Station Master** or the **Guard,** so far as the safe and proper working of his Engine will permit him to do.

131. No person, except the proper Engineman and his Fireman, will be allowed to ride on the Engine or Tender without permission of the Locomotive Superintendent, or in special cases, by an order in writing from one of the Chief Officers of the Company with a notice to the Superintendent.

132. When the Engine is motion, the Engineman is to stand where he can keep a good look out ahead. In approaching all Stations he must have his Engine well in command, so

as to be able to bring his Train to a stand at the Distant Signal.

133. The Fireman must also keep a sharp look out, especially for any signals from the Guard, Pointsmen, Gatemen, &c., which he will immediately communicate to the Enginemen.

134. Every Engineman shall have at all times on his Tender, or with him, the following articles:

1 Case of Detonating Signals.
1 Set of Signal Flags.
1 Set of Lamps for Engine and Tender.
1 Set of Screw Keys.
1 Large and Small Monkey wrench
1 Traversing Screw Jack.
Large and Small Crowbars.
2 Short Chains with Hooks.
2 Short Chains with Hooks.
2 Fire Buckets.
Hammers and chisels.
1 Large and 1 Small Punch.
3 Half-round Files.
1 Set of Oil Cans and Fillers.
4 Tube Plugs and 1 Driver
1 Spare Clock.
2 Syphon Cups.
2 Glass Gauges.
1 Shovel and Fire Iron.
2 Pairs of Scotches.
2 Pairs of Scotches.
A few spare Bolts and Nuts, Cord, 2 Spun Flax, Yarn and a Rope.

The Lamps are to be delivered into the Lamp-house when the journey is complete, and taken out again when required.

135. Enginemen are bound to **observe** all **Signals,** without exception, and under all circumstances, whether the **cause is known** to them, **or not.** Any Engineman neglecting a Signal is liable to dismissal and such other server punishment as may be provided under the Railway Act. On seeing a Red Signal, he must, if possible, bring his Engine or Train to a stand-still, short of such signal; he may then, if he can make himself perfectly acquainted with the circumstance under which the Signal is exhibited, move his Train slowly inside the Signal for protection, and having move sufficiently far to protect his Engine or Train, he must stand still until the "Danger" Signal is taken off.

136. An unlighted Distant Signal after dust must be considered as a Danger Signal. Enginemen must stop and examine the position of the aim at the post: if that be **all right**, they must proceed with **caution** to the Station and sound their whistle repeatedly; and then inform the **Station Master** that the lamp is not lighted, and report the circumstance at the end of their journey.

137. In addition to the Red Signal, if an Engineman passes over a **Detonating Signal**, or Two Detonating Signals close together, he must immediately **shut off steam** and proceed with the utmost caution until the either ascertains that the Line is clear, or passes over **another** Detonating Signal when he must immediately **stop** the Train and protect it by Signals as described in Rule 116, and at the same time send forward some one to ascertain how near he can drawn up his Train to the obstruction, or what assistance he can render.

138. As a general rule, Goods Trains must in all cases give way to and assist Passenger

Trains in keeping their proper time.

139. No special or extra Engine, with or without a Train, will be allowed to pass along a Railway without previous notice or a written order from the Locomotive Superintendent, and without strict observance of the provisions of Rule 3, Section I, so as to provide against any risk of a collision from one Engine meeting another or overtaking a Train.

140. When an Engine is sent out to **assist** a Train disable in any way, the speed shall not, on the section of the line that is blocked, exceed **5 miles an hour**, and a man shall move 600 yards in advance of the Engine, bearing a Red Signal flag by day, and a Red Light by night.

141. The particular attention of Enginemen, Firemen and Guards is directed to the Level Crossings on the Line, either private or public (as the inexperience of the natives renders them liable to accident); the whistle is therefore to be sounded on approaching such places and the Engine stopped, unless the Signal "All Right" be exhibited; and special orders will be issued regulating the speed of Engines or Trains over portions of the Line in which such Crossings occur.

142. Every Engineman on going out is to take with him his Book of Time Tables and Special Instructions, and regulate by it the speed of his Engine; and when not attached to a Train, he is not to exceed a speed of 20 miles an hour, nor to prolong his stay at any intermediate Station or place, unless otherwise instructed, or except when compelled to do so by accident or necessity.

143. When the road is obscured by steam or smoke from an Engine which has become disabled, and is stopping on a siding, no approaching Engine is allowed to pass quickly through such steam or smoke, and no meeting a broken-down or disabled Engine, the Driver must ascertain the cause of such stoppage, and report it to the next Station Master, and must render any necessary assistance.

144. In going down Inclines, Enginemen must take care that they have **complete control** over the Trains by applying their Brakes, and they must **on no account attempt to make up lost time in going down Inclines.**

145. Enginemen are responsible for having, in descending Inclines, a sufficient amount of Brake power to ensure complete control over the speed of their Train.

146. Enginemen with Pilot Engines must be prepared, while on duty, to start immediately on receiving an order from their superior Officer.

147. In case of an **accident to his Engine** or Tender when without a Train, the Engineman must immediately **send back** his **Fireman** 600 yards, or 800 yards on a descending gradient steeper than 1 in 100, with **Danger Signals** to stop any coming Engine or Train. These signals are to be used as directed in Rule 116.

148. Enginemen shall afford every assistance with their Engines that may be required for the arrangement and despatch of the Trains, and shall follow the instructions of the Guards in working them.

149. Guards will give Enginemen a Signal to start by waving a flag after previously drawing their attention by blowing a mouth whistle, which the Enginemen must answer before

starting by a short Whistle from the Steam Whistle. In every case when it is necessary for **all the Brakes** to be applied, he shall give **two short sharp whistles,** and shall attend to any **Signal** made by the Guard, whether by ringing the Bell attached to the back part of the Tender, by waving Flags, or by application of the Broke.

150. No Engineman with a Train is to start without the signal being given; he is to start cautiously to avoid the breakage of Couplings; he is also to exercise caution in the mode of stopping, and to be careful that it is not done suddenly, except in cases of emergency. He is to pay particular attention to the weight of the Train, the state of the Rails, and must not enter a Station so rapidly as to require a violent application of the Brakes.
151. No Engineman shall run his Engine Tender foremost (unless when shunting into a Siding), without the written order of the Locomotive Superintendent, or unless in case of unavoidable necessity, to be established by the Engineman; in such cases he shall not exceed a speed of **twelve miles an hour**.
152. In going through points at Junctions or Sidings no Engine is to run at a greater rate than **five miles an hour**.
153. An Engineman is never to get up steam, nor to leave an Engine in steam, without shutting the Regulator, putting the slides out of gear, and screwing up the Tender Brake, and he must **on no account leave his Engine** or Train on the Main Line, except in charge of the person.
154. No Engine shall cross the line of Railway at an intermediate Station without permission, and **no Engine shall stand on the Main Line** when not attached to a train.
155. Particular caution must be used in foggy weather, or during a dust storm or heavy rain, by all the Railway servants engaged on the Line.
156. Engineman must always sound their Whistle before putting their Engine in motion, and the Whistle is also to be sounded on approaching Stations, Level-Crossings and Junctions and all other places where obstructions are likely to take place.
157. Should **fire** be discovered in the Train, the Steam must be instantly shut off and the **train brought to a stand,** the proper Signals put on, and the burning Wagon or Carriages must be detached, and every exertion used to put out the fire with the least possible delay. **No attempt** must be made **to run** even to the nearest water-tank, if it is **more distant than 300 yards** from the place where the fire is discovered, as such a course is dangerous.
158. Every Engineman must frequently look back while on a journey on passing all posts where a Pointsman, Gateman, Platelayer, & c., is stationed, to observe any signal which he may give, and to see that no portion of his train has broken loose.
159. If any portion of a Train breaks loose when in motion, the Engineman will stop carefully to have it re-attached in such a way that the portion in front does not stop before the detached portion has stopped.
160. Every Engineman at the end of his journey is to report to the Locomotive. Superintendent or his Foreman: - 1st, the state of the Engine and Tender; 2nd, any defect in the Road, Works, Signals, or any unusual circumstances that may have taken

place during his journey, and he is to fill up such returns as may be required of him.

161. No Engine without a Train shall pass along the Line after sun-set unless a **Red Tail Lamp** shall be lighted at the back thereof, in addition to the Lamp in front, which on a single Line, will also be **Red.**

162. A **Red Board** or **Red Flag**, or an additional lighted **Red Tail Lamp**, placed at the back of the Engine or Train, denotes that an extra Train is to follow.

163. When two Engines are working together, the second Engineman must watch for and take his Signals from the leading Engineman; but should the second Engineman discover anything wrong, he must sound his Whistle to warn the Engineman in front, so that the two may always check each other and stop together.

164. When the assistance of a second Engine may be required to propel a Passenger or Goods Train, the Assistant Engine must invariably be attached in front.

165. **All Engines** running with or without trains must be brought to a **stand** at **every Station**, and are on no account to run through without stopping. Care must be taken by the Engineman to see that the facing points are all clear.

SECTION XIV
POLICEMEN, POINTSMEN, AND SIGNALMEN

166. Every man on duty is to stand upon the Line **clear of the Rails,** and give the proper Signal on the passing of an Engine or Train.

167. All points connected with the Main Line must be kept locked, and only opened for the passage of an Engine or Vehicle.

168. The Pointsman is to be careful in keeping his Points clean and well oiled, and the channels of the crossings raked out and swept, and whenever a Train or Engine has passed over, he is to remove any particle of coke or dirt that may have dropped between the Points, so as to prevent them from closing, and must also see that they are replaced in their proper position; he is to try his Points before the passage through of a Train, that he may be thoroughly satisfied that there is no impediment to their true working; and in any case where Facing Points exist, these precautions become doubly important.

169. Pointsmen are not to allow persons to frequent their Boxes, as the practice tends to withdraw attention from their important duties. The Boxes inside and outside are to be kept in a state of the utmost cleanliness.

170. Whenever the points, Crossing or Guide Rails receive injury or strain, or the Rails themselves are split, chipped, or crushed, the circumstance must immediately be reported by the person in charge of the points to his superior Officer, and to the nearest Platelayer.

171. If he is in charge of Signals, he must pay particular attention to the Rules for working Signals, and must report immediately any derangement in the Signal Lamps, or means of working them.

172. All Policemen, Pointsmen, Signalmen are responsible for all Lamps under their charge being trimmed, and showing a clear and distinct light, and also for a supply of detonating Signals and other necessaries being in their possession.

173. They are not to allow strangers to trespass on the Line without written authority, and are to be careful in carrying out the Regulations of the Railway.

174. Each man on duty will be supplied with a Whistle to aid him in calling the attention of the next official in communication with him, and such Signal is not to be considered as received until answered by the person to whom it is passed.

175. The attention of Policemen is called to the Rules for Enginemen in cases where the Line may be obstructed, and they must tender all assistance in their power under such circumstances.

176. The attention of Policemen is particularly directed to the several private Crossings in the Line (not Public Highways); they must see that the low for regulating such places is strictly carried out. See Abstract of Act, page 78.

177. Ten minutes must elapse between the passage of all Trains in the same direction, and the **Danger Signal** must be kept **on for 10 minutes,** and the **Caution Signal for 5 minutes subsequently, after the Train has passed.**

SECTION XV
GATEMEN AT LEVEL-CROSSINGS

178. All Level-Crossing Gates closing across the Line must be provided with **Red** Signal Boards, and with Lamps showing **Red** up and down the Line when the Gates are closed across the Lines.

179. Every Gateman will be provided with Day and Night Signals, viz., a Tri-coloured Hand-Lamp, Red and Green Flags, and 12 Detonating Signals, which he must keep in proper order, reporting immediately any defect he may observe to his superior Officer.

180. Unless specially ordered to the contrary, the Gates must always be kept open for the passage of Trains, and **shut and locked across the Road**, except when required to be opened for the Traffic across the Line, and must then again as quickly as possible, be closed across the Road.

181. The Gates are never to be closed across the Railway when a Train can be seen or heard approaching, or is due and expected, and Gatemen are enjoined to allow no person or thing within them at such times.

The **Danger Signal** must be exhibited **both up and down** the Line whenever the Gates are closed across the Railway.

182. In all cases the Gateman, when signalling, is to stand in a position clear of the rails where he can be seen by the approaching Engineman.

183. If the Gateman observe any Gates or fastenings to be out of order, he must immediately report to his superior Officer, and in case any part becomes deranged, he must immediately report to the nearest Platelayer, in order that the Gates may be made perfectly safe.

184. Gatemen are to prevent as much as possible any person trespassing upon the Railway, and every case of trespass must be immediately reported to their superior Officer; and they are also to report any irregularity of Signals or other infringements of the Railway Regulations, whether of Platelayers or others in the Railway service.

185. Gatemen must keep themselves, their clothes and huts **neat and clean**; they must also take care that the channel for the flange of the wheels is carefully raked out before the arrival of each Train; that the rails and way are clear and that no rubbish whatever is allowed to accumulate near the Hut and Crossings.
186. If one Train follow another within 10 minutes, **the Danger Signal to stop must be given**, and for the next **five minutes** the **Caution** Signal must be shown.
187. In the event of the road being from **any cause obstructed,** the Gateman is to do everything in his power to prevent an accident by **warning the approaching Train**.

SECTION XVI
FREE PASSES

188. Servants and others connected with the Railway are required to book and pay their Fare the same as other Passengers, except such Officers or persons to whom passes may have been granted in the proper forms.

SECTION XVII
FORMS TO BE SIGNED BY THE RAILWAY SERVANTS (NO STAMP REQUIRED)

Form to be signed by the Railway Servants engaged in England on their arrival in India

189. I, ____ a Servant of Her Majesty in the ____ Department of the ______ Railway, hereby declare that I have received a copy of all the Rules, Instructions and Regulations for the conduct of the Railway Servants in that ___ Department, that they have been read (by)* and fully explained to me, and that I clearly understand them. I have also read Circular Orders Nos. ___ to ___, inclusive, and I hereby accept and bind myself to obey and abide by these Regulations and Circular Orders.

Dated this day of 187 __
Signed in the presence of ________

(THIS FORM REQUIRES A STAMP ACCORDING TO THE AMOUNT OF SALARY AS PER CLAUSE 7, SCHEDULE A OF THE STAMP ACT)

Form to be signed by the Railway Servants engaged in India

190. I, ____ a Servant of Her Majesty in the ____ Department of the ______ Railway, hereby declare that I have received a copy of all the Rules, Instructions and Regulations for the conduct of the Railway Servants in that ___ Department, that they have been read (by)* and fully explained to me, and that I clearly understand them. I have also read Circular Orders Nos. ___ to ___, inclusive, and I hereby accept and bind myself to obey and abide by these Regulations and Circular Orders as

the terms on which I am personally to serve the Government for the hire of Rs. ___ ___ per month.

Dated this day of 18 __
Signed in the presence of __ __ __ __ __ __ __

SECTION XVIII

REGULATIONS FOR INSPECTORS, FOREMAN, MISTRIES AND LABOURERS ENGAGED IN REPAIRING THE PERMANENT-WAY AND WORKS

191. The Inspector or person in charge of each District of the Line will be held responsible for the condition of the Permanent-way and Works on his District. He must keep an account of all materials used, and must see that none are wasted.
192. He must take care that the Foremen and Mistries are supplied with copies of the Rules and Regulations. He shall furnish them also with proper Signals and Lamps and accurate Gauges for the Line, and all necessary Tools, which he must require them to produce once in every month for his inspection that he may ascertain if the Gauges are correct, the Tools and Signals in good order, and that no articles have been lost.
193. It will be his duty to see that the men employed under him are active and efficient in the discharge of their duties, and that they attend carefully to the Rules and Regulations laid down for their guidance, and to make such return of each man's time as may be ordered.
194. He must examine frequently the Bridges, Points, Crossings, Time-tables, Water-Cranes, Signals and all other works on the Line, and report upon them to the Engineer as occasion may require.
195. He must have a list of the names and abodes of every Foreman and Maistry in his District, so that in case of accident he may be called upon to summon his labourers immediately to assist in any way that may be deemed necessary; and should any obstruction or casualty take place, each Foreman or Maistry is instantly to collect the required strength to remove the obstacle, or render their assistance.
196. He must regulate the working of the Ballast and Earth Trains, and must take care that nothing is done which involves risk to the Trains, or danger to the men employed.
197. He must report to the Engineer all cases of neglect, accident or irregularity occurring upon his District.
198. He must promptly obey all the orders of the Engineer, and it will be his special duty to report to the Engineer any case in which these Rules have been infringed or disregarded.
199. He must thoroughly acquaint himself with the working of all these Rules and Regulations, and with the Code of Signals in use on the Railway, as he will be held responsible for any breach of them by his Subordinates.
200. The Foreman and Maistries of the Platelayers and Labourers will receive their instructions from the District Inspector, and will be under his charge.
201. Each Foreman and Maistry will be supplied with a copy of these "Rules and Regulations", which he is always to have with him while on duty. He must thoroughly

acquaint himself with them, and especially with the working of the Signals, and must read and explain them to the men under him, and must produce them when required to do so.

202. Each gang will be supplied with such Tools as are necessary, and the Foreman or Maistry will be responsible for the call of them.

203. Each Foreman or Maistry will be supplied with the following Signals: -

Two Red Flags
Two White Flags
Two Green Flags

Two Hand Lamps, each shewing Red, Green and White Lights and six Detonating Signals, all of which must be used as directed in the Rules for Signals.

204. He will be held responsible for the conduct of the men under him, and for the state of the Permanent way, the Gates, Fences, Ditches and all other works on the portion of the Line allotted to him.

205. No Trolly or Lorry is to be placed on the Line, except under the charge of the Inspector of the District, or of a Foreman with the permission of the Inspector, and notice must be given to the Station Masters at each of the nearest Stations.

206. When any Trolly or Lorry is upon the Main Line, it must be **preceded and followed** at intervals of **600 yards** except on a **descending gradient** steeper than I in 100 when the distance shall be **800 yards** by a man bearing a **Red** Signal, being a **Red Flag** by Day and a **Red Lamp** by Night, or in a Tunnel.

Trollies when not in use must have the **wheels chained and locked together,** and must never be left in such a position as to allow of their being tampered with.

207. Except in cases of emergency, the Platelayers are not to take out any Rails on the Main Line, or perform any other operation involving danger to the Trains, without the permission of the Inspector, under whose personal supervision the work is to be done, and notice must be given to the Station Masters at each of the nearest Stations. The Inspectors will be held responsible for the prevention of any unnecessary interruption of the ordinary traffic by repairs or other common work of the Permanent-way.

208. When any repairs or alternations of the road are to be done, which render it necessary to stop or slacken the speed of any Train, men must be stationed at a distance of **600 yards** (except on a **descending gradient** steeper than 1 in 100 when the distance shall be **800 yards**) both up and down the Line, from the point of interruption, and most show as conspicuously as possible their **Red or Green Signal,** as the case may require, and **in addition** must place **Detonating Signals** on the Line in darkness, or fog or stormy weather. They must keep a sharp look out for Trains, and must remain at their post until the Line is again clear and safe.

209. If the repairs or alternations are of a serious character, the Engineer must erect as soon as possible, **fixed Signals** at the above named distance from the interruption of the road, and the **Traffic Manager** is responsible for taking over **change of the working** of these fixed Signals must invariably be laid down at the above distance as an additional precaution.

210. During the time that any portion of the road is under repairs, Plate-layers must see that the gravel or ballast is swept from the surface of the Rail previous to the passing of a Train, and no **ballast** must be left higher than the **level of the top of the rails.**
211. All obstructions must be removed, and the Line made clear and safe, 15 minutes before any Train is due.
212. No impediment or obstruction of the Line is to be permitted in rainy or foggy weather, or during a dust-storm or at night, except by order of the Inspector.
213. In all cases of accident or emergency, the Foreman or Maistry, with his labourers, must hasten to render all the assistance in their power, and must inform the nearest Station Master as quickly as possible.
214. Each Foreman or Maistry must walk over the portion of the Permanent-way in his charge every day before the departure of the first Train, and more frequently, if necessary, to examine carefully the state of the road, and to tighten any loose keys or fastenings. Where fish-plates are used, he must see that the bolts are not loose, and if any are wanting, he must have them replaced.
215. The Plate-layers must see that all Occupation Gates are kept shut and fastened, and must take care that cattle and other animals do not stray upon the Line.
216. Plate-layers and Labourers must remove all grass, boughs of trees, creepers, or rubbish from the Electric Telegraph wires and posts. If any of the wires are broken, slack, entangled, or touching each other, or any building is in any way out of order, they are immediately to report the circumstance to the nearest Station Master.
217. Every Foreman or Maistries is required to order off all persons trespassing within the Fences on his District, and if such persons persist in remaining, he is to take them to the nearest station and give them into charge of the Station Master or Police.
218. Foreman or Maistries are to report if any Gates which the owners or occupiers of the land are requested to keep shut, have been left open, in order that the parties may be charged with the penalties.
219. He must take care that the permanent-way is not raised in greater lifts than 2 inches, and that both Rails are lifted at the same time, and to the same extent, and that sleepers are firmly packed as the lifting proceeds, so as to leave as short a space or possible in imperfect connection.
220. On every occasion when the lifting required, the Foreman or Maistry must send men back and forward **600 yards** (except on a **descending gradient** steeper than 1 in 100 when the distance shall be **800 yards**) from the place, with a **Green Signal** to slacken the speed of any coming Engine.
221. No Sleepers, Rails, Tools, or Materials are to be laid within 3 feet of the Rails, and the ballast is not to be thrown up in any place to a greater height than **the level of the top of the Rails.**
222. It is strictly prohibited to lay down or make use of Facing Points, unless a written order be given by the Engineer to do so, and a man approved by him be employed expressly to attend to such points. No siding or switches shall be laid down at all without express permission of the Engineer given in writing. No temporary switches

shall be used excepting of such construction as shall be approved of by the Engineer. When a temporary siding is used, a man to be approved of by the engineer shall be employed to attend to the switches, but the Engineer shall, or soon as possible, inform the Traffic Manager, who will at once appoint competent Pointsmen to take charge of the Points. No Siding is to be nearer than **6 feet** to the nearest Rail, and in a Station **8 feet**.

223. Plate-layers and Labourers must get out of the way of a Train when it is 400 yards distant, and the Foreman must order his men to move to the side of the road clear of the Line to secure the men from risk of injury by the train. If working in a Tunnel, when the Train approaches the men should lie down clear of the rails until the Train has passed.
224. Any Luggage, or Goods, or Articles of any kind, falling off the Train, are to be conveyed without delay to the nearest Station Master.
225. Each Foreman or Maistry must report to the Inspector of Permanent-way any case in which any of the Signals are disregarded by the Enginemen.
226. Each Foreman or Maistry is required, in the event of a flood, to examine carefully the action of the water through the Culverts and Bridges on his length, and should he see any cause to apprehend danger to the works, he must immediately exhibit the proper Signals for the Train to proceed cautiously, or to stop as necessity may require, and inform the Inspector thereof, and until the Inspector arrives, he must take all precautionary measures for securing the stability of the Line.
227. **Each Foreman or Maistry** must consider himself **responsible for the safety of the Line** in his District, and he must not permit any person, whether employed as a Plate-layer, or in any other capacity, or under any pretence whatever, to commit any breach of these Rules, or to do any thing by which danger is incurred. He must report all cases of neglect or disobedience to the Inspector.

SECTION XIX
REGULATIONS FOR BALLASTING

228. No, Ballast or Material Train shall move on the Line without one or more Brakevans, or without a competent Guard or Brakesman, who will be subject to the same Rules and Regulations as the Guards of Passenger or Goods Trains, and will be held responsible for their observance.
229. He must make himself acquainted with all the Railway Regulations and the use of the Signals.
230. The Guard or Brakesman of the Ballast Train has the authority to direct the Foremen and Maistries and others employed in repairing the Permanent-way and Works, to assist him in the proper working of the Signals.
231. No Ballasting is to be carried on except by the express permission of the Engineer.
232. Ballast Engines are prohibited from passing along the Main Line in a fog, or during a heavy rain or short-storm, except when authorized to do so under special circumstances, and shall not move faster than 15 miles an hour.

233. The Ballast Trains must be moved clear of the Main Line at least 15 minutes before any Goods or Passenger Train is due.

234. When the Ballast Wagons are left on a Siding, the Guard must lock a wheel of the Wagon nearest to the Points of the Siding with the chain and lock provided for that purpose, so as to prevent the Wagons being moved on the Main Line.

235. The guard must report to the Inspector any case in which a Plate-layer or other workman has refused to carry back a Signal, or to obey any other instructions.

236. Engines and Vehicles used by Contractors are under the inspection of the Railway Authorities, and any condemned by them as **unfit** to travel, must at once be **withdrawn** by the Contractor, and not re-placed without the permission in writing of the Engineer or Locomotive Superintendent.

C.H. DICKENS, Colonel, R.A.,
Secretary to the Govt. of India

---

1. As the catch words in the margin are not integral to the Rules, they are not reproduced here.

380

Act for the Indian Railway Companies to Issue and Register Shares and Securities in India, 1873

Source: H.E. Trevor: The Law Relating to Railways in British India, London, 1891

Gist: The Act, passed on 21 July 1873, enabled the Indian Railway Companies to issue, register, and transfer shares, stock, bonds, and securities, and the registration of shareholders in India.

PUBLIC GENERAL STATUTES

36 & 37 Vict., c. 43

An Act to enable Indian Railway Companies to issue and register Shares and Securities in India [21st July 1873]

Be it enacted by the Queen's most excellent Majesty, by and with the advice and consent of the Lord's Spiritual and Temporal, and Commons, in this present Parliament assembled, and by the authority of the same, as follows; (that is to say,)

1. Every company now formed, or which shall hereafter be formed, whether by the amalgamation or otherwise, for constructing, maintaining, and working railways in India, may establish at such places in India as they think fit an office for the issue, registration, and transfer of shares, stock, bonds, and securities of the company, and the registration of transfers of shares, stock, bonds, and securities, and the registration of shareholders, and may form time to time remove or alter the place of any such office, and may make such regulations, consistent with the provisions of this Act, as they think fit, for enabling and facilitating the issue, registration, and transfer of shares, stock, bonds, and securities, and the registration of transfers of shares, stock, bonds, and securities, and the registration of shareholders at such office, and all and every the powers and provisions in relation to the issue, transfer, and registration of shares, stock, bonds, and securities, and the registration of shareholders in Great Britain, contained in any deed of settlement or Act of Parliament under or by which the company shall be constituted or governed, shall apply and be in force as to the shares, stock, bonds, and securities, and the registration of transfers of thereof, and the registration of shareholders, to be issued, transferred, registered and made at such office in India, except so far as the same are inconsistent with the provision of this Act.

2. Every such company may keep at their office in India books to be called respectively "the Indian register of shareholders," "the Indian register of holders of consolidated stock," "the Indian shareholders address book," "the Indian register of transfers," and also books for the registration of bonds, debentures, mortgages, and the debenture stock, and the transfers thereof respectively, and the books so kept shall be of the like validity and effect as the books kept for the like purposes by the company in England, and accounts of all entries and alterations made in the books of the company in India shall be transmitted to the principal office of the same company in England.
3. Provided always, that if and when the company have offices in India at more places than one, then the company shall substitute for or add to the word "India" in the titles of the register kept at every such office, the name of the place at which the particular office is established.
4. All transfers of any such shares, stock, bonds, and securities as aforesaid shall be made at the office at which the same respectively shall for the time being be registered, and no share, stock, bond, or security shall be on the registry of more than one office at one and the same time: provided always, that the company may keep in England duplicates of any of its books of register kept in India, but no such duplicate book shall be deemed a register.
5. Subject to the regulations from time to time made by such companies respectively, with respect to the issue, register, and transfer of shares, stock, bonds, and securities respectively, and the registration of transfers of shares, stock, bonds, and securities respectively, every such company may and shall, on notice in writing by the holder of any share, stock, bond, or security to the person for the time being acting as secretary, managing director, or principal clerk at the office in England or in India where such share, stock, bond, or security shall then be registered, transfer the share, stock, bond, or security from the register thereof at that office to the corresponding register at any other office of the company where for the time being a register shall be kept to be appointed and named in such notice, and as soon as conveniently may be after the receipt of any such notice such secretary, managing director, or principal clerk shall transmit advice thereof to the office to which the transfer is directed to be made.
6. For the purpose of determining any question as to the place or jurisdiction within which any share, stock, bond, or security shall be deemed to be or to have been situated at any given time, the locality, whether in India or in Great Britain, of the register in which such share, stock, bond, or security shall be or have been actually registered for the time being, shall be deemed to be or have been at such time the locality of such share, stock, bond, or security, and so soon as notice shall have been given as aforesaid for the transfer of any share, stock, bond, or security from one register to another, the share, stock, bond, or security shall for the purpose of this section be deemed to be actually registered in the register to which it is so directed to be transferred.
7. Nothing in this Act shall interfere with or affect any powers, which are now vested in any Indian railway company by any Acts of Parliament by which the company is governed (a).

381

Public General Statutes for Indian Guaranteed Railway Companies, 1873

Source: Henry Edward Trevor: The Law Relating to Railways in British India, London, 1891

Gist: The Act, passed on 29 May 1868, enabled certain guaranteed railway companies to raise capital on shares and debentures for the construction of railways in India.

PUBLIC GENERAL STATUTES

31 Vict. c. 26.

An Act to enable certain guaranteed Indian Railway Companies to raise Money on Debenture Stock [29th May 1868]

Whereas the railway companies severally known as the Great Indian Peninsula Railway Company, the East Indian Railway Company, the Madras Railway Company, the Bombay, Baroda and Central India Railway Company, the Scinde Railway Company, the Eastern Bengal Railway Company, and the Oude and Rohilcund Railway Company, Limited, were constituted and incorporated by the Acts of Parliament, or by certificate under Act of Parliament, for the purpose of constructing, maintaining, and working railways in India; and the said companies have, under powers vested in them by their Acts, or otherwise vested in them, entered into terminable contracts and arrangements with the East India Company, or with the Secretary of State in Council of India, with respect to their undertakings, and they have in exercise of such powers, with the sanction of the East India Company, or the Secretary of State in Council of India, raised capital by the issue of shares or stock, and have borrowed money for their undertakings on the security of mortgages or bonds:

And whereas it is expedient that each of the said companies should be empowered to create, with the sanction of the Secretary of State in Council of India, debenture stock in lieu of borrowing or in substitution for, or for the discharge of, mortgages or bonds:

Be it therefore enacted by the Queen's most excellent Majesty, by and with the advice and consent of the Lords Spiritual and Temporal, and Commons, in this present Parliament assembled, and by the authority of the same, as follows:

1. Each of the said companies may from time to time, with the sanction of the Secretary of State in Council of India, and of three-fifths of the votes of its shareholders and stockholders entitled to vote in that behalf at meetings of the company, present in

person or by proxy at any extra ordinary meeting convened with notice of this purpose, raise all or any part of the money which for the time being the company has raised or is authorized to raise on mortgage or bond by the creation and issue at such times, in such amounts and manner, on such terms, at such price, subject to such conditions, and with such rights and privileges, as the Secretary of State in Council of India shall think fit, of stock to be called debenture stock, instead of and to the same amount as the whole or any part of the money which may for the time being be owing by the company on mortgage or bond, or which the company may from time to time have power to raise on mortgage or bond, and may, with such sanction of its shareholders and stockholders as aforesaid, attach to the stock so created such fixed and perpetual irredeemable, redeemable, variable, or other interest at such rate, payable half-yearly or otherwise, and commencing at once or at any future time or times, when and as the debenture stock shall be issued or otherwise, as the Secretary of State in Council of India shall think fit.

2. All the provisions following shall apply to every case of one of the said companies exercising the power hereinbefore given for raising money by the creation and issue of debenture stock; (that is to say,)

    1. The debenture stock, with the interest thereon, shall be a charge upon the undertaking of the company prior to all other stock or shares of the company, and shall be transmissible and transferable in the same manner and according to the same regulations and provisions as other stock of the company, and shall in all other respects have the incidents of personal estate.
    2. The interest on debenture stock shall have priority of payment over all dividends or interest on any other stock or shares of the company, and shall rank next to the interest payable on the mortgages or bonds for the time being of the company legally granted before the creation of such stock, but the holders of debentures stock shall not as among themselves be entitled to any preference or priority.
    3. The company shall cause entries of the debenture stock from time to time created to be made in a register to be kept for that purpose, wherein they shall enter the names and addresses of the several persons and corporations from time to time entitled to the debenture stock, with the respective amounts of the stock to which they are respectively entitled, and any instalments by which the price or subscription for any debenture stock may be made payable shall be recoverable as calls are recoverable under "The Companies Clauses Consolidation Act, 1854."
    4. The company shall deliver to every holder of debenture stock a certificate stating the amount of debenture held by him, and all regulations or provisions for the time being applicable to certificates of shares in the capital of the company shall apply, *mutatis mutandis*, to certificates of debenture stock.
    5. Nothing herein contained shall in any way affect any mortgage or bond at any time legally granted by the company before the creation of such stock, or any power of the company to raise money on mortgage or bonds, so far as such power is not by this Act expressly extinguished; but the holders of all such mortgages

and bonds shall, during the continuance thereof, respectively be entitled to the same priorities, rights, and privileges in all respects as they would have been entitled to in this Act had not been passed.

6. The debenture stock shall not entitle the holders thereof to be present or vote at any meeting of the company, or confer any qualification with reference to the Government thereof, but shall in all respects, not otherwise by this Act provided for, be considered as entitling the holders to the rights and powers of mortgages of the undertaking other than the right to require repayment of the principal money paid up in respect of the debenture stock: Provided always, that if on the issue of any such stock the company shall have agreed to repay the principal money at a fixed time, the holders thereof shall be entitled to be repaid their principal money at such fixed time.
7. The money raised by debenture stock shall be applied exclusively either in paying off money due by the company on mortgage or bond, or else for the purposes to which the same money would be applicable if it were raised on mortgage or bond instead of on debenture stock; provided always, that the receipt, disposal and application of all monies raised by the debenture stock shall be at all times and in all respects subject to the supervision, direction, and control of the Secretary of State in Council of India.
8. Separate and distinct accounts shall be kept by the company showing how much money has been received for or on account of debenture stock, and how much money borrowed or owing on mortgage or bond for which they have power so to borrow has been paid off by debenture stock or raised thereby instead of being borrowed on mortgage or bond.
9. The powers of borrowing and re-borrowing by the company shall, to the extent of the nominal amount of the debenture stock for the time being issued, be extinguished.

The Great Indian Peninsula Railway Company Rules for General Passengers, 1873

Source: The Gazette of India, Part 1, July-December 1873

Gist: The Rules sanctioned on 9 October 1873 by the Governor General in Council allows the Great Indian Peninsula Railway Company to fine and punish any passenger who makes use of the means of communication between the passengers and servants of the Company in charge of the train without reasonable and sufficient cause.

RAILWAY

The 9th October 1873

No. 3. In exercise of the power conferred by Section 26 of Act No., XVIII of 1854 (relating to Railway in India), as amended by Act XXV of 1871, the Great Indian Peninsula Railway Company has made the following rule; and such rule has been submitted to the Governor General in Council for sanction, and has received sanction, and is now published in the *Gazette of India*, pursuant to the said section: -

2. Whenever in any train worked by the Great Indian Peninsula Railway Company, and carrying passengers, means of communication between the passengers and servants of the Company in charge of the train shall have been provided, any passenger who makes use of the said means of communication without reasonable and sufficient cause, shall be liable for each offence to a fine not exceeding Rupees 50, or in default of payment of such fine, to simple or rigorous imprisonment for a term which may extend to two months.

C.H. DICKENS, *Colonel, R.A.*,
Secretary to the Government of India

383

The Repealing Act, 1874

Source: The Gazette of India, Part IV, 26th December 1874

Gist: The Repealing Act, 1874 (Act 16 of 1874) was enacted to repeal certain obsolete enactments. The earlier Acts and the extent of repeal are listed in the schedule of the Repealing Act. The whole of Act 12 of 1873, and minor portions of some sections of the Acts of 18 of 1854, 8 of 1860, 25 of 1871 and 8 of 1873 were repealed.

Act No. XVI of 1874

An Act for the repeal of certain Obsolete Enactments

WHEREAS it is expedient that the enactments mentioned in the schedule to this Act, which have ceased to be in force otherwise than by express and specific repeal, or have by lapse of time and change of circumstances become unnecessary, or which merely repeal prior enactments, should be expressly and specifically repealed; It is hereby enacted as follows: -

1. The enactments described in the schedule annexed to this Act are hereby repealed to the extent mentioned in the third column of the same schedule:

   Provided that the repeal by this Act of any enactment shall not affect any statute, Act or Regulation in which such enactment has been applied, incorporated, or referred to:

   And this Act shall not affect the validity or invalidity of anything already done or suffered, or any indemnity already granted, or any right or title already acquired or accrued, or any remedy or proceeding in respect thereof, or the proof of any past act or thing:

   Nor shall this Act affect any principle or rule of law, or established jurisdiction, form or course of pleading, practice or procedure, or existing usage, custom, privilege, restriction, exemption, office or appointment, notwithstanding that the same respectively may have been in any manner affirmed, recognised, or derived, by, in, or from any enactment hereby repealed:

   Nor shall this Act provide or restore any jurisdiction, office, custom, privilege, restriction, exemption, usage or practice not now existing or in force.
2. This Act may be cited as "The Repealing Act, 1874," it extends to the whole of British India; and it shall come into force on the passing thereof.

SCHEDULE

Number & Year	*Subject*	*Extent of repeal*
XVIII of 1854	Railways	In the preamble, the words "under the superintendence and control of the East India Company," and "in any part of the territories in the possession and under the Government of the said Company." In section two, the words "or of the East India Company." Sections thirty-two and thirty-three.
VIII of 1860	Telegraphs	In section eighteen, the words "or for the Settlement of Prince of Wales' Island, Singapore, and Malacca."
XXV of 1871	Railways	The third paragraph of section one.
VIII of 1873	Canals and Drainage	The third paragraph of section one.
XII of 1873	Repealing Act, 1873	The whole Act.

384

The Indian Railway Act, 1879

Source: The Calcutta Gazette, Part V, 19th March 1879

Gist: The Indian Railway Act, 1879 (Act 4 of 1879), which came in force from 1 July, is a comprehensive legislation with 54 sections, subsections and clauses under them, and two schedules, spread over six chapters dealing with carriage of passengers and goods, and offences by administration, servants and other persons and punishments and jurisdiction thereof, besides preliminaries and miscellaneous matters.

Act No. IV of 1879

THE INDIAN RAILWAY ACT, 1879

CHAPTER I
PRELIMINARY

1. This Act may be called "The Indian Railway Act, 1879:"
   It extends to the whole of British India and, so far as regards subjects of Her Majesty the Empress of India, to the dominions of Princes and States in India in alliance Her said Majesty;
   And it shall come into force on the first day of July 1879.
2. On and from that day, the Acts specified in the first schedule hereto annexed shall be repealed.
   All rules made, notifications published and powers conferred under any are of such Acts, or any enactment thereby repealed, shall (so far as they are consistent herewith) be deemed to have been respectively made, published and conferred under this Act.
   Nothing in the Carriers Act, 1865, shall apply to carriers by railway.
3. In this Act, unless there be something repugnant in the subject or context, –
   "Railway" means a railway for the public conveyance of passengers or goods.

It includes –

(a) all land within the fences or other boundary-marks prescribed under section fifty-two;

(b) all lines of rail, sidings or branches worked over for the purposes of, or in connection with, a Railway;
(c) all stations, offices, warehouses, fixed machinery and other works constructed for the purposes of, or in connection with, a Railway;
(d) all vessels and rafts used for the purpose of carrying on the traffic of a Railway.

In section four, "Railway" includes a railway under construction, and in the remaining part of this section and in the following sections (namely), six, eight, sixteen, twenty-five, thirty-three, thirty-four, forty to forty-six (both inclusive), fifty-two and fifty-three, "Railway" includes a Railway under construction and a Railway not used for the public conveyance of passengers or goods:

"Railway-administration" means in the case of a Railway worked by Government or a Native state, the Manager of such Railway, and in the case of a Railway worked by a Company or private individual, such Company or individual:

"Railway-servant" means any person employed by a Railway-Administration, to perform any function in connection with a Railway, and in section twenty-five, last clause, sections twenty six, twenty-seven, thirty-eight, and forty-two includes any person employed to perform any such function by any other person in execution of a contract into which he has entered with a Railway-Administration.

4. It shall be lawful, with the previous sanction of the Governor General in Council, use on every Railway locomotive engines or other motive power, and carriages and wagons to be drawn or propelled thereby.

CHAPTER II

Duties of the Railway-Administration

5. No Railway or portion or extension of, or addition to, a Railway shall be opened for the public conveyance of passengers until the Railway-Administration has given to the Governor General in Council notice in writing of the intention of opening the same and until an officer appointed by the Governor General in Council to inspect such Railway, portion, extension or addition has, after inspection thereof, reported in writing to the Governor General in Council that in his opinion the opening of the same would not be attended with danger to the public using the same.
6. Every Railway-Administration shall, within forty-eight hours after the occurrence upon the Railway of –

(a) any accident attended with loss of human life or serious injury to person or property,
(b) any accident of a description usually attended with such loss or injury, and
(c) any accident of any other description which the Governor General in Council may, form time to time, direct to be notified,

give notice thereof to the Local Government; and the Station-master nearest to the place at which the accident occurs, or, where there is no Station-master the officer in charge of the section of the Railway on which the accident occurs, shall without unnecessary delay give notice in writing or by telegraph of such accident to the nearest Magistrate and to the officer in charge of the Police-station in the jurisdiction of which the accident occurs or to such other Magistrate and Police-officer as the Local Government from time to time appoints in this behalf.

7. Every Railway-Administration shall make up and deliver to the Governor General in Council a return of accidents occurring in the course of the public traffic upon the Railway, whether attended with personal injury or not, in such form and manner and at such intervals of time, as the Governor General in Council from time to time directs.
8. Every Railway-Administration shall make general rules for the following purposes (that is to say):

   (a) for regulating the mode in which, and the speed at which, carriages and wagons used on the Railway are to be moved or propelled;
   (b) for regulating the maximum number of passengers which each carriage and compartment may carry, and the mode in which such number shall be denoted thereon;
   (c) for regulating the provision to be made for the accommodation and convenience of passengers;
   (d) for declaring what shall be deemed to be, for the purposes of this Act, dangerous goods; and
   (e) generally for regulating the travelling upon, and the use, working and management of, the Railway; and may, from time to time, alter any such rules.

   Any such rule may contain a provision that any person committing a breach of it shall be liable to a fine, which may extend to fifty rupees, or, in default of payment of such fine, to simple imprisonment for a term, which may extend to two months.

   No such rule shall take effect unless it is consistent with this Act and until it has received the sanction of the Governor General in Council.

   All rules made under this section shall be published in the Gazette of India, and shall be otherwise notified to the Railway-servants and the public in such manner as the Governor General in Council, from time to time directs.

   The Governor General in Council may at any time cancel any such rule.
9. An abstract of this Act, and a copy of the Time-tables and tariff of charges which may, from time to time, be published for any Railway by any Railway-Administration, shall be exhibited in some conspicuous place at each station of such Railway, so that they may be easily seen and read.

   All such documents shall be exhibited in English and in the principal vernacular language of the district in which the station is situated, and in such other language, if any, as the Governor General in Council may direct.

CHAPTER III

Carriage of Property

10. Every agreement purporting to limit the obligation or responsibility imposed on a carrier by Railway by the Indian Contract Act, 1872, sections 151 and 161, in the case of loss, destruction or deterioration of, or damage to, property shall, in so far as it purports to limit such obligation or responsibility, be void unless –

    (a) it is in writing signed by, or on behalf of, the person sending or delivering such property, and

    (b) is otherwise in a form approved by the Governor General in Council.

11. When any property mentioned in the second schedule hereto annexed is contained in any parcel or package delivered to a carrier by Railway, the carrier shall not be liable for loss, destruction or deterioration of, or damage to, such property, unless at the time of delivery the value and nature thereof have been declared by the person sending or delivering the same, and an increased charge for the safe conveyance of the same, or an engagement to pay such charge, has been accepted by some Railway-servant specially authorized in this behalf.

    When any property of which the value and nature have been declared under this section has been lost, destroyed or damaged, or has been deteriorated, the compensation recoverable for such loss, destruction, damage or deterioration shall not exceed the value so declared.

12. A carrier by Railway shall in no case be answerable for loss, destruction or deterioration of or damage to any passenger's luggage, unless a Railway-servant has booked and given a receipt for the same.

13. In any suit against a carrier by Railway for compensation for loss, destruction or deterioration of, or damage to, property delivered to a Railway-servant, it shall not be necessary for the plaintiff to prove in what manner such loss, destruction, deterioration, or damage was caused.

14. If any person fails to pay on demand any sum due by him to a carrier by Railway for conveyance of any property by Railway, or for the custody of any property or for demurrage or wharfage in respect of the same, the Railway-Administration may detain the whole or any part of such property or, if the same have been removed from the Railway, any other property of such person then on such Railway or thereafter coming into the possession of the Railway-Administration;

    and may also sell by public auction, in the case of perishable property at once, and in the case of other property on the expiration of at least fifteen days' notice thereof published in one or more of the local newspapers or, where there are no such newspapers, in such manner as the Local Government may, from time to time, direct, sufficient of such property to produce the sum payable as aforesaid, and all charges and expenses of such detention, notice and sale, or, if such person fails to remove from the Railway within a reasonable time any property so detained, the whole of such property;

and may, out of the proceeds of the sale, retain the sum so payable, together with all charges and expenses aforesaid, rendering the surplus, if any, of such proceeds, and so much of the property (if any) as remains unsold, to the person entitled thereto;

or such carrier may recover any such sum by suit.

15. The owner or person having the care of any property which has been carried upon any Railway, or is brought into any station or warehouse for the purpose of being carried upon a Railway, shall, on demand by any Railway-servant appointed in this behalf by the Railway-Administration, deliver to him an exact account in writing signed by such owner or person of the quantity and description of such property.

16. No passenger shall take with him on a railway, and no person shall deliver or tender for carriage upon any Railway, any dangerous luggage or goods delivered or tendered for carriage, distinctly marking their nature on the outside of the package containing the same.

Any Railway-servant may refuse to carry upon a Railway any luggage or parcel which he suspects to contain dangerous goods, and may require such luggage or parcel to be opened to ascertain the fact previously to carrying the same;

and in case any such luggage or parcel is received for the purpose of being carried upon a Railway, any Railway-servant may stop the transit thereof until he is satisfied as to the nature of its contents.

CHAPTER IV

Carriage of Passengers

17. Every person desirous of travelling on a Railway shall, upon payment of his fare, be furnished with a ticket specifying in English and the principal vernacular language of the district in which the ticket is issued, the class of carriage for which, and the place from and place to which, the fare has been paid, and the amount of such fare;

and every passenger shall, when required, show his ticket to any Railway-servant duly authorized to examine the same, and shall deliver up such ticket upon demand to any Railway-servant duly authorized to collect tickets.

18. At the intermediate stations, the fares shall be deemed to be accepted and the tickets furnished only upon condition that there be room in the train for which the tickets are furnished.

In case there is not room for all the passengers to whom tickets have been furnished, those who have obtained tickets for the longest distance shall have the preference; and those who have obtained tickets for the same distance shall have the preference according to the order in which they have received their tickets:

Provided that all officers and troops of Her Majesty on duty, and all other persons on the business of the Government who, by virtue of any contract with the Government or, in the case of a Railway worked by Government, of any direction of the Governor General in Council, are entitled to be conveyed on a Railway in preference to, or in priority over, the public, shall entitled to such preference and priority without reference to the distance for which, or the order in which, they have received their tickets.

Any passenger to whom a ticket has been furnished at any station and for whom there is no room shall, on returning the ticket within a reasonable time after its issue, be entitled to have his fare at once refunded.

19. Except with the permission of the Railway-Administration or of such officer as it appoints in this behalf, no person shall enter any carriage used on any Railway for the purpose of travelling therein without first paid his fare and obtained a ticket.

20. Any passenger found suffering from an infectious disease in a Railway-carriage or in any place on a railway may, if his remaining in such carriage or place is likely to spread the infection of such disease, be removed from such carriage or place by any railway-servant;

any passenger so removed who has paid his proper fare to or at the place at which he is so removed, shall be entitled, on returning his ticket, to have such fare refunded.

CHAPTER V

OFFENCES AND PROCEDURE

(A) Offences by the Railway-Administration

21. Any Railway-Administration opening, in contravention of section five, any Railway, or any portion or extension of, or addition to, a Railway shall forfeit to Government the sum of one thousand rupees for every day during which the same continues open in contravention of that section.

22. Any Railway-Administration omitting to give notice as required by section six, shall forfeit to Government the sum of one hundred rupees for every day during which such omission continues.

23. Any Railway-Administration failing to deliver any return mentioned in section seven within fourteen days after the same ought to be delivered, or to make or notify any rules as required by section eight, or to exhibit any abstract or copy mentioned in section nine in manner required by that section, shall forfeit to Government the same of fifty rupees for every day during which such failure continues.

(B) Offences by Railway-Servants

24. Any Station-master or other person omitting to give notice as required by section six, shall be punished with fine which may extend to fifty rupees.

25. Any Railway-servant who is in a state of intoxication whilst actually employed upon a Railway in the discharge of any duty, or who negligently omits to perform his duty, or who performs the same in an improper manner, shall be punished with fine which may extend to fifty rupees;

or if the duty in any of the cases aforesaid be such that the negligent omission or improper performance thereof would be likely to endanger the safety of any person travelling or being upon such Railway, such servant shall be punished with imprisonment for a term which may extend to one year, or with fine, or with both.

26. If any Railway-servant in the discharge of his duty endangers the safety of any person–

    (a) by disobeying any general rule sanctioned and published and notified in the manner prescribed by section eight; or
    (b) by disobeying any rule or order not inconsistent with the general rules aforesaid, and which such servant was bound by the terms of his employment to obey, and of which he had notice; or
    (c) by any rash or negligent act or omission, he shall be punished with imprisonment for a term which may extend to three years, or with fine which may extend to five hundred rupees, or with both.

27. Every Railway-servant shall be deemed a "public servant" within the meaning of sections 161, 162, 163, 164 and 165 of the Indian Penal Code.

    In the definition of legal remuneration contained in the said section 161, the word "Government" shall, for the purpose of this section, be deemed to include any employer of a Railway-servant as such.

28. Any Railway-servant who.compels or attempts to compel any passenger to enter a carriage or compartment containing the maximum number of passengers denoted thereon in accordance with a rule made and notified under section eight, shall be punished with fine which may extend to one hundred rupees.

(C) Offences by Persons generally

29. Any person required under section fifteen to give an account of the quantity and description of any property who neglects or refuses to give such account,

    or who wilfully gives a false account,

    shall be punished with fine which may extend to five rupees for every maund (of 3,200 tolahs) of such property; and such fine shall be in addition to any charge to which such property may be liable.

30. Whoever, in contravention of section sixteen, takes with him any dangerous goods on a Railway, or delivers or tenders any such goods for the purpose of being carried upon a Railway, shall be punished with fine which may extend to two hundred rupees.

31. Any passenger travelling on a railway without a proper ticket or having such a ticket and not showing or delivering up the same when so required under section seventeen, shall be liable to pay the fare of the class in which he is found travelling, from the place whence the train originally started, unless he can prove that he has travelled a less distance only, in which case he shall be liable to pay the fare of the class aforesaid only from the place whence he has travelled.

    Every such fare shall, on application by a Railway-servant to a Magistrate, and on proof on the passenger's liability, be recoverable from such passenger as if it were a fine, and shall, when recovered, be paid to the Railway-Administration.

32. Any person who defrauds, or attempts to defraud, any carrier by Railway –

    (a) by travelling, or attempting to travel, on any Railway without having previously paid his fare;

(b) by riding or attempting to ride in or on a carriage, or by a train, of a higher class than that for which he has paid his fare;

(c) by using or attempting to use a ticket on any day for which such ticket is not available;

(d) by continuing his journey in or upon any carriage beyond the place to which he has paid his fare, without previously paying the fare for the additional distance;

or who, in any other manner whatever, attempts to evade the payment of his fare,

or who wilfully alters or defaces his ticket so as to render the date, number or other material portion thereof illegible,

shall be punished with fine which may extend to fifty rupees, and shall also be liable to pay the fare (if any) which he ought to have paid; and such fare shall be recoverable in manner provided by section thirty-one and shall, when recovered, be paid to the Railway-Administration.

33. Any passenger who gets into or upon, or attempts to get into or upon, or quits, or attempts to quit, any carriage upon any Railway, while such carriage in motion, shall be punished with fine which may extend to twenty rupees;

and any passenger who rides, or attempts to ride, on the steps, or any other part of a carriage, upon any Railway, except on those parts which are intended for the accommodation of passengers,

shall be punished with fine which may extend to one hundred rupees.

34. Any person who, without the permission of the Railway-Administration, rides or attempts to ride upon any locomotive-engine or tender upon any Railway; or in or upon any vehicle not appropriated to the carriage of passengers,

shall be punished with fine which may extend to one hundred rupees.

35. Any person who, without the consent of his follow-passengers, if any, in the same compartment, smokes in or upon any Railway-carriage, except in a carriage or compartment specially provided for the purpose, shall be punished with fine which may extend to twenty rupees;

and any person who persists in so smoking (except as aforesaid) after being warned by any Railway-servant to desist may, in addition to incurring the liability above-mentioned, be removed by any Railway-servant from any such carriage, and from the premises of the Railway, and where he has paid his fare and obtained a ticket, shall forfeit such fare and ticket.

36. Any person who is in a state of intoxication, or who commits any nuisance or act of indecency in any Railway-carriage, or upon any part of any Railway;

or who wilfully and without lawful excuse interferes with the comfort of any passenger, or extinguishes any lamp in any Railway-carriage,

shall be punished with fine which may extend to fifty rupees; and may be removed by any Railway-servant from any such carriage, and also from the premises of the Railway, and where he has paid his fare and obtained a ticket, shall forfeit such fare and ticket.

37. If any carriage, compartment, room or place be reserved by the Railway-Administration for the exclusive use of females, any male person who without lawful excuse enters such carriage, compartment, room or place knowing the same to be reserved as aforesaid, or remains therein after having been informed of its having been so reserved, shall be punished with fine which may extend to one hundred rupees,

    and may be removed therefrom, and also from the premises of the Railway, by any Railway-servant,

    and where he has paid his fare and obtained a ticket, shall forfeit such fare and ticket.

38. Whoever wilfully obstructs or impedes any Railway-servant in the discharge of his duty, shall be punished with fine which may extend to one hundred rupees.

39. Any passenger wilfully entering a carriage or compartment containing the maximum number of passengers which has been denoted thereon in accordance with a rule made and notified under section eight, shall be punished with fine which may extend to one hundred rupees.

40. Any person who without authority or reasonable excuse makes, alters, shows, hides, removes or extinguishes any signal or light upon any Railway, or upon any engine, carriage, wagon or other vehicle upon a Railway,

    or who negligently damages any engine, carriage, wagon or other vehicle belonging to a Railway, or any warehouse, building, machine, fence or other thing so belonging,

    or who needlessly interferes with the means of communication provided in any train between the guard and the engine-driver or passengers,

    shall be punished with fine which may extend to one hundred rupees,

41. Any person who unlawfully enters upon a Railway shall be punished with fine which may extend to twenty rupees; and if any person so entering refuses to leave such Railway on being requested to do so by any Railway-servant, or by any other person on behalf of the Railway-Administration, he shall be punished with fine which may extend to fifty rupees, and may be immediately removed from such Railway by such servant or other person as aforesaid.

42. The owner or person in charge of any bulls, cows, bullocks, calves, elephants, camels, buffaloes, horses, mares, geldings, ponies, colts, fillies, mules, asses, pigs, rams, ewes, sheep, lambs, goats and kids straying on any Railway provided with fences suitable for the exclusion of such animals, shall be punished with fine which may extend to ten rupees for each animal, in addition to any amount that may be recovered under the Cattle Trespass Act, 1871.

    Whenever any such animals are wilfully and unlawfully driven, or knowingly and unlawfully permitted to be, on any Railway provided with fences suitable for the exclusion of such animals,

    and whenever any such animals are wilfully driven, or knowingly permitted to be, on any Railway not so provided, otherwise than for the purpose of lawfully crossing the Railway, or for any other lawful purpose,

    the person in charge of such animals, or if he cannot be identified, then the owner of the said animals, shall be punished with fine which may extend to fifty rupees for each animal, in addition to any amount that may be required under the same Act.

All fines imposed under this section may, if the convicting Magistrate so direct, be recovered in manner provided by section twenty five of the said Cattle Trespass Act, 1871, and may be appropriated in whole or in part in compensation for loss or damage proved to his satisfaction.

The expression "public road" in sections eleven and twenty-six of the same Act shall be deemed to include a Railway. And any Railway-servant may exercise the powers of seizure provided by the said section eleven.

43. Whoever knowing or having reason to believe that any engine or train is approaching along a Railway opens any gate which the Railway-Administration has set up on either side of the Railway across any road for the use or accommodation of any person, or passes or attempts to pass, or drives or takes, or attempts to drive or take, any vehicle, animal or other thing, across the Railway;

and whoever at any time, in the absence of a gate-keeper, omits to shut and fasten such gate as soon as he and any vehicle, animal or other thing under his charge have passed through the same,

shall be punished with fine which may extend to fifty rupees.

44. Whenever any minor under twelve years of age unlawfully –

(a) places or throws, or attempts to place or throw, upon or across a Railway any wood, stone or other thing, or

(b) removes or displaces, or attempts to remove or displace, any rail, sleeper, spike, key or other thing belonging to the permanent way of a Railway, or

(c) throws or causes to fall, or attempt to throw or cause to fall, against, into or upon any engine, tender, carriage or other vehicle used upon a Railway, any wood, stone or other thing,

such minor shall be deemed guilty of any offence, and the convicting Magistrate may, in his discretion, direct either that the minor, if a male, shall be punished with whipping, or that the father or guardian of the minor shall, within such reasonable time as the Magistrate may fix, execute a bond binding himself, in such penalty as the Magistrate may direct, to prevent the minor from repeating such offence.

The amount of such bond, if forfeited, shall be recoverable as if it were a fine.

Any person neglecting or refusing to execute a bond when required under this section so to do shall be punished with fine which may extend to fifty rupees.

45. Whoever wilfully does any act, or wilfully omits to do what he is legally bound to do, intending by such act or omission to endanger, or knowing that he is thereby likely to endanger, the safety of any person travelling or being upon any Railway, shall be punished with transportation (or in the case of an European or American, penal servitude) for a term of not less than seven years or with imprisonment for a term which may extend to ten years.

46. Whoever rashly or negligently does any act, or omits to do what he is legally bound to do, and such act or omission is likely to endanger the safety of any person travelling

or being upon a Railway, shall be punished with imprisonment for a term which may extend to one year, or with fine, or with both.

47. Every driver or conductor of an omnibus, carriage or other vehicle shall, while in or upon any station-yard or other premises forming part of a Railway, obey the reasonable directions of any Railway-servant duly authorized in this behalf; and every person offending against this section shall be punished with fine which may extend to twenty rupees.

(D) *Arrest of Offenders*

48. If any person commits any offence punishable under this Act and there is reason to believe that he will abscond or his name and address are unknown, and he refuses to give his name and address, or there is reason to believe that the name or address given by him is incorrect, any Railway-servant or Police-officer, or any other person whom such Railway-servant or Police-officer may call to his aid, may, without any warrant or written authority, arrest and detain such offender until he can be taken before a Magistrate or give sufficient security for his appearance before such Magistrate, or is otherwise discharged by due course of law.

49. Every person committing any offence mentioned in sections eight, twenty-five, twenty-six, thirty-six, thirty-seven, thirty-eight, forty-four, forty-five and forty-six may be arrested without any warrant or written authority by any Railway-servant or Police-officer, or by any other person whom such servant or officer may call to his aid;

    and every person so arrested shall, without unnecessary delay, be taken before a Magistrate authorized to punish him or to commit him for trial.

(E) *Jurisdiction*

50. No Magistrate other than a Presidency Magistrate and a Magistrate whose powers are not less than those of a Magistrate of the second class shall try any offence under this Act.

    Any person committing any offence against this Act or the rules made under it, shall be triable for such offence in any place in which he may be found or which the Local Government may, from time to time, notify in this behalf, as well as in any other place in which he might be tried under any law for the time being in force.

    Every notification under this section shall be published in the local official Gazette and a copy thereof shall also be exhibited in some conspicuous place at each of such Railway-stations as the Local Government may direct, so that it may be easily seen and read.

(F) *Saving of other Criminal Laws*

51. Nothing in this Act shall deemed to prevent any person from being arrested, prosecuted or punished under any other law for any act or omission which constitutes an offence against this Act or the rules made under it: Provided that no person shall be punished

twice for the same offence.

CHAPTER VI

MISCELLANEOUS

52. The Governor General in Council, or the Local Government with the previous sanction of the Governor General in Council, may, from time to time, make rules requiring –

(a) that boundary-marks or fences be provided for any Railway or any part thereof, and for roads constructed in connection therewith;
(b) that gates or bars be erected at places where any Railway crosses a road on the level; and
(c) that person be employed to open and shut such gates or bars;

and may be such rules determine what kind of fences shall, for the purposes of section forty-two, be deemed to be suitable for the exclusion of cattle,

and direct that any Railway-Administration wilfully neglecting or violating any rule made under this section, shall forfeit to Government a sum not exceeding five hundred rupees for every such neglect or violation, or, when such neglect or violation is continuous, for every day during which it continues.

53. The Governor General in Council may, from time to time by notification in the Gazette of India, declare what Government or other authority shall be deemed to be, for the purposes of this Act, the Local Government in respect of the whole or any part of a Railway.

54. The Governor General in Council may, by notification, extend this Act or any portion thereof to any tramway worked by steam.

THE FIRST SCHEDULE

ACTS REPEALED

(See section 2)

Number and Year	*Title*
XVIII of 1854	*An Act relating to Railway in India*
XXXI of 1867	*An Act to render penal certain offences committed by servants of Railway Companies*
XIII of 1870	*An Act to apply the provisions of Act No. XVIII of 1854 Railways belonging to, or worked by, Government*
XXV of 1871	*An Act to amend the Railway Act*

THE SECOND SCHEDULE

(See section 11)

(a) Gold or silver, coined or uncoined, manufactured or unmanufactured;
(b) Plated articles;

(c) Cloths and tissue and lace of which gold or silver forms part;
(d) Precious stones, jewellery, trinkets;
(e) Watches, clocks or time-pieces of any description;
(f) Government securities;
(g) Government stamps;
(h) Bills of exchange, hundies, promissory notes, bank-notes, orders or other securities for payment of money;
(i) Maps, writings, title-deeds;
(j) Paintings, engravings, lithographs, photographs, carvings, sculpture and other works of art;
(k) Glass, china, marble;
(l) Silks in a manufactured or unmanufactured state, and whether wrought up or not wrought up with other materials;
(m) Shawls;
(n) Lace;
(o) Opium;
(p) Ivory, ebony, sandalwood, sandalwood-oil;
(q) Musical and scientific instruments.

D. FITZPATRICK,
Secy. to the Govt. of India

Indian Guaranteed Railways Act, 1879

Source: H.E. Trevor: The Law Relating to Railways in British India, London, 1891

Gist: Indian Guaranteed Railways Act, 1879, passed on 11 August 1879, with eight sections and some clauses under them, enabled the guaranteed railway companies and the Secretary of State for India to enter into agreement with respect to the working of railways and telegraphs and to confer upon these companies additional powers with respect to their undertakings.

INDIAN GUARANTEED RAILWAYS ACT, 11 AUGUST 1879

(42 & 43 Vict. c. 41)

An Act to enable Guaranteed Railway Companies in India and the Secretary of State for India in Council to enter into Agreements with respect to the working of Railways, and with respect to Telegraphs, and to confer upon those Companies additional powers with respect to their undertakings.

[11th August 1879]

BE it enacted by the Queen's most Excellent Majesty, by and with the advice and consent of the Lords Spiritual and Temporal, and Commons, in this present Parliament assembled, and by the authority of the same, as follows:

1. In and for the purpose of this Act, –

The term "guaranteed company" means any of the companies specified in the schedule to this Act, and any railway company which for the time being constructs, maintains or works a railway under any guarantee from or arrangement with the Secretary of State for India in Council.

The term "Railway Company" includes any person or body of persons being the owner or lessee of or working a railway,

(a) Local and Personal Act, 18 Vict. ch. XL (Madras Railway Company); Local and Personal Act, 22 & 23 Vict. ch. CII (Bombay, Baroda and Central India Railway Company), ss. 61-66,

except the East Indian Railway Company, and except any railway company of which the undertaking is after the passing of this Act purchased by the Secretary of State for India in Council.

The term "railway" means a railway constructed before or after the passing of this Act, and belonging to the Secretary of State for India in Council, or situate in her Majesty's territories in India, or in any territory in the East Indies belonging to any native prince or state in alliance with her Majesty or to any European power, and includes any tramway so belonging or situate and worked by steam power, and any ferry so belonging or situate and worked or used in connection with a railway.

2. A guaranteed company may from time to time make with the Secretary of State for India in Council, and carry into effect, or, with the sanction of the Secretary of State for India in Council, make with any railway company and carry into effect, any agreement with respect to any of the following purposes; namely,

   (a) The working, use, management, and maintenance of any railway or part of a railway;
   (b) The supply of rolling stock and machinery necessary for any of the purposes hereinbefore mentioned, and of officers and servants for the conduct of the traffic of any such railway or part:
   (c) The payments to be made and the conditions to be performed with respect to such working, use, management, and maintenance:
   (d) The interchange, accommodation, and conveyance of traffic on, coming from, or destined for the respective railways of the contracting parties, and the fixing, collecting, apportionment, and appropriation of the revenues arising from the traffic:
   (e) Generally, the giving effect to any such provisions or stipulations with respect to any of the purposes hereinbefore mentioned as the contracting parties may think fit and mutually agree on.

3. A guaranteed company may from time to time make with the Secretary of State for India in Council, and carry into effect, any agreement with respect to any of the following purposes; namely,

   (a) The surrendering, selling, or letting by the company to the Secretary of State of all or any part of the telegraphs belonging to the company:
   (b) The doing of any thing connected with the working, use, management, or maintenance of or otherwise relating to any telegraphs in India which belong to the Secretary of State in Council or a guaranteed company, or in which the Secretary of State in Council or any such company is for the time being interested, including the application of the revenue to arise from any such telegraphs:
   (c) Generally the giving effect to any such provisions or stipulations with respect to any such telegraphs as the Secretary of State in Council and any such company may think fit and mutually agree on.

4. A guaranteed company may from time to time, with the sanction of the Secretary of State for India in Council, exercise all or any of the following powers:

(a) They may use, maintain, farm, or work and take tolls in respect of any bridge or ferry used in connection with their railway:

(b) They may construct, use, maintain, and take tolls in respect of any road in connection with a railway bridge:

(c) They may provide any means of transport which may be required for the reasonable convenience of persons or goods carried or to be carried on their railway, but not between any places between which any company shall for the time being be carrying on the business of carriers by water:

Provided always, that the capital outlay on the works mentioned in the three preceding sub-sections shall not in the case of any guaranteed company exceed in all ten lacs of rupees:

(d) They may make and carry into effect agreements with the Secretary of State for India in Council, for the construction of rolling stock, plant, or machinery used on or in connection with railways, or for leasing or taking on lease any rolling stock, plant, machinery, or equipments required for use on railway.

A guaranteed company shall have, for the purpose of recovering any tolls which they are authorized to take under this section, such powers as may be conferred upon them by laws and regulations made by the Governor-General of India in Council.

5. The Secretary of State for India in Council may from time to time, with respect to any case or class of cases, delegate to the Governor-General of India in Council the power to give any sanction required under this Act.
6. The powers conferred by this Act shall be in addition to and not in derogation of any powers existing independently of this Act.
7. Any agreement made before the passing of this Act by a guaranteed company for any of the purposes specified in this Act shall be as valid as if it had been made after the passing of this Act.
8. This Act may be cited as the Indian Guaranteed Railways Act, 1879.

SCHEDULE

The Great Indian Peninsula Railway Company.
The Madras Railway Company.
The Bombay Baroda and Central India Railway Company.
The Scinde, Punjab, and Delhi Railway Company.
The Eastern Bengal Railway Company.
The South Indian Railway Company.
The Oudh and Rohilcund Railway Company (Limited).

386

The Darjeeling Steam Tramway Act, 1879

Source: H.E. Trevor: The Law Relating to Railways in British India, London, 1891

Gist: The Darjeeling Steam Tramway Act, 1879 (Act 6 of 1879), which got the assent of the Lieutenant-Governor of Bengal on the 16th April 1879, and of the Governor-General on the 20th May 1879, provided for the construction of a steam tramway between Darjeeling and Siligoree

ACT OF THE LIEUTENANT-GOVERNOR OF BENGAL IN COUNCIL

Act No. VI of 1879

PASSED BY THE LIEUTENANT-GOVERNOR OF BENGAL IN COUNCIL

(*Received the assent of the Lieutenant-Governor on the 16th April 1879, and of the Governor-General on the 20th May 1879*)

An Act to provide for the construction of a Steam Tramway between Siligoree and Darjeeling

WHEREAS a company has been formed, called the Darjeeling Steam Tramway Company, Limited, hereinafter called the company for the purpose of constructing, maintaining, and working a steam tramway from Siligoree to Darjeeling; and whereas an agreement bearing date the eighth day of April eighteen hundred and seventy-nine, has been entered into between Franklin Prestage, Esq., as trustee on behalf of the company, and the Secretary of State for India in Council, for the above purpose; and whereas it is expedient that the company should be authorized to construct, maintain, and work a steam tramway upon the existing cart road between Siligoree and Darjeeling as aforesaid, and to do all things necessary in that behalf; it is enacted as follows: –

1. This Act may be called The Darjeeling Steam Tramway Act; and it shall come into force from the date on which it may be published in the *Calcutta Gazette* with the assent of the Governor-General.
2. The company may construct and maintain upon the said existing cart road between Siligoree and Darjeeling a tramway, conformable to the specification and conditions set forth in the hereinbefore mentioned agreement between the said trustee for the

company and the said Secretary of State, or any agreement which may hereafter be entered into between the company and the said Secretary of State, with all proper rails, sidings, stations, offices, warehouses, fixed machinery and other works connected therewith or for the purposes thereof, and use and employ upon such tramway such locomotive engines or other moving power, and such carriages or wagons to be drawn or propelled thereby, as they may deem fit.

3. The company may, with the permission of such officer as the local government may from time to time empower in that behalf, obstruct the said cart road; but in such case the company shall provide such accommodation for the local traffic during such obstruction as the said officer shall direct.

387

East Indian Railway Company Purchase Act, 1879

Source: H. E. Trevor: The Law Relating to Railways in British India, London, 1891

Gist: Section 27 of the East Indian Railway Company Purchase Act, 1879 enables the company to enter into and conclude with the Secretary of State any contract for any of the purposes cited in the section and empowers to carry out it.

EAST INDIAN RAILWAY COMPANY PURCHASE ACT, 1879

(Local and Personal), (42 & 43 Vict. ch. CCVI)

Sect. 27. "From and after the commencement of this Act, the company may enter into and conclude with the Secretary of State any contract or contracts for any of the following purposes; that is to say –

(a) The carrying into effect the memorandum of terms come to between the company and the Secretary of State, and any addition thereto or modification thereof, as may be agreed upon between them, not being contrary to or at variance with the provisions of this Act;
(b) The maintenance and management of the East Indian Railway, or any part thereof;
(c) The improving and enlarging the East Indian Railway, or any part thereof, and the constructing deviation or auxiliary railways, and other works in connection therewith;
(d) The use and working of the East Indian Railway, or any part thereof, and the conveyance of traffic thereon;
(e) The granting running powers and other facilities and accommodation of whatever description to other railway companies or to State railways;
(f) The use by the company of running powers and other facilities and accommodation of whatever description that any other railway company or the Secretary of State may at any time have power to grant to the company;
(g) The maintenance and management of railways in connection with but not forming part of the East Indian Railway, and the use and working of such railways, and the conveyance of traffic thereon;

(h) The control and supervision of the Secretary of State in respect of the matters aforesaid, including the appointment of one or more Government directors;

(i) The doing all things necessary or incidental to the matters provided for by this Act, or any of them;

and the Secretary of State and the company are hereby authorized and empowered to carry any such contract or contracts into effect."

388

General Rules and Regulations for all Railways in India, 1880

Source: The Gazette of India, Part 1, 18th September 1880.

Gist: General Rules and Regulations for all Railways in India, 1880 were formulated in conformity with section 8 of the Indian Railway Act, 1879. The Rules, 394 paragraphs and subparagraphs in 19 sections, were held applicable to all lines of railway in India used for the public conveyance of passengers or goods. Each railway administration were allowed to make subsidiary rules if found necessary or expedient, provided that these would not be inconsistent with the general rules. Section II, dealing with the general management, lists the dangerous goods in paragraph 31. Section III provides rules generally applicable to railway servants, while sections IV and V deal with various signals and signalling in foggy or tempestuous weather, or during dust-storms. Sections from VI to IX lay down duties of station masters and clerks in charge of stations, of pointmen and signalmen, of guards, and of drivers and firemen. The Rules specify the responsibilities of inspectors, platelayers, gangers, and others employed on the permanent way, and provide regulations for ballasting and level-crossings. It also provides (sections XIII to XIX) general rules for specific problems mentioned in rule 3, section II.

GENERAL RULES FOR ALL RAILWAYS IN INDIA MADE IN CONFORMITY WITH SECTION 8 OF "THE INDIAN RAILWAY ACT, 1879"

The rules comprised in this code shall be held applicable to, and are to be observed on, all lines of Railway in India used for the public conveyance of passengers or goods, unless specially exempted by the Governor General in Council.

Each Railway administration may hereafter make such subsidiary rules as may be found necessary or expedient, provided that no such subsidiary rule shall be inconsistent with these general rules.

Every Railway servant is bound by the terms of his employment to obey both the general and subsidiary rules.

SECTION I
INTERPRETATION CLAUSES AND DEFINITIONS

The catchwords in the margin of this code have been added merely for the purpose of facilitating reference; they are not to be held either as an integral part of the code, or in any way giving an interpretation to the clauses to which they are annexed.

2. In the rules comprised in this code unless there is something repugnant in the subject or context: -

"Written" instructions, orders, forms, &c., include documents which are printed, lithographed, or prepared by other processes, and instructions which are sent by telegram;

"Main line" means the line ordinarily used by trains to run through and between stations on any part of a Railway;

"Train" means an engine with or without vehicles attached;

"Passenger train" means a train intended for the conveyance of passengers and other coaching traffic;

"Goods train" means a train intended for the conveyance of general merchandize;

And includes -

(a) trains carrying livestock;
(b) trains carrying minerals;
(c) trains carrying materials;

"Mixed train" means a train intended to convey both passengers and goods;

"Ordinary train" means a train, whether passenger, goods, or mixed which is entered in the working time-tables;

"Special train" means any train not classed as an "Ordinary train";

"System of working" means the system adopted for the time being on any portion of a Railway as prescribed in Rule 3 and as detailed in Sections XIII to XIX;

"Station" means any place -

(i) at which traffic is booked, and where authority is given for trains to proceed;
(ii) at which authority is given for trains to proceed under the "System of working";

"Station limits" include all traffic lines and premises within the distant signal or signals if such be provided:

Where no distant signal is provided, the "Station limits" extend to the outside points:

Where there are no points and no distant signal the "Station limits" extend to the ends of the platform, or other positions fixed in each case;

"Authorized Officer" means the person who usually issues instructions of the nature referred to in each case;

"Special instructions" means instructions given by the "authorized officer";

"Station Master" means the person on duty responsible for the time being for working the trains and traffic within "Station limits";

And includes -

(a) Assistant Station Master;
(b) Inspector;
(c) Clerk in charge;
(d) Any other person appointed to the charge of a Station;

"Ganger" means the man in charge of a gang of men employed on repairing the permanent way whatever he may be called on any particular Railway;

"Driver" means the person in charge for the time being of a working locomotive engine;

"Station signal" means the signal which on some Railways is called "Main" or "Home" or "Platform" signal;

"Guard" includes the under Guard, and any Brakesman or other person who may, for the time being, be performing the duties of the Guard;

"Servant" means any person employed to perform any function in connection with Railway.

SECTION II
GENERAL MANAGEMENT

3. Every Line of Railway upon which engine power is used, for the public conveyance of passengers or goods, must be worked on one of the following system, viz. -

"Line clear and caution message,"
"Absolute block,"
"Train Following,"
"Train Staff and Ticket,"
"Train Despatching,"
"Pilot Guard,"
"One Engine only,"

in accordance with the rules laid down in Sections XIII to XIX for the system adopted.

4. On a double line trains must invariably be run on the left hand road, except under special instructions to the contrary and in accordance with rule 28.

On a single line no engine, with or without a train, shall be permitted to leave one station for another until it shall have been ascertained that the line between those stations is clear of engines and trains coming from the opposite direction, and of all impediments as far as can be known.

When allowable under the system adopted for working, trains may follow one another between stations in the same direction under special instructions on both single and double lines in accordance with rules 23 and 24.

5. Except when necessary to carry passengers in goods vehicles, no passenger or mixed train shall be allowed to move from any station unless it be provided with an arrangement by which the Guard can communicate with, make his way, or otherwise get access to every passenger carriage in the train.
6. No engine shall be allowed to push a train, or portion of a train, or fuel truck, unless within station limits, or under special instructions.
7. Except in the case of an engine running without vehicles, no train shall be despatched from any station without one or more brake-vans, and one or more Guards, and all the necessary lamps and other appliances.
8. Whenever any train or engine is timed to run, or from any cause is expected to run, on any portion of the line later than sunset and before sunrise, the signal lamps must be lighted at sunset. During twilight in the mornings and evenings, both day and night signals must be used. The signal lights must not be put out until broad day-light except under instructions from an authorized officer.

   In foggy or stormy weather when the day signals cannot be seen plainly, the signal lamps must be lighted, and kept burning, and at such times both the day and night signals must be used.
9. No engine shall be driven tender, or fuel truck, foremost, except within station limits, without a written order, or unless in cases of unavoidable necessity to be established by the Driver.
10. No special train, or light engine, shall leave a station unless previous notice shall have been given, when practicable, to all stations concerned.
11. Madras time, or such time as is adopted on each Railway in India, shall be sent to the principal stations in accordance with authorized instructions.
12. No person suffering from an infectious disease shall enter a Railway carriage or premises without previously notifying to the Station Master that he is so suffering, and obtaining from him permission to enter under special instructions.
13. Any one being in attendance on a person suffering from an infectious disease is subject to the same restrictions, while travelling by Railway, as if he himself were suffering from the disease.
14. The maximum number of passengers that may be carried in each compartment of every description of carriage must be fixed by the Railway Administration with the approval of Government, and such number must be distinctly exhibited, inside each first and second class compartment in the English language, and both inside and outside of each compartment of all classes inferior to the second class, in conspicuous places in English and in the vernacular language most commonly used in the districts through which the Railway passes.
15. Tickets are only available from the date and for the period specified by the Railway Administration by which they are issued.
16. Any person found smoking, or having an open light or fire, in good-sheds, store yards,

or, who persists in smoking, after being warned by a Railway servant or Police Officer to desist, on any other portion of the Railway premises, where such practice may be deemed dangerous by the authorized officer, shall be liable to immediate removal from the Railway premises, and to a fine which may extend to fifty rupees, or, in default of payment of such fine, to simple imprisonment for a term which may extend to two months.

17. In the event of any person being drunk and disorderly, or causing annoyance to others, the Station Master is to use all reasonable means to stop the annoyance, and if the offender persists, the Station Master is to have him removed from the Railway premises, and the offender is liable to prosecution under the Railway Act.

18. Every person desirous of travelling on a Railway shall, upon payment of his fare, be furnished with a ticket specifying in English and the principal vernacular language of the district in which the ticket is issued, the class of carriage for which, and the place from and place to which, the fare has been paid, and the amount of such fare.

    And every passenger shall when required, show his ticket to any Railway servant duly authorized to examine the same, and shall deliver up such ticket upon demand to any Railway servant duly authorized to collect tickets.

19. At the intermediate stations, the fares shall be deemed to be accepted and the tickets furnished only upon condition that there be room in the train for which the tickets are furnished.

    In case there is no room for all the passengers to whom tickets have been furnished, those who have obtained tickets for the longest distances shall have the preference; and those who have obtained tickets for the same distance shall have the preference according to the order in which they have received their tickets.

20. Any passenger to whom a ticket has been furnished at any station and for whom there is no room shall, on returning the ticket within a reasonable time after the issue, be entitled to have his fare at once refunded.

21. No trespassing upon the Railway shall be allowed, and no person, other than a Railway servant, shall be permitted to walk on the line, unless provided with a license to do so, signed by an authorized officer of the Railway. If the trespasser, on being requested to quit, persists in remaining, he may be immediately removed from the Railway by any Railway servant or by any other person, and is liable to prosecution under the Railway Act.

22. No carriage door shall be opened while the train is in motion.

23. Where the block system is not in operation, no train or engine shall be allowed to follow any other train or engine on the same line within ten minutes, unless it has been ascertained that the preceding train has arrived at the next station in advance.

24. Where the line is not worked under the block system, no passenger train shall follow a goods train, nor shall a fast goods train follow a stopping passenger train from a station within fifteen minutes, nor even then, until the engine driver has been properly warned of the time of the departure of the preceding train and where it will next stop. But in case the distance to the next station in advance exceeds ten miles, the interval

must be increased under special instruction of the authorized officer.

25. Fixed distant signals must be constructed to exhibit danger in case of any failure of their connections.
26. Every portion of the permanent-way must be inspected daily on foot by some authorized person responsible for its condition; and bridges and all other works (including signals and signal wires) must be regularly inspected in accordance with rules laid down by the authorized officer.
27. Special rules shall be laid down by the authorized Officer for dealing with cases of fires in trains.
28. On the double line should an accident block one of the lines of Railway, so as to necessitate the passing of all up and down trains on a single line, immediate steps must be taken to establish single line working, on the rules adopted by each Railway for working in such cases.
29. Drivers with engines or trains must run within the limits of speed fixed for the section of the line upon which they are running.

    These limits are not on any line to exceed, on the 5 feet 6 inch gauge, for passenger trains, sixty (60) miles an hour, and for goods and mixed trains thirty (30) miles an hour. On the metre gauge, or other narrow gauge, these limits are not to be exceeded - for passenger trains, forty (40) miles an hour, and for goods and mixed trains, twenty (20) miles an hour.
30. Drivers with engines or trains must not make up between any two stations more time than is allowed to be made up in that distance by an authorized officer.
31. For the purposes of the Railway Act, the following are declared to be dangerous goods:

Carbolic Acid
Fusel Oil
Kerosine Oil
Naphthalin
Paraffin
Petroleum and other Hydrocarbon Oils
Rangoon Oil
Wood Naphtha
Muriate of Tin
Nitrate of Iron
Perchloride of Iron
Solution of Ammonia
Sulphate of Indigo, concentrated
Aquafortis
Bromine
Chloride of Sulphur
Chloroform
Chloroform

Coloured Fires
Congreve Matches
Cracker
Combustibles
Cotton powder
Chlorate mixture
Detonators
Dynamite
Fire work Composition
Fire works
Fog Signals
Fuze
Gun-cotton
Gun-powder
Gun-cotton-power
Lathofracteur
Lucifer Matches
Nitrated gun-cotton

Fluoric Acid

Glacial Acetic Acid
Mineral Acid, such as
Muriatic Acid;
Nitric Acid;
Sulphuric Acid or Oil of Vitriol
Ammunition
Amorphous Phosphorus
Cartridges

Nitroglycerine and its compounds
Phosphorous
Percussion caps
Schultze gun-powder
Tubes for firing explosives.
Vesuvians
War rockets
Exclusive Chemicals
All other explosives

32. Copies of the General Rules and Regulations must be supplied to Railway servants in accordance with rules 39 and 40.

SECTION III
RULES GENERALLY APPLICABLE TO RAILWAY SERVANTS

33. Each person in Railway service must devote himself exclusively to the service of the Railway on which he is employed, residing at whatever place may be appointed, attending at such hours as may be required, paying prompt obedience to all persons placed in authority over him, and confirming to all the rules and regulations of the Railway.
34. Any Railway servant who shall quit the service without having given one month's previous notice in writing, or the notice required by his agreement of service, shall forfeit all claims for pay due, and shall also be subject on conviction to the penalty prescribed in Rule 55.
35. When any one leaves the service he must deliver up all Railway property in his charge; and no money due for wages will be paid until all articles, which have been supplied to him, shall have been delivered up in accordance with existing regulations. If not delivered up, or if any article be missing, or be damaged from neglect or by improper use, the cost of such article, or of the repair of such damage shall be deducted from any pay due to him or from any moneys held for him by the Railway Authorities, and if such moneys should be insufficient to meet the claim, the balance will become a debt recoverable at law.
36. All Railway servants are subject to immediate dismissed, or suspension without pay, for refusal of duty, disobedience of orders, negligence, misconduct, absence without leave, or for any neglect of those regulations; and may be held liable for all damages occasioned by misconduct or negligence, and are also subject on conviction to the penalty prescribed in Rule 55.
37. The pay of every servant always includes his services during all hours, whether early or late, as may be determined from time to time by his superior.
38. Intoxication on duty renders the offender liable to dismissal; and also to criminal prosecution under the Railway Act.

39. A copy of these rules and regulations shall be supplied to each Railway servant who understands English, and who is in any way connected with the out-door working of the Railway, or with the working of trains.

    Each native subordinate who is in any way connected with the out-door working of the Railway or with the working of trains, and who may be unacquainted with the English language, shall be provided with a translation, in such language as he understands of these rules, or of the section relating to his duties.

40. Every servant must make himself acquainted with the rules or sections of the rules supplied to him, and must produce his copy when required. If the copy be lost, defaced or torn, he must apply to his immediate superior for a new one which will be supplied at the cost of the servant. Any Railway servant who should have a copy and is found without one is liable to punishment.

    Station Masters, Foremen, and Gangers or Mistries of Platelayers, are responsible that the subordinates working under them are acquainted with all the rules relating to their respective duties.

41. Every servant is required to assist in carrying out the rules and regulations, and must immediately report to his superior any infringement thereof, or any occurrence affecting the safe and proper working of the Railway which may come under his notice.
42. The safety of the public must, under all circumstances, be the chief care of Railway servants.
43. No servant may, under any circumstances, absent himself from duty without proper permission.
44. Every person required to wear uniform is to appear in it, clean and neat when on duty.
45. The conduct of all servants must be prompt, civil, and obliging. They must at all times afford every proper facility for the business to be performed, and be careful to give correct information.
46. Swearing and immoral language, and violent altercations and threats, are strictly prohibited.
47. No Railway servant is allowed to travel on the Railway unless provided with a proper ticket, or free pass; nor is he allowed to ride on the engine, or in the brake-van, or in any vehicle in which luggage or parcels are conveyed, unless in the execution of his duty, without written permission from an authorized officer.
48. No money or gratuity, in the shape of fee, or reward, is allowed to be taken from passengers, or other persons, by any Railway servant, even although the regular hours of duty shall have expired, without the permission of the Railway Administration. Any infringement of this rule renders the offender liable to immediate dismissal and on conviction to imprisonment for three years or to fine, or to both under sections 161 to 165 of the Indian Penal Code.
49. Drivers, Guards and others directly connected with the working of trains, shall not, when on duty, be supplied with spirituous liquors at refreshment-rooms, except under rules framed by an authorized officer.

50. No trespassing upon the Railway shall be allowed, and no person other than a Railway servant shall be permitted to walk on the line unless provided with a license to do so, signed by the authorized officer of the Railway. If the trespasser, on being requested to quit, persists in remaining, he may be immediately removed from the Railway by any Railway servant or by any other person, and is liable to prosecution under the Railway Act.
51. In the case of accident or obstruction the safety of passengers must be deemed of the first importance. The most prompt mode of communicating the circumstance to the next station, and to head-quarters, must be adopted, and all possible assistance may be demanded from, and must be promptly rendered by, any Railway servant where services may be needed.
52. Any lost article found on the Railway line and premises must be immediately made over to the nearest Station Master to be dealt with in accordance with special instructions. See Rule 139.
53. The stuff along the line must always be prepared for special trains without previous notice.
54. Drivers, Guards, and others must invariably report to the nearest Station Master any defective signals, or obstruction of them, or neglect in working them.
55. Any person committing a breach of Rules 34, 36, 43, 46, and 47 shall be liable to a fine which may extend to fifty rupees, or, in default of payment of such fine, to simple imprisonment for a term which may extend to two months.

SECTION IV
SIGNALS

56. RED is a signal of "Danger" - Stop.
GREEN is a signal "CAUTION" - Go slowly.
WHITE is a signal of "ALL RIGHT" - Go on.

Hand Signals

57. The hand signals shall be made by flags in the day and by lights at night or in foggy weather or in tunnels.
58. When the line is clear, the signalman must either stand erect with his flag in his hand, thus -

ALL CLEAR.

or display a white flag, or white light.

59. If it be necessary to proceed with "Caution" the green flag will be elevated thus -

CAUTION.

or the green light shown.

60. If it be necessary to proceed with "Caution" from any defect on the road or rails, the green flag will be depressed thus -

CAUTION (RAILS).

or the green light shown.

61. If it be necessary to stop, the red flag will be shown and waved to and fro, the signalman facing the engine thus -

DANGER.

or the red light shown.

62. In the absence of flags -
Both arms raised above the head denotes "Danger" thus -

One arm raised with the hand above the head denotes "Caution" thus -

CAUTION.

One arm held in a horizontal position across the line of rails denotes "All Right" thus

ALL RIGHT.

63. In the absence of a green light, a white light waved slowly from side to side denotes "Caution" - Go slowly.
64. In the absence of a red light, any light moved up and down or waved violently denotes "Danger" - Stop.

Fixed Signals

65. The fixed signals are for the most part, constructed with one or more Semaphore arms for day signals, and with one or more lamps for night, but disc and other signals are in some cases used.

    The day signal is invariably made by the arm on the left hand side of the post as seen by the Driver of an approaching engine.
66. The "Danger signal" is shown in the day time by the arm on the left hand side of the post being raised to the horizontal position thus -

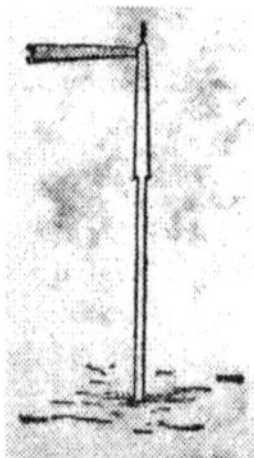

DANGER.

and by the exhibition of "*red*" light by right.

67. The "Caution Signal" is shown in the day time by the arm on the left hand side of the post being placed half-way to the horizontal position thus -

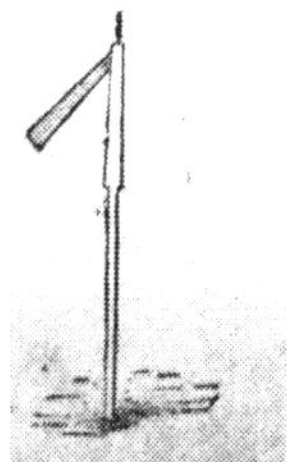

CAUTION.

and by the exhibition of a *"green"* light by night.

68. The "All Right Signal" is shown in the day time by the arm on the left hand side being lowered to the post, thus -

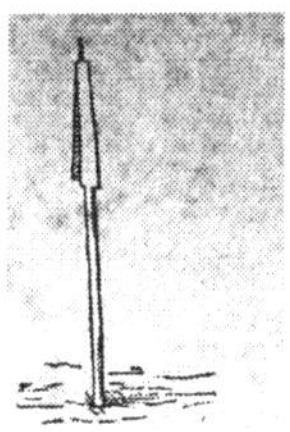

ALL RIGHT.

and by the exhibition of a *"white"* light by night

69. Except at level crossings worked under rule 336, fixed signals are always to be kept at "Danger" and lowered or reversed only to allow a train or engine to pass.

Station Signals

(Also called "Main" or "Home," or "Platform" Signals)

70. Station signals are placed at stations, junctions, sidings outside station limits, and signal boxes, and when at "Danger," no train or engine must pass them, or foul the crossings or points to which they apply, except as prescribed in Rules 72 and 77.
71. Station signals at junctions must never be passed when at "Danger" by the train to which the signal applies.
72. Station signals at stations, sidings, and signal boxes (other than at junctions) must never be passed when at "Danger" unless the Driver is signalled past by hand by a person duly appointed by an authorized officer.
73. Station signals must invariably stand at "Danger" except when lowered for an approaching train.

Distant Signals

74. Distant signals are fixed at a considerable distance from the station, and are constructed to exhibit the "Danger" and "All Right" signals only, or "Danger" and "Caution" signals only.

75. Distant signals must be replaced at "Danger" immediately they are passed by an engine.
76. When a distant signal is at "Danger," the Driver of an approaching train must bring his train to a "*dead stop*" outside of it, and must then ascertain if the line is clear to admit the train within it. If the line be clear, he must at once draw the train cautiously within the distant signal so as to be protected by it, and then stop until signalled into the station in accordance with rules prescribed by the authorized officer. If, however, there is any obstruction on the line so near to the distant signal as to prevent the whole of the train from passing safely within it, the rules for the protection of trains when stopped outside station limits must be immediately carried out See Rules 179 and 240.
77. Station and distant signals apply only to trains or engines running in the proper direction, and must not be used for any other purpose. Trains or engines shunting from one main line to another, or shunting into, or out of, sidings connected with the main line, must, unless special signals are provided for the purpose of signalling such operations, be signalled past the station signal, either verbally, or by hand lamp, or flags as occasion may require; it being necessary in such cases, that the Danger signal should be exhibited at the station signal as well as at the distant signal, for the protection of the train or engine so employed.
78. Every Station Master, or other person, must in the event of any signal under his charge becoming defective, immediately report the case to his immediate superior, and to the nearest Permanent Way Inspector; and the Station Master shall place a competent man or men with the necessary hand signals and detonators to signal in lieu of such defective signal, until it is again in proper working order.

    When the Station Master cannot provide proper men from his own staff, he must apply to the nearest Permanent Way Inspector for competent men.
79. Except at places specially exempted upon each railway, the absence of a signal at a place where a signal is ordinarily shown, or signal imperfectly exhibited, must be considered a Danger signal, and treated accordingly, and the fact reported to the station Master.
80. Drivers, Guards, and others must invariably report to the nearest Station Master any defective signals, or obstruction of them, or neglect in working them.

Detonating Signals

81. Every Guard, Driver, Foreman of works, and Ganger or Mistry of Platelayers will be provided with detonators of fog signals which they are always to have ready for use whilst on duty; and every person in charge of a station must keep a supply of those signals in a suitable place, easy of access.
82. In trick, foggy, or tempestuous weather, and in cases of obstruction, detonators must be used in addition to the regular day and night signals, in accordance with Rules 86, 87, 88 and 179.
83. Detonators must be carefully handled, as they are liable to explode if roughly treated. It is necessary to keep them well protected from damp. Al least one from each person's

stock must be tested, at intervals of not more than one month to ensure that they are in good condition. Station Masters in charge of stations, where extra supplies are kept for Guards and others, shall test at least one from each box before issue.

84. Detonators must be placed on the rail (label or brand upwards) and secured by bending the clasp round the upper flange of the rail. A detonator explodes with a loud report, when the engine passes over it and the Driver must stop as quickly as possible, and then proceed cautiously to the place of obstruction, or until he receives an "All Right" signal.

Train Signals

85. On both double and single line between sunset and sunrise and during foggy weather, every train must exhibit a Red Tail Light and two Red Side Lights in rear of the train, and every engine running alone must exhibit at least one Red Tail Light; in both cases Head Lights prescribed by the authorized officer must be exhibited.

In the case of two or more engines running coupled together without a train, the first engine only must exhibit the prescribed Head Light, and the last engine only must exhibit at least one Red Tail Light.

This rule does not apply to engines and trains doing station work.

SECTION V
SIGNALLING IN FOGGY OR TEMPESTUOUS WEATHER, OR DURING DUST-STORMS

86. In foggy or tempestuous weather two detonators 10 yards apart must be placed on the rail by the signalman or other trained servant selected by the Station Master at least one hundred yards outside the distant signal post, or, in the absence of a distant signal, at least seven hundred yards from the outside points. Drivers and Guards must report all cases of omission to do this.
87. On the double line, detonators must be renewed immediately after a train has passed over them; and on the single line they must be placed before an approaching train is due or expected.
88. The Station Master must see that fresh supplies of signals are sent to the men in place of those exploded, and in case it is necessary to keep a man out for any length of time, he must be relieved every six hours, and visited as often as practicable to ensure that he is on the alert.
89. In foggy weather or in dust-storms, when the day signals cannot be seen plainly, the signal lamps must be lighted and kept burning.

SECTION VI
STATION MASTERS AND CLERKS IN CHARGE OF STATIONS

90. Every Station Master, or person in charge of a station, is answerable for the security and protection of the office and buildings, and of the Railway property there. He is

responsible for the faithful and efficient discharge of the duties devolving upon all the Railway servants, either permanently or temporarily employed at the station, or within its limits, and all such servants are subject to his authority and directions in the working of the line and station. He is also responsible for the general working of the station being carried out in strict accordance with all rules, regulations, and orders.

91. Station Masters will receive their orders from, and report to, such Traffic Officer as may be placed over them.

92. It is the special duty of every Station Master, or such other person as may be appointed for the purpose by an officer of the Traffic Department, to attend to the arrival and departure of trains.

93. The Station Master must always appear in uniform when on duty, if required.

94. The Station Master, or such other person as may be appointed for the purpose must daily inspect the station, and see that all rooms, latrines, and other offices, and platforms, &c., are kept neat and clean.

95. The Station Master must see that all orders and instructions are duly entered and executed, and that all books are regularly and neatly kept, and all returns properly prepared and submitted.

96. The Station Master must take care that all the servants at his station behave respectfully and civilly to the public and passengers of every class.

97. The Station Master must take care that all the servants at his station come on duty at proper times in a clean and tidy state, and in uniform when so required.

98. Every exertion must be made for the expeditious despatch of the station duties, and for ensuring the safety of the public and punctuality of the trains. But no train conveying passengers must be started before the advertised time.

99. The Station Master must report, without delay, to his superior officer, neglect of duty or other misconduct on the part of any of the Railway servants within station limits, and must also forward to his superior officer particulars of any complaint made by the public.

100. The Station Master must see that the proper time-bills and notices are exhibited and renewed when necessary, and that they are removed when out of date.

101. The Station Master must not be absent without leave from his immediate superior; and in cases of illness he must inform his superior officer and take care that some competent person is entrusted with his duties.

102. The Station Master must be careful that all stores supplied for the station are prudently and economically used, and that there is no waste of oil, stationery, &c.

103. The greatest care must be exercised in the cleaning, trimming, and lighting of signal lamps, and Station Masters will be held responsible that this work is efficiently performed. The signal lamps must be lighted and extinguished in accordance with Rule No. 104.

104. Whenever any train or engine is timed to run, or from any cause is expected to run, or any portion of a line later than sunset and before sunrise, the signal lamps must be lighted at sunset. During twilight in the mornings and evenings, both day and night

signals must be used. The signal lights must not be put out until broad day light, except under instructions from an authorized officer.

In foggy or stormy weather, when the day signals cannot be seen plainly, the signal lamps must be lighted, and kept burning, and at such times both day and night signals must be used.

105. The Station Master on duty must look at the head and tail lamps of every passing train, and, if necessary and possible, must see that they are retrimmed. But if the train does not stop at the station, and any of the lamps require trimming, he must immediately telegraph to the station in advance to stop the train and re-trim the lamps.

106. At stations where roof lamps are supplied to trains, Station Masters are responsible that the lamps are properly cleaned and trimmed, and that no smoky, defective, or badly burning lamp is placed in the train.

107. The Station Master is responsible that, immediately on the stopping of each passenger train, the name of the station is called out along the train in a distinct and audible manner, and that the station servants pay immediate attention to any indication shown by the passengers of their desire to alight.

108. No carriage door shall be opened while the train is in motion.

109. When a passenger or mixed train has come to a stand at a station - whether alongside, beyond, or short of the platform – the Driver must not move it for any purpose whatever except upon instructions from the guard, under orders of the person in charge of the Station. The signal for the train to again move must not be given by the Guard until he has satisfied himself that no passenger is getting into, or out of, the train, and that all the carriage doors are closed. Before moving his train the Driver must sound his whistle sharply and distinctly.

110. The Station Master must leave it to the discretion of the Driver to determine what load the engine can take, but every instance of refusal to take the regulation load must be reported to the Traffic Officer.

111. The Station Master is responsible that vehicles standing at the station or sidings are properly secured in accordance with rules prescribed by the authorized officer, and scotch blocks, where provided, fastened.

112. The Station Master is responsible that all safety points and catch sidings, when it is not necessary that they should be opened, are closed against the line which they are intended to protect.

113. Facing points must in all cases be securely fastened or held for the passage of trains or vehicles.

114. No vehicle which is pronounced unfit by the Carriage and Wagon Examiner shall be run on a train; and no vehicle which has been off the road shall be allowed to run on the line between stations unit it has been examined and passed by a competent Examiner, except in this case of derailment outside station limits, when, if the Driver considers it safe, the vehicle may be taken slowly to the next station.

115. No vehicle shall be loaded beyond its marked carrying capacity.

116. Before the commencement of any loading or other operation by which any line of

rails, in use for traffic purposes, may be fouled or obstructed, the person in charge of such operation must obtain the permission of the Station Master, who must see that all necessary steps are taken for the protection of traffic during such obstructions.

117. Carriages, machinery, timber, and other large articles in open trucks must be loaded within the authorized loading dimensions.

118. When the jib of a crane or a load projects beyond its truck, whether standing in a yard or on a running train, it must be protected by a dummy, which dummy may be loaded.

119. Station Masters must see that the shunting of trains, or crossing from one line to another, is performed only at such times and in such manner as will not incur danger.

120. No engine or vehicle must be shunted or moved so as to obstruct the main line until the proper signals have been exhibited, in one or both directions as may be necessary; and care must be taken when the main line is about to be obstructed, after a distant signal has been placed at "Danger" for the purpose of protecting it, that sufficient time is allowed to elapse for any approaching engine or train (which may have been near to or within such signal before it was so placed at "Danger") to pass before the obstruction takes place.

121. Should any vehicle or portion of a train escape from a station, immediate steps must be taken to warn the other station concerned, and prevent accident as far as practicable.

122. When vehicles are shunted at places situated on steep gradients, proper precautions must be taken to prevent any vehicle from running down the incline; a sufficient number of brakes must be put on, and sprags or hand-scotches used, when necessary, to prevent the possibility of any vehicle running away. At such place a supply of scotches must be kept for the purpose. See Rule 210.

123. Fly shunting of vehicles against loaded passenger trains, or of vehicles containing passengers or live stock, is strictly prohibited.

124. The Station Master is responsible that all points, gates, and signals at his station are in proper working order. He must report the particulars of any defects to the nearest Permanent Day Inspector, and must advise his immediate superior.

125. All vehicles shunted off at stations as empties must be carefully searched. The windows and lamp holes of all empty compartments must be closed when the carriages are standing or the sidings at the stations. See Rule 200.

126. Before a train starts, care must be taken that all carriage doors are fastened. The signal to the Driver to start must be given by the Guard, upon receiving intimation from the person in charge of the station, that all is right for the train to proceed. But no train shall be started until the rules of the system of working have been complied with. See Rule 171.

127. Where the block system is not in operation, no train or engine shall be allowed to follow any other train or engine on the same line within ten minutes, unless it has been ascertained that the preceding train has arrived at the next station in advance.

128. When the line is not worked under the block system, no passenger train shall follow a goods train, nor shall a fast goods train follow a stopping passenger train, from a station within fifteen minutes, nor even then, until the Driver has been properly warned

of the time of the departure of the preceding train, and where it will next stop. But in case the distance to the next station in advance exceeds ten miles, the interval must be increased under special instructions of the authorized officer.

129. No passenger train shall be stopped at the station where it is not timed to call, for the purpose of taking up or setting down passengers, without special authority.

130. At stations where Carriage Examiners are kept, the Station Master, before starting the train, must satisfy himself that the examination of it has been completed, and that the train is all right and fit to proceed. Where Examiners are not kept, steps must be taken to remedy any defects that may be observed in the running of vehicles by supplying oil or grease to the axle boxes where required, or removing the defective vehicle from the train when necessary.

131. In case of obstruction or accident, the Station Master must obtain all necessary assistance as soon as possible, and report the occurrence by telegraph, or by the most expeditious means, to the next station on the other side of the accident, so that notice may be given to the Drivers and Guards of approaching trains. See Rule 186.

132. The Station Master nearest to the place at which any accident attended with loss of human life or serious injury to person or property or any accident of a description usually attended with such loss of injury, occurs, must, without unnecessary delay, give notice in writing or by telegraph of such accident to the nearest Magistrate and to the officer incharge of the Police Station in the jurisdiction of which the accident occurs, or to such other Magistrate or Police Officer as the Local Government from time to time appoints in this behalf.

The Station Master must also report to officers of the Railway all accidents in accordance with special instructions.

133. In case a train may have to stop between stations, to take up or put down material, the permission of the Station Master of the last station before the stoppage has to be made, must be obtained, before the train leaves such station. The Station Master must take care to give all necessary instructions.

134. No person shall be allowed, without proper authority, to enter any carriage for the purpose of travelling therein unless the fare has been paid and a ticket obtained. See Rule 199.

135. If any passenger shall refuse, or be unable, to produce a proper ticket, or shall commit any other offence, the case must be immediately investigated by the Station Master, and he is to exercise his discretion as to the proceedings to be taken, always reporting to his immediate superior.

136. The power of arrest and detention is to be exercised with the greatest caution, and never where the address is given, and there is no good and sufficient reason to doubt its correctness; or adequate security is offered for appearance to answer a charge. When it shall be necessary to detain any person, such detention shall not continue for a longer period than is absolutely necessary, but such person must be conveyed before a Magistrate with as little delay as possible.

137. As it is the intention which constitutes the offence, caution and discretion must be

used in treating different cases, as it frequently occurs that passengers travel, unintentionally, beyond the distance for which they have paid their fares. In such cases they may be allowed to return to the station for which they booked on payment of the ordinary single fare for the distance overridden, provided they return by the next train, and do not in the interval, leave the railway premises.

138. Passengers not producing their tickets are required to pay the fare from whence the train started, until enquiry can be made in order to ascertain whether the fare had been previously paid or not; in every case the circumstance must be enquired into without delay and reported. See Rule 199.

139. An account of all unclaimed luggage, and any lost property found on the line and on the Railway premises must be kept by the Station Master, and all such must be dealt with in accordance with special instructions. See Rule 52.

140. In the event of any person being drunk and disorderly, or causing annoyance to others, the Station Master is to use all reasonable means to stop the annoyance, and if the offender persists, the Station Master is to have him removed from the Railway premises, and the offender is liable to prosecution under the Railway Act.

141. Any person found smoking or having an open light or fire in goods sheds or store yards, or who persists in smoking often being warned by a Railway servant or Police Officer to desist on any other portion of the Railway premises where such practice may be deemed dangerous by the authorized officer, shall be liable to immediate removal from the Railway premises, and to a fine which may extend to fifty rupees or, in default of payment of such fine, to simple imprisonment for a term which may extend to two months.

142. No unprotected light shall be allowed in any Railway vehicles.

143. No person suffering from an infectious disease shall enter a Railway carriage or premises without previously notifying to the Station Master that he is so suffering, and obtaining from him permission to enter under special instructions.

144. Any one being in attendance on a person suffering from an infectious disease is subject to the same restrictions while travelling by Railway as if he himself were suffering from the disease.

145. No person suffering from an infections disease is to be allowed to travel in the same compartment with other passengers, but must take and pay for reserved accommodation, and special precaution is to be taken against the infection being communicated to other persons on the Railway premises.

146. Any person found suffering from an infectious disease in a Railway carriage or in any place on a Railway where there is likelihood of the infection spreading, and who has not obtained the permission of the Station Master under Rule 12, is to be removed from the Railway premises, and shall, on conviction under section 268 of the Indian Penal Code, be liable to imprisonment for six months, or to fine, or to both, or on conviction under section 270 of the Indian Penal Code be liable to imprisonment for two years, or to fine, or to both.

147. If any Railway carriage has been entered by a person suffering from an infectious

disease, such carriage must be disinfected immediately after it has arrived at its destination, and no passenger shall be allowed into it until the disinfection has been completed.

148. Prisoners and persons afflicted with insanity must not be allowed to mix with other passengers, but must be placed, with their escort, in a prison-van or separate compartment, upon reserved accommodation being paid for.

149. No engine, or other vehicle, the property of a private owner, shall be allowed to enter upon the main line, except under special arrangement.

SECTION VII
POINTSMEN AND SIGNALMEN

150. Pointsmen must be careful to keep their points clear, and whenever a train or engine has passed, they must remove anything that may have got within the points so as to prevent them from closing.

151. Facing points must, in all cases, be securely fastened or held for the passage of trains or vehicles.

152. Points must not under any circumstances be fastened in any other than the manner prescribed by an authorized officer.

153. Whenever points, crossings, or guide rails are injured, or damaged, the Pointsman must immediately report the circumstance to his superior officer, and, if possible, to the nearest Permanent Way Inspector.

154. Signalmen and Pointsmen must not leave the signals or points of which they have charge during their period of duty.

155. Men in charge of signals must pay particular attention to the rules for working signals.

156. All signals must be kept ready for immediate use. Every man who has charge of, or uses, signals must bring any defect to the notice of his superior.

157. Signalmen and pointsmen must have with them, when on duty, flags and hand signal lamps which must be lighted when necessary.

158. Station signals at junctions must never be passed when at "Danger" by the train to which the signal applies.

159. Station signals at stations, sidings, and signal-boxes (other than at junctions) must never be passed when at "Danger" unless the Driver is signalled past by hand by a person duly appointed by an authorized officer.

160. No line shall be obstructed or occupied by shunting or otherwise, until the signals applicable to it have been placed at "Danger."

161. Should any impediment or obstruction exist upon the line within the sight or knowledge of the Pointsman or Signalman, he must exhibit the "Danger" signals, and must not allow any train or engine to pass in that direction, until such impediment or obstruction has been removed, and the line made clear and safe; and he must, as soon as practicable, take steps to report the obstruction to his superior officer.

162. Whenever any train or engine is timed to run, or from any cause is expected to run, or any portion of a line later than sunset and before sunrise, the signal lamps must be

used lighted at sunset. During twilight in the mornings and evenings, both the day and night signals must be used. The signal light must not be put out until broad day light, except under instructions from an authorized officer.

In foggy weather, when the day signals cannot be seen plainly, the signal lamps must be lighted, and kept burning, and at such times both the day and night signals must be used.

163. If a Signalman or Pointsman observes anything wrong or unusual in a passing train, he must report the circumstance to his superior, but if it is of such a nature as to involve danger to the train or public, he must at once take all practicable steps to stop the train.

SECTION VIII
GUARDS

164. Every Guard must be at the station from which he is to start at the time appointed for his attendance, and must have with him a copy of these regulations and of the working time-tables of the lines over which he has to run.

165. Every Guard must have with him the equipment and stores prescribed by the authorized officer.

166. Guards will receive instructions from the Station Master, or other authorized officer to whom they must apply for anything necessary for the working of their trains.

167. Guards are responsible that their brakes and lamps are in good working order, and that the lamps are trimmed and lighted and brightly burning between sunset and sunrise, and during a fog; also that the vehicles of the train are in good order, and properly coupled up, and that the cord or other appliance for communication between Guard and Driver, if provided, is in order and properly arranged throughout.

168. The train when in motion is under the control of the Guard when there is only one, and of the Head Guard when there are more than one. The passengers and property in the train are under his charge; he is responsible for the safety and regularity of the whole; he must regulate his time-piece in accordance with authorized rules.

169. When there are two or more Guards or Brakesmen with a train, they must obey the instructions of the Head Guard.

170. Each Guard must ride in his proper van and not on the Engine, nor in a carriage or wagon, except under special circumstances.

171. The signal for starting a train must be given to the Driver by the Guard upon receiving the necessary authority in accordance with the system adopted for working the Railway. See Rule 126.

172. After each train has left the platform, and before it reaches the distant signal, the Guard and the Driver must exchange signals with each other. This exchange of signals must also be made whenever a train runs through a station without stopping. The Driver must stop if the proper signals are not exchanged.

173. Every Guard when travelling must keep a good look-out, and should he see any reason to apprehend danger, he must use his best endeavours to attract the attention of the

Driver and give notice to him of the apprehended danger.

174. In the absence of special rules to the contrary, when the Driver gives three or more short sharp whistles, or sounds the brake whistle (when a special whistle is supplied for that purpose), or applies the communication, where such exists, the Guard, or Guards must immediately apply the brakes.

175. In travelling down steep inclines, Guards must, in order to steady the train, assist the Driver, with their brakes of required.

176. The Guards must not allow any person to ride outside the carriages, nor must they permit any unauthorized person to ride in any compartment or vehicle not intended for the conveyance of passengers, except under special arrangements.

177. Guards must see that the doors of the carriages are properly closed.

178. Guards must exert themselves to prevent any breach of the regulation by passengers or others, and report any such breach that comes to their notice.

179. Except as provided in Rule 180, when a train has been stopped, from any cause, outside station limits on the double line, the head Guard must go, or see that a competent person be sent back, showing danger hand signals, having with him detonators (to be used by day as well as by night) to stop any train approaching on the same line of rails.

The person going to protect the train must place upon the rails, on which the train has been running, two detonators ten yards apart, at a distance of three quarters of a mile on a gradient of one in two hundred and fifty or steeper, falling in the direction of the train, or half a mile on any flatter gradient, or on the level, and he must also, on his way out, place one detonator at half those distances respectively. He must remain exhibiting his hand danger signal at the further distance until recalled by engine whistle, or otherwise, when he must leave down the two most distant detonators, taking up the other on his way back.

On a double line, should both roads be found, detonators and hand signals must be used on each line in the manner prescribed, and all trains approaching from either direction must be stopped.

In the case of a single line the train must be protected, in the same manner, in front as well as in rear.

If one, or more, trains approach the obstruction, the train which last arrives must be protected in the rear in the manner prescribed, and when the other train or trains are thus protected in that direction, the person, or persons who protected such other trains can return, and the intermediate detonators may be removed.

When the mixed gauge is laid, detonators must be placed on each rail, both for the broad and the narrow gauge trains.

On the single line the rear of a train must be protected first, and in cases, on the double line when both roads are obstructed and men are not available to send out in both directions at the same time, the Guard must use his discretion as to which road should be first protected.

When necessary a Fireman must be sent out with the signals for the protection of the train.

Should the stoppage occur to an engine not attached to a train, the Driver must take the prescribed precautions for its protection.

On the double road, should both lines be fouled, the Driver must aid the Guard, and at once display a "Danger signal" to the front, and, if the engine is not disabled, it should be used to convey the person who goes forward to the proper distance.

When starting a train which has stopped outside station limits, the Guards and Drivers must exchange signals. Unless these signals are exchanged the Driver must stop.

180. Ballast or other trains, the working of which requires that they must stop outside station limits, may be protected by special regulations; but unless so especially provided for in each case, they must be protected as prescribed in Rule 179.

181. Should an accident to a train cause an obstruction and the Driver run forward without being aware of it, the Guard must take steps in accordance with Rule 179 to protect either or both lines as may be necessary.

182. When a portion of a train is left on the line outside station limits from accident or inability of the engine to take the whole forward, the Guard must put down the brakes and carefully secure the rear portion, so that it will remain stationary, and it must be protected in the manner prescribed in Rule 179. The Driver must not return for the second portion on the same line except upon written instructions from the Guard, and if, upon the double road, no such written instructions are given, the engine must return upon the proper line under the rules of the system adopted for working, and cross at the nearest points to the rear of the part left, which he must work to a station or siding where he can again shunt to the front of the train. If it is necessary for the engine to return to the rear portion of the train on the same line, the Driver must, before starting with the front portion, obtain from the Guard the necessary written instructions authorising him to do so, and the Guard must in such cases continue to protect his train in the rear, and must not permit a following train to move it.

When there are two Guards with a train so divided, the second Guard, or, if there is only one Guard, the Fireman must if practicable, and safe to do so, ride upon the last vehicle of the front portion until it is placed in a siding.

183. No engine shall be allowed to push a train or portion of a train, or fuel truck, unless within station limits, or under special instructions.

184. No engine or vehicle must be shunted or moved so as to obstruct the main line, until the proper signals have been exhibited in one or both directions, as may be necessary; and care must be taken when the main line is about to be obstructed after a Distant Signal has been placed at "Danger" for the purpose of protecting it, that sufficient time is allowed to elapse for any approaching engine or train (which may have been near to or within such signal before it was so placed at "Danger") to pass before the obstruction takes place.

185. Should any part of a train become detached when in motion, care must be taken not to stop the front part before the rear portion has been stopped, and the rear Guard must

promptly apply his brake to prevent a collision with the front portion.

186. In the case of accident or obstruction to trains the Guard must take steps to report in the quickest possible manner to the nearest Station Master, and if the telegraph be injured, or if there be no telegraph, the report must be sent to the Stations on both sides. See Rule 131.

187. When a train is shunted for another train to pass, the side Lamps must be reversed, or so disposed of as not to exhibit the Red Light to a following train.

188. Fly shunting of vehicles against loaded passenger trains, or of vehicles containing passengers or live-stock, is strictly prohibited.

189. Should a Guard observe any irregularity in the working of signals, or any obstruction on the line, or any defect in the signals, works, permanent way, or telegraph, he must report the same at the first station at which the train stops, and also in his journal: and must further report any unusual circumstance which he may have observed during the journey. But should the circumstance involve danger, he must use every endeavour to stop the train at the next station or signal box in order to report it.

190. Except at places specially exempted upon each Railway, the absence of a Signal at a place where a Signal in ordinarily shown, or a Signal imperfectly exhibited, must be considered a Danger Signal and treated accordingly, and the fact reported to the Station Master.

191. Every Guard must make himself acquainted with all instructions requiring his attention on those parts of the line over which he has to work.

192. A brake must be placed at the rear of every train unless special instructions are given to the contrary.

193. When a passenger or mixed train has come to a stand at a station - whether alongside, beyond, or short of the platform - the Driver must not move it for any purpose whatever, except upon instructions from the Guard under orders from the person in charge of the Station. The signal for the train to again move must not be given by the Guard until he has satisfied himself that no passenger is getting into, or out of, the train, and that all the carriage doors are closed. Before moving his train, the Driver must sound his whistle sharply and distinctly.

194. The Guard must take care that passengers enter the proper carriages for the places to which they are booked, and that no passenger is allowed to leave train for the purpose of re-booking by the same train with a view to evade payment of the proper fare.

195. Should a vehicle be attached to, or detached from, the rear of a train at an intermediate station, the Guard, or if there be more than one, the Guard in the rear van, must see that the Tail and Side Lamps are in their proper places on the train.

196. Should complaint be made of the running of any carriage, the Guard must report it to the Station Master, and enter the particulars in his Journal, giving the number and class of carriage; but if the Guard has reason to apprehend danger from such carriage before it can be inspected, he must have it detached from the train.

197. No carriage door shall be opened while the train is in motion.

198. When ladies are travelling alone, the Guards are to pay every attention to their comfort,

and in placing them in the train they must, if requested, endeavour to select a carriage (according to the class of their tickets) in which other ladies are travelling.

199. The Guard must not allow any passenger or parcel to be conveyed by the train unless properly booked; and, if he has reason to suppose that any passenger is without a ticket, or is not in the proper carriage, he must request the passenger to show his ticket, reporting to the Station Master, or person in charge, any irregularity he may detect. When a passenger is desirous of changing from an inferior to a superior class or carriage, on payment of the difference in fare, the Guard must have this arranged by the Station Master or person in charge. See Rules 134 and 138.

200. The windows and lamp-holes of all empty compartments must be closed not only while the carriages are standing at stations, but also when the trains are running. See Rule 125.

201. In case a train may have to stop between stations, to take up or put down material, the permission of the Station Master of the last station before the stoppage has to be made must be obtained before the train leaves such station. The Station Master must take care to give all necessary instructions.

202. No person suffering from an infectious disease shall enter a railway carriage or premises without previously notifying to the Station Master that he is so suffering, and obtaining from him permission to enter under special instructions.

203. Any one being in attendance on a person suffering from an infectious disease is subject to the same restrictions while travelling by railway as if he himself were suffering from the disease.

204. No person suffering from an infectious disease is to be allowed to travel in the same compartment with other passengers, but must take and pay for reserved accommodation, and special precaution is to be taken against the infection being communicated to other persons on the railway premises.

205. Any person found suffering from an infectious disease in a railway carriage or in any place on a railway where there is likelihood of the infection spreading and who has not obtained the permission of the Station Master under Rule 12, is to be removed from the railway premises, and shall, on conviction under section 269 of the Indian Penal Code, be liable to imprisonment for six months, or to fine, or to both, or on conviction under section 270 of the Indian Panel Code, be liable to imprisonment for two years, or to fine, or to both.

206. If any railway carriage has been entered by a person suffering from an infectious disease, such carriage must be disinfected immediately after it has arrived at its destination, and no passenger shall be allowed into it until the disinfection has been completed.

207. Prisoners and persons afflicted with insanity must not be allowed to mix with other passengers, but must be placed with their escort in a prison-van or separate compartment upon reserved accommodation being paid for.

208. In the event of any passenger being drunk or disorderly, or causing annoyance to others, the Guard is to use all reasonable means to stop the annoyance; failing which,

he must, for the safety and convenience of all, have him removed from the train at the first station, and the offender is liable to prosecution under the Railway Act.

209. The Guard in charge must satisfy himself before starting, and during the journey, that the train is properly loaded, marshalled, coupled, lamped, greased or oiled, and sheeted, that lashings and chains are secure, also that the brakes are in good working order, and, as far as he can ascertain, that the train is in a state of efficiency for travelling, and has the proper signals attached to it. He must carefully examine the loading of any vehicles he may attach on the way, and should any vehicle become unsafe from the shifting or derangement of the load, he must, at once, have the load readjusted, or the vehicle removed from the train.

210. When from any cause a train has been brought to a stand on the line, where the line is not level, and it is necessary for the engine to be detached from the train for the purpose of attaching or detaching vehicles, the Guard must, before the engine is uncoupled, satisfy himself that the van-brakes have been put on securely, and, as an additional precaution, must pin down a sufficient number of other brakes, or carry out such other instructions as may be prescribed. See Rule 122.

When the line is level, the van-brakes must be put on securely.

211. Before attaching any travelling crane, the Guard must see that the jib is properly lowered and secured. It must, when practicable, be so placed that the jib will point towards the rear of the train.

212. When a jib of a crane or a load projects beyond its truck, whether standing in a yard or on a running train, it must be protected by dummy, which dummy may be loaded.

213. Guards must not leave their trains until they have been properly handed over.

SECTION IX
DRIVERS AND FIREMEN

214. Drivers and Firemen must be with their engines at such time before starting as the Locomotive Superintendent may require, and must satisfy themselves that their engines are in proper order.

215. Every Driver must have with him, at all times when on duty, such flags, lamps, tools and other appliances or may be ordered by the Locomotive Superintendent from time to time.

He must also have with him a copy of these Regulations, and the working time-tables in force upon the lines over which his engine has to run.

216. No person other than the Driver and Fireman is to ride on the engine or tender without permission from a properly authorized officer.

217. Drivers must always sound the whistle before putting an engine in motion.

218. No engine shall be allowed to be in motion outside station limits unless both the Driver and Fireman are upon it.

219. Every Driver must make himself acquainted with all instructions requiring his attention on those parts of the line over which he has to work.

220. The Driver must place his engine in front of the train not less than five minutes before

the time of starting; after that time, and until the end of the journey, he will receive his orders from the Guard in all matters affecting the starting, stopping or movement of the train; and he must promptly obey all orders or signals given to him, whether by the Station Master or the Guard, so far as the safe and proper working of his engine will allow.

221. The Driver must afford such assistance with his engine as may be required for the formation, arrangement and despatch of his train.

222. Fireman must obey the orders of the Driver in all particulars, and they are held jointly responsible with the Driver for the proper observance of all Rules and Regulations.

223. The Driver and Fireman must, frequently, during the journey, look back and see that the whole of the train is following in a safe and proper manner.

224. The signal for starting a train must be given to the Driver by the Guard, but before starting the Driver must have the permission prescribed by the rules of the system adopted for working the line and must satisfy himself that the line before him is clear, and he must sound the whistle.

225. No engine shall enter upon or cross the main line without the permission of the person in charge of the points and signals, and the Driver must satisfy himself that the proper signal has been exhibited.

226. The Driver must, before starting, see that his lamps are in good order, and that his engine carries the proper distinguishing lights, or other indicators of the train. At and after sunset, and during foggy weather, he must have the necessary lamps lighted. He is responsible that they are always in proper order and trimmed, and that, when lighted, they burn brightly.

227. The Driver must keep a good look-out all the time the engine is in motion, and Firemen must also keep a look-out, when not necessarily otherwise engaged.

228. The Driver and Fireman must carefully observe all signals; and when from fog or storm, or any cause, the fixed signals are not visible, as soon as usual, every possible precaution must be used, especially in approaching stations and junctions, so that the train can be stopped short of any obstruction, should the signals be against it.

229. The Driver must regulate the running of his engine as accurately as practicable, according to the Working Time-Table, so as to avoid extreme speed, or loss of time.

230. No Driver shall run his engine with tender, or any portion of a train, or fuel-truck, foremost (except within station limits), without written order, or unless in cases of unavoidable necessity, to be established by the Driver.

231. Station signals are placed at stations, junctions, sidings outside station limits, and signal boxes, and when at "Danger", no train or engine must pass them, or foul the crossings or points to which they apply, except as prescribed in Rules 233 and 235.

232. Station signals at junctions must never be passed when at "Danger" by the train to which the signal applies.

233. Station signals at stations, sidings, and signals-boxes (other than at junctions) must never be passed when at "Danger", unless the Driver is signalled post by hand by a person duly appointed by an authorized officer.

234. When a distant signal is at "Danger," the engine-driver of an approaching train must bring his train to a "*dead stop*" outside of it, and must then ascertain if the line is clear to admit the train within it. If the line be clear he must at once draw the train cautiously within the distant signal so as to be protected by it, and then stop until signalled into the station in accordance with rules prescribed by the authorized Officer. If, however, there is any obstruction on the Line so near to the distant signal as to prevent the whole of the train from passing safely within it, the rules for the protection of trains when stopped outside station limits, must be immediately carried out. See Rule 240.

235. Station and distant signals apply only to trains or engines running in the proper direction, and must not be used for any other purpose. Trains or engines shunting from one main line to another, or shunting into, or out of, sidings connected with the main line, must, unless special signals are provided for the purpose of signalling such operations, be signalled past the station signal, either verbally, or by hand lamp or flag, as occasion may require; it being necessary, in such cases, that the danger signal should be exhibited at the station signal, as well as at the distant signal, for the protection of the train or engine so employed.

236. The Driver and Fireman must pay immediate attention to and obey all signals, whether the cause of the signal being shown is known to them or not. The Driver must not, however, trust entirely to signals, but must, on all occasions, be vigilant and cautious.

237. A detonator explodes with a loud report when an engine passes over it, and the Driver must stop as quickly as possible, and then proceed cautiously to the place of obstruction, or until he receives he "All Right" signal. See Rule 84.

238. Except at places specially exempted upon each Railway, the absence of a signal at a place where a signal is ordinarily shown, or a signal imperfectly exhibited, must be considered a danger signal, and treated accordingly, and the fact reported to the Station Master.

239. When, from any cause, an engine, or train without a Guard, is stopped upon the line outside station limits unprotected by fixed signals, the Driver must send his Fireman, or some other competent person with signals, to protect the engine or train during the time it is in such a position, in the manner prescribed for the Guards in Rule 240.

240. Except as provided in Rule 241, when a train has been stopped, from any cause, outside station limits on the double line, the head Guard must go, or see that a competent person be sent back, showing danger hand signals, having with him detonators (to be used by day as well as by night), to stop any train approaching on the same line of rails.

The person going to protect the train must place upon the rails on which the train has been running, two detonators 10 yards apart, at a distance of three quarters of a mile on a gradient of one in two hundred and fifty (1/250) or steeper, falling in the direction of the train, or half a mile on any flatter gradient, or on the level, and he must also, on his way out, place one detonator at half those distances respectively. He must remain exhibiting his hand danger signal at the further distance until recalled by engine whistle, or otherwise, when he must leave down the two most distant detonators, taking up the other on his way back.

On a double line, should both roads be folded, detonators and hand signals must be used on each line in the manner prescribed, and all trains approaching from either direction must be stopped.

In the case of a single line the train must be protected, in the same manner, in front as well as in rear.

If one, or more, trains approach the obstruction, the train which last arrives must be protected in the rear in the manner prescribed, and when the other train or trains are thus protected in that direction, the person or persons, who protected such other trains can return, and the intermediate detonators may be removed.

When the mixed gauge is laid, detonators must be placed on each rail, both for the broad and the narrow gauge trains.

On the single line the rear of a train must be protected first, and in cases on the double line, when both roads are obstructed and men are not available to be sent out in both directions at the same time, the Guard must use his discretion as to which road should be first protected.

When necessary a Fireman must be sent out with the signals for the protection of the train.

Should the stoppage occur to an engine not attached to a train, the Driver must take the prescribed precautions for its protection.

On the double road, should both lines be fouled, the Driver must aid the Guard and at once display a "danger signal" to the front, and, if the engine is not disabled, it should be used to convey the person who goes forward to the proper distance.

When starting a train which has stopped outside station limits, the Guard and Driver must exchange signals. Unless these signals are exchanged the Driver must stop.

241. Ballast or other trains the working of which requires that they must stop outside station limits may be protected by special regulations; but unless so specially provided for in each case they must be protected as prescribed in rule 240.

242. Should any part of a train become detached when in motion, care must be taken not to stop the front part before the rear portion has been stopped, and the rear Guard must promptly apply his brake to prevent a collision with the front portion.

243. When a portion of a train is left on the line outside station limits from accident or inability of the engine to take the whole forward, the Guard must put down the brakes and carefully secure the rear portion, so that it will be remain stationary, and it must be protected in the manner prescribed in rule 240. The Driver must not return for the second portion on the same line except upon written instructions from the Guard, and if, upon the double road, no such written instructions are given, the engine must return upon the proper line under the rules of the system adopted for working, and cross at the nearest points to the rear of the part left, which he must work to a station or siding where he can again shunt to the front of the train. If it is necessary for the engine to return to the rear portion of the train on the same line, the Driver must,

before starting with the front portion, obtain from the Guard the necessary written instructions authorizing him to do so, and the Guard must in such cases continue to protect his train in the rear, and must not permit a following train to move it.

When there are two Guards with a train so divided, the second Guard, or, if there is only one Guard, the Fireman must, if practicable and safe to do so, ride upon the last vehicle of the front portion until it is placed in a siding.

244. Drivers must not pass through facing points at a speed exceeding ten (10) miles per hour.

245. In the absence of special rules to the contrary, when a Driver requires the assistance of the Guards brake, he must give three or more short, sharp whistles, or sound the brake whistle (when a special whistle is supplied for that purpose), and apply the communication, where such exists. See Rule 174.

246. No engine shall be allowed to push a train, or portion of a train or fuel truck, unless within station limits, or under special instructions.

247. When two or more engines are employed in drawing the same train, the Driver and Fireman of the leading engine are responsible for the observance of signals; the Drivers of the other engines must watch for and take signals from the Driver of the leading engine.

248. On both double and single line between sunset and sunrise and during foggy weather, every train must exhibit a red tail light and two red side lights in rear of the train; and every engine running alone must exhibit at least one Red Tail Light; in both cases Head Lights prescribed by the authorized Officer must be exhibited.

In the case of two or more engines running coupled together without a train, the first engine only must exhibit the prescribed Head Lights and the last engine only must exhibit at least one Red Tail Light.

This rule does not apply to engines and trains doing station work.

249. Whenever on the double line a Driver observes any thing wrong on the road opposite to that on which he is running, he must sound his whistle and exhibit "Danger" signal to any train he may meet, and stop at the first signal-box or station in order to report that which he has observed.

250. Whenever on the double line a Driver observes a train following too closely any preceding train on the road opposite to that on which he is running, he must sound his whistle and exhibit a caution or danger signal, as occasion may require, to warn the Driver of such following train.

251. The Driver must start and stop his train steadily and without a jerk.

He must exercise care in approaching all stations at which his train is required to stop and in passing stations at which he is not required to stop. In stopping his train he must pay particular attention to the state of the weather and the condition of the rails, as well as to the length of the train; and these circumstances must have due weight in determining when the shut off steam.

252. Should another train be approaching, stopping at, or leaving the station, on the opposite line, or should shunting operations be going on, the Driver must, on approaching and

whilst passing through a station, sound the engine whistle.

The whistle must also be sounded on entering a tunnel, and repeated in long tunnels.

253. On the double line trains must invariably be run on the left hand road except under special instructions to the contrary.

254. When a passenger or mixed train has come to a stand at a station-whether alongside, beyond, or short of the platform- the Driver must not move it for any purpose whatever except upon instructions from the Guard under order of the person in charge of the station. The signal for the train to again move must not be given by the Guard until he has satisfied himself that no passenger is getting into, or out of, the train, and that all the carriage doors are closed. Before moving his train, the Driver must sound his whistle sharply and distinctly.

255. When the block system is not in operation, no train or engine shall be allowed to follow any other train or engine on the same line within ten minutes, unless it has been ascertained that the preceding train has arrived at the next station in advance.

256. When the line is not worked under the block system, no passenger train shall follow a goods train, nor shall a fast goods train follow a stopping passenger train from a station within fifteen minutes, nor even then, until the Driver has been properly warned of the time of the departure of the preceding train, and where it will next stop. But in case the distance to the next station in advance exceeds ten miles, the interval must be increased under special instructions of the authorized Officer.

257. Should a Driver observe any irregularity in the working of signals, or any obstruction on the line or defect in the signals, or any defect in the works, permanent way or telegraph, he must report the same at the first station at which he stops, and at the end of his journey he must also report any other unusual circumstance that he may have observed.

But should the circumstance involve danger he must stop at the next station or signal-box in order to report; and should it be necessary for the safety of the traffic he must stop at once.

258. Fly shunting of vehicles against loaded passenger trains, or of vehicles containing passengers or live-stock, is strictly prohibited.

259. If an engine is running without a Guard, the Driver is responsible for carrying out all rules and for taking all necessary precautions which the Guard is required to observe for the safe working and protection of trains.

260. Should a Driver observe a train or engine obscured by steam or smoke, on the opposite line to that on which he is travelling or on a siding, he must sound his whistle and approach it cautiously so as to be able to stop if necessary.

261. A green flag or a green light exhibited by Platelayers indicates that speed must not exceed fifteen miles an hour, or such lower speed as may be ordered, over the portion of line protected by such signal.

262. Shunting engines employed in station yards and signals must, after sunset and in foggy weather, carry the prescribed head and tail lights.

263. After taking water from tanks or water columns, Drivers must be careful to leave the hose or water crane clear of the main line and properly secured.
264. The Driver when on duty at stations or on the line must not leave his engine unless it is absolutely necessary for him to do so, and, under no circumstances, without a man being left in charge of it.
265. Drivers with trains or engines must run within the limits of speed fixed for the section of the line upon which they are running.
266. Drivers with engines or trains must not make up between any two stations more time than is allowed to be made up in that distance by an authorized officer.

SECTION X
INSPECTORS, PLATELAYERS, GANGERS, AND OTHERS EMPLOYED ON THE PERMANENT WAY

267. The Inspector or person in charge of each district of the line will be held responsible for the condition of the permanent way and works in his district. He must keep an account of all materials used, and must see that none are wasted. He must also report promptly to the Engineer in charge of the district all accidents, and all defects in the road or works that may interfere with the safe running of trains.
268. In each gang of platelayers or men repairing the permanent way, there shall be a Foreman, Ganger or Mistry; and the inspector of permanent way for the district must take care that every such man in charge of a gang is provided with a copy in the vernacular of the section of these Regulations which relates to his duties, also with proper signals, a permanent-way gauge, and all necessary tools which he must inspect at least once a month and ascertain that the gauges are correct, and the tools and signals are in good order, and that no articles have been lost.
269. Each Foreman, Ganger or Mistry is responsible that the subordinates working under him are acquainted with all the rules relating to their respective duties.
270. Each gang of platelayers or labourers must be supplied by the Inspector of permanent way for the district with two sets of flag signals, two hand signal lamps, and a proper number of detonators. Such Ganger will be held responsible for having his signals constantly in proper order and ready for use.
271. The Inspector must take care that all Regulations are observed, and report any departure from them to the Engineer.
272. Each Inspector must have a register of the name and place of residence of all the Foremen and Gangers employed in his district, so that, in case of accident, he may be enabled to call upon them to summon their men immediately to assist in any way that may be required; and should any obstruction take place, caused by slips, or other sudden emergency, each Foreman or Ganger must immediately collect the men required.
273. The signals to be used by the men engaged in repairing the permanent way are red and green flags, and hand lamps and detonators. The flags must be used during day light, the lamps after sunset and in foggy weather, and the detonators when necessary,

by day and night.

The red and detonating signals indicate "Danger," and must be used only when it is necessary to stop a train. The green signal indicates "Caution," and must be used when it is necessary to slacken the speed of a train.

274. A green flag or a green light, exhibited by Platelayers, indicates that speed must not exceed fifteen miles an hour, or such lower speed as may be ordered over the position of the line protected by such signal.

275. The permanent-way staff or others must not put in points and crossings without the written authority of the Engineer in charge of the district, and must not being or perform any operation which will involve danger to trains or traffic without the previous permission of the Permanent-way Inspector, or other authorized competent persons, who must himself be present to superintend such operation, and who is responsible that all necessary signals are shown and other precautions taken as prescribed in Rules 276 and 277, as the case may be, before the commencement of work, and that such signals and precautions are continued until the line is again clear for trains or traffic. But in case of emergency when it may be necessary for safety to replace to turn any rail or otherwise obstruct traffic before the Inspector can arrive, the Ganger or other person in charge of the gang must take all necessary steps to protect trains and traffic as prescribed in Rules 276 and 277.

276. When it is necessary within station limits to change or turn a rail, or in any manner to obstruct the line, or to do any work of a character to make the exhibition of a signal necessary, the permission of the Station Master must be first obtained by the Foreman, Platelayer or Ganger, and, the work must not be commenced until all necessary signals have been placed at "Danger," and the signals must remain in that position until the Station Master, or Ganger, is informed by the same Platelayer that the line is again clear and safe for traffic.

The Platelayers must, in addition, protect their operations by hand signals.

277. When outside station limits a rail has to be taken out, or the line is not safe from any cause, a "Danger" signal must be exhibited, and two detonators placed on the line, ten yards apart, at a distance of at least three-quarters of a mile on a gradient of one in two hundred and fifty or steeper, falling in the direction of the obstruction, and half a mile on a flatter gradient or on the level, in rear of the place of obstruction on the double line, and in both directions on a single line; and hand signals must also be exhibited at the place where the work is being done.

278. Platelayers and labourers must not, except in case of emergency, or as provided in Rule 276, avail themselves of the Fixed Signals, and must, in all cases, use their own special signals for their own purposes.

279. In case a train may have to stop between stations to take up or put down material, the permission of the Station Master of the last station before the stoppage has to be made must be obtained before the train leaves such station. The Station Master must take care to give all necessary instructions.

280. When repairing, lifting the line or performing any operation so as to make it necessary

for a train to proceed cautiously, the Foreman or Ganger must send a man back at least quarter of mile and as much further as the circumstances of the case render necessary, exhibit the "Caution" Signal so as to be plainly visible to the Driver of an approaching train.

281. In no case, except when absolutely necessary, is a rail to be displaced or any other work to be performed, by which an obstruction may be made to the passage of the trains during a fog or storm; and the times for effecting repairs which involve the stopping of trains must, as far as practicable, be so selected as to interfere as little as possible with the passage of the traffic.

282. A lorry or truck, loaded or empty, used for conveying materials, must be taken in the same direction as that in which the trains run on double line, and must be followed at a distance of not less than half a mile by a man with Danger hand-signals and detonators. In the case of a single line where trains run in both directions, the lorry or truck must be protected in both directions.

On no occasion must a lorry be run in the wrong direction on a double line.

283. No lorry, used for the conveyance of material, or trolly for the conveyance of men, may, in any case, be placed on the line, except by the authorized person who is responsible for its proper protection and use according to the rules in force on the Railway.

284. No lorry or trolly shall, under any circumstances, be attached to a train, and all lorries and trollies, when not in use, must be taken off the rails, placed well clear of the line, and the wheels secured with chain and padlock.

285. No Ballast train, wagon, truck, lorry, or other impediment shall be allowed to be on any part of the main line within ten minutes of a train being due, except on lines worked on the block system when the time must not be less than five minutes; and excepting in cases of accident, or absolute necessity, all repairs must be effected, and the line made clear and safe for the passage of trains not less than ten, or five minutes, as the case may be, before a train is due. See Rule 317.

286. All persons in charge of Ballast trains must obey the orders of Station Masters so far as relates to the time of their running on the line, and no Driver of a ballast train must leave a siding without the necessary permission.

287. Guards of Ballast trains are responsible for carrying out Rules 179 and 180, and all other regulations prescribed for Guards for the protection of trains.

288. Ballast trains must not work between stations in a fog except when authorized under special circumstances, and no Ballast train, wagon, truck or lorry must be run, if it can be avoided, except during daylight, and when the weather is sufficiently clear for a signal to be distinctly seen at a distance of half a mile. But when necessary to run a Ballast train at night, or during a fog, it must be protected by the prescribed lights. See Rules 313.

289. Any accident of a train or engine, or failure of any part of the works affecting the safety of the line, must be reported as soon as possible to the nearest Inspector of permanent way and to the Station Masters on both sides of the point at which the

accident or failure has occurred.

290. Every portion of the permanent way must be inspected daily on foot by some authorized person responsible for its condition; and bridges and all other works (including signals and signal wires) must be regularly inspected in accordance with rules laid down by the authorized officer.

291. Each Foreman, Ganger or Mistry must report to the Inspector of permanent way when any telegraph post appears to be in an unsafe state, or any of the signal or telegraph wires are broken slack, entangled, or touching each other or any building. He must also see that all grass, creepers, boughs of trees, and rubbish are removed from the wires.

Where the maintenance of the telegraph posts and wires is under the control of the Government Telegraph Department, the removal of grass, creepers, boughs of trees, and rubbish will be carried out by the Government Telegraph Officers, and all reports of defects in posts and wires should be made to the officers of the Department by the Inspector.

292. In lifting the permanent way, no lift must be greater than three inches at once, and then it must be effected in such a manner as not to occasion any sudden change of gradient. Both rails must be raised equally and at the same time, and if possible the ascent must be made in the direction in which the trains run.

293. No Ballast shall be thrown up to a higher level between the rails than three inches on the 5 feet 6 inch gauge, and not higher than rail level on the metre or other narrow gauge, and it must be thrown as much as possible on the outside of each line, or between the two roads. The rails must be kept clear of gravel, ballast, or any other material.

294. No vehicle shall be left in any siding outside station limits without the wheels being properly secured, clear of all running lines.

295. No blasting shall be allowed on or near to the Railway, without the authority of the Engineer in charge.

296. Gangers must close and fasten all gates they find open, and report the circumstances.

297. Each Foreman, Ganger or Mistry must, in the event of a flood, carefully examine the action of the water through culverts and bridges on his length of line; and should he see any cause to apprehend danger to the works, he must immediately exhibit the proper signals for the trains to proceed cautiously, or to stop, as necessity may require, and inform the Inspector thereof; and until the Inspector arrives he must take precautionary measures for securing the safety and stability of the line.

298. In the event of any fire upon or near the line, the men employed on the line must take immediate measures for putting it out.

299. Gangers must keep clean the working parts of points and signals, unless the duty is otherwise specially provided for.

300. Each Foreman or Ganger must keep his portion on the line clear and safe and the fences in repair; and if any sheep, cattle, or other animals be on the line or within the fences, he must immediately remove them, and report the circumstance to the Inspector

of permanent way.

301. Foremen or Gangers must see that all broken chairs, rails, sleepers, or other defective materials, are removed from the road with the least possible delay, and sound materials substituted.

All tools, rails, sleepers, pieces of iron or wood, or other implements or materials, must be carefully placed so as to be quite clear of the line, and not within three feet of the rails.

302. Each Inspector of permanent way will be held responsible for the security of all rails, chairs, sleepers, and other permanent way materials, in his district. They must be kept clear of both lines and properly stacked.

303. Each Foreman or Ganger is responsible on his own length of line for the security of tools and implements supplied to him.

304. When a train is approaching, Platelayers and labourers must stop work and stand clear of all the lines.

305. Each Foreman or Ganger will be responsible for collecting any coupling chains, hooks, pins, iron, or other materials which may be found on the line, and for having them conveyed to the nearest station.

306. All luggage, goods, or articles found on the line, must be taken to the nearest station, and a report made containing the best information that can be obtained respecting the train from which they may have fallen.

307. Gangers and others employed on the line must order of the Railway all trespassers, who, if they persist in remaining, may be immediately removed from the Railway by any Railway servant or by any other person.

SECTOIN XI
REGULATIONS FOR BALLASTING

308. Ballast trains must, except where specially exempted, be worked under the same rules and regulations as other trains.

309. Guards and Brakesman of Ballast trains shall be experienced men selected from the Train Guards.

310. A Guard or Brakesman must accompany each Ballast train.

311. The Guard or Brakesman of a Ballast train has authority to require those employed in repairing the permanent way and works to assist him in working signals.

312. No Ballasting is to be carried on except with the permission of the Engineer in charge of the section of the Railway.

313. Ballast trains are prohibited from passing along the main line at night, or in a fog, or during a heavy rain, except when authorized to do so under special circumstances, and then must not move faster than fifteen miles an hour. But when necessary to run a Ballast train at night, or during a fog, it must be protected by the prescribed lights. See Rule 288.

314. The Guard of a Ballast train is held responsible for keeping clear of all other trains. When a Ballast train has to work on the line between two stations, the Guard must,

when practicable, arrange with both Station Masters where and when the next train is to be passed.

315. In case a train may have to stop between stations to take up or put down material, the permission of the Station Master of the last station before the stoppage has to be made must be obtained before the train leaves such station. The Station Master must take care to give all necessary instructions.

316. The Guard must, before leaving a station, receive a line clear message with the necessary instructions endorsed upon it, or the usual authority for leaving a station in accordance with the system in force for working the traffic.

317. No Ballast train, wagon, truck, lorry, or other impediment shall be allowed to be on any part of the main line within ten minutes of a train being due, except on lines worked on the block system, when the time must be not less than five minutes. See Rule 285.

318. When a Ballast train is intended to run through from one station to another, without working between them, it must be treated as an ordinary or special train.

319. When Ballast wagons are left on a siding outside station limits, the Guard must secure a wheel of the wagon nearest to the points of the siding, and he is responsible that the vehicles are properly secured in accordance with rules prescribed by the authorized officer, and that the scotch blocks, were provided, are fastened.

320. Ballast trains, the working of which requires that they must stop outside station limits, may be protected by special regulations; but unless so specially provided for in each case they must be protected as prescribed in Rule 179.

321. Ballast trains may be run with a pushing engine on a written order, but in such cases the speed must not exceed fifteen miles an hour, or such lower speed as may be ordered.

322. Guards in charge of Ballast trains must, before giving the starting signal, tell the coolies working with the train and riding in the open trucks to sit down.

SECTION XII
GATEMEN AT LEVEL-CROSSINGS

323. All level-crossings of which the gates close across the Railway must be provided with red signal boards, and with lamps showing red, up and down the line, when the gates are closed across the line. The lamps must be kept lighted from sunset to sunrise and during foggy weather.

324. Every Gateman must be provided with day and night signals, which he must keep in proper order, reporting immediately any defect he may observe to his superior officer.

325. Unless specially ordered to the contrary, the gates at all thoroughfares must be kept open for the passage of trains, and securely closed across the thoroughfare, except when required to be opened for the road traffic, and must then as quickly as possible be closed again across the thoroughfare. Before opening the gates the gateman must look up and down the line to assure himself that no train is approaching.

326. Where special authority is given, gates made to close across the Railway may be kept open to the public thoroughfare; except when an engine or train is due or expected, at

which time such gates must be closed and fastened across the public thoroughfare; and until such engine or train has passed, the gates must be kept closed, and no person or thing is to be allowed within them. While the gates are closed across the Railway and open to the thoroughfare, the "Danger" signal must be exhibited both up and down the line. In opening double gates closing across the Railway for an approaching train where there is only one signal lamp to each gate, the half with the signal lamp attached is not to be moved until the other half is shut across the thoroughfare.

327. The gate towards which road traffic is approaching must not be opened until the opposite gate has been opened, so as to allow it to cross over without stopping upon the line.

328. Every gateman must take particular notice of each train, and if he should see anything wrong, he must show a "Danger" signal to the Guard and Driver.

329. In all cases the Gateman, when signalling, is to stand in a position clear of the rails where he can be seen by the approaching Driver.

330. All Gateman must have a knowledge of hand signals.

331. If any gates or fastenings are out of order, the Gateman must immediately report to his superior officer, and to the nearest Platelayer, in order that the gates may be made safe.

332. Gatemen are to prevent as much as possible any trespassing on the Railway, and every case of the trespass must be immediately reported; and they are also to report any irregularity in the signals, or their working, or other infringement of the Railway Regulations.

333. Gateman must keep themselves, and their clothes and hats, neat and clean; they must also take care that the channel for the flange of the wheels is always clear before passage of each train; that the rails and way are clear, and that rubbish is not allowed to accumulate near the hut and crossings.

334. In the event of the road being from any caused obstructed, the Gateman must do everything in his power by warning approaching trains to prevent accident.

335. At the level crossings where fixed signals are provided, the Gateman must satisfy himself of the proper working of his signals both by day and by night, and must report immediately any defect to the Inspector of permanent way, or other person in charge of the repair of signals, and also to the Station Master, or other person, under whose supervision he acts.

336. At level-crossings where the block system is not in operation, and where there are fixed signals, the "Danger" signal must be exhibited for at least five minutes after the passing of any train, after which, if the gates are open for the passage of trains, a "Caution" signal must be exhibited for a further period of five minutes.

SECTION XIII

GENERAL RULES FOR WORKING A LINE ON THE SYSTEM TERMED "LINE CLEAR AND CAUTION MESSAGE" IN RULE 3, SECTION II

337. The working of trains on the "Line clear and caution message" system does not in any

way dispense with the use of station distant or other signals whenever and wherever such signals may be requisite.

338. On a single line no engine with or without a train shall be permitted to leave one station for another until it shall have been ascertained by means of electric telegraph that the line between those stations is clear of engines and trains coming in the opposite direction, and of all impediments as far as can be known.

Trains may follow one another between stations in the same direction, on both single and double line, under the following rules; and in accordance with Rule 339.

(a) No train or engine shall be allowed to follow any other train or engine on the same line of rails within ten minutes, unless "Line clear" has been received.

(b) No passenger train shall follow a goods train, nor shall a fast goods train follow a stopping passenger train from a station within fifteen minutes; and in case the distance to the next station in advance exceeds ten miles, the interval must be increased under special instructions of the authorized officer.

339. When one train follows another at an interval exceeding the limits laid down in Rule 338, it must run under the authority of a "Caution message" obtained in the manner prescribed in the rules in force on each Railway.

340. No one except the Station Master or other duly authorized person is to give or seek a line clear or caution message.

341. A Station Master must not apply for a line clear message from the station in advance, until he has received advice that the approaching train has left the station in rear.

342. No engine or train shall be moved from any station until the Driver has in his possession a "Line clear," "Caution message" or other permission written on the authorized from showing that he can proceed to the next station. The Driver is to receive this written permission from no other person than the Guard of his own train, and must also receive from him the usual starting signal before moving.

343. The Station Master is to hand the written permission to the Guard, who must satisfy himself that it is properly filled up and dated, with the time added and is signed in full and in ink, and that it applies to the particular train or engine for which it is given and received, before handing it to the Driver. The Driver must also satisfy himself on these points before starting.

This written permission is never to be given to the Driver until the train is to start, and when waiting to pass another train, it must not be given to the Driver until the whole of such other train has come in and is clear of the points.

344. No forms other than those specially provided from time to time for the purpose are to be used in working under this system. And each station must keep the regular books provided for by the working orders in force.

345. The leaves of these books are to be progressively numbered in type, and when any message has from any caused to be cancelled, the form to which it applies must also be marked as cancelled both on the form and counterfoil, and must be carefully preserved by doubling it on the counterfoil.

346. In addition to the progressive printed number every message from each station must be numbered to stations on each side from midnight to midnight, commencing with number one to each station, and this number is to be treated as a portion of the message and entered on the counterfoil.
347. When a message is in reply to another, each station number must be quoted at the beginning of the message.
348. When the message bears reference to a former message in the same direction, the number of that message must also be quoted at the beginning.
349. In train messages the engine or train must be distinctly described, as, for instance, "No. 2 Down ballast," "No. 4 Up goods," and so on; and for every train a separate enquiry and reply must be sent, but an enquiry and reply message must never be sent on one form.
350. In line clear enquiries, the time of arrival of the last train in the opposite direction must always be given. If the train follows another on a caution message, the time of departure of the proceeding train must be endorsed on the message.
351. After a line clear message has been given and has been subsequently cancelled, no train is to be started in the opposite direction on a single line until a telegram has been received stating that the train for which the line clear had been first given is and will be detained, and that the message has been cancelled.
352. No part of any message affecting the passage of trains must be forwarded or acted upon until the whole is written out, except when an accident may be prevented, or in other case of emergency.
353. Line clear or caution permissions are not to be written out in full or in part, or signed, before they are required.
354. All messages connected with train working, including line clear authorities, are to be written in ink or other indelible substance, and are also to be signed in full by the Station Master or other authorized person.
355. Line clear and enquiry messages must be written for at least a fort-night.
356. In case of failure or interruption of telegraph communication, trains must be worked between stations in accordance with prescribed rules.

SECTION XIV
RULES FOR WORKING ON THE SYSTEM TERMED "TRAIN FOLLOWING" IN RULE 3, SECTION II

357. This system is applicable only to double line working.
358. Trains may follow one another in accordance with the following rules.
359. No train or engine shall be allowed to follow another train or engine on the same line of rails within ten minutes unless it has been ascertained by the telegraph that the preceding train has arrived at the next station in advance.
360. No passenger train shall follow a goods train, nor shall a fast goods train follow a stopping passenger train, from a station within fifteen minutes, nor even then until the Driver has been warned in accordance with Rule 362. And in case the distance to

the next station in advance exceeds ten miles, the interval must be increased under special orders.

361. Should a train arrive at a station within the limits of time in Rules 359 and 360, it must be stopped until the prescribed interval has elapsed.

362. When one train follows another before the first has reached the next station, the Station Master must caution the Guard and Driver of the second train, giving them the time of departure of the preceding train. The order to proceed must be given in writing, and an acknowledgement in writing must be obtained from the Driver, the train being stopped act of course if not booked to stop.

SECTION XV
GENERAL REGULATIONS FOR WORKING ON THE SYSTEM TERMED "ABSOLUTE BLOCK" IN RULE 3, SECTION II

363. The object of the system of Electric Train-signalling is to prevent more than one train or engine being between any two Signal Stations on the same line at the same time. This is accomplished by not allowing any train or engine to leave a Signal Stations till the previous train or engine has been signalled clear.

364. The Block System of train working by Electric Train-signalling does not in any way dispense with the use of outdoor and hand signals, whenever and wherever such signals may be requisite.

365. The Special Electric train Instruments, if provided, are exclusively for the signalling of trains, and must not, under any circumstances, be used for conversing nor for any purpose other than block working in strict accordance with prescribed rules, and they must only be used by the person appointed for the duty.

366. On those portions of any Railway which are worked on the Absolute Block System, a train or engine must not be allowed to enter any section until it has been ascertained by telegraph that the section is clear of trains or engines.

Except when otherwise specified, a section is to be understood to be the line between two stations outside station limits.

367. Should there be reason to suppose that from accident or otherwise either or both lines are obstructed, care must be taken to advise other stations concerned so as to prevent trains from entering the section.

368. In the event of any failure of the instruments so that the necessary signals cannot be forwarded and received, trains must be worked under Rule 338, and if telegraph communication is entirely interrupted, trains must be worked between stations in accordance with the prescribed rules.

SECTION XVI
REGULATIONS FOR WORKING SINGLE LINE OF RAILWAY ON THE SYSTEM TERMED "TRAIN STAFF AND TICKET" IN RULE 3, SECTION II

369. The Train staff and Ticket System of train working does not in way dispense with the

use of outdoor and hand signals, whenever and wherever such signals may be requisite.

370. The Working Time-tables will contain the necessary information from time to time as to the places which are appointed staff stations.

371. A Train Staff or Train Staff Ticket must be carried with each train or engine, and without this staff or ticket, no train or engine must be allowed to leave any station.

372. No train or engine shall be permitted to leave any staff station unless the staff for that portion of the line over which it is to travel is then at the station.

373. The person in charge of the station for the time being is the only person authorized to receive and deliver the staff or ticket, and all tickets must be cancelled directly they are handed to him after use.

374. When a train or engine is ready to start from a station, and no second train or engine is intended to follow before the staff will be required for a train in the opposite direction, it is the duty of the person in charge of the station to give the staff to the Driver, who shall then place it in a conspicuous place provided for that purpose on the engine.

375. If other trains or engines are intended to follow in succession before the staff can be returned, a Ticket indicating that the staff is following must be given by the person in charge of the station to the Driver of the first train or engine, the staff for the section being shown to him and so on with any other train or engine, except the last the staff itself being given to the Driver of the last train or engine, as directed in Rule 374. After the staff has been sent away, no other train or engine must, under any circumstances, leave the station to follow in the same direction until the staff for that station has been returned.

376. No Driver with a train or engine shall leave a station until he has received the proper staff or ticket for that section of the line over which he is about to travel, and he must not take the staff or ticket from any other than the person in charge of the station for the time being. After receiving the staff or ticket, he must not start until the proper signals have been exhibited, nor, when with a train, until a signal has also be given by the Guard. But he must not accept a Ticket in any case unless he sees the staff at the same time in the possession of the person who gives him such ticket. On arriving at the station to which the staff or ticket extends, such staff or ticket must immediately be given up to the person in charge of the station and all tickets, so given up, must be immediately cancelled.

377. Each staff must have shown upon it the name of the staff station at each end of the portion of line to which it applies. The staff, boxes, and tickets for the different portions of the line must be distinguished by different colours.

378. The tickets must be kept in the proper ticket-box fastened by an inside spring, the key to open the box being the staff to which the tickets apply.

379. The Station Master must keep a record in a book of each ticket issued, showing the number of tickets and the particular train or engine for which it is issued.

380. The staff, whom at the station, must not be left in the box, but must be in the safe custody of the Station Master.

381. Drivers must not take the staff or ticket beyond the station at which it ought to be left.

382. When trains are assisted by a second engine in the front, the leading engine must carry the staff or ticket; but when the assisting engine is pushing the train, the train engine must carry a ticket, and the assisting engine the staff, except in cases where the train and assisting engine are travelling over the entire length of line to which the staff applies, and have to be followed by another train or engine, when the train and assisting engine must each have a ticket. When the assisting engine is intended to return to the station from which it is started, without running through the entire portion of line to which the staff applies, it must always carry the staff.

383. In the event of an engine which carries the staff breaking down between two stations, the Fireman must take the staff to the staff station in the direction whence assistance can be obtained in order that the staff may be at the station on arrival of the engine. Should the engine that fails be in possession of a ticket instead of the staff, assistance must only come from the station at which the staff has been left. But if assistance can be more readily obtained at a station other than that where the staff is, immediate steps must be taken to have the staff transferred to the other end of the section. Fireman must accompany the assisting engine to the place where he has left his own engine.

384. When a Ballast train has to work between stations, the staff must be given to the Driver in charge of it. This will close the line whilst the Ballast train is at work. The Ballast train must proceed afterwards to one of the staff stations to open the line, before the ordinary traffic can be resumed.

Ballast trains not stopping to work between stations may run with staff on ticket as ordinary or special trains.

Sample form of Train Staff Ticket

Ticket No.____________________

__________________________ *Railway.*

TRAIN STAFF TICKET

DOWN

*Train No.*_______________

________*h.*________*m. from*____________________*to*____________

To Driver and Guard.

You are authorized to proceed from

____

to

____

And the Train Staff will follow.

*Train No.*__________________*in front left*____________*h.*__________*m.*

*Signed*____

Office in charge at

Date.

(Back of Ticket)

When this ticket is given to the Driver, he must, before starting, see the Train Staff for the portion of line which he is about to enter.

This ticket is to be given up by the Driver immediately on arrival to the person in charge of the station which he is authorized to proceed, and such person will be responsible that this ticket is at once cancelled.

SECTION XVII

REGULATIONS FOR WORKING SINGLE LINES OF RAILWAY ON THE SYSTEM TERMED "TRAIN DESPATCHING" IN RULE 3, SECTION II

This system is not to be extended to any Railway on which it is not now in force, and it is to be understood to be sanctioned only as an *"ad interim" arrangement until one of the systems described in Sections XIII to XVI can be brought into use on the Railway.*

385. The working of all ordinary trains shall be regulated by Time-tables, and no departure from the regular running shall be made without the order of an authorized officer, and such order shall be conveyed in writing, or in an attested copy of a telegram.
386. No special train, or Pilot engine, except in case of accident, shall leave a station or pass along the Railway, unless previous notice in writing shall have been given to each station, or notice shall have been sent by electric telegraph, and shall have been acknowledged at every station throughout the distance to which such engine or train is intended to proceed.
387. These rules will not prevent a Locomotive Foreman, or other servant acting in that capacity (should he be unable to communicate with the Traffic Officer in charge of the Division, or, if by so doing, unnecessary time would be lost) from sending, with the concurrence of the principal officer at the station, an engine to assist a disabled train, provided that both have satisfied themselves that there is no danger in such act.

SECTION XVIII

REGULATION FOR WORKING SINGLE LINE OF RAILWAY ON THE SYSTEM TERMED "PILOT GUARD" IN RULE 3, SECTION II

This system is only to be held as applicable to short Branch Lines.

388. The Pilot Guard will be distinguished by a red dress or badge; and no train or engine shall, under any circumstances, be allowed to run on the line unless it is either accompanied or personally started by the Pilot Guard wearing such dress or badge.
389. The Pilot Guard will, when practicable, accompany every train; but when it is necessary to start two or more trains from one end of the portion of line under his control before a train has to be started from the other end, the Pilot Guard must furnish the Guard in charge of each train not accompanied by himself with printed Pilot Guard's ticket, where such are provided, properly filled up and signed, and personally start such train, and must himself accompany the last train. The ticket will apply only to the single journey to the station named on it, where it must be immediately given up to the person in charge of the station, and all tickets so given up must be immediately cancelled.
390. The Driver must not start his train without seeing the Pilot Guard. But if the Pilot Guard does not accompany the train, the Driver must not start until he has received from the Guard of his train the Pilot Guard's ticket authorising him to proceed. A Driver working on engine, unaccompanied by a Guard, must observe the same regulations as herein laid down for a Guard with a train.

SECTION XIX

REGULATIONS FOR WORKING SINGLE LINES ON THE SYSTEM TERMED "ONE ENGINE ONLY" IN RULE 3, SECTION II

This system is only to be held as applicable to short Branch Lines.

391. Only one engine in steam, or two or more coupled together, which are then to be treated so one engine or train, must be allowed to be on the line at one and the same time, except as provided in Rule 292.
392. In the case of an engine or train becoming disabled and requiring assistance, or an accident occurring which renders it impossible for the engine to proceed, the Guard in charge must instruct the Driver to keep the engine stationary until his return, and then make the best of his way to the station whence assistance can be obtained, and inform the person in charge there of the circumstances, who will, or receipt of such information, allow a second engine to enter the line. The second engine must be accompanied by the Guard of the disabled engine or train, who must explain it the Driver where, and under what circumstances, the disabled engine or train is situated.
393. The Guard of the disabled engine or train will be held responsible for the safe and proper working of the line until both engines have left it, and it is again clear.

394. Should an engine without a Guard become disabled, the Fireman, or, if necessary, the Driver, must perform the duties prescribed for the Guard.

The 13th September, 1880.

No. 300. Mr. G.A.D. Anley, Executive Engineer, 1st Grade, Bengal, is appointed to officiate as Superintending Engineer of the Eastern Circle, *vice* Major Smyth, R.E., on furlough. While so officiating, Mr. Anley will have the temporary rank of a Superintending Engineer, 3rd Class.

This cancels Public Works Notification No. 103. dated the 19th March 1880.

The 14th September, 1880.

No. 301. The services of Lieutenant J.H.C. Harrison, R.E., Assistant Engineer, 1st Grade, Railway Branch, are places at the disposal of the Government of the North-Western Provinces and Oudh for employment as Assistant Principal of the Thomason College.

The 10th September, 1880.

No. 302. Colonel W.S. Trevor, V.C., R.E., Chief Engineer, Class II, British Burmah, is transferred to the office of the Director General of Railways.

Mr. W.C. Furnivall, Chief Engineer, Class III, is transferred from the office of the Director General of Railways to be Chief Engineer and Secretary to the Chief Commissioner of British Burmah in the Public Works Department.

No.303. Mr. F.G. Teale, Superintendent, 1st Grade, Indian Telegraph Department, having proceeded on privilege leave, with effect from the 15th of August 1880, the following officiating appointments are made: -

Mr. T.C. Hill, Superintendent, 3rd Grade, to officiate as Superintendent, 2nd Grade.

Mr. W.P. Johnston, Assistant Superintendent, 1st Grade, to act as Superintendent, 3rd Grade.

No. 304. Honorary Captain and Deputy Commissary H.E. Mitchell, Assistant Engineer, 3rd Grade, Military Works Branch, is promoted to Assistant Engineer, 2nd Grade.

The 16th September, 1880.

No. 305. The Governor General in Council is pleased to make the following promotions in the Engineer Establishment attach to Local Administrations, with effect from the 6th August 1880, *vice* Mr. D.E.H. Noyes, Executive Engineer, 4th Grade resigned.

PERMANENT

From Assistant Engineer, 1st Grade, to Executive Engineer, 4th Grade.

Lieutenant R.O. Lloyd, R.E., Executive Engineer, 4th Grade, temporary rank, British Burmah.

From 2nd to 1st Grade, Assistant Engineer.

Mr. Bhagat Singh, Rajputana.

TEMPORARY

From Assistant Engineer, 1st Grade, to Executive Engineer, 4th Grade.
Mr. J. Rollo, Assam, *vice* Lieutenant Lloyd, R.E., confirmed.

No. 306. Mr. J.E. Ives, Apprentice Engineer, Punjab Public Works Department, is promoted to Assistant Engineer, 3rd Grade, with effect from 1st July 1880.

The 17th September 1880.

No. 307. To fill a vacancy existing in the Engineer Establishment, Railway Branch, Mr. W. McHutchin is promoted from 2nd to 1st Grade Assistant Engineer, with effect from 14th September 1880.

ALEX FRASER, *Major Genl., R.E.*
Secy. to the Govt. of India

389

The Indian Railway Act, 1883

Source: Preliminary Administration Report on the Railways in India for 1882-83, Simla, 1883

Gist: Indian Railway Act, 1883 (Act 4 of 1883) was passed for amending certain sections of the Indian Railway Act, 1879 for opening of new lines for conveyance of passengers. Sections 5 and 22 are substituted, while section 8 is amended.

Act No. IV of 1883

Passed by the Governor-General of India in Council

(Received the assent of the Governor General on the 16th February 1883)

An Act to amend the Indian Railway Act, 1879

Whereas it is expedient to amend the Indian Railway Act, 1879, in manner hereinafter appearing; it is hereby enacted as follows: –

1. This Act may be called the Indian Railway Act, 1883; and it shall come into force at once.
2. For section five of the said Act the following sections shall be substituted, namely: – "5. A Railway, or portion or extension of, or addition to, a Railway, shall not be opened for the public conveyance of passengers until the Railway Administration has given to the Governor General in Council notice in writing of the intention of opening the same, and until the Governor General in Council has by order sanctioned the opening of the same.

   "5A. The Governor General in Council may from time to time appoint, by name or by virtue of their office, officers to be inspecting-officers under this Act.

   "5B. (1) The sanction referred to in section five shall not be given until an officer appointed under section 5A has, after inspection of the Railway, portion, extension or addition, as the case may be, reported to the Governor General in Council that in his opinion of the same would not be attended with danger to the public using it.

   "(2) Notwithstanding anything hereinbefore contained, the Governor General in Council may, in any particular case or any particular class of cases, by special order, confer on any officer appointed under section 5A power to sanction the opening of a Railway, portion, extension or addition, if in the officer's opinion the opening of the same will not be attended with danger to the public using it.

"(3) In such case it shall not be necessary to make the report required by sub-section (4); but the Governor General in Council may by order cancel the sanction given under sub-section (2), or direct that the sanction shall be subject to such conditions as he thinks fit.

"(4) The sanction given under this section may be either absolute or subject to such conditions as the Governor General in Council, or the officer appointed under section 5A, as the case may be, thinks necessary for the safety of the public.

"(5) When sanction for the opening of any Railway, or portion, or extension of, or addition to, any Railway is given subject to conditions, and the Railway Administration fails or neglects to fulfil, or comply with, these conditions, the sanction shall on the failure or neglect forthwith be deemed to be void, and the Railway, or portion, or extension, or addition, as the case may be, shall be used unless and until sanction is again obtained under this section for the opening thereof.

"5C. If, after a Railway has been opened as hereinbefore provided, any portion of it is so altered by the Railway Administration as to cause danger to, or affect the safety of, passengers carried thereon, the portion so altered shall not be used for public conveyance of passengers, unless and until sanction is obtained, in accordance with the provisions of section 5B, for the opening of it.

"5D.(1) Every officer appointed under section 5A shall, for the purpose of the inspection, be deemed to be a public servant within the meaning of the Indian Penal Code, and shall, subject to the control of the Governor General in Council, have the following powers, namely: –

"(a) he may enter on and inspect any Railway, or portion thereof which has been opened for the public conveyance of passengers, or such rolling stock used thereon.

"(b) he may, by an order in writing under his hand, require the attendance of any Railway servant whom he thinks fit to call before him and examine for the said purpose, and may require any such servant to answer, or furnish returns regarding, such inquiries for the said purpose as he thinks fit to make.

"(c) he may require and enforce the production of all books, papers and documents belonging to or in the possession of any Railway Administration which in his opinion are necessary for the said purpose.

"(2) Every Railway Administration where Railway or rolling-stock is being inspected under this Act shall afford all reasonable facilities for making the inspection to the officer making it.

"5E. When after inspecting any Railway or portion of a Railway, or any rolling stock used thereon, any officer appointed under section 5A reports to the Governor

General in Council that in his opinion the use of the Railway or portion or any specified rolling stock will be attended with danger to the public using it, the Governor General in Council may, by order, direct that the Railway or portion be closed for public conveyance of passengers, or that the rolling-stock so specified shall no longer be used, as the case may be.

"5F. (1) When a Railway or portion of a Railway has been closed under section 5E, it shall not be reopened for the public conveyance of passengers unless and until it has been inspected, and its opening sanctioned, in accordance with the provisions of section 5B.

"(2) When the Governor General in Council has directed under section 5E that any rolling-stock shall not be used, the rolling-stock shall not be used unless and until an officer appointed under section 5A reports that it is fit for use and the Governor General in Council sanction its use."

3. In section eight of the said Act, in clause (d), the word "and" shall be omitted, and after clause (d) the following clause shall be, and be deemed to have always been, inserted: –

"(dd) for regulating the conduct of the Railway servants, and."

4. For section twenty-one of the said Act the following section shall be substituted: –

"21. Any Railway Administration opening or using, in contravention of section five, section 5B, or section 5C, any Railway, or any portion or extension of, or addition to, a Railway, or keeping, in contravention of an order of the Governor General in Council under section 5E, any Railway, or portion thereof open, or re-opening, in contravention of section 5F, sub-section (1), any Railway or portion thereof, or using, in contravention of section 5F, sub-section (2), any rolling-stock, shall forfeit to the Government the sum of one thousand rupees for every day during which the Railway, portion, extension or addition remains open or is used in contravention of any of those sections or of the order of the Governor General in Council, as the case may be, or during which the rolling-stock is so used."

390

The Sindh-Pishin Railway Act, 1887

Source: H.E. Trevor: The Law Relating to Railways in British India, London, 1891

Gist: The Sindh-Pishin Railway Act, 1887 (Act 11 of 1887), which received the assent of the Governor-General on 25 February 1887, was passed for the regulation of traffic on the Sindh-Pishin section of the North-Western Railway.

Act No. XI of 1887[1]

PASSED BY THE GOVERNOR-GENERAL OF INDIA IN COUNCIL

(Received the assent of the Governor-General on the 25th February 1887)

An Act to provide for the regulation of traffic on the Sindh-Pishin Section of the North-Western Railway

WHEREAS it is inexpedient that the Indian Railway Act, 1879, should apply in its entirety to that part of the Sindh-Pishin section of the North-Western Railway which lies beyond the province of Sindh; It is hereby enacted as follows: –

1. (1) This Act may be called the Sindh-Pishin Railway Act, 1887.
   (2) It shall extend to all persons for whom the Governor General in Council has power to make laws and regulations at meetings for that purpose; and
   (3) It shall come into force at once.
2. In the following sections of this Act, "railway" means that part of the Sindh-Pishin section of the North-Western Railway which, whether completed at the commencement of this Act or not, lies beyond the province of Sindh.
3. (1) Unless and until extended under this section, no portion of the Indian Railway Act, 1879, shall apply to any part of the railway.
   (2) The Governor General in Council may, by notification in the Gazette of India, extend to the railway or any part thereof such portions of the Act as he thinks fit.
   (3) In extending any portion of that Act the railway or any part thereof the Governor General in Council may extend it subject to such modifications as he thinks fit.
4. (1) No person shall be entitled, as of right, to be carried on the railway or to have property carried thereon.
   (2) But the carriage of passengers and property on the railway shall be permitted subject to such conditions and restrictions as the Governor General in Council may prescribe.

5. Where any person or property is permitted to be carried on the railway, the Government shall not be responsible for any injury which may happen to the person, or for any loss or damage which may occur in respect of the property, unless the injury happens, or the loss or damage occurs, on a part of the railway with respect to which the Governor General in Council has, by notification in the Gazette of India, announced that the Government accepts responsibility, to such extent as may be described in the notification, for injury happening, or loss or damage occurring, thereon.

---

1. The Act XI of 1887 was amended later by the Act IX of 1890.

391

The Indian Railways Act, 1890

Source: The Gazette of India, Part IV, 22 March 1890

Gist: The Indian Railways Act, 1890 (Act 9 of 1890), passed by the Governor General of India on 21 March 1890, has 150 sections, subsections and clauses under them, and two schedules, spread over 10 chapters. The Act has detailed provisions specifying inspection of railways, construction and maintenance of works, opening of railways, railway commissions and traffic facilities, general working of railways, carriage of property and passengers, responsibility of railway administration as carriers, measures if accidents occur, offences and penalties including those for forfeitures by railway companies and other offences. The first schedule is on repealed enactments (read with section 2) and the second schedule lists the articles to be declared and insured (read with section 75).

The Indian Railways Act, 1890[1]

An Act to consolidate, amend and add to the law relating to Railways in India

WHEREAS it is expedient to consolidate, amend and add to the law relating to railways in India; it is hereby enacted as follows: -

CHAPTER I
PRELIMINARY

1. (1) This Act may be called the Indian Railways Act, 1890.
   (2) It extends to the whole of British India, inclusive of Upper Burma and (in so far as it has been or may be extended under the provisions of the Sindh-Pishin Railway Act, 1887) of British Baluchistan, and applies also to all subjects of Her Majesty within the dominions of Princes and States in India in alliance with Her Majesty, and to all Native subjects of Her Majesty without and beyond British India and those dominions; and
   (3) It shall come into force on the first day of May 1890.
2. (1) On and from that day the enactments specified in the first schedule are repealed to the extent mentioned in the third column thereof.
   (2) But all rules, declarations and appointments made, sanctions and directions given, forms approved, powers conferred and notifications published under any of those enactments, or under any enactment repealed by any of them, shall, so far as

they are consistent with this Act, be deemed to have been respectively made, given, approved, conferred and published under this Act.

(3) Any enactment or document referring to any of those enactments or to any enactment repealed by any of them, shall, so far as may be, be construed to refer to this Act or to the corresponding portion thereof.

3. In this Act, unless there is something repugnant in the subject or context, -

(1) "tramway" means a tramway constructed under the Indian Tramways Act, 1886, or any special Act relating to tramways:

(2) "ferry" includes a bridge of boats, pontoons or rafts, a swing-bridge, a flying bridge and a temporary bridge, and the approaches to, and landing places of, a ferry:

(3) "inland water" means any canal, river, lake or navigable water in British India:

(4) "railway" means a railway, or any portion of a railway, for the public carriage of passengers, animals or goods, and includes -

(a) all land within the fences or other boundary-marks indicating the limits of the land appurtenant to a railway;

(b) all lines of rails, sidings or branches worked over for the purposes of, or in connection with, a railway;

(c) all stations, offices, warehouses, wharves, workshops, manufactories, fixed plant and machinery and other works constructed for the purposes of, or in connection with, a railway; and

(d) all ferries, ships, boats and rafts which are used on inland waters for the purposes of the traffic of a railway and belong to or are hired or worked by the authority administering the railway:

(5) "railway company" includes any persons, whether incorporated or not, who are owners or lessees of a railway or parties to an agreement for working a railway :

(6) "railway administration" or "administration" in the case of a railway administered by the Government or a Native State, means the Manager of the railway and includes the Government or the Native State, and, in the case of a railway administered by a railway company, means the railway company:

(7) "railway servant" means any person employed by a railway administration in connection with the service of a railway:

(8) "Inspector" means an Inspector of Railways appointed under this Act:

(9) "goods" includes inanimate things of every kind:

(10) "rolling-stock" includes locomotive engines, tenders, carriages, wagons, trucks and trolleys of all kinds:

(11) "traffic" includes rolling-stock of every description as well as passengers, animals and goods:

(12) "through traffic" means traffic which is carried over the railways of two or more railway administrations:

(13) "rate" includes any fare, charge or other payment for the carriage of any

passenger, animal or goods:

(14) "terminals" includes charges in respect of stations, sidings, wharves, depots, warehouses, cranes and other similar matters, and of any services rendered thereat:

(15) "pass" means an authority given by a railway administration, or by an officer appointed by a railway administration in this behalf, and authorising the person to whom it is given to travel as a passenger on a railway gratuitously:

(16) "ticket" includes a single ticket, a return ticket and a season ticket:

(17) "maund" means a weight of three thousand two hundred tolas, each tola being a weight of one hundred and eighty grains Troy: and

(18) "Collector" means the chief officer in charge of the land-revenue administration of a district, and includes any officer specially appointed by the Local Government to discharge the functions of a Collector under this Act.

CHAPTER II
INSPECTION OF RAILWAYS

4. (1) The Governor General in Council may appoint persons, by name or by virtue of their office, to be Inspectors of Railways.

(2) The duties of an Inspector of Railways shall be -

(a) to inspect railways with a view to determine whether they are fit to be opened for the public carriage of passengers, and to report thereon to the Governor General in Council as required by this Act;

(b) to make such periodical or other inspections of any railway or of any rolling-stock used thereon as the Governor General in Council may direct;

(c) to make inquiry under this Act into the cause of any accident on a railway;

(d) to perform such other duties as are imposed on him by this Act or any other enactment for the time being in force relating to railways.

5. An inspector shall, for the purpose of any of the duties which he is required or authorised to perform under this Act, be deemed to be a public servant within the meaning of the Indian Penal Code, and, subject to the control of the Governor General in Council, shall for that purpose have the following powers, namely: -

(a) to enter upon and inspect any railway or any rolling-stock used thereon;

(b) by an order in writing under his hand addressed to the railway administration, to require the attendance before him of any railway servant, and to require answers or returns to such inquiries as he thinks fit to make from such railway servant or from the railway administration;

(c) to require the production of any book or document belonging to or in the possession or control of any railway administration (except a communication between a railway company and its legal advisers) which it appears to him to be necessary to inspect.

6. A railway administration shall afford to the Inspector all reasonable facilities for

performing the duties and exercising the powers imposed and conferred upon him by this Act.

CHAPTER III
CONSTRUCTION AND MAINTENANCE OF WORKS

7. (1) Subject to the provisions of this Act and, in the case of immovable property not belonging to the railway administration, to the provisions of any enactment for the time being in force for the acquisition of land for public purposes and for companies, and, subject also, in the case of a railway company, to the provisions of any contract between the company and the Government, a railway administration may, for the purpose of constructing a railway or the accommodation or other works connected therewith, and notwithstanding anything in any other enactment for the time being in force, -

   (a) make or construct in, upon, across, under or over any lands, or any streets, hills, valleys, roads, railways or tramways, or any rivers, canals, brooks, streams or other waters, or any drains, water-pipes, gas-pipes or telegraph lines, such temporary or permanent inclined planes, arches, tunnels, culverts, embankments, aqueducts, bridges, roads, ways, passages, conduits, drains, piers, cuttings and fences as the railway administration thinks proper;

   (b) alter the course of any rivers, brooks, streams or watercourses, for the purpose of constructing and maintaining tunnels, bridges, passages or other works over or under them, and divert or alter, as well temporarily as permanently, the course of any rivers, brooks, streams or water-courses or any roads, streets or ways, or raise or sink the level thereof, in order the more conveniently to carry them over or under or by the side of the railway, as the railway administration thinks proper;

   (c) make drains or conduits into, through or under any lands adjoining the railway for the purpose of conveying water from or to the railway;

   (d) erect and construct such houses, warehouses, offices and other buildings and such yards, stations, wharves, engines, machinery, apparatus and other works and conveniences as the railway administration thinks proper;

   (e) alter, repair or discontinue such buildings, works and conveniences as aforesaid or any of them, and substitute others in their stead; and

   (f) do all other acts necessary for making, maintaining, altering or repairing and using the railway.

   (2) The exercise of the powers conferred on a railway administration by sub-section (1) shall be subject to the control of the Governor General in Council.

8. A railway administration may, for the purpose of exercising the powers conferred upon it by this Act, alter the position of any pipe for the supply of gas, water or

compressed air or the position of any electric wire or of any drain not being a main drain:

Provided that -

(a) when the railway administration desires to alter the position of any such pipe, wire or drain it shall give reasonable notice of its intention to do so, and of the time at which it will begin to do so, to the local authority or company having control over the pipe, wire or drain, or, when the pipe, wire or drain is not under the control of a local authority or company, to the person under whose control the pipe, wire or drain is;

(b) a local authority, company or person receiving notice under proviso (a) may send a person to superintend the work, and the railway administration shall execute the work to the reasonable satisfaction of the person so sent and shall make arrangements for continuing during the execution of the work the supply of gas, water, compressed air or electricity or the maintenance of the drainage, as the case may be.

9. (1) The Governor General in Council may authorise any railway administration, in case of any slip or other accident happening or being apprehended to any cutting, embankment or other work under the control of the railway administration, to enter upon any lands adjoining its railway for the purpose of repairing or preventing the accident, and to do all such works as may be necessary for the purpose.

(2) In case of necessity the railway administration may enter upon the lands and do the works aforesaid without having obtained the previous sanction of the Governor General in Council, but in such a case shall, within seventy-two hours after such entry, make a report to the Governor General in Council, specifying the nature of the accident or apprehended accident, and of the works necessary to be done, and the power conferred on the railway administration by this subsection shall cease and determine if the Governor General in Council, after considering the report, considers that the exercise of the power is not necessary for the public safety.

10. (1) A railway administration shall do as little damage as possible in the exercise of the powers conferred by any of the three last foregoing sections, and compensation shall be paid for any damage caused by the exercise thereof.

(2) A suit shall not lie to recover such compensation, but in case of dispute the amount thereof shall, on application to the Collector, be determined and paid in accordance, so far as may be, with the provisions of sections 11 to 15, both inclusive, and sections 18 to 42, both inclusive, of the Land-acquisition Act, 1870, and the provisions of sections 57 and 58 of that Act shall apply to the award of compensation.

11. (1) A railway administration shall make and maintain the following works for the accommodation of the owners and occupiers of lands adjoining the railway, namely: -

(a) such and so many convenient crossings, bridges, arches, culverts and passages over, under or by the sides of, or leading to or from, the railway as may, in the opinion of the Governor General in Council, be necessary for the purpose of making good any interruptions caused by the railway to the use of the lands through which the railway is made, and

(b) all necessary arches, tunnels, culverts, drains, watercourses or other passages, over or under or by the sides of the railway, of such dimensions as will, in the opinion of the Governor General in Council, be sufficient at all times to convey water as freely from or to the lands lying near or affected by the railway as before the making of the railway, or as nearly so as may be.

(2) Subject to the other provisions of this Act, the works specified in clauses (a) and (b) of sub-section (1) shall be made during or immediately after the laying out or formation of the railway over the lands traversed thereby and in such manner as to cause as little damage or inconvenience as possible to persons interested in the lands or affected by the works.

(3) The foregoing provisions of this section are subject to the following provisos, namely: -

(a) a railway administration shall not be required to make any accommodation works in such a manner as would prevent or obstruct the working or using of the railway, or to make any accommodation works with respect to which the owners and occupiers of the lands have agreed to receive and have been paid compensation in consideration of their not requiring the works to be made;

(b) save as hereinafter in this Chapter provided, a railway administration shall not, except on the requisition of the Governor General in Council, be compelled to defray the cost of executing any further or additional accommodation works for the use of the owners or occupiers of the lands after the expiration of ten years from the date on which the railway passing through the lands was first opened for public traffic;

(c) where a railway administration has provided suitable accommodation for the crossing of a road or stream, and the road or stream is afterwards diverted by the act or neglect of the person having the control thereof, the administration shall not be compelled to provide other accommodation for the crossing of the road or stream.

(4) The Governor General in Council may appoint a time for the commencement of any work to be executed under sub-section (1), and if for fourteen days next after that time the railway administration fails to commence the work or, having commenced it, fails to proceed diligently to execute it in a sufficient manner, the Governor General in Council may execute it and recover from the railway administration the cost incurred by him in the execution thereof.

12. If an owner or occupier of any land affected by a railway considers the works made

under the last foregoing section to be insufficient for the commodious use of the land, or if the Local Government or a local authority desires to construct a public road or other work across, under or over a railway, he or it, as the case may be, may at any time require the railway administration to make at his or its expense such further accommodation works as he or it thinks necessary and are agreed to by the railway administration or as, in case of difference of opinion, may be authorised by the Governor General in Council.

13. The Governor General in Council may require that, within a time to be specified in the requisition or within such further time as he may appoint in this behalf, -

(a) boundary-marks or fences be provided or renewed by a railway administration for a railway or any part thereof and for roads constructed in connection therewith;
(b) any works in the nature of a screen near to or adjoining the side of any public road constructed before the making of a railway be provided or renewed by a railway administration for the purpose of preventing danger to passengers on the road by reason of horses or other animals being frightened by the sight or noise of the rolling-stock moving on the railway;
(c) suitable gates, chains, bars, stiles or handrails be erected or renewed by a railway administration at places where a railway crosses a public road on the level;
(d) persons be employed by a railway administration to open and shut such gates, chains or bars.

14. (1) Where a railway administration has constructed a railway across a public road on the level, the Governor General in Council may at any time, if it appears to him necessary for the public safety, require the railway administration, within such time as he thinks fit, to carry the road either under or over the railway by means of a bridge or arch, with convenient ascents and descents and other convenient approaches, instead of crossing the road on the level, or to execute such other works as, in the circumstances of the case, may appear to the Governor General in Council to be best adapted for removing or diminishing the danger arising from the level-crossing.

(2) The Governor General in Council may require, as a condition of making a requisition under sub-section (1), that the local authority, if any, which maintains the road shall undertake to pay the whole of the cost to the railway administration of complying with the requisition or such portion of the cost as the Governor General in Council thinks just.

15. (1) In either of the following cases, namely: -

(a) where there is danger that a tree standing near a railway may fall on the railway so as to obstruct traffic,
(b) when a tree obstructs the view of any fixed signal,

the railway administration may, with the permission of any Magistrate, fell the tree or deal with it in such other manner as will in the opinion of the railway administration avert the danger or remove the obstruction, as the case may be.

(2) In case of emergency, the power mentioned in sub-section (1) may be exercised by a railway administration without the permission of a Magistrate.

(3) Where a tree felled or otherwise dealt with under sub-section (1) or sub-section (2) was in existence before the railway was constructed or the signal was fixed, any Magistrate may, upon the application of the persons interested in the tree, award to those persons such compensation as he thinks reasonable.

(4) Such an award, subject, where made in a presidency-town by any Magistrate other than the Chief Presidency Magistrate or where made elsewhere by any Magistrate other than the District Magistrate, to revision by the Chief Presidency Magistrate or the District Magistrate, as the case may be, shall be final.

A Civil Court shall not entertain a suit to recover compensation for any tree felled or otherwise dealt with under this section.

CHAPTER IV
OPENING OF RAILWAYS

16. (1) A railway administration may, with the previous sanction of the Governor General in Council, use upon a railway locomotive engines or other motive power, and rolling-stock to be drawn or propelled thereby.

(2) But rolling-stock shall not be moved upon a railway by steam or other motive power until such general rules for the railway as may be deemed to be necessary have been made, sanctioned and published under this Act.

17. (1) Subject to the provisions of sub-section (2), a railway administration shall, one month at least before it intends to open any railway for the public carriage of passengers, give to the Governor General in Council in writing of its intention.

(2) The Governor General in Council may in any case, if he thinks fit, reduce the period of, or dispense with, the notice mentioned in sub-section (1).

18. A railway shall not be opened for the public carriage of passengers until the Governor General in Council, or an Inspector empowered by the Governor General in Council in this behalf, has by order sanctioned the opening thereof for that purpose.

19. (1) The sanction of the Governor General in Council under the last foregoing section shall not be given until an Inspector has, after inspection of the railway, reported in writing to the Governor General in Council -

(a) that he has made a careful inspection of the railway and rolling-stock;

(b) that the moving and fixed dimensions prescribed by the Governor General in Council have not been infringed;

(c) that the weight of rails, strength of bridges, general structural character of the works, and the size of and maximum gross load upon the axles of any rolling-stock are such as have been prescribed by the Governor General in Council;

(d) that the railway is sufficiently supplied with rolling-stock;

(e) that general rules for the working of the railway when opened for the public carriage of passengers have been made, sanctioned and published under this Act; and

(f) that, in his opinion, the railway can be opened for the public carriage of passengers without danger to the public using it.

(2) If in the opinion of the Inspector the railway cannot be so opened without danger to the public using it, he shall state that opinion together with the grounds therefor to the Governor General in Council, and the Governor General in Council may thereupon order the railway administration to postpone the opening of the railway.

(3) An order under the last foregoing sub-section must set forth the requirements to be complied with as a condition precedent to the opening of the railway being sanctioned, and shall direct the postponement of the opening of the railway until those requirements have been complied with or the Governor General in Council is otherwise satisfied that the railway can be opened without danger to the public using it.

(4) The sanction given under this section may be either absolute or subject to such conditions as the Governor General in Council thinks necessary for the safety of the public.

(5) When sanction for the opening of a railway is given subject to conditions and the railway administration fails to fulfil those conditions, the sanction shall be deemed to be void and the railway shall not be worked or used until the conditions are fulfilled to the satisfaction of the Governor General in Council.

20. (1) The provisions of sections 17, 18 and 19 with respect to the opening of a railway shall extend to the opening of the works mentioned in sub-section (2) when those works form part of, or are directly connected with, a railway used for the public carriage of passengers and have been constructed after the inspection which preceded the first opening of the railway.

(2) The works referred to in sub-section (1) are additional lines of railway, deviation lines, stations, junctions and crossings on the level, and any alteration or re-construction materially affecting the structural character of any work to which the provisions of sections 17, 18 and 19 apply or are extended by this section.

21. When an accident has occurred resulting in a temporary suspension of traffic, and either the original line and works have been rapidly restored to their original standard, or a temporary diversion has been laid for the purpose of restoring communication, the original line and works so restored, or the temporary diversion, as the case may be, may, in the absence of the Inspector, be opened for the public carriage of passengers, subject to the following conditions, namely: -

(a) that the railway servant in charge of the works undertaken by reason of the accident has certified in writing that the opening of the restored line and works, or of the temporary diversion, will not in his opinion be attended with danger to the public using the line and works or the diversion; and

(b) that notice by telegraph of the opening of the line and works or the diversion shall be sent, as soon as may be, to the Inspector appointed for the railway.

22. The Governor General in Council may make rules defining the cases in which, and in those cases the extent to which, the procedure prescribed in sections 17 to 20 (both inclusive) may be dispensed with.

23. (1) When, after inspecting any open railway used for the public carriage of passengers, or any rolling-stock used thereon, an Inspector is of opinion that the use of the railway or of any specified rolling-stock will be attended with danger to the public using it, he shall state that opinion, together with the grounds therefor, to the Governor General in Council; and the Governor General in Council may thereupon order that the railway be closed for the public carriage of passengers, or that the use of the rolling-stock so specified be discontinued, or that the railway or the rolling-stock so specified be used for the public carriage of passengers on such conditions only as the Governor General in Council may consider necessary for the safety of the public.

(2) An order under sub-section (1) must set forth the grounds on which it is founded.

24. (1) When a railway has been closed under the last foregoing section, it shall not be re-opened for the public carriage of passengers until it has been inspected, and its re-opening sanctioned, in accordance with the provisions of this Act.

(2) When the Governor General in Council has ordered under the last foregoing section that the use of any specified rolling-stock be discontinued, that rolling-stock shall not be used until an Inspector has reported that it is fit for use and the Governor General in Council has sanctioned its use.

(3) When the Governor General in Council has imposed under the last foregoing section any conditions with respect to the use of any railway or rolling-stock, those conditions shall be observed until they are withdrawn by the Governor General in Council.

25. (1) The Governor General in Council may, by general or special order, authorise the discharge of any of his functions under this Chapter by an Inspector, and may cancel any sanction or order given by an Inspector discharging any such function or attach thereto any condition which the Governor General in Council might have imposed if the sanction or order had been given by himself.

(2) A condition imposed under sub-section (1) shall for all the purposes of this Act have the same effect as if it were attached to a sanction or order given by the Governor General in Council.

CHAPTER V
RAILWAY COMMISSIONS AND TRAFFIC FACILITIES

Railway Commissions

26. (1) For the purposes of this Chapter the Governor General in Council shall, as occasion may in his opinion require, appoint a commission, styled a Railway Commission

(in this Act referred to as the Commissioners) and consisting of one Law Commissioner and two Lay Commissioners.

(2) The Commissioners shall sit at such times and in such places as the Governor General in Council appoints.

(3) The Law Commissioner shall be such Judge of the High Court having jurisdiction in reference to European British subjects under the Code of Criminal Procedure, 1882, in the place where the Commissioners are to sit as, in the case of a High Court established under the Statute 24 and 25 Victoria, chapter 104, the Chief Justice or, in the case of the Chief Court of the Punjab, the Senior Judge or, in the case of the Court of the Recorder of Rangoon, the Chief Commissioner of Burma may, on the request of the Governor General in Council, assign by writing under his hand.

(4) The Lay Commissioners shall be appointed by the Governor General in Council, and one at least of them shall be of experience in railway business.

27. The Commissioners shall take cognisance of such cases only as are referred to them by the Governor General in Council.

28. In any of the following circumstances, namely: -

(a) where complaint is made to the Governor General in Council of anything done or any omission made by a railway administration in violation or contravention of any provision of this Chapter;

(b) where any difference which is under the provisions of any agreement required or authorised to be referred to arbitration arises between railway administrations, and the railway administrations apply to the Governor General in Council to have it referred to the Commissioners;

(c) where any other difference, being a difference between railway administrations or one to which a railway administration is a party, arises, and the parties thereto apply to the Governor General in Council to have it referred to the Commissioners;

the Governor General in Council may, if he thinks fit, refer the case to the Commissioners for decision.

29. The three Commissioners shall attend at the hearing of any case referred to them for decision under this Chapter, and the Law Commissioner shall preside at the hearing.

30. (1) In hearing any such case the Commissioners shall have all the powers which may be exercised in the hearing of an original civil suit by a High Court.

(2) The decision shall, if the Commissioners differ in opinion, be in accordance with the opinion of the majority, and the final order in the case shall be by way of injunction and not otherwise.

(3) At the hearing the Commissioners may permit any party to appear before them either by himself or by any legal practitioner entitled to practise in any High Court.

31. (1) An appeal shall not lie from any order of the Commissioners upon any question of fact on which two of the Commissioners are agreed.

(2) Subject to the provisions of sub-section (1), an appeal shall lie from an order of

the Commissioners -

(a) where the Law Commissioner was the Recorder or Additional Recorder of Rangoon, to the High Court of Judicature at Fort William in Bengal, and

(b) in any other case, to the High Court of which the Law Commissioner was a member.

(3) Such an appeal must be presented within six months from the date of the order appealed from, and shall be heard by a bench of as many Judges, not being fewer than three, as the High Court may by rule prescribe.

(4) In the hearing of the appeal the High Court shall, subject to the other provisions of this Chapter, have all the powers which it has as an Appellate Court under the Code of Civil Procedure, and may make any order which the Commissioners could have made.

32. Notwithstanding any appeal to the High Court from an order of the Commissioners, the order shall, unless the Commissioners or the majority of them see fit to suspend it, continue in operation until it is reversed or varied by that Court.

33. (1) The Commissioners, in the exercise of their jurisdiction under this Chapter, may from time to time, with the general or special sanction of the Governor General in Council, call in one or more persons of engineering or other technical knowledge to act as assessors.

(2) There shall be paid to such persons such remuneration as the Governor General in Council upon the recommendation of the Commissioners may direct.

34. The Governor General in Council may make rules regulating proceedings before the Commissioners and enabling the Commissioners to carry into effect the provisions of this Chapter, and prescribing fees to be taken in relation to proceedings before the Commissioners.

35. The costs of and incidental to any proceedings before the Commissioners or the High Court under this Chapter shall be in the discretion of the Commissioners or the High Court, as the case may be, and the payment of costs awarded by the Commissioners may be enforced by the Court of which the Law Commissioner was a Judge as if the payment had been ordered by a decree of a High Court.

36. (1) The Court of which the Law Commissioner was a Judge may, if it appears on the application of any person who was a party to the proceedings before the Commissioners or on appeal before the High Court, or of the representative of any such person, that an injunction made under this Chapter by the Commissioners or by a High Court has not been obeyed by the party enjoined, order such party to pay a sum not exceeding one thousand rupees for every day during which the injunction is disobeyed after the date of the order directing such payment.

(2) The payment of such sum may be enforced by the Court which made the order as if that Court had given a decree for the same, and the Court may direct that the whole or any part of the sum shall be paid to the person making the application under sub-section (1) or to the Government.

37. A document purporting to be signed by the Commissioners, or any of them, shall be received in evidence without proof of the signature, and shall, until the contrary is proved, be deemed to have been so signed and to have been duly executed or issued by the Commissioners.
38. The Commissioners shall, as soon as may be after the disposal of each case referred to them, submit to the Governor General in Council a special report on the case, and the Governor General in Council shall cause the report to be published in such manner as he thinks fit for the information of persons interested in the subject-matter thereof.
39. Except for the purpose of the last foregoing section, a Railway Commission shall be deemed to be dissolved at the close of the last of the sittings of the Commissioners for the decision of the cases referred to them:

    Provided that, on the application of any person who was a party to the proceedings before the Commissioners, or of the representative of any such person, the Governor General in Council may, if he thinks fit, in any case in which the order passed by the Commissioners is not open to appeal, re-appoint the Commissioners for the purpose of hearing an application for a review of their decision and of granting the same and re-hearing the case if they think that the case should be re-heard.
40. Subject to the foregoing provisions of this Chapter and to any direction of Her Majesty in Council, an order of the Commissioners shall be final and shall not be questioned in or restrained by any Court.
41. Except as provided in this Act, no suit shall be instituted or proceeding taken for anything done or any omission made by a railway administration in violation or contravention of any provision of this Chapter or of any order made thereunder by the Commissioners or by a High Court.

Traffic Facilities

42. (1) Every railway administration shall, according to its powers, afford all reasonable facilities for the receiving, forwarding and delivering of traffic upon and from the several railways belonging to or worked by it and for the return of rolling-stock.

    (2) A railway administration shall not make or give any undue or unreasonable preference or advantage to or in favour of any particular person or railway administration, or any particular description of traffic, in any respect whatsoever, or subject any particular person or railway administration or any particular description of traffic to any undue or unreasonable prejudice or disadvantage in any respect whatsoever.

    (3) A railway administration having or working railways which form part of a continuous line of railway communication, or having its terminus or station within one mile of the terminus or station of another railway administration, shall afford all due and reasonable facilities for receiving and forwarding by one of such railways all the traffic arriving by the other at such terminus or station, without any unreasonable delay, and without any such preference or advantage or prejudice

or disadvantage as aforesaid, and so that no obstruction may be offered to the public desirous of using such railways as a continuous line of communication, and so that all reasonable accommodation may by means of such railways be at all times afforded to the public in that behalf.

(4) The facilities to be afforded under this section shall include the due and reasonable receiving, forwarding and delivering by every railway administration, at the request of any other railway administration, of through traffic to and from the railway of any other railway administration at through rates:

Provided as follows: -

(a) the railway administration requiring the traffic to be forwarded shall give written notice of the proposed through rate to each forwarding railway administration, stating both its amount and its apportionment and the route by which the traffic is proposed to be forwarded. The proposed through rate for animals or goods may be per truck or per maund;

(b) each forwarding railway administration shall, within the prescribed period after the receipt of such notice, by written notice inform the railway administration requiring the traffic to be forwarded whether it agrees to the rate, apportionment and route, and, if it has any objection, what the grounds of the objection are;

(c) if at the expiration of the prescribed period no such objection has been sent by any forwarding railway administration, the rate shall come into operation at the expiration of that period;

(d) if an objection to the rate, apportionment or route has been sent within the prescribed period, the Governor General in Council, may, if he thinks fit, on the request of any of the railway administrations, refer the case to the Commissioners for their decision;

(e) if the objection is to the granting of the rate or to the route, the Commissioners shall consider whether the granting of the rate is a due and reasonable facility in the interests of the public, and whether, regard being had to the circumstances, the route proposed is a reasonable route, and shall allow or refuse the rate accordingly or fix such other rate as may seem to the Commissioners to be just and reasonable;

(f) if the objection is only to the apportionment of the rate, and the case has been referred to the Commissioners, the rate shall come into operation at the expiration of the prescribed period, but the decision of the Commissioners as to its apportionment shall be retrospective : in the case of any other objection the operation of the rate shall be suspended until the Commissioners make their order in the case;

(g) the Commissioners in apportioning the through rate shall take into consideration all the circumstances of the case, including any special expense incurred in respect of the construction, maintenance or working of the route or any part of the route, as well as any special charges which any railway administration is entitled to make in respect thereof;

(h) the Commissioners shall not in any case compel any railway administration to accept lower mileage rates than the mileage rates which the administration may for the time being legally be charging for like traffic carried by a like mode of transit on any other line of communication between the same points, being the points of departure and arrival of the through route;

(i) subject to the foregoing provisions of this sub-section, the Commissioners shall have full power to decide that any proposed through rate is due and reasonable, notwithstanding that a less amount may be allotted to any forwarding railway administration out of the through rate than the maximum rate which the railway administration is entitled to charge, and to allow and apportion the through rate accordingly;

(j) the prescribed period mentioned in this sub-section shall be one month, or such longer period as the Governor General in Council may by general or special order prescribe.

43. (1) Whenever it is shown that a railway administration charges one trader or class of traders or the traders in any local area lower rates for the same or similar animals or goods or lower rates for the same or similar services, than it charges to other traders or classes of traders, or to the traders in another local area the burden of proving that such lower charge does not amount to an undue preference shall lie on the railway administration.

(2) In deciding whether a lower charge does or does not amount to an undue preference, the Commissioners may, so far as they think reasonable, in addition to any other consideration affecting the case, take into consideration whether such lower charge is necessary for the purpose of securing, in the interests of the public, the traffic in respect of which it is made.

44. Where a railway administration is a party to an agreement for procuring the traffic of the railway to be carried on any inland water by any ferry, ship, boat or rail which does not belong to or is not hired or worked by the railway administration, the provisions of the two last foregoing sections applicable to a railway shall extend to the ferry, ship, boat or raft in so far as it is used for the purposes of the traffic of the railway.

45. A railway administration may charge reasonable terminals.

46. (1) The Governor General in Council may, if he thinks fit, refer to the Commissioners for decision any question or dispute which may arise with respect to the terminals charged by a railway administration, and the Commissioners may thereupon decide what is a reasonable sum to be paid to the railway administration in respect of terminals.

(2) In deciding the question or dispute the Commissioners shall have regard only to the expenditure reasonably necessary to provide the accommodation in respect of which the terminals are charged, irrespective of the outlay which may have been

actually incurred by the railway administration in providing that accommodation.

CHAPTER VI
WORKING OF RAILWAYS

General

47. (1) Every railway company and, in the case of a railway administered by the Government, an officer to be appointed by the Governor General in Council in this behalf, shall make general rules consistent with this Act for the following purposes, namely: -

(a) for regulating the mode in which, and the speed at which, rolling-stock used on the railway is to be moved or propelled;
(b) for providing for the accommodation and convenience of passengers and regulating the carriage of their luggage;
(c) for declaring what shall be deemed to be, for the purposes of this Act, dangerous or offensive goods, and for regulating the carriage of such goods;
(d) for regulating the conditions on which the railway administration will carry passengers suffering from infectious or contagious disorders, and providing for the disinfection of carriages which have been used by such passengers;
(e) for regulating the conduct of the railway servants;
(f) for regulating the terms and conditions on which the railway administration will warehouse or retain goods at any station on behalf of the consignee or owner; and,
(g) generally, for regulating the travelling upon, and the use, working and management of, the railway.

(2) The rules may provide that any person committing a breach of any of them shall be punished with fine which may extend to any sum not exceeding fifty rupees, and that, in the case of a rule made under clause (e) of sub-section (1), the railway servant shall forfeit a sum not exceeding one month's pay, which sum may be deducted by the railway administration from his pay.

(3) A rule made under this section shall not take effect until it has received the sanction of the Governor General in Council and been published in the Gazette of India :

Provided that, where the rule is in the terms of a rule which has already been published at length in the Gazette of India, a notification in that Gazette referring to the rule already published and announcing the adoption thereof shall be deemed a publication of a rule in the Gazette of India within the meaning of this sub-section.

(4) The Governor General in Council may cancel any rule made under this section, and the authority required by sub-section (1) to make rules thereunder may at

any time, with the previous sanction of the Governor General in Council, rescind or vary any such rule.

(5) Every rule purporting to have been made for any railway under section 8 of the Indian Railway Act, 1879, and appearing from the Gazette of India to be intended to apply to the railway at the commencement of this Act, shall, notwithstanding any irregularity in the making or publication of the rule, be deemed to have been made and to have taken effect under this section.

(6) Every railway administration shall keep at each station on its railway a copy of the general rules for the time being in force under this section on the railway, and shall allow any person to inspect it free of charge at all reasonable times.

48. Where two or more railway administrations whose railways have a common terminus or a portion of the same line of rails in common, or form separate portions of one continued line of railway communication, are not able to agree upon arrangements for conducting at such common terminus, or at the point of junction between them, their joint traffic with safety to the public, the Governor General in Council, upon the application of either or any of the administrations, may decide the matters in dispute between them, so far as those matters relate to the safety of the public, and may determine whether the whole or what proportion of the expenses attending on such arrangements shall be borne by either or any of the administrations respectively.

49. Any railway company, not being a company for which the Statute 42 and 43 Victoria, chapter 41, provides, may from time to time make and carry into effect agreements with the Governor General in Council for the construction of rolling-stock, plant or machinery used on, or in connection with, railways, or for leasing or taking on lease any rolling-stock, plant, machinery or equipments required for use on a railway, or for the maintenance of rolling-stock.

50. Any railway company, not being a company for which the Statute 42 and 43 Victoria, chapter 41, provides, may from time to time make with the Governor General in Council, and carry into effect, or, with the sanction of the Governor General in Council, make with any other railway administration, and carry into effect, any agreement with respect to any of the following purposes, namely: -

(a) the working, use, management and maintenance of any railway;

(b) the supply of rolling-stock and machinery necessary for any of the purposes mentioned in clause (a) and of officers and servants for the conduct of the traffic of the railway;

(c) the payments to be made and the conditions to be performed with respect to such working, use, management and maintenance;

(d) the interchange, accommodation and conveyance of traffic being on, coming from or intended for the respective railways of the contracting parties, and the fixing, collecting, apportionment and appropriation of the revenues arising from that traffic;

(e) generally, the giving effect to any such provisions or stipulations with respect to any of the purposes hereinbefore in this section mentioned as the contracting parties may think fit and mutually agree on :

Provided that the agreement shall not affect any of the rates which the railway administrations parties thereto are from time to time respectively authorised to demand and receive from any person, and that every person shall, notwithstanding the agreement, be entitled to the use and benefit of the railways of any railway administrations, parties to the agreement, on the same terms and conditions, and on payment of the same rates, as he would be if the agreement had not been entered into.

51. Any railway company, not being a company for which the Statute 42 and 43 Victoria, chapter 41, provides, may from time to time exercise with the sanction of the Governor General in Council all or any of the following powers, namely: -

(a) it may establish, for the accommodation of the traffic of its railway, any ferry equipped with machinery and plant of good quality and adequate in quantity to work the ferry;
(b) it may work for purposes other than the accommodation of the traffic of the railway any ferry established by it under this section;
(c) it may provide and maintain on any of its bridges roadways for foot-passengers, cattle, carriages, carts or other traffic;
(d) it may construct and maintain roads for the accommodation of traffic passing to or from its railway;
(e) it may provide and maintain any means of transport which may be required for the reasonable convenience of passengers, animals or goods carried or to be carried on its railway;
(f) it may charge tolls on the traffic using such ferries, roadways, roads or means of transport as it may provide under this section, according to tariffs to be arranged from time to time with the sanction of the Governor General in Council.

52. Every railway administration shall, in forms to be prescribed by the Governor General in Council, prepare, half-yearly or at such intervals as the Governor General in Council may prescribe, such returns of its capital and revenue transactions and of its traffic as the Governor General in Council may require, and shall forward a copy of such returns to the Governor General in Council at such times as he may direct.

Carriage of Property

53. (1) Every railway administration shall determine the maximum load for every wagon or truck in its possession, and shall exhibit the words or figures representing the load so determined in a conspicuous manner on the outside of every such wagon or truck.

(2) Every person owning a wagon or truck which passes over a railway shall

similarly determine and exhibit the maximum load for the wagon or truck.

(3) The gross weight of any such wagon or truck bearing on the axles when the wagon or truck is loaded to such maximum load shall not exceed such limit as may be fixed by the Governor General in Council for the class of axle under the wagon or truck.

54. (1) Subject to the control of the Governor General in Council, a railway administration may impose conditions, not inconsistent with this Act or with any general rule thereunder, with respect to the receiving, forwarding or delivering of any animals or goods.

(2) The railway administration shall keep at each station on its railway a copy of the conditions for the time being in force under sub-section (1) at the station, and shall allow any person to inspect it free of charge at all reasonable times.

(3) A railway administration shall not be bound to carry any animal suffering from any infectious or contagious disorder.

55. (1) If a person fails to pay on demand made by or on behalf of a railway administration any rate, terminal or other charge due from him in respect of any animals or goods, the railway administration may detain the whole or any of the animals or goods, or, if they have been removed from the railway, any other animals or goods of such person then being in or thereafter coming into its possession.

(2) When any animals or goods have been detained under sub-section (1), the railway administration may sell by public auction, in the case of perishable goods at once, and in the case of other goods or of animals on the expiration of at least fifteen days' notice of the intended auction, published in one or more of the local newspapers or, where there are no such newspapers, in such manner as the Governor General in Council may prescribe, sufficient of such animals or goods to produce a sum equal to the charge and all expenses of such detention, notice and sale, including, in the case of animals, the expenses of the feeding, watering and tending thereof.

(3) Out of the proceeds of the sale the railway administration may retain a sum equal to the charge and the expenses aforesaid, rendering the surplus, if any, of the proceeds, and such of the animals or goods (if any) as remain unsold, to the person entitled thereto.

(4) If a person on whom a demand for any rate, terminal or other charge due from him has been made fails to remove from the railway within a reasonable time any animals or goods which have been detained under sub-section (1), or any animals or goods which have remained unsold after a sale under sub-section (2), the railway administration may sell the whole of them and dispose of the proceeds of the sale as nearly as may be under the provisions of sub-section (3).

(5) Notwithstanding anything in the foregoing sub-sections, the railway administration may recover by suit any such rate, terminal or other charge as aforesaid or balance thereof.

56. (1) When any animals or goods have come into the possession of a railway

administration for carriage or otherwise and are not claimed by the owner or other person appearing to the railway administration to be entitled thereto, the railway administration shall, if such owner or person is known, cause a notice to be served upon him requiring him to remove the animals or goods.

(2) If such owner or person is not known, or the notice cannot be served upon him, or he does not comply with the requisition in the notice, the railway administration may within a reasonable time, subject to the provisions of any other enactment for the time being in force, sell the animals or goods as nearly as may be under the provisions of the last foregoing section, rendering the surplus, if any, of the proceeds of the sale to any person entitled thereto.

57. Where any animals, goods or sale-proceeds in the possession of a railway administration are claimed by two or more persons or the ticket or receipt given for the animals or goods is not forthcoming, the railway administration may withhold delivery of the animals, goods or sale-proceeds until the person entitled in its opinion to receive them has given an indemnity, to the satisfaction of the railway administration, against the claims of any other person with respect to the animals, goods or sale-proceeds.

58. (1) The owner or person having charge of any goods which are brought upon a railway for the purpose of being carried thereon, and the consignee of any goods which have been carried on a railway, shall, on the request of any railway servant appointed in this behalf by the railway administration, deliver to such servant an account in writing signed by such owner or person, or by such consignee, as the case may, be, and containing such a description of the goods as may be sufficient to determine the rate which the railway administration is entitled to charge in respect thereof.

(2) If such owner, person or consignee refuses or neglects to give such an account, and refuses to open the parcel or package containing the goods in order that their description may be ascertained, the railway administration may, (a) in respect of goods which have been brought for the purpose of being carried on the railway, refuse to carry the goods unless in respect thereof a rate is paid not exceeding the highest rate which may be in force at the time on the railway for any class of goods or, (b) in respect of goods which have been carried on the railway, charge a rate not exceeding such highest rate.

(3) If an account delivered under sub-section (1) is materially false with respect to the description of any goods to which it purports to relate, and which have been carried on the railway, the railway administration may charge in respect of the carriage of the goods a rate not exceeding double the highest rate which may be in force at the time on the railway for any class of goods.

(4) If any difference arises between a railway servant and the owner or person having charge, or the consignee, of any goods which have been brought to be carried or have been carried on a railway, respecting the description of goods of which an account has been delivered under this section, the railway servant may detain

and examine the goods.

(5) If it appears from the examination that the description of the goods is different from that stated in an account delivered under sub-section (1), the person who delivered the account, or, if that person is not the owner of the goods, then that person and the owner jointly and severally, shall be liable to pay to the railway administration the cost of the detention and examination of the goods, and the railway administration shall be exonerated from all responsibility for any loss which may have been caused by the detention or examination thereof.

(6) If it appears that the description of the goods is not different from that stated in an account delivered under sub-section (1), the railway administration shall pay the cost of the detention and examination and be responsible to the owner of the goods for any such loss as aforesaid.

59. (1) No person shall be entitled to take with him, or to require a railway administration to carry, any dangerous or offensive goods upon a railway.

(2) No person shall take any such goods with him upon a railway without giving notice of their nature to the station-master or other railway servant in charge of the place where he brings the goods upon the railway, or shall tender or deliver any such goods for carriage upon a railway without distinctly marking their nature on the outside of the package containing them or otherwise giving notice in writing of their nature to the railway servant to whom he tenders or delivers them.

(3) Any railway servant may refuse to receive such goods for carriage and, when such goods have been so received without such notice as is mentioned in sub-section (1) having to his knowledge been given, may refuse to carry them or may stop their transit.

(4) If any railway servant has reason to believe any such goods to be contained in a package with respect to the contents whereof such notice as is mentioned in sub-section (2) has not to his knowledge been given, he may cause the package to be opened for the purpose of ascertaining its contents.

(5) Nothing in this section shall be construed to derogate from the Indian Explosives Act, 1884, or any rule under that Act, and nothing in sub-sections (1), (3) and (4) shall be construed to apply to any goods tendered or delivered for carriage by order or on behalf of the Government or to any goods which an officer, soldier, sailor or police-officer or a person enrolled as a volunteer under the Indian Volunteers Act, 1869, may take with him upon a railway in the course of his employment or duty as such.

60. At every station at which a railway administration quotes a rate to any other station for the carriage of traffic other than passengers and their luggage, the railway servant appointed by the administration to quote the rate shall, at the request of any person, show to him at all reasonable times, and without payment of any fee, the rate-books or other documents in which the rate is authorised by the administration or administrations concerned.

61. (1) Where any charge is made by and paid to a railway administration in respect of the carriage of goods over its railway, the administration shall, on the application of the person by whom or on whose behalf the charge has been paid, render to the applicant an account showing how much of the charge comes under each of the following heads, namely: -

(a) the carriage of the goods on the railway;
(b) terminals;
(c) demurrage; and
(d) collection, delivery and other expenses; but without particularising the several items of which the charge under each head consists.

(2) The application under sub-section (1) must be in writing and be made to the railway administration within one month after the date of the payment of the charge by or on behalf of the applicant, and the account must be rendered by the administration within two months after the receipt of the application.

Carriage of Passengers

62. The Governor General in Council may require any railway administration to provide and maintain in proper order, in any train worked by it which carries passengers, such efficient means of communication between the passengers and the railway servants in charge of the train as the Governor General in Council has approved.

63. Every railway administration shall fix, subject to the approval of the Governor General in Council, the maximum number of passengers which may be carried in each compartment of every description of carriage, and shall exhibit the number so fixed in a conspicuous manner inside or outside each compartment, in English or in one or more of the vernacular languages in common use in the territory traversed by the railway, or both in English and in one or more of such vernacular languages, as the Governor General in Council, after consultation with the railway administration, may determine.

64. (1) On and after the first day of January, 1891, every railway administration shall in every train carrying passengers reserve for the exclusive use of females one compartment at least of the lowest class of carriage forming part of the train.

(2) One such compartment so reserved shall, if the train is to run for a distance exceeding fifty miles, be provided with a closet.

65. Every railway administration shall cause to be posted in a conspicuous and accessible place at every station on its railway, in English and in a vernacular language in common use in the territory where the station is situate, a copy of the time-tables for the time being in force on the railway, and lists of the fares chargeable for travelling from the station where the lists are posted to every place for which card-tickets are ordinarily issued to passengers at that station.

66. (1) Every person desirous of travelling on a railway shall, upon payment of his fare, be supplied with a ticket, specifying the class of carriage for which, and the place from and the place to which, the fare has been paid, and the amount of the fare.
(2) The matters required by sub-section (1) to be specified on a ticket shall be set forth-

(a) if the class of carriage to be specified thereon is the lowest class, then in a vernacular language in common use in the territory traversed by the railway, and
(b) if the class of carriage to be so specified is any other than the lowest class, then in English.

67. (1) Fares shall be deemed to be accepted, and tickets to be issued, subject to the condition of there being room available in the train for which the tickets are issued.
(2) A person to whom a ticket has been issued and for whom there is not room available in the train for which the ticket was issued shall on returning the ticket within three hours after the departure of the train be entitled to have his fare at once refunded.
(3) A person for whom there is not room available in the class of carriage for which he has purchased a ticket and who is obliged to travel in a carriage of a lower class shall be entitled on delivering up his ticket to a refund of the difference between the fare paid by him and the fare payable for the class of carriage in which he travelled.

68. No person shall, without the permission of a railway servant, enter any carriage on a railway for the purpose of travelling therein as a passenger unless he has with him a proper pass or ticket.
69. Every passenger by railway shall, on the requisition of any railway servant appointed by the railway administration in this behalf, present his pass or ticket to the railway servant for examination, and at or near the end of the journey for which the pass or ticket was issued or, in the case of a season pass or ticket, at the expiration of the period for which it is current, deliver up the pass or ticket to the railway servant.
70. A return ticket or season ticket shall not be transferable and may be used only by the person for whose journey to and from the places specified thereon it was issued.

71. (1) A railway administration may refuse to carry, except in accordance with the conditions prescribed under section 47, sub-section (1), clause (d), a person suffering from any infectious or contagious disorder.
(2) A person suffering from such a disorder shall not enter or travel upon a railway without the special permission of the station-master or other railway servant in charge of the place where he enters upon the railway.
(3) A railway servant giving such permission as is mentioned in sub-section (2) must arrange for the separation of the person suffering from the disorder from other persons being or travelling upon the railway.

CHAPTER VII

RESPONSIBILITY OF RAILWAY ADMINISTRATIONS AS CARRIERS

72. (1) The responsibility of a railway administration for the loss, destruction or deterioration of animals or goods delivered to the administration to be carried by railway shall, subject to the other provisions of this Act, be that of a bailee under sections 151, 152 and 161 of the Indian Contract Act, 1872.

(2) An agreement purporting to limit that responsibility shall, in so far as it purports to effect such limitation, be void unless it -

(a) is in writing signed by or on behalf of the person sending or delivering to the railway administration the animals or goods, and

(b) is otherwise in a form approved by the Governor General in Council.

(3) Nothing in the common law of England or in the Carriers Act, 1865, regarding the responsibility of common carriers with respect to the carriage of animals or goods, shall affect the responsibility as in this section defined of a railway administration.

73. (1) The responsibility of a railway administration under the last foregoing section for the loss, destruction or deterioration of animals delivered to the administration to be carried on a railway shall not in any case exceed, in the case of elephants or horses, five hundred rupees a head or, in the case of camels or horned cattle, fifty rupees a head or, in the case of sheep, goats, dogs or other animals, ten rupees a head, unless the person sending or delivering them to the administration caused them to be declared, or declared them, at the time of their delivery for carriage by railway, to be respectively of higher value than five hundred, fifty or ten rupees a head, as the case may be.

(2) Where such higher value has been declared, the railway administration may charge, in respect of the increased risk, a percentage upon the excess of the value so declared over the respective sums aforesaid.

(3) In every proceeding against a railway administration for the recovery of compensation for the loss, destruction or deterioration of any animal the burden of proving the value of the animal and, where the animal has been injured, the extent of the injury shall lie upon the person claiming the compensation.

74. A railway administration shall not be responsible for the loss, destruction or deterioration of any luggage belonging to or in charge of a passenger unless a railway servant has booked and given a receipt therefor.

75. (1) When any articles mentioned in the second schedule are contained in any parcel or package delivered to a railway administration for carriage by railway, and the value of such articles in the parcel or package exceeds one hundred rupees, the railway administration shall not be responsible for the loss, destruction or deterioration of the parcel or package unless the person sending or delivering the parcel or package to the administration caused its value and contents to be declared

or declared them at the time of the delivery of the parcel or package for carriage by railway, and, if so required by the administration, paid or engaged to pay a percentage on the value so declared by way of compensation for increased risk.

(2) When any parcel or package of which the value has been declared under sub-section (1) has been lost or destroyed or has deteriorated, the compensation recoverable in respect of such loss, destruction or deterioration shall not exceed the value so declared, and the burden of proving the value so declared to have been the true value shall, notwithstanding anything in the declaration, lie on the person claiming the compensation.

(3) A railway administration may make it a condition of carrying a parcel declared to contain any article mentioned in the second schedule that a railway servant authorised in this behalf has been satisfied by examination or otherwise that the parcel actually contains the article declared to be therein.

76. In any suit against a railway administration for compensation for loss, destruction or deterioration of animals or goods delivered to a railway administration for carriage by railway, it shall not be necessary for the plaintiff to prove how the loss, destruction or deterioration was caused.

77. A person shall not be entitled to a refund of an overcharge in respect of animals or goods carried by railway or to compensation for the loss, destruction or deterioration of animals or goods delivered to be so carried; unless his claim to the refund or compensation has been preferred in writing by him or on his behalf to the railway administration within six months from the date of the delivery of the animals or goods for carriage by railway.

78. Notwithstanding anything in the foregoing provisions of this Chapter, a railway administration shall not be responsible for the loss, destruction or deterioration of any goods with respect to the description of which an account materially false has been delivered under sub-section (1) of section 58 if the loss, destruction or deterioration is in any way brought about by the false account, nor in any case for an amount exceeding the value of the goods if such value were calculated in accordance with the description contained in the false account.

79. Where an officer, soldier or follower, while being or travelling as such on duty upon a railway belonging to, and worked by, the Government, loses his life or receives any personal injury in such circumstances that if he were not an officer, soldier or follower being or travelling as such on duty upon the railway compensation would be payable under Act No. XIII of 1855 or to him, as the case may be, the form and amount of the compensation to be made in respect of the loss of his life or his injury shall, where there is any provision in this behalf in the military regulations to which he was immediately before his death, or is, subject, be determined in accordance with those regulations, and not otherwise.

80. Notwithstanding anything in any agreement purporting to limit the liability of a railway administration with respect to traffic while on the railway of another administration, a suit for compensation for loss of the life of, or personal injury to, a passenger, or for

loss, destruction or deterioration of animals or goods, where the passenger was or the animals or goods were booked through over the railways of two or more railway administrations, may be brought either against the railway administration from which the passenger obtained his pass or purchased his ticket or to which the animals or goods were delivered by the consignor thereof, as the case may be, or against the railway administration on whose railway the loss, injury, destruction or deterioration occurred.

81. Where a railway administration under contract to carry animals or goods by any inland water procures the same to be carried in a vessel which is not a railway as defined in this Act, the responsibility of the railway administration for the loss, destruction or deterioration of the animals or goods during their carriage in the vessel shall be the same as if the vessel were such a railway.

82. (1) When a railway administration contracts to carry passengers, animals or goods partly by railway and partly by sea, a condition exempting the railway administration from responsibility for any loss of life, personal injury or loss of or damage to animals or goods which may happen during the carriage by sea from the act of God, the King's enemies, fire, accidents from machinery, boilers and steam and all and every other dangers and accidents of the seas, rivers and navigation of whatever nature and kind so ever shall, without being expressed, be deemed to be part of the contract, and, subject to that condition, the railway administration shall, irrespective of the nationality or ownership of the ship used for the carriage by sea, be responsible for any loss of life, personal injury or loss of or damage to animals or goods which may happen during the carriage by sea, to the extent to which it would be responsible under the Merchant Shipping Act, 1854, and the Merchant Shipping Act Amendment Act, 1862, if the ship were registered under the former of those Acts and the railway administration were owner of the ship, and not to any greater extent.

(2) The burden of proving that any such loss, injury or damage as is mentioned in sub-section (1) happened during the carriage by sea shall lie on the railway administration.

CHAPTER VIII
ACCIDENTS

83. When any of the following accidents occurs in the course of working a railway, namely:-

(a) any accident attended with loss of human life, or with grievous hurt as defined in the Indian Penal Code, or with serious injury to property;
(b) any collision between trains of which one is a train carrying passengers;
(c) the derailment of any train carrying passengers, or of any part of such a train;
(d) any accident of a description usually attended with loss of human life or with such grievous hurt as aforesaid or with serious injury to property;
(e) any accident of any other description which the Governor General in Council

may notify in this behalf in the Gazette of India;

the railway administration working the railway and, if the accident happens to a train belonging to any other railway administration, the other railway administration also shall, without unnecessary delay, send notice of the accident to the Local Government and to the Inspector appointed for the railway; and the station-master nearest to the place at which the accident occurred or, where there is no station-master, the railway servant in charge of the section of the railway on which the accident occurred shall, without unnecessary delay, give notice of the accident to the Magistrate of the district in which the accident occurred, and to the officer in charge of the police-station within the local limits of which it occurred, or to such other Magistrate and police-officer as the Governor General in Council appoints in this behalf.

84. The Governor General in Council may make rules, consistent with this Act and any other enactment for the time being in force, for all or any of the following purposes, namely: -

(a) for prescribing the forms of the notices mentioned in the last foregoing section, and the particulars of the accident which those notices are to contain;

(b) for prescribing the class of accidents of which notice is to be sent by telegraph immediately after the accident has occurred;

(c) for prescribing the duties of railway servants, police-officers, Inspectors and Magistrates on the occurrence of an accident.

85. Every railway administration shall send to the Governor General in Council a return of accidents occurring upon its railway, whether attended with personal injury or not, in such form and manner and at such intervals of time as the Governor General in Council directs.

86. Whenever any person injured by an accident on a railway claims compensation on account of the injury, any Court or person having by law or consent of parties authority to determine the claim may order that the person injured be examined by some duly qualified medical practitioner named in the order and not being a witness on either side, and may make such order with respect to the costs of the examination as it or he thinks fit.

CHAPTER IX
PENALTIES AND OFFENCES

Forfeitures by Railway Companies

87. If a railway company fails to comply with any requisition made under section 13, it shall forfeit to the Government the sum of two hundred rupees for the default and a further sum of fifty rupees for every day after the first during which the default continues.

88. If a railway company moves any rolling-stock upon a railway by steam or other motive power in contravention of section 16, sub-section (2), or opens or uses any railway or work in contravention of section 18, section 19, section 20 or section 21, or re-opens any railway or uses any rolling-stock in contravention of section 24, it shall forfeit to the Government the sum of two hundred rupees for every day during which the motive power, railway, work or rolling-stock is used in contravention of any of those sections.
89. If a railway company fails to comply with the provisions of section 47, sub-section (6), section 54, sub-section (2), or section 65, with respect to the books or other documents to be kept open to inspection or conspicuously posted at stations on its railway, it shall forfeit to the Government the sum of fifty rupees for every day during which the default continues.
90. If a railway company fails to comply with the provisions of section 47 with respect to the making of general rules, it shall forfeit to the Government the sum of fifty rupees for every day during which the default continues.
91. If a railway company refuses or neglects to comply with any decision of the Governor General in Council under section 48, it shall forfeit to the Government the sum of two hundred rupees for every day during which the refusal or neglect continues.
92. If a railway company fails to comply with the provisions of section 52 or section 85, with respect to the submission of any return, it shall forfeit to the Government the sum of fifty rupees for every day during which the default continues after the fourteenth day from the date prescribed for the submission of the return.
93. If a railway company contravenes the provisions of section 53 or section 63, with respect to the maximum load to be carried in any wagon or truck, or the maximum number of passengers to be carried in any compartment, or the exhibition of such load on the wagon or truck or of such number in or on the compartment, or knowingly suffers any person owning a wagon or truck passing over its railway to contravene the provisions of the former of those sections, it shall forfeit to the Government the sum of twenty rupees for every day during which either section is contravened.
94. If a railway company fails to comply with any requisition of the Governor General in Council under section 62 for the provision and maintenance in proper order, in any train worked by it which carries passengers, of such efficient means of communication as the Governor General in Council has approved, it shall forfeit to the Government the sum of twenty rupees for each train run in disregard of the requisition.
95. If a railway company fails to comply with the requirements of section 64 with respect to the reservation of compartments for females or the provision of closets therein, it shall forfeit to the Government the sum of twenty rupees for every train in respect of which the default occurs.
96. If a railway company omits to give such notice of an accident as is required by section 83 and the rules for the time being in force under section 84, it shall forfeit to the Government the sum of one hundred rupees for every day during which the omission continues.

97. (1) When a railway company has through any act or omission forfeited any sum to the Government under the foregoing provisions of this Chapter, the sum shall be recoverable by suit in the District Court having jurisdiction in the place where the act or omission or any part thereof occurred.

(2) The suit must be instituted with the previous sanction of the Governor General in Council, and the plaintiff therein shall be the Secretary of State for India in Council.

(3) The Governor General in Council may remit the whole or any part of any sum forfeited by a railway company to the Government under the foregoing provisions of this Chapter.

98. Nothing in those provisions shall be construed to preclude the Government from resorting to any other mode of proceeding instead of, or in addition to, such a suit as is mentioned in the last foregoing section, for the purpose of compelling a railway company to discharge any obligation imposed upon it by this Act.

Offences by Railway Servants

99. If a railway servant whose duty it is to comply with the provisions of section 60 negligently or wilfully omits to comply therewith, he shall be punished with fine which may extend to twenty rupees.

100. If a railway servant is in a state of intoxication while on duty, he shall be punished with fine which may extend to fifty rupees, or, where the improper performance of the duty would be likely to endanger the safety of any person travelling or being upon a railway, with imprisonment for a term which may extend to one year, or with fine, or with both.

101. If a railway servant, when on duty, endangers the safety of any person -

(a) by disobeying any general rule made, sanctioned, published and notified under this Act, or

(b) by disobeying any rule or order which is not inconsistent with any such general rule, and which such servant was bound by the terms of his employment to obey, and of which he had notice, or

(c) by any rash or negligent act or omission,

he shall be punished with imprisonment for a term which may extend to two years, or with fine which may extend to five hundred rupees, or with both.

102. If a railway servant compels or attempts to compel, or causes, any passenger to enter a compartment which already contains the maximum number of passengers exhibited therein or thereon under section 63, he shall be punished with fine which may extend to twenty rupees.

103. If a station-master or a railway servant in charge of a section of a railway omits to give such notice of an accident as is required by section 83and the rules for the time being in force under section 84, he shall be punished with fine which may extend to

fifty rupees.

104. If a railway servant unnecessarily -

(a) allows any rolling-stock to stand across a place where the railway crosses a public road on the level, or

(b) keeps a level-crossing closed against the public,

he shall be punished with fine which may extend to twenty rupees.

105. If any return which is required by this Act is false in any particular to the knowledge of any person who signs it, that person shall be punished with fine which may extend to five hundred rupees, or with imprisonment which may extend to one year, or with both.

Other Offences

106. If a person requested under section 58 to give an account with respect to any goods gives an account which is materially false, he and, if he is not the owner of the goods, the owner also shall be punished with fine which may extend to ten rupees for every maund or part of a maund of the goods, and the fine shall be in addition to any rate or other charge to which the goods may be liable.

107. If in contravention of section 59 a person takes with him any dangerous or offensive goods upon a railway, or tenders or delivers any such goods for carriage upon a railway, he shall be punished with fine which may extend to five hundred rupees, and shall also be responsible for any loss, injury or damage which may be caused by reason of such goods having been so brought upon the railway.

108. If a passenger, without reasonable and sufficient cause, makes use of or interferes with any means provided by a railway administration for communication between passengers and the railway servants in charge of a train, he shall be punished with fine which may extend to fifty rupees.

109. (1) If a passenger, having entered a compartment which is reserved by a railway administration for the use of another passenger or which already contains the maximum number of passengers exhibited therein or thereon under section 63, refuses to leave it when required to do so by any railway servant, he shall be punished with fine which may extend to twenty rupees.

(2) If a passenger resists the lawful entry of another passenger into a compartment not reserved by the railway administration for the use of the passenger resisting or not already containing the maximum number of passengers exhibited therein or thereon under section 63, he shall be punished with fine which may extend to twenty rupees.

110. (1) If a person, without the consent of his fellow-passengers, if any, in the same compartment, smokes in any compartment except a compartment specially provided for the purpose, he shall be punished with fine which may extend to

twenty rupees.

(2) If any person persists in so smoking after being warned by any railway servant to desist, he may, in addition to incurring the liability mentioned in sub-section (1), be removed by any railway servant from the carriage in which he is travelling.

111. If a person, without authority in this behalf, pulls down or wilfully injures any board or document set up or posted by order of a railway administration on a railway or any rolling-stock, or obliterates or alters any of the letters or figures upon any such board or document, he shall be punished with fine which may extend to fifty rupees.

112. If a person, with intent to defraud a railway administration, -

(a) enters in contravention of section 68 any carriage on a railway, or

(b) uses or attempts to use a single pass or single ticket which has already been used on a previous journey or, in the case of a return-ticket, a half thereof which has already been so used,

he shall be punished with fine which may extend to one hundred rupees in addition to the amount of the single fare for any distance which he may have travelled.

113. (1) If a passenger travels in a train without having a proper pass or a proper ticket with him, or, being in or having alighted from a train, fails or refuses to present for examination or to deliver up his pass or ticket immediately on requisition being made therefor under section 69, he shall be liable to pay, on the demand of any railway servant appointed by the railway administration in this behalf, the excess charge hereinafter in this section mentioned, in addition to the ordinary single fare for the distance which he has travelled or, where there is any doubt as to the station from which he started, the ordinary single fare from the station from which the train originally started, or, if the tickets of passengers travelling in the train have been examined since the original starting of the train, the ordinary single fare from the place where the tickets were examined or, in case of their having been examined more than once, were last examined.

(2) If a passenger travels or attempts to travel in or on a carriage, or by a train, of a higher class than that for which he has obtained a pass or purchased a ticket, or travels in or on a carriage beyond the place authorised by his pass or ticket, he shall be liable to pay, on the demand of any railway servant appointed by the railway administration in this behalf, the excess charge hereinafter in this section mentioned, in addition to any difference between any fare paid by him and the fare payable in respect of such journey as he has made.

(3) The excess charge referred to in sub-section (1) and sub-section (2) shall, -

(a) where the passenger has immediately after incurring the charge and before being detected by a railway servant notified to the railway servant on duty with the train the fact of the charge having been incurred, be one rupee, two annas or eight annas, and

(b) in any other case, be six rupees, one rupee or three rupees, according as the passenger is travelling or has travelled or has attempted to travel in a carriage of the highest class or in a carriage of the lowest class or in a carriage of any other class or kind:

Provided that such excess charge shall in no case exceed, -

(a) where the liability to pay it arises under sub-section (1), the amount of the ordinary single fare which the passenger incurring the charge is liable to pay under that sub-section, or

(b) where such liability arises under subsection (2), the amount of the difference between the fare paid by the passenger incurring the charge and the fare payable in respect of such journey as he has made.

(4) If a passenger liable to pay the excess charge and fare mentioned in sub-section (1), or the excess charge and any difference of fare mentioned in sub-section (2), fails or refuses to pay the same on demand being made therefor under one or other of those sub-sections, as the case may be, the sum payable by him shall, on application made to any Magistrate by any railway servant appointed by the railway administration in this behalf, be recovered by the Magistrate from the passenger as if it were a fine imposed on the passenger by the Magistrate and shall, as it is recovered, be paid to the railway administration.

114. If a person sells or attempts to sell, or parts or attempts to part with the possession of, the return half of a return ticket in order to enable any other person to travel therewith, or purchases such half of a return ticket, he shall be punished with fine which may extend to fifty rupees, and, if the purchaser of such half of a return ticket travels or attempts to travel therewith, he shall be punished with an additional fine which may extend to the amount of the single fare for the return journey authorised by the ticket.

115. That portion of any fine imposed under section 112 or the last foregoing section which represents the single fare therein mentioned shall, as the fine is recovered, be paid to the railway administration before any portion of the fine is credited to the Government.

116. If a passenger wilfully alters or defaces his pass or ticket so as to render the date, number or any material portion thereof illegible, he shall be punished with fine which may extend to fifty rupees.

117. (1) If a person suffering from an infectious or contagious disorder enters or travels upon a railway in contravention of section 71, sub-section (2), he, and any person having charge of him upon the railway when he so entered or travelled thereon, shall be punished with fine which may extend to twenty rupees, in addition to the forfeiture of any fare which either of them may have paid and of any pass or ticket which either of them may have obtained or purchased, and may be removed from the railway by any railway servant.

(2) If any such railway servant as is referred to in section 71, sub-section (2), knowing that a person is suffering from any infectious or contagious disorder, wilfully

permits the person to travel upon a railway without arranging for his separation from other passengers, he shall be punished with fine which may extend to one hundred rupees.

118. (1) If a passenger enters or leaves, or attempts to enter or leave, any carriage while the train is in motion, or elsewhere than at the side of the carriage adjoining the platform or other place appointed by the railway administration for passengers to enter or leave the carriage, or opens the side-door of any carriage while the train is in motion, he shall be punished with fine which may extend to twenty rupees.

(2) If a passenger, after being warned by a railway servant to desist, persists in travelling on the roof, steps or footboard of any carriage or on an engine, or in any other part of a train not intended for the use of passengers, he shall be punished with fine which may extend to fifty rupees and may be removed from the railway by any railway servant.

119. If a male person, knowing a carriage, compartment, room or other place to be reserved by a railway administration for the exclusive use of females, enters the place without lawful excuse, or, having entered it, remains therein after having been desired by any railway servant to leave it, he shall be punished with fine which may extend to one hundred rupees, in addition to the forfeiture of any fare which he may have paid and of any pass or ticket which he may have obtained or purchased, and may be removed from the railway by any railway servant.

120. If a person in any railway carriage or upon any part of a railway -

(a) is in a state of intoxication, or

(b) commits any nuisance or act of indecency, or uses obscene or abusive language, or

(c) wilfully and without lawful excuse interferes with the comfort of any passenger or extinguishes any lamp,

he shall be punished with fine which may extend to fifty rupees, in addition to the forfeiture of any fare which he may have paid and of any pass or ticket which he may have obtained or purchased, and may be removed from the railway by any railway servant.

121. If a person wilfully obstructs or impedes any railway servant in the discharge of his duty, he shall be punished with fine which may extend to one hundred rupees.

122. (1) If a person unlawfully enters upon a railway, he shall be punished with fine which may extend to twenty rupees.

(2) If a person so entering refuses to leave the railway on being requested to do so by any railway servant, or by any other person on behalf of the railway administration, he shall be punished with fine which may extend to fifty rupees, and may be removed from the railway by such servant or other person.

123. If a driver or conductor of a tramcar, omnibus, carriage or other vehicle while upon the premises of a railway disobeys the reasonable directions of any railway servant or

police-officer, he shall be punished with fine which may extend to twenty rupees.

124. In either of the following cases, namely: -

(a) If a person, knowing or having reason to believe that an engine or train is approaching along a railway, opens any gate set up on either side of the railway across a road, or passes or attempts to pass, or drives or takes, or attempts to drive or take, any animal, vehicle or other thing across the railway,

(b) if, in the absence of a gatekeeper, a person omits to shut and fasten such a gate as aforesaid as soon as he and any animal, vehicle or other thing under his charge have passed through the gate,

the person shall be punished with fine which may extend to fifty rupees.

125. (1) The owner or person in charge of any cattle straying on a railway provided with fences suitable for the exclusion of cattle shall be punished with fine which may extend to five rupees for each head of cattle, in addition to any amount which may have been recovered or may be recoverable under the Cattle-trespass Act, 1871.

(2) If any cattle are wilfully driven, or knowingly permitted to be, on any railway otherwise than for the purpose of lawfully crossing the railway or for any other lawful purpose, the person in charge of the cattle or, at the option of the railway administration, the owner of the cattle shall be punished with fine which may extend to ten rupees for each head of cattle, in addition to any amount which may have been recovered or may be recoverable under the Cattle-trespass Act, 1871.

(3) Any fine imposed under this section may, if the Court so directs, be recovered in manner provided by section 25 of the Cattle-trespass Act, 1871.

(4) The expression "public road" in sections 11 and 26 of the Cattle-trespass Act, 1871, shall be deemed to include a railway, and any railway servant may exercise the powers conferred on officers of police by the former of those sections.

(5) The word "cattle" has the same meaning in this section as in the Cattle-trespass Act, 1871.

126. If a person unlawfully -

(a) puts or throws upon or across any railway any wood, stone or other matter or thing, or

(b) takes up, removes, loosens or displaces any rail, sleeper or other matter or thing belonging to any railway, or

(c) turns, moves, unlocks or diverts any points or other machinery belonging to any railway, or

(d) makes or shows, or hides or removes, any signal or light upon or near to any railway, or

(e) does or causes to be done or attempts to do any other act or thing in relation to any railway,

with intent, or with knowledge that he is likely, to endanger the safety of any person travelling or being upon the railway, he shall be punished with transportation for life or with imprisonment for a term which may extend to ten years.

127. If a person unlawfully throws or causes to fall or strike at, against, into or upon any rolling-stock forming part of a train any wood, stone or other matter or thing with intent, or with knowledge that he is likely, to endanger the safety of any person being in or upon such rolling-stock or in or upon any other rolling-stock forming part of the same train, he shall be punished with transportation for life or with imprisonment for a term which may extend to ten years.

128. If a person, by any unlawful act or by any wilful omission or neglect, endangers or causes to be endangered the safety of any person travelling or being upon any railway, or obstructs or causes to be obstructed or attempts to obstruct any rolling-stock upon any railway, he shall be punished with imprisonment for a term which may extend to two years.

129. If a person rashly or negligently does any act, or omits to do what he is legally bound to do, and the act or omission is likely to endanger the safety of any person travelling or being upon a railway, he shall be punished with imprisonment for a term which may extend to one year, or with fine, or with both.

130. (1) If a minor under the age of twelve years is with respect to any railway guilty of any of the acts or omissions mentioned or referred to in any of the four last foregoing sections, he shall be deemed, notwithstanding anything in section 82 or section 83 of the Indian Penal Code, to have committed an offence, and the Court convicting him may, if it thinks fit, direct that the minor, if a male, shall be punished with whipping, or may require the father or guardian of the minor to execute, within such time as the Court may fix, a bond binding himself, in such penalty as the Court directs, to prevent the minor from being again guilty of any of those acts or omissions.

(2) The amount of the bond, if forfeited, shall be recoverable by the Court as if it were a fine imposed by itself.

(3) If a father or guardian fails to execute a bond under sub-section (1) within the time fixed by the Court, he shall be punished with fine which may extend to fifty rupees.

Procedure

131. (1) If a person commits any offence mentioned in section 100, 101, 119, 120, 121, 126, 127, 128 or 129 or in section 130, sub-section (1), he may be arrested without warrant or other written authority by any railway servant or police-officer, or by any other person whom such servant or officer may call to his aid.

(2) A person so arrested shall, with the least possible delay, be taken before a Magistrate having authority to try him or commit him for trial.

132. (1) If a person commits any offence under this Act other than an offence mentioned in the last foregoing section, or fails or refuses to pay any excess charge or other sum demanded under section 113, and there is reason to believe that he will abscond, or his name and address are unknown and he refuses on demand to give his name and address, or there is reason to believe that the name or address given by him is incorrect, any railway servant or police-officer, or any other person whom such railway servant or police-officer may call to his aid, may, without warrant or other written authority, arrest him.

(2) The person arrested shall be released on his giving bail, or, if his true name and address are ascertained, on his executing a bond without sureties, for his appearance before a Magistrate when required.

(3) If the person cannot give bail and his true name and address are not ascertained, he shall with the least possible delay be taken before the nearest Magistrate having jurisdiction.

(4) The provisions of Chapters XXXIX and XLII of the Code of Criminal Procedure, 1882, shall, so far as may be, apply to bail given and bonds executed under this section.

133. No Magistrate other than a Presidency Magistrate or than a Magistrate whose powers are not less than those of a Magistrate of the second class shall try any offence under this Act.

134. (1) Any person committing any offence against this Act or any rule thereunder shall be triable for such offence in any place in which he may be or which the Local Government may notify in this behalf, as well as in any other place in which he might be tried under any law for the time being in force.

(2) Every notification under sub-section (1) shall be published in the local official Gazette, and a copy thereof shall be exhibited for the information of the public in some conspicuous place at each of such railway stations as the Local Government may direct.

CHAPTER X
SUPPLEMENTAL PROVISIONS

135. Notwithstanding anything to the contrary in any enactment, or in any agreement or award based on any enactment, the following rules shall regulate the levy of taxes in respect of railways and from railway administrations in aid of the funds of local authorities, namely:-

(1) A railway administration shall not be liable to pay any tax in aid of the funds of any local authority unless the Governor General in Council has, by notification in the official Gazette, declared the railway administration to be liable to pay the tax.

(2) While a notification of the Governor General in Council under clause (1) of this section is in force, the railway administration shall be liable to pay to the local

authority either the tax mentioned in the notification or, in lieu thereof, such sum, if any, as an officer appointed in this behalf by the Governor General in Council may, having regard to all the circumstances of the case, from time to time determine to be fair and reasonable.

(3) The Governor General in Council may at any time revoke or vary a notification under clause (1) of this section.

(4) Nothing in this section is to be construed as debarring any railway administration from entering into a contract with any local authority for the supply of water or light, or for the scavenging of railway premises, or for any other service which the local authority may be rendering or be prepared to render within any part of the local area under its control.

(5) "Local authority" in this section means a local authority as defined in the General Clauses Act, 1887, and includes any authority legally entitled to or entrusted with the control or management of any fund for the maintenance of watchmen or for the conservancy of a river.

136. (1) None of the rolling-stock, machinery, plant, tools, fittings, materials or effects used or provided by a railway administration for the purpose of the traffic on its railway, or of its stations or workshops, shall be liable to be taken in execution of any decree or order of any Court without the previous sanction of the Governor General in Council.

(2) Nothing in sub-section (1) is to be construed as affecting the authority of any Court to attach the earnings of a railway in execution of a decree or order.

137. (1) Every railway servant shall be deemed to be a public servant for the purposes of Chapter IX of the Indian Penal Code.

(2) In the definition of "legal remuneration" in section 161 of that Code the word "Government" shall, for the purposes of sub-section (1) be deemed to include any employer of a railway servant as such.

(3) A railway servant shall not -

(a) purchase or bid for, either in person or by agent, in his own name or in that of another, or jointly or in shares with others, any property put up to auction under section 55 or section 56, or,

(b) in contravention of any direction of the railway administration in this behalf, engage in trade.

(4) Notwithstanding anything in section 21 of the Indian Penal Code, a railway servant shall not be deemed to be a public servant for any of the purposes of that Code except those mentioned in sub-section (1).

138. If a railway servant is discharged or suspended from his office, or dies, absconds or absents himself, and he or his wife or widow, or any of his family or representatives, refuses or neglects, after notice in writing for that purpose, to deliver up to the railway administration, or to a person appointed by the railway administration in this behalf,

any station, dwelling-house, office or other building, with its appurtenances, or any books, papers or other matters, belonging to the railway administration and in the possession or custody of such railway servant at the occurrence of any such event as aforesaid, any Magistrate of the first class may, on application made by or on behalf of the railway administration, order any police officer, with proper assistance, to enter upon the building and remove any person found therein and take possession thereof, or to take possession of the books, papers or other matters, and to deliver the same to the railway administration or a person appointed by the railway administration in that behalf.

139. Any notice, determination, direction, requisition, appointment, expression of opinion, approval or sanction to be given or signified on the part of the Governor General in Council, for any of the purposes of, or in relation to, this Act, or any of the powers or provisions therein contained, shall be sufficient and binding if in writing signed by a Secretary, Deputy Secretary, Under-Secretary or Assistant Secretary to the Government of India, or by any other officer or servant authorised to act on behalf of the Governor General in Council in respect of the matters to which the same may relate, and the Governor General in Council shall not in any case be bound in respect of any of the matters aforesaid unless by some writing signed in manner aforesaid.

140. Any notice or other document required or authorised by this Act to be served on a railway administration may be served, in the case of a railway administered by the Government or a Native State, on the Manager and, in the case of a railway administered by a railway company, on the Agent in India of the railway company -

(a) by delivering the notice or other document to the Manager or Agent, or
(b) by leaving it at his office, or
(c) by forwarding it by post in a prepaid letter addressed to the Manager or Agent at his office and registered under Part III of the Indian Post Office Act, 1866.

141. Any notice or other document required or authorized by this Act to be served on any person by a railway administration may be served -

(a) by delivering it to the person, or
(b) by leaving it at the usual or last known place of abode of the person, or
(c) by forwarding it by post in a prepaid letter addressed to the person at his usual or last known place of abode and registered under Part III of the Indian Post Office Act, 1866.

142. Where a notice or other document is served by post, it shall be deemed to have been served at the time when the letter containing it would be delivered in the ordinary course of post, and in proving such service it shall be sufficient to prove that the letter containing the notice or other document was properly addressed and registered.

143. (1) A rule under section 22, section 34 or section 84, or the cancellation, rescission or variation of a rule under any of those sections or under section 47, sub-section (4), shall not take effect until it has been published in the Gazette of India.

(2) Where any rule made under this Act, or the cancellation, rescission or variation of any such rule, is required by this Act to be published in the Gazette of India, it shall, besides being so published, be further notified to persons affected thereby in such manner as the Governor General in Council, by general or special order, directs.

(3) The Governor General in Council may cancel or vary any rule made by him under this Act.

144. (1) The Governor General in Council may, by notification in the Gazette of India, invest, absolutely or subject to conditions, any Local Government with any of the powers or functions of the Governor General in Council under this Act with respect to any railway, and may, by that or a like notification, declare what Local Government shall, for the purposes of the exercise of powers or functions so conferred, be deemed to be the Local Government in respect of the railway.

(2) The provisions of section 139 with respect to proceedings of the Governor General in Council shall, so far as they can be made applicable, apply to proceedings of a Local Government exercising the powers or discharging the functions of the Governor General in Council in pursuance of a notification under sub-section (1).

145. (1) The Manager of a railway administered by the Government or a Native State, and the Agent in India of a railway administered by a railway company, may, by instrument in writing, authorise any railway servant or other person to act for or represent him in any proceeding before any Civil, Criminal or other Court.

(2) A person authorised by a Manager or Agent to conduct prosecutions on behalf of a railway administration shall, notwithstanding anything in section 495 of the Code of Criminal Procedure, 1882, be entitled to conduct such prosecutions without the permission of the Magistrate.

146. The Governor General in Council may, by notification in the Gazette of India, extend this Act or any portion thereof to any tramway worked by steam or other mechanical power.

147. The Governor General in Council may, by a like notification, exempt any railway from any of the provisions of this Act.

148. (1) For the purposes of section 3, clauses (5), (6) and (7), and sections 4 to 19 (both inclusive), 47 to 52 (both inclusive), 59, 79, 83 to 92 (both inclusive), 96, 97, 98, 100, 101, 103, 104, 107, 111, 122, 124 to 132 (both inclusive), 134 to 138 (both inclusive), 140, 141, 144, 145 and 147, the word "railway", whether it occurs alone or as a prefix to another word, has reference to a railway or portion of a railway under construction and to a railway or portion of a railway not used for the public carriage of passengers, animals or goods as well as to a railway falling within the definition of that word in section 3, clause (4).

(2) For the purposes of sections 5, 21, 83, 100, 101, 103, 104, 121, 122, 125 and 137, sub-sections (1), (2) and (4), and section 138, the expression "railway servant" includes a person employed upon a railway in connection with the service thereof by a

person fulfilling a contract with the railway administration.

149. In sections 194 and 195 of the Indian Penal Code, for the words "by this Code or the law of England" the words "by the law of British India or England" shall be substituted.

150. For that portion of the preamble to the Sindh-Pishin Railway Act, 1887, which begins with the words "so far as it applies" and ends with the words "in its entirety", the words "should apply in its entirety to that part of the Sindh-Pishin section of the North-Western Railway which lies beyond the Province of Sindh" shall be substituted.

THE FIRST SCHEDULE
ENACTMENTS REPEALED

(See section 2)

Number and year	Title	Extent of repeal
	Acts of the Governor General in Council	
III of 1865	Carriers Act, 1865	Section 7 (so far as it relates to railways) and section 10
IV of 1879	Indian Railway Act, 1879	The whole
IV of 1883	Indian Railway Act, 1883	The whole
XI of 1886	Indian Tramways Act, 1886	Section 49
XX of 1886	Upper Burma Laws Act, 1886	So much as relates to Acts IV of 1879 and IV of 1883
	Act of the Lieutenant-Governor of Bengal in Council	
II of 1882	Bengal Embankment Act, 1882	Section 16, and in section 17 the proviso to the first paragraph of that section, the words "or under the section last preceding" and the words "or railroad" wherever they occur.

THE SECOND SCHEDULE
ARTICLES TO BE DECLARED AND INSURED

(See section 75)

(a) gold and silver, coined or uncoined, manufactured or unmanufactured;
(b) plated articles;

(c) cloths and tissue and lace of which gold or silver forms part, not being the uniform or part of the uniform of an officer, soldier, sailor, police-officer or person enrolled as a volunteer under the Indian Volunteers Act, 1869, or of any public officer, British or foreign, entitled to wear uniform;

(d) pearls, precious stones, jewellery and trinkets;

(e) watches, clocks and timepieces of any description;

(f) Government securities;

(g) Government stamps;

(h) bills of exchange, hundis, promissory-notes, bank-notes and orders or other securities for payment of money;

(i) maps, writings and title-deeds;

(j) paintings, engravings, lithographs, photographs, carvings, sculpture and other works of art;

(k) art pottery and all articles made of glass, china or marble;

(l) silks in a manufactured or unmanufactured state, and whether wrought up or not wrought up with other materials;

(m) shawls;

(n) lace and furs;

(o) opium;

(p) ivory, ebony, coral and sandalwood;

(q) musk, sandalwood-oil and other essential oils used in the preparation of *itr* or other perfume;

(r) musical and scientific instruments;

(s) any article of special value which the Governor General in Council may, by notification in the Gazette of India add to this schedule.

S. HARVEY JAMES,
Secy. to the Govt. of India

1. See Appendices to Part II for (1) memorandums by the Great Indian Peninsula Railway Company, East Indian Railway Company, and Madras Railway Company submitted to the Secretary of State for India, (2) the statement of the Bombay, Baroda and Central India Railway Company, on the Indian Railways Act IX of 1890, (3) the two notes by the Legal Adviser of the India Office, London regarding the implications of the Act, and for the letter from the Secretary of State for India, the India Office, London to the Governor General of India in Council, forwarding the above referred items.

392

General Rules for all Railways in India, 1890

Source: H. E. Trevor: The Law Relating to Railways in British India, London, 1891

Gist: General Rules for all Railways in India, 1890 were brought in through a resolution of the Government of India, Public Works Department (published in the *Gazette of India*, August 30, 1890). The General Rules were formulated under sections 8 and 47 of the Indian Railways Acts, 1879 and 1890 respectively. Theses rules are a result of certain modifications in the General Rules for Indian Railways, 1880. Many of the General Rules concern railway servants only. Those that appear to be of general interest are given below here.

GENERAL RULES

Under section 8 and 47 of the Indian Railways Acts, 1879 and 1890 respectively

By a resolution of the Government of India, Public Works Department (published in the *Gazette of India*, August 30, 1890), sanction was given to the application to certain specified railways of certain modifications in the General Rules for Indian railways, and it was ordered that the General Rules in question, which had already been published in the *Gazette of India*, dated 18th September, 1880, should be further notified to the railway servants and to the public by a copy thereof, as in the resolution modified, being open to inspection, free of any charge, in the office of the station master of every station on the said railways.

Many of the General Rules concern railway servants only: such as appear to be of general interest are given below. None of them are affected by any of the modifications referred to, but all are applicable to all railways used for the public conveyance of passengers or goods, unless specially exempted by the Governor-General in Council.

GENERAL RULES FOR ALL RAILWAYS IN INDIA

Made in conformity with Section 8 of "The Indian Railway Act, 1879"

The rules comprised in this code shall be held applicable to, and are to be observed on, all lines of Railway in India used for the public conveyance of passengers or goods, unless specially exempted by the Governor-General in Council.

Each railway administration may hereafter make such subsidiary rules as may be found necessary or expedient, provided that no such subsidiary rule shall be inconsistent with these general rules.

Every railway servant is bound by the terms of his employment to obey both the general rules and the subsidiary rules.

5. Except when necessary to carry passengers in goods vehicles, no passenger or mixed train shall be allowed to move from any station unless it be provided with an arrangement by which the guard can communicate with, make his way, or otherwise got access to every passenger carriage in the train.

12. No person suffering from an infectious disease shall enter a railway carriage or premises without previously notifying to the station master that he is so suffering, and obtaining from him permission enter under special instructions.

13. Any one being in attendance on a person suffering from an infectious disease is subject to some restrictions, while travelling by railway, as if he himself were suffering from the disease.

14. The maximum number of passengers that may be carried in each compartment of every description of carriage must be fixed by the railway administration with the approval of Government; and such number must be distinctly exhibited, inside each first and second class compartment in the English language, and both inside and outside of each compartment of all classes inferior to the second class, in conspicuous places in English and in vernacular language most commonly used in the districts through which the railway passes.

15. Tickets are only available from the date and for the period specified by the railway administration by which they are issued.

16. Any person found smoking, or having an open light or fire, in goods-sheds, store yards, or who persists in smoking, after being warned by a railway servant or police officer to desist, on any other portion of the railway premises, where such practice may be deemed dangerous by the authorized officer, shall be liable to immediate removal from the railway premises and to a fine which may extend to fifty rupees, or, in default of payment of such fine, to simple imprisonment for a term which may extend to two months.

17. In the event of any person being drunk and disorderly, or causing annoyance to others, the station master is to use all reasonable means to stop the annoyance, and if the offender persists, the station master is to have him removed from the railway premises, and the offender is liable to prosecution under the Railway Act.

18. Every person desirous of travelling on a railway shall, upon payment of his fare, be furnished with a ticket specifying in English and the principal vernacular language of the district on which the ticket is issued, the class of carriage for which, and the place from and place to which, the fare has been paid, and the amount of such fare.

And every passenger shall, when required, show his ticket to any railway servant duly authorized to examine the same, and shall deliver up such ticket upon demand to any railway servant duly authorized to collect tickets.

19. At the intermediate stations, the fares shall be deemed to be accepted and the tickets furnished, only upon condition that there be room in the train for which the tickets are furnished.

In case there is no room for all the passengers to whom tickets have been furnished, those who have obtained tickets for the longest distance shall have the preference; and those who have obtained tickets for the same distance shall have the preference according to the order in which they have received their tickets.

20. Any passenger to whom a ticket has been furnished in any station and for whom

there is no room shall, on returning the ticket within a reasonable time after its issue, be entitled to have his fare at once refunded.

21. No trespassing upon the railway shall be allowed, and no person, other than a railway servant, shall be permitted to walk on the line, unless provided with a licence to do so, signed by an authorized officer of the railway. If the trespasser, on being requested to quit, persists in remaining, he may immediately be removed from the railway by any railway servant or by any other person, and is liable to prosecution under the Railway Act.

22. No carriage door shall be opened while train is in motion.

31. For the purposes of the Railway Act, the following are declared to be dangerous goods:–

Carbolic Acid
Fusel oil
Kerosene oil
Naphthalin
Paraffin
Petroleum and other hydrocarbon oils
Rangoon oil
Wood naphtha
Muriate of tin
Nitrate of iron
Perchloride of iron
Solution of ammonia
Sulphate of indigo, concentrated
Aquafortis
Bromine
Chloride of sulphur
Chloroform
Fluoric acid
Glacial acetic acid
Mineral acids such as -
Muriatic acid
Nitric acid
Cartridges
Coloured fires
Congreve matches
Crackers
Combustibles
Cotton powder
Chlorate mixture
Detonators
Dynamite
Firework composition
Fireworks
Fog signals
Fuze
Gun-cotton
Gun-powder
Gun-cotton-powder
Lithofracteur
Lucifer matches
Nitrated gun-cotton
Nitro-glycerine and its compounds
Phosphorus
Percussion-caps
Schultzo gun-powder
Sulphuric acid or
Oil of vitriol
Ammunition
Amorphous phosphorus
Tubes for firing explosives
Vesuvians
War rockets
Explosive chemicals
All other explosives

48. No money or gratuity, in the shape of fee, or reward, is allowed to be taken from passengers, or other persons, by any railway servant, even although the regular hours of duty shall have expired, without the permission of the railway administration. Any infringement of this rule renders the offender liable to immediate dismissal and on conviction to imprisonment

for three years or to fine, or to both under sections 161 to 165 of the Indian Penal Code.

98. Every exertion must be made for the expeditious despatch of the station masters, and for ensuring the safety of the public, and punctuality of the trains. But no train conveying passengers must be started before the advertised time.

107. The station master is responsible that, immediately on the stopping of each passenger train, the name of the station is called out along the train in a distinct and audible manner, and that the station servants pay immediate attention to any indication shown by the passengers of their desire to alight.

109. When a passenger or mixed train has come to a stand at a station- whether alongside, beyond, or short of the platform - the driver must not move for any purpose whatever except upon instructions from the guard under orders of the person in charge of the station. The signal for the train to again move must not be given by the guard until he has satisfied himself that no passenger is getting into, or out of, the train, and all the carriage doors are closed. Before moving his train, the driver must sound his whistle sharply and distinctly.

129. No passenger train shall be stopped at a station where it is not timed to call, for the purpose of taking up or setting down passengers, without special authority.

131. No person shall be allowed without proper authority, to enter any carriage for the purpose of travelling therein unless the fare has been paid and a ticket obtained. See Rule 199.

135. If any passenger shall refuse, or be unable, to produce a proper ticket, or shall commit any other offence, the case must be immediately investigated by the station master, and he is to exercise his discretion as to the proceedings to be taken, always reporting to his immediate superior.

136. The power of arrest and detention is to be exercised with the greatest caution, and never where the address is given, and there is no ground and sufficient reason to doubt its correctness; or adequate security is offered for appearance to answer a charge. When it shall be necessary to detain any person, such detention shall not continue for a longer period than is absolutely necessary, but such person must be conveyed before a Magistrate with as little delay as possible.

137. As it is the intention which constitutes the offence, caution and discretion must be used in treating different cases, as it frequently occurs that passengers travel unintentionally beyond the distance for which they have paid their fares. In such cases they may be allowed to retain to the station for which they booked on payment of the ordinary single fare for the distance overridden, provided they return by the next train, and do not, in the interval, leave the railway premises.

138. Passengers not producing their tickets are required to pay the fare from whence the train started until enquiry can be made in order to ascertain whether the fare had been previously paid, or not; in every case the circumstance must be enquired into without delay and reported. See Rule 199.

142. No unprotected light shall be allowed in any railway vehicle.

145. No person suffering from an infectious disease is to be allowed to travel in the same compartment with other passengers, but must take and pay for reserved accommodation, and special precaution is to be taken against the infection being communicated to other persons on the railway premises.

146. Any person found suffering from an infectious disease in a railway carriage or in any place on a railway where there is likelihood of the infection spreading, and who has not obtained the permission of the station master under Rule 12, is to be removed from the railway premises, and shall on conviction, under section 269 of the Indian Penal Code be liable to imprisonment for six months, or to fine, or to both, or on conviction under section 270 of the Indian Penal Code be liable to imprisonment for two years, or to fine, or to both.

147. If any railway carriage has been entered by a person suffering from an infectious disease, such carriage must be disinfected immediately after it has arrived at its destination, and no passenger shall be allowed into it until the disinfection has been completed.

148. Prisoners and persons afflicted with insanity must not be allowed to mix with other passengers, but must be placed, with their escort, in a prison-van or separate compartment, upon reserved accommodation being paid for.

149. No engine or other vehicle, the property of a private owner, shall be allowed to enter upon the main line, except under special arrangement.

177. Guards must see that the doors of the carriages are properly closed.

178. Guards must exert themselves to prevent any breach of the regulations by passengers or others, and report any such breach that comes to their notice.

198. When ladies are travelling alone, the guards are to pay every attention to their comfort, and in placing them in the train they must, if requested, endeavour to select a carriage (according to the class of their tickets) in which other ladies are travelling.

199. The guard must not allow any passenger or parcel to be conveyed by the train unless properly booked; and if he has reason to suppose that any passenger is without a ticket, or is not in the proper carriage, he must request the passenger to show his ticket, reporting to the station master, or person in charge, any irregularity he may detect. When a passenger is desirous of changing from an inferior to a superior class of carriage, on payment of the difference in fare the guard must have this arranged by the station master or person in charge. See Rules 134 and 138.

208. In the event of any passenger being drunk or disorderly, or causing annoyance to others, the guard is to use all reasonable means to stop the annoyance; failing which, he must, for the safety and convenience of all, have him removed from the train at the first station, and the offender is liable to prosecution under the Railway Act.

323. All level-crossings of which the gates close across the railway must be provided with red signal boards, and with lamps showing red, up and down the line, when the gates are closed across the line. The lamps must be kept lighted from sunset to sunrise and during foggy weather.

324. Every gateman must be provided with day and night signals, which he must keep in proper order, reporting immediately any defect he may observe to his superior officer.

325. Unless specially ordered to the contrary, the gates at all thoroughfares must be kept open for the passage of trains, and securely closed across the thoroughfare except when required to be opened for the road traffic, and must then as quickly as possible be closed again across the thoroughfare. Before opening the gates the gateman must look up and down the line to

assure himself that no train is approaching.

326. Where special authority is given, gates made to close across the railway may be kept open to the public thoroughfare, except when an engine or train is due or expected, at which time such gates must be closed, and fastened across the public thoroughfare; and until such engine or train has passed, the gates must be kept closed, and no person or thing is to be allowed within them. While the gates are closed across the railway and open to the thoroughfare, the "danger" signal must be exhibited both up and down the line. In opening double gates closing across the railway for an approaching train where there is only one signal lamp to each gate, the half with the signal lamp attached is not to be moved until the other half is shut across the thoroughfare.

336. All level-crossings where the block system is not in operation, and where there are fixed signals, the "danger" signal must be exhibited for at least five minutes after the passing of any train; after which, if the gates are open for the passage of trains, a "caution" signal must be exhibited for a further period of five minutes.

393

The Indian Railway Companies Act, 1895

Source: Suranjan Chakravarty: The Indian Railways Act, 1890, Appendix D; Calcutta, 1961

Gist: The Indian Railway Companies Act, 1895 (Act 10 of 1895) deals with the provisions related to the payment by railway companies registered under the Indian Companies Act of 1882, of interest out of capital during construction.

Act No. X of 1895

7th March 1895

An Act to provide for the payment by Railway Companies registered under the Indian Companies Act, 1882, of interest out of capital during construction.

WHEREAS it is expedient to provide for the payment by Railway Companies registered under the Indian Companies Act, 1882 (VI of 1882), of interest out of capital during construction; It is hereby enacted as follows:-

1. *Title and extent.* (1) This Act may be called the Indian Railway Companies Act, 1895.

   (2) It extends to the territories which, immediately before the 1st November 1956, were comprised in Part B States.

2. *Definitions.* In this Act, unless there is something repugnant in the subject or context,

   (1) "railway" means a railway as defined in section 3, clause (4), of the Indian Railways Act, 1890 (IX of 1890) :

   (2) "the railway" means the railway in relation to the construction of which interest out of capital is permitted to be paid as hereinafter provided : and

   (3) "Railway Company" means a Company registered under the Indian Companies Act, 1882 (VI of 1882), and formed for the purpose of making and working, or making or working, a railway in India, whether alone or in conjunction with other purposes.

3. *Payment of interest out of capital.* A Railway Company may pay interest on its paid-up share capital out of capital, for the period, and subject to the conditions and restrictions in this section mentioned, and may charge the same to capital as part of the cost of construction of the railway: -

(1) Such interest shall be paid only for such period as shall be determined by the Central Government; and such period shall in no case extend beyond the close of the half-year next after the half-year during which the railway shall be actually completed and opened for traffic.

(2) No such payment shall be made unless the same is authorised by the Company's memorandum of association or by a special resolution of the Company.

(3) No such payment, whether authorised by the Company's memorandum of association or by special resolution as aforesaid, shall be made without the previous sanction of the Central Government.

(4) The amount so paid out of capital by way of interest, in respect of any period, shall in no case exceed a sum which shall, together with the net earnings of the railway during such period, make up the rate of four per cent per annum.

(5) No such payment of interest shall be made until such Railway Company has satisfied the Central Government that two-thirds at least of its share capital, in respect whereof interest is to be so paid, has been actually issued and accepted, and is held by shareholders who, or whose representatives, are legally liable for the same.

(6) No such interest shall accrue in favour of any shareholder for any time during which any call on any of his shares is in arrear.

(7) The payment of such interest shall not operate as a reduction of the amount paid up on the shares in respect of which it is paid.

4. *Provisions of section 3 applicable to additional share capital for extensions.* A railway in course of construction and intended to be made or worked by a Railway Company in addition to or by way of extension of any railway owned or worked by such Company, shall be deemed to be the railway of such Company for the purposes of this Act, and all the provisions of the last preceding section shall apply to such railway and to the share capital issued for the purposes of its construction.

5. *Notice in prospectus and other documents.* When a Railway Company has power to pay interest under this Act, notice to that effect shall be given in every prospectus, advertisement or other document inviting subscriptions for shares therein, and in every certificate of such shares.

6. *Accounts.* When any interest has been paid by a Railway Company under this Act, the annual or other accounts of such Company shall show the amount on which, and the rate at which, interest has been so paid.

7. *Construction of borrowing powers.* If by any memorandum of association, articles of association or other document any power of borrowing money is conferred on a Railway Company, or on its Directors, with or without the sanction of any meeting, and if such power of borrowing is limited to an amount bearing any proportion to the capital of such Company, the amount of the capital applied or to be applied in payment of interest under this Act shall, for the purpose of ascertaining the extent of such power of borrowing, be deducted from the capital of such Company.

---

* See now the Companies Act, 1956 (1 of 1956).

394

Repealing of Acts on Indian Railways passed between 1854 and 1890 by the Governor General of India

Source: H. E. Trevor: The Law Relating to Railways in British India, London, 1891

Gist: This document summarizes the history of repealing of Acts on Indian Railways by the Governor General in Council between 1854 and 1890.

ACTS OF THE GOVERNOR-GENERAL IN COUNCIL

REPEALED ACTS

The first Railway Act was Act XVIII of 1854, intituled "An Act relating to Railways in India," which applied to all railways which had then been or should be opened by any railway company under the superintendence and control of the East India Company for the public conveyance of passengers or goods in any part of the territories in the possession and under the government of the said Company. This Act was amended by Act LII of 1860, so as to enable police magistrates in certain circumstances to try offences punishable under sects. 27 and 28 of the Act with imprisonment.

By Act XIII of 1870, sects. 1 and 2, it was enacted that the provisions of Act XVIII of 1854 should apply to all railways then or thereafter belonging to government, but worked by a railway company, in the same manner as if such railways belonged to the company, and had been opened by the company, in manner mentioned in the preamble to the said Act. And that, subject to the modifications thereinafter mentioned, the said Act should apply to all railways then or thereafter worked by government, in the same manner as if such railways had been opened by a railway company in manner aforesaid.

Act XVIII of 1854 was further amended by the Railway Act Amendment Act XXV of 1871.

Sect. 39 of Act XVIII of 1854 was repealed by Act XIV of 1870; sects. 32 and 33 by Act XVI of 1874, and the remainder of the Act, together with Acts XIII of 1870 and XXV of 1871, was repealed by the second Railway Act, IV of 1879. Act XXXI of 1867, intituled "An Act to render penal certain Offences committed by Servants of Railway Companies," was also repealed by Act IV of 1879. Act IV of 1879, in its turn, after having been amended by Act IV of 1883, and extended to Upper Burmah by Act XX of 1886, was repealed, with its amending and extending Acts, by the third and present Railway Act, IX of 1890.

395

The Indian Telegraph Act, 1885

Source: The Gazette of India, Part IV, 25th July 1885

Gist: The Indian Telegraph Act, 1885 (Act 13 of 1885), which received the assent of the Governor-General on the 22 July 1885, has 33 sections in five parts. The Act repeals the Indian Telegraph Act, 1876 and provides for establishment and maintenance of telegraph, right to use any telegraph established, maintained or worked by any person licensed under this Act on the occurrence of any public emergency, or in the interest of the public safety, right of the telegraph authority to place and maintain a telegraph line under, over, along or across, and posts in or upon, any immovable property, and also measures to penalize offences. Sections 6 and 22 relate to railway companies. Any railway company, on being required, shall permit the Government to establish and maintain a telegraph upon any part of the land of the company, and shall give every reasonable facility for working the same. If neglects or refuses to comply with, the company or officer shall be punished with fine, which may extend to one thousand rupees for every day during which the neglect or refusal continues.

Act No. XIII of 1885

Passed by the Governor-General of India in Council

(Received the assent of the Governor-General on the 22nd July 1885)

An Act to amend the law relating to Telegraphs in India

Whereas it is expedient to amend the law relating to telegraphs in India; It is hereby enacted as follows: –

PART I
Preliminary

1. (1) This Act may be called the Indian Telegraph Act, 1885.
   (2) It extends to the whole of British India, and, so far as regards subjects to Her Majesty, to the dominions of princes and states in India in alliance with Her Majesty; and
   (3) It shall come into force on the first day of October 1885.
2. The Indian Telegraph Act, 1876, is hereby repealed. That all licenses granted and rules

made under that Act or any Act thereby repealed, and now in force, shall, so far as they could be granted or made under this Act, be deemed to have been respectively granted and made hereunder.

3. In this Act unless there is something repugnant in the subject or context,

   (1) "Telegraph" means electric, galvanic or magnetic telegraph, and includes appliances and apparatus for transmitting or making telegraphic, telephonic or other communications by means of electricity, galvanism or magnetism;

   (2) "Telegraph officer" means any person employed either permanently or temporarily in connection with a telegraph established, maintained or worked by the Government or by a person licensed under this Act;

   (3) "Message" means any communication sent by telegraph, or given to a telegraph officer to be sent by telegraph or to be delivered;

   (4) "Telegraph line" means a wire or wires used for the purpose of a telegraph, with any casing, coating, tube or pipe enclosing the same, and any appliances and apparatus connected therewith for the purpose of fixing or insulating the same;

   (5) "Post" means a post, pole, standard, stay, strut or other above-ground contrivance for carrying, suspending or supporting a telegraph line;

   (6) "Telegraph authority" means the Director-General of Telegraphs, and includes in any officer empowered by him to perform all or any of the functions of the telegraph authority under this Act;

   (7) "Local authority" means any municipal committee, district board, body of port commissioners or other authority legally entitled to, or entrusted by the Government with, the control or management of any municipal or local fund.

PART II

Privileges and Powers of the Government

4. Within British India, the Governor-General in Council shall have the exclusive privilege of establishing, maintaining and working telegraphs:

   Provided that the Governor-General in Council may grant a license, on such conditions and in consideration of such payments as he thinks fit, to any person to establish, maintain or work a telegraph within any part of British India.

5. (1) On the occurrence of any public emergency, or in the interest of the public safety, the Governor-General in Council or a Local Government, or any officer specially authorized in this behalf by the Governor-General in Council, may –

   (a) take temporary possession of any telegraph established, maintained or worked by any person licensed under this Act; or

   (b) order that any message or class of messages to or from any person or class of persons, or relating to any particular subject, brought for transmission by or transmitted or received by any telegraph, shall not be transmitted or shall be intercepted or detained, or shall be disclosed to the Government or an officer thereof mentioned in the order.

(2) If any doubt arises as to the existence of a public emergency, or whether any act done under sub-section (1) was in the interest of the public safety, a certificate signed by a secretary to the Government of India or to the Local Government shall be conclusive proof on the point.

6. Any railway company, on being required so to do by the Governor-General in Council, shall permit the Government to establish and maintain a telegraph upon any part of the land of the company, and shall give every reasonable facility for working the same.

7. (1) The Governor-General in Council may, from time to time, by notification in the Gazette of India, make rules consistent with this Act for the conduct of all or any telegraphs established, maintained or worked by the Government or by persons licensed under this Act.

(2) Rules under this section may provide for all or any of the following, among other matters, that is to say: –

(a) the rates at which, and the other conditions and restrictions subject to which, messages shall be transmitted;

(b) the precautions to be taken for preventing the improper interception or disclosure of messages;

(c) the period for which, and the conditions subject to which, telegrams and other documents belonging to, or being in the custody of, telegraph officers shall be preserved; and

(d) the fees to be charged for searching for telegrams or other documents in the custody of any telegraph officer.

(3) When making rules for the conduct of any telegraph established, maintained or worked by any person licensed under the Act, the Governor-General in Council may by the rules prescribe fines for any breach of the same:

Provided that the fines so prescribed shall not exceed the following limits, namely: –

(1) When the person licensed under this Act is punishable for the breach, one thousand rupees, and in the case of a continuing breach, a further fine of two hundred rupees for every day after the first during the whole or any part of which the breach continues;

(2) When a servant of the person so licensed, or any other person, is punishable for the breach, one-fourth of the amounts specified in clause (1).

8. The Governor-General in Council may, at any time, revoke any license granted under section 4, on the breach of any of the conditions therein contained, or in default of payment of any consideration payable thereunder.

9. The Secretary of State for India in Council shall not be responsible for any loss or damage which may occur in consequence of any telegraph officer failing in his duty

with respect to the receipt, transmission or delivery of any message; and no such officer shall be responsible for any such loss or damage, unless he causes the same negligently, maliciously or fraudulently.

PART III

Power to Place Telegraph Lines and Posts

10. The telegraph authority may, from time to time, place and maintain a telegraph line under, over, along or across, and posts in or upon, any immovable property; Provided that –

    (a) the telegraph authority shall not exercise the powers conferred by this section except for the purpose of a telegraph established or maintained by the Government, or to be so established or maintained;

    (b) the Government shall not acquire any right other than that of user only in the property under, over, along, across, in or upon which the telegraph authority places any telegraph line or post; and

    (c) except as hereinafter provided, the telegraph authority shall not exercise those powers in respect of any property vested in or under the control or management of any local authority, without the permission of that authority; and

    (d) in the exercise of the powers conferred by this section, the telegraph authority shall do as little damage as possible, and, when it has exercised those powers in respect of any property other than that referred to in clause (c), shall pay full compensation to all persons interested for any damage sustained by them by reason of the exercise of those powers.

11. The telegraph authority may, at any time for the purpose of examining, repairing, altering or removing any telegraph line or post, enter on the property under, over, along, across, in or upon which the line or post has been placed.

Provisions applicable to Property vested in or under the Control or Management of Local Authorities

12. Any permission given by a local authority under section 10, clause (c), may be given subject to such reasonable conditions as that authority thinks fit to impose, as to the payment of any expense to which the authority will necessarily be put in consequence of the exercise of the powers conferred by that section, or as to the time or mode of execution of any work, or as to any other thing connected with or relative to any work undertaken by the telegraph authority under those powers.

13. When, under the foregoing provisions of this Act,a telegraph line or post has been placed by the telegraph authority under, over, along, across, in or upon any property vested in or under the control or management of a local authority, and the local authority, having regard to circumstances which have arisen since the telegraph line or post was so placed, considers it expedient that it should be removed or that its position should be altered, the local authority may require the telegraph authority to remove it or alter its position, as the case may be.

14. The telegraph authority may, for the purpose of exercising the powers conferred upon it by this Act in respect of any property vested in or under the control or management of a local authority, alter the position thereinunder of any pipe (not being a main) for the supply of gas or water, or of any drain (not being a main drain):

Provided that –

(a) when the telegraph authority desires to alter the position of any such pipe or drain it shall give reasonable notice of its intention to do so, specifying the time at which it will begin to do so, to the local authority, and, when the pipe or drain is not under the control of the local authority, to the person under whose control the pipe or drain is;

(b) a local authority or person receiving notice under clause (a) may send a person to superintend the work, and the telegraph authority shall execute the work to the reasonable satisfaction of the person so sent.

15. (1) If any dispute arises between the telegraph authority and a local authority in consequence of the local authority refusing the permission referred to in section 10, clause (c), or prescribing any condition under section 12, or in consequence of the telegraph authority omitting to comply with a requisition made under section 13, or otherwise in respect of the exercise of the powers conferred by this Act, it shall be determined by such officer as the Local Government may appoint either generally or specially in this behalf.

(2) An appeal from the determination of the officer so appointed shall lie to the Local Government; and the order of the Local Government shall be final.

Provisions applicable to other Property

16. (1) If the exercise of the powers mentioned in section 10 in respect of property referred to in clause (d) of that section is resisted or obstructed, the District Magistrate may, in his discretion, order that the telegraph authority shall be permitted to exercise them.

(2) If, after the making of an order under sub-section (1), any person resists the exercise of these powers or, having control over the property, does not give all facilities for their being exercised, he shall be deemed to have committed an offence under section 188 of the Indian Penal Code.

(3) If any dispute arises concerning the sufficiency of the compensation to be paid under section 10, clause (d), it shall, on application for that purpose by either of the disputing parties to the District Judge within whose jurisdiction the property situates, be determined by him.

(4) If any dispute arises as to the persons entitled to receive compensation, or as to the proportions in which the persons interested are entitled to share in it, the telegraph authority may pay into the Court of the District Judge such amount as

he deems sufficient or, where all the disputing parties have in writing admitted the amount tendered to be sufficient or the amount has been determined under sub-section (3), that amount; and the District Judge, after giving notice to the parties and hearing such of them as desire to be heard, shall determine the persons entitled to receive the compensation or, as the case may be, the proportions in which the persons interested are entitled to share in it.

(5) Every determination of a dispute by a District Judge under sub-section (3) or sub-section (4) shall be final:

Provided that nothing in this sub-section shall affect the right of any person to recover by suit the whole or any part of any compensation paid by the telegraph authority, from the person who has received the same.

17. (1) When, under the foregoing provisions of this Act, a telegraph line or post has been placed by the telegraph authority under, over, along, across, in or upon any property, not being property vested in or under the control or management of a local authority, and any person entitled to do so desires to deal with that property in such a manner as to render it necessary or convenient that the telegraph line or post should be removed to another part thereof or to a higher or lower level or altered in form, he may require the telegraph authority to remove or alter the line or post accordingly:

Provided that, if compensation has been paid under section 10, clause (d), he shall when making the requisition, tender to the telegraph authority the amount requisite to defray the expense of the removal or alteration, or half of the amount paid as compensation, whichever may be the smaller sum.

(2) If the telegraph authority omits to comply with the requisition, the person making it may apply to the District Magistrate within whose jurisdiction the property is situate to order the removal or alteration.

(3) A District Magistrate receiving an application under sub-section (2) may, in his discretion, reject the same or make an order, absolutely or subject to conditions, for the removal of the telegraph line or post to any other part of the or to a higher or lower level or for the alteration of its form, and the order so made shall be final.

Provisions applicable to all Property

18. (1) If any tree standing or lying near a telegraph line interrupts, or is likely to interrupt, telegraphic communication, a Magistrate of the first or second class may, on the application of the telegraph authority, cause the tree to be removed or dealt with in such other way as he deems fit.

(2) When disposing of an application under sub-section (1), the Magistrate shall, in the case of any tree in existence before the telegraph line was placed, award to the persons interested in the tree such compensation as he thinks reasonable, and the award shall be final.

19. Valong, across, in or upon any property, for the purpose of a telegraph established

or maintained by the Government, shall be deemed to have been placed in exercise of the powers conferred by, and after observance of all the requirements of, this Act.

PART IV
Penalties

20. If any person establishes, maintains or works a telegraph within British India, otherwise than as permitted by a license granted under section 4, or breaks any condition contained in such a license, he shall be punished with fine which may extend to one thousand rupees, and with a further fine which may extend to five hundred rupees for every week during which the line is maintained or worked or the breach of the condition continues.
21. If any person, knowing or having reason to believe that a telegraph has been established or is maintained or worked in contravention of this Act, transmits or receives any message by such telegraph, or performs any service incidental thereto, or delivers any message for transmission by such telegraph or accepts delivery of any message sent thereby, he shall be punished with fine which may extend to fifty rupees.
22. If a Railway Company or an officer of a Railway Company neglects or refuses to comply with the provisions of section 6, it or he shall be punished with fine which may extend to one thousand rupees for every day during which the neglect or refusal continues.
23. If any person –

    (a) without permission of competent authority, enters the signal-room of a telegraph office of the government, or of a person licensed under this Act, or
    (b) enters a fenced enclosure round such a telegraph office in contravention of any rule or notice not to do so, or
    (c) refuses to quit such room or enclosure on being requested to do so by any officer or servant employed therein, or
    (d) wilfully obstructs or impedes any such officer or servant in the performance of his duty,

    he shall be punished with fine which may extend to five hundred rupees.

24. If any person does any of the acts mentioned in section 23 with the intention of unlawfully learning the contents of any message, or of committing any offence punishable under this Act, he may (in addition to the fine with which he is punishable under section 23) be punished with imprisonment for a term which may extend to one year.
25. If any person, intending –

    (a) to prevent or obstruct the transmission or delivery of any message, or
    (b) to intercept or to acquaint himself with the contents of any message, or
    (c) to commit mischief, damages, removes, tampers with or touches any battery,

machinery, telegraph line, post or other thing whatever, being part of or used in or about any telegraph or in the working thereof,

he shall be punished with imprisonment for a term which may extend to three years, or with fine, or with both.

26. If any telegraph officer, or any person, not being a telegraph officer but having official duties connected with any office which is used as telegraph office, –

(a) wilfully secretes, make away with or alters any message which he has received for transmission or delivery, or

(b) wilfully, and otherwise than in obedience to an order of the Governor-General in Council or of a Local Government, or of an officer specially authorised by the Governor-General in Council to make the order, omits to transmit, or intercepts or detains, any message or any part thereof, or otherwise than in pursuance of his official duty or in obedience to the direction of a competent Court, discloses the contents or any part of the contents of any message, to any person not entitled to receive the same, or

(c) divulges the purport of any telegraphic signal to any person not entitled to become acquainted with the same, he shall be punished with imprisonment for a term which may extend to three years, or with fine, or with both.

27. If any telegraph officer transmits by telegraph any message on which the charge prescribed by the government, or by a person licensed under this Act, as the case may be, has not been paid, intending thereby to defraud the Government or that person, he shall be punished with imprisonment for a term which may extend to three years, or with fine, or with both.

28. If any telegraph officer, or any person not being a telegraph officer but having official duties connected with any office which is used as a telegraph office, is guilty of any act of drunkenness, carelessness or other misconduct whereby the correct transmission or the delivery of any message is impeded or delayed, or if any telegraph officer loiters or delays in the transmission or delivery of any message, he shall be punished with imprisonment for a term which may extend to three months, or with fine which may extend to one hundred rupees, or with both.

29. If any person transmits or causes to be transmitted by telegraph a message which he knows to be false or fabricated, he should be punished with imprisonment for a term which may extend to three years, or with fine, or with both.

30. If any person fraudulently retains, or wilfully secretes, makes away with or detains a message which ought to have been delivered to some other person, or, being required by a telegraph officer to deliver up any such message, neglects or refuses to do so, he shall be punished with imprisonment for a term which may extend to two years, or with fine, or with both.

31. A telegraph officer shall be deemed a public servant within the meaning of sections 161, 162, 163, 164 and 165 of the Indian Penal Code; and in the definition of "legal remuneration" contained in the said section 161, the word "Government" shall, for

the purpose of this Act, be deemed to include a person licensed under this Act.

32. Whoever attempts to commit any offence punishable under this Act shall be punished with punishment herein provided for the offence.

PART V

Supplemental Provision

33. (1) Whenever it appears to the Local Government that any act causing or likely to cause wrongful damage to any telegraph is repeatedly and maliciously committed in any place, and that the employment of an additional police-force in that place is there by rendered necessary, the Local Government may send such additional police-force as it thinks fit to the place, and employ the same therein so long as, in the opinion of that government, the necessity of doing so continues.

(2) The inhabitants of the place shall be charged with the cost of the additional police-force, and the District Magistrate shall subject to the order of the Local Government, assess the proportion in which the cost shall be paid by the inhabitants according to his judgement of their respective means.

(3) All moneys payable under sub-section (2) shall be recoverable either under the warrant of a Magistrate by distress and sale of the movable property of the defaulter within the local limits of his jurisdiction, or by suit in any competent Court.

(4) The Local Government may, by order in writing, define the limits of any place for the purpose of this section.

D. FITZPATRICK,
Secy. to the Govt. of India

396

The Indian Telegraph Act, 1888

Source: The Gazette of India, Part IV, October 6, 1888

Gist: The Indian Telegraph Act, 1888 (Act 11 of 1888) is enacted to add section 34 with 3 subsections to the Indian Telegraph Act, 1885, clarifying some juridical authorities.

Act No. XI of 1888

An Act to make an addition to the Indian Telegraph Act, 1885

WHEREAS it is expedient to make an addition to the Indian Telegraph Act, 1885; It is hereby enacted as follows: -

I. The following section shall be added to that Act, namely: -

"34. (1) This Act, in its application to the presidency-towns, shall be read as if for the words 'District Magistrate' in section 16, sub-section (1), and section 17, sub-sections (2) and (3), for the words 'Magistrate of the first or second class' in section 18, sub-section (1), and for the word 'Magistrate' in section 18, sub-section (2), there had been enacted the words 'Commissioner of Police', and for the words 'District Judge' in section 16, sub-sections (3), (4) and (5), the words 'Chief Judge of the Court of Small Causes'.

(2) Section 16, in its application to the town of Rangoon, shall be read as if for the words 'District Judge', wherever they occur in that section, there had been enacted the words 'Judge of the Court of Small Causes'.

(3) The fee in respect of an application to the Chief Judge of a Presidency Court of Small Causes under sub-section (3) of section 16 shall be the same as would be payable under the Court-fees Act, 1870, in respect of such an application to a District Judge beyond the limits of a presidency-town, and fees for summonses and other processes in proceedings before the Chief Judge under sub-section (3) or sub-section (4) of that section shall be payable according to the scale set forth in the fourth schedule to the Presidency Small Cause Courts Act, 1882".

S. HARVEY JAMES,
Secretary to the Government of India

397

Memorandum from the Great Indian peninsula Railway Company dated 27 June 1890, upon the Indian Railways Act, 1890 submitted to the Secretary of State for India

Source: Other Series Records, Great Indian Peninsula Railway Company, 7 July 1890

Gist: Memorandum from the Great Indian peninsula Railway Company dated 27 June 1890, upon the Indian Railways Act, 1890 submitted to the Secretary of State for India deals with the protest lodged by the Board of Directors of the company against infringement of their rights under their agreement with the Government of India. The memorandum very firmly contended that the Act is altogether ultra vires as far as it interferes with the rights of the companies under their contracts. They declared that the proposed Act was a deliberate and serious breach of contracts made under the express authority of Acts of the Imperial Legislature and in all respects mischievous. They urged the Secretary of State for India to withdraw the Act IX of 1890.

MEMORANDUM ON THE INDIAN RAILWAYS ACT, 1890 SO FAR AS IT AFFECTS THE GREAT INDIAN PENINSULA RAILWAY COMPANY

(*Prepared in accordance with the suggestion made by the Secretary of State on Thursday, 19th June* 1890)

1. The proposed Indian Railways Act, if allowed to stand, will throw upon (amongst others) the Great Indian Peninsula Railway Company a number of onerous duties and liabilities to which the Company has not been hitherto subject; it will convert into statutory duties with penalties attached a number of duties to which the Company has hitherto been bound only by Contract, enforceable only in the ordinary manner; it contains provisions taking away the Company's right to justice in the ordinary tribunals, and compels reference to arbitration or other irregular tribunals on matters far other than those voluntarily dealt with by the Contract of 1849 or any subsequent Contract by which the Company is bound ; and it seriously restricts the Company's stipulated and assured control over its own rates, in all these respects violating the rights of the Company under its Contract with the Government, against all which the Company very respectfully protest.

2. It is very confidently contended that the proposed Act is altogether ultra vires, so far as it interferes with the rights of the Companies under their Contracts with the Government.

3. This Company was established and incorporated by an Act of the Imperial Parliament, which received the Royal Assent on the 1st August 1849. Under the powers of this Act, a Contract dated the 17th August 1849, was entered into between the East India Company and this Railway Company, which Contract defines the relations between the Government and the Railway Company.

4. The Act of 1849 does more than merely authorise the Railway Company to enter into Contracts with the Government, it declares (Section 5) that such Contracts shall be valid and effectual and binding to all intents and purposes whatsoever, and full effect shall be given to the same accordingly. The Contract when made has the force of an Act of the Imperial Legislature, and can only be modified against the will of the Railway Company by the like authority and in such cases as the present; where no power whatever is reserved of subsequent variation, such a course, though of course within the power of Parliament, is so harsh and oppressive that it is without precedent.

The nearest approach to it is the reservation in recent Acts of Parliament conferring powers on companies which declare that nothing in the Act contained shall exempt the Company from any future general Act, not *"of general application,"* but *"relating to railways."*

It is submitted that but for this reservation the general railways Acts of England could not have passed.

There is no such stipulation in India.

5. Again, the objects of the Company, the objects for which the Directors are empowered to expend the funds of the Company and to pledge its credit, are confined by the Act of 1849 to the carrying out of certain agreements with the Government of India. Any attempt on the part of the Directors to use their powers for the furtherance of any other object would be *ultra vires*, and might be objected to by any single dissentient shareholder. The Railway Company is an English Company, not an Indian Company and any such dissentient shareholder might take proceedings in the English Courts against the Directors to prevent ultra vires action on their part; and if such proceedings in England were otherwise justified, what defence would it be to set up a mere ordinance of the Indian Legislative Council?

6. But apart from the legal and technical objections to the proposed infringement of the Railway Company's rights, the injustice thereof is flagrant.

7. There was nothing to compel either of the two parties to the Agreement of 1849 to enter into that or any other agreement, and the result is that the relations between the Government and the Railway Company depend entirely on the voluntary bargain between the parties.

8. On the faith of the Contract of 12th August, 1849, the shareholders' money was originally asked for, and from that time to the present, whenever any alteration of the relations between the Government and the Railway Company has been found desirable, such alteration has always been made by mutual consent of both parties and has been the subject of stipulation and free agreement on both sides.

9. It appears from the Act of 1849 itself that the negotiations which resulted in the Contract were in progress at the time of the passing of the Act but had not then been concluded (see

the third recital in Act). The 5th Section authorises the Railway Company to enter into and conclude with the East India Company on account of the Government of India such Contracts, Agreements and Arrangements as the respective parties may think fit and agree upon, including (among other things) provisions for giving to the East India Company *"any absolute or other rights"* of control, and "any provisions for referring disputes to arbitration." It is therefore perfectly clear that at the time the Act was passed it was contemplated that the Government might demand and the Railway Company might agree to any degree of control on the part of the Government, from an absolute right downwards. When the Contract is referred to, and is found under these circumstances to provide for a carefully limited power of control on the part of the Government, and a very restricted power of compulsory reference to arbitration, it can hardly be denied that an attempt on the part of the Government to extend its powers of control and of reference against the will of the Company would be a clear breach of Contract.

10. That the proposed Act does in fact violate the contractual rights of the Great Indian Peninsula Railway Company is virtually admitted by the Select Committee which advised the Government of India to pass the Act. The Report of the Select Committee is dated the 12th February 1890. Alluding to previous railway Bills, which had contained clauses protecting in some degree (though most inadequately) the contractual rights of Railway Companies, the report proceeds as follows: –

"After much consideration we have been compelled to the conclusion that a clause saving existing Contracts such as has been proposed by several Railway Companies, ought not to be inserted in the Bill."

Breach of Contract is therefore deliberately intended and openly confessed.

11. The report gives the reasons of the Committee for this course as follows:

"Such a clause might bring each Railway Company under a different law, and would certainly cause great inconvenience. Each company might claim to interpret the Act according to its view of its rights under its Contract, and the attempt to do this even if not successful, might very seriously impair the operation of those parts of the proposed Act, which deal with the creation of traffic facilities, and with the prevention of undue preference."

The meaning of this is that if the Contracts are allowed to stand, the operation of the Act will be seriously impaired. In the contrary event, the Contracts will be seriously impaired. Thus the breach of Contract is by the admission of the Select Committee serious as well as deliberate.

12. The control of the Government over the rates which the Railway Company may charge, is a matter to which the Railway Company attached extreme importance, and accordingly the Contract of 1849 contains the clearest demarcation of the control of the Government on the one hand, and of the freedom of action of the Railway Company on the other hand.

13. By clause 8 of the Contract of 1849 it was stipulated as follows:

> "The Railway Company shall be authorised and empowered to charge such fares for the carriage of passengers and goods, and such tolls for the use of the said railway as shall have been approved by the East India Company, and shall not in any case charge any higher or different fares or tolls whatsoever without such approval being first obtained, but such fares and tolls shall, *when such net receipts*

as are hereinafter mentioned shall in any year have exceeded 10 per cent upon the outlay, be reduced in accordance with any requisition of the East India Company in that behalf, *but only with a view of limiting the said fares and tolls so far that the net receipts shall not exceed 10 per cent as aforesaid."*

14. The 10 per cent has not yet been reached, so that the time for Government interference has not yet arrived. And it is submitted that the Secretary of State cannot and ought not by means of this proposed Act to improve the position of the Government as one of the parties to the Contract of his own mere motion, against the will and in spite of the formal protest of the Great Indian Peninsula Railway Company. If the Government desire to anticipate the stipulated period for interfering with the fares, they ought at least in common fairness to guarantee the 10 per cent. to the Shareholders, or come to some other agreement by way of compensation with the Company.

15. It may be alleged that the proposed breach of Contract is justified by public policy. It is not easy to imagine in what way public policy can be served by the proposed Act. It is submitted that a deliberate and serious breach of Contract is of itself contrary to the best interests of both Government and people. Even if there were no question of breach of Contract, the success achieved by the Great Indian Peninsula Railway Company under the existing system has been such that any prospect of increased power of interference and compulsion on the part of the Government is calculated to excite great anxiety and alarm. The proposal is neither just nor expedient.

16. It is put forward by the Select Committee that public policy will be served by the proposed Act as calculated to produce uniformity among the different Railway Companies. Absolute uniformity, however, is by no means an unmixed advantage, and in any event the Government is not entitled to require the Company to pay the cost of it.

17. The cause of such want of uniformity as there may be is not the fault of the Great Indian Peninsula Railway Company. Their Contract was made in 1849, before all the other Contracts with other Railway Companies and now remaining in force were made. In such other Contracts it was open to the Government, but not to the Great Indian Peninsula Railway Company, to secure uniformity with the Contract previously made with the Great Indian Peninsula Railway Company.

18. But the uniformity which the proposed Act would produce is in the first place an uniformity of confusion.

19. There is a great contrast between the 31 intelligible clauses of the Contract of 1849, and the tortuous and involved phraseology of the 150 sections (many of them including several sub-sections) of the proposed Act, and it may fairly be questioned whether the loss of simplicity and clearness will not of itself be a considerable set-off against the proposed gain in uniformity. It would seem that some of the clauses are contradictory of one another.

20. In illustration of the character of the Act reference may be made to the following sample:

By Section 47. Every Railway Çompany shall make general rules for (among other things) regulating the use, working and management of the Railway. By Section 90. If a Railway Company fails to comply with the provisions of Section 47 with respect to the making of general rules, it shall forfeit to the Government the sum of 50 rupees for every day during which the default continues. By Section 3, Sub-section 5, "Railway Company" includes any persons, whether incorporated or not, who are owners or lessees of a Railway or parties to an agreement for working a Railway, unless there is something repugnant in the subject or context. The result is that a Railway Company that has leased, or otherwise parted with the entire control over its Railway is liable to a penalty for not making rules for the management of that Railway, although rules may have been duly made by the lessee Company; because there is not necessarily any repugnance, seeing that the control of the Governor-General in Council under Section 47, Sub-section 3, may be supposed to prevent it. Nay, more; by Section 3, Sub-section 4 (*b*), "Railway" includes a portion of a Railway, and also a siding in connection with a Railway; therefore a manufacturer who constructs a siding connected with the Railway, and enters into an agreement relating to the traffic thereon, becomes a party to an agreement for working a Railway, and similarly liable to a penalty for not making general rules, though whether for the whole Railway system, or only for a part thereof, it would be difficult to say. These are but examples of the difficulties and confusion to be caused by the proposal.

21. The Great Indian Peninsula Railway Company have the strongest cause for insisting on the maintenance of their Contract, when the alternative is that their relations to the Government and the public are to be thrown into such confusion and uncertainty as will assuredly be produced by the proposed Act.

22. In the next place this uniformity is not a real uniformity, for by Section 147 the Governor-General in Council may exempt any Railway from any of the provisions of the Act; and besides, where so much is left to be provided for by rules to be made separately for each Railway, the Act cannot be said in any sense to ensure uniformity. Further, if disputes arise as to the interpretation of Chapter V of the Act, they are to be decided not by a fixed tribunal which might possibly adhere to some general principle, but by an irregular tribunal to be constituted on each occasion for that occasion only. See Section 39.

23. To the constitution of this tribunal there are the strongest objections. The Government of India have a great pecuniary interest in every one of the Railways in India, and some they actually administer. In the character of Railway owners, they might raise disputes as to traffic facilities and through rates. They could then nominate two members out of three, a majority of whom would have sole jurisdiction to decide the dispute. The tribunal is to be dissolved when the dispute is decided. How is uniformity to be attained? The only possible way would be one which the Company would hardly like even to suggest as probable, viz., for the Government to give instructions beforehand to their nominees as to how the dispute should be decided. In any event if this irregular and possibly unjust tribunal should decide against the Government, it is hardly likely that the same members would be again nominated. The Select Committee whose report is above cited say, " The powers which it is proposed to take in India are the same as it has been found necessary to take in England." It would have been more in accordance with the facts if the Select Committee had reported that the powers which it is proposed to take are without parallel or precedent either in England or in any civilised country. In England the Railway Commissioners are a permanent tribunal, not removable by the Crown at pleasure; and they are required to get rid of every semblance of interest, and to part with every Railway share they possess. The alleged resemblance to the English provisions would be greater if the

majority of the English Railway Commissioners were to be nominated by the London and North-Western Railway Company separately for the occasion of each separate dispute arising, including disputes to which the London and North-Western Railway Company was a party. And even then the parallel would be inadequate; for there is not a single Railway Company in India in which the Government of India have not a pecuniary interest. In particular they have under the Contract a power exercisable in the year 1899 of taking over the undertaking of the Great Indian Peninsula Railway Company at the market price of the shares. If, therefore, any special tribunal at all were to be constituted, even greater precautions and guarantees should be taken in India than in England for the impartiality and irremovability of the judges and their absolute freedom from any possible Government influences. It is contrary to the most elementary principles of justice that the Government should have the appointment of the tribunal on whose decisions the future prosperity of the Railway Company is to depend.

24. The Contracts between the Railway Company and the Government are English Contracts made in England, deriving their validity and binding force from an Act of the Imperial Parliament, and regulated by English law. It is submitted that it is utterly incompetent to the Indian Legislature, without the express authority of the Imperial Parliament, to force a Company in the position of the Great Indian Peninsula Railway Company against their will to refer their disputes to arbitration or to any special tribunal. And when the tribunal is one which in its constitution violates the principles of natural justice the legal arguments against the proposal are reinforced as well as the moral arguments against its propriety.

25. It is of the utmost importance to the Great Indian Peninsula Railway Company, having regard to the views entertained by the Indian Government as to the importance of their contractual obligations, to preserve free access to the public tribunals.

26. By Clause 30 of the Contract of 17th August 1849, the Government bound itself to promote the passing by the Governor-General of India in Council of any Act or Acts which shall be necessary or convenient for enabling the Railway Company to fulfil in India the objects of their undertaking according to the terms and provisions of that Contract. Whatever may be the effect of this clause, it is inconsistent with the promotion or allowance by the Secretary of State in Council of Acts of the Government of India intended to override the terms and provisions of the Contract.

27. By exercising their right of purchase at the stipulated time the Government can obtain without injustice all the control and all the advantages over the Great Indian Peninsula Railway that they may desire. In the lowest view of the case it seems hardly worthwhile, in order to anticipate that time by a few years, to commit a deliberate and serious breach of faith.

28. Under the circumstances, if ever any attempt should be made to take action under the Act in question, it would become the duty of the Great Indian Peninsula Railway Company to contest the validity of the proposed Indian legislation by all the means in their power; but having regard to the importance of the issues involved, it cannot be disguised that if litigation were once begun, the end of it could not be easily foreseen, and would import acrimony and friction into the hitherto harmonious relations between the guaranteed Companies and the Government of India. This in itself would more than outweigh any supposed benefits from the proposed legislation.

29. On the whole, the Great Indian Peninsula Railway Company submit that they have clear right to beg the Secretary of State to hold that the proposed Act will be deliberate and serious breach of the Contracts made under the express authority of Acts of the Imperial Legislature, that the proposal is in all respects mischievous, and to advise Her Majesty to exercise the powers of Sec. 21 of the Statute 24 and 25 Vic., c. 67 (for which there is no time limited), by signifying in the manner therein prescribed Her disallowance thereof.

27th June, 1890

R.D.M. LITTLER
GEORGE II BLAKESLEY

At a meeting of the Board of Directors of the Great Indian Peninsula Railway Company held on the 4th July 1890.

T. R. Watt, Eso., in the Chair

"*It was resolved* –

"That the Memorandum dated the 27th June 1890 signed by Counsel now submitted be adopted, and that it be forwarded to the Secretary of State for India in Council as expressing the views of the Board."

(Signed) T.R. WATT
Chairman

398

Memorandum from the East Indian Railway Company dated 10 July 1890, upon the Indian Railways Act, 1890 submitted to the Secretary of State for India

Source: Other Series Records, East Indian Railway Company, 10th July 1890

Gist: Memorandum from the East Indian Railway Company dated 10 July 1890, upon the Indian Railways Act, 1890 submitted to the Secretary of State for India deals with the protest lodged by the Board of Directors of the company against the infringement of their rights under their agreement with the East India Company. The Board unanimously remarked that the passing of the Act IX of 1890 was ultra vires of the Governor General of India. They stated that the Select Committee of the Council of the Governor General of India frankly opined that the passing of this Act might bring each railway company under a different law and would certainly cause great inconvenience. The said Act was an ill-advised attempt to transplant into India legislation not adapted to its conditions and requested the Secretary of State for India to disallow the present Act.

MEMORANDUM ON BEHALF OF THE EAST INDIAN RAILWAY COMPANY UPON THE INDIAN RAILWAYS ACT, 1890

1. The East Indian Railway Company was incorporated by a British Act of Parliament (12 and 13 Vict. c. 93) in the year 1849.
2. Under that Act the Company was empowered to make contracts with the East India Company on behalf of the Government of India for making railways in India and for other purposes.
3. The Company constructed their railways under divers contracts made in pursuance of the said Act.
4. One or more of such contracts contained a provision that on the conditions therein mentioned the East India Company should be entitled to purchase the undertaking of the Company.
5. The rights and liabilities of the East India Company under the said contracts were subsequently transferred to Her Majesty.
6. In pursuance of the right so vested in Her Majesty in that behalf the Secretary of State

for India in Council arranged with the Company for the purchase of their undertaking.

7. The said purchase was duly carried out by an Act of the Imperial Parliament (being the 42 and 43 Vict. c. 206) in the year 1879, intituled "The East Indian Railway Company Purchase Act, 1879."
8. The said Act recites the Memorandum of Terms under which the Secretary of State for India in Council had offered to the Company, and the Company had agreed to undertake, the working of the East Indian Railway.
9. The said Act, amongst other things, contained powers for the Company to enter into contracts with the Secretary of State for India in Council for (amongst other things) any of the following purposes: –

   The entering into and concluding with the said Secretary of State contracts as therein mentioned for deferring the payment of a portion of the annuity created under the said Act not exceeding one-fifth, and for the participation by the Company to an extent not exceeding one-fifth in the surplus profits of the undertaking, with the object of providing for the carrying on of the Company's undertaking by the Company itself under contracts for that purpose to be made between the Company and the said Secretary of State.

   The carrying into effect the said Memorandum of Terms come to between the Company and the Secretary of State for India in Council and any addition thereto, or modification thereof, as might be agreed upon between them, not being contrary to or at variance with the provisions of the said Act.

   The maintenance and management of the East Indian Railway.

   The improvement and enlargement and the construction of auxiliary railways and other works in connection therewith.

   The use and working thereof conveyance of traffic thereon.

   The grant of running powers and other facilities, and accommodation to other railway companies or to State railways.

   The control and supervision of the said Secretary of State in respect of the matters aforesaid.

10. The said powers are contained in Sections 13, 27, and 28 of the said last-mentioned Act.
11. In pursuance of the said last-mentioned powers the Company and the Secretary of State for India in Council did enter into and duly execute a contract on the 22nd of December 1879.
12. We beg to refer to the several Articles of the said Contract, and particularly to the following – namely:

    Article 3, by which, in accordance with the provisions of the said Section 13 of the Purchase Act, the payment of one-fifth of the annuity of £1,473,750 mentioned in the said Purchase Act is deferred during the continuance of the Contract, and in lieu thereof interest at the rate of 4 percent per annum on the sum of £6,550,000 is to be paid by the Secretary of State to the Company in London by half-yearly payments.

Article 36, Subsection 7, by which the surplus, if any, as defined by the same Article, shall be applied in the manner therein indicated, that is to say, four-fifths thereof shall belong to the said Secretary of State, and one-fifth thereof shall belong to the Company for distribution among the persons entitled thereto under the said Purchase Act of 1879.

Articles 10, 11, and 12, by which the Company undertake to maintain the undertaking, and to provide, keep, and execute all such rolling stock, plant, machinery, staff and works respectively as the said Secretary of State may deem necessary and sufficient for the purposes of the undertaking.

Article 13, which provides that the Company shall carry out such alterations, improvements, and additions to the undertaking as the said Secretary of State shall think necessary for the safety of passengers and the public, and for the effectual working of the undertaking.

Articles 15 and 16, which provide for the fixing and arrangement by the Company, with the approval of the said Secretary of State, of the number, speed, and destination of trains on the said Railway, and of the rates and fares for passengers and goods, besides special provision as to the rates for agricultural produce and mineral traffic, and for a certain class of passenger fares.

Articles 37, 38, and 41, which provide, on the requirement of the Secretary of State, for the exercise by other companies and by the State railways of running powers over the railways of the Company; for the loan, on reasonable terms and conditions, to such other companies and State railways of the rolling stock of the Company; for the interchange with them of traffic and rolling stock and for the use by them of the stations of the Company.

Article 44, which provides for arbitration in the event of any requirement by the said Secretary of State, under the three last-mentioned Articles, and certain other Articles combined therewith being deemed unreasonable by the Company.

Article 47, which provides that in all matters relating to the undertaking and not in the said Contract provided for the Company shall be subject to the supervision and control of the said Secretary of State.

Article 55, which provides that the said Secretary of State shall promote the passing by the Legislature in India of any Act or Acts which may be required to enable the Company to carry the said Contract into effect.

Article 56, which provides that no claim shall be made upon the said Secretary of

State by the Company for compensation in respect of any Act of the Indian Legislature of *general applicability* which may prejudicially affect the undertaking or the profits thereof.

Article 61, which amply provides for the settlement of all differences or difficulties arising between the Company and the said Secretary of State, in reference to the said Contract or the operation of it, or as to the duties, rights, or liabilities of either party in relation to it.

Article 36, which specifies and sets forth the money consideration for which the Company undertook their various duties and liabilities under the said Contract.

13. The said Contract so made and entered into as aforesaid is in fact part and parcel of and has and ought to have the full force and effect of an Act of the Imperial Parliament.
14. Notwithstanding the terms and provisions of the foregoing Purchase Act and Contract an Act has lately been passed by his Excellency the Governor-General of India in Council and has received his assent entituled "The Indian Railways Act of 1890, being Act No. IX of 1890." That such Act was considered by a Select Committee of the Council of the Governor-General of India assembled for legislative purposes, and the said Committee frankly reported as follows: "After much consideration we have been compelled to the conclusion that a clause saving existing contracts, such as has been proposed by several railway companies, ought not to be inserted in the Bill. Such a clause might bring each railway company under a different law, and would certainly cause great inconvenience. *Each company might claim to interpret the Act according to its view of its rights under its contract, and the attempt to do this, even if not successful, might very seriously impair the operation of those parts of the proposed Act which deal with the creation of traffic facilities and with the prevention of undue preference.*"
15. The said Act is divided into chapters and clauses, the whole of which purport to be made applicable to the undertaking of the Company.
16. All of the provisions in the said Act so made applicable other than those which are in conformity with the provisions of Acts of the Indian Legislature passed before the 1st January, 1880, or with arrangements to which the Company have agreed with the Secretary of State for India in Council, constitute, not only an infringement of the rights of the Company in respect of the profits to which they are entitled under the said Contract, but also alterations and increases of its duties and liabilities and changes in the manner in which questions arising in relation to the constitution and operation of the said Contract, and the rights, duties, and liabilities of the Company and the Secretary of State for India in Council in relation to each other respectively, are to be determined.
17. We beg to refer to the various chapters and clauses of the said Act, but especially to the following – namely:

    Chapter II, which provides for the appointment by the Governor-General of inspectors of railways; and specifies the powers and duties of such inspectors.

Chapter III, §§ 11, 12, 13, and 14, which throws on railways certain extensive burdens and obligations with regard to accommodation works, fences, and bridges.

Chapter IV, which gives to the Governor-General extensive powers with regard to the sanction of the opening of new lines, or of altered portions of existing lines, and with regard to the closing of lines already opened.

Chapter V, which constitutes a Railway Commission with powers so extensive with regard to rates, fares, interchange of traffic, and other matters that the said Chapter by itself constitutes a virtual repeal of many of the most important stipulations of the said Contract of the 22nd of December 1870.

Chapters VI, VII, VIII, IX, and *X*, which similarly alter and enlarge the duties and liabilities of the Company to a very serious extent, as a detailed reference to their contents would abundantly show.

18. We respectfully insist that the passing of the last-mentioned Act, as applicable to the undertaking of the Company, as stated in paragraph 16 of this Memorandum (and so over-riding as it does in fact a British Act of Parliament), was *ultra vires* of the Governor-General of India in Council, and that the said Act ought, so far as it is applicable to the Company's undertaking, to be disallowed by the Secretary of State for India in Council.
19. We respectfully urge that to do anything short of this would be for the Secretary of State for India in Council to permit a serious breach or rather a supersession of one of his own contracts to the detriment of those with whom it was made.
20. The said Act is incompatible with the relations between the Secretary of State for India in Council and the railway companies which have contracts with him, and is an ill-advised attempt to transplant into India legislation not adapted to its conditions.
21. The Railway and Canal Traffic Act of the United Kingdom is on the other hand compatible with the conditions under which British railway companies exist, the said British companies being merely statutory commercial companies with which the Government have neither privity nor contract.
22. Moreover, in all, or nearly all, of the Acts constituting such companies, or authorising the construction of any railways by them, the alteration of their statutory rights by Acts of Parliament specially affecting railways is expressly provided for.
23. The said Act is not an Act of general applicability within the meaning of Article 56 of the said Contract.
24. We desire to point out as a matter of detail in connection with the said Act that many of its provisions if insisted on would involve considerable expenditure of money, and that the Company have no powers under their Contract to raise or expend money except with the consent of the Secretary of State for India in Council.
25. The Company object most strongly to the alteration of their rights, duties, and liabilities involved in the application to the Company and its undertaking of the said Act as hereinbefore mentioned, and amongst other things especially to the

substitution of the control and supervision of the Governor-General of India in Council and an occasional Commission to be appointed from time to time under the said Act for that of the Secretary of State for India in Council, to which alone under the said Contract the Company are now subject, and to the chance of reduction of those profits to which the Company is entitled under the Contract, in consideration of the reduction to 4 percent. of the interest on the capital sum above mentioned, and of the management of the undertaking by the Company on behalf of the said Secretary of State, and to the loss of the power to refer to arbitration all matters of difficulty and difference arising under the said Contract, and all questions as to the conduct, duties, rights, and obligations of the Company and the Secretary of State for India in Council respectively thereunder in manner provided by Article 61 of the said Contract.

26. For these and other reasons we respectfully urge that either the said Act should be disallowed or that the undertaking of the Company should be excepted from its operation by legislation adequate for the purpose.

27 We earnestly request that we may be heard before the Secretary of State for India in Council in support of the allegations and arguments contained in this Memorandum.

7th July, 1890.

EDWARD HENRY PEMBER,
JOHN II CRAWFORD

At a Meeting of the Board of Directors of the East Indian Railway Company held this day, it was

Resolved:

"That the Memorial as signed by Counsel be and is hereby adopted by the Company, and that it be sent in to the Secretary of State under a covering letter to be signed by Messrs. Freshfields & Williams on behalf of the Board."

By order of the Board,

10th July, 1890.

A. P. DUNSTAN,
Secretary

399

Memorandum from the Madras Railway Company dated 14 July 1890, upon the Indian Railways Act, 1890 submitted to the Secretary of State for India

Source: Other Series Records, Madras Railway Company, 14th July 1890

Gist: Through the memorandum from the Madras Railway Company dated 14 July 1890, upon the Indian Railways Act, 1890 submitted to the Secretary of State for India, the Board of Directors of the company most strongly object to the alteration of their rights, duties and liabilities involved in the application of the Act to the Company and its undertaking. They viewed that the Act IX of 1890 was incompatible with the relations between the Secretary of State for India and the railway companies and it was an ill-advised attempt to transplant into India legislation not adapted to its conditions. They argued that the Railway and Canal Traffic Act of the U.K. was compatible with the conditions under which British railway companies existed, as they were merely statutory commercial companies with which the Government had neither privity nor contract. They urged that the passing of this Act would be for the Secretary of State for India to permit a serious breach or rather supersession of one of his won contracts to the detriment of those with whom it was made. They unanimously urged the Secretary of State to disallow the Act.

MEMORANDUM ON BEHALF OF THE MADRAS RAILWAY COMPANY UPON THE INDIAN RAILWAYS ACT, 1890

1. The Madras Railway Company were established by a deed of settlement dated the 26th July 1852, for the purpose (inter alia) of making, acquiring and working railways in India.
2. Under the powers in that behalf contained in the said deed of settlement, a contract was entered into between the East India Company of the one part and the Madras Railway Company of the other part, dated the 22nd December, 1852, for the construction, working, and maintenance of an experimental line of railway, which railway the Company have constructed.
3. The Company beg to refer to the several Articles of the said contract and particularly to the following, viz.: –

Article 4, which provides for the construction by the Company, under the supervision and control in the said contract aftermentioned, of the said experimental line of railway, and of all such stations, offices, warehouses, fixed machinery, and other works and conveniences as in the opinion of the East India Company (such opinion to be certified in writing) should be necessary or expedient, as well with reference to *the original construction of the said railway and the working thereof as with reference to the permanent maintenance thereof;*

Articles 6 and 7 provide for the raising and application of the capital of the Company;

Article 8, which provides that the Company shall, subject to the supervision and control in the said contract aftermentioned, provide to the satisfaction of the East India Company a good and sufficient working stock of engines, carriages, and other plant and machinery for working the said railway, and that the Company shall cause to be run on the said railway so many trains at such times, and at such rates of speed, and between such places, and with such conveniences and accommodations, as the East India Company shall from time to time require, and that the Company shall allow the use of the said railway to the public on such terms as shall be approved by the East India Company, and that the Company shall be authorised and empowered to charge such fares for the carriage of passengers and goods, and such tolls for the use of the said railway, as shall have been approved by the East India Company, and shall not in any case charge any higher or different fares or tolls without such approval being first obtained, but that such fares or tolls shall, when such net receipts as are in the said contract after mentioned shall in any year have exceeded ten per cent upon the outlay, be reduced in accordance with any requisition of the East India Company in that behalf, *but only with a view of limiting the said fares and tolls so far that the net receipts shall not exceed ten per cent as aforesaid;*

Article 10, which provides for and specifies in great detail the right of supervision and control of the Company, to be vested in and exercised by the East India Company;

Article 11, which provides that all the expenses of the Company shall from time to time be stated and submitted to the East India Company for their sanction and approval, and, as between the Company and the East India Company, *shall be allowed so far only as the same shall from time to time have been sanctioned and approved by the East India Company;*

Article 13, which provides for the maintenance and equipment of the said railway by the Company to the satisfaction of the East India Company;

Articles 16 and 17 provide for the payment of interest at the rate of 4½ per cent. per annum by the East India Company on the capital of the Company;

Article 20, which prescribes the terms upon and rates at which the Company are to carry mails, post-office servants, troops, and other persons in the article mentioned, and are to render to the East India Company the services therein specified;

Article 28, which provides that any notice, approval, or sanction to be given or signified on the part of the East India Company for any of the purposes of the said contract, shall be sufficient and binding if signed by the Secretary or Deputy-Secretary of the East India Company in London, or by the Secretary of Government at Madras, or by any other officer or servant of the East India Company duly authorised to act on behalf of the East India Company in respect of the matters to which the same shall relate; *and that the East India Company shall not in any case be bound in respect of the matters aforesaid, unless by some writing signed in the manner aforesaid;*

Article 30, which provides that the East India Company and the Company shall promote the passing by Parliament and the Governor-General of India in Council, of any Act or Acts which shall be necessary or convenient for enabling the Company to fulfil the objects of their undertaking, *according to the terms and provisions of the said contract.*

4. The Company were incorporated by an Act of the Imperial Parliament, 16 Vic., Cap. XLVI (1853).
5. By that Act the said contract of the 22nd December, 1852, was confirmed, and the Company were empowered from time to time to enter into and conclude with the East India Company, on account of the Government of India, such contracts, agreements, and arrangements as the respective parties might think fit and agree upon for making any railway and railways in India, and any telegraphs connected therewith, and for maintaining and working the same, and for the other objects and purposes therein before mentioned, including, so far as the said respective parties might agree thereto, all or any of the provisions following, that is to say:– Any provisions for securing to the East India Company any facilities, rights, and advantages in relation to the said railways and premises respectively, and any provisions as to the tolls, receipts, and profits thereof, and the deposit, custody, and application of such tolls, receipts, and profits and any provisions for giving to the East India Company, or to any of their officers, servants, or agents any absolute or other right of supervising, controlling, directing, regulating and ordering the Company, and the works, contracts, accounts, by-laws, acts, proceedings, transactions, and affairs of the Company, as well in England as elsewhere, and any provisions for enabling the East India Company to appoint an *ex officio* Director of the said Railway Company, whether qualified by holding share's or not, in the place of any one of the ordinary Directors of the said Railway Company or otherwise, and any provisions for regulating the powers, including even a right of veto at the Board of Directors, and the duties and proceedings, and the liabilities of any such official Director, and any provisions for binding the

said Railway Company to conform to and fulfil all or any of the directions which might be given by the East India Company, or their authorised officers and agents, touching all or any of the matters aforesaid, and any provisions for the appointment of agents of the said Railway Company in India or elsewhere, and for determining and regulating the powers and duties of such agents as aforesaid, and any provisions for depositing with or paying to the East India Company all or any part of the subscribed capital of the said Railway Company, upon any terms as to interest or otherwise to be agreed upon, and any provisions with regard to any land which might be granted or leased to the said Railway Company by the East India Company or otherwise, and any provisions for charging all or any part of the property of the said Railway Company with any sum or sums of money upon any terms to be agreed upon, and any provisions for the surrender or sale to the East India Company, or to any other person or persons; of the said railway or railways or any part thereof, and of all or any part of the property of the said Railway Company at any future period, and any provisions for referring disputes to arbitration, and any provisions intended to enforce or secure the due performance of any contract or engagement to be made by the said Railway Company, and generally all such provisions and stipulations in relation to the matters aforesaid and any of them, and in relation to the undertakings of the said Railway Company and the encouragement and promotion thereof, and the eventual or continual transfer of the same undertakings, and the property of the said Railway Company or any part thereof to the East India Company as the said respective parties should think fit and agree upon from time to time to vary and alter such contracts, agreements, and arrangements, and to enter into new or other contracts, agreements, and arrangements in relation to the premises; all which contracts, agreements, and arrangements, whether the same should or not be within the objects originally contemplated by the said Railway Company, or in accordance with the provisions and clauses by which the said Railway Company would otherwise be governed, should, subject to the provisions of the said Act, be valid and effectual and binding to all intents and purposes whatsoever, and full effect should be given for the same accordingly.

6. By an Act, 17 Vic., Cap. XXIX (1854), the Company were empowered to enter into and conclude with the East India Company on account of the Government of India such contract or contracts, agreements, and arrangements, as the respective parties might think fit and agree upon for the extension as therein mentioned of the said experimental line of railway, and for any other or others of the purposes or objects contemplated by the said Act incorporating the Company, and from time to time to vary and alter such contracts, agreements, and arrangements, and to enter into such new or other contracts, agreements, and arrangements for, or preparatory to, the construction and maintenance of any other railway or railways in the East Indies as should from time to time be deemed expedient.
7. In pursuance of the said last-mentioned Act, the Company entered into further contracts with the East India Company, dated respectively the 19th December, 1855, and the 13th August, 1858, and have constructed the railways therein respectively

provided for. The provisions of these contracts respectively are in the main in all essential particulars the same those contained in the said contract of the 22nd December 1852. The contract of 1855 contains provisions for the payment by the East India Company of interest at the rate respectively of 5 per cent per annum, 4¾ per cent per annum, and 4½ per cent per annum on the capital of the Company then raised, or thereafter to be raised, for the railways therein provided for. And the contract of 1858 contains provisions for the payment by the East India Company of interest at the rate of £5 per cent per annum upon the sum of £1,000,000 then raised or to be raised by the Company for the purposes of the railway therein provided for, and of interest, at such rate as might be agreed upon, upon any excess above £1,000,000 to be raised by the Company for such last-mentioned railway.

8. Each of the said last-mentioned contracts provides (Article 29): –

> "That the said East India Company shall promote the passing by the Governor-General of India in Council of any Act or Acts which shall be necessary or convenient for enabling the said Railway Company to fulfil in India the objects of their undertaking *according to the terms and provisions of these presents.*"

9. Since the passing of the said Acts, and the making of the said contracts, the rights, duties, and liabilities of the East India Company under such contracts have been transferred to the Secretary of State for India in Council.
10. By a contract dated the 2nd January, 1871, made between the Secretary of State and the Company, the several undertakings of the Company comprised in the said contracts before mentioned were, as from the 1st July, 1870, consolidated into one undertaking, upon the terms and subject to the conditions in the said contract after contained or referred to.
11. The Company beg to refer to the several articles of the said last-mentioned contract, and particularly to the following, viz.: –

> *Article* 3, which provides for the keeping of a capital account by the Company, to which account all moneys paid by the Company, the expenditure of which has or shall have received the sanction and approval of the Secretary of State, shall from time to time be carried; and which further provides that upon any additions, alterations, or improvements, such as shall be properly chargeable to the capital account, being at any time made *with the sanction and approval of the Secretary of State,* to, of, or, in, the said railways, or any of them, or the works, conveniences, telegraphs, engines, carriages, plant, or machinery, the cost necessarily incurred shall be added to the said capital account;
>
> *Article* 4, which provides for the keeping of a revenue account;
>
> *Article* 5, which provides that all the earnings of all the said railways received by or on account of the Company in India shall be paid at such times and in such manner as the Secretary of State shall direct, without any deduction under any pretence whatever, into the Treasury of the Government of India at Madras; and

that when any money shall be required by the Company for any purposes in connection with the said railways or any of them *sanctioned by the Secretary of State*, such money may be drawn as therein mentioned;

Article 6, which provides that the net receipts of the said railways remaining after paying and providing for the several charges and liabilities therein specified shall belong to the Secretary of State, provided always that in case in any half year such net receipts shall exceed the aggregate amount of interest payable for such half year by the Secretary of State under the contracts for the time subsisting guaranteeing the payment of interest, then, and in every such case, a moiety of such excess shall belong and be paid to the Company for their own use and benefit;

Article 9, which vests in the Secretary of State at the time, and in the manner therein prescribed, the right to purchase the said railways and works, with the rolling stock, plant, and machinery, and provides that the Secretary of State, in the event of his electing so to purchase the same, shall be bound to pay in London for the purchase of all the same premises a sum equal to the full amount of the value of all the shares or capital stock, but not including debenture stock (if any) in the said Railway Company, *calculated according to the mean market value in London of such shares or stock during the three years immediately preceding such purchase;*

Article 10, which vests in the Secretary of State in case of default by the Company in the performance of their covenants under the said contracts before referred to, the right at the time and in the manner mentioned to resume possession of the said railways, and provides that in the event of his so resuming possession the Secretary of State shall be liable to repay to the Company in London the capital expended by the Company;

Article 14, provides that such of the provisions of the said contracts of 1852, 1855, and 1858, as are not by the said contract rescinded and were then capable of effect, and could be applied to the consolidated undertaking should, as from the 1st July, 1870, apply to such undertaking.

12. The contract made and now subsisting between the Company and the Secretary of State, under the powers of the said Acts, 16 Vic., Cap. XLVI and 17 Vic., Cap. XXIX, and embodied in the said several indentures of 22nd December, 1852, 19th December, 1855, 13th August, 1858, and 2nd January, 1871, is, under the circumstances hereinbefore set out, in fact part and parcel of, and has and ought to have the full force and effect of, an Act of the Imperial Parliament, and cannot be altered, except by mutual consent, without the authority of the Imperial Parliament.
13. Notwithstanding the terms and provisions of the foregoing Acts and contracts, an Act has lately been passed by His Excellency the Governor-General of India in Council, and has received his assent, intituled "The Indian Railways Act of 1890, being Act No. IX of 1890." Such Act was considered by a Select Committee of the Council of the Governor-General of India, assembled for legislative purposes, and the said Committee

frankly reported as follows: "After much consideration, we have been compelled to the conclusion that a clause saving existing contracts, such as has been proposed by several railway companies, ought not to be inserted in the Bill. Such a clause might bring each railway company under a different law, and would certainly cause great inconvenience. Each Company might claim to interpret the Act according to its view of its rights under its contract, and the attempt to do this, even if not successful, might very seriously impair the operation of those parts of the proposed Act which deal with the creation of traffic facilities, and with the prevention of undue preference."

14. The said Indian Railways Act is divided into chapters and clauses, the whole of which purport to be made applicable to the undertaking of the Company.
15. All of the provisions in the said Indian Railways Act so made applicable, other than those which are in conformity with the provisions of Acts of the Indian Legislature passed before the 22nd December, 1852, or with arrangements to which the Company have agreed with the Secretary of State, constitute not only an infringement of the rights of the Company in respect of the profits to which they are entitled under the said contract, but also alterations and increases of their duties and liabilities and changes in the manner in which questions arising in relation to the construction and operation of the said contracts, and the mutual rights, duties and liabilities of the Company and the Secretary of State are to be determined. The effect, moreover, of the application of many of the provisions of this Act to the undertaking of the Company might, and probably would, most prejudicially affect the rights and interests of the Company, as secured to them by the 9th Article of the said contract of the 2nd January, 1871, and their position and the value of their property to be acquired and paid for by the Secretary of State in the event of his exercising the right of purchase vested in him by such last-mentioned article.
16. The Company beg to refer to the various chapters and clauses of the said Railways Act, but especially to the following, viz.: –

Chapter II, which provides for the appointment by Governor-General of Inspectors of Railways, and specifies the powers and duties of such inspectors;

Chapter III, Sections 11, 12, 13, and 14, which throws on railways certain extensive burdens and obligations with regard to accommodation works, fences and bridges;

Chapter IV, which gives to the Governor-General extensive powers with regard to the sanction of the opening of new lines, or of altered portions of existing lines, and with regard to the closing of lines already opened.

Chapter V, which constitutes a Railway Commission with powers so extensive with regard to rates, fares, interchange of traffic, and other matters that the said chapter by itself constitutes a virtual repeal of many of the most important stipulations of the subsisting contracts between the Secretary of State and the Company;

Chapters VI, VII, VIII, IX, and X, which similarly alter and enlarge the duties and liabilities of the Company to a very serious extent, as a detailed reference to their contents would abundantly show.

17. The Company respectfully insist that the passing of the Indian Railways Act, as applicable to the undertaking of the Company, as stated in paragraph 15 of this Memorandum, and so overriding as it does in fact a British Act of Parliament, was *ultra vires* of the Governor-General of India in Council, and that the said Act ought, so far as it is applicable to the Company's undertaking, to be disallowed by the Secretary of State for India in Council.
18. The Company respectfully urge that, to do anything short of this would be for the Secretary of State to permit a serious breach, or rather a supersession of one of his own contracts to the detriment of those with whom it was made, and who on the faith of the strict observance and performance of the terms and conditions in the said several contracts contained, and on the part of the East India Company and the Secretary of State to be observed and performed, have from time to time subscribed the capital necessary for the construction of the said railways.
19. The said Act is incompatible with the relations between the Secretary of State and the Railway Companies which have entered into contracts with him, and is an ill-advised attempt to transplant into India legislation not adapted to its conditions.
20. The Railway & Canal Traffic Act of the United Kingdom on the other hand is compatible with the conditions under which British Railway Companies exist, the said British Companies being merely statutory commercial companies, with which the Government have neither privity nor contract.
21. Moreover, in all, or nearly all, of the Acts constituting such companies, or authorising the construction of any railways by them, the alteration of their statutory rights by Acts of Parliament specially affecting railways, is expressly provided for.
22. The Company desire to point out as a matter of detail in connection with the said Act that many of its provisions if insisted on would involve considerable expenditure of money, and that the Company have no powers to raise further capital, nor to expend money in any way except with the consent of the Secretary of State.
23. The Company object most strongly to the alteration of their rights, duties, and liabilities, involved in the application to the Company and its undertaking of the said Indian Railways Act, and amongst other things especially to the substitution of the control and supervision of the Governor-General of India in Council, and an occasional Commission to be appointed by him from time to time under the said Act, for that of the Secretary of State, to which alone under their contracts the Company are now subject, and to the chance of reduction of those profits to which the Company are entitled under such contract, and to the consequent depreciation in value of their property and capital stock.
24. For these and other reasons the Company respectfully urge that the Indian Railways Act, 1890, should be disallowed, or that the undertaking of the Company should be excepted from the operation of the said Act by legislation adequate for the purpose, or should, by direction of the Secretary of State, be exempted from all the provisions

thereof under the powers contained in Section 147 of the Act.

25. The Company earnestly request that they may be heard before the Secretary of State for India in Council, in support of the allegations and arguments contained in this Memorandum.

July 14, 1890

JOHN II CRAWFORD

At a meeting of the Board of Directors of the Madras Railway Company held on the 11th July 1890,

It was resolved –

That the Memorandum prepared by Counsel, and to be signed by him, be approved, and that Messrs. Freshfields & Williams be requested to forward the same to the Secretary of State for India in Council, as expressing the views of the Board.

G.N. TAYLOR
Chairman

400

Statement of the Bombay, Baroda and Central India Railway Company dated 14 1890, upon the Indian Railways Act, 1890 submitted to the Secretary of State for India

Source: Other Series Records, Bombay, Baroda and Central India Railway Company, 1890

Gist: Statement of the Bombay, Baroda and Central India Railway Company dated 14 July 1890, upon the Indian Railways Act, 1890 submitted to the Secretary of State for India deals with the protest lodged against the infringement of the company's rights and duties under their agreement with the Government of India. The Board of Directors of the company stated that the implementation of the Act would automatically disturb the amicable and friendly relations so long maintained between the railway companies and the Government of India. They warned that any attempt to enforce the Act against the interest of the railway companies would invite litigation both in India and England and drive the companies to stand upon their strict rights in all cases. They unanimously urged the Secretary of State to disallow the Act as he had absolute legal control over the Indian Legislature..

STATEMENT ON BEHALF OF THE BOMBAY, BARODA AND CENTRAL INDIA RAILWAY COMPANY

1. The Bombay, Baroda and Central India Railway Company was originally formed by Deed of Settlement dated the 24th day of April 1855, for the construction of railways in India.
2. On the 2nd July 1855, an Act, the short title of which is "The Bombay, Baroda and Central India Railway Act, 1855," received the Royal assent.

   By this Act the Bombay Company was incorporated and authorised to enter into contracts with the East India Company on behalf of the Government of India.
3. On the 21st November 1855, a contract was entered into between the Honourable East India Company and the Bombay, Baroda and Central India Railway Company with reference to the construction of a railway from Surat to Baroda and from thence to Ahmedabad in Guzerat.
4. On the 13th August 1859, a further Act, the short title of which is "The Bombay, Baroda

and Central India Railway Act, 1859," received the Royal assent.

By this Act the Deed of Settlement of the 24th April, 1855, was annulled, and the Bombay, Baroda and Central India Railway Act, 1855, was repealed, but it was enacted that the Company should remain incorporated, and the Act also provided that the contract of the 21st November, 1855, should be effectual to all intents for, against and with respect to the Company and might be proceeded on and enforced accordingly.

By the 19th Section of this Act it is enacted that the Company from time to time may negotiate for, conclude and enter into with the Secretary of State in Council of India and carry into effect contracts and agreements with respect to all or any of the matters mentioned in that section, to wit, the making, maintaining, regulating, working and using by the Company of a railway from Bombay to Baroda and Ahmedabad, or any railway or railways in India, and any works and conveniences connected therewith, the acquiring by the Company of lands in India for the purposes of their undertakings, the obtaining by the Company from the Secretary of State in Council of India of any guarantee of interest on the Capital of the Company, and any other support, countenance, and facilities for the purposes of their undertakings, the making of provision as to the tolls, charges, revenue, and profits of the Company, and the deposit, custody, and application thereof respectively, the surrendering or selling at any future period to the Secretary of State in Council of India on behalf of Her Majesty, or to any other persons, of the railways, or any railway of the Company, or any part thereof, the making of provision for enforcing or securing the due performance of any contract or arrangement made by the Company, and generally all such provisions and stipulations with respect to the matters provided for by the Act as the respective parties should think fit and mutually agree upon.

By the 21st section of the same Act it is enacted that the Company and the Secretary of State in Council of India respectively from time to time may negotiate for, conclude, and enter into any contracts and agreements for the purposes of the Act in addition to or by way of repeal or modification of the existing indentures of agreement or of any contracts or agreements theretofore entered into by them for the purposes of the Act.

5. On the 2nd February 1859, a contract was entered into between the Secretary of State in Council of India and the Bombay, Baroda and Central India Railway Company for the construction of a line of railway from Bombay to Surat. The 8th clause of the said agreement contains the following contract by the Secretary of State in Council: – "And the said Railway Company shall be authorised and empowered to charge such fares for the carriage of passengers and goods, and such rates for telegrams and such tolls as shall have been approved by the Secretary of State in Council, and shall not in any case charge any higher or different fares, rates, or tolls whatsoever without such approval being first obtained, but the fares, rates, or tolls to be taken under the said Indenture of the 21st day of November, 1855, and these presents, shall, when such net receipts as are hereinafter mentioned shall in any year have exceeded 10 per cent upon the whole outlay, be reduced in accordance with any requisition of the Secretary of State in Council in that behalf, but only with a view of limiting the said fares,

rates, and tolls, so far that the net receipts shall not exceed 10 per cent as aforesaid, and this present clause shall be in substitution for the corresponding clause of the said Indenture of the 21st day of November, 1855."

The Secretary of State in Council duly approved a schedule of maximum rates, fares, and tolls referred to in this clause in the year 1869, and that schedule has remained unaltered ever since.

The 22nd clause of the same agreement empowers the Secretary of State in Council to purchase the undertaking of the railway company in 1905, at a price calculated according to the mean market value in London of the stock and shares of the company during the three years immediately preceding.

The 29th clause of the same agreement contains a contract by the Secretary of State in Council to promote the passing by the Governor-General of India in Council of any Act or Acts which shall be necessary or convenient for enabling the Railway Company to fulfil in India the objects of the undertaking, according to the terms and conditions of the said agreement.

6. On the 17th of November 1871, a further contract was entered into between the Secretary of State in Council and the Bombay, Baroda and Central India Railway Company, as to the construction of a line from the River Sabarmuttee to Veerumgaum and Wudwan. This contract contains clauses similar to those above set out from the agreement of 2nd February 1859.

   Several other contracts have been entered into between the Secretary of State in Council of India and the Bombay, Baroda and Central India Railway Company, with reference to extensions and additions to the line of the Company, and to all these extensions and additions the schedule of maximum rates sanctioned in 1869 has, with the approval of the Secretary of State in Council, been applied as they have successively been opened for traffic as part of the Company's line.

7. Under agreements dated the 24th of September 1884, and 16th March 1888, respectively, made between the Secretary of State in Council of the one part, and the Company of the other part, the Company also maintain and work the Rajputana-Malwa and the Cawnpore-Achnera State Railways.
8. The lines now owned by the Bombay, Baroda and Central India Railway Company are 460 miles and 4,772 feet, and the State lines now worked by the Company are 1,671 miles and 4,990 feet in length.
9. The Share Capital (now the Consolidated Stock) of the Bombay, Baroda and Central India Railway Company now stands at £7,550,300 and the Company have borrowed on Debenture bonds £1,238,500 making a total Capital outlay of £8,788,800.
10. The Secretary of State in Council of India has under various contracts guaranteed a dividend of 5 per cent on the Share Capital (now the Consolidated Stock) of the Company, and has also guaranteed interest at various rates on the Debenture Capital of the Company.

    The contracts also provide for the appointment by the Secretary of State of an *ex-officio* Director with a right of veto, and give the Secretary of State in Council great power as to the regulation of the line, supervision over the construction, and control over the revenue and capital expenditure.

11. The shares and bonds of the Bombay, Baroda and Central India Railway Company are largely held by trustees.

12. By the Act for the better Government of India, 21 and 22 Vic. Cap. 106, and the Indian Councils Act, 24 and 25 Vic. Cap. 67, and subsequent Acts amending these Acts, the Governor-General of India in Council has power to make laws relating to the Government of India as provided for in the Statutes.

    By the Statutes before referred to it is provided that the Secretary of State may contract, sue and be sued, and shall stand in the same position as the Old East India Company (21 and 22 Vic. c. 106 s. 40, 22 and 23 Vic. c. 41 s. 2).

13. The Acts also confer on the Secretary of State a power to annul or disallow any Act passed by the Governor-General in Council. His sanction is not required by the Acts or any of them as a condition precedent to the validity of any such Act, but he has power at any time to veto it (24 and 25 Vic., c. 67, ss. 21 and 22).

14. The Act of the Governor-General of India in Council, called the Indian Railways Act, 1890, very seriously affects the contracts hereinbefore mentioned between the Bombay, Baroda and Central India Railway Company and the East India Company and the Secretary of State of India in Council. As instances: –

    (*a.*) Chapter III provides for the execution by the Company of additional accommodation and other works at any time on the requisition of the Governor-General in Council. The Company has already, under its contracts with the Secretary of State in Council, duly completed to his satisfaction all their railways with such works and conveniences as the Secretary of State considered necessary or expedient.

    (*b.*) Chapter V virtually repeals the provisions in the said contracts of 1855, 1859 and 1871 as regards rates and tolls and the management of the railways, and creates a new tribunal with absolute powers over the rates and tolls to be charged by the Company, and over their management of their lines.

    (*c.*) Chapters VI, VII, VIII, IX, and X also interfere with the rights of the Company under their contracts.

15. The Bombay, Baroda and Central India Railway Company desire to submit to the Secretary of State in Council the following reasons for putting his veto on his Act unless all contracts made between any Railway Company and the Secretary of State in Council are exempted from its operation: –

    (1) The Secretary of State in Council has entered into express contracts with the Railway Company on the faith of which very large sums have been expended. It is impossible to suppose that the Secretary of State would desire to repudiate these contracts or any of them. These contracts were made under powers created by the Imperial Legislature. No powers, therefore, inferior to that of the Imperial Legislature can abrogate these contracts or release the Secretary of State in

Council therefrom. The Governor-General in Council has no such power.

(2.) The Secretary of State in Council has power to prevent the attempt of the Indian Legislature to destroy his contracts. Inasmuch as he would not himself commit a breach of any such contract, it follows that he should prevent anyone over whom he has absolute legal control from doing or attempting to do for him that which he would not do for himself. He has absolute legal control over the Indian Legislature.

(3) It would be very unfortunate if the amicable relations that have subsisted for the last 35 years between the Secretary of State in Council and the Company with advantage to both parties should now be disturbed by litigation, and it would be very injurious to the interests of the Company and to the credit of the Secretary of State in Council that any litigation should take place between them for breach of contract by the Secretary of State in Council. But if it is attempted to inforce the provisions of the Indian Railways Act, 1890, against the Company, litigation both in India and in England appears inevitable. Such litigation would put an end to the friendly relations so long maintained, and would drive the Company to stand upon their strict rights in all cases, instead of doing their best (as they have hitherto done) to meet the wishes of the Secretary of State in Council as far as possible.

(4) On general principles and apart from the particular contractual rights of the Company, it is submitted that there is no fair analogy between Indian and English Railways. In England the State owns no railway, and the Railway Commission applies equal justice to all. But in India the State is the owner of thousands of miles of railway, and, in particular, the railways leading to Kurrachee compete directly with the railways of the Company for the export and import trade of the Punjab. It would be inexpedient to give one competitor absolute power over his rivals, even although the recipient of such power is the Indian Government.

(5) The inevitable effect of the Act, if allowed to affect this Company, will be to depreciate the value of its shares, and this will enable the Government to purchase the undertaking of the Company in 1905 at a depreciated value. It is submitted that this would have a most prejudicial effect on the credit of the Indian Government.

14th July, 1890.

GEO FARWELL

401

Letter from the Secretary of State for India, the India Office, London to the Governor General of India in Council (the Government of India) dated 28 August 1890

Source: P.W.D. Proceedings, Nos. 22 to 24, Railway Traffic, Simla Records, May 1891 (Despatches from and to Secretary of State)

Gist: Forwarding the copies of Memorandums delivered by four guaranteed railway companies protesting against the Indian Railway Act IX of 1890 together with two notes by the Legal Adviser of the India Office, London, the Secretary of State for India, in a letter dated 28 August 1890, requested the Governor General of India in Council that before deciding on the implementation of the Act, whether the opinion of the Law Officers of the Crown should be taken, and he might also be furnished with any observations the Government of India might have to make on the case.

India Office,
London, 28th August 1890.

Railway,

No. 95.

To His Excellency The Most Honourable The Governor General of India in Council

My Lord Marquis,

1. I have to inform your Excellency that, on the 19th June last, I received a deputation from various Railway Companies, with whom contracts have been made for constructing and working railways in India, who wished to make representations to me as to the effects of the Indian Railways Act No. IX of 1890 on their respective undertakings.
2. I declined to comply with their requests that they should be heard by Counsel, but invited them to put in writing whatever they might desire to bring before me in Council.
3. I now forward, for your information, copies of the memoranda which have been prepared and delivered in on behalf of the East Indian, the Great Indian Peninsula, the Bombay, Baroda, and Central India, and the Madras Railway Companies, in which several of the Railway Companies have intimated their concurrence.

4. Their general complaint is that the passing of the Act was ultra vires of the Governor General in Council, as far as regards the Guaranteed Companies, and that it interferes with their rights, duties, and responsibilities under their contracts with the Secretary of State.
5. I transmit herewith, for your information, two notes by the Legal Adviser of this Office on the legal position of the Companies. You will see that Mr. Pontifex suggests that the opinion of the Law Officers of the Crown should be taken on the case; but, before deciding whether this course is desirable, I shall be glad to receive any observations which you may have to make in connection herewith.

I have the honour to be,

My Lord Marquis,

Your Lordship's most obedient humble Servant,

(Signed) Cross.

ENCLOSURES[1]

- Note by Legal Adviser, India Office, dated 18th June 1890.
- Note by Legal Adviser, India Office, dated 30th July 1890.
- Protest memorandums or statements of the East Indian, Great Indian Peninsula, Bombay, Baroda and Central India, and Madras Railway Companies against the Indian Railways Act No. IX of 1890.

1. Editor prepared the list of enclosures, as given above.

402

Note by Legal Adviser, India Office dated 18 June 1890 regarding the Indian Railway Act IX of 1890

Source: P.W.D. Proceedings, Nos. 22 to 24, Railway Traffic, Simla Records, May 1891 (Despatches from and to Secretary of State)

Gist: The legal adviser is of the opinion that the legislation is for the general benefit, not of the public only, but of all the railways; and its result will be to increase general traffic and profits. However, as interference being unreasonable, the Government of India and the Secretary of State in Council, in their executive capacities, will continue to have an overruling discretion, and the Railway Companies ought to be satisfied that such discretion will be reasonably and fairly exercised.

NOTE 1

The anomalous position which, under the statutes relating to India, the Secretary of State in Council and the Governments of India separately and jointly fill, necessarily gives rise to questions like that now raised by the Railway Companies.

Subject to the veto and overriding control of the Secretary of State in Council, the Government of India performs triple functions: –

It exercises very wide executive authority.

(1.) It is (in its capacity of Governor General in Council for making laws and regulations) the sole legislative power.

(2.) As agent for the Secretary of State in Council it has large powers of contracting with concessionaires, &c.

(3.) As representing the Secretary of State in Council it is the commercial owner of the State Railways.

While the Secretary of State in Council has veto and control over functions (1) and (2), he is with respect to (3) the actual contracting party. And with respect to railway contracts generally he is so in fact, and not merely because the Government of India is his agent, though it is not likely that he would enter into such contracts without full consultation with the Government of India.

The argument of the Railway Companies who have contracted with the Secretary of State is virtually that the terms of their contracts having been presumably approved by the Government of India, that Government is debarred from authorizing the infraction of any of the terms of their contracts by the exercise of either of its functions (1) or (2); and further, that the Secretary of State in Council, having actually bound himself to the precise terms of any contract, ought, by his veto or otherwise, to prevent the exercise by the Government of India of its legislative function so as to cause any such infraction.

I apprehend, however, that, even apart from any clause in the contracts providing for this contingency, parties who contract with the Secretary of State must be taken to be aware of the nature of the Government of India, and that their contracts are subject to a liability to the general legislation of India; and, therefore, that they are not entitled even to complain unless some very unreasonable interference with their particular contract is enacted.

In the cases of all except three Companies – the Great Indian Peninsula, the Bombay, Baroda, and Central India, and the Madras Railway – (see Mr Scoble's observations of 21st March 1890 on moving the consideration of the Report) clauses were, for greater caution, inserted in the various contracts expressly to meet this difficulty.

But even with respect to the three Companies above mentioned I am of opinion that their contracts must be held to be subject to the provisions of general legislation, though of course legislative interference with a contract ought not to be sanctioned without reasonable consideration. The Companies cannot, in my opinion, put their cases higher than the cases of English Companies, who, having obtained special Acts of Parliament, are nevertheless liable to be interfered with by subsequent legislation.

In this case, so far from interference being unreasonable, the legislation is for the general benefit, not of the public only, but of all the railways; and its result will be to increase general traffic and profits, though possibly in some instances by the diminution of the charges of an individual Company upon particular business which would not otherwise have come to that individual Company at all.

The Government of India and the Secretary of State in Council, in their executive capacities, will continue to have an overruling discretion; and it seems to me that the Railway Companies ought to be satisfied that such discretion will be reasonably and fairly exercised.

18th June 1890

(Signed)

CHARLES PONTIFEX

403

Note by Legal Adviser, India Office dated 30 July 1890 regarding the Indian Railway Act IX of 1890

Source: P.W.D. Proceedings, Nos. 22 to 24, Railway Traffic, Simla Records, May 1891 (Despatches from and to Secretary of State)

Gist: The legal adviser suggests placing the various memoranda before the English Law Officers for an authoritative opinion, drawing their attention to certain specific clauses of the memoranda, and expects that this alone will satisfy the Companies.

NOTE 2

I have nothing to add, as far as my own opinion is concerned, to my observations of 18th June 1890.

No doubt the matter is complicated by the fact that the Government of India is itself largely interested, both as owner and as guarantor of railways in India; and the objections of the Railway Companies to the arbitration of the Railway Commission (see, e.g., paragraph 23 of the Great Indian Peninsula's Memorandum) are theoretically sound.

The Government of India deliberately enacted the Indian Railways Bill in the face of the Company's objections. These objections were fully considered by the Law Member of Council, and I presume the Indian Law Officers were consulted.

It seems to me the only course now to be taken is to place the various memoranda before the English Law Officers for an authoritative opinion, which alone will satisfy the Companies.

This course will be expensive.

In the case to be submitted to the Law Officers their attention will have to be drawn specifically to the contentions of the East Indian Railway Company in the 13th and 18th clauses of its Memorandum, of the Great Indian Peninsula Railway Company in the 4th and 24th clauses of its Memorandum, of the Madras Railway Company in the 12th clause of its Memorandum, and of the Bombay, Baroda, and Central India Railway Company in Clause 15 (1) of its Statement, which, no doubt, raise a substantial question; and to the fact that in three of the railway contracts no clause is contained providing that the Company shall not be entitled to make any claim for compensation in respect of any act of the Indian Legislature of "general applicability;" and with respect to the other contracts they must be asked to determine whether the construction of the words "general applicability" can be confined in the manner suggested in Clauses 22 and 23 of the Memorandum of the East Indian Railway Company.

30th July 1890

(Signed)
CHARLES PONTIFEX

PART III

Land Acquisition Acts and Rules (1857-1894)

404. Land Acquisition Act VI of 1857 for Railways and Public Purposes
405. Land Acquisition Act XXII of 1863 for Railways and Other Public Works
406. The Land Acquisition Act, 1870
407. Land Acquisition Declaration, 1889 under Section 6 of the Land Acquisition Act X of 1870 for the Assam-Behar State Railway
408. Rules for Land Acquisition for Railways and other Public Purposes Promulgated by the Government of India in 1889 under Section 59 of Act X of 1870
409. The Land Acquisition Act, 1894

404

Land Acquisition Act VI of 1857 for Railways and Public Purposes

Source: The Calcutta Gazette, 16 May 1857

Gist: The land acquisition Act (Act 6 of 1857) deals with the procedures to be followed for the acquisition of land and determination of the amount of compensation to be made to the owner or owners of the acquired land. This Act with 39 sections repealed relevant parts or completely the earlier Acts and Codes from 1824 to 1854, and provides adequate powers to the authorities to acquire land.

Act No. VI of 1857

An Act for the acquisition of land for public purposes

WHEREAS it is expedient to make better provision for the acquisition of land needed for public purposes within the territories in the possession and under the Government of the East India Company, and for the determination of the amount of compensation to be made for the same: It is enacted as follows: -

I. Sections I to VII inclusive, Regulation I, 1824 of the Bengal Code; so much of Act XXVIII of 1839 as is in force; Act 1 of 1850; Act XVII of 1850; Act XLII of 1850; Act XX of 1852; and Act 1 of 1854 - are hereby repealed, except so far as they repeal the whole or any part of any other Regulation or Act, and except as to suits or proceedings commenced, contracts made, acts done, and liabilities incurred before the passing of this Act.

II. Whenever it appears to the Local Government that any land is required to be taken by Government at the public expense for a public purpose, a declaration shall be made to that effect under the signature of a Secretary to the Government or of some Officer duly authorized to certify the orders of the Government, and such declaration shall be conclusive evidence that the purpose for which the land is needed is a public purpose; and after making such declaration, the Government may take any such land in the manner hereinafter provided.

III. Whenever any land shall have been declared to be so required for a public purpose, the Government shall direct the Collector of the District or some other Officer specially appointed in that behalf, to take order for the acquisition of the land in the manner hereinafter provided.

IV. The Collector or other Officer shall thereupon cause the land to be marked out and measured, and a plan to be made of the same. After the land has been so marked out and measured, he shall cause a notice to be affixed in some conspicuous place upon the land, and published by proclamation in the neighbouring bazaars and villages, to the effect that the land is about to be taken by Government for a public purpose; and shall also give notice to the same effect to the occupier (if any) of such land, and to all such persons known or believed to be interested therein or to be entitled by Section XXXVIII of this Act to act for persons so interested as shall reside or have agents within the Collectorate or other Revenue District in which the land is situate by serving such notice on such persons or their agents. Such notice shall contain a citation calling on all persons interested in the land to appear personally or by agent at a time and place therein mentioned, such time not being less than fifteen days after the date of publication of the notice, and to state the nature of their interests in the land and the amount and particulars of their claims to compensation for the same.

V. On the day fixed, the Collector or other Officer shall proceed to enquire summarily into the value of the land and the amount of compensation to be awarded: and if he and all the persons interested who have attended in pursuance of the notice agree as to the amount of compensation to be allowed, shall make an award for the same; and if the said persons agree also in the apportionment of the compensation, such apportionment shall be specified in the award. The award shall be final and conclusive in regard to the value of the land and the amount of compensation for the same; and also in regard to the apportionment (if any) of the compensation among the persons who have agreed thereto. The Collector or other Officer may, if no claimant shall attend pursuant to the notice, or, if he shall think fit for any other cause, postpone the enquiry to a day to be fixed by him and notified in the manner provided in the preceding Section.

VI. When the Collector or other Officer proceeds to make the enquiry as aforesaid, whether on the day originally fixed for the enquiry or on the day to which the enquiry may have been postponed, if no claimant shall attend, or if the said Collector or other Officer shall be unable to agree with the persons interested who have attended in pursuance of the notice as to the amount of compensation to be allowed, the matter shall be referred to the determination of arbitrators to be appointed in the manner hereinafter provided.

VII. If upon the said enquiry any question arise, respecting the title to the land or any rights or interests therein, between two or more persons making conflicting claims in respect thereof, the person deemed by the Collector or other Officer to be in possession as owner, or in receipt of the rents as being entitled thereto, shall, for the purpose only of taking such measures as may be necessary for fixing the value of the land and the amount of compensation to be allowed for the same, be held as between such persons to be the person interested in the land.

VIII. When the Collector or other Officer has made an award or directed a reference to arbitration, he may take immediate possession of the land which shall thenceforward be vested absolutely in the Government, free from all other estates, rights, titles, and interests.

IX. If the Collector or other Officer is opposed or impeded in taking possession of such land, he shall apply to the Magistrate who shall enforce the surrender of the land.

X. Clause 1. When any case is referred to arbitration, the Collector or other Officer, and the person interested in the land, shall, unless they concur in the appointment of a single arbitrator, each appoint one arbitrator; if there be several persons having a joint interest in the land, and they can not agree in the appointment of an arbitrator, such disagreement shall be deemed a refusal to appoint within the meaning of the next following Section.

Clause 2. If there be several persons having distinct and separate interests in the land, and they can not agree in the appointment of an arbitrator on their behalf, it shall be competent to the Collector or other Officer (subject to the orders of the Commissioner or other superior Revenue authority) to refer the question of the compensation to be allowed for each of such distinct and separate interests to a separate arbitration, or to select any one of the persons interested whose interest appears to him to qualify such person to represent the others; and the person so selected shall appoint an arbitrator on behalf of all the persons interested.

In every case the appointment shall be in writing, and neither of the parties to the arbitration shall have power to revoke the same without the consent of the order.

XI. If no claimant shall have attended, or if the persons interested in the matter in dispute or authorized to act in that behalf, refuse or neglect for the period of fifteen days to appoint an arbitrator, then a single arbitrator appointed by the Collector or other Officer shall arbitrate the matter. Provided that the person so appointed shall not be an Officer of Government.

XII. When more than one arbitrator shall be appointed, the arbitrators shall, before they enter upon the matter referred to them, nominate and appoint by writing a third person to act with them as arbitrator; and in case the arbitrators shall neglect to appoint such third person for a period of one week after having been required to do so, the Collector or other Officer shall appoint a third arbitrator.

XIII. If any person, or being appointed an arbitrator, shall refuse to act, or, after accepting the appointment, shall die or become incapable of acting, another person shall be appointed in his stead, in the same manner in which the first person was appointed.

XIV. When the amount of compensation is referred to arbitration, it shall be competent to the Collector or other Officer, with the written consent of all the persons interested, to require the arbitrators to determine the proportions in which all such persons are entitled to share in the amount awarded.

XV. When the Collector or other Officer and the persons interested in the land agree as to the amount of compensation, or when such amount shall have been settled by arbitration, if any dispute shall arise as to the apportionment of the same or any part thereof, it shall be competent to the Collector or other Officer, with the written consent of all persons interested in the matter in dispute, to refer the same to arbitration. If the parties can not agree with respect to the nomination of the arbitrators, or if the persons nominated by them shall refuse to accept the arbitration, or, having accepted it, shall refuse to act, and the parties are desirous that the nomination shall be made by the Collector or other Officer, he shall appoint some proper person or persons to arbitrate the matter. The provisions of this Act relating to arbitrators appointed under Sections X and XI and to the proceedings of such arbitrators shall be applicable to persons appointed arbitrators under this Section.

XVI. After the arbitrators have accepted the appointment, the Collector or other Officer shall be competent to exercise towards them such powers and authority for securing their attendance and the due completion of their award, as the Collector may legally exercise towards witnesses summoned before him when acting judicially for the purpose of compelling them to attend and give evidence.

XVII. If no award be made within a period to be fixed for that purpose by the Collector or other Officer, he may order that the matter shall be referred to another arbitrator or other arbitrators to be chosen in the same manner and subject to the same rules as the first.

XVIII. The Collector or other Officer shall furnish the arbitrators, or so far as may be in his power procure for them, any information which his records or those of any public department may afford connected with the subject of enquiry. He shall, on the application of the arbitrators, summon any witnesses whom the arbitrators may call for and whom the parties may not be able to produce before them without such process, and require the persons so summoned to bring and produce before them all such books, papers, deeds, writings, maps, and plans as they shall require. Persons so summoned shall be subject to all the provisions of the laws in force regarding persons summoned as witnesses before the Collector when acting judicially.

XIX. Every witness examined before the arbitrators shall be examined upon oath or affirmation to be administered by or made before the said arbitrators.

XX. On the close of the enquiry, the arbitrators or a majority of them shall deliver a full and complete award in respect of the matter referred to them, and shall therein specify (as the nature of the case may require) the amount and particulars of compensation awarded by them, the persons entitled to compensation, and the proportions in which they are so entitled.

XXI. The arbitrators on making their award shall be entitled to reasonable fees for their services, the amount of which shall be fixed by the Collector or other Officer subject to the orders of the Commissioner or other superior Revenue authority.

XXII. The award shall declare the costs of the arbitration and by whom and in what proportion they shall be paid. All costs, including the fees of the arbitrators, incurred for the purpose only of determining the amount of compensation to be allowed for the land, shall be charged to the Government, unless the arbitrators shall award as compensation the same or a less sum than shall have been offered by the Collector or other Officer, in which case each party shall bear his own costs so incurred and shall also pay a moiety of the fees of the arbitrators. Costs incurred for determining the apportionment of the compensation among the persons interested shall be paid by such persons in such proportions as the arbitrators shall direct.

XXIII. The proceedings of the arbitration shall be deposited in the office of the Collector or other Officer; and every person interested therein shall be entitled to a copy of the award on plain paper under seal and signature of the Collector or other Officer, which copy shall be prima facie evidence thereof.

XXIV. When any land is taken under the provisions of this Act, the amount of compensation to be awarded shall include any damage which may be sustained by any of the persons interested therein in respect of any adjoining land held therewith.

XXV. If any compensation beyond the value of the land be awarded on account of any damage which may be sustained by any person interested in the land, the award shall specify the value of the land and the amount of such damage separately, and also the name of the person to whom compensation for damage is awarded.

XXVI. When any land is taken under this Act forms part of an estate paying revenue to Government, the award shall specify the net rent of the land including the Government Revenue, and the computed value of such rent: and it shall be at the discretion of the Revenue authorities either to pay over the whole of such value to the owner of the estate on the condition of his continuing to pay the jumma thereof without abatement; or to determine what proportion of the net rent shall be allowed as a remission of revenue, in which case a deduction shall be made from the said value proportionate to the value of such remission.

XXVII. When the amount of compensation to be paid for land taken under the provisions of this Act is determined by the award of the Collector or other Officer under Section V, he shall pay the amount awarded at the time when possession is taken of the land on account of Government. When the compensation is determined by the award of arbitrators under Section XX, the Collector or other Officer shall pay the amount awarded with interest at the rate of six per cent per annum from the time when possession was taken of the land on account of Government.

XXVIII. Except, as provided in the next following Section, payment of the compensation shall be made, according to the award, to the persons named therein. Provided always that nothing in this Act contained shall affect the liability of any person who may receive the compensation awarded for any land or any portion of such compensation to pay the same to the person lawfully entitled thereto.

XXIX. If there exists any ground which, in the judgement of the Collector or other Officer, renders it improper to make immediate payment of the compensation, or of any portion thereof, to any of the persons having or claiming any interest in the land or in the compensation awarded in respect thereof, the amount, or such portion of the amount as he may deem sufficient, shall be invested in Government Securities, and held in deposit until an order of Court shall be obtained for the payment thereof. Such order shall be obtained in the Court which would have had jurisdiction in respect of the land taken.

XXX. If the land taken be within the local limits of any Her Majesty's Supreme Courts of Judicature, and the amount of compensation awarded do not exceed five hundred Rupees, the order may be made by the Court of Small Causes.

XXXI. No award of arbitrators made in accordance with the provisions of this Act, shall be liable to be reversed or altered, except by the decision of a Civil Court on the ground of corruption or misconduct of the arbitrators. In case the award shall be so reversed, the matter shall be referred to another arbitrator or other arbitrators to be appointed in the same manner as the first. All suits to set aside an award under this Act shall be instituted within three months from the date of the award.

XXXII. The provisions of this Act shall not be put in force for the purpose of acquiring a part only of any house or other building or manufactory, if the owner desires that the whole of such house, building, or manufactory shall be taken.

XXXIII. Whenever any land is needed for a road, canal, railway, or the like, and the local Government makes the declaration provided in Section II, it shall not be necessary to specify the extent, limits or position of the land, but it shall be sufficient to declare the general direction of the line of the work and the average breadth of the land required for the same.

XXXIV. When any declaration has been made under the provisions of Section II of this Act, the Collector or other Officer may authorize any person, with his servants and workmen, to enter upon the land for the purpose of making a survey thereof; and in the case of a road, canal, or railway, to set out the intended line thereof, and to mark such line by cutting a trench or placing land-marks; and where otherwise the survey can not be completed, and the line marked, to cut down and clear away any part of any jungle or tope of trees in the direction of the intended line. Provided that no person shall enter into any house or building or upon the curtilage of any house or any enclosed garden (unless with the consent of the occupier thereof) without previously giving the said occupier twenty-four hours' notice of his intention to do so.

XXXV. It shall be the duty of the Collector or other Officer to take account of all necessary damage done as aforesaid, and forthwith to offer payment for the same to the persons interested. In case the offer is not accepted, the damage shall be allowed for in the compensation to be awarded.

XXXVI. Whoever wilfully obstructs any person in lawfully setting out the line of any road, canal, or railway, or wilfully destroys, damages, or displaces any land-mark, or effaces or fills any trench intended to mark such line, shall, on conviction, be liable to be imprisoned for any term not exceeding six months, or to fine not exceeding two hundred Rupees, or to both.

XXXVII. The powers of this Act shall extend, in the case of any road, canal, or railway, to authorize the temporary occupation of any land not more than one hundred yards from the centre line of the road, canal, or railway, as marked on the ground, for taking earth or other materials for making or repairing the road, canal, or railway, or for depositing thereon superfluous earth or other materials, or erecting temporary buildings and workshops thereon, and of any land which may be needed for making temporary roads, from any public road to the intended line of railway; and for the temporary occupation of any such land, and for any permanent damage done by such occupation and use of the land, including the full value of all clay, stone, gravel, sand and other materials taken thence, compensation shall be paid to and among all persons having an interest therein, to be ascertained, in case of disagreement, in the same manner as compensation for land permanently taken.

XXXVIII. In any proceedings under this Act the following persons shall be deemed persons entitled to act as and to the extent hereinafter provided, (that is to say) - a trustee or trustees for other persons beneficially interested shall in all cases be deemed the person or persons entitled to act with reference to any such proceedings, and that to the same extent as the persons beneficially interested could have acted if free from disability. A married woman, in cases to which the English law is applicable, shall be deemed the person so entitled to act, and, whether of full age or not, to the same extent as if she were unmarried and of full age. The guardians of minors and the Committees of lunatics or idiots shall be deemed respectively the persons so entitled to act to the same extent as the minors, lunatics, or idiots themselves, if free from disability, could have acted.

XXXIX. The following words and expressions in this Act shall have the several meanings hereby assigned to them, unless there be something either in the subject or context repugnant to such construction (that is to say) -

The words "the local Government" shall mean the person or persons for the time being immediately administering the Executive Government of that portion of the territories in the possession and under the Government of the East India Company in which the land in question is situate; and shall include any Chief Commissioner or other Chief Civil Officer of a Province whom the Governor General in Council may authorize to exercise the powers vested by this Act in the local Government.

The word "land" shall extend to tenements and hereditaments of any tenure, and all houses, buildings, trees, or appurtenances thereupon, as well as land.

The expression "person interested in the land" shall include all persons interested in the land either for life or for years, or in remainder, reversion, or succession, and all mortgagees, leaseholders, or tenants, not being tenants by the month or at will, of such land.

Words importing the singular number only shall include the plural, and words importing the plural number only shall include the singular.

Words importing the masculine gender only shall include females.

The word "person" shall include a corporation.

W. MORGAN,
Clerk of the Council

405

Land Acquisition Act XXII of 1863 for Railways and Other Public Works

Source: The Calcutta gazette, 25 March 1863

Gist: The Land Acquisition Act XXII of 1863 for Railways and Other Public Works has 53 sections. It deals with the official procedures to be followed by the railway companies or promoters to acquire any land for any constructional work for public utility from the Government of India. The Act deals also with the authority of the government to inspect and supervise whether the construction of roads, railroads, tramroads, bridges, canal for irrigation and navigation, drainage and electric telegraphs, on the acquired land would cause any danger to the public.

Act No. XXII of 1863

An Act to provide for taking land for works of public utility to be constructed by private persons or Companies, and for regulating the construction and use of works on land so taken.

WHEREAS it is expedient to enable the Government to take land for the construction of works of public utility by private persons or Companies; and whereas it is proper at the same time to protect the rights of all persons from whom land shall be so taken, or be proposed to be taken, and also to determine the manner in which such works may be undertaken, and shall be managed after their construction, as well as to secure to the public under suitable regulations the use of works constructed on land so taken; It is enacted as follows: -

AS TO THE CONSTRUCTION OF THE ACT

I. The following words and expressions shall have the several meanings hereby assigned to them, unless when a contrary intention appears from the context.

Words in the singular number shall include the plural, and words in the plural shall include the singular.

Words importing the masculine gender shall include females.

The words "the work" shall signify the public work proposed to be undertaken.

The words "Local Government" shall mean the head of the Executive

Administration of the Province in which the public work is proposed to be constructed.

The words "the Collector" shall include any Officer exercising by authority of Government the duties of a Collector of Land Revenue by whatever name his office may be designated.

The words "the Promoters" shall mean the person or persons who propose to construct the work, or are empowered to construct it, whether a single person or a Company.

The words "Work under this Act" shall imply a work definitively registered as hereinafter provided by this Act.

The words "the Owners" or "the Company" shall signify the parties in charge of any public work under this Act, or referred to in this Act, whether as promoters, proprietors, lessees, agents, assignees, or otherwise, and whether a single person or a Company.

The word "Lands" shall include messuages, lands, tenements, and hereditaments of any tenure.

The word "Conditions" shall signify the special conditions of agreement between the promoters or owners of a work under this Act, and the Government, referred to in Section XV of this Act.

The word "Toll" shall include any rate or charge or other payment to be made for any use of a work under this Act, or for any service performed in connection with the use of any such work.

II. A work of public utility within this Act shall be held to mean any bridge, road, railroad, tramroad, canal for irrigation or navigation, work for the improvement of a river or harbour, dock, quay, jetty, drainage work, or electric telegraph; also all works subsidiary to any such work. It shall be lawful for the Governor-General in Council, from time to time by a declaration to be made to that effect and published in the Official Gazette, to order that any other class of works, or any particular work other than those named above, shall be included among works of public utility within this Act.

III. It shall be lawful for the Governor-General of India in Council to vest the principal Executive Officer of any territory under the immediate administration of the Governor-General in Council with any or all of the powers vested by this Act in the Local Government of such territory.

AS TO THE PRELIMINARY PROCEEDINGS TO BE TAKEN, AND THE REGISTRATION OF WORKS

IV. The promoters of any work of public utility, who shall desire to proceed under this

Act, shall make a preliminary application in writing to the Local Government, explaining the general object and nature of the work, and its intended locality. Every such application shall further be accompanied by a statement of the estimated cost of the construction of the said work, and the mode in which the promoters propose to provide the funds for constructing, maintaining and working the same.

V. If the Local Government shall not be satisfied with any such application or statement, it may reject it, or it may call on the promoters to supply any further information, or to amend such application or statement on any point on which such further information or amendment shall to the Local Government seem requisite.

VI. If the promoters shall desire to undertake any preliminary survey on account of the proposed work, before preparing and submitting the statement aforesaid, they shall declare the same in their preliminary application, and it shall be lawful for the Local Government, if satisfied of the expediency of permitting such survey, to issue a certificate authorizing the same. Such certificate shall declare the names of the promoters entitled to use it, the time for which it shall be in force, and the District or Districts or locality for which it shall be valid, and shall contain such further regulations for the guidance of the persons using the said certificate as to the Local Government shall seem fit. The promoters named in such certificate, and such other persons as the promoters shall name in a list to be furnished to the Chief Officer charged with the Executive Administration of each District in which the proposed work is to be constructed, shall be authorized to enter upon any lands, in the manner and for the time declared in such certificate, to undertake any survey or other investigation necessary for the proper prosecution of the proposed work; and while acting under the authority given in the said certificate, such promoters and other persons aforesaid shall be deemed to be public servants whose duty it is to make a survey under Clause 10 of Section 21 of the Indian Penal Code.

Provided that such promoters and other persons shall not be authorized to enter any house or building, or the curtilage of any house or enclosed garden, without the assent of the occupier, or to cut down any tree or otherwise injure or destroy any property. Provided also that such promoters and other persons aforesaid shall, while acting under the authority of such certificate, be liable as public servants for any offence described in Chapter IX of the said Indian Penal Code, to the penalty provided in the said Chapter for such offence.

VII. It shall be lawful for the Local Government, before issuing a certificate as aforesaid, to call on the promoters to deposit, as caution money, such sum and in such manner as the Local Government shall in each case determine, to be applied by the Local Government to make good any damage done in the course of such survey by the promoters or other persons using the said certificate. The promoters shall be entitled on their demand to receive back, after the expiry of such certificate, and after the payment of any claim for damage which shall have been proved to the satisfaction of the Local Government, any surplus remaining in the hands of such Government.

VIII. It shall be lawful for the Local Government, at any time prior to the provisional registration of a public work under this Act as hereinafter provided, to cancel a certificate granted under Section VI of this Act, if it shall appear to such Local Government that the powers granted by such certificate have been abused, or for any other sufficient reason.

IX. The promoters shall, at the time when they submit their preliminary application to the Local Government, publish the same, and if they so desire, the statement that accompanies it, in the Official Gazette, and also, if possible, in at least two Newspapers (one of which shall be in English) in the Province in which the work is proposed to be executed, and shall repeat such publication at least six times within a period of two months from the date of submission of such application to the Local Government; the promoters shall further cause to be delivered, with all reasonable despatch and within a period not exceeding two months, to the Collector of every district in which any part of such work is proposed to be constructed, or such other Officer as the Local Government shall from time to time direct, six copies of such application, with a faithful translation of the same into the vernacular language of the District; and shall in like manner publish from time to time and deliver as aforesaid, copies and translations of any amended applications submitted to the Local Government.

X. The Collector or other Officer as aforesaid shall, on receipt of the preliminary application, publish the same in English and in the vernacular language of the District, in the localities where the work is proposed to be constructed, in such manner as to him seems best.

XI. At any time not sooner than four months after receipt of the said application, or if the application be amended then within four months after the receipt of such amended application, the Local Government, on being satisfied by the promoters that the above conditions have been complied with, shall be authorized to consider finally such application, and any objections that shall have been raised against the construction of the proposed work, and to declare whether the said work may be provisionally registered under this Act or not.

XII. Before declaring that any work may be provisionally registered under this Act, being a railway or tramway in continuation of or forming a branch of any existing line, or being a line that might reasonably be expected to be united with any existing railway either as a continuation or a branch, and at the same time being at some one point within fifty miles distance of such existing railway, the Local Government shall afford to the owners of such existing line reasonable time and opportunity to declare whether they offer any opposition to the registration of the proposed line, and on a full consideration of such opposition, and of the application of the promoters, and of any objections aforesaid, and of the relative public advantages of all proposals made in the matter, the Local Government shall be authorized to declare its decision on the said application.

XIII. Previously to deciding that the said work shall be provisionally registered under this Act, it shall be lawful for the Local Government, if it shall think fit, to appoint a

Commission of one or more persons who may be Government Officers to enquire into the general object and nature of the said work, its intended locality and probable utility, its estimated cost, the grounds of any opposition to the said work, and any other matter connected with the said work, on which such Local Government shall desire to be satisfied. For the purposes of such enquiry, such Commission shall have power to take evidence, and for obtaining the attendance and for the examination of witnesses, may exercise the powers of a Civil Court under the Code of Civil Procedure.

XIV. On the receipt of the Report of the Commission appointed under the last proceeding Section, the Local Government shall decide if the said work shall be provisionally registered.

XV. Before declaring its decision as aforesaid, the Local Government shall, subject to such general or special instructions as the Governor-General of India in Council shall from time to time lay down, prescribe the conditions which such Local Government shall consider it necessary to impose on the promoters, having regard to the special circumstances of each case, in respect to the provision and payment of the price of the land for the proposed work, the construction, maintenance, or working of the same, the regulation of the use of the work as regards the security and convenience of the public, and such other matters as to the Local Government may from time to time seem right, and the Local Government shall inform the promoters of such conditions.

XVI. The Local Government, on causing a work to be provisionally registered under this Act, shall determine for what period, being not less than six months, such registry shall be in force. And at any time within such period the promoters may claim to have the registry made definitive as hereinafter provided.

XVII. Unless for any cause the Local Government shall otherwise determine, the promoters, before they are entitled to claim the definitive registry of the proposed work, shall deposit with the Government, in such manner as shall be approved by the Local Government, a sum to be fixed in each case by the Local Government, but not exceeding ten percent on the whole estimated cost of the said work, as caution money, to be deposed of in the manner agreed in the said conditions, unless it be otherwise dealt with as hereinafter provided. And any sum remaining in the hands of the Local Government from any caution money lodged under Section VII of this Act shall be held to be a payment in part of the caution money required under this Section.

XVIII. The promoters, before such claim for definitive registry shall be admitted, shall further complete an agreement with the Secretary of State for India in Council through the Government, under the conditions aforesaid, or under such other conditions as may be agreed between the said promoters and the Local Government. And thereupon the Local Government shall cause such agreement with the conditions thereof to be published in the Official Gazette, and shall declare that the work is definitively registered as a public work under this Act.

XIX. It shall be lawful for the Local Government, on the application of the promoters of any public work under this Act, to cause to be definitively registered under this Act, any public work undertaken by such promoters under an agreement entered into previously to the passing of this Act with the Secretary of State, or the Government of India, or any Local Government, as though such work had been proposed to be undertaken under the provisions of this Act hereinbefore contained. Provided that, at the time of so registering any work, the Local Government shall cause the said contract to be published in the Official Gazette, with all the conditions attaching thereto, and declare that the said work has been so registered definitively.

XX. It shall be lawful for the Local Government to apply any land in its lawful possession, also any public road or place, for the purposes of any public work under this Act, to be constructed at the expense and risk of the promoters of such work. Provided that every such work shall be definitively registered accordingly, and that the conditions under which such work is undertaken shall be published in the Official Gazette; also that the prosecution and construction of every such work shall be subject to the provisions of Section XII of this Act.

XXI. The Local Government may from time to time, with the assent of the owners of any work under this Act, vary the conditions to be agreed to under Section XV of this Act. Provided that such variation shall forthwith be published in the Official Gazette, and that after such publication the amended conditions shall be in force in supersession of those first made.

XXII. After the definitive registry of any work under this Act, it shall be lawful for the Local Government from time to time, in such wise as to it shall appear fit, to issue certificates to authorize the promoters, their servants, and agents to enter upon any lands, and to undertake such surveys or levels or other examinations as may be necessary for the proper prosecution of the said work; also to dig and bore into the sub-soil, and to indicate the intended boundaries of the land to be taken, and the positions of the proposed works, by suitable land-marks, and to perform all other necessary preliminary acts of the like nature; and such certificates shall declare the names of the persons entitled to use them, the time for which they shall be in force, and the Districts or locality for which they shall be valid, and shall contain such further regulations for the guidance of the persons using them as to the Local Government shall seem fit. And while acting under the authority given in the said certificate, such persons shall be deemed to be public servants, whose duty it is to make a survey under Clause 10 of Section 21 of the Indian Penal Code. Provided, however, that such persons shall not enter any house, or building, or the curtilage of any house, or enclosed garden without giving twenty four hours' notice, or without the assent of the occupier thereof, nor shall they cut down any tree, or otherwise injure or destroy any property, unless the same be essentially necessary. Provided also that such persons, while acting under the authority of such certificate, shall be liable as public servants for any offence described in Chapter IX of the said Indian Penal Code, to the penalty provided in the said Chapter for such offence.

XXIII. The promoters shall, on the completion of the necessary surveys and the like, submit to the Local Government such drawings, maps, and plans of the proposed work, as well as the land required for it, as the Local Government shall in each case require.

And thereupon the Local Government shall appoint one or more Commissioners, who may be Government Officers, to examine the said drawings, maps and plans, and to determine finally, in concert with the promoters or their agents, all matters of detail in respect of the exact position of the work, or of the parts thereof, as well as the boundaries of the land to be taken for the said work, and shall notify such appointment in the Official Gazette, and shall cause such notification to be published in the District where the work is proposed to be undertaken in such manner as shall seem best to the Local Government.

XXIV. The Commissioners appointed under the last preceding Section shall proceed at any time, but not sooner than thirty days after such notification, to settle, in concert with the promoters or their agents, the exact position of the work or of the parts thereof, and thereafter with all practicable despatch to examine the boundaries of the land proposed to be taken for the work; and the said Commissioners may call upon the promoters to make any variation in their project, and in the position of the works or any part of them, and in the boundaries of the land proposed to be taken, that may to the said Commissioners seem necessary to secure the safety or convenience of the public, or to prevent any undue interference with private property, or for any other reasonable cause, and any such variation, if agreed to by the promoters, shall thereon be considered to be finally adopted; but if the promoters shall not agree, the question in dispute shall be submitted to the Local Government, and the decision of the Local Government shall be final, provided that the promoters shall not be bound to carry out the proposed work if any variation be insisted upon by the Local Government to which the promoters will not assent.

XXV. The Local Government shall be authorized to extend the periods allowed for giving any notices, or for performing any acts required under the foregoing Sections, as from time to time may seem to it proper.

AS TO THE TAKING LANDS, THE TITLE THEREIN, AND THE PAYMENT THEREFOR

XXVI. When the boundaries of the land required for the work shall have been settled as aforesaid, and the promoters shall have caused the said land to be measured, and suitable land-plans to be prepared of the same, the Local Government shall cause a declaration to be made, under the signature of a Secretary to such Government or some Officer duly authorized to certify the orders of the Local Government that the land aforesaid is required for the said work, and such declaration, shall be conclusive that the land may be taken under this Act. After making such declaration the Local Government may proceed to take any such land as though it had been required to be taken at the public expense, and for a public purpose, and as though a declaration had been made as required under Act VI of 1857 (*for the acquisition of land for public purposes.*)

XXVII. The boundaries as determined by the Commissioners, and the plans and measurements aforesaid of the said land, when verified and found to be correct, or when duly corrected by the Collector or other Officer appointed to proceed under the said Act VI of 1857, shall be held to be the boundaries, plans, and measurements required under Section IV of the said Act, so far as the said lands are concerned.

XXVIII. If at any time land shall be required for any necessary or reasonable extension of or addition to any work under this Act, it shall be lawful for the Local Government to make all requisite declarations for the purpose of obtaining such land under this Act, after such and only such of the preliminary proceedings and enquiries herein before required, as to the Local Government shall in each case seem sufficient for the protection of the rights of the public and of individuals concerned.

Provided that nothing shall be done contrary to the provisions of Section XII of this Act, and that all proceedings for the actual taking possession of the land shall be conducted in accordance with the provisions of the said Act VI of 1857.

XXIX. Land may be taken under this Act for a temporary purpose in like manner as under the said Act VI of 1857.

XXX. All land taken under this Act shall vest absolutely in the Local Government as though it had been taken for a public purpose under the said Act VI of 1857, and it shall be lawful for the Local Government to dispose of any land taken under this Act, the whole or any part of which shall not be required for the purpose for which it was taken, in any manner that it may think fit. The Local Government alone shall be responsible for the payment of all claims on account of such land to all persons whatever, and the promoters shall in no wise be responsible for any such payment otherwise than to the Local Government, and then only as is herein declared and provided, and as shall be specially agreed in the conditions aforesaid.

XXXI. When all the conditions as aforesaid applicable to the transfer of the land to the promoters shall have been fully complied with, and not till then, the Government shall cause the promoters to be placed in possession of such land in accordance with such conditions. The title of the Local Government or of the promoters to such land shall not be liable to be questioned on account of any informality in any proceeding taken under this Act.

XXXII. All expenses attending the proceedings of the Commissioners to be appointed under Section XXIII of this Act, and all expenses incurred by the Local Government in taking up the land required for the promoters under the said Act VI of 1857, shall be paid by the said promoters, unless otherwise specially agreed. The Local Government shall determine the sum due on account of such expenses, and shall be authorized to deduct such amount from any sum lodged as caution money as aforesaid, and any sum remaining unpaid both as aforesaid, if it be not otherwise paid by the promoters, and any sum remaining unpaid both as aforesaid, and on account of land or compensation for which the promoters are liable under the said conditions, may, on the order of the Local Government to that effect, be levied by distress and sale on the said promoters, in the manner provided for distress and sale under Civil process.

XXXIII. The promoters shall further be liable for all damage done in any of their preliminary operations, and shall duly satisfy and pay all claims of this description; and if at the time of taking possession of the land required for the promoters, it shall appear that any such claim remains unsatisfied, the Collector or other Officer acting under the said Act VI of 1857 in respect of such land shall be authorized to determine all such claims summarily, as though they had been claims arising under the said Act, and all payments on account of such claims shall be made good by the promoters as under the last preceding Section.

AS TO THE PUBLIC USE OF WORKS

XXXIV. Every work under this Act shall be available for the use of the public in accordance with and to the extent provided by the conditions aforesaid, or any Act at the time being in force, but not otherwise; and after the publication of the conditions relating to any such works in the Official Gazette, all Courts may take judicial notice of the same, and it shall be lawful for any person whatsoever to sue the owners of such work for any damage he may incur by reason of any neglect of the said conditions by the said owners, in respect of any such public use of such work, as though such person had been a party to the said conditions.

XXXV. The owners of any work under this Act shall be authorized to levy such tolls, in such manner, as shall be fixed in accordance with the conditions aforesaid, also to refuse the use of such work, and to refuse to perform any service in connection therewith, unless such tolls shall be paid in the manner fixed aforesaid, as well as to detain any thing or animal on which such tolls shall be due, and to sell the same if the said tolls shall remain unpaid after a reasonable time has been allowed to elapse for payment of the same. Provided that no such tolls shall be demanded or taken at any place unless proper tables and lists of such tolls be exhibited at such place in the manner fixed as aforesaid.

AS TO THE CONSTRUCTION OF THE WORKS, AND THE INSPECTION OF THE SAME

XXXVI. The Local Government may appoint Inspectors to inspect any work under this Act, also all things appertaining thereto, and to the working of the same; but not books or documents otherwise than as shall be provided in the conditions aforesaid. The owners of such work, and all persons authorized by them to use the same in connection with any public use of the said work, and their servants and agents, shall be bound to afford to such Inspectors all reasonable facility for their inspection, and all such information as may be reasonably required by them.

XXXVII. If it appear to the Local Government, upon the report of any Inspector, that the use of any work under this Act can not be continued without danger to the public or to the persons employed thereon, or that rules adequate to the protection of the public under the provisions of this Act have not been framed and put in force, or that the conditions agreed upon under Section XV of this Act have not been carried out, the Local

Government may order that all defects shall be made good within a reasonable specified time; and in default of the owners of such work complying with such order within such time, or such further time as the Local Government shall appoint, the Local Government shall be empowered to direct that the use of such work shall be suspended, until the defects aforesaid shall be remedied to the satisfaction of the Local Government.

XXXVIII. The Local Government may at any time, on the report of an Inspector during the construction of any work under this Act, direct the promoters to construct in connection therewith such culverts, bridges, tunnels, drains or other works as may be considered by the Local Government to be necessary to continue to the public any roads, or rights of way, or easements, or the use of any water theretofore available, and to make due provision for the irrigation and drainage of the country, so as to prevent the same from being impeded or unnecessarily altered by the construction of the said work. If default be made in complying with any directions given under the provisions of this Section, the Local Government may order the prosecution of the work to be stopped until such directions shall be complied with to the satisfaction of the Local Government.

XXXIX. Nothing in the last preceding Section shall be construed to render the promoters liable to construct any work, or to undertake any thing, at variance with the special conditions of agreement under Section XV of this Act.

XL. The owners of every Railway under this Act, being of the gauge of five feet six inches, shall be bound, unless specially exempted by the Governor-General of India in Council, to erect all the fixed structures, and to construct all the rolling stock, in conformity with the standard dimensions determined in that behalf from time to time by the Governor-General of India in Council, and it shall be lawful for the Local Government to order the said owners to make good all defects in such structures or rolling stock, and to suspend their use until such defects shall be made good to the satisfaction of the Local Government.

XLI. The provisions of Act XVIII of 1854 (relating to Railways in India) shall apply to all Railways under this Act; provided that in respect of such Railways the Local Government shall be authorized to determine, from time to time, the extent to which fences shall be constructed under Section XX of the said Act XVIII of 1854, and that the owners of such Railways shall not be liable to maintain fences under the said Section otherwise than as shall be so determined.

XLII. In case any doubt shall at any time arise, as to the necessity for constructing or altering any work to ensure the safety of the public, or to provide for established public rights of way, or other public rights of any sort in connection with any work under this Act, the decision of the Local Government on such subject shall be final, and shall not be liable to be called in question in any Court of Justice.

XLIII. If the owners of a Railway under this Act shall desire to form a connection with any existing Railway of the same gauge, the owners of the new line shall be authorized to call on the owners of the old line to effect the junction, and if the owners of the old line shall not proceed to effect the junction within a reasonable time, the Local Government, on being satisfied that the junction may be made with safety to the public, and without injury to the existing Railway, or determent to the traffic thereon, may authorize the owners of the proposed line to form the junction, and to do all necessary acts in that behalf, and to lay down such additional lines of rails, points, and crossings as may be necessary for the purpose, at such time and in such manner as the Local Government shall direct. Provided that if the junction be effected by the owners of the previously existing Railway, the expense of forming the junction, of supplying all necessary works, and of keeping in repair and renewing the same, shall be paid by the owners of the new line.

XLIV. If any difference shall arise as to the terms on which the traffic of a branch or junction line of Railway under this Act shall pass over or upon any other line with which it shall be connected, or as to the manner and times of conducting the traffic, or of regulating the same, over the two lines or either of them, or as to any matter touching any line under this Act used in common by two or more Companies, the Local Government shall be authorized, on the application of either or any one of the said Companies, to hear and determine all such differences, and any order given by the Local Government in such a case shall be final and binding on all parties, provided that no order shall be so given at variance with any condition of any agreement between the Government and any of the said Companies, that shall be applicable to the said lines of Railway.

AS TO THE MAKING OF BYE-LAWS

XLV. It shall be lawful for the owners of any work under this Act to make Bye-Laws and Regulations for the guidance of their servants and agents, and of persons employed by them, and for the maintenance of order in the use of such work, and to provide for the safety and convenience of the public, or of the persons employed on such work; and all such Bye-Laws and Regulations shall be subject to the approval of the Local Government, and when so approved all Courts and Magistrates shall take judicial notice of the same, and the Local Government shall be authorized to cause any alterations to be made in the Bye-Laws and Regulations so made and approved, as to the Local Government shall from time to time seem proper. Provided that such Bye-Laws and Regulations be not repugnant to any Law in force in the British Territories in India, and that no penalty shall be attached to the infringement of any such Bye-Law or Regulation exceeding a fine of fifty Rupees.

XLVI. Such Bye-Laws and Regulations affecting the public shall be published, and the substance of them shall be notified, in such places on the said work and in such manner as the Local Government shall from time to time approve or direct, and no penalty shall be recoverable under such Bye-Laws or Regulations unless the same shall have been published and kept published as aforesaid.

XLVII. In the case of a Railway under this Act, being of the gauge of five feet and six inches, it is further provided that the Bye-Laws and Regulations shall, unless the Governor-General of India in Council shall otherwise permit, conform in every respect to the Regulations for Railway Companies under the said Act XVIII of 1854.

AS TO THE LIEN OF THE GOVERNMENT ON ANY WORK

XLVIII. No lands taken or supplied by Government for any work under this Act; no tree, building, or structure standing on such lands; no machinery nor permanent way fixed to the soil on such lands; nor anything whatsoever on which the Local Government shall be entitled to re-enter, or of which it shall be entitled to take possession without payment on the determination from any cause of the agreement between the Local Government and the promoters under the conditions aforesaid, shall without the consent of the Local Government be liable to be seized or applied in satisfaction of any debts or liabilities of any sort of the promoters, nor without such consent shall the promoters alienate the same, or any part thereof, in any way not provided for, or consonant with such agreement or conditions.

XLIX. ŭ If the owners of a work under this Act shall voluntarily determine to wind up their affairs, or shall be so directed by an order of Court, or shall abandon or determine to abandon such work, or shall commit an act of Bankruptcy or Insolvency, it shall be lawful for the Local Government thereupon to terminate all contracts then existing between it and the promoters in respect of such work, and to re-enter upon and take possession of all things whatsoever, to which the Local Government shall be so entitled under the conditions of such contracts; all of all lands taken at the public expense, or supplied to the said promoters free of cost, together with all trees, buildings, and structures standing on such lands, as well as all machinery and permanent way fixed to the soil on such lands; provided that nothing shall be so taken which shall be expressly excluded from such liability under the conditions aforesaid. But the Local Government shall be bound to surrender to a lawful claimant all moveable property of which it shall at any time obtain possession from the promoters otherwise than by purchase, which shall not have been fully paid for by the promoters; or in lieu of such surrender, if the Local Government shall so determine, to satisfy all just outstanding claims on account of such property; provided that no such surrender shall be obligatory, and no such claim shall be entertained, in respect of any thing that shall have been delivered to the said promoters more than twelve months before the date of such surrender being required, or of such claim being made known to the Local Government.

AS TO MINES NEAR ANY WORK

L. Whenever land shall be taken under this Act for the construction of any work, the taking thereof shall not be held to convey or include the right to any mine of coal or other minerals lying under such land, except only such part thereof as shall be necessary to be dug or carried away or used in the construction of the works, unless compensation for the same shall have been expressly allowed in the award made in favour of the persons interested in the land.

LI. If the owner, lessee, or occupier of any mine of coal, or of any other mineral, lying immediately under any work under this Act, or within forty yards therefrom, shall work the same, it shall be competent to the Local Government, on the application of the promoters of such work, to require such person to abandon such working, or so to work the same as not to endamage the said work, and to construct the works necessary to make it safe. Provided that compensation shall be awarded to such owner, lessee, or occupier, in the manner provided for in the said Act VI of 1857, for any loss sustained by him from being compelled to abandon or alter his mode of working to mine, and also for any necessary works constructed by him (when so required as aforesaid) in order to prevent damage to the said work, but all damage or loss to the promoters, arising from any improper working of such mines, shall be at the risk of the owners, lessees, or occupiers of the said mines, and shall be made good by them.

AS TO OFFENCES, AND THE RECOVERY OF PENALTIES

LII. Whoever shall obstruct or commit any contempt of the lawful authority of any public servant in the discharge of any function or in the performance of any thing undertaken under this Act, or shall commit mischief by destroying, defacing, or removing any land-mark fixed by the authority of any such public servant shall be punishable under the provisions of the Indian Penal Code.

LIII. All penalties for offences under the Bye-Laws and Regulations aforesaid shall be recoverable in the manner provided for offences punishable by fine only in the said Act XVIII of 1854 (*relating to Railways in India*).

M. WYLIE,
Deputy Secy. to the Govt. of India,
Home Department

406

The Land Acquisition Act, 1870

Source: The Calcutta Gazette, Part V, 1870

Gist: The Land Acquisition Act, 1870 (Act 10 of 1870) has 59 sections in eight parts. It was enacted for the acquisition of land for public purposes and for companies. Though the Act received assent on 1 April 1870, it was made effective from 1 June 1870. The Act extended to the whole of British India. The Act provides for proceedings of acquisition such as preliminary investigation, declaration of intended acquisition, enquiry into value and claims, compensation award by collector, taking possession, reference to court and procedure thereon, apportionment of compensation where there are several persons interested, and temporary occupation of land. Part VII deals with the acquisition of land for companies.

Act No. X of 1870

PASSED BY THE GOVERNOR-GENERAL OF INDIA IN COUNCIL

(Received the assent of the Governor-General on the 1st April, 1870)

An Act for the Acquisition of Land for Public Purposes and for Companies

WHEREAS it is expedient to consolidate and amend the law for the acquisition of land needed for public purposes and for companies, and for determining the amount of compensation to be made on account of such acquisition; It is hereby enacted as follows:-

PART I
PRELIMINARY

1. This Act may be called "The Land Acquisition Act, 1870:" It extends to the whole of British India;

   And it shall come into force on the first day of June 1870.

2. On and from such day Act No. VI of 1857 (*for the acquisition of land for public purposes*), Act No. II of 1861 (*to amend Act No. VI of 1857*), and Act No. XXII of 1863 (*to provide for taking land for works of public utility to be constructed by private persons or companies, and for regulating the construction and use of works on land so taken*) shall be repealed.

   All references made to any of the said Acts in subsequent Acts, orders or, contracts shall be read as if made to this Act.

3. In this Act: –

The expression "land" includes benefits to arise out of land, and things attached to the earth or permanently fastened to anything attached to the earth:

The expression "person interested" includes all persons claiming an interest in compensation to be made on account of the acquisition of land under this Act:

The expression "collector" means the collector of a district, and includes a deputy commissioner and any officer specially appointed by the Local Government to perform the functions of a collector under this Act:

The expression "court" means, in the Regulation Provinces, British Burma and Sindh, a principal civil court of original jurisdiction, and in the Non-regulation Provinces other than British Burma and Sindh, the court of a commissioner of a division, unless when the Local Government has appointed (as it is hereby empowered to do), either specially for any case, or generally within any specified local limits, a judicial officer to perform the functions of a judge under this Act, and then the expression "court" means the Court of such officer:

The expression "company" means a company registered under the Indian Companies' Act, 1866, or formed in pursuance of an Act of Parliament or by Royal Charter or letters patent;

And the following persons shall be deemed persons "entitled to act" as and to the extent hereinafter provided (that is to say) –

Trustees for other persons beneficially interested shall be deemed the persons entitled to act with reference to any such case, and that to the same extent as the persons beneficially interested could have acted if free from disability:

A married woman, in cases to which the English law is applicable, shall be deemed the person so entitled to act, and, whether of full age or not, to the same extent as if she were unmarried and of full age; and

The guardians of minors and committees of lunatics or idiots shall be deemed respectively the persons so entitled to act, to the same extent as the minors, lunatics, or idiots themselves, if free from disability, could have acted.

PART II
ACQUISITION

Preliminary Investigation

4. Whenever it appears to the local government that land in any locality is likely to be needed for any public purpose, a notification to that effect shall be published in the

local gazette, and the collector shall cause public notice of the substance of such notification to be given at convenient places in the said locality. Thereupon it shall be lawful for any officer either generally or specially authorized by such government in this behalf, and for his servants and workmen;

To enter upon and survey and take levels of any land in such locality:

To dig or bore into the subsoil:

To do all other acts necessary to ascertain whether the land is adapted for such purpose:

To set out the boundaries to the land proposed to be taken and the intended line of the work (if any) proposed to be made thereon:

To mark such levels, boundaries and line by placing marks and cutting trenches:

And where otherwise the survey cannot be completed and the levels taken and the boundaries and line marked, to cut down and clear away any part of any standing crop, fence or jungle.

Provided that no person shall enter into any building or upon any enclosed court or garden attached to a dwelling house (unless with the consent of the occupier thereof) without previously giving such occupier at least seven days' notice in writing of his intention to do so.

5. The officer so authorized shall at the time of such entry pay on tender payment for all necessary damage to be done as aforesaid, and in case of dispute as to the sufficiency of the amount so paid or tendered, he shall at once refer the dispute to the decision of the collector, and such decision shall be final.

Declaration of Intended Acquisition

6. Subject to the provisions of Part VII of this Act, whenever it appears to the local government that any particular land is needed for a public purpose, or for a company, a declaration shall be made to that effect under the signature of a secretary to such government or of some officer duly authorized to certify its orders:

Provided that no such declaration shall be made unless the compensation to be awarded for such property is to be paid out of public revenues, or out of some municipal fund, or by a company.

The declaration shall be published in the local official gazette and shall state the district or other territorial division in which the land is situate, the purpose for which it is needed, its approximate area, and, where a plan shall have been made of the land, the place where such plan may be inspected.

The said declaration shall be conclusive evidence that the land is needed for a public purpose or for a company, as the case may be; and after making such declaration, the local government may acquire the land in manner hereinafter appearing.

7. Whenever any land shall have been so declared to be needed for a public purpose, or for a company, the local government, or some officer authorized by the local government in this behalf, shall direct the collector to take order for the acquisition of the land.
8. The collector shall thereupon cause the land (unless it has been already marked out under section 4) to be marked out. He shall also cause it to be measured, and (if no plan has been made thereof) a plan to be made of the same.
9. The collector shall then cause public notice to be given at convenient places on or near the land to be taken, stating that the Government intends to take possession of the land, and that claims to compensation for all interests in such land may be made to him.

Such notice shall state the particulars of the land so needed and shall require all persons interested in the land to appear personally or by agent before the collector at a time and place therein mentioned (such time not being earlier than fifteen days after the date of publication of the notice) and to state the nature of their respective interests in the land and the amount and particulars of their claims to compensation for such interests.

The collector shall also serve notice to the same effect on the occupier (if any) of such land and on all such persons known or believed to be interested therein, or to be entitled to act for persons so interested, as reside, or have agents authorized to receive service on their behalf, within the Revenue District in which the land is situate.

In case any person so interested resides elsewhere, and has no such agent, the notice shall be sent to him by post.

10. The collector may also require any such person to deliver to him a statement containing, so far as may be practicable, the name of every other person possessing any interest in the land or any part thereof as co-proprietor, sub-proprietor, mortgagee, tenant or otherwise, and of the nature of such interest, and of the rents and profits (if any) received or receivable on account thereof for the year next preceding the date of the statement.

Every person required to make or deliver a statement under this section or section nine, shall be deemed to be legally bound to do so within the meaning of sections one hundred and seventy-five and one hundred and seventy-six of the Indian Penal Code.

Enquiry into Value and Claims

11. On the day so fixed, the collector shall proceed to enquire summarily into the value of the land and to determine the amount of compensation which in his opinion should be allowed therefor, and shall tender such amount to the persons interested who have attended in pursuance of the notice.

    For the purpose of such enquiry, the collector shall have power to summon and enforce the attendance of witnesses and to compel the production of documents by the same means and (as far as may be) in the same manner as is provided in the case of a Civil Court under the Code of Civil Procedure.

12. The collector may, if no claimant attends pursuant to the notice, or if for any other cause he thinks fit, from time to time postpone the enquiry to a day to be fixed by him.
13. In determining the amount of compensation the collector shall take into consideration the matters mentioned in section twenty-four and shall not take into consideration any of the matters mentioned in section twenty-five.

Award by Collector

14. If the collector and the persons interested agree as to the amount of compensation to be allowed, the collector shall make an award under his hand for the same.

    Such award shall be filed in the collector's office and shall be conclusive evidence as between the collector and the persons interested, of the value of the land and the amount of compensation allowed for the same.

15. When the collector proceeds to make the enquiry as aforesaid, whether on the day originally fixed for the enquiry or on the day to which it may have been postponed,

    If no claimant attends,

    Or if the collector considers that further enquiry as to the nature of the claim ought to be made by the Court,

    Or if any person whom the collector has reason to think interested does not attend,

    Or if the collector is unable to agree with the persons interested who have attended in pursuance of the notice as to the amount of compensation to be allowed,

    Or if upon the said enquiry any question respecting the title to the land or any rights thereto or interests therein arise between or among two or more persons making conflicting claims in respect thereof,

    the collector shall refer the matter to the determination of the Court in manner hereinafter appearing.

Taking Possession

16. When the collector has made an award under section fourteen or a reference to the Court under section fifteen, he may take possession of the land, which shall thereupon vest absolutely in the Government free from all encumbrances.
17. In cases of urgency, whenever the local government so directs, the collector (though no such reference has been directed or award made) may, on the expiration of fifteen days from the publication of the notice mentioned in the first paragraph of section nine, take possession of any waste or arable land needed for public purposes or for a company.

Such land shall thereupon vest absolutely in the Government free from all encumbrances.

The collector shall offer to the persons interested compensation for the standing crops and trees (if any) on such land; and in case such offer is not accepted, the value of such crops and trees shall be allowed for in awarding compensation for the land under the provisions herein contained.

PART III
REFERENCE TO COURT AND PROCEDURE THEREON

18. In making a reference under section fifteen, the collector shall state for the information of the Court, in writing under his hand –
    (*a*) The situation and extent of the land needed;
    (*b*) The names of the persons whom he has reason to think interested in such land;
    (*c*) The amount awarded for damages and paid or tendered under sections five and seventeen, or either of them, the amount of compensation tendered for the land under section eleven, or, if no claimant has attended pursuant to the notice mentioned in section nine, the amount of compensation which the collector is willing to give to the persons interested; and
    (*d*) The grounds on which the amount of compensation was determined.
19. The Court shall thereupon cause to be served on each of the persons so named a notice requiring him (if he has not made a claim under section nine) to state to the Court, on or before a day to be therein mentioned, the sum which he claims as compensation for his interest in the land so needed.

    The Court shall also cause a notice to be served on the collector and each of such persons requiring them to appoint, on or before a day to be therein mentioned, two qualified assessors (one to be nominated by the collector and the other by the persons interested) for the purpose of aiding the judge in determining the amount of the compensation.

If no claimant has attended pursuant to the notice mentioned in section nine, the Court shall cause to be affixed on some conspicuous place on or near the land needed a notice to the effect that, if the persons interested in such land do not, on or before a day to be therein mentioned, appear in Court and state the nature of their respective interests in the land and the amount and particulars of their claims to compensation, and nominate a qualified assessor, the Court will proceed to determine such amount.

20. In case of failure to nominate either of such assessors within the time so specified, the judge shall himself appoint an assessor in his stead.
21. As soon as the assessors have been appointed, the judge and the assessors shall proceed to determine the amount of compensation.
22. If before such amount is determined, any of the assessors dies or desires to be discharged, or refuses or neglects, or becomes incapable to act, the party by whom he was appointed may appoint some other qualified person to act in his place.

If the assessor so dying or desiring to be discharged, or refusing, or neglecting, or becoming incapable were appointed by the judges,

Or, in the case of an assessor appointed by either party, if for the space of seven days after notice from the Court for that purpose the party who appointed such assessor fails to appoint another,

the judge shall appoint some other qualified person in his stead.

Every assessor so substituted shall have the same powers as were vested in the former assessor at the time of his so dying or desiring to be discharged, or refusing or neglecting or becoming incapable.

23. Every proceeding under section twenty-one shall take place in open Court, and all persons entitled to practise in any Civil Court shall be entitled to appear, plead, and act, or to appear and act (as the case may be), in such proceeding.
24. In determining the amount of compensation to be awarded for land acquired under this Act, the judge and assessors shall take into consideration –

First, the market-value, at the time of awarding compensation, of such land:

Secondly, the damage (if any) sustained by the person interested, at the time of awarding compensation, by reason of severing such land from his other land:

Thirdly, the damage (if any) sustained by the person interested, at the time of awarding compensation, by the reason of the acquisition injuriously affecting his other property, whether moveable or immoveable, in any other manner, or his earnings; and

Fourthly, if, in consequence of the acquisition, he is compelled to change his residence, the reasonable expenses (if any) incidental to such change.

25. But the judge or assessors shall not take into consideration –

First, the degree of urgency which has led to the acquisition:

Secondly, any disinclination of the person interested to part with the land acquired:

Thirdly, any damage sustained by him which, if caused by a private person, would not render such person liable to a suit:

Fourthly, any damage which, after the time of awarding compensation, is likely to be caused by or in consequence of the use to which the land acquired will be put:

Fifthly, any increase to the value of the land acquired likely to accrue from the use to which it will be put when acquired:

Sixthly, any increase to the value of the other land of the person interested, likely to accrue from the use to which the land acquired will be put; or

Seventhly, any outlay or improvements on such land made, commenced, or effected with the intention of enhancing the compensation to be awarded therefore under this Act.

26. Where the person interested has made a claim to compensation, pursuant to any notice mentioned in section nine or in section nineteen, the amount awarded to him shall not exceed the amount so claimed, or be less than the amount tendered by the collector under section eleven.

Where the person interested has refused to make such claim, or has omitted without sufficient reason (to be allowed by the judge) to make such claim, the amount awarded may be less than, and shall in no case exceed, the amount so tendered.

Where the person interested has omitted for a sufficient reason (to be allowed by the judge) to make such claim, the amount awarded to him shall not be less than, and may exceed, the amount so tendered.

The provisions of this and the two preceding sections shall be read to every assessor, in a language which he understands, before he gives his opinion as to the amount of compensation to be awarded under this Act.

27. The opinion of each assessor shall be given orally and shall be recorded in writing by the judge.

28. In case of a difference of opinion between the judge and the assessors or any of them upon a question of law or practice or usage having the force of law, the opinion of the judge shall prevail, and there shall be no appeal therefrom.

29. In case the judge and one or both of the assessors agree as to the amount of compensation, their decision thereon shall be final.

30. In case of difference of opinion between the judge and both of the assessors as to the amount of compensation, the decision of the judge shall prevail, subject to the appeal

allowed under section thirty-five.

31. Every assessor appointed under this Act, not being an officer of Government, shall receive such fee for his services as the judge shall direct, provided that such fee shall not exceed five hundred rupees.

Such fee shall be deemed to be costs in the proceeding.

32. The costs of all proceedings taken under this part by order of the Court shall, in the first instance, be paid by the collector.

33. Where the amount awarded does not exceed the sum tendered by the collector, the costs of all proceedings under this part shall be paid by the person interested.

Where the amount awarded exceeds the sum so tendered, such costs shall be paid by the collector.

34. Every award made under this part shall be in writing signed by the judge and the assessors or assessor concurring therein, and shall specify the amount awarded under the first clause of section twenty-four, and also the amounts (if any) respectively awarded under the second, third and fourth clauses of the same section, together with the grounds of awarding each of the said amounts.

It shall also state the amount of costs incurred in the proceedings under this part, and by what persons and in what proportions they are to be paid.

The costs (if any) payable by the person interested and not deducted under section forty-two may be recovered as if they were costs incurred in a suit, and as if the award were the decree therein.

35. If the judge differs from both the assessors as to the amount of compensation, he shall pronounce his decision, and the collector or the person interested (as the case may be) may appeal therefrom to the Court of the district judge, unless the judge whose decision is appealed from is the district judge, or unless the amount which the judge proposes to award exceeds five thousand rupees, in either of which cases the appeal shall lie to the High Court.

Every appeal under this section shall be presented within the time and in manner provided by the code of civil procedure for regular appeals in suits.

36. The following provisions of the Code of Civil Procedure

(*a*) as to adding parties,
(*b*) as to adjournment,
(*c*) as to death, marriage and bankruptcy or insolvency of parties,
(*d*) as to summoning witnesses and their attendance,
(*e*) as to examination of parties and witnesses,
(*f*) as to production of documents, and
(*g*) as to commissions to examine absent witnesses and to make local inquiries,

shall apply, so far as may be, to proceedings before the Court.

PART IV
APPORTIONMENT OF COMPENSATION

37. Where there are several persons interested, if such persons agree in the apportionment of the compensation, the particulars of such apportionment shall be specified in the award, and as between such persons the award shall be conclusive evidence of the correctness of the apportionment.

38. When the amount of compensation has been settled under section fourteen, if any dispute arises as to the apportionment of the same or any part thereof, the collector shall refer such dispute to the decision of the Court.

39. When the amount of compensation has been settled by the Court, and there is any dispute as to the apportionment there of, or when a reference tc the Court has been made under section thirty-eight, the judge sitting alone shall decide the proportions in which the persons interested are entitled to share in such amount.

An appeal shall lie from such decision to the High Court, unless the judge whose decision is appealed from is not the district judge, in which case the appeal shall lie in the first instance to the district judge.

Every appeal under this section shall be presented within the time and in manner provided by the Code of Civil Procedure for regular appeals in suits.

PART V
PAYMENT

40. Payment of the compensation shall be made by the collector according to the award to the persons named therein, or, in the case of an appeal under section thirty-nine, according to the decision on such appeal:

Provided that nothing herein contained shall affect the liability of any person who may receive the whole or any part of any compensation awarded under this Act, to pay the same to the person lawfully entitled thereto.

41. When the amount of the compensation has been settled under section fourteen, if the persons interested shall so desire, the collector shall on the making of the said award pay the amount of such compensation and take possession of the land:

Provided that, in any case where immediate possession is not required, he may allow the occupants (if any) of the land to remain in occupation of the same, upon such terms as he and they may agree on, until possession of the land is required.

42. In addition to the amount of any compensation awarded under Part II or Part III of this Act, the collector shall in consideration of the compulsory nature of the acquisition, pay fifteen per centum on the market value mentioned in section twenty-four.

When the amount of such compensation is not paid on taking possession, the collector shall pay the amount awarded and the said percentage with interest on such amount and percentage at the rate of six per centum per annum from the time of so taking possession:

Provided that the costs, if any, payable to the collector by the person interested, shall be deducted from such amount and percentage.

Provided that, in cases where the decision of the Court under Part III or Part IV of this Act is liable to appeal, the collector shall not pay the amount of compensation, or the percentage, or any part thereof, until the time for appealing against such decision has expired and no appeal shall have been presented against such decision, or until any such appeal shall have been disposed of.

PART VI
TEMPORARY OCCUPATION OF LAND

43. Subject to the provisions of Part VII of this Act, whenever it appears to the local government that the temporary occupation and use of any waste or arable land are needed for any public purpose, or for a company, the local government may direct the collector to procure the occupation and use of the same for such term as it shall think fit, not exceeding three years from the commencement of such occupation.

The collector shall thereupon give notice in writing to the persons interested in such land of the purpose for which the same is needed, and shall, for the occupation and use thereof for such term as aforesaid, and for the materials (if any) to be taken therefrom, pay to them such compensation, either in a gross sum of money, or by monthly or other periodical payments, as shall be agreed upon in writing between him and such persons respectively.

In case the collector and the persons interested differ as to the sufficiency of the compensation, the collector shall refer such difference for the final order of the Court.

44. On payment of such compensation,

or on executing such agreement,

or on making a reference under section forty-three,

the collector may enter upon and take possession of the land, and use or permit the use thereof in accordance with the terms of the said notice.

And on the expiration of the term, the collector shall make or tender to the persons interested compensation for the damage (if any) done to the land and not provided for by the agreement, and shall restore the land to the persons interested therein:

Provided that, if the land has become permanently unfit to be used for the purpose for which it was used immediately before the commencement of such term, and if the persons interested shall so require, the local government shall proceed under this Act to acquire the land as if it was needed permanently for a public purpose or for a company.

45. In case the collector and persons interested differ as to the condition of the land at the expiration of the term, or as to any matter connected with the said agreement, the collector shall refer such difference for the final order of the Court, and on such reference, or on a reference under section forty-three, the judge sitting alone shall decide the difference referred.

PART VII
ACQUISITION OF LAND FOR COMPANIES

46. Subject to such rules as the Governor-General of India in Council may from time to time prescribe in this behalf, the local government may authorize any officer of any company desiring to acquire land for its purposes to exercise the powers conferred by section four.

In every such case section four shall be construed as if, for the words "for such purpose", the words "for the purposes of the company" were substituted, and section five shall be construed as if, after the words "the officer," the words "of the company" were inserted.

47. The provisions of section six to section forty-five (both inclusive) shall not be put in force in order to acquire land for any company, unless with the previous consent of the local government, and unless the company shall have executed the agreement herein after mentioned.

48. Such consent shall not be given unless the local government be satisfied, by an enquiry held as hereinafter provided –

(1) that such acquisition is needed for the construction of some work, and
(2) that such work is likely to prove useful to the public.

Such enquiry shall be held by such officer and at such time and place as the local government shall appoint.

Such officer may summon and enforce the attendance of witnesses, and compel the production of documents by the same means and, as far as possible, in the same manner as is provided by the Code of Civil Procedure in the case of a Civil Court.

49. Such officer shall report to the local government the result of the enquiry, and if the local government is satisfied that the proposed acquisition is needed for the construction of a work, and that such work is likely to prove useful to the public, it shall, subject to such rules as the Governor-General of India in Council may from time to time prescribe in this behalf, require the company to enter into an agreement with

the Secretary of State for India in Council providing to the satisfaction of the local government for the following matters, namely:–

(1) The payment to Government of the cost of the acquisition:
(2) The transfer, on such payment, of the land to the company:
(3) The terms on which the land shall be held by the company:
(4) The time within which, and the conditions on which, the work shall be executed and maintained; and
(5) The terms on which the public shall be entitled to use the work.

50. Every such agreement shall, as soon as may be after its execution, be published in the *Gazette of India* and also in the local official gazette, and shall thereupon (so far as regards the terms on which the public shall be entitled to use the work) have the same effect as if it had formed part of this Act.

PART VIII
MISCELLANEOUS

51. Service of any notice under this Act shall be made by delivering or tendering a copy thereof signed, in the case of a notice under section four, by the officer therein mentioned, and, in the case of any other notice, by or by order of the collector or the judge.

Whenever it may be practicable, the service of the notice shall be made on the person therein named.

When such person can not be found, the service may be made on any adult male member of his family residing with him; and if no such adult male member can be found, the notice may be served by fixing the copy on the outer door of the house in which the person therein named ordinarily dwells or carries on business.

52. Whoever wilfully obstructs any person in doing any of the acts authorized by section four or section eight, or wilfully fills up, destroys, damages, or displaces any trench or mark made under section four shall, on conviction before a magistrate, be liable to imprisonment for any term not exceeding one month, or to fine not exceeding fifty rupees, or to both.

53. If the collector is opposed or impeded in taking possession under this Act of any land, he shall, if a magistrate, enforce the surrender of the land to himself, and if not a magistrate, he shall apply to a magistrate or (within the towns of Calcutta, Madras and Bombay) to the commissioner of police, and such magistrate or commissioner (as the case may be) shall enforce the surrender of the land to the collector.

54. Except in the case provided for in section forty-four, nothing in this Act shall be taken to compel the Government to complete the acquisition of any land unless an award shall have been made or a reference directed under the provisions herein before contained.

But whenever the Government declines to complete any such acquisition, the collector shall determine the amount of compensation due for the damage (if any) done to such land under section four or section eight, and not already paid for under section five, and shall pay such amount to the person injured.

55. The provisions of this Act shall not be put in force for the purpose of acquiring a part only of any house, manufactory or other building, if the owner desire that the whole of such house, manufactory or building shall be so acquired.
56. Where the provisions of this Act are put in force for the purpose of acquiring land at the cost of any municipal fund, or of any company, the charges incurred by the collector in such acquisition shall be defrayed from or by such fund or company.
57. No award or agreement made under this Act shall be chargeable with stamp duty and no person claiming under any such award or agreement shall be liable to pay any fee for a copy of the same.
58. No suit shall be brought to set aside an award under this Act.

And no suit or other proceeding shall be commenced or prosecuted against any person for anything done in pursuance of this Act, without giving to such person a month's previous notice in writing of the intended proceeding, and of the cause thereof, nor after tender of sufficient amends, nor after the expiration of three months from the accrual of the cause of suit or other proceeding.

59. The local government shall have power to make rules consistent with this Act for the guidance of officers in all matters connected with its enforcement, and may from time to time after and add to the rules so made.

All such rules, alterations and additions shall, when sanctioned by the Governor-General in Council, be published in the local official gazette, and shall thereupon have the force of law.

407

Land Acquisition Declaration, 1889 under Section 6 of the Land Acquisition Act X of 1870 for the Assam-Bihar State Railway

Source: The Calcutta Gazette, Part 1, 27th March 1889

Gist: Land Acquisition Declaration, 1889 under Section 6 of the Land Acquisition Act X of 1870 for the Assam-Bihar State Railway has 51 specific declarations (numbered 91 to 141) by Lieutenant-Governor of Bengal, acquiring lands in standard measurements such as acre, roods and poles for public purposes, viz. the construction of huts for the permanent-way gangmen, for repairing banks, etc.

RAILWAY

The 25th March 1889

No. 91. Declaration. Whereas it appears to the Lieutenant-Governor of Bengal that land is required to be taken up by Government at the public expense for a public purpose, viz., for the construction of huts for the permanent-way Gangmen on the main line of the Tirhoot State Railway at miles 33, 41, 47, and 51, in the respective mouzahs of Mahespatti, Ismailnagar-Pitonjia, Sirampur-Ajodhya, and Misrowlia, in Pergunnah Sarisa, in the district of Durbhunga, it is hereby declared that for the above purpose four plots of land measuring, more or less, 3 roods and 6.59 poles, equivalent to 2 bighas 7 cottahs and 14 chittacks of standard measurement in all, are required within the aforesaid mouzahs as per detail below –

Number of mile	*District*	*Pergunnah*	*Mouzah*	*Approximate area to be acquired*					
				A.	R.	P.	B.	C.	Ch.
33	Durbhunga	Sarisa	Mahespatti	0	0	25.28	0	9	9
41	Ditto	Do	Ismailnagar-Pitonjia.	0	0	36.03	0	13	10
47	Ditto	Do	Sirampur- Ajodhya.	0	0	38.18	0	14	7
51	Ditto	Do	Misrowlia.	0	0	27.10	0	10	4
				0	3	6.59	2	7	14

This declaration is made, under the provisions of section 6 of Act X of 1870, to all whom it may concern.

No. 92. Declaration. Whereas in appears to the Lieutenant-Governor of Bengal that land is required to be taken up by Government at the public expense for a public purpose, viz., for the construction of huts for the permanent-way Gangmen on the main line of the Tirhoot State Railway at miles 93, 98, 103, 108, 113, 118, 123, 128, 133, 138 and 143, in the respective mouzahs of Chupra Muzahid and Chakia, in Pergunnahs Mahesi and Kunria, Kumarpur, Surajpurtola Mudda Chak, Gopalpur, Panch-Rukha, Chupra, Baharupia, Baithnia, and Dutcheeara, in pergunnah Majhowa in the district of Chumparun, it is hereby declared that for the above purpose 11 plots of land measuring, more or less, 1 acre 2 roods and 32.71 poles, equivalent to 5 bighas 3 cottahs and 3 chittacks of standard measurement in all, are required within the aforesaid mouzahs as per detail below –

Number of mile	*District*	*Pergunnah*	*Mouzah*	*Approximate area to be acquired*					
				A.	R.	P.	B.	C.	Ch.
93	Chumparun	Mahesi	Chupra Muzahid	0	0	20.96	0	7	15
98	Ditto	Do	Chakia	0	0	23.14	0	8	12
103	Ditto	Majhowa	Kunria	0	0	23.62	0	8	15
108	Ditto	Ditto	Kumarpur	0	0	24.29	0	9	3
113	Ditto	Ditto	Surajpurtola Mudda Chak	0	0	19.80	0	7	8
118	Ditto	Ditto	Gopalpur	0	0	29.08	0	11	0
123	Ditto	Ditto	Panch Rukha	0	0	31.23	0	11	13
128	Ditto	Ditto	Chupra	0	0	9.89	0	3	12
133	Ditto	Ditto	Baharupia	0	0	28.25	0	10	11
138	Ditto	Ditto	Baithnia	0	0	29.40	0	11	2
143	Ditto	Ditto	Dutcheeara	0	0	33.05	0	12	8
				1	2	32.71	5	3	3

This declaration is made, under the provisions of section 6 of Act X of 1870, to all whom it may concern.

No. 93. Declaration. Whereas it appears to the Lieutenant-Governor of Bengal that land is required to be taken up by Government at the public expense for a public purpose, viz., for the construction huts for the permanent-way gangmen at miles 57, 67, 83, and 88 on the main line, and at miles

15 and 29 on the Hajipore Branch of the Tirhoot State Railway, in the respective mouzahs of Rupanpatti and Serpur in pergunnah Bisara, and Ghoswar in pergunnah Hajipur, in the district of Mozufferpore, it is hereby declared that for the above purpose six plots of land measuring, more or less, 3 roods and 23.23 poles, equivalent to 2 bighas 14 cottahs and 3 chittacks of standard measurement in all, are required within the aforesaid mouzahs as per detail below:

Number of mile	*District*	*Pergunnah*	*Mouzah*	*Approximate area to be acquired*					
				A.	R.	P.	B.	C.	Ch.
Main Line	Mozuffer-	Bisara	Rupanpatti						
57	pore			0	0	37.02	0	14	0
67	Ditto	Do	Serpur	0	0	36.67	0	13	14
83	Ditto	Bhadsara	Nuryar	0	0	19.17	0	7	4
88	Ditto	Do	Mahammadpur Kusai	0	0	27.10	0	10	4
Hajipore Branch									
15	Ditto	Bisara	Bakhtargunge	0	0	18.34	0	6	15
29	Ditto	Hajipore	Ghoswar	0	0	4.93	0	1	14
				0	3	23.23	2	14	3

This declaration is made, under the provisions of section 6 of Act X of 1870, to all whom it may concern.

No. 94. Declaration. Whereas it appears to the Lieutenant-Governor of Bengal that land is required to be taken up at the public expense for a public purpose, viz., for repairing banks, &c., for the Assam-Bihar State Railway, in the mouzah of Bhomrah, pergunnah Tajpore, Zillah Dinagepore, it is hereby declared that for the above purpose a plot of land measuring, more or less, 3 acres and 20 poles of standard measurement, bounded on the east by Gottur village, west by Mohanbatee village, and on one side by the railway line, is required within the aforesaid mouzah.

This declaration is made, under the provisions of section 6 of Act X of 1870, to all whom it may concern.

No. 95. Declaration. Whereas it appears to the Lieutenant-Governor of Bengal that land is required to be taken up at the public expense for a public purpose, viz., for repairing banks, &c., for the Assam-Behar State Railway, in the mouzah of Mohanbatee, pergunnah Dilivarpore, Zillah Dinagepore, it is hereby declared that for the above purpose, a plot of land measuring, more or less, 38 poles of standard measurement, bounded on the east by Bhomrah village, west by Raigunge village, and on one side by the railway line, is required within the aforesaid mouzah.

This declaration is made, under the provisions of section 6 of Act X of 1870, to all whom it may concern.

No. 96. Declaration. Whereas it appears to the Lieutenant-Governor of Bengal that land is required to be taken up at the public expense for a public purpose, viz., for repairing banks, &c., for the Assam-Behar State Railway, in the mouzah of Raigunge, pergunnah Sujahnagar, Zillah Dinagepore, it is hereby declared that for the above purpose, a plot of land measuring, more or less, 2 roods and 5 poles of standard measurement, bounded on the east by Bhomrah village, west by Kolgaon village, and Koollick river, and on one side by the railway line, is required within the aforesaid mouzah.

This declaration is made, under the provisions of section 6 of Act X of 1870, to all whom it may concern.

No. 97. Declaration. Whereas it appears to the Lieutenant-Governor of Bengal that land is required to be taken up at the public expense for a public purpose, viz., for repairing banks, &c., for the Assam-Behar State Railway, in the mouzah of Mohanbatee, pergunnah Dilivarpore, Zillah Dinagepore, it is hereby declared that for the above purpose a plot of land measuring, more or less, 1 rood and 10 poles of standard measurement, bounded on the east by Bhomrah village, west by Raigunge village, and on one side by railway line, is required within the aforesaid mouzah.

This declaration is made, under the provision of section 6 of Act X of 1870, to all whom it may concern.

No. 98. Declaration. Whereas it appears to the Lieutenant-Governor of Bengal that land is required to be taken up at the public expense for a public purpose, viz., for repairing banks and triangle siding at Raigunge station for the Assam-Behar State Railway, in the mouzah of Raigunge, pergunnah Sujahnugur, Zillah Dinagepore, it is hereby declared that for the above purpose a plot of land measuring, more or less, 5 acres 2 roods and 3 poles of standard measurement, bounded on the east by Bhomrah village, west by Kolgaon and the Koollick river, and on one side by the railway line, is required within the aforesaid mouzah.

This declaration is made, under the provisions of section 6 of Act X of 1870, to all whom it may concern.

No. 99. Declaration. Whereas it appears to the Lieutenant-Governor of Bengal that land is required to be taken up at the public expense for a public purpose, viz., for repairing banks, &c., for the Assam-Behar State Railway, in the mouzah of Raigunge, pergunnah Sujahnugur, Zillah Dinagepore, it is hereby declared that for the above purpose a plot of land measuring, more or less, 2 acres 2 roods and 13 poles of standard measurement, bounded on the east by Bomrah village, west by Kolgaon and Koollick river, and on one side by the railway line, is required within the aforesaid mouzah.

This declaration is made, under the provisions of section 6 of Act X of 1870, to all whom it may concern.

No. 100. Declaration. Whereas it appears to the Lieutenant-Governor of Bengal that land is required to be taken up at the public expense for a public purpose, viz., for repairing banks,

&c., for the Assam-Behar State Railway, in the mouzah of Kolgaon, pergunnah Tajpore, Zillah Dinagepore, it is hereby declared that for the above purpose a plot of land measuring, more or less, 2 acres 1 rood and 37 poles of standard measurement, bounded on the east by Raigunge village and the Koollick river, west by Chapdoar and Nasrathpur villages, and on one side by the railway line, is required within the aforesaid mouzah.

This declaration is made, under the provisions of section 6 of Act X of 1870, to all whom it may concern.

No. 101. Declaration. Whereas it appears to the Lieutenant-Governor of Bengal that land is required to be taken up at the public expense for a public purpose, viz., for repairing banks, &c., for the Assam-Behar State Railway, in the mouzah of Nasrathpore, pergunnah Tajpore, Zillah Dinagepore, it is hereby declared that for the above purpose a plot of land measuring, more or less, 5 poles of standard measurement, bounded on the east by Kolgaon village, west by Kismat Maharajpore, and on one side by the railway line, is required within the aforesaid mouzah.

This declaration is made, under the provisions of section 6 of Act X of 1870, to all whom it may concern.

No. 102. Declaration. Whereas it appears to the Lieutenant-Governor of Bengal that land is required to be taken up at the public expense for a public purpose, viz., for repairing banks, &c., for the Assam-Behar State Railway, in the mouzah of Kismat Maharajpore, pergunnah Tajpore, Zillah Dinagepore, it is hereby declared that for the above purpose, a plot of land measuring, more or less, 1 pole of standard measurement, bounded on the east by Nasrathpore village, west by Marjada Maharajpore, and on one side by the railway line, is required within the aforesaid mouzah.

This declaration is made, under the provisions of section 6 of Act X of 1870, to all whom it may concern.

No. 103. Declaration. Whereas it appears to the Lieutenant-Governor of Bengal that land is required to be taken up at the public expense for a public purpose, viz., for repairing banks, &c., for the Assam-Behar State Railway, in the mouzah of Kismat Maharajpore, pergunnah Tajpore, Zillah Dinagepore, it is hereby declared that for the above purpose a plot of land, measuring, more or less, 2 poles of standard measurement, bounded on the east by Nasrathpore, on the west by Marjada Maharajpore village, and on one side by the railway line, is required within the aforesaid mouzah.

This declaration is made, under the provisions of section 6 of Act X of 1870, to all whom it may concern.

No. 104. Declaration. Whereas it appears to the Lieutenant-Governor of Bengal that land is required to be taken up at the public expense for a public purpose, viz., for repairing banks, &c., for the Assam-Behar State Railway, in the mouzah of Nasrathpore, pergunnah Tajpore, Zillah Dinagepore, it is hereby declared that for the above purpose, a plot of land measuring, more or less, 12 poles of standard measurement, bounded on the east by Kolgaon, west by Marjada

Maharajpore, and on one side by the railway line, is required within the aforesaid mouzah.

This declaration is made, under the provisions of section 6 of Act X of 1870, to all whom it may concern.

No. 105. Declaration. Whereas it appears to the Lieutenant-Governor of Bengal that land is required to be taken up at the public expense for a public purpose, viz., for repairing banks, &c., for the Assam-Behar State Railway, in the mouzah of Marjada Maharajpore, pergunnah Tajpore, Zillah Dinagepore, it is hereby declared that for the above purpose, a plot of land measuring, more or less, 1 acre 2 roods and 20 poles of standard measurement, bounded on the east by Kismat Maharajpore and Nasrathpore villages, west by Marjada Maharajpore, and on one side by the railway line, is required within the aforesaid mouzah.

This declaration is made, under the provisions of section 6 of Act X of 1870, to all whom it may concern.

No. 106. Declaration. Whereas it appears to the Lieutenant-Governor of Bengal that land is required to be taken up at the public expense for a public purpose, viz., for repairing banks, &c., for the Assam-Behar State Railway, in the mouzah of Chapdoar, pergunnah Tajpore, Zillah Dinagepore, it is hereby declared that for the above purpose a plot of land measuring, more or less, 32 poles of standard measurement, bounded on the east by Marjada Maharajpore village, west by Hatmani village, and on one side by railway line, is required within the aforesaid mouzah.

This declaration is made, under the provisions of section 6 of Act X of 1870, to all whom it may concern.

No. 107. Declaration. Whereas it appears to the Lieutenant-Governor of Bengal that land is required to be taken up at the public expense for a public purpose, viz., for repairing banks, &c., for the Assam-Behar State Railway, in the mouzah of Chapdoar, pergunnah Tajpore, Zillah Dinagepore, it is hereby declared that for the above purpose a plot of land measuring, more or less, 3 roods and 22 poles of standard measurement, bounded on the east by Kolgaon village, west by Kismat Maharajpore village, and on one side by the railway line, is required within the aforesaid mouzah.

This declaration is made, under the provisions of section 6 of Act X of 1870, to all whom it may concern.

No. 108. Declaration. Whereas it appears to the Lieutenant-Governor of Bengal that land is required to be taken up at the public expense for a public purpose, viz., for repairing banks, &c., for the Assam-Behar State Railway, in the mouzah of Hatmani, pergunnah Tajpore, Zillah Dinagepore, it is hereby declared that for the above purpose a plot of land measuring, more or less, 1 acre, 1 rood and 21 poles of standard measurement, bounded on the east by Chapdoar village, west by Sonegaon or Sangram village, and on one side by the railway line, is required within the aforesaid mouzah

This declaration is made, under the provisions of section 6 of Act X of 1870, to all whom it may concern.

No. 109. Declaration. Whereas it appears to the Lieutenant-Governor of Bengal that land is required to be taken up at the public expense for a public purpose, viz., for repairing banks, &c., for the Assam-Behar State Railway, in the mouzah of Sonegaon or Sangram, pergunnah Tajpore, Zillah Dinagepore, it is hereby declared that for the above purpose a plot of land measuring, more or less, 1 rood and 18 poles of standard measurement, bounded on the east by Hatmani village, west by Jhatkia village, and on one side by the railway line, is required within the aforesaid mouzah.

This declaration is made, under the provisions of section 6 of Act X of 1870, to all whom it may concern.

No. 110. Declaration. Whereas it appears to the Lieutenant-Governor of Bengal that land is required to be taken up at the public expense for a public purpose, viz., for repairing banks, &c., for the Assam-Behar State Railway, in the mouzah of Sonegaon or Sangram, pergunnah Tajpore, Zillah Dinagepore, it is hereby declared that for the above purpose a plot of land measuring, more or less, 1 rood and 11 poles of standard measurement, bounded on the east by Hatmani village, west by Jhatkia village, and on one side by the railway line, is required within the aforesaid mouzah.

This declaration is made, under the provisions of section 6 of Act X of 1870, to all whom it may concern.

No. 111. Declaration. Whereas it appears to the Lieutenant-Governor of Bengal that land is required to be taken up at the public expense for a public purpose, viz., for repairing banks, &c., for the Assam-Behar State Railway, in the mouzah of Jhatkia, pergunnah Tajpore, Zillah Dinagepore, it is hereby declared that for the above purpose a plot of land measuring, more or less, 3 acres 1 rood and 13 poles of standard measurement, bounded on the east by Sonegaon or Sangram village, west by Makra village, and on one side by the railway line, is required within the aforesaid mouzah.

This declaration is made, under the provisions of section 6 of Act X of 1870, to all whom it may concern.

No. 112. Declaration. Whereas it appears to the Lieutenant-Governor of Bengal that land is required to be taken up at the public expense for a public purpose, viz., for repairing banks, &c., for the Assam-Behar State Railway, in the mouzah of Jhatkia, pergunnah Tajpore, Zillah Dinagepore, it is hereby declared that for the above purpose a plot of land measuring, more or less, 2 acres 3 roods and 8 poles of standard measurement, bounded on the east by Sonegaon or Sangram village, west by Makra village, and on one side by the railway line, is required within the aforesaid mouzah.

This declaration is made, under the provisions of section 6 of Act X of 1870, to all whom it may concern.

No. 113. Declaration. Whereas it appears to the Lieutenant-Governor of Bengal that land is required to be taken up at the public expense for a public purpose, viz., for repairing banks, &c., for the Assam-Behar State Railway, in the mouzah of Makra, pergunnah Mathurapore, Zillah Dinagepore, it is hereby declared that for the above purpose a plot of land measuring, more or less, 4 acres 18 poles of standard measurement, bounded on the east by Jhatkia village, west by the Nagor river, and on one side by the railway line, is required within the aforesaid mouzah.

This declaration is made, under the provisions of section 6 of Act X of 1870, to all whom it may concern.

No. 114. Declaration. Whereas it appears to the Lieutenant-Governor of Bengal that land is required to be taken up at the public expense for a public purpose, viz., for repairing banks, &c., for the Assam-Behar State Railway, in the mouzah of Makra, pergunnah Mathurapore, Zillah Dinagepore, it is hereby declared that for the above purpose a plot of land measuring, more or less, 1 rood and 19 poles of standard measurement, bounded on the east by Jhatkia village, west by Nagor river, and on one side by the railway line, is required within the aforesaid mouzah.

This declaration is made, under the provisions of section 6 of Act X of 1870, to all whom it may concern.

No. 115. Declaration. Whereas it appears to the Lieutenant-Governor of Bengal that land is required to be taken up at the public expense for a public purpose, viz., for repairing banks, &c., for the Assam-Behar State Railway, in the mouzah of Pedasun, pergunnah Bulrampore, Zillah Purneah, it is hereby declared that for the above purpose a plot of land measuring, more or less, 5 acres and 14 poles of standard measurement, bounded on the east by Nagor river, west by Kutchna village, and on one side by the railway line, is required within the aforesaid mouzah.

This declaration is made, under the provisions of section 6 of Act X of 1870, to all whom it may concern.

No. 116. Declaration. Whereas it appears to the Lieutenant-Governor of Bengal that land is required to be taken up at the public expense for a public purpose, viz., for repairing banks, &c., for the Assam-Behar State Railway, in the mouzah of Pedasun, pergunnah Bulrampore, Zillah Purneah, it is hereby declared that for the above purpose a plot of land measuring, more or less, 15 poles of standard measurement, bounded on the east by Nagor river, west by Kutchna village, and on one side by the railway line, is required within the aforesaid mouzah.

This declaration is made, under the provisions of section 6 of Act X of 1870, to all whom it may concern.

No. 117. Declaration. Whereas it appears to the Lieutenant-Governor of Bengal that land is required to be taken up at the public expense for a public purpose, viz., for repairing banks, &c., for the Assam-Behar State Railway, in the mouzah of Kutchna, pergunnah Barool, Zillah Purneah, it is hereby declared that for the above purpose a plot of land measuring, more or less, 2 acres 3 roods and 7 poles of standard measurement, bounded on the east by Kutchna village, west by Rusool village, and on one side by the railway line, is required within the aforesaid mouzah.

This declaration is made, under the provisions of section 6 of Act X of 1870, to all whom it may concern.

No. 118. Declaration. Whereas it appears to the Lieutenant-Governor of Bengal that land is required to be taken up at the public expense for a public purpose, viz., for repairing banks, &c., for the Assam-Behar State Railway, in the mouzah of Chachora, pergunnah Bador, Zillah Purneah, it is hereby declared that for the above purpose a plot of land measuring, more or less, 2 acres 2 roods and 7 poles of standard measurement, bounded on the east by Kutchna village, west by Rusool village, and on one side by the railway line, is required within the aforesaid mouzah.

This declaration is made, under the provisions of section 6 of Act X of 1870, to all whom it may concern.

No. 119. Declaration. Whereas it appears to the Lieutenant-Governor of Bengal that land is required to be taken up at the public expense for a public purpose, viz., for repairing banks, &c., for the Assam-Behar State Railway, in the mouzah of Chachora, pergunnah Bador, Zillah Purneah, it is hereby declared that for the above purpose a plot of land measuring, more or less, 9 acres 3 roods and 4 poles of standard measurement, bounded on the east by Kutchna village, west by Rusool village, and on one side by the railway line, is required within the aforesaid mouzah.

This declaration is made, under the provisions of section 6 of Act X of 1870, to all whom it may concern.

No. 120. Declaration. Whereas it appears to the Lieutenant-Governor of Bengal that land is required to be taken up at the public expense for a public purpose, viz., for repairing banks, &c., for the Assam-Behar State Railway, in the mouzah of Rusool, pergunnah Bador, Zillah Purneah, it is hereby declared that for the above purpose a plot of land measuring, more or less, 1 acre 1 rood and 27 poles of standard measurement, bounded on the east by Chachora village, west by Buleara village, and on one side by the railway line, is required within the aforesaid mouzah.

This declaration is made, under the provisions of section 6 of Act X of 1870, to all whom it may concern.

No. 121. Declaration. Whereas it appears to the Lieutenant-Governor of Bengal that land is required to be taken up at the public expense for a public purpose, viz., for repairing banks, &c., for the Assam-Behar State Railway, in the mouzah of Buleara, pergunnah Barool, Zillah Purneah, it is hereby declared that for the above purpose a plot of land measuring, more or less 3 acres 3 roods and 35 poles of standard measurement, bounded on the east by Rusool village, west by Bansbhita village, and on one side by the railway line, is required within the aforesaid mouzah.

This declaration is made, under the provisions of section 6 of Act X of 1870, to all whom it may concern.

No. 122. Declaration. Whereas it appears to the Lieutenant-Governor of Bengal that land is required to be taken up at the public expense for a public purpose, viz., for repairing banks, &c., for the Assam-Behar State Railway, in the mouzah of Bansbhita, pergunnah Dilalpore, Zillah Purneah, it is hereby declared that for the above purpose a plot of land measuring, more or less, 2 acres 2 roods and 32 poles of standard measurement, bounded on the east by Buleara village, west by Chandpura village, and on one side by the railway line, is required within the aforesaid mouzah.

This declaration is made, under the provisions of section 6 of Act X of 1870, to all whom it may concern.

No. 123. Declaration. Whereas it appears to the Lieutenant-Governor of Bengal that land is required to be taken up at the public expense for a public purpose, viz., for repairing banks, &c., for the Assam-Behar State Railway, in the mouzah of Bansbhita, pergunnah Dilalpore, Zillah Purneah, it is hereby declared that for the above purpose a plot of land measuring, more or less, 247 square feet of standard measurement, bounded on the east by Buleara village, west by Chandpura village, and on one side by the railway line, is required within the aforesaid mouzah.

This declaration is made, under the provisions of section 6 of Act X of 1870, to all whom it may concern.

No. 124. Declaration. Whereas it appears to the Lieutenant-Governor of Bengal that land is required to be taken up at the public expense for a public purpose, viz., for repairing banks, &c., for the Assam-Behar State Railway, in the mouzah of Chandpura, pergunnah Sujahnugur, Zillah Purneah, it is hereby declared that for the above purpose a plot of land measuring, more or less, 1 acre and 37 poles of standard measurement, bounded on the east by Bansbhita village, west by Dutchna village, and on one side by the railway line, is required within the aforesaid mouzah.

This declaration is made, under the provisions of section 6 of Act X of 1870, to all whom it may concern.

No. 125. Declaration. Whereas it appears to the Lieutenant-Governor of Bengal that land is required to be taken up at the public expense for a public purpose, viz., for repairing banks, &c., for the Assam-Behar State Railway, in the mouzah of Dutchna, pergunnah Tajpore, Zillah Purneah, it is hereby declared that for the above purpose a plot of land measuring, more or less, 1 rood and 9 poles of standard measurement, bounded on the east by Chandpura village, west by Raghunathpore village, and on one side by the railway line, is required within the aforesaid mouzah.

This declaration is made, under the provisions of section 6 of Act X of 1870, to all whom it may concern.

No. 126. Declaration. Whereas it appears to the Lieutenant-Governor of Bengal that land is required to be taken up at the public expense for a public purpose, viz., for repairing banks, &c., for the Assam-Behar State Railway, in the mouzah of Dutchna, pergunnah Tajpore, Zillah Purneah, it is hereby declared that for the above purpose a plot of land measuring, more or less, 1 acre and 36 poles of standard measurement, bounded on the east by Chandpura, west by Raghunathpore village, and on one side by the railway line, is required within the aforesaid mouzah.

This declaration is made, under the provisions of section 6 of Act X of 1870, to all whom it may concern.

No. 127. Declaration. Whereas it appears to the Lieutenant-Governor of Bengal that land is required to be taken up at the public expense for a public purpose, viz., for repairing banks, &c., for the Assam-Behar State Railway, in the mouzah of Dutchna, pergunnah Tajpore, Zillah Purneah, it is hereby declared that for the above purpose a plot of land measuring, more or less, 2 roods and 20 poles of standard measurement, bounded on the east by Chandpura, west by Raghunathpore, and on one side by the railway line, is required within the aforesaid mouzah.

This declaration is made, under the provisions of section 6 of Act X of 1870, to all whom it may concern.

No. 128. Declaration. Whereas it appears to the Lieutenant-Governor of Bengal that land is required to be taken up at the public expense for a public purpose, viz., for repairing banks, &c., for the Assam-Behar State Railway, in the mouzah of Raghunathpore, pergunnah Raghunathpore, Zillah Purneah, it is hereby declared that for the above purpose a plot of land measuring, more or less, 1 rood and 2 poles of standard measurement, bounded on the east by Dutchna village, west by Mahanuddy river, and on one side by the railway line, is required within the aforesaid mouzah.

This declaration is made, under the provisions of section 6 of Act X of 1870, to all whom it may concern.

No. 129. Declaration. Whereas it appears to the Lieutenant-Governor of Bengal that land is required to be taken up at the public expense for a public purpose, viz., for repairing banks, &c., for the Assam-Behar State Railway, in the mouzah of Raghunathpore, pergunnah Raghunathpore, Zillah Purneah, it is hereby declared that for the above purpose a plot of land measuring, more or less, 12 acres 1 rood and 2 poles of standard measurement, bounded on the east by Dutchna, west by Mahanuddy river, and on one side by the railway line, is required within the aforesaid mouzah.

This declaration is made, under the provisions of section 6 of Act X of 1870, to all whom it may concern.

No. 130. Declaration. Whereas it appears to the Lieutenant-Governor of Bengal that land is required to be taken up at the public expense for a public purpose, viz., for repairing banks, &c., and erecting temporary staff-quarters, &c., for the Assam-Behar State Railway, in the mouzah of Raghunathpore, pergunnah Raghunathpore, Zillah Purneah, it is hereby declared that for the above purpose a plot of land measuring, more or less, 88 acres 1 rood and 12 poles of standard measurement, bounded on the east by Dutchna, west by Mahanuddy river, and on one side by the railway line, is required within the aforesaid mouzah.

This declaration is made, under the provisions of section 6 of Act X of 1870, to all whom it may concern.

No. 131. Declaration. Whereas it appears to the Lieutenant-Governor of Bengal that land is required to be taken up at the public expense for a public purpose, viz., for bund on Mahanuddy east bank for the Assam-Behar State Railway, in the mouzah of Ematpore, pergunnah Raghunathpore, Zillah Purneah, it is hereby declared that for the above purpose a plot of land measuring, more or less, 3 acres and 16 poles of standard measurement, bounded on the east by Hatunpore village, west by Mahanuddy river, south by Raghunathpore and railway line, and north by Bajeetpore, is required within the aforesaid mouzah.

This declaration is made, under the provisions of section 6 of Act X of 1870, to all whom it may concern.

No. 132. Declaration. Whereas it appears to the Lieutenant-Governor of Bengal that land is required to be taken up at the public expense for a public purpose, viz., for repairing banks, &c., for the Assam-Behar State Railway, in the mouzah of Nurrungah, pergunnah Sujahnugur, Zillah Purneah, it is hereby declared that for the above purpose a plot of land measuring, more or less, 5 acres and 1 rood of standard measurement, bounded on the east by Mahanuddy river, west by Mudunpore village, and on one side by the railway line, is required within the aforesaid mouzah.

This declaration is made, under the provisions of section 6 of Act X of 1870, to all whom it may concern.

No. 133. Declaration. Whereas it appears to the Lieutenant-Governor of Bengal that land is required to be taken up at the public expense for a public purpose, viz., for repairing banks, &c., for the Assam-Behar State Railway, in the mouzah of Mudunpore, pergunnah Berar, Zillah Purneah, it is hereby declared that for the above purpose a plot of land measuring, more or less, 2 acres 1 rood and 9 poles of standard measurement, bounded on the east by Nurrungah village, west by Tajpore village, and on one side by the railway line, is required within the aforesaid mouzah.

This declaration is made, under the provisions of section 6 of Act X of 1870, to all whom it may concern.

No. 134. Declaration. Whereas it appears to the Lieutenant-Governor of Bengal that land is required to be taken up at the public expense for a public purpose, viz., for repairing banks, &c., for the Assam-Behar State Railway, in the mouzah of Mudunpore, pergunnah Berar, Zillah Purneah, it is hereby declared that for the above purpose a plot of land measuring, more or less, 4 poles of standard measurement, bounded on the east by Nurrungah village, west by

Tajpore village, and on one side by the railway line, is required within the aforesaid mouzah.

This declaration is made, under the provisions of section 6 of Act X of 1870, to all whom it may concern.

No. 135. Declaration. Whereas it appears to the Lieutenant-Governor of Bengal that land is required to be taken up at the public expense for a public purpose, viz., for repairing banks, &c., for the Assam-Behar State Railway, in the mouzah of Tajpore, pergunnah Tajpore, Zillah Purneah, it is hereby declared that for the above purpose a plot of land measuring, more or less, 8 acres 2 roods and 20 poles of standard measurement, bounded on the east by Mudunpore village, west by Teghra village, and on one side by the railway line, is required within the aforesaid mouzah.

This declaration is made, under the provisions of section 6 of Act X of 1870, to all whom it may concern.

No. 136. Declaration. Whereas it appears to the Lieutenant-Governor of Bengal that land is required to be taken up at the public expense for a public purpose, viz., for repairing banks, &c., for the Assam-Behar State Railway, in the mouzah of Tajpore, pergunnah Tajpore, Zillah Purneah, it is hereby declared that for the above purpose a plot of land measuring, more or less, 4 acres 2 roods and 16 poles of standard measurement, bounded on the east by Mudunpore village, west by Teghra village, and on one side by the railway line is required within the aforesaid mouzah.

This declaration is made, under the provisions of section 6 of Act X of 1870, to all whom it may concern.

No. 137. Declaration. Whereas it appears to the Lieutenant-Governor of Bengal that land is required to be taken up at the public expense for a public purpose, viz., for repairing banks, &c., for the Assam-Behar State Railway, in the mouzah of Teghra, pergunnah Tajpore, Zillah Purneah, it is hereby declared that for the above purpose a plot of land measuring, more or less, 11 poles of standard measurement, bounded on the east by Tajpore village, west by Shepore or Gobindpore village, north by Tengri village, and on one side by the railway line, is required within the aforesaid mouzah.

This declaration is made, under the provisions of section 6 of Act X of 1870, to all whom it may concern.

No. 138. Declaration. Whereas it appears to the Lieutenant-Governor of Bengal that land is required to be taken up at the public expense for a public purpose, viz., for repairing banks, &c., for the Assam-Behar State Railway, in the mouzah of Teghra, pergunnah Tajpore, Zillah Purneah, it is hereby declared that for the above purpose a plot of land measuring, more or less, 11 poles of standard measurement, bounded on the east by Tajpore village, west by Shepore or Gobindpore village, south by Tengri village, and on one side by the railway line, is required within the aforesaid mouzah.

This declaration is made, under the provisions of section 6 of Act X of 1870, to all whom it may concern.

No. 139. Declaration. Whereas it appears to the Lieutenant-Governor of Bengal that land is required to be taken up at the public expense for a public purpose, viz., for repairing banks, &c., for the Assam-Behar State Railway, in the mouzah of Tengri, pergunnah Tajpore, Zillah Purneah, it is hereby declared that for the above purpose a plot of land measuring, more or less, 1 acre and 23 poles of standard measurement, bounded on the east by Teghra village, west and south by Shepore or Gobindpore villages, and on one side by the railway line, is required within the aforesaid mouzah.

This declaration is made, under the provisions of section 6 of Act X of 1870, to all whom it may concern.

No. 140. Declaration. Whereas it appears to the Lieutenant-Governor of Bengal that land is required to be taken up at the public expense for a public purpose, viz., for repairing banks, &c., for the Assam-Behar State Railway, in the mouzah of Shepore or Gobindpore, pergunnah Tajpore, Zillah Purneah, it is hereby declared that for the above purpose a plot of land measuring, more or less, 25 poles of standard measurement, bounded on the east by Teghra or Tengri villages, west by Gurnadamudarpore village, and on one side by the railway line, is required within the aforesaid mouzah.

This declaration is made, under the provisions of section 6 of Act X of 1870, to all whom it may concern.

No. 141. Declaration. Whereas it appears to the Lieutenant-Governor of Bengal that land is required to be taken up at the public expense for a public purpose, viz., for repairing banks, &c., for the Assam-Behar State Railway, in the mouzah of Teldangir, pergunnah Tajpore, Zillah Purneah, it is hereby declared that for the above purpose a plot of land measuring, more or less, 5 acres and 37 poles of standard measurement, bounded on the east by Tajpore village, west by Gobindpore and Luskurpore villages, south by Tengri village, and on one side by the railway line, is required within the aforesaid mouzah.

This declaration is made, under the provisions of section 6 of Act X of 1870, to all whom it may concern.

408

Rules for Land Acquisition for Railways and other Public Purposes Promulgated by the Government of India in 1889 under Section 59 of Act X of 1870

Source: L.R., Head A.E., Coll. 1, Proceedings 100-101, August 1890

Gist: Rules for Land Acquisition for Railways and other Public Purposes Promulgated by the Government of India in 1889 under Section 59 of Act X of 1870 contain two sections. Section I provides general rules issued under the authority of the Board of Revenue for the guidance of public officers in the administration of the Land Acquisition Act X of 1870. Section II, in four parts, provides special rules issued under the authority of the Board of Revenue for the guidance of public officers in taking up land for (1) guaranteed railways and railways to be constructed or assisted by private companies, (2) state railways, (3) all railways, roads and canals, and (4) special rules issued after consideration of the contract of January 1880, entered into between the secretary of state for India in council, and the East Indian Railway Company. The Rules uses 31 appendices. However, the present document has attached only two of them (appendices XI and XXXI).

LAND ACQUISITION FOR PUBLIC PURPOSES

The following rules have been promulgated by Government under section 59 of Act X of 1870 (vide Calcutta Gazette of 6th November 1889, pages 898-900), and have the force of law:

WHEREAS the basis of compensation to be awarded for revenue-paying lands taken up under the provisions of Act X of 1870 is intended by the said Act to be the actual price for which the land, subject to all its burdens, and among others to the burden of the payment of land revenue, would sell in the market, it is necessary that the exact amount of the revenue demand should be ascertained and recorded before the award of compensation can be determined; and whereas, under the provisions of the existing law, the Revenue authorities, and none other, can regulate the amount of the revenue charge to be enforced against an estate, or a portion of an estate; and whereas some of the rules already promulgated under section 59 of the said Act proceed on assumptions which are at variance with the principle above enunciated, the following revised rules are issued by the Government of Bengal, with the sanction of the Governor-General in Council, in supersession of those previously in force:-

I. Whenever any revenue-paying land shall be acquired under the Act, the proprietor shall, except as provided in rule VI, be relieved of liability to pay revenue to the extent of the Government demand upon the said land, and such relief shall have effect from the date on which the Collector may take possession of the land on account of Government.

II. In such cases the Collector shall, before making a tender or a reference to a Court regarding compensation, ascertain in accordance with the following rule, and record the amount of Government revenue which is to be taken as payable in respect of the acquired portion, and shall, in the event of a reference being made to a Court, furnish the Court, at the time of making the reference, with particulars of the amount of the share so ascertained and recorded.

III. If the land to be acquired be an entire estate or tenure assessed with a specific amount of revenue, the whole of such amount shall be remitted.

IV. If the land be not liable for a specific amount of revenue, but be a portion of an estate or tenure which is liable for a specific amount, the proportion of Government revenue to be deemed payable in respect of the land taken shall be ascertained under the following rules: -

1st. When an estate has, within twenty years next preceding the date of the commencement of proceedings for the acquisition of any land situate therein, been subjected to a detailed settlement, or has formed portion of an estate brought under division under Regulation XIX of 1814,* made after inquiry into and record of the assets of the estate, the Government revenue to be deemed payable in respect of the said land shall bear to the assets of the said land the same proportion as the Government revenue of the whole estate bears to the assets of the whole estate, as shown in the settlement or division proceedings.

2nd. When there may have been no such settlement or division as aforesaid, then, if the area of the estate is known with accuracy, the amount of Government revenue to be deemed payable in respect of the portion of the land taken shall bear to the Government revenue of the whole estate the same proportion as the area of the said portion bears to the area of the whole estate.

3rd. When the Government revenue deemed payable in respect of the land taken cannot be determined by either of the above rules, one-fourth of the net rent (i.e., the gross rental less a deduction of 10 per cent for the expenses of collection) of the said land shall be taken to be the amount of Government revenue thereon chargeable.

V. In determining the amount of compensation to be tendered, the Collector shall take into consideration the fact that the land acquired is subject to the burden of the payment of Government revenue.

VI. In the event of the proprietor declining to accept an abatement of revenue, such circumstance shall not entitle him to any compensation over and above the amount tendered on the original basis of calculation. In cases, however, in which the area of

* In the territories under the Lieutenant Governor of Bengal, this Act has been superseded by Act VIII (B.C.) of 1876.

the portion of land acquired does not exceed one-twentieth part of the area of the estate, it shall be competent to the Revenue authorities, if the proprietor of the estate so desire, to pay to the proprietor the computed value of the revenue deemed payable in respect of such portion, on the condition of his continuing to pay the revenue of the entire estate without abatement: provided that in computing the value of the revenue so assigned, the basis of calculation shall not exceed the number of years' purchase (if known) upon which the market value of the proprietor's profits, i.e., the tender of compensation, has been determined. Thus, if the market value of the said profits has been computed at 12 years' purchase, the capitalized value of the revenue deemed payable in respect of the portion of land acquired shall be calculated at not more than 12 years' purchase of the amount of revenue in question.

VII. When there is any doubt whether the land to be acquired is part of a revenue-paying estate, or is revenue-free, the Collector shall, before making the reference to the Court, which under the circumstances he would be required to make by section 15 of the Act, determine the amount of revenue which would be deemed payable in respect of the land acquired in the event of the land being adjudged by the Court to be a portion of the revenue-paying estate of which it is alleged to form a part.

VIII. To enable the Collector to calculate accurately the additional compensation to be given under section 42 of the Act, and to enable him to keep up fully and clearly his registers of all lands occupied and compensation paid for them, the Collector shall invariably record separately his finding under the first head of section 24 of the Act, which concerns the market value of the land, and also the specific portion of the compensation which he may award for any houses, trees, or crops upon the land.

IX. The procedure laid down for a reference under section 15 shall be held applicable to a reference under section 43.

X. The procedure to be followed in the apportionment of the compensation awarded on account of lands taken up for temporary occupation shall be in accordance with the provisions of Part IV of the Act.

XI. On the date on which payment of compensation in any case may become due under section 41 of the Act, the Collector shall tender the amount to such of the persons entitled to receive it as may be present at his office in person, or by agent duly authorized to receive the same, informing them at the same time that in the event of their refusal to accept the amount tendered no claim to interest will be entertained. Should any such person be absent and have no authorized agent at the Collector's Court, the Collector shall serve a notice upon him, calling upon him to attend in person or by agent, within one week of his receipt of the notice, to receive the amount due to him, and warning him that on failure to appear, within the period above named, no interest whatever will be paid to him. The Collector shall satisfy himself of the due service of the notice, and should endeavour, from time to time, to secure the presence of the parties to receive payment, so as to avoid, as far as possible, payment into the treasury on deposit. In the event of the payees not presenting themselves for payment within a year from the date of the award, the amounts due may be paid into the

Treasury on revenue deposit and vouched for in the form prescribed by Rule 5 on page 30a of the Civil Account Code, vol. I, 4th edition (vide Appendix XI of the Board's Land Acquisition Rules). When the payees ultimately claim payment of sums placed on deposit, the amounts will be paid to them in the same manner as ordinary revenue deposits, under the authority of the Collector.

Section I

GENERAL RULES ISSUED UNDER THE AUTHORITY OF THE BOARD OF REVENUE FOR THE GUIDANCE OF PUBLIC OFFICERS IN THE ADMINISTRATION OF THE LAND ACQUISITION ACT, X OF 1870

1. By the definition in section 3 of the Act, the expression "Collector" means the Collector of a district, or a Deputy Commissioner, or "any officer specially appointed by the local Government to perform the functions of a Collector under this Act." The Collector cannot delegate to another any of his judicial functions, but he can make over any of his ministerial functions. For instance, he may depute a subordinate to map the ground or make a local inquiry, but he cannot delegate to another the duty of determining the amount of compensation. Whenever, therefore, it may be necessary to employ an Assistant or Deputy Collector to perform duties under the Act involving the exercise of judicial functions, the Collector of the district must apply through the Commissioner to the Board to have him vested by the local Government with the necessary powers under section 3. It is usual to vest officers with the powers of a Collector under the Act either in a particular district or place, or for the purpose of taking up land for a particular object. An officer once vested with powers in a particular district, can exercise those powers whenever he may be retransferred to that district.
2. No officer should be recommended for investment with powers under the Act unless the Collector to whom such officer is subordinate is satisfied that he is well acquainted with the provisions of the law, and the rules and instructions promulgated thereunder.
3. Though an indefeasible title is secured by proceeding under the Land Acquisition Act, X of 1870, and the procedure therein provided is in most cases calculated to save Government from the risk of paying more than the true market value for land, cases may occur (especially in localities where the tenure of land is of a simple character) in which there is no risk, with respect to title, in securing land by private bargain, and in which the land may, in this way, be more speedily and cheaply secured than by proceeding under the Act. Local officers should bear this in mind when deciding what course to propose in any particular case. It must, however, be borne in mind that the interests of any one of the claimants to compensation cannot be purchased by private bargain, and the interests of the other claimants dealt with under the Act.
4. Sections 4 and 5 lay down certain rules under which preliminary investigation may be made into the condition and circumstances of lands which the local Government may consider likely to be needed for any public purpose. These sections, however, seldom come into operation, and are only required in cases in which uncertainty may exist as to the position of the land to be taken up or its suitability for the

purpose for which it is required, or when operations on a large scale are in contemplation and it is necessary to determine the line of a road, canal, or other important work. The form of notification is given in form I. Attention is called to the words italicised above; and it should be observed that whenever a notification has been issued under section 4, it must be followed by a declaration under section 6, as soon as it is decided to proceed with the acquisition, and the position and boundaries of the land to be acquired have been fixed and determined.

5. The conduct of the preliminary investigation will be entrusted to such officer as the Government may generally or especially authorize for the purpose.
6. The chief local representative of the Department which proposes the work will prepare a draft notification under section 4, and submit it for publication in the Calcutta Gazette. After publication of the notification, due notice of its substance will be publicly given by the Collector at convenient places in the locality, and the Collector must invariably apprise the officer entrusted with the preliminary investigation of the issue of the Gazette notification. No officer should commence preliminary investigation until he is certified of the issue of notice.
7. After receipt of intimation of the issue of the public notice from the Collector, the officer entrusted with the preliminary investigation will then proceed, as necessary, to examine the land, survey, dig, bore, and otherwise ascertain the suitability of the land for the purpose required, and will prepare such a preliminary map or plan of the land, and collect such further information, as will assist the Collector in forming an estimate of the probable cost of taking up the land. A memorandum accompanying the map should specify generally the character of the land, e.g., whether waste, cultivated, or jheel, &c., and the number and character of buildings, trees, &c.
8. The map and memorandum will be made over to the Collector, who will prepare an estimate of the probable cost of the land, and of the houses and other properties on it. In making this estimate the Collector will consult his records, and use all the means at his command to obtain the nearest approximation to the probable outlay which can be obtained without a detailed valuation of the property. Detailed and final valuation can only be made after the declaration has been issued and the regular survey required by section 8 has been completed; but the Collector must bear in mind the explanation given in clause 27 below of the mode in which the value of the land (when revenue-paying) is to be arrived at. No fixed rule can be laid down for determining the value, but generally it will be convenient to adopt the following illustration: -

	Rs.	An.	Ps.	Rs.	An.	Ps.
Gross rental of...............acres of land				....		
Deduct Government revenue ascertained under (rule III or rule IV, clause, of the						

Government rules as
the case may be) ....
Deduct cost of collection
at 10 per cent ....
Net profit ....
years' purchase of the net profit ....
Add value of houses, emblements, &c. ....
Add additional compensation at 15 per
cent, under section 42 of the Act, on
the above items ....
Add damages under section 24 of the
Act ....
Add capitalized value of the Government
revenue at years' purchase (under rule
VI of the Government Rules, or clause
58, section 1 of the Board's Rules, as
the case may be) ....
Add contingencies ....
Add cost of establishment (when
necessary) ....
Totals Rs. ....

9. The Investigation to be made by the Collector in cases referred to him under section 5 is a summary one. The law gives him no power to take evidence on oath in conducting it. He may order a local inquiry, which he is at liberty to make either in person or by deputy who, if the claim be for any sum exceeding Rs. 300, should be a Covenanted Officer or a Deputy Collector. The responsibility for the proceedings and for the award will, however, in all cases rest with the Collector.
10. If the land is required for public works purposes, the Collector will forward the preliminary map with his memorandum or estimate of cost, and also a draft of declaration in form II for issue under section 6, to the Executive Engineer, for submission of the declaration to Government through the usual channel and for preparation of the Public Works estimate required by paragraph 20, chapter IX of the Public Works Code; but if the land is required for other departments or for a company, the Collector will (unless otherwise ordered) forward the documents to the chief local representative of the department or company for which it is required, for submission to Government through the head of the Department.
11. When no preliminary investigation has been made under sections 4 and 5, the Collector, if the land is required for the Revenue Department, will prepare the necessary preliminary estimate and draft declaration in form II for publication under section 6, and forward them through the Commissioner and the Board for the orders of Government. If the land be required for any other department or for a company, some

duly authorized officer on behalf of the department or company must supply the Collector with the particulars, so far as known, of the land required. But in all cases the Collector will verify the information given by inquiry on the spot, and attach a certificate to his estimate of value, to the effect that "the rates have been arrived at after local inquiry and inspection of the ground." The illustration given in clause 8 above is applicable to the preparation of the estimate required by this clause also.

12. If the land be required for public works purposes, the Collector will then forward an estimate of the cost of the land and a draft of declaration in form II, for issue under section 6, to the Executive Engineer, for submission to Government through the usual channel; but if the land is required for other departments or for a company, the Collector will (unless otherwise ordered) forward the documents to the chief local representative of the department or Company for which it is required for submission to Government through the head of the department.
13. When the land required is known or purposed to overlie mines of coal, iron-stone or other mineral, the draft declaration under clauses 10 to 12 above, should be drawn up in the form given in the Appendix marked III.
14. The special attention of Collectors is drawn to the necessity for making their initial estimates (whether under clause 8 or clause 11 above) of the cost of land to be taken up as accurate as possible. Careless estimates not only throw out the calculations of the department for which the land is to be acquired, but, if they err by excess, are likely, though in no way binding on Government, to prejudice the public interests by giving colour to extravagant claims at a later stage of the proceedings. As plots of land similar to those to be acquired change hands from time to time, and records of many, if not all, of these transactions are to be found in the several Registrars' offices, the Collector should test the valuation by a careful examination of the registration records. He should also consult the road cess records and all other sources of information available.
15. The law does not require that the declaration under section 6 shall specify the precise boundaries or area of the land to be taken. This, however, is advisable when no doubt exists as to the actual quantity which is required; but where there is a doubt, the declaration should be so generally worded that no impediment may afterwards arise from its terms to prevent the appropriation of all the land that can possibly be required. In the case of land required for a road, canal, distributary, railway, &c., unless there is any reason to the contrary, it will be sufficient to give in the declaration the approximate area, length, breadth, and the general direction of the land for the line or channel with the names of the district, pergunnahs, and villages through which it will pass.
16. When issuing the declaration, Government will also sanction the estimate, and communicate this sanction to the chief office of the department through which the reference has been made, and also to the Board of Revenue and the Examiner of Accounts concerned, or the Accountant-General, as the case may be; and will also state against what particular item of the budget the expenditure is to be charged.
17. After the issue of the declaration, the officer who was entrusted with the preliminary

investigation or, in case no such investigation shall have been held, some officer on behalf of the department or company for which the land is required - such Department not being the Revenue Department - will if this has not already been done, mark out, on the requisition of the Collector, the boundaries of the land, and furnish the Collector with a plan or map of it. The Collector will then proceed to make a detailed survey of the land. For this purpose he may employ any of his subordinate staff who may be acquainted with surveying. In important cases sanction to a special establishment must be applied for. The cost of this establishment and all other charges incurred for the purposes of the acquisition will be costs in the case. Wherever practicable, the survey should be made by chain and prismatic compass and be plotted by scale, and the officer conducting it should prepare a detailed record of his survey and measurements and an abstract, or khatian, grouping together the plots of lands and other property found in the possession of each person interested. The officer who has conducted the preliminary investigation, or some other competent officer deputed by the Department for which the land is to be occupied - if that Department be other than the Revenue Department - will, on the requisition of the Collector, point out the boundaries of the land to be taken up, whether such boundaries have been demarcated under section 4 or not. On receipt of the plan and measurement papers, the Collector should test them by comparison with the map and specification of area supplied by the Department for which the land is required, and in case of discrepancy have an inquiry made, and, if necessary, call on such Department to point out the boundaries a second time. The plan or map should be prepared on paper of the same quality as that used by the Survey Department for village maps or on tracing cloth, and should be on a scale of 150 feet to an inch. When possible, the size of the map should not exceed that of an ordinary page of foolscap paper. It may be that in some infrequent cases the details will be so minute as to make it necessary to plot them on a larger scale. When this is so, the particular parts containing these details should be shown on a larger scale on the same map. It should show in one or more clearly coloured blocks the land acquired under the declaration and the scale on which it has been prepared. In the margin of the plan it should be stated that "the land acquired for (specify the purpose) as shown in this plan is coloured (pink or blue or green), and contains an area of so many acres, and is bounded as follows:- * * * * The description, where possible, should enumerate the boundaries on all sides, so as to leave no doubt of the particular plot required to be occupied. These particulars should be transcribed in English in the Collector's Office.

18. If the land be required for the Revenue Department, the necessary demarcation and the preparation of the map will be, of course, carried out by an officer deputed for the purpose by the Collector.

19. When the Collector has satisfied himself that the two plans represent the same land, he ought, where this appears advisable, to have the survey tested on the spot, making on such testing any alteration that may seem necessary. He will also ascertain the rates of rent paid, and record them, and appraise the quality of the land and the

value of the houses, trees, or crops upon it. The Collector may delegate to a Covenanted Officer or Deputy Collector, or in certain cases to a Sub-Deputy Collector or other duly qualified subordinate, the conduct of the inquiry into rates and values contemplated in this clause.

20. With the data thus obtained, the Collector will be in a position to revise the initial estimate referred to in clauses 8 and 11. Too great care cannot be taken in making the examination. The amount of the revised estimate should be recorded, and if it materially exceed the amount of the original estimate, the Collector should at once stay proceedings and report the probability of such excess to the Executive Engineer, in the case of land required for Public Works purposes, or, in the case of land required for any other Department or for a Company, to the chief local representative of the Department or Company for which it is required, that it may be ascertained whether the object sought cannot be otherwise secured, either by obtaining some other plot of land than that originally contemplated, or in some other way. The same course should be followed if at any time before award or reference to the Civil Court the Collector has reason to believe that the cost of acquisition will considerably exceed the estimate.

21. In preparing the revised estimate, the Collector should take into account the matters specified in section 24 of the Act, as well as the additional compensation of 15 per cent which is payable on the market value under section 42. When the land is revenue-paying, he should carefully observe the directions in clause 27 below as to the mode in which the --- --- --- --- amount of Government revenue which is to be deemed payable in respect of the land, and state by which of the modes mentioned in rules III and IV of the Government rules the amount has been ascertained; and where the area of the land does not exceed one-twentieth of the area of the parent estate, he should note the amount of the capitalized value of the revenue which will have to be paid to the proprietor, in addition to the market value, in the event of the arrangement described in rule VI of the Government rules being agreed upon between the Collector and the proprietor.

22. As soon as the operations prescribed by the last preceding clause have been completed, the Collector will proceed under section 9 of the Act. When he issues notices on the persons interested in the land, or on an occupier (if any) of such land, he shall at the same time inform the Municipal body, Railway or any other Company, who have under section 56 to defray the charges of the land acquisition, of the day on which the enquiry under section 11 is to be held or to which it may be postponed, and give such body or company an opportunity of contesting the claims of the claimants to compensation before the Collector makes his tender. Should the land be occupied by, or any portion of it belong to, or be in the possession of, Government, the personal notice required by the law should be served on the chief local representative of the Department interested. Forms of notice will be found in appendices IV and V. A form of requisition under section 10 is given in Appendix VI.

23. The attention of Revenue Officers is called to the provisions of clause 2 of section 10 of the Act, recourse to which will obviate delay, when the Collector has not the

information required to enable him to serve the necessary notices under section 9.

24. An occupancy ryot is undoubtedly entitled to compensation for his right of occupancy in a holding taken up for public purposes. Even a tenant with a lease of two or three years only is entitled to some compensation, though less than what would be due to an occupancy ryot. This claim of the ryots, although capable of valuation, is believed to be seldom put forward or pressed, the compensation money being usually shared among the superior tenure-holders and the zemindars. The attention of Revenue Officers is therefore drawn to the fact that ryots having a right of occupancy, as well as ryots holding under unexpired leases, are "persons interested" in the land, and entitled to share in the compensation, and that their names should be entered in any notice under section 9 of Act X of 1870, and in any reference to the Civil Court under sections 15 and 18, or under section 38. The ryot will frequently not be able to obtain his share unless the Collector intervenes in his behalf, and he should therefore be distinctly and officially recognized in all stages of the proceedings.

25. Whenever the proprietor of any land, which may be required to be taken up by Government officers to make an absolutely free gift of it, or to give it provisionally for a particular purpose, on the understanding that when no longer wanted for that purpose it shall revert to him, it will not always be necessary to carry out the procedure prescribed by the Act; but the following rule will apply. In cases in which all the interests in the land are given free of cost, i.e., where a zemindar agrees to hand over the land free of all encumbrances to Government, himself settling with the under-tenants, the donor should be required to execute and register a deed of gift, the cost of stamping and registering such deed being borne by Government. When, however, some interests, but not all, are given, it will be a matter for consideration whether it is worth while to accept the gift, and the Collector should report such cases for the orders of the Board. If the Board determine to accept the gift, a deed of gift will be taken from the donor and acquisition proceedings under the Act will then be carried out, Government taking the donor's place in respect of the interest conveyed by the deed of gift. If the Board decide to decline the gift, it will of course be necessary to carry out the procedure laid down in the Act in respect of the whole of the interests concerned.

26. All officers employed in acquiring land are to keep a register of Land Acquisition cases in the form given in appendix VII.

27. Sections 11 to 15 lay down the rules according to which the Collector is to conduct his enquiry into the value of the land and into the amount of compensation to be awarded to the persons interested in it, and the conditions upon which he is either to make the award himself or to refer the matter to the decision of the Court. The Collector's attention has already been directed to the rules promulgated under section 59 of the Act, and having the force of law, which are published at the beginning of these instructions. It will be observed that the procedure in the case of revenue-paying land has by these rules been materially altered. In every case, as the rules now stand, acquisition of land under the Act entitles the proprietor to release from liability for any revenue charge upon it, and it is the duty of the Collector, before determining the

amount of compensation to be tendered or allowed in the case of any revenue-paying land which is under acquisition, to ascertain, in the manner laid down in rules III and IV of the Government rules, the amount of Government revenue which is to be deemed payable in respect of such land, and to record this for the purposes of the subsequent proceedings. He will then determine the market value of the land, i.e., the price which it would command in the market while continuing subject to the payment of the ascertained amount of land revenue. It is upon this market value, and upon this only, that the additional compensation of 15 per cent under section 42 must be calculated and paid. The proprietor receiving the market value is also entitled to have his revenue abated by the amount of revenue to which his estate is liable if the land acquired be a whole estate or tenure assessed with a specific amount of revenue, or by the amount assessed by the Collector as above upon the land acquired, and this abatement must in every case be offered. If the proprietor declines to receive an abatement of revenue, he is not at liberty to claim its capitalized value or to demand any further compensation on that account. It is only in cases where the area of the land acquired does not exceed one-twentieth of the area of estate that the Collector is at liberty, if the proprietor desires this, to pay to him the capitalized value of the revenue demand on the land on condition of his continuing to pay the revenue of the entire estate without abatement. The capitalized value will be calculated in the way prescribed in rule VI of the Government rules.

28. Section 15 specifies five separate conditions, on the occurrence of any one of which the inquiry is taken out of the Collector's hands. Four of these conditions, viz., the first, third, fourth, and fifth, read together with that specified in section 14, limit his jurisdiction to the single instance in which all persons whom he may have reason to believe interested in the land have presented themselves, raise no question among themselves as to their several rights and interests in the land, and accept the amount of compensation offered. Even in the absence of any difficulties or objections on the part of the persons interested, the Collector can, under the second condition specified in section 15, hand the matter over to the Court, if for any good reason he considers that further inquiry as to the nature of any claim preferred before him ought to be made by the Court. References under section 15 should, as far as possible, be made in accordance with each separate and distinct proprietary interest (a separate and distinct proprietary interest may be composed of several claims) one reference being made for one or more plot or plots of land subject to each interest.

29. It is not always necessary, or even desirable, to treat the whole land covered by a declaration as a single case, the objection to doing so being that if a single claimant or interested person fails to attend, the whole matter must be sent to the Court, very often greatly to the inconvenience and expense of those parties who have attended and agreed to the Collector's tender. The land may ordinarily be divided into separate portions or plots, and separate proceedings be held as regards each plot, provided only that the basis of division be land, and land alone. It is not permissible to divide off the separate interests in a particular plot and treat each as a separate case. The

general practice should be to split up the block of the land covered by the declaration into a number of separate and distinct plots, each plot representing not a separate interest, but a separate claim. There is a wide difference between a separate interest and a separate claim. A may be interested in a piece of land as a zemindar, B as a putnidar, C as an under-tenant, but the three interests of A, B, and C make up only one claim. The Collector has nothing to do with the separate interests A, B, and C: he awards compensation calculated on the market value of the land, and if A, B, and C cannot agree to divide among themselves the total sum awarded in proportion to their separate interests, the Civil Court must apportion the amount under part IV of the Act. The point for inquiry, it should always be borne in mind, is the whole value of the land.

30. Section 38 provides that even after the amount of compensation has been settled with the parties, if any dispute arises about the apportionment of that amount, the Collector shall refer such dispute to the decision of the Court - the award, however, as regards the total amount of compensation remaining final. If no such dispute occurs, the particulars of the apportionment are, under section 37, to be specified in the award.
31. There is a distinction between section 38 and section 15, clause 5. The object of the fifth clause of section 15 is to provide for a reference in a case where the Collector cannot settle the compensation because of a dispute as to the right or title. He has therefore not been able to make any award. Section 38 applies to cases in which the Collector has settled the compensation, although such a dispute exists; but he has made an award and is obliged to refer the case to the Civil Court for an apportionment.
32. In conducting his proceedings as to the award, the Collector should invariably explain carefully to the parties before him the provisions of sections 24 and 25, informing them that on the principles therein enunciated his own award and that of the Court, if reference be made to it, must be based; and that if the case goes to the Court, and the sum ultimately awarded as compensation by the Court does not exceed the amount tendered by himself, the whole costs of the proceeding before the Court will fall on them under section 33.
33. The award to be made by the Collector must of course include the value of any buildings and trees standing upon the land, and of such crops as the parties interested shall not agree to remove.
34. The law (section 14) distinctly requires that the award shall be made under the hand of the Collector, and under section 40 it is laid down that "compensation shall be made by the Collector according to the award to the persons named therein." Section 41 also authorizes the Collector to make payment after the award has been made. It is illegal, therefore, to pay compensation before making an award, and a mere verbal award subsequently recorded in writing is not sufficient to comply with the provisions of the law in this respect. It is necessary that in all cases a formal award should be recorded, and signed and dated by the Collector before making payment.
35. When a reference has been made by the Collector under section 15 to the Court, the Collector should defend the case exactly as he would a Government suit. The claimant

in such cases is to be regarded as the plaintiff and the Government as defendant; and it is the duty of the Collector to see that evidence is forthcoming to show the fairness of the amount which --- --- --- --- files his written statement in the case in Court, the Government Pleader should apply to the Court for a copy of it for the information of the Collector, to enable the Collector to meet the case set up by the plaintiff with suitable evidence. The Collector must remember that the Court will decide on the evidence before it what amount of compensation is to be given, and he must; therefore, be prepared with reliable evidence at the trial. In important cases he should consult the Legal Remembrances as in ordinary civil suits. At the time of the award of the Court being declared, the Collector, or the officer who appears on his behalf, should request the Judge to state the amount of costs incurred in the proceedings, and by what persons and in what proportions they are to be paid.

36. In the case of lands taken up for a canal, road, or railway, the reference to be made by the Collector to the Court under section 15 or 43 must in no one case cover more land than is included in any one of the mile plans prepared by the surveyor in measuring lands of this description.
37. A separate finding under the first head of section 24 of the Act, for the calculation of the additional compensation, must be recorded, in accordance with the instructions given in rule VIII of the Government rules.
38. An award made by a Collector cannot, if it is made in accordance with the provisions of the law, be subsequently amended by any authority. Officers should, therefore, be most careful, before making an award, to take all precautions to avoid error or oversight.
39. Proceedings and awards under sections 11 and 14 of the Act, and references to the Civil Court under sections 15 and 38, should be drawn up in the form given in Appendices VIII, IX and X.
40. Whenever proceedings under the Act are conducted by an Assistant or Deputy Collector empowered, under the provisions of section 3, to act as a Collector, such officer may, if the amount of his intended award be within the sanctioned estimate, make the award without further reference. If it be beyond the amount of the sanctioned estimate, or if the amount of compensation which it is proposed to tender exceeds in any one case Rs. 10,000, he must consult the Collector of the district demi-officially, and will make his final award according to the instructions received from that officer. The Collector, however, is at liberty, if he sees fit, to require a reference to be made to him in all cases before the award is given. The completion report of every case under the Act, and every progress report, when such reports are submitted, must be subscribed with a certificate signed by the officer making an award under section 14, that "the prices awarded are not in excess of those for which similar lands are actually sold in the same parts of the district;" or in case such officer should be unable to find evidence of the circumstances of actual sales, that "the prices awarded are not greater than those which similar lands in the same parts of the district might be reasonably expected to command."

41 In special cases it is competent to the Commissioner to exempt officers empowered to take up land under the Act from the obligation of referring their proceedings for the approval and confirmation of the Collector of the district.

42. Commissioners and Collectors will be held responsible for these references being disposed of with despatch. Any unnecessary delay in dealing with such cases not only embarrasses the department for which the land is required, but may seriously enhance the cost; for it has been ruled that, on a reference to the Civil Court, the Judge and assessors are bound to consider the market value of the land at the time of the award of compensation by the Court. Hence if, from any --- --- --- --- papers are under consideration of the Commissioner or Collector, as the case may be, the original estimate may be greatly exceeded. The knowledge that proceedings are pending may of itself tend to enhance the market value of land.

43. Section 16 empowers the Collector to take possession of the land as soon as he has made an award or a reference to the Court, and the Act empowers no one else to do so. He may also take possession, before making an award or a reference to the Court, with the written consent of the parties interested, provided formal possession be subsequently taken as laid down in clause 44 below. It is to be distinctly understood that occupation of the land by any other officer or person without written authority from the Collector is illegal. When land has been taken up for the use of the Public Works Department, possession will be given by the Collector to the Executive Engineer, or to some person duly authorized in writing by the Executive Engineer to receive it, and to no other person. Where a reference has been made to a Court, the Collector, if the land is not required for immediate use, may at his discretion defer taking possession of it until the award of the Court has been declared.

44. In cases of urgency, section 17 allows occupation by the Collector, under special orders from the local Government, before award or reference; but the Collector should be careful to obtain the orders of Government before taking possession, and should wait until the expiry of 15 days from the date of the publication of the notice mentioned in the first paragraph of section 9. It is also necessary, in regard to this section, to observe that it applies to "waste and arable" land only, and not to land occupied by roads, tanks, buildings, &c. There is, however, no objection to land and buildings being informally occupied if necessary, provided all the parties interested consent in writing to the land being occupied in anticipation of the formal orders, and that it is understood at the time that the taking of such possession is without prejudice to the right of Government to be acquired under the Act in respect of such land or building. Formal possession must, however, be afterwards taken under the Act in supersession of the previous possession acquired by consent. Care should be taken that no land which may reasonably be supposed to contain workable mines is occupied under section 17.

It must be remembered that neither section 16 nor section 17 is applicable to the case of temporary occupation of land under Part VI of the Act, as the proprietary right in the land taken up under those sections vests absolutely in the State.

45. Sections 18 to 36 regulate the procedure to be adopted by the Court in the

investigation of cases referred by the Collector. The only sections among them, other than sections 24 and 25 already referred to, which concern the Collector, are sections 18, 19, and 35, and their provisions call for no special remark, except that the assessor to be nominated by the Collector under section 19 should be, as a rule, a gazetted officer of Government not below the grade of a Sub-Deputy Collector, and that all the rules in force relating to appeals in civil suits in which Government is concerned apply to appeals instituted against or on behalf of Government under section 35.

46. Under section 18, a reference is made by the Collector to the Civil Court. The words "reason to think interested" in that section refer to the result of enquiries made by the Collector. That officer first conducts a local enquiry on the spot at the time of measurement, when he ascertains the market value of the land: he then receives claims after the due notices have been published. And under section 10, he has the power to require any interested person to deliver to him a statement containing the names and interests of all other persons interested. The information which the Collector may be able to obtain by these means should be furnished in his statement of reference to the Judge. The statement should also contain the boundaries of the land which is the subject-matter of each case and the names and addresses of the persons whom the Collector has reason to think interested. When maps of the locality have been prepared, the number of the plot in the map should be stated in the reference.

47. When the amount of compensation has been settled under section 14, if any dispute arises as to the apportionment of the same, or any part thereof, the Collector shall refer such dispute to the decision of the Civil Court under section 38. The cost of serving processes or any other costs should not fall on the Government in such cases; but as interest under section 42 is payable by Government when cases are referred under section 38 as well as when they are referred under section 15, it is necessary to take steps to expedite the proceedings in all cases alike, and the costs of the service of notice to the persons interested must therefore always be paid into Court by the Collector in the first instance.

48. The rules for payment are contained in sections 40 to 42 of the Act, and rule XI of the rules promulgated under section 59. Rule XI has been framed in accordance with the principle that section 42 of the Act cannot be construed to give a claimant a right to any interest if the non-receipt of the principal is due to his own neglect. The Collector is, however, personally responsible for the disbursement of the amount, as soon as it falls due, under the provisions of those sections, and is properly applied for; and neglect or carelessness in this respect may render him liable to pay any interest which may accrue under section 42 of the Act. All compensation, save, at the discretion of the Land Acquisition Officer, petty sums awarded to the owners of huts, shall be paid by cheque when land is acquired in Calcutta or the immediate neighbourhood or at the head-quarters of districts or sub-divisions. In other cases payment of all sums exceeding Rs. 20 shall be made by cheques, payable at head-quarters or at sub-divisional treasuries, according to the convenience of the parties interested. Cheques must be drawn by the Land Acquisition Officer himself at the time of payment, and

handed over by him or in his presence to the claimant, from whom a receipt will then be taken. If inconvenience is likely to be caused in the case of any project in consequence of the parties interested being at a great distance from a treasury, the Commissioner may, on the application of the Collector, direct the payment of compensation in cash up to a limit of Rs. 100. The discretion thus left to the Commissioner must be exercised in exceptional cases only, as it is very desirable that cash payment should be very generally restricted to sums not exceeding Rs. 20. In cases in which the amount of a single payment does not exceed Rs. 100, the Collector or special officer should, if he fail to secure the attendance of the payee to receive the money as required by Rule XI, forward to him the amount by postal money-order, whenever his residence for the time being is situated at a greater distance than 10 miles from the Collector or other officer's head-quarters. If the amount to be disbursed is likely to exceed the funds at the Collector's command, he should take timely steps for obtaining, in accordance with departmental instructions, the necessary supply of money before the date on which the payment becomes due; but that payment must in any case be made when due and properly applied for. The amount which may be paid under rule VI of the Government rules is not liable to any interest charge under section 42, as it does not form part of the award of compensation.

49. Land required for the Public Works Department is taken up under the Act either by the Collector or by some special officer who is placed at the disposal of the Public Works Department and vested with the powers of a Collector under the Act: the procedure differs in the two cases.

50. Officers who are specially employed for this work, being vested with the powers of a Collector under the Act and placed at the disposal of the Public Works Department, are regarded as Public Works disbursers, and are supplied with funds by means of letters of credit issued in their favour on the application of the Examiner of Accounts concerned.

51. The rules for payment of compensation are contained in pages 30a to 30e of the Civil Account Code, Volume I, 4th edition, and are reproduced in Appendix XI. The vouchers in Form B, referred to in those rules, will be supplied by the Accountant-General in books containing each one hundred vouchers. These vouchers will be printed with consecutive printed numbers, and each book will contain its own serial number. These books should be kept under lock and key by the Land Acquisition Officer himself, who should make a periodical comparison of the pass-books from the treasury with the counterfoils.

52. On receipt of the treasury advice list referred to in Rule 11, page 30b, of the Civil Account Code, volume I, the officer who issued the orders of payment should himself carefully see that the amounts paid are those for which orders were issued by him. When advances are drawn for payment to the payees, they should be separate for each declaration under which the land is acquired, and the receipts for the advances must mention the account officer to whom the corresponding award statements have been sent; when the payee's receipts are forwarded to the treasury officer in adjustment of

the advances, they should be accompanied by a statement showing the amounts drawn and paid; and if there remain any balance in hand which is not required for payments for the lands acquired under the declaration, it should at once be refunded into the treasury, and should not, under any circumstances, be paid for lands taken up under another declaration.

53. In any case in which land is acquired for a Municipality or other body financially independent of Government, the Collector or Deputy Collector employed is responsible for the whole of the land acquisition proceedings, but the Government may direct that the payments instead of being made and audited in the same manner as the ordinary payments of such body, shall be made and audited as if the land were being acquired for Government. If the Government issues such an order, the Collector or other officer who makes payments on account of the land acquired, shall draw funds from the treasury and make payments in the manner laid down in the rules in appendix XI, using the forms prescribed, and shall render his accounts to the Civil Accountant-General. In the event of the payees not presenting themselves to receive payment within a year from the date of the award, the amounts due may be placed in revenue deposit and receipts taken in form C referred to in Appendix XI, in the same manner as is provided in clause XI of the rules promulgated under section 59 of the Act. The Municipality or other body will pay the estimated cost of the compensation to the credit of Government in advance on such dates and in such instalments as the Government may direct, further payment to Government being required as soon as the Accountant-General reports that the payments made exceed the amount received in advance. The Accountant-General will deal with the accounts and payments as prescribed in these rules, debiting the payments against the advances received from the Municipality or other body.

54. The account officers to whom the statements of awards (from A referred to in Appendix XI) should be sent are given below:

Examiner of Public Works Accounts, Bengal	If the land is acquired for any purposes of the Public Works Department under a declaration of the Government of Bengal in the Public Works Department.
Examiner of State Railway Accounts concerned	If the land is for a State Railway
Examiner of Military Works Accounts	If the land is for the Military Works Department
Controller of Military Accounts	If the land is for any purposes of the Military Department

Comptroller of Post Office Accounts	If the land is for the Postal Department.
Examiner of Telegraph Accounts	If the land is for the Telegraph Department
Accountant-General, Bengal, ...	If the land is for any Civil Department, or for any local fund of which the charges are under the audit of the Accountant-General.

55. When the lands have been held heretofore free of rent in cash or kind, or on a quit-rent on condition of the performance of some public service, the Collector for, in cases of doubt as to the proper procedure, should refer the matter to the Board, in view to obtain instructions for the due protection of the Government interest in the apportionment of the compensation, in respect to its lien for the purposes of the public service, and to enable him to represent this where necessary before the Civil Court.

56. In cases in which the land held free or on a quit-rent is held by a paik, or village chowkidar, or patwari, the value of the holding should be separately assessed and recorded, and should be included in the total amount of compensation to be allowed in the award. The value so ascertained should not be paid to the service-holder, but should be applied for the purpose of purchasing another piece of land, similar in quality and quantity to the first piece, and situated adjacent to it, or in its immediate neighbourhood. If the amount is not sufficient to purchase the land required to compensate the holder of the service land, the difference should be made good by Government, and the amount charged to land revenue, care being taken that due economy is observed and unreasonable claims are not admitted. This second piece of land should be acquired under the provisions of the Act, and should be made over to the holder of the service land to be held by him on the same terms as the original holding was held at the time of its acquisition. Meanwhile, interest at the rate of 6 per cent per annum should be paid to the service-holder from the date on which he was dispossessed of his service land to the date on which the new piece of land is made over to him, the amount being charged to land revenue, and the bill submitted to the Board, for transmission to the Accountant-General, Bengal, for audit.

In Orissa this rule is applicable only to cases occurring subsequent to the 31st December 1887.

57. The Collector must disburse all costs of measurement under section 8. Costs when incurred under section 4 will be disbursed by the officer entrusted with the preliminary investigation.

58. Whenever land is acquired for any purpose which is not strictly a Government purpose, as for a Municipality, a District Board, a District Road Committee, or a Company, or the like, the whole cost of acquisition should be charged to such Municipality, Committee, Company or other body of persons as the case may be. The cost of

establishment, including therein a proportionate share of the salary of the Deputy Collector employed on the work, shall be separately estimated for, and proceedings shall not be commenced until the amount of the estimate, inclusive of the estimated cost of establishment, has been paid into the treasury in the manner provided for in clause 53. Provided that when the land is revenue-paying land in respect of which an abatement of revenue has been granted, in addition to the cost of acquisition, the Municipality, Committee, Company, or other persons concerned shall be required to pay to Government the capitalized value of the revenue assigned to the land, calculated at the current rate for capitalizing annual payments made to or by Government.

59. As soon as possession of the land has been taken, the Collector should give effect to any abatement of revenue which may have been determined on in connection with it.

60. The attention of Collectors is called to the provisions of section 42, by which an additional compensation of 15 per cent on the market value, not the total award, is to be paid to the owners of the land occupied. In other words, 15 per cent is not to be added to compensation awarded in consideration of any of the matters specified in clauses 2, 3, and 4 of section 24. Nor is it to be added to the amount which may be paid under rule VI of the Government rules as the capitalized value of the revenue deemed payable in respect of the land acquired as that amount does not form part of the market value of the land. A table is given in appendix XII, for calculating the additional compensation. Collectors should be careful, when making an offer for the land to be taken, to see that that offer is based strictly on the grounds prescribed by the law. They should also, at the time of making the offer, inform the proprietors that they will receive 15 per cent over and above the market value of the land. If this be not borne in mind, it will sometimes happen that 15 per cent will go to the proprietors in excess of what they agreed to, or of what the Collector intended to award.

61. As under section 3, trees, houses, and other immoveable things standing on land under acquisition for public purposes are included in the definition of the ward "land," the value of such things minus the cost of repairs of houses should always be included in the Collector's estimate of the market value of the land, and the additional compensation under section 42 must be paid on the lump sum.

62. It should be borne in mind that it is a presumption of law that the surrender of land acquired under the Act in compulsory. The additional compensation of 15 per cent must therefore be paid in all cases, except where, under special agreement, the parties have accepted a lump sum, and distinctly waived or included therein the claim to any additional compensation under section 42. In all such cases this agreement must be taken in writing, and filed with the proceedings.

63. Sections 43 to 45 prescribe the procedure to be followed in procuring temporary occupation of waste or arable land. In these cases no declaration is required by the law, but with this reservation, all the procedure prescribed above will apply as far as the case requires.

64. Sections 46 to 50, making special provision for the terms on which Government will take up lands for the use of Companies, need no particular comment. The officer of

any Company for whom Government may undertake to acquire land will, when authorized under section 4, proceed according to the instructions already given. Under section 50 the agreement must appear in the Gazette of India, as well as in the local official Gazette before proceedings can be taken under section 8 of the Act.

65. The amount of compensation under section 54, as under section 5, will be fixed by the Collector on a summary inquiry, and without record of evidence on oath, and is final.
66. Collectors should be very careful in dealing with cases under section 55. When the cases are of importance or difficulty, the Board should be consulted before the claims are admitted.
67. The Collector will prepare and submit to the Commissioner a final report of his proceedings for each project in the form of Appendix XIII. This report, accompanied by Appendix XIV, and, in the case of land taken up for a railway, by Appendix XV when necessary, should be submitted to the Board for confirmation of the proceedings. When the proceedings have been confirmed, Appendices XIV and XV will be recorded in the Board's office, and the final report will be returned.
68. Deputy Collectors employed in acquiring land for irrigation and railway purposes are empowered to meet law charges incurred by them, and the Examiner of Accounts concerned will admit the charges in the monthly contingent bills, when duly supported by vouchers, provided that the bills have first been passed by the Collector of the district.
69. Costs decreed to Government, although realised from the owner of the land by deduction from the amount of compensation paid, being of the nature of advances recovered, should not be taken in abatement of the price paid for the land.
70. When land is taken up for a road, railway or any other purpose that necessitates the consecutive acquisition of several plots of land abatement statements in the form of Appendix XVI should be submitted monthly until the work is completed. District. officers will regard the Board's sanction to the abatements of revenue shown in these statements as sufficient authority for including in their quarterly return No. IX the amounts so sanctioned, the Board's orders being quoted in each instance.
71. Alienations of land from revenue-paying estates under this Act should be carefully noted against the estates in the Collector's general register (A). Similar entries in the rent-free land register should be made for lakhiraj lands taken.
72. Under section 16 of the Act the land acquired vests absolutely in the Government, free from all encumbrances. The title of Government is not derived from the former owner, but created under the Act. The receipt for compensation is, therefore, a simple receipt for money paid, and registration under clause (c), section 17 of Act III of 1877, is unnecessary.
73. The receipt for payments due under the award should be taken in form B referred to in Appendix XI. The receipts should be forwarded with the monthly accounts to the officer whose duty it is to audit those accounts, and the counterfoil should be kept with the records of the case.
74. The Commissioner and Board of Revenue cannot set aside or modify any order

passed by the Collector under this Act.

75. The following returns are required to be submitted periodically to the Board:

Return No. XVIII. Progress in taking up land for public purposes.

Return No. XVIII (a). Progress made in the temporary occupation, under section 43 of the Act, of land required for public purposes.

These statements should be submitted monthly in cases of land for the acquisition of which a special officer is employed, and quarterly in all other cases, including embankments under Act II (B.C.) of 1882.

NOTE. No case should be struck out of any of the Monthly or Quarterly Returns till the proceedings have been reported to, and confirmed by the Board.

Annual Return No. XXIV. Estimate of compensation for land to be taken up for public purposes.

Forms of these returns are given in Appendices XVII, XVIII and XIX. The Monthly and Quarterly Returns are to be submitted through the Commissioner; the Annual Return to the Board direct.

Commissioners should insist upon the punctual submission of Returns, and should see that the Returns are submitted to the Board with all possible despatch from their own offices.

SECTION II

Special Rules Issued Under The Authority of The Board of Revenue, for The Guidance of Public Officers in Taking up Land for Guaranteed Railways; for Railways to be Constructed by Assisted, or Private Companies; for State Railways, and for Canals and Roads.

PART I

GUARANTEED RAILWAYS AND RAILWAYS TO BE CONSTRUCTED BY ASSISTED OR PRIVATE COMPANIES

1. Land required for guaranteed railways and railways to be constructed by assisted or private Companies is divided into four classes - A, B, C, and D. First, class A, land which a Railway Company receives free of charge, under the contract with the Government, for permanent occupation; second, class B, land also provided free of cost, but only for temporary occupation; third, class C, land which the Railway Company has to provide at its own cost; fourth, class D, land provided free of cost, but which does not come directly into the possession of the Railway Company at all.
2. Class A comprises the land required for the permanent works of a railway, including the road with its bridges, &c., and all stations, workshops, permanent store-houses, and the like, necessary for the line when opened, and which, under the contract, is to

be provided by Government free of cost to the Railway Companies. The occupation of this land by a Railway Company is so far permanent that it only ceases when their contract is terminated or surrendered, and the whole lapses to Government. It is all provided free of charge.

3. Class B contains land essential for the execution of the permanent works of a railway, but not required after the completion of the line, in part or in whole such as land for spoil banks, for extra excavation to make banks for river diversion, and for the storage of railway materials held in stock by the Railway Company, pending the construction of the line or their despatch to the works. *It also is provided free of charge. The occupation of this class of land will be temporary.
4. Class C contains the land which a Railway Company has to provide at its own cost. This is the land which is required for the provision or preparation of materials, for purposes contingent on the actual execution of the works on the line, or for other miscellaneous objects which the Government recognizes as falling legitimately within the scope of the Railway Company's operations, though not giving the Company a claim to the provision of land free of charge. As a Railway Company is bound to pay for the construction of all works out of its capital, only receiving from Government, without charge, the land on which the works stand, the provision of all materials, and the means of facilitating the execution of all works, are to be at the cost of the Railway Company.[ϒ] It is proper to bear in mind, in fixing the rent, that this land will in part deteriorate by the use to which it is put, and in part will not so deteriorate. In all cases, however, it will be most convenient to deal with the land in the first instance in the same manner. It will be taken possession of by

---

* The last sort of land is allowed free under the Right Hon'ble the Secretary of State's letter No. 25 of 30th November 1858.

ϒ The following words were also in the original rules and in the rules for taking up land for railway purposes by the Government of India, issued 29th June 1861:
"In this class, therefore, will fall all land for brickmaking, for quarrying ballast (*a*) for houses for persons employed on the work, &c.; so also land for houses for engine-drivers and the like on the line when opened, and for other similar purposes, will come under Class C."
But Her Majesty's Secretary of State for India thought that any particularization in the rule might raise questions as to the power of Government to alter or vary the terms of the contract (a power which the Government has no intention of claiming). It has therefore been thought best to give these words in a note, simply for the guidance of the officers of Government and parties interested, as to the construction which Government puts on the contract in regard to certain points of frequent practical application.

(*a*) In the original rules, the words "for roads to works in progress" here found place, but they have been struck out as calculated to mislead. It is clear a road may be required from a site used temporarily for storage of materials itself in class B. This would easy the road itself into the same class. A road from a brickfield or quarry would be in the same category as the brickfield or quarry, viz. class C; whereas a road from a detached but permanent store-yard, although leading "to works in progress, would not the less come under class D, should such road still be necessary after the — — — — particular works. Thus, generally, the circumstances of the tenure — — — — — — — —.

Government, and handed over to the Railway Company for occupation at a fair rental. When the necessity for occupation ceases, the land will be restored to the Government by the Railway Company, the proper time for the relinquishment being determined by the Railway officer and Consulting Engineer.

5. Class D contains that land which, being required in consequence of the works of a railway, still does not come directly into the occupation of the Railway Company. It will be provided free of charge. It will be exclusively land for roads, either new roads leading to railway stations, or to permanent store-yards or workshops detached from the main works, diversions, or changes of old roads made necessary by railway works.
6. Inconvenience would arise if Railway Companies were permitted to hold land on their own account, or otherwise than is above explained. By causing them to rent from the Government all land to which they are not entitled free, in the manner above explained, simplicity in the tenure of their property is secured, which will be a matter of importance at a future time when the railway may be transferred to Government. The determination of the value to be paid by the Government for any land not included in class A, which might be held by a Railway Company, would certainly be in such an event a great embarrassment.
7. Houses, trees, tanks, or other property on land which is not provided free of charge, and for which special payment or compensation is necessary must be paid for at once by the Railway Company, and the Revenue officers will be held strictly responsible for the regular adjustment by the Railway Companies of all charges on this account and on account of land, to be determined in the manner above explained. In the case of land provided free of charge, the materials, &c., derived from the "clearance" of the surface which then will be at the expense of Government, will be disposed of by the Revenue officers to the best advantage.
8. The annual rent on lands in class C, occupied by any Railway Company, shall be fixed at 5 per cent on the outlay incurred by Government in taking up the land, plus any revenue or rent payable to Government in respect of the said land.
9. In the case of land already belonging to, and in the occupation of, Government, the rent shall be fixed at 5 per cent on the value of the land estimated by the Collector.
10. In the event of the land being required for purposes through which its letting value will be diminished, the Railway Company, on relinquishing it, shall pay, in addition to any rent paid during the occupation of the land under the previous instructions, the estimated difference between the actual value of the land when relinquished and the value that the land would have had if the rent remained at the amount that was paid during the occupancy of the Company.
11. When land, presented in free gift by private individuals for the purpose of a railway, is made over to a Railway Company in class C, no rent shall be charged by Government for the land.

12. Under clause 10 above, the real value of the land to the Government, before it was handed over to the company, would be properly estimated on the basis of the rent charged for it. But when land has been actually paid for by the Company already, no re-opening of the old transactions should take place, and the adjustment can be made when any land is given up.
13. Compensation paid for surrender of a lease or any other charge should be considered in fixing the rent. If the land is not in the occupation of the Government, and therefore cannot be transferred to the Company without charge of some sort, it comes under clause 8, above.
14. It will be necessary for the Government to see that all rents or other payments for clearances, &c., chargeable on behalf of Government against --- --- --- ---.
15. All contemplated changes in the land in possession of a railway company should be promptly reported by the Railway Agent to the Consulting Engineer to Government, who will notify the same to the Local Government. It will be for the latter to see that the necessary steps are taken by the Revenue authorities for entering such changes in their records, and for carrying out all further proceedings that are requisite on such an occurrence.
16. The several classes of land required for guaranteed railways, and railways to be constructed by assisted or private companies will be coloured pink, yellow, purple, and green, respectively, in the plans, and the exact purpose to which each parcel of land is to be devoted will be noticed in the schedule.
17. The subjoined form of schedule should be used for all guaranteed railways and railways constructed by assisted or private companies:

Form of Schedule

Plan sheet No. ________________________

Railway ________________________

District ________________________

Schedule of land required for the use of the railway in -

Village

Pergunnah

District

Number of plan		Payable by Government.			Payable by Railway Company.
	Purpose for which required.	A. (Pink.) Land for permanent occupation by Railway Company.	B. (Yellow.) Land for temporary occupation by Railway Company.	D. (Green.) Land to be occupied by Government permanently.	C. (Purple.) Land for occupation by Railway Company permanently or temporarily.

Consulting Engineer to Government. *Chief Engineer-Railway.*

PART II
STATE RAILWAYS

1. Acquisition work should not be delayed because sanction has not been specifically accorded to the estimate of cost of taking up the land prepared by the revenue officers. The Secretary of State's general sanction to the estimate of the entire cost of the line covers this and all other detailed estimates. The Engineer-in-Chief includes the Collector's estimate of the market value of the land and cost of acquisition in his estimate of the total cost of the railway, and the Secretary of State's sanction to the whole estimate covers the cost of the land, which is only a fraction of the entire cost of the undertaking. When the general sanction of the Secretary of State to the estimate is received, the Government will forward a copy of it to the Board for communication to the local officers.
2. Land acquisition officers employed in taking up land for State Railways, although under the direct orders of the District Collector as regards procedure and purely revenue matters, should be in regular communication with the Railway authorities concerned upon such subjects as when and where land should have priority of acquisition and upon questions of funds.
3. Land acquired for State Railways may be divided into two classes-A and B.
4. Class A. Land required permanently, or land necessary for the railway when it is open for public traffic, and when the works of construction are finished. Such lands are the sites of bridges, embankments, cuttings, fencings, and other works; the cess or berm introduced for the sake of safety between the limits of the works and the adjacent spoil bank, bazaar, or side-cutting; roads permanently required and immediately in the neighbourhood of stations, over-bridges, under-bridges, or level-crossings on the railway; land or water required for the water-supply; land wanted for the preparation and reception of such materials as are used in maintenance, as ballast-pits; land for the lasting diversion of water-courses and all space permanently required at the stations,

whether for traffic, storage, workshops, dwellings, or recreation.

5. Class B. Land required temporarily, or land necessary to be taken up, but not permanently wanted. Such land will be for roads required for access to works while in progress, but which will subsequently be abandoned; land for side-cutting and spoil banks occupied during construction for the preparation and reception of materials used in constructing the railway, as brick-fields, quarries, or ballast-pits; the temporary diversion of streams and highways. The sites of overseers' dwellings to be occupied only during construction will come in this class.
6. All transfers of land belonging to a State Railway are reported by the Executive Engineer to the Engineer-in-Chief, who is required to notify the same to Government for such orders as will ensure the changes being entered by the Revenue officers in the records, and for carrying out all further proceedings that are requisite on such an occasion.
7. Land required permanently under class A for a State Railway will be coloured pink in the plans; those temporarily under class B will be coloured yellow.
8. Subjoined is the form of schedule of lands taken for State Railways:

State Railway ____________________
Plan No. ____________________
District ____________________
Schedule of land taken for the use of the Railway in -
Zillah
Pergunnah
Mouzah

Number of plan.	Purpose for which required.	Class A. coloured pink		Class B. coloured yellow	
		Occupation permanent		Occupation temporary	
		Land for the regular works of the railway, including land for high roads and rivers, &c.		Land for excavations, spoil, and for contingencies of construction, for dwelling-houses, &c., &c.	
		Acres.	R.P.	Acres.	R.P.
	Total... ...				

Executive Engineer *Engineer-in-Chief*

PART III

GENERAL - FOR ALL RAILWAYS, ROADS, AND CANALS

1. All land required for any line of railway, road or canal should be applied for in continuous portions; the measurements and areas being recorded in accordance with the fiscal divisions of villages, estates or mouzahs, pergunnahs and zillahs. In the case of land required for a railway, these details should be given in schedules for form of which vide clause 17, part 1, and clause 8, part 2, showing in detail the several classes to which the land belongs.
2. Plans furnished by Railway officers of lands required for a guaranteed or state railway, or for a line to be constructed by assisted or private companies, will be drawn on a scale of 400 feet to the inch or, where a larger scale is required, 100 feet to the inch. Plans for roads should be drawn on a scale of 150 feet to the inch, but it may be that in some infrequent cases the details will be so minute as to make it necessary to plot them on a larger scale. When this is so, the particular parts containing these details should be shown on a larger scale on the same map. Plans for canals should be on a scale of 300 feet to the inch. Each plan should consist of the length of one mile, and they should be numbered consecutively. The area of the land to which each plan refers should be noted, in acres, roods and poles, and in standard beeghas of 14,400 square feet, on the face of the plan, as well as in an accompanying reference sheet or schedule. Where lands situated in different villages are covered by the plan, the boundaries of each different village, when intersected, should be distinctly shown; and the area of the portion included in each village is to be shown separately in the plan and schedule. Each plan and schedule shall also bear a note stating the purpose for which the land is required.
3. The boundary of a district will of course seldom or never coincide with the termination of a mile. Unless it does so, a separate plan should be prepared for each of the broken parts of a mile on either side of the boundary, so as to keep the records of each district separate.
4. Detached portions of land should be referred to some fixed point on one of the main sheets, with such distances and compass or other bearings as will enable the land to be identified at once. A corresponding entry should also be made on the main sheet to draw attention to the detached portion.
5. The general correctness of the plans and schedules furnished by the Engineer for guaranteed railways and railways to be constructed by assisted or private companies will be attested by the Consulting Engineer to the Government of India: those for State Railways, by the Engineers-in-Chief or other controlling officers; and the attesting officers will in each case forward them with the application for the land, through Government, to the Board of Revenue to be dealt with as may be necessary by the Revenue authorities.
6. The instructions laid down in clauses 8 to 22, section I, for the preparation and submission of plans and estimates, and for the issue of declarations and notices, will apply. When issuing orders for the acquisition of land for a new railway, Government

will inform the Board from whom funds are to be obtained and to whom accounts are to be furnished.

7. After issue of the declaration, the Collector, or the officer appointed to take up the land, will call on the officer who conducted the preliminary investigation, or some other officer to be appointed on the Collector's requisition by the department or company on account of which the land is to be occupied, to mark out the boundaries of the land. These marks, whether pegs or trenches, must be in exact accordance with the plans or instructions, and the termination of each mile must be clearly defined by side pegs and a cross nicking. The numbers (reckoned consecutively from the starting point of the line) of the miles of which they severally mark the termination and commencement should be painted on the front and back of each peg respectively. The --- --- --- --- should himself mark the spot where the line passes out of one district into another.
8. The officer appointed to take up the land will then appoint an ameen or surveyor to make the measurements necessary for fixing the value of the land and for preparing schedules.
9. The Ameen's maps for all railways, roads, and canals, should be prepared on paper or tracing-cloth and should correspond each to each with those of the professional officer, and each one should represent a mile according to the marks on the ground where the termination of each mile is represented by a cross nicking. The maps must show the different holdings, and the boundaries of each village differently coloured, and should be on the scale of 100 feet to the inch. Each plot or dag of the ameen's measurement is to be numbered consecutively from the beginning of each mile; and the area of each plot (in standard beeghas of 14,400 square feet, and in acres, roods and poles,) with the name of the proprietor should be noted on the face of the plan. In the cases of lands required for railways, a separate series of numbers must be given for each class of land (A, B, C, or D), and a separate schedule of each class of land in each mouzah should also be given on the face of the plan.
10. From each separate plan is to be prepared a separate schedule in the form given in Appendix XX. A separate plan and schedule must be prepared for each of the broken parts of a mile on either side of the boundary, so as to keep the records of each district separate. Similarly when the termination of a mile does not coincide precisely with the boundary of a holding, the holding must be broken up into the portions lying on either side of the termination of a mile, and entered in the schedule accordingly.
11. As soon as the plan and schedule of each mile, or portion of a mile, is completed, it should be submitted by the ameen to the officer appointed to take up the land, who will immediately test the correctness of the ameen's work in every particular, making any alterations that he may think necessary in red ink, and returning the rough copy to the ameen to be copied fair, as finally approved. The officer will, at the same time, himself appraise the quality of the land and the value of the houses, trees, or crops upon it.
12. The ameen will prepare the usual abstract or khatian of his survey and measurements

as directed in clause 17, section I.

13. The officer appointed to take up the land will then issue the notices prescribed by section 9 of the Act, and prepare a register in the form given in Appendix XXI, in which he will enter the particulars of each case separately. It is desirable, as far as possible, to treat as one case all the land in one plan for which compensation is to be paid to one person or set of persons.* The cases should be entered in separate groups according to the nature of the tenure as "revenue free," "revenue paying," &c.
14. There should be a separate register for each separate mile, or portion of a mile, to correspond with the separate plan and schedule of the ameen or surveyor. The register cannot be completed until the proceedings are finally closed, but the officer should at once test the correctness of the areas entered in it by comparing the total area which it shows (which must of course be identical with that shown in the corresponding plan and schedule of the ameen or surveyor) with the gross area of the whole mile as shown in the original plan (see clause 2 above). If the result be a difference of more than 2½ per cent, the cause must be investigated and (if correction is impossible) recorded. But correction must always be made where practicable, as a difference of area is a proof that one of the two plans is incorrect.
15. As soon as the register and records of each mile are as complete as the officer can make them, they shall be forwarded to the Collector of the district, who, when he has received all the records of the portion of the line which passes through his district, will prepare an abstract in the form given in Appendix XXII.
16. The abstract should be bound up with the registers and schedules, and with the counterfoils of the receipts given for the compensation paid, and should be deposited in the record-room with a proper label upon it.
17. The Engineer's mile plans should be sent, with the copies of the ameen's mile plans which are forwarded to the Board with the final reports for confirmation of the proceedings taken, only in the case of lands acquired for railways. Neither of these

---

* Vide clause 36, section 1, which provides that "the reference to be made by the Collector to the Court under section 15 or 43 shall in no one case cover more land than is included in any one of the mile plans prepared by the surveyor." The course to be adopted will be better understood from the following illustration:-

Let AB, BC, CD, DE, be mile sections of a strip of land required for a road. Let AX, XY, YZ, ZE represent the portions of the strip which are severally included in distinct estates, and let 0 marks the intersection of the strip and the district boundary.

A B C D E

X Y Z O

Then the compensation for the lands comprised in AB, BX, XY, YC, CZ, ZD, DO, OE, respectively, must be determined in separate and distinct cases, whether the award be made by the Collector or the case be referred to the Court of adjudication. And in this illustration the cases comprising the lands from A to O and O to E severally will of course be disposed of by the authorities of the district in which the areas in question are respectively included.

plans should be submitted when lands are taken for roads or canals.

18. All lands required for any railway under class B will, in the first instance, be permanently acquired by Government in accordance with the general rules, except in the neighbourhood of towns and other places of importance where the land is above the ordinary value. Such portions of B class lands as will not suffer deterioration while in the possession of the Railway officers may, to secure economy, be taken temporarily.
19. No Railway officer shall obtain possession of land whether by purchase, lease, or on simple toleration, except through the Revenue authorities. As soon as land is made over to the Railway officer, a certificate of possession should be taken from him, and a copy of it should be sent to the Board for information.
20. When the necessity for occupation ceases the land belonging to any railway will be restored to Government, the proper time for this being determined by the Consulting Engineer in the case of lands relinquished by Companies, and by the Engineer-in-Chief when no longer required for State Railways, or other controlling officers.
21. When the land is restored, Government will issue orders to the Board for its resumption and sale, and on receipt of these orders, the Board will depute a competent officer to verify on the spot the plans prepared by the officer who acquired the land and by the Engineers of the Railway.
22. The Manager or Agent of the Railway, as the case may be, may, on receipt of an application from the Board, at his discretion help the officer deputed to verify the plans by allowing him the use of a trolly, with men, and in any other way that may be necessary to enable him to carry on the work of verification as completely and expeditiously as possible.
23. In verifying the plans, the officer will first, in communication with the Manager or Agent, as the case may be, ascertain if any portion of the resumed land is required by the Railway. If so, the orders of Government for the retention of the land should be obtained by the Manager or Agent, and a copy forwarded to the Board.
24. On the completion of the verification, the officer will prepare two sets of verified plans with schedules written on them, and one of these sets will be forwarded by the Board to the Collector with instructions to sell the land not required. This set of plans will be used by the Collector for the purpose of dividing the land into lots for sale. When this is done, the lots should be numbered consecutively, and as each lot is sold, the particulars of the price realized, &c., should be entered in the several columns of the Lotbundee Register (Appendix XXIII) and the signature of the purchaser taken in the column intended for the purpose.
25. Ordinarily, Collectors will use their own discretion as to the time and place of sale, but in no case should land be sold until the final report of the proceedings taken for the acquisition of the land has been prepared, or if the land has been taken up by a special officer, until the final report has been submitted to the Collector.
26. The date of sale should be fixed at least six weeks after the date of the first publication in the Calcutta Gazette of the advertisement of sale. Local publicity, by beat of drum

and by all other means considered necessary, should be given of the intended sale. The advertisement of sale (in the form given in Appendix XXIV) should be forwarded by the Collector to the Superintendent of Government Printing, Bengal, for publication.

27. A statement, in the form of Appendix XXV, of the lots sold and of the sale proceeds, should be submitted quarterly to the Commissioner for approval of the sales, a copy being at the same time sent to the Manager or Agent, in order that he may, if he considers the prices realized unreasonably low, refer the matter to the Board. The Commissioner should submit this statement to the Board, with an expression of his opinion whether the sales should be confirmed or not. A note should be made by the Collector in the last statement that no more land remains to be sold.

28. After the confirmation of the sales by the Board, the proceeds should be credited to the Railway concerned in the case of State Railways, and to Government in the Civil Department in the case of Guaranteed Railways and Railways constructed by assisted or private companies, and the purchasers should be put in possession of the land by the Collector and supplied with a certificate of sale (Appendix XXVI), together with an attested extract from the lot-bundee plan, referred to in clause 24, showing the exact position of the particular lot as well as its measurement. The certificate should be in duplicate; and the original, which should be given to the purchaser, should bear the ad valorem stamp required, the cost of which will be borne by the purchaser.

29. Two complete sets of plans are prepared at the time the verification takes place, and one of them is sent to the Collector, vide clause 24 above. In order to secure a correct record of title for all Railway lands, two more sets of plans will be prepared in the Board's office from the remaining set, and after the confirmation of the sales by the Board, three sets of schedules and three copies of registers of title will also be prepared, in the forms given in Appendices XXVII and XXVIII for State Railways and in Appendices XXIX and XXX for Guaranteed Railways and Railways constructed by assisted or private companies. One set of plans and schedules and a copy of the register of title will be sent, in the case of State Railways, to the Manager, and in the case of Guaranteed Railways and Railways constructed by assisted or private companies, to the Consulting Engineer to the Government of India. Of the remaining two sets, one will be sent to the Collector of the district, and the other will be kept in the office of the Board of Revenue. All these three sets will be attested by the Secretary to the Board, the Manager of the Railway, and the Under-Secretary to the Government of Bengal, Public Works Department, Railway Branch, if for a State Railway, and by the Secretary to the Board, the Agent or Chief Engineer of the Railway, and the Consulting Engineer to the Government of India if for a Guaranteed Railway or a Railway constructed by an assisted or a private company. All subsequent additions or alterations should be carefully noted in these records by the officers concerned.

30. It will be advisable for the Railway officers, in order to prevent any doubts arising as to the exact boundaries of permanent lands, to raise masonry pillars at convenient distances on either side of the line.

31. It is the duty of the Consulting Engineer to the Government of India for Railways,

and the Engineer-in-Chief or other controlling officers of State Railways, in conjunction with Engineers in charge of railways and the revenue authorities, periodically to adjust the boundaries, the controlling officers being held specially responsible for any excess or deficiency in the land held for railway purposes, as well as for the punctual fulfilment of the foregoing rules in their several departments, and for the careful record of correct registers, plans and schedules in their respective offices.

PART IV

Special Rules Issued after Consideration of The Contract of January 1880, Entered Into Between the Secretary of State for India in Council, and The East Indian Railway Company

1. All distinctions as to classes of land in the possession of the East Indian Railway Company that existed prior to the 1st of January 1880 shall cease from that date.
2. From and after the 1st January 1880, the East Indian Railway Company, when taking up land, shall pay the value of the land, including cost of clearances and compensation to owners and occupiers, plus the capitalized value of the abatement of land revenue, and the expenditure necessary in the different processes required in the taking up of the land.
3. The capitalized value of the abatement of land revenue is the amount which, invested in 4 per cent Government securities, at the market rate of the day, will produce interest equal to the abatement.
4. If the land required for the East Indian Railway Company be the property of the State, its value shall be the value as appraised by the revenue authorities at the time of its transfer to the undertaking, inclusive of incidental expenditure.
5. All lands required under these rules shall be taken up through the principal revenue officer of the district within which such lands are situated. If the land be the property of private individuals, payment shall be made for it to its owners in the manner described in rules 4 and 5 of chapter 6 of the Civil Account Code, volume I, 4th edition. If the land be the property of the State, the principal revenue officer of the district aforesaid shall complete his valuation and award, and shall communicate the same to the Provincial Accountant-General or Comptroller, as the case may be, for recovery from the East Indian Railway Company.
6. The amounts declared recoverable from the East Indian Railway Company, in respect of lands taken up under these rules, shall be adjusted according to rule 8, chapter 62 of the Civil Account Code, Volume II, 4th edition.

APPENDIX XI

[SEE SECTION I, CLAUSES 51 TO 54 AND 73]

Rules for the payment of compensation for land taken up under the Land Acquisition Act of 1870

1. After all preliminaries in respect to estimate, &c., that may be required under departmental rules in force for the time being have been duly carried out, the land will be taken up under the Act either by the Collector or by some special officer who is placed at the disposal of the Public Works Department, and invested with the powers of a Collector under the Act; the procedure differs in the two cases.
2. Officers who are especially employed for this work, being invested with the powers of a Collector under the Act and placed at the disposal of the Public Works Department, are regarded as Public Works disbursers, and are supplied with funds in the same manner as an Executive Engineer, as described in Chapter 24 of the Civil Account Code. The following procedure shall be observed by such officers.
3. When the amount of compensation is accepted by the persons the amounts payable to each person under the award, and shall on the day the award is made forward a copy of the statement, signed by himself, to the Examiner of Public Works Accounts with whom he is in account. Before signing the copy, the officer should carefully satisfy himself that it correctly shows the amounts due under the award, and should himself, both in the original and copy, enter the total of column 6 of the statement in words.
4. In paying the amounts due under the award, the officer shall take the receipt of each person to whom money is paid on a separate voucher in the accompanying form (marked B), containing a reference to the item showing the amount due to that person in the statement prescribed in the preceding paragraph: the date of payment should also be noted on the voucher. The officer shall forward the receipts of the payees to the Examiner of Public Works Accounts with whom he is in account when forwarding to him the account of the month in which the payments are made.
5. In the event of the payees not presenting themselves for payment within a year from the date of the award, the amounts due may be paid into the Treasury on Revenue deposit and vouched for in the accompanying form (marked C). Every endeavour should, however, be made to secure the presence of the payees to receive payment, so as to avoid as far as possible payment into the Treasury on deposit. When the payees ultimately claim payment of sums placed on deposit, the amounts will be paid to them in the same manner as ordinary Revenue deposits, under the authority of the Collector.
6. When the compensation offered is not accepted by the persons interested, and the amounts payable are consequently settled by the award made by the Court under the provisions of part III of the Act, the special officer shall, as soon as he ascertains what the award of the Court is, prepare a statement in form A showing the amounts

due under the award and forward a copy to the Examiner in the same manner as prescribed in rule 3. In paying the amounts due under such award, the officer shall take from each person to whom a payment is made a receipt in Form B, or in the event of the payees not presenting themselves for payment within a year from the date of the award, from the Treasury Officer in Form C, containing a reference to the entry showing the amount due in the statement just referred to, and shall forward those receipts to the Examiner of Public Works Accounts in forwarding to him the accounts of the month in which the payments are made.

7. The special officer should, as far as possible, arrange to make the payments due in or near the village to which the payees belong. This will make it more easy to secure the attendance of the payees, and so reduce the number of sums which it will be necessary to place on deposit under rule 5.
8. In any case in which a reference is made to the Civil Court, and the award of the Court is not made till after the special officer has been relieved of his special duties, the payments due under the award shall be made by the Collector, who will observe the same procedure as if the reference to the Civil Court had been made by himself, as prescribed in rules 9 and 10 below.
9. When the land is taken up by the Collector or other Civil Officer not specially employed for the work, such Collector or Civil Officer is not a Public Works disburser, but draws money for payment due under the award made by him or by the Civil Court from the Civil Treasury. Such Collector or Civil Officer shall as soon as he makes the award or as soon as he ascertains that an award has been made by the Civil Court, prepare a statement in Form A showing the amounts due, and forward a copy thereof to the Examiner of Public Works Accounts concerned in the manner prescribed in rules 3 and 6.
10. In making the payments due under the award, the Collector shall take from each person to whom payment is made a receipt in Form B containing a reference to the particular entry in the award showing the amount due to the payee. These receipts will be the Treasury Officer's vouchers for the payments, and shall be forwarded by him with the accounts of the month to the Accountant-General of the province, who will in ordinary course forward them to the Examiner of Public Works Accounts. In the event of the payees not presenting themselves to receive payment within a year from the date of the award, the amounts due may be placed on Revenue deposit, and receipts taken in Form C in the same manner as is provided in Rule 5.
11. The Treasury Officer has no concern with the award or with the award statement; he makes the payments on the authority of the Collector or other officer assessing compensation. The Collector may either draw the amount due to each payee separately, in which case he should countersign the receipt in form B, and make it payable at the Treasury to the payee, altering the words "Paid in my presence to in cash/by cheque "Pay"; or he may draw the total amount due under the award on his own receipt as an advance, and after making the payments forward the receipts of the payees to the Treasury Officer in adjustment of the advance. In the former case, an advice list of

the forms passed for payment should be sent to the Treasury Officer, who in turn should send weekly an advice of orders paid.

12. Whether the payment is made by special officer or by the Collector (or other Civil Officer), the audit of the Examiner of Public Works Accounts shall consist in seeing that every payment is supported by a receipt in Form B or C, and that the amount paid on such receipt is the amount payable to the payee under the award, as shown in the statements of which he will have received copies under the preceding orders. The Examiner will also note in the last column of Form A the date on which possession is --- --- --- ---.
13. The Examiner will, as he receives the vouchers, fill in the entries in column 8 of the award statement (Form A); and as he receives the reports of possession he will fill in the entries in column 9: when all the vouchers showing either payment to the payee or payment into the Treasury on deposit and the reports of possession have been received, he will forward a copy of the completed statement in Form A to the Chief Revenue authority. This will complete the audit of the Examiner; any other or further returns or reports from the officers who assess or pay compensation, and any reports regarding the payment of sums placed on deposit under Rules 5 and 10 above, will be disposed of by the Chief Revenue Authority without reference to the Examiner.
14. When the land is acquired for and the cost is debitable to the Military Works Department, the procedure above laid down will be observed, the Examiner of Military Works Accounts being substituted for the Examiner of Public Works Accounts.
15. When the land is acquired for and the cost is debitable to any other Department than the Public Works Department or Military Works Department, the procedure will also be the same, the Account Officer who will audit the payments being substituted for the Examiner of Public Works Accounts.
16. In any case in which land is acquired for a Municipality or other body financially independent of Government, the Local Government may direct that the payments instead of being made and audited in the same manner as the ordinary payments of such body, shall be made and audited as if the land were being acquired for Government. If the Local Government issues such an order, the Collector or other officer who makes payments on account of the land acquired shall draw funds from the Treasury and make payments in the manner laid down in these rules, using the forms prescribed, and shall render his accounts to the Civil Accountant-General. The Municipality or other body will pay the estimated cost of the compensation to the credit of Government in advance on such dates and in such instalments as the Local Government may direct, further payment to Government being required as soon as the Accountant-General reports that the payments made exceed the amount received in advance. The Accountant-General will deal with the accounts and payments as prescribed in these rules, debiting the payments against the advances received from the Municipality or other body.

APPENDIX XXXI

Rules of the Government of India for the acquisition of land for State Railways [received with Bengal Government order No. 2319R, dated the 18th December 1885]

I. The general course of procedure laid down in the Public Works Code, Chapter XV, paragraph 92, is to be followed on State Railways.

II. Railway officers shall not obtain possession of land, whether by purchase, lease, or on simple toleration, except through the proper Revenue authorities.

III. Engineers in preparing land plans for submission will divide their applications under two heads, viz.-

(a) Land required permanently or land necessary for the railway when it is opened for public traffic and when the works of construction are finished. Such lands are the sites of bridges, embankments, cuttings, fences, and other works, the cess or berm introduced for the sake of safety between the limit of the works and the adjacent spoil bank, bazaar, or side-cuttings; roads permanently required, such as those immediately in the neighbourhood of stations, over-bridges, under-bridges, or level crossings on the railway; land or water required for the water-supply; land wanted for the preparation and reception of such materials as are used in maintenance, as ballast pits; land for the permanent diversion of water-courses, all space permanently required at the stations, whether for traffic, storage, workshops, dwellings, or recreation, and also, as a general rule, land required for side cuttings and spoil banks.

(b) Land required temporarily or land necessary to be taken up, but not permanently wanted. Such land will be for side-cuttings and spoil banks, for roads, for access to works while in progress, but which will subsequently be abandoned; for the preparation and reception of materials used in constructing the railway, as brick-fields, quarries, ballast pits, or the temporary diversions of streams and highways. The sites of such dwellings as will be occupied only during construction will also come in this class.

IV. The land to be taken up permanently for the through line of railway will be, in the first instance, sufficient for a double line, so as to allow of a cart-road to exist parallel to the railway inside the fence. This road will be useful not only during construction for service purposes, but afterwards for access to the stations, for maintenance purposes, and for stacking materials.

V. The enclosed sections, which are not intended to be used as a type for fencing, but merely as an illustration showing the amount of land to be taken up, show the widths to be allowed for different purposes, and the relative position of the road, fence and ditch with reference to the railway. The boundary of the railway land permanently acquired is in every case to be considered as the outside edge of the ditch. Beyond the ditch a clear space or berm of not less than 6 feet must be left free from the spoil bank or side-cutting nearest to the railway, the cutting or bank being sloped off at an angle of not less than 2 to 1 to prevent any encroachment on this berm from the effects of weather. It will be seen from the section that the width of land to be permanently acquired for a line on the 5 feet 6 inches gauge will be for embankments 70 feet, for cuttings 76 feet, in addition to the width required in each case for the bases of the slopes. For a line on the metre gauge the widths will be for embankments 64 feet, for cuttings 70 feet, in addition to the slopes.

VI. Land for side-cuttings and spoil banks will, as a rule, be permanently taken up by Government, and subsequently disposed of when no longer required. Estimates will provide and be sanctioned for the full cost of purchase, and should also exhibit the sum which it is estimated may be realised by the ultimate sale of the land.

Embankments under 3 feet in height will only require side-cutting on one side of the railway. Slopes of side-cutting will be generally 2 to 1 all round, but care must be taken to provide for exceptional cases when a flatter slope may be needed. Similarly, the contents of cuttings under 3 feet high will be laid to spoil on one side only. Side-cuttings should not be too deep; a depth of 6 feet may be estimated for in calculating the width of land required for side-cuttings. They should be formed into well-defined tanks of moderate length; and should not, as a rule, be connected with each other or with adjacent water-courses. Valuable land should not be taken up for side-cuttings or for temporary purposes. A sufficient water-course should be provided at right angles to the centre line of railway for each culvert or bridge, and on either side of this water-course, land will be left clear of the side-cuttings sufficient to prevent the water from the river running into the side-cuttings. The precaution of leaving land uncut in this manner is necessary to prevent the formation of a dangerous stream parallel to the railway.

VII. In the neighbourhood of towns or other places, where land is above the ordinary value, the width of land to be taken for slopes, fence, &c., must be specially considered to secure economy.

VIII. All land will be applied for in continuous portions, and shown when practicable, mile by mile or village by village, on each sheet. The plans will be drawn to a scale of 150 feet to an inch; the centre line of railway will be shown divided into chains of 100 feet, and all dimensions will be figured in feet. The name of each zillah, pergunnah, and mouzah will be shown on each sheet. On curves the tangential point on the centre line will be marked and the radius of curvature given. The areas in acres, roods, and poles will be recorded in accordance with fiscal divisions in a schedule (form the same as that issued with circular No. 10 (Railway) of 1871); showing in detail the class to which the land belongs, and the purpose to which it is to be devoted. Land required permanently will be coloured pink; land required for temporary occupation will be coloured yellow; although, as pointed out in Rule VI, it will as a rule be acquired by Government permanently.

IX. Detached portions of land should be referred to some fixed point on one of the main sheets with distances and compass or other bearings, or such reference to the published maps of the neighbourhood as will ensure a ready identification of the land. A corresponding entry should be made on the main sheet to draw attention to the detached plot.

X. As a general rule, three complete sets of land plans and schedules will suffice for record, viz., one for the Engineer in charge of the railway, one for the local Government or Administration, and one for the Revenue authorities; but should more be required, they will be supplied by the Railway Engineers.

XI. The general correctness of the plans and schedules submitted by the Railway Engineer in charge being attested by the Engineer-in-Chief or Manager of the State Railway, the application will be forwarded to the Revenue authorities, and will be dealt with by them under the orders of the local Government or Administration.

XII. The land plans and schedules will be rectified from time to time as changes occur, and local Governments will see that a correct register of all railway lands is maintained.

XIII. When land is no longer required for the railway, it will be retransferred to the Revenue authorities and disposed of by them. All contemplated changes in the land occupied by a railway should be reported to the local Government, and it will be for the latter to see that the necessary steps are taken by the Revenue authorities for entering such changes in their records and for carrying out all further requisite proceedings.

XIV. In Native States all land will be obtained through the Political Agent, and the distinction of temporary and permanent need not be observed; but this will not make it the less incumbent on the officials concerned to see that all land not permanently required for the purposes of the railway is restored when no longer wanted, and to keep as complete records of the land retained for railway purposes in Native States as in British Territory. Such plans and schedules as the Political Agent may require will be supplied by the Railway Engineers.

The Land Acquisition Act, 1894

Source: The Gazette of India Calcutta, Part IV, 1894

Gist: The Land Acquisition Act, 1894 came into force on 1 March 1894 and was applicable to the whole of British India. The Act was to amend the law for the acquisition of land needed for public purposes and Companies and also for determining the compensation to be paid thereof. The Land Acquisition Act, 1870, and section 74 of the Punjab Courts Act, 1884, stood repealed with this Act. The Act, divided into 55 sections and further subsections in eight parts, has provisions for survey and testing of soil, etc, for the purpose of acquisition, provided no person shall enter into any building or upon any enclosed court or garden attached to a dwelling-house (unless with the consent of the occupier thereof) without previously giving such occupier at least seven days' notice in writing of his intention to do so. The Act provides that the Collector shall at the time of taking possession offer to the persons interested compensation for the standing crops and trees (if any) on such land and for any other damage sustained by them caused by such sudden dispossession. It also provides for Court proceedings in case of dispute. Separate provisions are given in Part VII to acquire land for any Company, with the consent of the Local Government.

The Land Acquisition Act, 1894

An Act to amend the law for the acquisition of land for public purposes and for Companies

WHEREAS it is expedient to amend the law for the acquisition of land needed for public purposes and for Companies and for determining the amount of compensation to be made on account of such acquisition; It is hereby enacted as follows:-

PART I
PRELIMINARY

1. *(1)* This Act may be called the Land Acquisition Act, 1894.
   (2) It extends to the whole of British India;
   (3) It shall come into force on the first day of March, 1894.
2. *(1)* The Land Acquisition Act, 1870, and section 74 of the Punjab Courts Act, 1884, are hereby repealed.
   (2) But all proceedings commenced, officers appointed or authorised, agreements

published and rules made under the said Land Acquisition Act shall, as far as may be, be deemed to have been respectively commenced, appointed or authorized, published and made under this Act.

(3) Any enactment or document referring to the said Land Acquisition Act or to any enactment thereby repealed shall, so far as may be, be construed to refer to this Act or to the corresponding portion thereof.

3. In this Act, unless there is something repugnant in the subject or context:-

(a) the expression "land" includes benefits to arise out of land, and things attached to the earth or permanently fastened to anything attached to the earth:

(b) the expression "person interested" includes all persons claiming an interest in compensation to be made on account of the acquisition of land under this Act; and a person shall be deemed to be interested in land if he is interested in an easement affecting the land:

(c) the expression "Collector" means the Collector of a district, and includes a Deputy Commissioner and any officer specially appointed by the Local Government to perform the functions of a Collector under this Act:

(d) the expression "Court" means a principal Civil Court of original jurisdiction, unless the Local Government has appointed (as it is hereby empowered to do) a special judicial officer within any specified local limits to perform the functions of the Court under this Act:

(e) the expression "Company" means a Company registered under the Indian Companies Act, 1882, or under the (English) Companies Acts, 1862 to 1890, or incorporated by an Act of Parliament or of the Governor General in Council, or by Royal Charter or Letters Patent:

(f) the expression "public purpose" includes the provision of village-sites in districts in which the Local Government shall have declared by notification in the official Gazette that it is customary for the Government to make such provision: and

(g) the following persons shall be deemed persons "entitled to act" as and to the extent hereinafter provided (that is to say) -
trustees for other persons beneficially interested shall be deemed the persons entitled to act with reference to any such case, and that to the same extent as the persons beneficially interested could have acted if free from disability:

a married woman, in cases to which the English law is applicable, shall be deemed the person so entitled to act, and, whether of full age or not, to the same extent as if she were unmarried and of full age; and

the guardians of minors and the committees or managers of lunatics or idiots shall be deemed respectively the persons so entitled to act, to the same extent as the minors, lunatics or idiots themselves, if free from disability, could have acted:

Provided that -

(i) no person shall be deemed "entitled to act" whose interest in the subject-matter shall be shown to the satisfaction of the Collector or Court to be adverse to the interest of the person interested for whom he would otherwise be entitled to act;

(ii) in every such case the person interested may appear by a next friend, or, in default of his appearance by a next friend, the Collector or Court, as the case may be, shall appoint a guardian for the case to act on his behalf in the conduct thereof;

(iii) the provision of Chapter XXXI of the Code of Civil Procedure shall, *mutatis mutandis,* apply in the case of persons interested appearing before a Collector or Court by a next friend, or by a guardian for the case, in proceedings under this Act; and

(iv) no person "entitled to act" shall be competent to receive the compensation money payable to the person for whom he is entitled to act, unless he would have been competent to alienate the land and receive and give a good discharge for the purchase money on a voluntary sale.

PART II
ACQUISITION

Preliminary Investigation

4\. *(1)* Whenever it appears to the Local Government that land in any locality is likely to be needed for any public purpose a notification to that effect shall be published in the official Gazette, and the Collector shall cause public notice of the substance of such notification to be given at convenient places in the said locality.

(2) Thereupon it shall be lawful for any officer either generally or specially authorized by such Government in this behalf, and for his servants and workmen, -

to enter upon and survey and take levels of any land in such locality;

to dig or bore into the subsoil;

to do all other acts necessary to ascertain whether the land is adapted for such purpose;

to set out the boundaries of the land proposed to be taken and the intended line of the work (if any) proposed to be made thereon;

to mark such levels, boundaries and line by placing marks and cutting trenches;

and, where otherwise the survey can not be completed and the levels taken and the boundaries and line marked, to cut down and clear away any part of any standing crop, fence or jungle;

Provided that no person shall enter into any building or upon any enclosed court or garden attached to a dwelling-house (unless with the consent of the occupier thereof) without previously giving such occupier at least seven days' notice in writing of his intention to do so.

5. The officer so authorized shall at the time of such entry pay or tender payment for all necessary damage to be done as aforesaid, and, in case of dispute as to the sufficiency of the amount so paid or tended, he shall at once refer the dispute to the decision of the Collector or other chief revenue-officer of the district, and such decision shall be final.

Declaration of Intended Acquisition

6. *(1)* Subject to the provision of Part VII of this Act, whenever it appears to the Local Government that any particular land is needed for a public purpose or for a Company, a declaration shall be made to that effect under the signature of a Secretary to such Government or of some officer duly authorized to certify its orders:

   Provided that no such declaration shall be made unless the compensation to be awarded for such property is to be paid by a Company, or wholly or partly out of public revenues or some fund controlled or managed by a local authority.

   (2) The declaration shall be published in the official Gazette and shall state the district or other territorial division in which the land is situate, the purpose for which it is needed, its approximate area, and, where a plan shall have been made of the land, the place where such plan may be inspected.

   (3) The said declaration shall be conclusive evidence that the land is needed for a public purpose or for a Company, as the case may be; and, after making such declaration, the Local Government may acquire the land in manner hereinafter appearing.

7. Whenever any land shall have been so declared to be needed for a public purpose, or for a Company, the Local Government, or some officer authorized by the Local Government in this behalf, shall direct the Collector to take order for the acquisition of the land.

8. The Collector shall thereupon cause the land (unless it has been already marked out under section 4) to be marked out. He shall also cause it to be measured, and (if no plan has been made thereof) a plan to be made of the same.

9. *(1)* The Collector shall then cause public notice to be given at convenient places on or near the land to be taken, stating that the Government intends to take possession of the land, and that claims to compensation for all interests in such land may be made to him.

   (2) Such notice shall state the particulars of the land so needed, and shall require all persons interested in the land to appear personally or by agent before the Collector at a time and place therein mentioned (such time not being earlier than fifteen days after the date of publication of the notice), and to state the nature of their respective interests in the land and the amount and particulars of their claims to

compensation for such interests, and their objections (if any) to the measurements made under section 8. The Collector may in any case require such statement to be made in writing and signed by the party or his agent.

(3) The Collector shall also serve notice to the same effect on the occupier (if any) of such land and on all such persons known or believed to be interested therein, or to be entitled to act for persons so interested, as reside, or have agents authorized to receive service on their behalf, within the revenue district in which the land is situate.

(4) In case any person so interested resides elsewhere, and has no such agent, the notice shall be sent to him by post in a letter addressed to him at his last known residence, address or place of business and registered under Part III of the Indian Post Office Act, 1866.

10. *(1)* The Collector may also require any such person to make or deliver to him, at a time and place mentioned (such time not being earlier than fifteen days after the date of the requisition), a statement containing, so far as may be practicable, the name of every other person possessing any interest in the land or any part thereof as co-proprietor, sub-proprietor, mortgagee, tenant or otherwise, and of the nature of such interest, and of the rents and profits (if any) received or receivable on account thereof for three years next preceding the date of the statement.

(2) Every person required to make or deliver a statement under this section or section 9 shall be deemed to be legally bound to do so within the meaning of sections 175 and 176 of the Indian Penal Code.

Enquiry into Measurements, Value and Claims, and Award by the Collector

11. On the day so fixed, or on any other day to which the enquiry has been adjourned, the Collector shall proceed to enquire into the objections (if any) which any person interested has stated pursuant to a notice given under section 9 to the measurements made under section 8, and into the value of the land, and into the respective interests of the persons claiming the compensation, and shall make an award under his hand of -

(i) the true area of the land;

(ii) the compensation which in his opinion should be allowed for the land; and

(iii) the apportionment of the said compensation among all the persons known or believed to be interested in the land, of whom, or of whose claims, he has information, whether or not they have respectively appeared before him.

12. *(1)* Such award shall be filed in the Collector's office and shall, except as hereinafter provided, be final and conclusive evidence, as between the Collector and the persons interested, whether they have respectively appeared before the Collector or not, of the true area and value of the land, and the apportionment of the compensation among the persons interested.

(2) The Collector shall give immediate notice of his award to such of the persons

interested as are not present personally or by their representatives when the award is made.

13. The Collector may, for any cause he thinks fit, from time to time adjourn the enquiry to a day to be fixed by him.
14. For the purpose of enquiries under this Act, the Collector shall have power to summon and enforce the attendance of witnesses, including the parties interested or any of them, and to compel the production of documents by the same means, and (so far as may be) in the same manner, as is provided in the case of a Civil Court under the Code of Civil Procedure.
15. In determining the amount of compensation, the Collector shall be guided by the provisions contained in sections 23 and 24.

Taking Possession

16. When the Collector has made an award under section 11, he may take possession of the land, which shall thereupon vest absolutely in the Government, free from all circumstances.
17. *(1)* In cases of urgency, whenever the Local Government so directs, the Collector, though no such award has been made, may, on the expiration of fifteen days from the publication of notice mentioned in section 9, sub-section (1), take possession of any waste or arable land needed for public purposes or for a Company. Such land shall thereupon vest absolutely in the Government, free from all encumbrances.

    (2) Whenever, owing to any sudden change in the channel of any navigable river or other unforeseen emergency, it becomes necessary for any Railway Administration to acquire the immediate possession of any land for the maintenance of their traffic or for the purpose of making thereon a river-side or ghat station, or of providing convenient connection with or access to any such station, the Collector may, immediately after the publication of the notice mentioned in sub-section *(1)* and with the previous sanction of the Local Government, enter upon and take possession of such land, which shall thereupon vest absolutely in the Government free from all encumbrances:

    Provided that the Collector shall not take possession of any building or part of a building under this sub-section without giving to the occupier thereof at least forty-eight hours' notice of his intention so to do or such longer notice as may be reasonably sufficient to enable such occupier to remove his moveable property from such building without unnecessary inconvenience.

    (3) In every case under either of the preceding sub-section the Collector shall at the time of taking possession offer to the persons interested compensation for the standing crops and trees (if any) on such land and for any other damage sustained by them caused by such sudden dispossession and not excepted in section 24; and, in case such offer is not accepted, the values of such crops and trees and the

amount of such other damage shall be allowed for in awarding compensation for the land under the provisions herein contained.

PART III

REFERENCE TO COURT AND PROCEDURE THEREON

18. *(1)* Any person interested who has not accepted the award may, by written application to the Collector, require that the matter be referred by the Collector for the determination of the Court, whether his objection be to the measurement of the land, the amount of the compensation, the persons to whom it is payable, or the apportionment of the compensation among the persons interested.

(2) The application shall state the grounds on which the objection to the award is taken:

Provided that every such application shall be made, -

(a) if the person making it was present or represented before the Collector at the time when he made his award, within six weeks from the date of the Collector's award;

(b) in other cases, within six weeks of the receipt of the notice from the Collector under section 12, sub-section (2), or within six months from the date of the Collector's award, whichever period shall first expire.

19. *(1)* In making the reference, the Collector shall state, for the information of the Court, in writing under his hand, -

(a) the situation and extent of the land, with particulars of any trees, buildings or standing crops thereon;

(b) the names of the persons whom he has reason to think interested in such land;

(c) the amount awarded for damages and paid or tendered under sections 5 and 17, or either of them, and the amount of compensation awarded under section 11; and,

(d) if the objection be to the amount of the compensation, the grounds on which the amount of compensation was determined.

(2) To the said statement shall be attached a schedule giving the particulars of the notices served upon, and of the statements in writing made or delivered by, the parties interested respectively.

20. The Court shall thereupon cause a notice, specifying the day on which the Court will proceed to determine the objection, and directing their appearance before the Court on that day, to be served on the following persons, namely:-

(a) the applicant;

(b) all persons interested in the objection, except such (if any) of them as have consented without protest to receive payment of the compensation awarded; and,

(c) if the objection is in the regard to the area of the land or to the amount of the compensation, the Collector.

21. The scope of the inquiry in every such proceeding shall be restricted to a consideration of the interests of the persons affected by the objection.

22. Every such proceeding shall take place in open Court, and all persons entitled to practise in any Civil Court in the province shall be entitled to appear, plead and act (as the case may be) in such proceeding.

23. *(1)* In determining the amount of compensation to be awarded for land acquired under this Act, the Court shall take into consideration—

first, the market-value of the land at the date of the publication of the declaration relating thereto under section 6;

secondly, the damage sustained by the person interested, by reason of the taking of any standing crops or trees which may be on the land at the time of the Collector's taking possession thereof;

thirdly, the damage (if any) sustained by any person interested, at the time of the Collector's taking possession of the land, by reason of serving such land from his other land;

fourthly, the damage (if any) sustained by any person interested, at the time of the Collector's taking possession of the land, by reason of the acquisition injuriously affecting his other property, moveable or immoveable, in any other manner, or his earnings;

fifthly, if, in consequence of the acquisition of the land by the Collector, the person interested is compelled to change his residence or place of business, the reasonable expenses (if any) incidental to such change; and

sixthly, the damage (if any) *bona fide* resulting from diminution of the profits of the land between the time of the publication of the declaration under section 6 and the time of the Collector's taking possession of the land.

(2) In addition to the market-value of the land, as above provided, the Court shall in every case award a sum of fifteen per centum on such market-value, in consideration of the compulsory nature of the acquisition.

24. But the Court shall not take into consideration, -

first, the degree of urgency which has led to the acquisition;

secondly, any disinclination of the person interested to part with the land acquired;

thirdly, any damage sustained by him which, if caused by a private person, would not render such person liable to a suit;

fourthly, any damage which is likely to be caused to the land acquired, after the date of the publication of the declaration under section 6, by or in consequence of the use to which it will be put;

fifthly, any increase to the value of the land acquired likely to accrue from the use to which it will be put when acquired;

sixthly, any increase to the value of the other land of the person interested likely to accrue from the use to which the land acquired will be put; or,

seventhly, any outlay or improvements on, or disposal of, the land acquired, commenced, made or effected without the sanction of the Collector after the date of the publication of the declaration under section 6.

25. *(1)* When the applicant has made a claim to compensation, pursuant to any notice given under section 9, the amount awarded to him by the Court shall not exceed the amount so claimed or be less than the amount awarded by the Collector under section 11.

(2) When the applicant has refused to make such claim, or has omitted without sufficient reason (to be allowed by the Judge) to make such claim, the amount awarded by the Court shall in no case exceed the amount awarded by the Collector.

(3) When the applicant has omitted for a sufficient reason (to be allowed by the Judge) to make such claim, the amount awarded to him by the Court shall not be less than, and may exceed, the amount awarded by the Collector.

26. Every award under this Part shall be in writing signed by the Judge, and shall specify the amount awarded under clause *first* of sub-section (1) of section 23, and also the amounts (if any) respectively awarded under each of the other clauses of the same sub-section, together with the grounds of awarding each of the said amounts.

27. *(1)* Every such award shall also state the amount of costs incurred in the proceedings under this Part, and by what persons and in what proportions they are to be paid.

(2) When the award of the Collector is not upheld, the costs shall ordinarily be paid by the Collector, unless the Court shall be of opinion, that the claim of the applicant was so extravagant or that he was so negligent in putting his case before the Collector that some deduction from his costs should be made or that he should pay a part of the Collector's costs.

28. If the sum which, in the opinion of the Court, the Collector ought to have awarded as compensation is in excess of the sum which the Collector did award as compensation, the award of the Court may direct that the Collector shall pay interest on such excess at the rate of six per centum per annum from the date on which he took possession of the land to the date of payment of such excess into Court.

PART IV
APPORTIONMENT OF COMPENSATION

29. Where there are several persons interested, if such persons agree in the apportionment

of the compensation, the particulars of such apportionment shall be specified in the award, and as between such persons the award shall be conclusive evidence of the correctness of the apportionment.

30. When the amount of compensation has been settled under section 11, if any dispute arises as to the apportionment of the same or any part thereof, and as to the persons to whom the same or any part thereof is payable, the Collector may refer such dispute to the decision of the Court.

PART V
PAYMENT

31. *(1)* On making an award under section 11, the Collector shall tender payment of the compensation awarded by him to the persons interested entitled thereto according to the award, and shall pay it to them unless prevented by some one or more of the contingencies mentioned in the next sub-section.

(2) If they shall not consent to receive it, or if there be no person competent to alienate the land, or if there be any dispute as to the title to receive the compensation or as to the apportionment of it, the Collector shall deposit the amount of the compensation in the Court to which a reference under section 18 would be submitted:

Provided that any person admitted to be interested may receive such payment under protest as to the sufficiency of the amount:

Provided also that no person who has received the amount otherwise than under protest shall be entitled to make any application under section 18:

Provided also that nothing herein contained shall affect the liability of any person, who may receive the whole or any part of any compensation awarded under this Act, to pay the same to the person lawfully entitled thereto.

(3) Notwithstanding anything in this section, the Collector may, with the sanction of the Local Government, instead of awarding a money compensation in respect of any land, make any arrangement with a person having a limited interest in such land, either by the grant of other lands in exchange, the remission of land-revenue on other lands held under the same title, or in such other way as may be equitable having regard to the interests of the parties concerned.

(4) Nothing in the last foregoing sub-section shall be construed to interfere with or limit the power of the Collector to enter into any arrangement with any person interested in the land and competent to contract in respect thereof.

32. *(1)* If any money shall be deposited in Court under sub-section (2) of the last preceding section and it appears that the land in respect whereof the same was awarded belonged to any person who had no power to alienate the same, the Court shall -

(a) order the money to be invested in the purchase of other lands to be held under the like title and the conditions of ownership as the land in respect of which such money shall have been deposited was held, or

(b) if such purchase can not be effected forthwith, then in such Government or other approved securities as the Court shall think fit;

and shall direct the payment of interest or other proceeds arising from such investment to the person or persons who would for the time being have been entitled to the possession of the said land, and such moneys shall remain so deposited and invested until the same be applied -

(i) in the purchase of such other lands as aforesaid; or
(ii) in payment to any person or persons becoming absolutely entitled thereto.

(2) In all cases of moneys deposited to which this section applies the Court shall order the costs of the following matters, including therein all reasonable charges and expenses incident thereto, to be paid by the Collector, namely:-

(a) the costs of such investments as aforesaid;
(b) the costs of the orders for the payment of the interest or other proceeds of the securities upon which such moneys are for the time being invested, and for the payment out of Court of the principal of such moneys, and of all proceedings relating thereto, except such as may be occasioned by litigation between adverse claimants.

33. When any money shall have been deposited in Court under this Act for any cause other than that mentioned in the last preceding section, the Court may, on the application of any party interested or claiming an interest in such money, order the same to be invested in such Government or other approved securities as it may think proper, and may direct the interest or other proceeds of any such investment to be accumulated or paid in such manner as it may consider will give the parties interested therein the same benefit therefrom as they might have had from the land in respect whereof such money shall have been deposited or as near thereto as may be.

34. When the amount of such compensation is not paid or deposited on or before taking possession of the land, the Collector shall pay the amount awarded with interest thereon at the rate of six per centum per annum from the time of so taking possession until it shall have been so paid or deposited.

PART VI
TEMPORARY OCCUPATION OF LAND

35. *(1)* Subject to the provisions of Part VII of this Act, whenever it appears to the Local Government that the temporary occupation and use of any waste or arable land are needed for any public purpose, or for a Company, the Local Government may direct the Collector to procure the occupation and use of the same for such term as it shall think fit, not exceeding three years from commencement of such occupation.

(2) The Collector shall thereupon give notice in writing to the persons interested in such land of the purpose for which the same is needed, and shall, for the occupation and use thereof for such term as aforesaid, and for the materials (if any) to be taken therefrom, pay to them such compensation, either in a gross sum of money, or by monthly or other periodical payments, as shall be agreed upon in writing between him and such persons respectively.

(3) In case the Collector and the persons interested differ as to the sufficiency of the compensation or apportionment thereof, the Collector shall refer such difference to the decision of the Court.

36. *(1)* On payment of such compensation, or on executing such agreement, or on making a reference under section 35, the Collector may enter upon and take possession of the land, and use or permit the use thereof in accordance with the terms of the said notice.

(2) On the expiration of the term, the Collector shall make or tender to the persons interested compensation for the damage (if any) done to the land and not provided for by the agreement, and shall restore the land to the persons interested therein:

Provided that, if the land has become permanently unfit to be used for the purpose for which it was used immediately before the commencement of such term, and the persons interested shall so require, the Local Government shall proceed under this Act to acquire the land as if it was needed permanently for a public purpose or for a Company.

37. In case the Collector and persons interested differ as to the condition of the land at the expiration of the term, or as to any matter connected with the said agreement, the Collector shall refer such difference to the decision of the Court.

PART VII
ACQUISITION OF LAND FOR COMPANIES

38. *(1)* Subject to such rules as the Governor General of India in Council may from time to time prescribe in this behalf, the Local Government may authorize any officer of any Company desiring to acquire land for its purposes to exercise the powers conferred by section 4.

(2) In every such case section 4 shall be construed as if for the words "for such purpose" the words "for the purposes of the Company" were substituted; and section 5 shall be construed as if after the words "the officer" the words "of the Company" were inserted.

39. The provisions of sections 6 to 37 (both inclusive) shall not be put in force in order to acquire land for any Company, unless with the previous consent of the Local Government, nor unless the Company shall have executed the agreement hereinafter mentioned.

40. *(1)* Such consent shall not be given unless the Local Government be satisfied, by an

enquiry held as hereinafter provided, -

(a) that such acquisition is needed for the construction of some work, and
(b) that such work is likely to prove useful to the public.

(2) Such enquiry shall be held by such officer and at such time and place as the Local Government shall appoint.

(3) Such officer may summon and enforce the attendance of witnesses and compel the production of documents by the same means and, as far as possible, in the same manner as is provided by the Code of Civil Procedure in the case of a Civil Court.

41. Such officer shall report to the Local Government the result of the enquiry, and, if the Local Government is satisfied that the proposed acquisition is needed for the construction of a work, and that such work is likely to prove useful to the public, it shall, subject to such rules as the Governor General of India in Council may from time to time prescribe in this behalf, require the Company to enter into an agreement with the Secretary of State for India in Council, providing to the satisfaction of the Local Government for the following matters, namely:-

(1) the payment to Government of the cost of the acquisition;
(2) the transfer, on such payment, of the land to the Company;
(3) the terms on which the land shall be held by the Company;
(4) the time within which, and the conditions on which, the work shall be executed and maintained; and
(5) the terms on which the public shall be entitled to use the work.

42. Every such agreement shall, as soon as may be after its execution, be published in the Gazette of India, and also in the local official Gazette, and shall thereupon (so far as regards the terms on which the public shall be entitled to use the work) have the same effect as if it had formed part of this Act.

43. The provisions of sections 39 to 42, both inclusive, shall not apply, and the corresponding sections of the Land Acquisition Act, 1870, shall be deemed never to have applied, to the acquisition of land for any Railway or other Company, for the purposes of which, under any agreement between such Company and the Secretary of State for India in Council, the Government, or was, bound to provide land.

44. In the case of the acquisition of land for the purposes of a Railway Company, the existence of such an agreement as is mentioned in section 43 may be proved by the production of a printed copy thereof purporting to be printed by order of Government.

PART VIII
MISCELLANEOUS

45. *(1)* Service of any notice under this Act shall be made by delivering or tendering a copy thereof signed, in the case of a notice under section 4, by the officer therein

mentioned, and, in the case of any other notice, by or by order of the Collector or the Judge.

(2) Whenever it may be practicable, the service of the notice shall be made on the person therein named.

(3) When such person can not be found, the service may be made on any adult male member of his family residing with him; and, if no such adult member can be found, the notice may be served by fixing the copy on the outdoor of the house in which the person therein named ordinarily dwells or carries on business, or by fixing a copy therein some conspicuous place in the office of the officer aforesaid or of the Collector or in the Court house, and also in some conspicuous part of the land to be acquired:

Provided that, if the Collector or Judge shall so direct, a notice may be sent by post, in a letter addressed to the person named therein at his last known residence, address or place of business and registered under Part 111 of the Indian Post Office Act, 1866, and service of it may be proved by the production of the addressee's receipt.

46. Whoever wilfully obstructs any person in doing any of the acts authorized by section 4 or section 8, or wilfully fills up, destroys, damages or displaces any trench or mark made under section 4, shall, on conviction before a Magistrate, be liable to imprisonment for any term not exceeding one month, or to fine not exceeding fifty rupees, or to both.

47. If the Collector is opposed or impeded in taking possession under this Act of any land, he shall, if a Magistrate, enforce the surrender of the land to himself, and, if not a Magistrate, he shall apply to a Magistrate or (within the towns of Calcutta, Madras and Bombay) to the Commissioner of Police, and such Magistrate or Commissioner (as the case may be) shall enforce the surrender of the land to the Collector.

48. *(1)* Except in the case provided for in section 36, the Government shall be at liberty to withdraw from the acquisition of any land of which possession has not been taken.

(2) Whenever the Government withdraws from any such acquisition, the Collector shall determine the amount of compensation due for the damage suffered by the owner in consequence of the notice or of any proceedings thereunder, and shall pay such amount to the person interested, together with all costs reasonably incurred by him in the prosecution of the proceedings under the Act relating to the said land.

(3) The provisions of Part III of this Act shall apply, so far as may be, to the determination of the compensation payable under this section.

49. *(1)* The provisions of this Act shall not be put in force for the purpose of acquiring a part only of any house, manufactory or other building, if the owner desire that the whole of such house, manufactory or building shall be so acquired:

Provided that the owner may, at any time before the Collector has made his award under section 11, by notice in writing, withdraw or modify his expressed desire that the whole of such house, manufactory or building shall be so acquired:

Provided also that, if any question shall arise as to whether any land proposed to be taken under this Act does or not form part of a house, manufactory or building within the meaning of this section, the Collector shall refer the determination of such question to the Court and shall not take possession of such land until after the question has been determined.

In deciding on such a reference the Court shall have regard to the question whether the land proposed to be taken is reasonably required for the full and unpaired use of the house, manufactory or building.

(2) If, in the case of any claim under section 23, sub-section (1), thirdly, by a person interested, on account of the serving of the land to be acquired from his other land, the Local Government is of opinion that the claim is unreasonable or excessive, it may, at any time before the Collector has made his award, order the acquisition of the whole of the land of which the land first sought to be acquired forms a part.

(3) In the case lest hereinbefore provided for, no fresh declaration or other proceedings under sections 6 to 10, both inclusive, shall be necessary; but the Collector shall without delay furnish a copy of the order of the Local Government to the person interested, and shall thereafter proceed to make his award under section 11.

50. *(1)* Where the provisions of this Act are put in force for the purpose of acquiring land at the cost of any fund controlled or managed by a local authority or of any Company, the charges of and incidental to such acquisition shall be defrayed from or by such fund or Company.

(2) In any proceeding held before a Collector or Court in such cases the local authority or Company concerned may appear and adduce evidence for the purpose of determining the amount of compensation:

Provided that no such local authority or Company shall be entitled to demand a reference under section 18.

51. No award or agreement made under this Act shall be chargeable with stamp-duty, and no person claiming under any such award or agreement shall be liable to pay any fee for a copy of the same.

52. No suit or other proceeding shall be commenced or prosecuted against any person for anything done in pursuance of this Act, without giving to such person a month's previous notice in writing of the intended proceeding, and of the cause thereof, nor after tender of sufficient amends.

53. Save in so far as they may be inconsistent with anything contained in this Act, the provisions of the Code of Civil Procedure shall apply to all proceedings before the Court under this Act.

54. Subject to the provisions of the Code of Civil Procedure applicable to appeals from original decrees, an appeal shall lie to the High Court from the award or from any part of the award of the Court in any proceedings under this Act.

55. *(1)* The Local Government shall have power to make rules consistent with this Act for the guidance of officers in all matters connected with its enforcement, and may from time to time alter and add to the rules so made.

(2) The power to make, alter and add to rules under sub-section (1) shall be subject to the condition of the rules being made, altered or added to after previous publication.

(3) All such rules, alterations and additions shall, when sanctioned by the Governor General in Council, be published in the official Gazette, and shall thereupon have the force of law.

S. HARVEY JAMES,
Secretary to the Government of India

Select Bibliography

PRIMARY SOURCES

A. Governments of India Records, NAI, New Delhi

Home Department (Public), Proceedings, 1832-59
Foreign Department Proceedings, 1840-1900
Pulic Works Department Proceedings, 1855-59
Public Works Department (Railway Branch) Proceedings, 1860-79
Accounts of Guaranteed Railway Branch
    'A'   Proceedings, 1871-79
    'B'   Proceedings, 1871-79
Account Railway Branch
    'A'   Proceedings, 1864-1900
    'B'   Proceedings, 1870-1904
Guaranteed Railway Branch
    'A'   Proceedings, 1871-76
    'B'   Proceedings, 1871-76
Railway Construction Branch
    'A'   Proceedings, 1879-1905
    'B'   Proceedings, 1879-1905
Railway Establishment Branch
    'A'   Proceedings, 1869-1905
    'B'   Proceedings, 1869-1905
Railway Establishment Accounts Branch
    'A'   Proceedings, 1872-94
Railway Project Branch
    'A'   Proceedings, 1898-1905
    'B'   Proceedings, 1898-1905
Railway Statistics Branch
    'A'   Proceedings, 1891-1905
    'B'   Proceedings, 1893-1905
Railway Stores Branch
    'A'   Proceedings, 1879-1905

'B' Proceedings, 1879-1905

Railway Traffic Branch

'A' Proceedings, 1879-1905

'B' Proceedings, 1879-1905

State Railway Branch

'A' Proceedings, 1872-73

'B' Proceedings, 1872-74

Despatches to the Secretary of State for India, 1861-71

B. Record Series (Company Period), 1848-59, NAI

Body Sheets (Railway), 1854-59
Diary of Letters Received, 1855-59
Diary of Railway, General Letters from the Court of Directors, 1851-58
Index to Railway, Letters from Court of Directors, 1852-61
Index to Railway Proceedings, 1853-59
P.W.D. Financial and Railway Department, Register of Letters, 1856
P.W.D. Letters to Court of Directors, 1855-58
Railway Consultations Nos. 83-106, 1853
Railway General, Letters to Court of Directors, 1850-61
Railway Letters, From Court of Directors, 1852-59
Railway Proceedings, 1858-59

C. P.W.D. (Miscellaneous) Records, 1858-1941, NAI

Governor General's Diary, 1860-63
Indian Railways : Capital and Revenue Accounts, 1897-1940
P.W.D. (General), State Railway, 1885-96
Register of State Railway Capital, 1894-1933

D. P.W.D. (Local Government) Records, 1850-88, NAI

Bombay Public and Railway Diary, 1853-58
Madras Public and Railway Diary, 1855-58
N.W.P. Railway Papers, 1859-62
P.W.D. Bombay (Railway), Letters to Court of Directors, 1850-59
P.W.D. Financial (Railway), Letters from Court of Directors to Government of Bombay 1856-58
P.W.D. (Railway), Letters from Court of Directors to Government of Bombay, 1851-59
P.W.D. Madras (Railway), Letters to Court of Directors, 1856-60

E. Crown Period Records, 1860-84, NAI

Bombay P.W.D. (Railway), Despatches from Secretary of State for India, 1860-71
Bombay P.W.D. (Railway), Despatches from and to Secretary of State for India, 1867-69

Bombay P.W.D. (Railway), Despatches to Secretary of State for India, 1860-71
Index to the Proceedings of P.W.D. (Railway), Madras Government, 1868
Madras P.W.D. (Railway) Despatches from and to Secretary of State for India, 1871
Madras P.W.D. (Railway) Despatches to Secretary of State for India, 1860-64
Madras Railway : Letters from Secretary of State for India, 1861-70
Madras Railway : Letters to Secretary of State for India, 1860-71

F. Other Series of Records (Railway Companies), NAI

Assam Bengal Railway Company, 1892-1921
Bengal Doars Railway Company, 1897-1916
Bengal and North Western Railway Company, 1883-1923
Bengal Nagpur Railway Company, 1887-1923
Bengal Central Railway Company, 1881-1902
Bombay Baroda and Central India Railway Company, 1855-1992
Calcutta South Eastern Railway Company, 1859-74
Delhi Umbala Kalka Railway Company, 1889-1917
East Indian Railway Company,1851-1923
Eastern Bengal Railway Company, 1857-83
Great Indian Peninsula Railway Company, 1848-1923
Great South India Railway Company,1858-1921
Indian Tramway Company, 1867-74
Indian Branch Railway Company, 1848-71
Indian Midland Railway Company, 1885-1907
Madras Railway Company, 1852-1906
Madras Southern Mahratta Railway Company, 1908-1921
Oudh and Rohilkhand Railway Company, 1867-1917
Rohilkhand and Kumaon Railway Company, 1882-1923
Sind Railway Company, 1875-77
Sind, Punjab and Delhi Railway Company, 1877-1907
South Mahratta Railway Company, 1882-1908
South Bihar Railway Company, 1895-1910

G. Residency (Native States) Records, NAI

Baroda Residency
Bhopal Political Agency
Bundelkhand Agency
Eastern Rajputana State Agency
Gwalior Residency
Hyderabad Residency
Hyderabad Residency (Political)
Jaipur Agency

Western Ghat State Agency

H. British Parliamentary Papers, 1832-1901, NAI

Microfilm Reel No. 28, Affairs of the East India Company; Rail Roads, 1831-32

Microfilm Reel No. 44, East India, 1854

Microfilm Reel No. 44, Railways (India), 1845

Microfilm Reel No. 46, Railways in India : Copy of Railway Report from India, 1847

Microfilm Reel No. 54, Railway Communication in India, 1850

Microfilm Reel No. 59, Madras Railway Company, 1852-53

Microfilm Reel No. 60, Copies of Correspondence between the Government of India and the Court of Directors, and of Documents received from India relating to the lines to be selected for the system of Railway Constructions in the Country; Railways (India), 1853-54

Microfilm Reel No. 67, Report of the Select Committee on East India (Railways) : together with the Proceedings of the Committee, Minutes of Evidence and Appendices, 1857-58

Microfilm Reel No. 70, Memorandum of A. Cotton on Railway, 1857-59

Microfilm Reel No. 72, East India (Railways), 1859-89

Microfilm Reel No. 74, East India (Guaranteed Companies), Railway in India; 1859-60

Microfilm Reel No. 77, Railway in India, 1860-61

Microfilm Reel No. 78, Railway in India, 1862-63

Microfilm Reel No. 79, East India (Railway Consulting Engineer), Railways in India, 1862-63

Microfilm Reel No. 81, Railways in India, 1863-64

Microfilm Reel No. 82, South Eastern of Bengal and Multan Railway Company, 1865-66

Microfilm Reel No. 83, Railways in India, 1865-66

Microfilm Reel No. 84, East Indian Railway Company, 1886-88

Microfilm Reel No. 85, Indian Railway Companies, A Bill to enable certain/Guaranteed Indian Railway Company to raise money on Debenture Stock, Railways in India, 1866-68

Microfilm Reel No. 87, Statistical Abstract relating to British India from 1857-1866; Indian Railway Companies, Bill, Power to each Company to create and issue Debenture Stock with sanction of the Secretary of State in Council of India: Indian Railway Companies; East India (Railways); Copies of Despatch from the Government of India, and Minutes by the Governor General, and Despatch to the Government of India on the subject of Railway extension in India; East India (Railway); Correspondence of the subject of the extension of Railways in India, and their future construction and management, 1867-69

Microfilm Reel No. 88, Statistical Abstracts relating to British India from, 1858-67; Despatch from the Governor General relating to Railway (India), 1868-69

Microfilm Reel No. 89, Railways in India, 1869-70

Microfilm Reel No. 90, East India (Railway Extension), 1870-71

Microfilm Reel No. 93, Railways in India, 1870-71 : East India (Khundwah & Indore Railway); Copy of Letter from the Board of Directors of the Great Indian Peninsula Railway Company to the Under Secretary of States for India with enclosed Report from their Consulting Engineer, Mr. Berkley, on the subject of the proposed Narrow Gauge Line of Railway between Khundwah and Indore, 1871-72

Microfilm Reel No. 94, Railways in India, 1872-73

Microfilm Reel No. 96, Railways in India, 1872-73; East Indian Railway (Break of Gauge); Copies of Correspondence between the Secretary of State for India in Council and the Governor General of India, with respect of the proposed Break of Gauge on the Main line of Railway to Peshawur; East India (Guaranteed Railways), 1872-73

Microfilm Reel No. 97, East India (Railway Gauge), Correspondence on the Question of the Gauge of the Punjab Northern and Indus Valley Railways

Microfilm Reel No. 98, Railways in India, 1873, Statistical Abstract relating to British India, 1864-1873

Microfilm Reel No. 100, Statistical Abstract relating to British India, 1865-1874

Microfilm Reel No. 102, Railways in India for the year 1875-76

Microfilm Reel No. 104, Victorian Railways, Report on Observation on Railways made during a tour in 1874-75 by Thomas Higinbotham; Statistical Abstract relating to India from 1866-67 to 1875-76

Microfilm Reel No. 106 Report from the Select Committee on East India (Public Works); together with Proceedings of the Committee, Minutes of Evidence and Appendices, 1878

Microfilm Reel No. 107, Railways in India, 1877-78

Microfilm Reel No. 108, East Indian Railway Company; East Indian Railway: Extracts from the Agreement between the East India Company and the Government of India respectively for the construction of Railways in India; Report from the Select Committee on East India (Public Works); East India (Rajputana Railway), 1878-79

Microfilm Reel No. 109, Railways in India, 1878-79; Statistical Abstract Relating to British India from 1868-69 to 1877-78; East Indian Railway; Redumption of Annuities; Report form the Select Committee on East India (Public Works), together with the Proceedings of the Committee, Minutes of Evidence and Appendix; East Indian Loan (East Indian Railway Debentures Bill), 1878-79

Microfilm Reel No. 110, 1880-81, East India (Frontier Raiway Company)

Microfilm Reel No. 111, Statistical Abstract Relating to British India from 1870-71 to 1879-80

Microfilm Reel No. 113, Report from the Select Committee on standing order No. 167 together with Proceedings of Committee, Minutes of Evidence, and Appendices; East India (Souhern Mahratta Railway); East India Railways; Statements showing the lengths open, the average age, and the general result of working of Railways, for the years from 1876 to 1882

Microfilm Reel No. 115, Report from the Select Committee on East India Railway Communication with the Poceedings of the Committee, 1883-84

Microfilm Reel No. 116, Report from the Select Committee on East India Railway Communication with the Proceedings of the Committee, 1883-84; Statistical Abstract relating to British India, 1884

Microfilm Reel No. 117, Report from the Select Committee on East Indian Railway Comunication; together with the Proceedings of the Committee, Minutes of Evidence,

and Index; East India (Frontier Railway Company), 1884-85
Microfilm Rell No. 119, Statistical Abstract relating to British India from 1874-75 to 1883-84.
Microfilm Reel No. 123, East India (Purchase and Construction of Railway), 1888
Microfilm Reel No. 124, South Indian Railway Purchase, 1890
Microfilm Reel No. 128, East India and Burma Railway Concession, 1893-94
Microfilm Reel No. 132, Statistical Abstracts relating to British India from 1881-85
Microfilm Reel No. 136, East India (Extension of Railways by Private Agency), 1897-98
Microfilm Reel No. 137, Statistical Abstract relating to British India from 1886-87 to 1895-96
Microfilm Reel No. 140, East India (Railways and Irrigation Works), 1889-1900
Microfilm Reel No. 142, Statistical Abstract relating to British India from 1889-90 to 1898-99

I. India Office Library Records, London

Railway Letters and Enclosures from Bengal and India, 1845-79 (Received from India Office in Microfilm Reel No. IOLR 31478 L PWD/2/43, ICHR)

SECONDARY SOURCES

A. Newspapers and Periodicals

Asiatic Journal
Bombay Gazette
Calcutta Gazette
Calcutta Review
Conservative
Economist
Englishman
Friends of India
Herapath's Railway Journal
Madras Gazette
Madras Herald
Manchester Guardian
Standard
Times

B. Reports

J.S. Trevor, *Administration Reports on Railway in India, 1879-80,* Calcutta, 1881
J.S. Trevor, *Administration Reports on Railway in India, 1880-81,* Roorkee, 1882
F.S. Stanton, *Administration Reports on Railway in India, 1881-82,* Simla, 1882
F.S. Stanton, *Administration Reports on Railway in India, 1882-83,* Simla, 1883
F.S. Stanton, *Administration Reports on Railway in India, 1883-84,* Simla, 1884

F.S. Stanton, *Administration Reports on Railway in India, 1884-85,* Simla, 1885
Conway Gordon, *Administration Reports on Railway in India, 1885-86,* Simla, 1886
Conway Gordon, *Administration Reports on Railway in India, 1886-87,* Simla, 1887
Conway Gordon, *Administration Reports on Railway in India, 1887-88,* Calcutta, 1888
Conway Gordon, *Administration Reports on Railway in India, 1888-89,* Calcutta, 1889
R.A. Sargeaunt, *Administration Reports on Railway in India, 1889-90,* Calcutta, 1891
R.A. Sargeaunt, *Administration Reports on Railway in India, 1890-91,* Simla, 1891
R.A. Sargeaunt, *Administration Reports on Railway in India, 1891-92,* Calcutta, 1892
R.A. Sargeaunt, *Administration Reports on Railway in India, 1892-93,* Simla, 1893
W.S.S. Bisset, *Administration Reports on Railway in India, 1893-94,* Simla, 1894
T.Gracy, *Administration Reports on Railway in India, 1894-95,* Simla, 1895
T.Gracy, *Administration Reports on Railway in India, 1895-96,* Calcutta, 1896
G.A. Anderson, *Administration Reports on Railway in India, 1896-97,* Calcutta, 1897
A. Brereton, *Administration Reports on Railway in India, 1897-98,* Simla, 1898
A. Brereton, *Administration Reports on Railway in India, 1898-99,* Calcutta, 1900
F.R. Upcott, *Administration Reports on Railway in India, 1899-1900,* Calcutta, 1900
F.R. Upcott, *Administration Reports on Railway in India, 1900-1901,* Simla, 1901
A. Brereton, *Administration Reports on Railway in India, 1901-02,* Simla, 1902

C. Private Papers on Microfilm Reels, NAI

Hardinge Papers, 1844-48
Dalhousie Papers, 1848-56
Lawrence Papers, 1864-69
Mayo Papers, 1869-72
Lytton Papers, 1876-80
Ripon Papers, 1880-84
Dufferin Papers, 1884-88
Lansdowne Papers, 1888-94
Elgin Papers, 1894-99
Curzon Papers, 1899-05
Salisbury Papers, 1874-81
Fowler Papers, 1894
Hamilton Papers, 1894-1904
Durand Papers, 1885-95

D. Articles

De Cosson, A.F.C., "The Early Days of the East Indian Railway, A. Side-Light on the Mutiny", *Bengal Past and Present,* V (January-June 1910), pp. 261-72.
Derbyshire, I.D., "Economic Change and the Railways in North India, 1860-1914", *Modern Asian Studies,* 21:3 (July 1987), pp. 521-45.
Dowden, T.F., "Notes on Railways, Bombay", *Indian Economic and Social History Review,* 25:1

(January-March 1988), pp. 79-96.

Harrison, John, "The Records of Indian Railways: A Neglected Resource", *South Asia Research,* 7:2 (November 1987), pp. 105-21.

Huddleston, G., "The Opening of the East India Railway", *Bengal Past and Present,* II: 1 (January-July 1908), pp. 55-61.

Hughes, H.C., "India Office Railway Records", *Journal of Transport History,* VI: 4 (November 1964), pp. 241-8.

Hughes, H.C., "The Scinde Railway", *Journal of Transport History,* 5:4 (November 1962), pp. 219-25.

Kerr, Ian J., "Constructing Railway in India—An Estimate of the Numbers Employed, 1850-80", *Indian Economic and Social Review,* 20:3 (July-September 1983), pp. 317-39.

Kerr, Ian J., "Working Class Protest in 19th Century India, Example of Railway Workers", *Economic and Political Weekly,* xx : 4 (26 January 1985)

Macpherson, W.J., "Investment in Indian Railways, 1845-1875", *Economic History Review,* 2nd series, VIII: 2 (1995), pp. 177-86.

Morris, David Morris and Clyde B. Dudley, "Selected Railway Statistics for the Indian Subcontinent (India, Pakistan and Bangladesh), 1853-1946-47", *Artha Vijnana,* XVII: 3 September 1975, pp. 187-298.

Morris, Morris David, "Values as an Obstacle to Economic Growth in South Asia: An Historical Survey", *Journal of Economic History* (December 1967), pp. 588-607.

Mukherjee, Hena, "The Early History of the East Indian Railway, 1845-1879", Ph.D. dissertation, University of London, School of Oriental and African Studies, July 1966.

Parry, J.W., "Some Features of Indian Railways", *Engineering Magazine* (July 1898)), pp. 558-74.

Ray, Bharati, "The Genesis of Railway Development in Hyderabad State: A Case of Nineteenth Century British Imperialism", *Indian Economic and Social History Review,* 21:1, January-March, 1894, pp. 45-69.

"Robertson, Murray, The Railways of India: Their Policy and Finance", *The Nineteenth Century and After,* LXX (July 1911), pp. 84-103.

Thorner Daniel, "Great Britain and the Development of India's Railways", *Journal of Economic History,* XI:4 (Fall, 1951), pp. 389-402.

E. Pulished Works

Aitken, Bill, *Exploring Indian Railways,* Oxford, 1994.

Amsteu, V., *The Economic Development of India,* London, 1952.

Andrew, W.P., *Indian Railways and their Probable Results,* London, 1848.

Antia, K.F., *Railway Track Design, Construction Maintenance, and Renewal of Permanent Way with Notes on Signalling and Bridge Maintenance,* Bombay, 1945.

Awasthi, Aruna, *History and Development of Railways in India,* New Delhi, 1994.

Bell, Horace, *Railway Policy in India,* London, 1894.

Berridge, P.S.A., *Couplings to the Khyber: The Story of the North Western Railway,* New York, 1969.

Bernstein, H.T., *Steam Boats on the Ganges*, Bombay, 1960.
Bhatia, B.M., *Famines in India*, New Delhi, 1963.
Bourne, J., *Railways in India*, London, 1848.
Chakravarti, A.K., *Railway for Developing Countries (with special emphasis on India)*, New Delhi, 1966.
Chapman, J., *The Cotton and Commerce of India*, London, 1851.
Charlesworth, Neil, *British Rule and the Indian Economy 1800-1914*, London, 1982.
Chattopadhyaya, H., *The Sepoy Mutiny: A Special Study and Analysis*, Calcutta, 1957.
Clapham, J.H., *Economic Development of France and Germany*, Cambridge, 1945.
Cotton, C.W.E., *Handbook of Commercial Information for India*, Calcutta, 1919.
Curzon, Lord, *British Government in India*, London, 1925.
Davidson, Edward, *The Railways in India*, London, 1868
Davis, Lance E. & Robert A. Huttenback, *Mammon and the Pursuit of Empire: The Economic of British Imperialism*, Cambridge, 1988.
Dickinson, John, *Remarks on the Indian Railway Reports Published by the Government and Reasons for a Change of Policy in India*, London, 1862.
Epstien, T.S., *Economic Development and Social Change in South India*, Manchester, 1962.
Ford, P. & Ford, G. (ed.), *British Parliamentry Papers*, Shannon (Ireland), 1970.
Furnivall, W.C., *Rajputana State Railway*, Simla, 1875.
Gadgil, D.R., *The Industrial Evolution of India*, Calcutta, 1950.
Ghose, S.C., *Lectures on Indian Railway Economics*, Calcutta, 1923.
Hawke, G.R., *Railways and Economic Growth in England and Wales*, 1840-70, Oxford, 1970.
Headrick, Daniel R., *The Tentacles of Progress, Technology Transfer in the Age of Imperialism, 1850-1940*, New York, 1988.
Huddleston, G., *History of the East Indian Railway*, Calcutta, 1906.
Jackman, W.T., *The Development of Transportation*, London, 1962.
Jenks, Leland H., *The Migration of British Capital, 1857-1927*, London, 1971.
Johnson, J., *The Economics of Indian Rail Transport*, Bombay, 1863.
Kaye, J., *The Administration of the East India Company*, London, 1853.
Kellett, John R., *Railway and Victorian Cities*, London, 1979.
Lee-Warner, Sir William, *The Life of the Marquis of Dalhousie*, London, 1904.
MacGeorge, G.W., *Ways and Works in India*, London, 1894.
Malik, M.B.K., *Hundred Years of Pakistan Railways*, Karachi, 1962.
Martin, R.M., *Our Indian Empire*, London, 1881.
McCulloch, J.R.M., *A Dictionary of Commerce and Commercial Navigation*, London, 1871.
Mill, James, *History of British India*, New Delhi, 1972.
Mukherjee, Hena, *The Early History of East Indian Railways*, 1845-1879, Calcutta, 1994.
Natesan, L.A., *State Management and Control of Railways in India*, Calcutta, 1946.
Nock, D.S., *Railways of Asia and the Far East*, New Delhi, 1978.
Pande, Ram, *Railways in Rajputana*, Jaipur, 1972.
Prasad, Amba, *Indian Railways: A Study in Public Utility Administration*, London, 1960.
Rao, Y. Saraswathy, *The Railway Board: A Study in Administration*, New Delhi, 1978.

Reed, M.C., (ed.), *Railway in the Victorian Economy: Studies in Finance and Economic Growth*, London, 1969.

Reid, C.L., *Commerce and Conquest*, London, 1947.

Robertson, Thomas, *Report on the Administration and Working of Indian Railway*, Calcutta, 1903.

Saul, S.B., *Studies in British Overseas Trade*, 1870-1914, Liverpool, 1960.

Shah, K.T., *Trade, Tariffs and Transport in India*, Bombay, 1923.

Sahni, J.N., *Indian Railways: One Hundred Years*, 1853 to 1953, New Delhi, 1953.

Sanyal, N., *The Development of Indian Railways*, Calcutta, 1930.

Satow, Michael and Desmond Ray, *Railways of the Raj*, New York, 1980.

Sharma, S.N., *History of the Great Indian Peninsula Railway*, Bombay, 1990.

Simmons, Jack, *The Railways of England and Wales*, 1830-1914, Leicester, n.d.

Stone, E. Herbert, *The Nizam's State Railway*, London, 1876.

Strachey, J. and Strachey, R., *The Finances and Public Works of India from 1869 to 1881*, London, 1988.

Strachey, R., *Report of India Famine Commission, 1880-1885*, New Delhi, 1889.

Sulivan, R.F.J., *One Hundred Years of Bombay*, Bombay, 1937.

Taylor, G.R., *The Transportation Revolution, 1815-1860*, New York, 1957.

Thorner, Daniel, *Investment in Empire, British Railway and Steam Shipping Enterprise in India, 1825-1849*, Philadelphia, 1950.

Thorner, Daniel, *The Shaping of Modern India*, Bombay, Allied Publishers, 1980.

Trevor, Henrey Edward, *Railway in British India: Including Indian Railway Act 1890*, London, 1891.

Tyson, G.W., *The Bengal Chamber of Commerce and Industry*, 1853-1953, Calcutta, 1953.

Walker, Charles, *Thomas Brassey: Railway Builder*, London, 1969.

Westwood, J.N., *Railway of India*, London, 1974.

INDEX